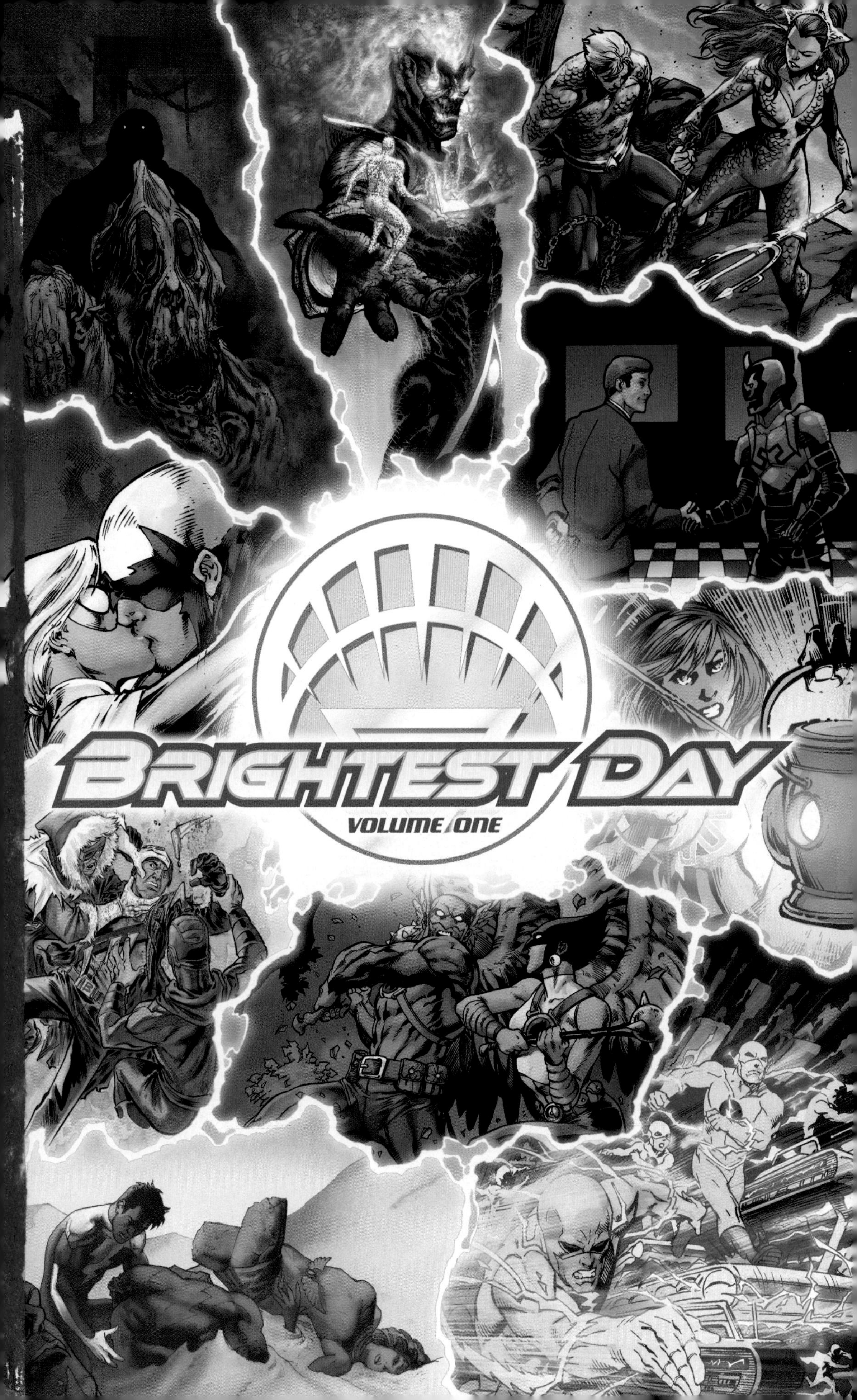
BRIGHTEST DAY
VOLUME ONE

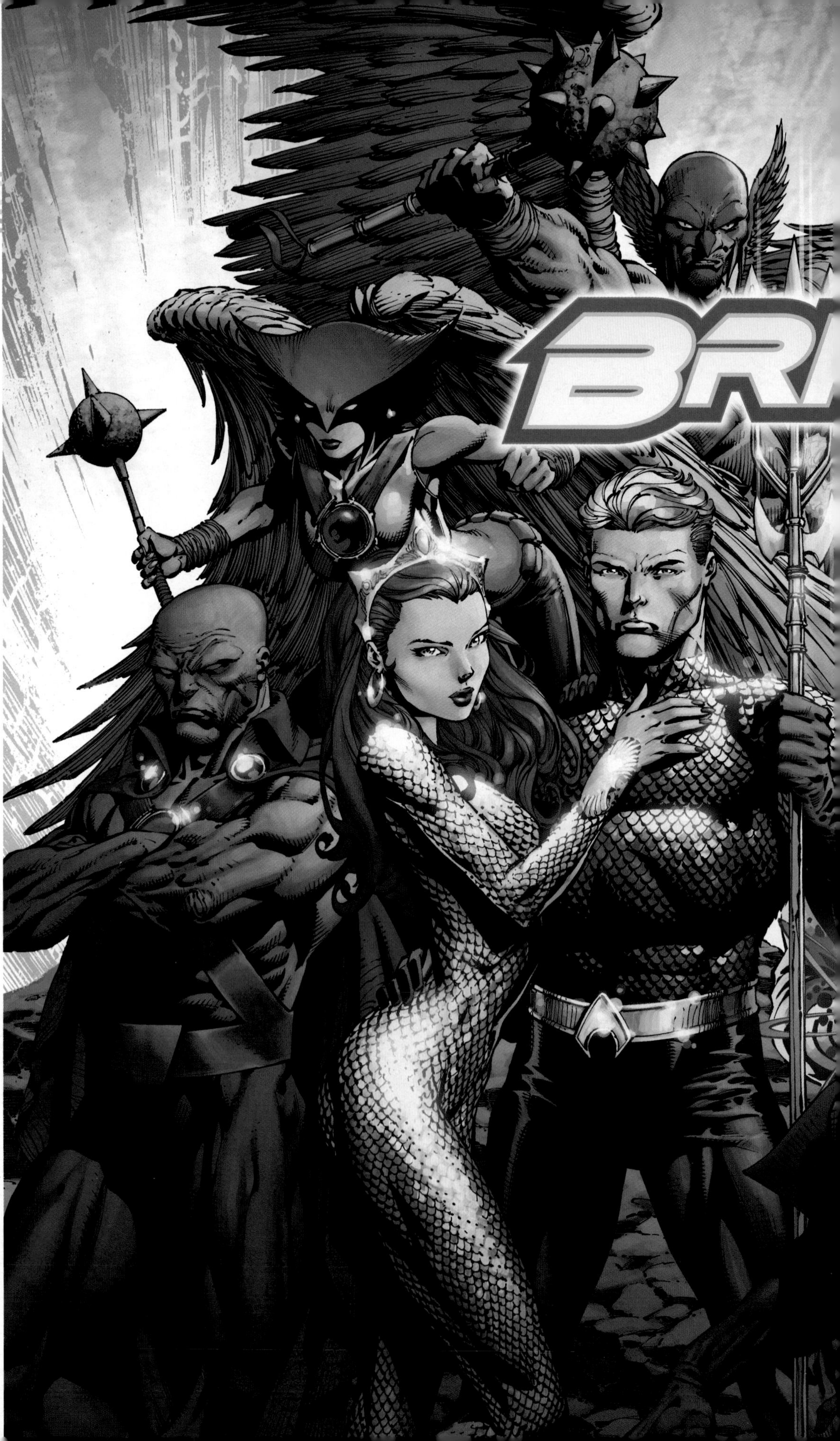

# GHTEST DAY

## VOLUME ONE

**GEOFF JOHNS**
**& PETER J. TOMASI**
WRITERS

**IVAN REIS**
**PATRICK GLEASON**
**FERNANDO PASARIN**
**ARDIAN SYAF**
**SCOTT CLARK**
**JOE PRADO**
ARTISTS

| | |
|---|---|
| **CHRISTIAN ALAMY** | **OCLAIR ALBERT** |
| **DAVID BEATY** | **REBECCA BUCHMAN** |
| **VICENTE CIFUENTES** | **JOHN DELL** |
| **TOM NGUYEN** | **MARK IRWIN** |
| **CAM SMITH** | **PRENTIS ROLLINS** |
| **ART THIBERT** | **DEXTER VINES** |

INKERS

| | |
|---|---|
| **MARK BAGLEY** | **ED BENES** |
| **FABRIZIO FIORENTINO** | **ROB HUNTER** |
| **ANDY KUBERT** | **AARON LOPRESTI** |
| **FRANCIS MANAPUL** | **MIKE MAYHEW** |
| **MATT RYAN** | |

GUEST ARTISTS

**ASPEN MLT'S PETER STEIGERWALD**
WITH **BETH SOTELO & JOHN STARR**
COLORISTS

**ROB CLARK JR.**
**NICK J. NAPOLITANO**
LETTERERS

**DAVID FINCH, SCOTT WILLIAMS**
**& PETER STEIGERWALD**
COVER ARTISTS

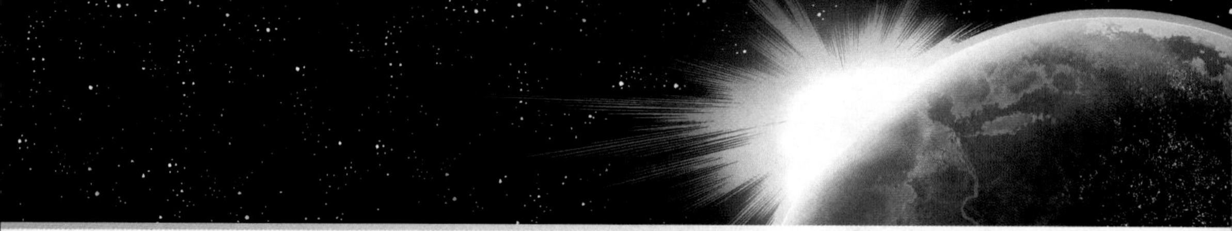

Eddie Berganza *Editor-original series* / Adam Schlagman *Associate Editor-original series*
Rex Ogle *Assistant Editor-original series* / Bob Harras *Group Editor-Collected Editions*
Sean Mackiewicz *Editor* / Robbin Brosterman *Design Director-Books* / Curtis King Jr. *Senior Art Director*

**DC COMICS** / Diane Nelson *President* / Dan DiDio and Jim Lee *Co-Publishers*
Geoff Johns *Chief Creative Officer* / Patrick Caldon *EVP–Finance and Administration*
John Rood *EVP–Sales, Marketing and Business Development* / Amy Genkins *SVP–Business and Legal Affairs*
Steve Rotterdam *SVP–Sales and Marketing* / John Cunningham *VP–Marketing*
Terri Cunningham *VP–Managing Editor* / Alison Gill *VP–Manufacturing* / David Hyde *VP–Publicity*
Sue Pohja *VP–Book Trade Sales* / Alysse Soll *VP–Advertising and Custom Publishing*
Bob Wayne *VP–Sales* / Mark Chiarello *Art Director*

**BRIGHTEST DAY VOLUME 1** Published by DC Comics.


**DC COMICS** 1700 Broadway, New York, NY 10019 A Warner Bros. Entertainment Company

Printed by Quad/Graphics, Versailles, KY, USA. 11/3/10. First printing.

HC ISBN: 978-1-4012-2966-5
SC ISBN: 978-1-4012-3092-0

SUSTAINABLE FORESTRY INITIATIVE
Certified Chain of Custody
Promoting Sustainable Forest Management
www.sfiprogram.org
Fiber used in this product line meets the sourcing requirements of the SFI program. www.sfiprogram.org PWC-SFICOC-260

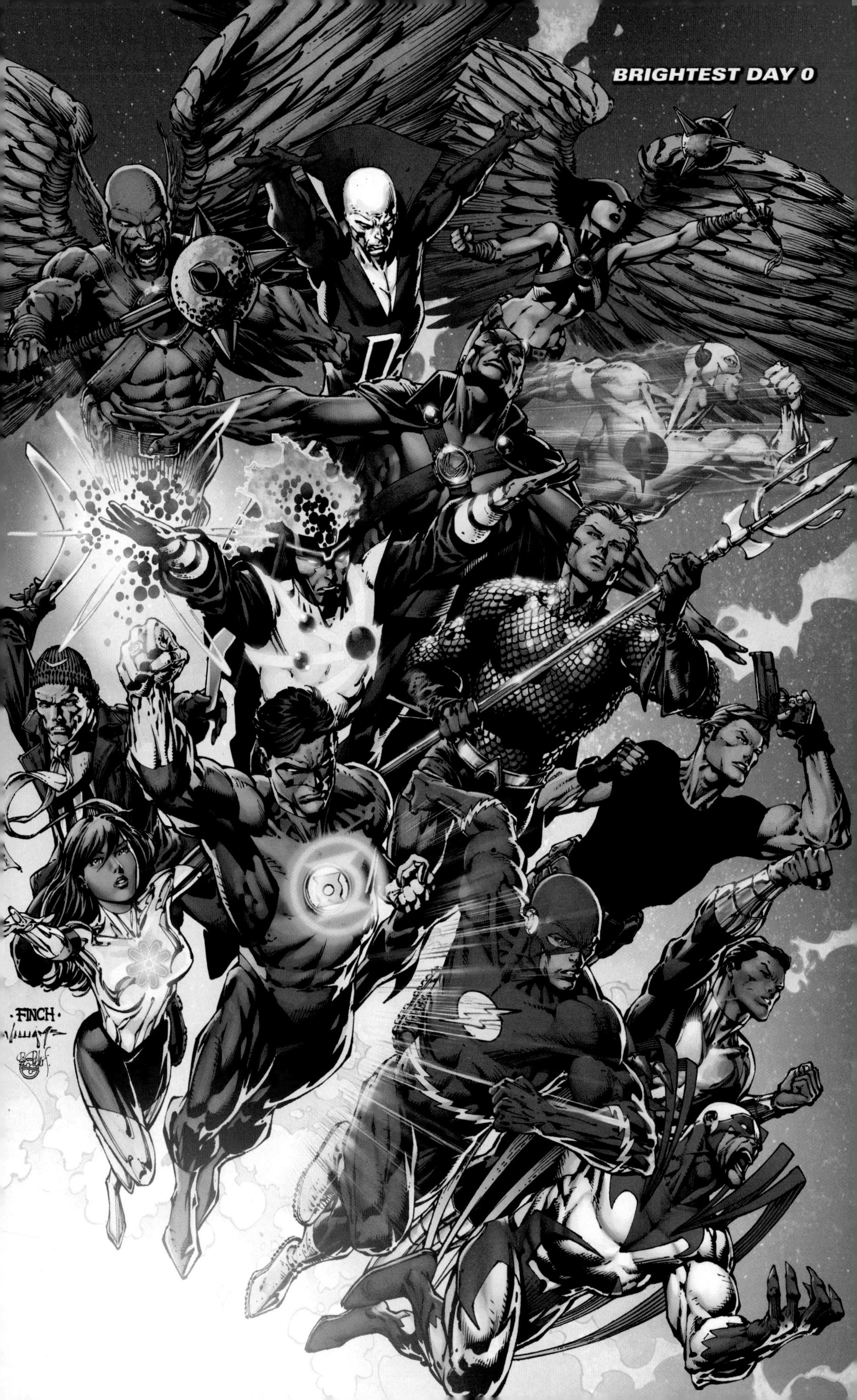
BRIGHTEST DAY 0
FINCH

# CARPE DIEM

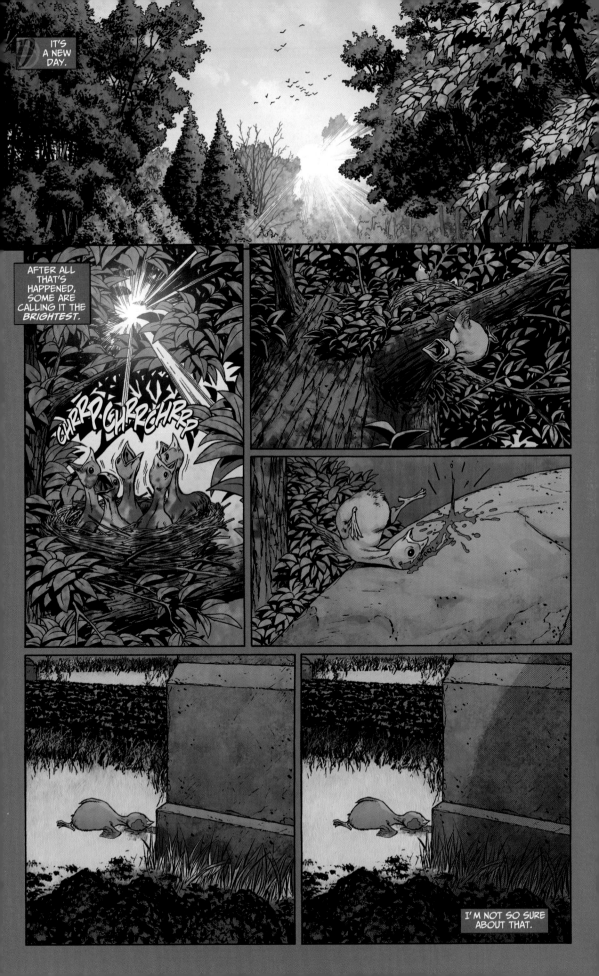

IT'S A NEW DAY.

AFTER ALL THAT'S HAPPENED, SOME ARE CALLING IT THE BRIGHTEST.

CHRRP CHRR CHRR.

I'M NOT SO SURE ABOUT THAT.

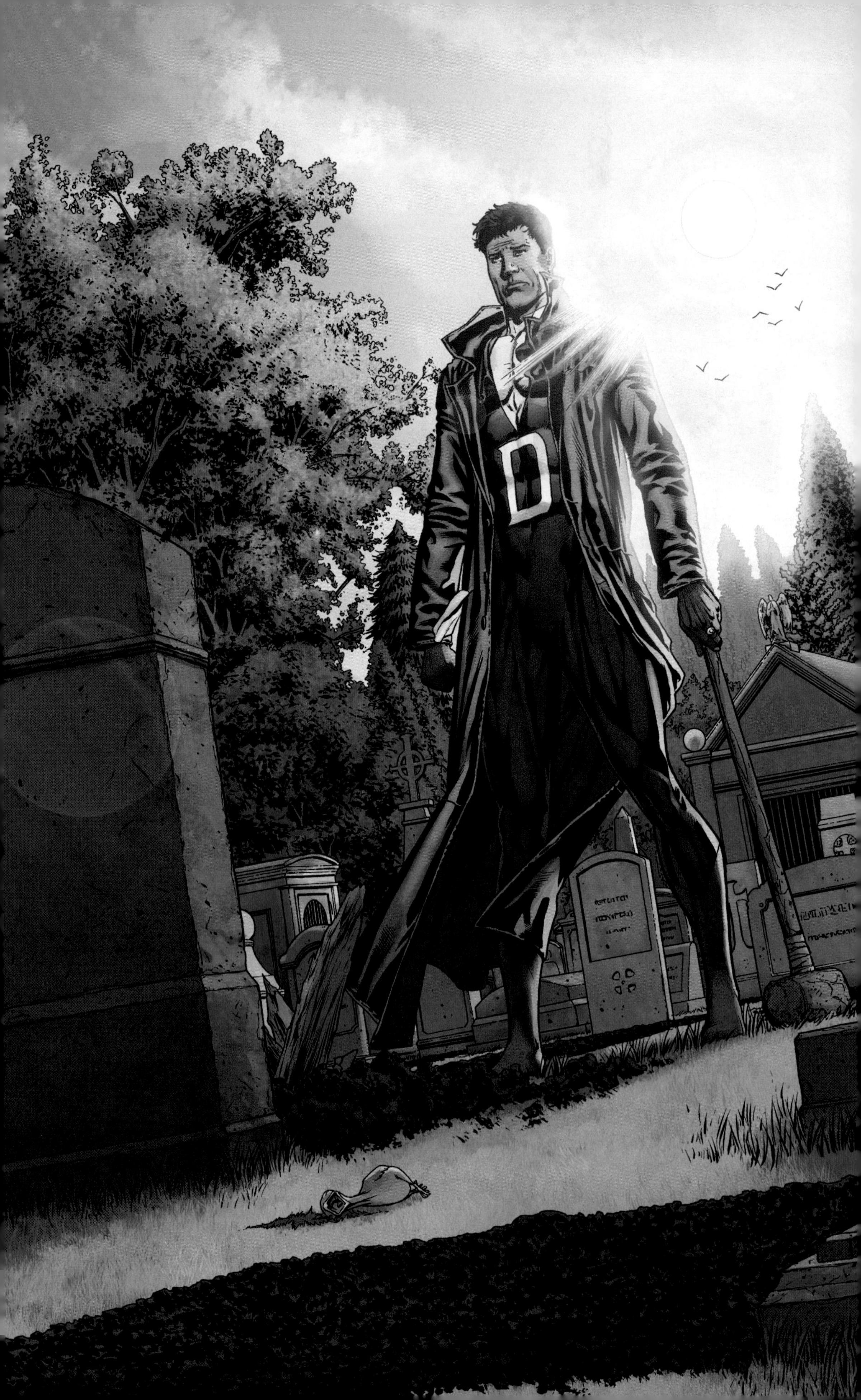

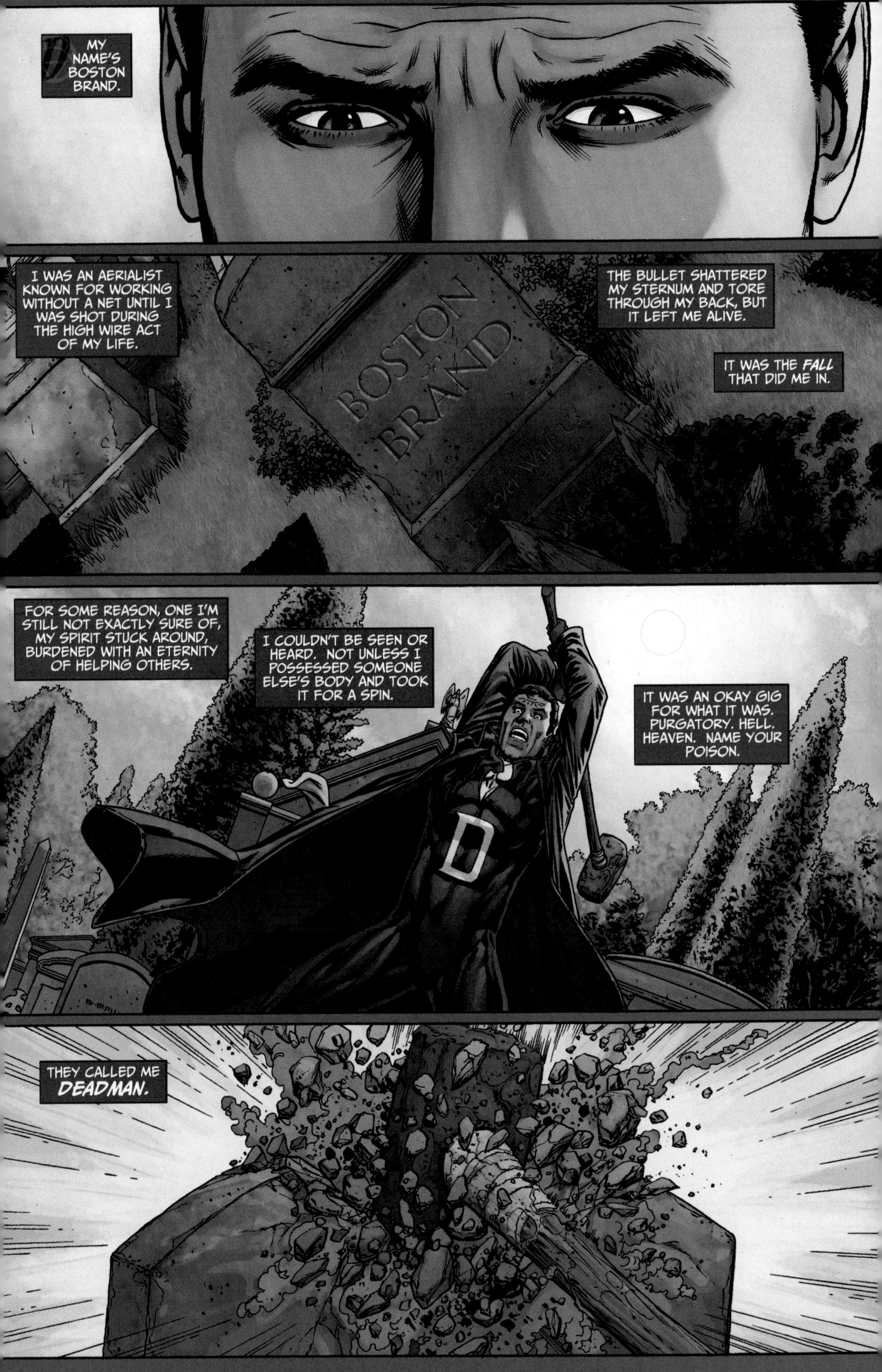

MY NAME'S BOSTON BRAND.
I WAS AN AERIALIST KNOWN FOR WORKING WITHOUT A NET UNTIL I WAS SHOT DURING THE HIGH WIRE ACT OF MY LIFE.
BOSTON BRAND
THE BULLET SHATTERED MY STERNUM AND TORE THROUGH MY BACK, BUT IT LEFT ME ALIVE.
IT WAS THE FALL THAT DID ME IN.
FOR SOME REASON, ONE I'M STILL NOT EXACTLY SURE OF, MY SPIRIT STUCK AROUND, BURDENED WITH AN ETERNITY OF HELPING OTHERS.
I COULDN'T BE SEEN OR HEARD. NOT UNLESS I POSSESSED SOMEONE ELSE'S BODY AND TOOK IT FOR A SPIN.
IT WAS AN OKAY GIG FOR WHAT IT WAS. PURGATORY. HELL. HEAVEN. NAME YOUR POISON.
THEY CALLED ME DEADMAN.

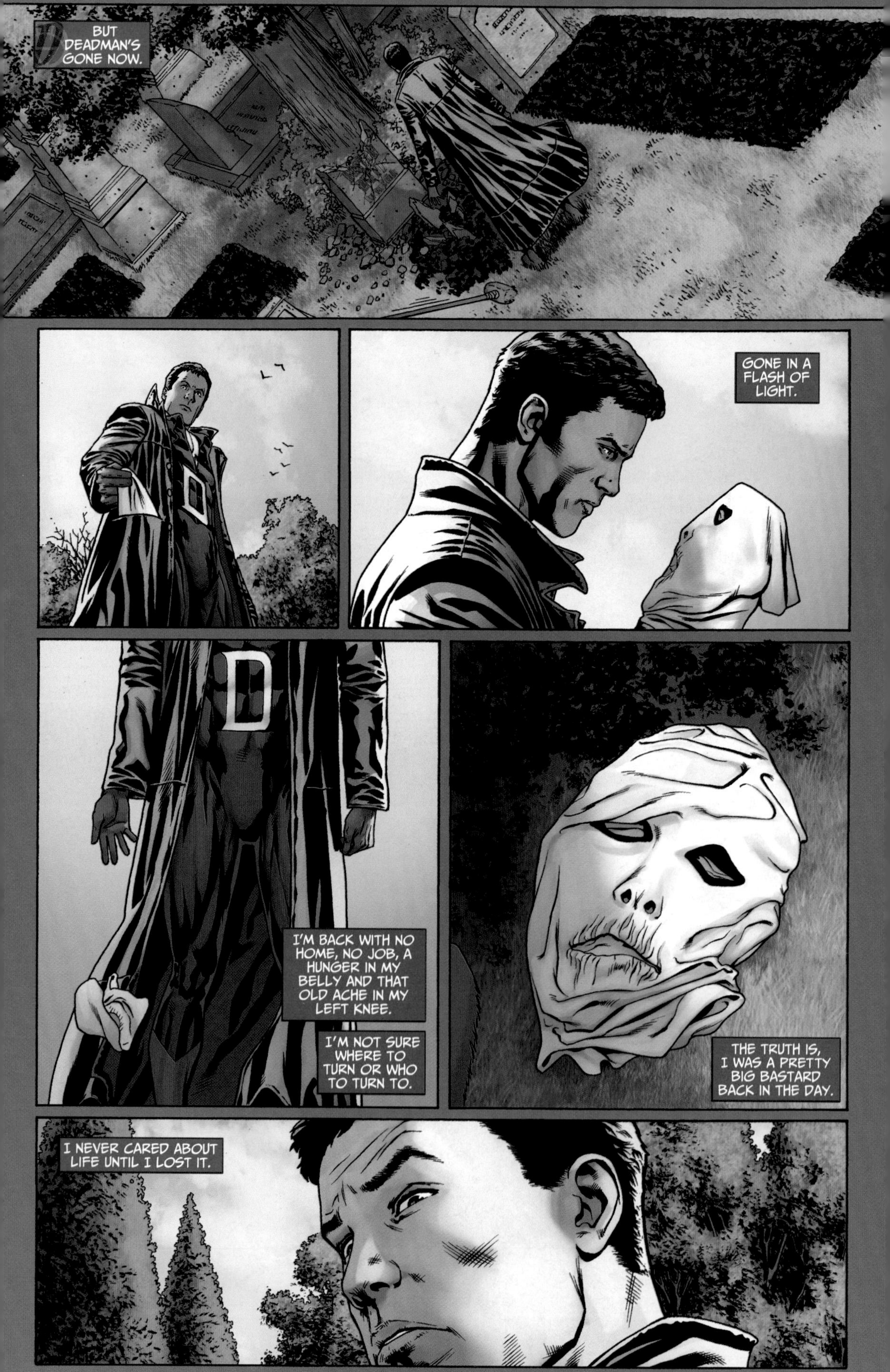
BUT DEADMAN'S GONE NOW.
GONE IN A FLASH OF LIGHT.
I'M BACK WITH NO HOME, NO JOB, A HUNGER IN MY BELLY AND THAT OLD ACHE IN MY LEFT KNEE.
I'M NOT SURE WHERE TO TURN OR WHO TO TURN TO.
THE TRUTH IS, I WAS A PRETTY BIG BASTARD BACK IN THE DAY.
I NEVER CARED ABOUT LIFE UNTIL I LOST IT.

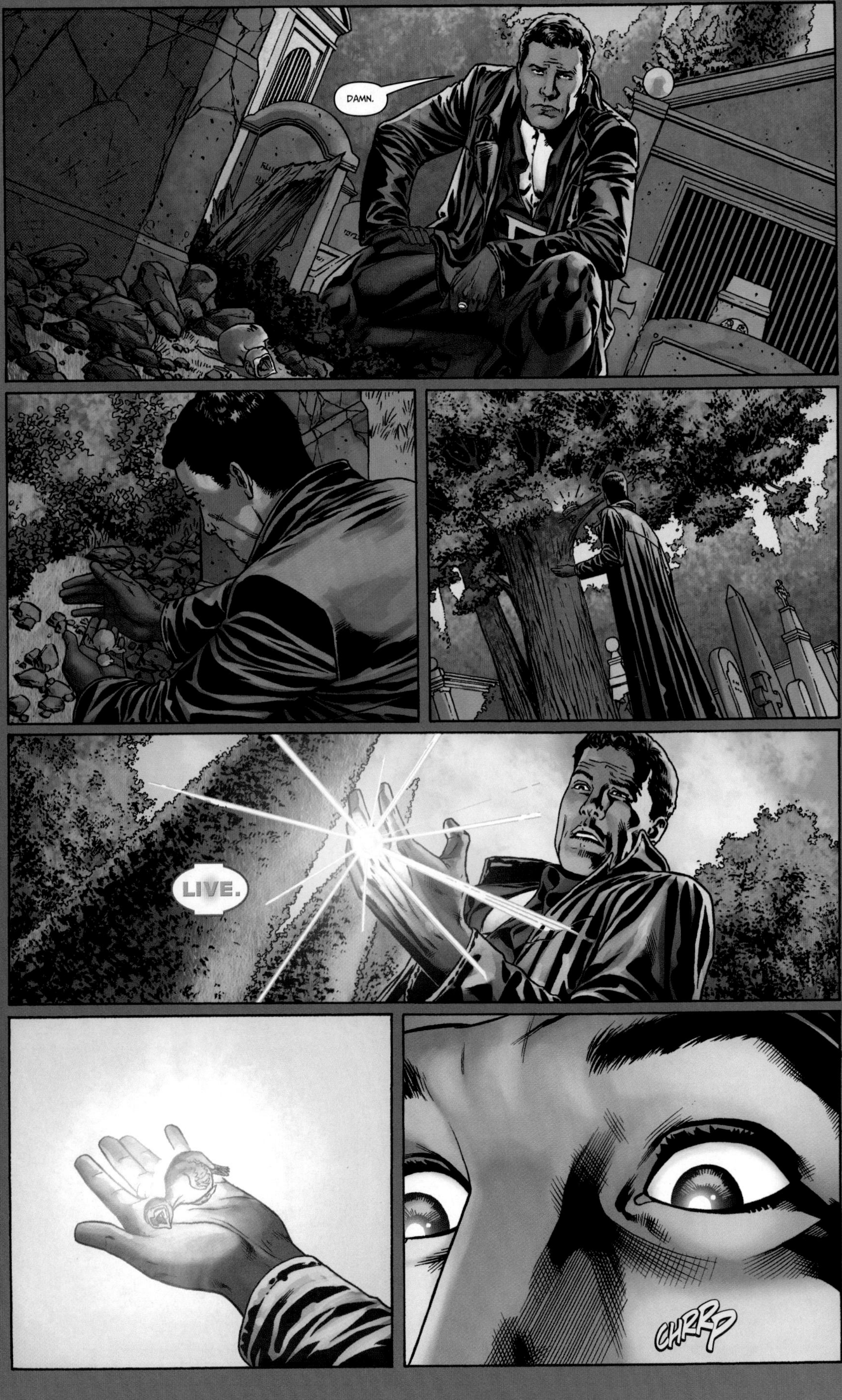
DAMN.
LIVE.
CHRRP

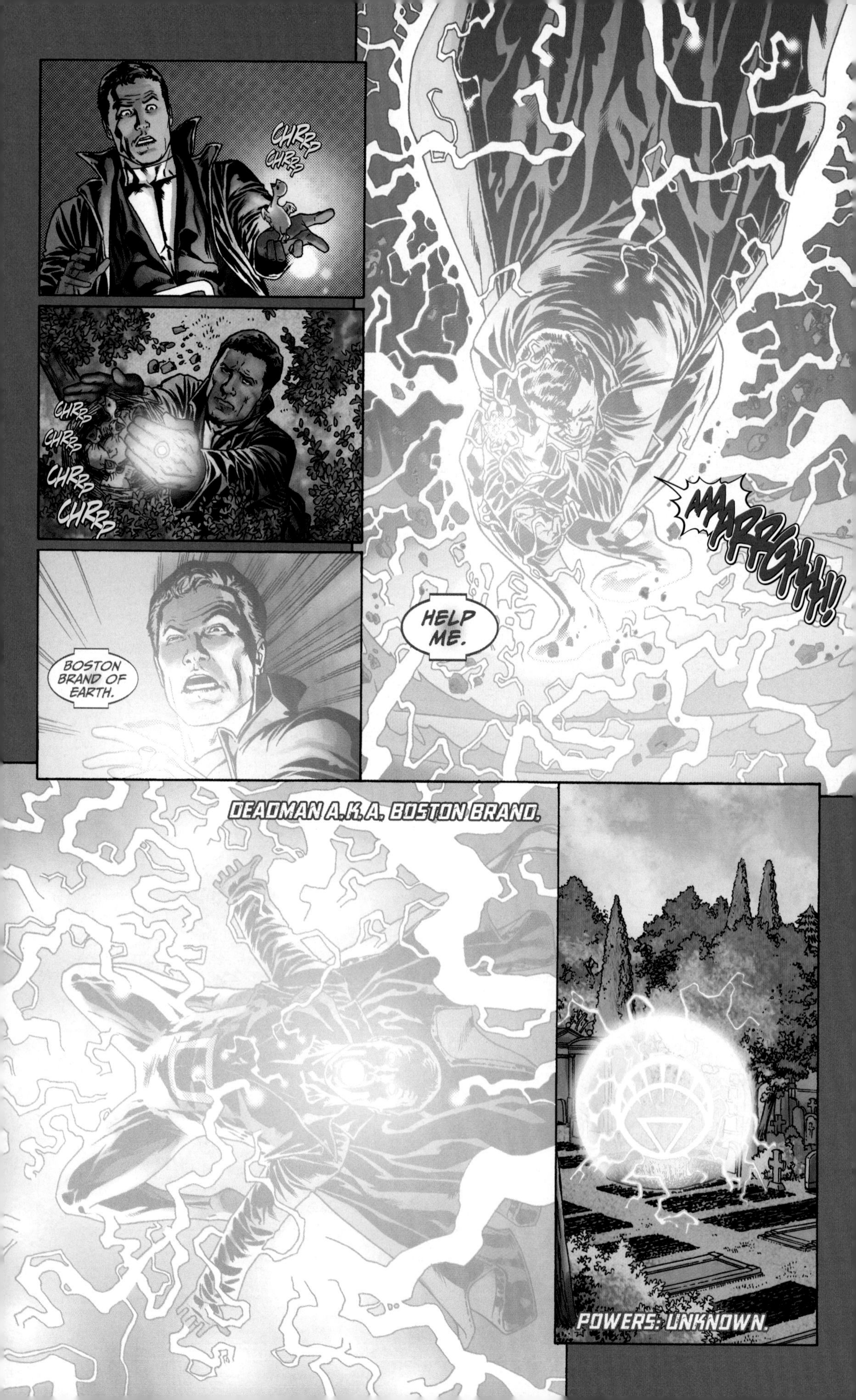

CHRRP CHRRP
CHRRP CHRRP CHRRP CHRRP
BOSTON BRAND OF EARTH.
HELP ME.
AAAARRRGHHH!
DEADMAN A.K.A. BOSTON BRAND.
POWERS: UNKNOWN.

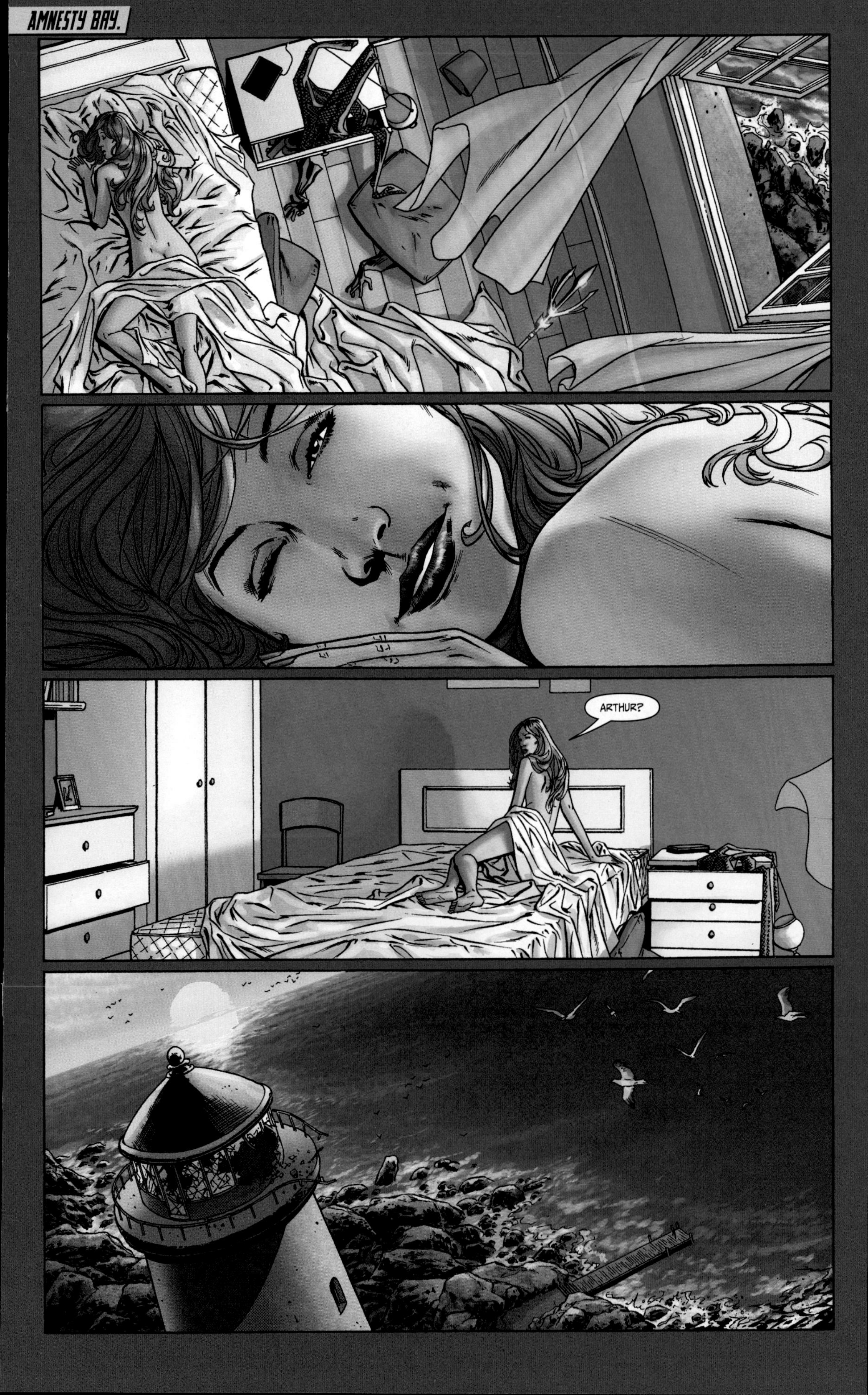
AMNESTY BAY.
ARTHUR?

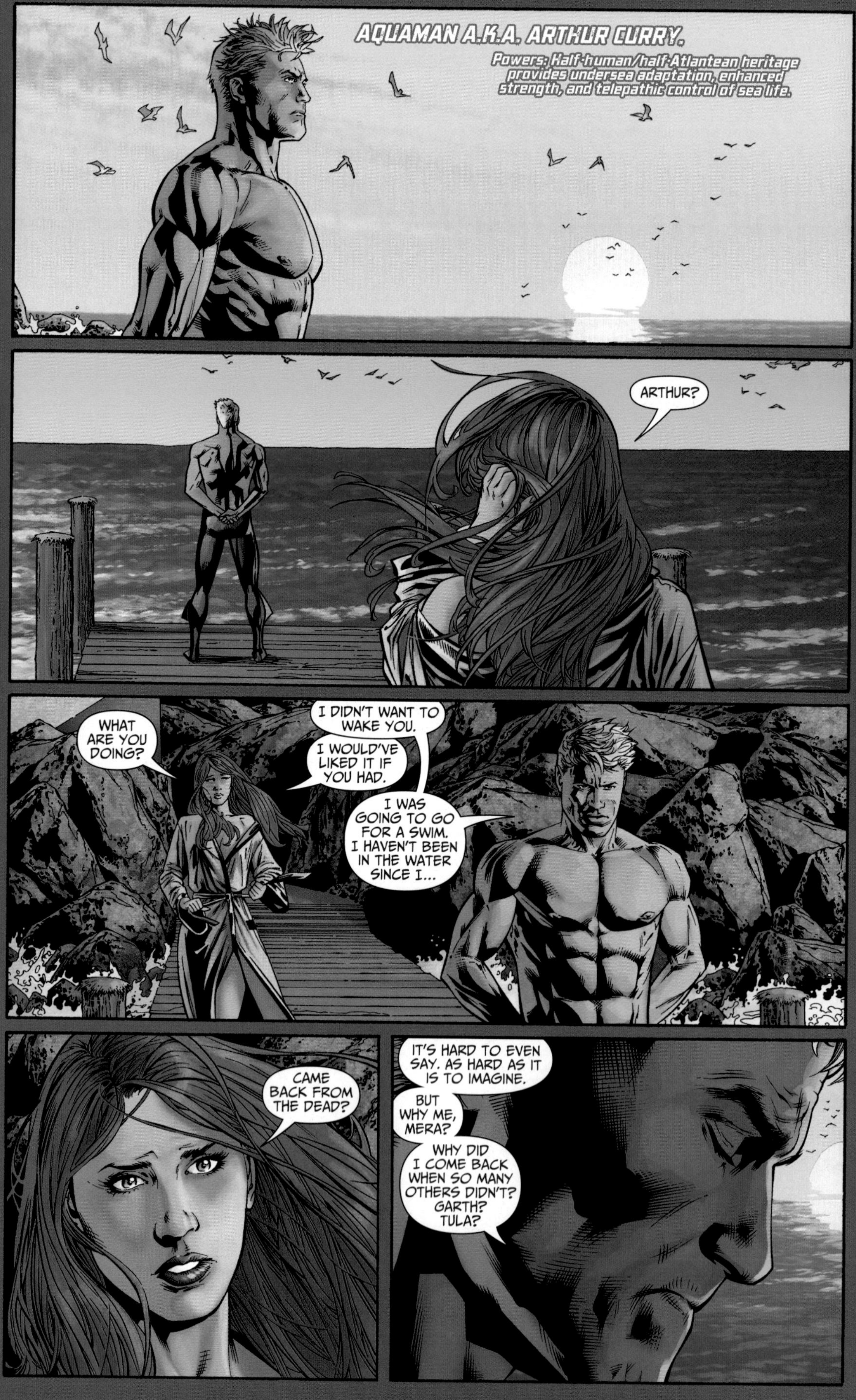
AQUAMAN A.K.A. ARTHUR CURRY.
Powers: Half-human/half-Atlantean heritage provides undersea adaptation, enhanced strength, and telepathic control of sea life.
ARTHUR?
WHAT ARE YOU DOING?
I DIDN'T WANT TO WAKE YOU.
I WOULD'VE LIKED IT IF YOU HAD.
I WAS GOING TO GO FOR A SWIM. I HAVEN'T BEEN IN THE WATER SINCE I...
CAME BACK FROM THE DEAD?
IT'S HARD TO EVEN SAY. AS HARD AS IT IS TO IMAGINE.
BUT WHY ME, MERA?
WHY DID I COME BACK WHEN SO MANY OTHERS DIDN'T? GARTH? TULA?

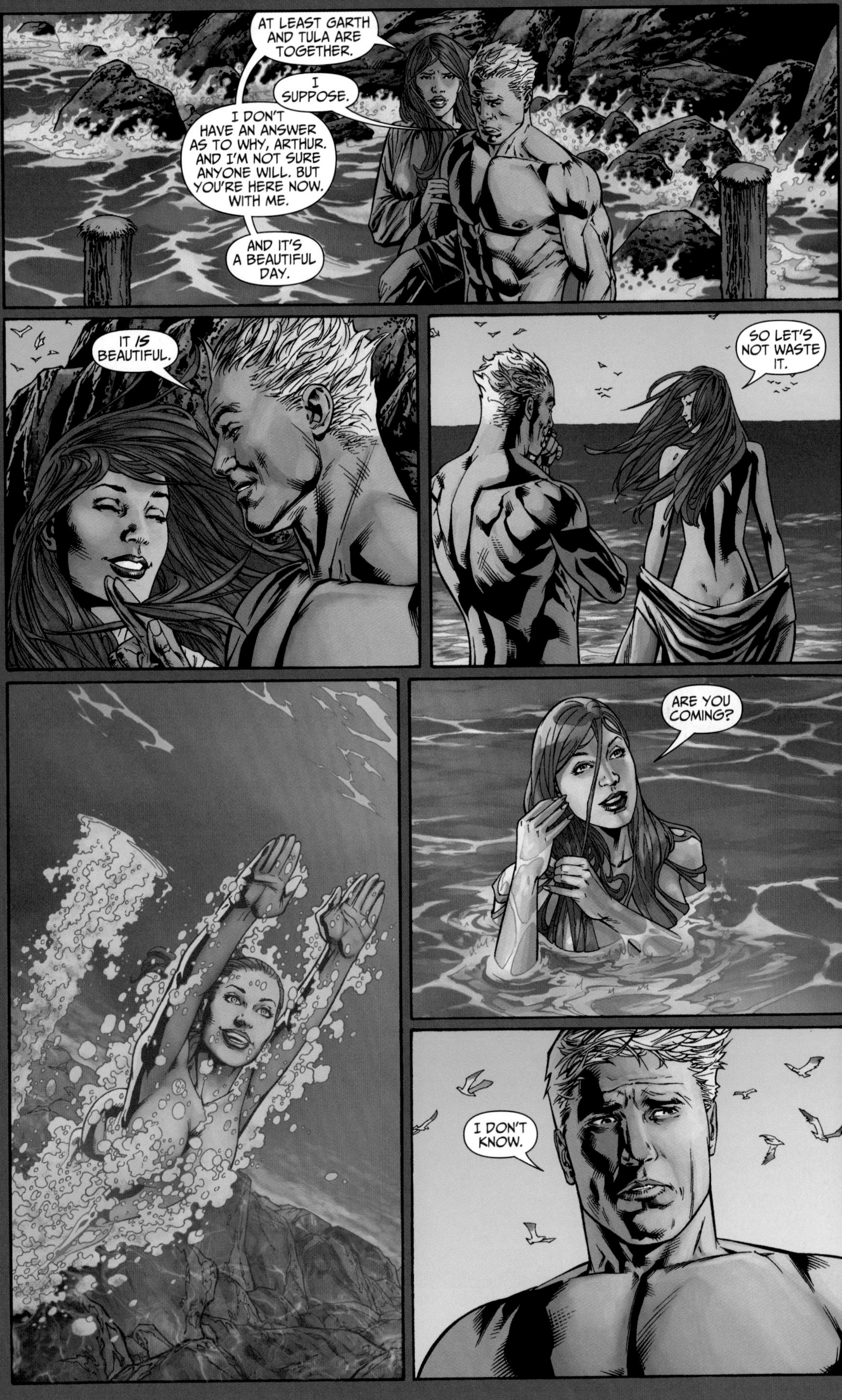
AT LEAST GARTH AND TULA ARE TOGETHER.
I SUPPOSE.
I DON'T HAVE AN ANSWER AS TO WHY, ARTHUR. AND I'M NOT SURE ANYONE WILL. BUT YOU'RE HERE NOW. WITH ME.
AND IT'S A BEAUTIFUL DAY.
IT *IS* BEAUTIFUL.
SO LET'S NOT WASTE IT.
ARE YOU COMING?
I DON'T KNOW.

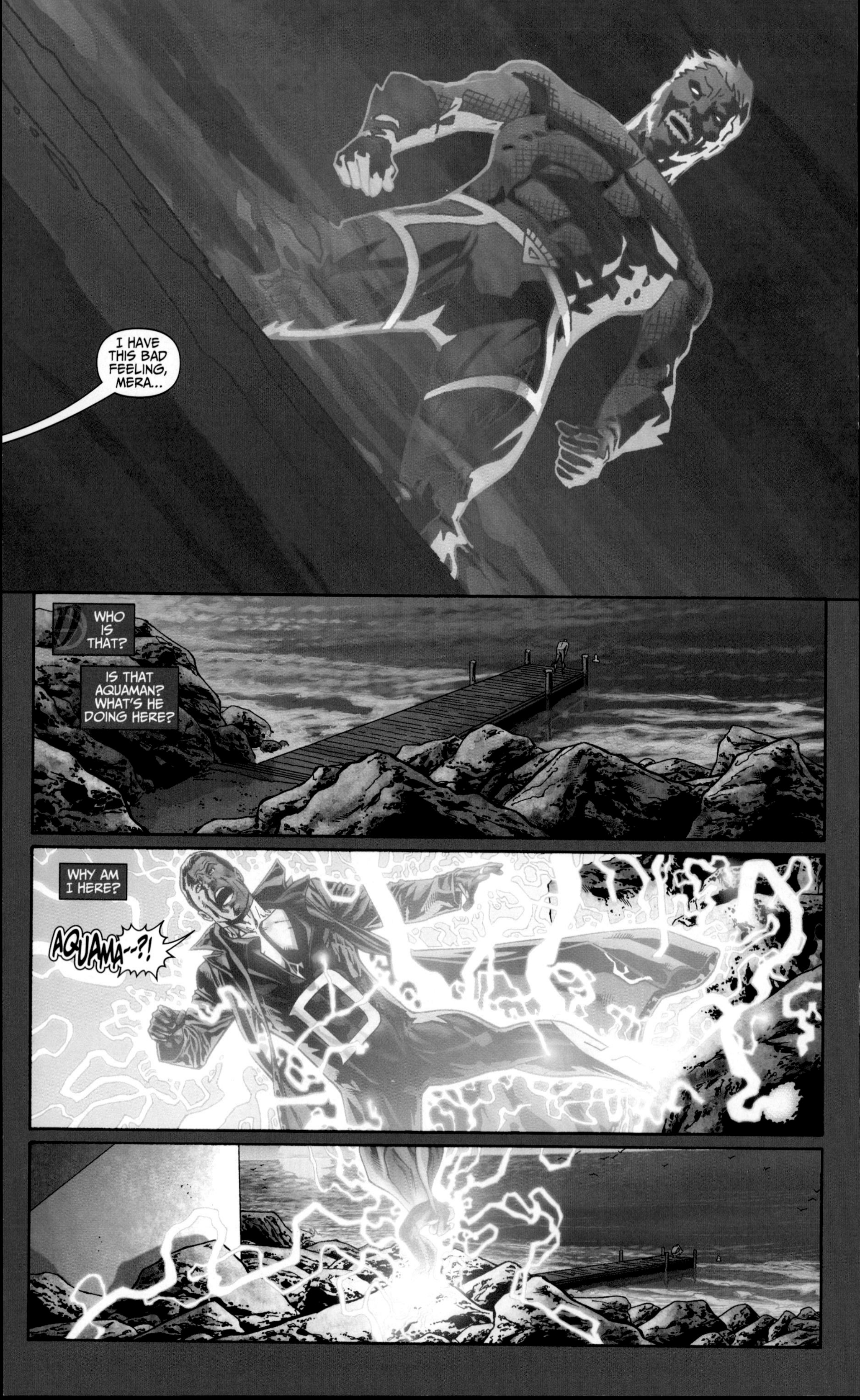
I HAVE THIS BAD FEELING, MERA...
WHO IS THAT?
IS THAT AQUAMAN? WHAT'S HE DOING HERE?
WHY AM I HERE?
AQUAMA--?!

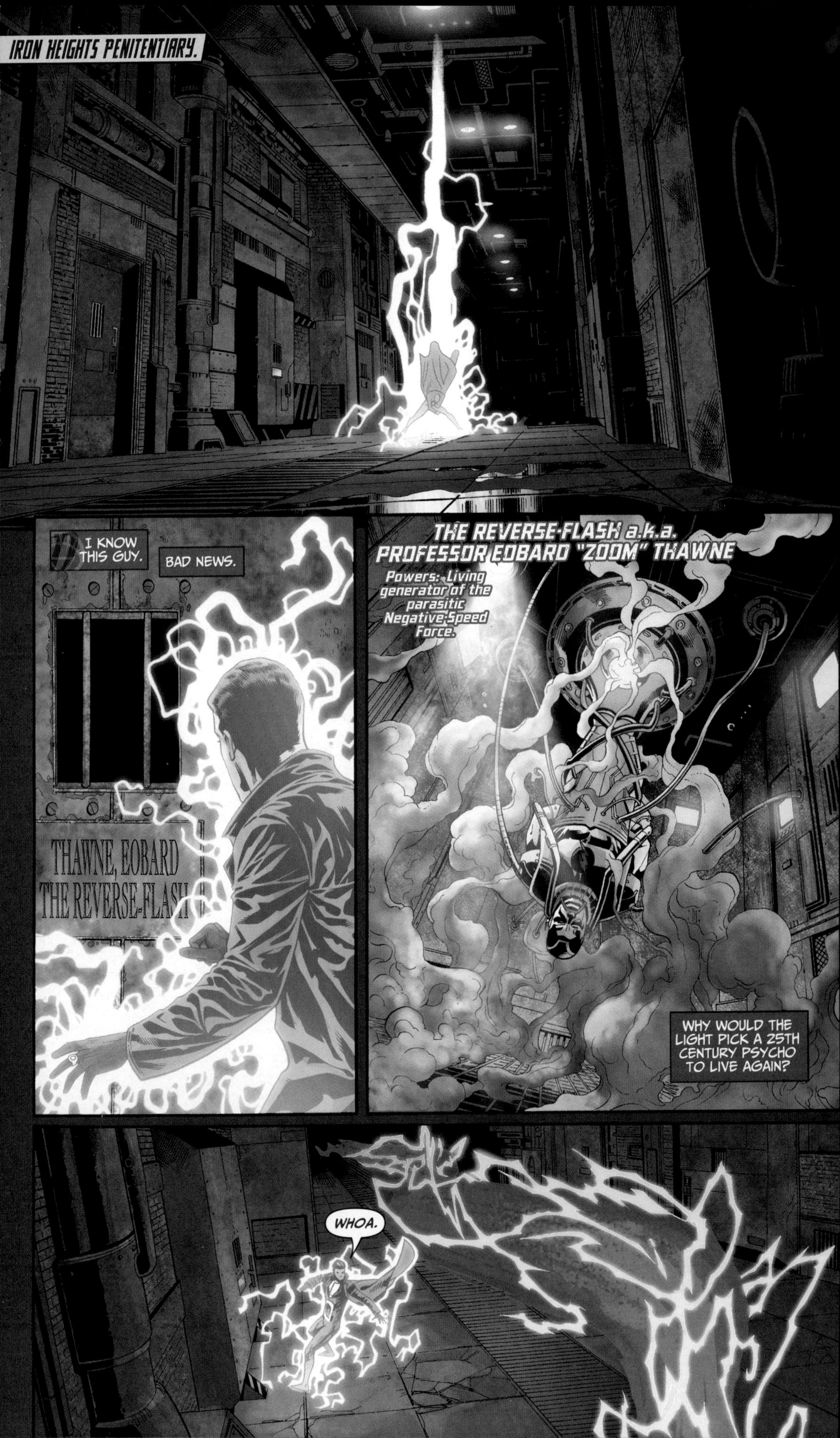
IRON HEIGHTS PENITENTIARY.
I KNOW THIS GUY.
BAD NEWS.
THAWNE, EOBARD
THE REVERSE-FLASH
THE REVERSE-FLASH a.k.a. PROFESSOR EOBARD "ZOOM" THAWNE
Powers: Living generator of the parasitic Negative-Speed Force.
WHY WOULD THE LIGHT PICK A 25TH CENTURY PSYCHO TO LIVE AGAIN?
WHOA.

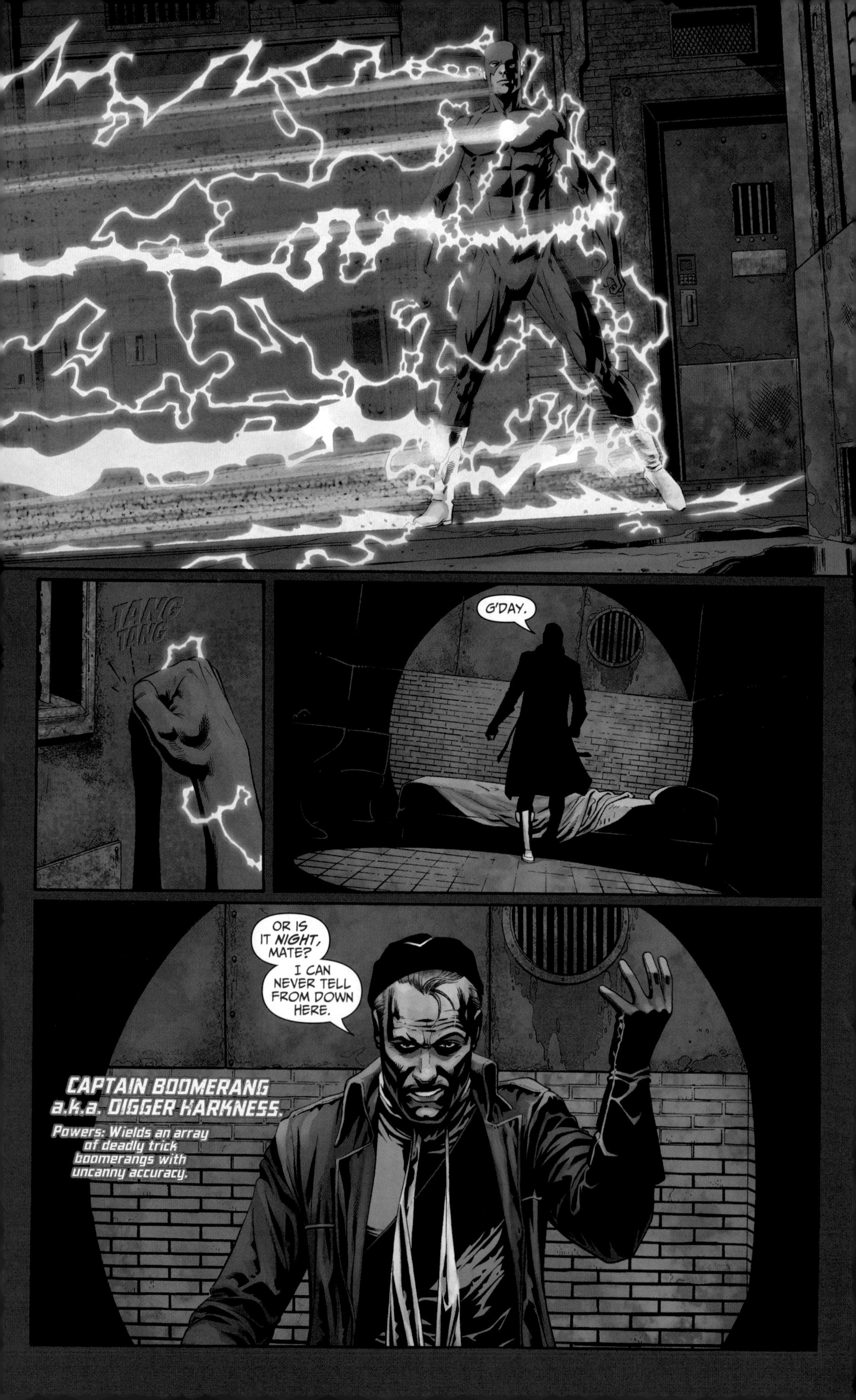
TANG
TANG
G'DAY.
OR IS IT *NIGHT*, MATE?
I CAN NEVER TELL FROM DOWN HERE.
CAPTAIN BOOMERANG a.k.a. DIGGER HARKNESS.
Powers: Wields an array of deadly trick boomerangs with uncanny accuracy.

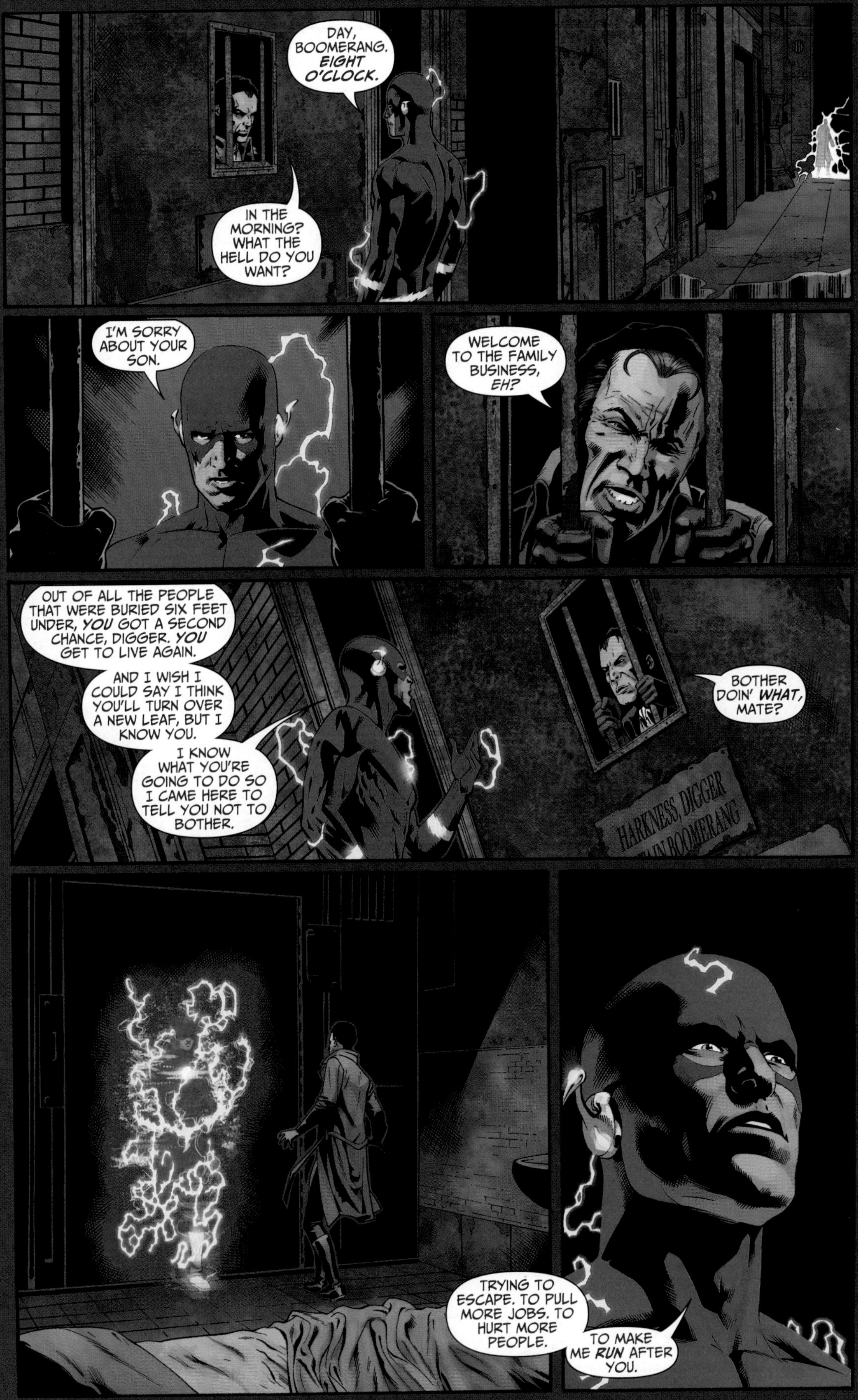
DAY, BOOMERANG. EIGHT O'CLOCK.
IN THE MORNING? WHAT THE HELL DO YOU WANT?
I'M SORRY ABOUT YOUR SON.
WELCOME TO THE FAMILY BUSINESS, EH?
OUT OF ALL THE PEOPLE THAT WERE BURIED SIX FEET UNDER, YOU GOT A SECOND CHANCE, DIGGER. YOU GET TO LIVE AGAIN.
AND I WISH I COULD SAY I THINK YOU'LL TURN OVER A NEW LEAF, BUT I KNOW YOU.
I KNOW WHAT YOU'RE GOING TO DO SO I CAME HERE TO TELL YOU NOT TO BOTHER.
BOTHER DOIN' WHAT, MATE?
HARKNESS, DIGGER
TRYING TO ESCAPE. TO PULL MORE JOBS. TO HURT MORE PEOPLE.
TO MAKE ME RUN AFTER YOU.

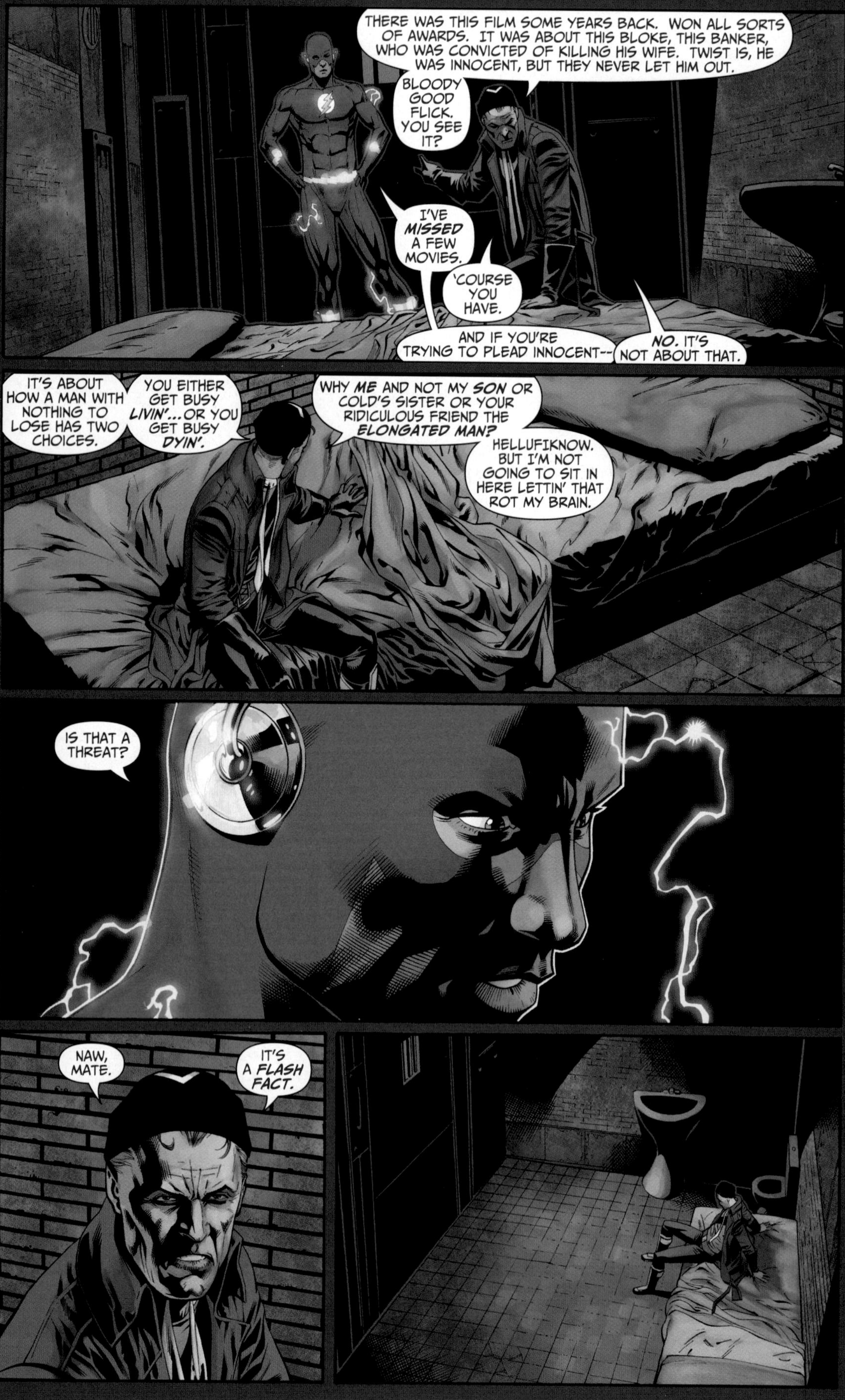
THERE WAS THIS FILM SOME YEARS BACK. WON ALL SORTS OF AWARDS. IT WAS ABOUT THIS BLOKE, THIS BANKER, WHO WAS CONVICTED OF KILLING HIS WIFE. TWIST IS, HE WAS INNOCENT, BUT THEY NEVER LET HIM OUT.
BLOODY GOOD FLICK. YOU SEE IT?
I'VE MISSED A FEW MOVIES.
'COURSE YOU HAVE.
AND IF YOU'RE TRYING TO PLEAD INNOCENT--
NO. IT'S NOT ABOUT THAT.
IT'S ABOUT HOW A MAN WITH NOTHING TO LOSE HAS TWO CHOICES.
YOU EITHER GET BUSY LIVIN'...OR YOU GET BUSY DYIN'.
WHY ME AND NOT MY SON OR COLD'S SISTER OR YOUR RIDICULOUS FRIEND THE ELONGATED MAN?
HELLUFIKNOW. BUT I'M NOT GOING TO SIT IN HERE LETTIN' THAT ROT MY BRAIN.
IS THAT A THREAT?
NAW, MATE.
IT'S A FLASH FACT.

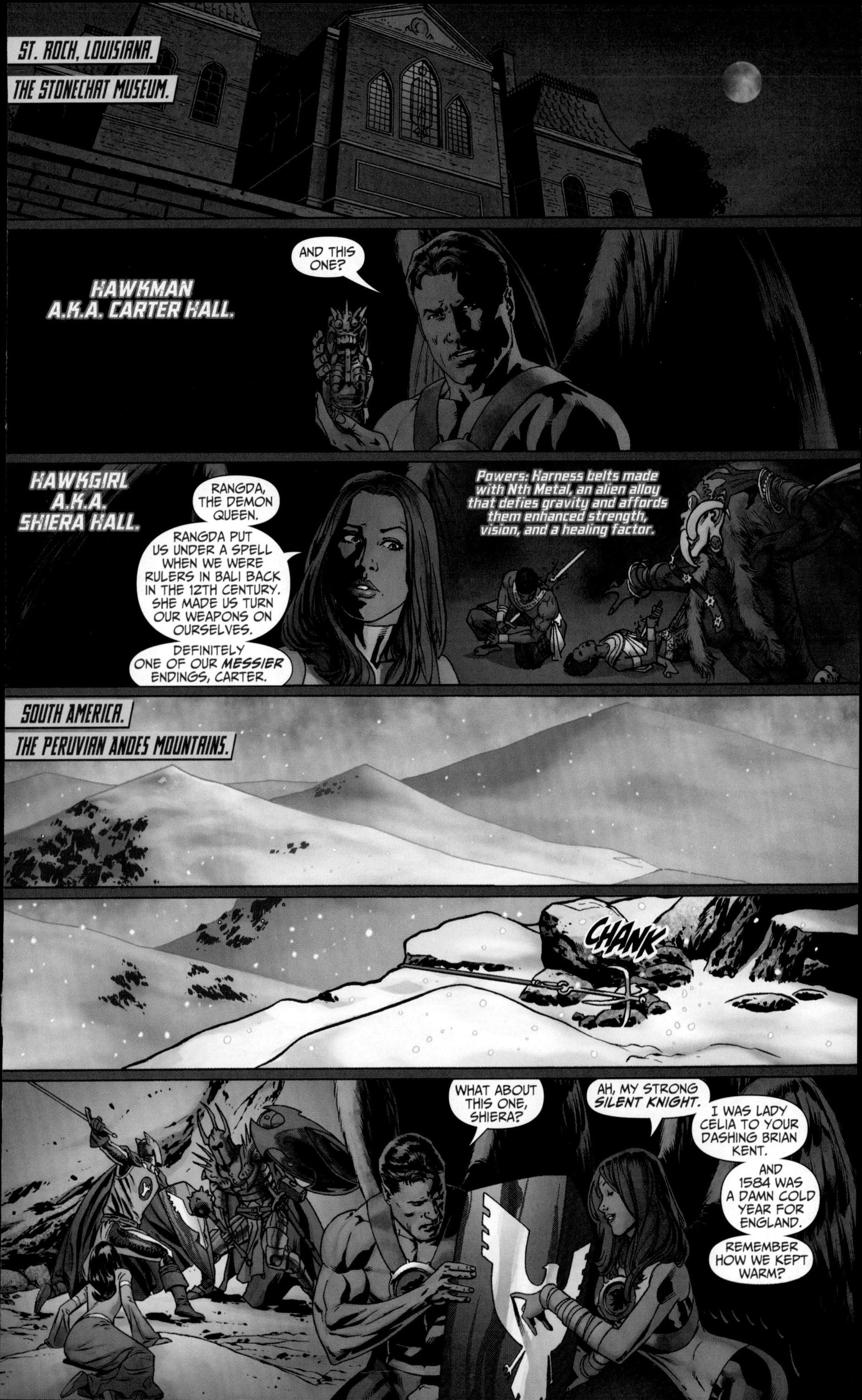
ST. ROCH, LOUISIANA.
THE STONECHAT MUSEUM.
AND THIS ONE?
HAWKMAN A.K.A. CARTER HALL.
HAWKGIRL A.K.A. SHIERA HALL.
RANGDA, THE DEMON QUEEN.
RANGDA PUT US UNDER A SPELL WHEN WE WERE RULERS IN BALI BACK IN THE 12TH CENTURY. SHE MADE US TURN OUR WEAPONS ON OURSELVES.
DEFINITELY ONE OF OUR MESSIER ENDINGS, CARTER.
Powers: Harness belts made with Nth Metal, an alien alloy that defies gravity and affords them enhanced strength, vision, and a healing factor.
SOUTH AMERICA.
THE PERUVIAN ANDES MOUNTAINS.
CHANK
WHAT ABOUT THIS ONE, SHIERA?
AH, MY STRONG SILENT KNIGHT.
I WAS LADY CELIA TO YOUR DASHING BRIAN KENT.
AND 1584 WAS A DAMN COLD YEAR FOR ENGLAND.
REMEMBER HOW WE KEPT WARM?

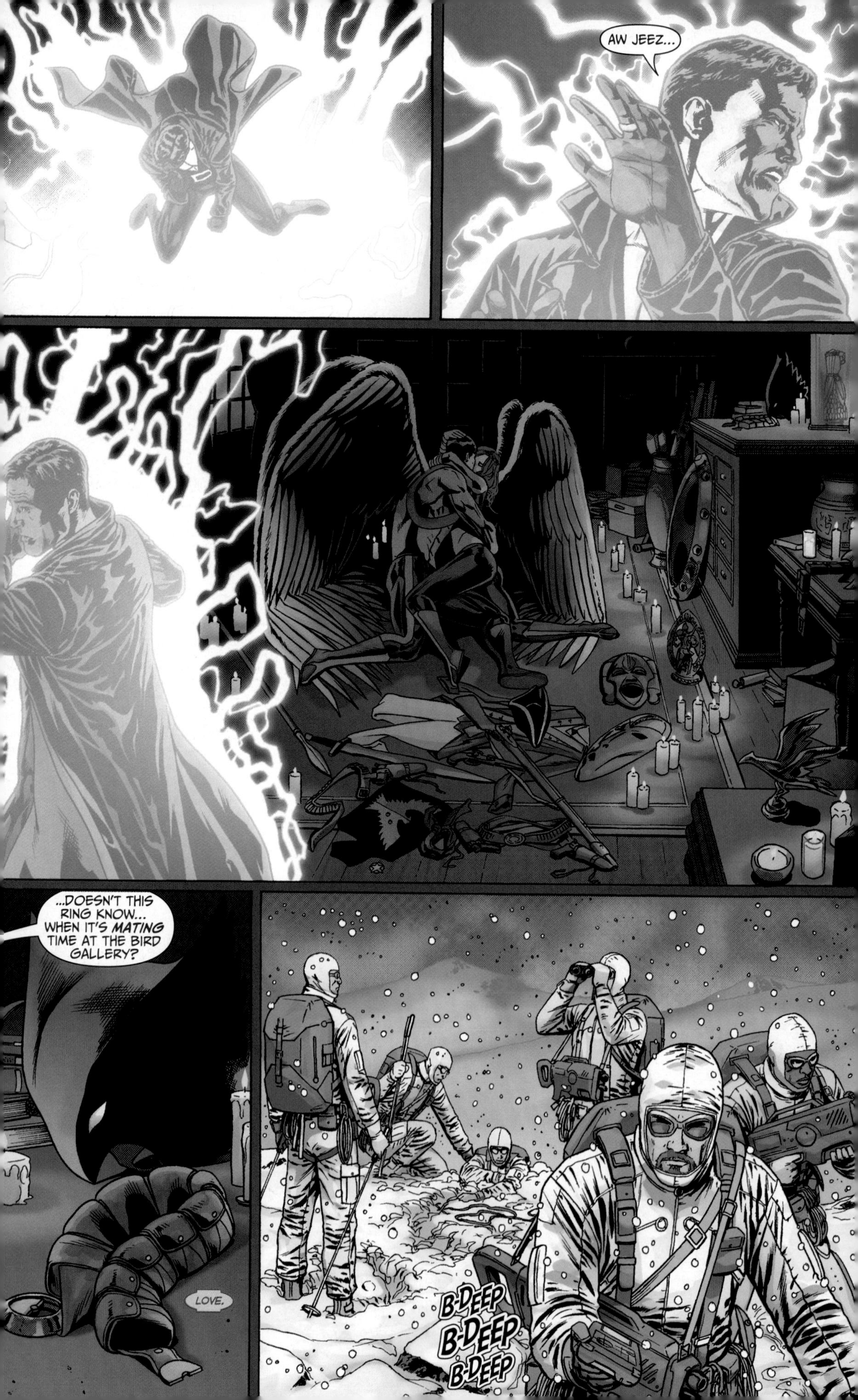
AW JEEZ...
...DOESN'T THIS RING KNOW... WHEN IT'S *MATING* TIME AT THE BIRD GALLERY?
LOVE.
B-DEEP
B-DEEP
B-DEEP

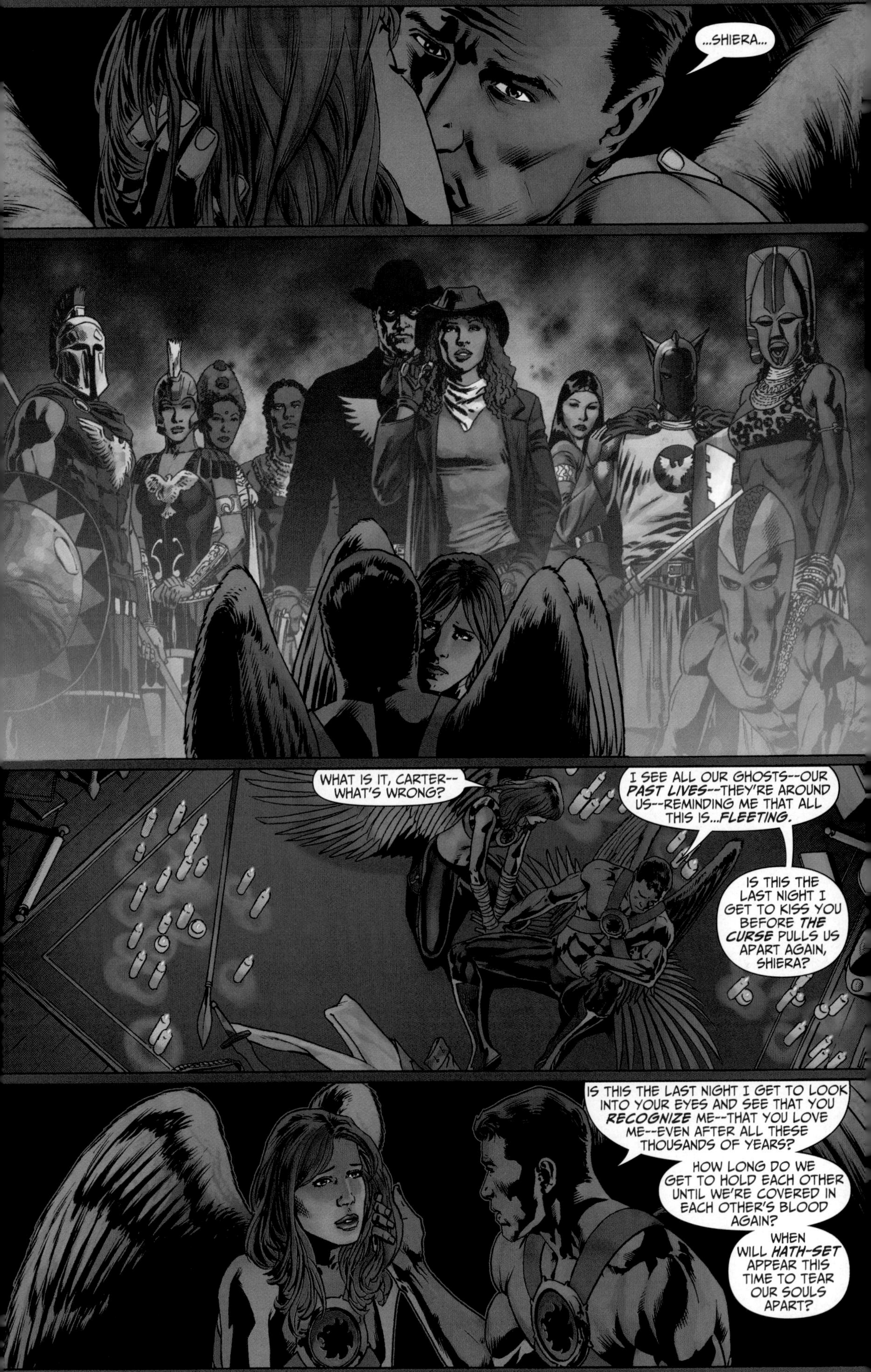
...SHIERA...
WHAT IS IT, CARTER--WHAT'S WRONG?
I SEE ALL OUR GHOSTS--OUR PAST LIVES--THEY'RE AROUND US--REMINDING ME THAT ALL THIS IS...FLEETING.
IS THIS THE LAST NIGHT I GET TO KISS YOU BEFORE THE CURSE PULLS US APART AGAIN, SHIERA?
IS THIS THE LAST NIGHT I GET TO LOOK INTO YOUR EYES AND SEE THAT YOU RECOGNIZE ME--THAT YOU LOVE ME--EVEN AFTER ALL THESE THOUSANDS OF YEARS?
HOW LONG DO WE GET TO HOLD EACH OTHER UNTIL WE'RE COVERED IN EACH OTHER'S BLOOD AGAIN?
WHEN WILL HATH-SET APPEAR THIS TIME TO TEAR OUR SOULS APART?

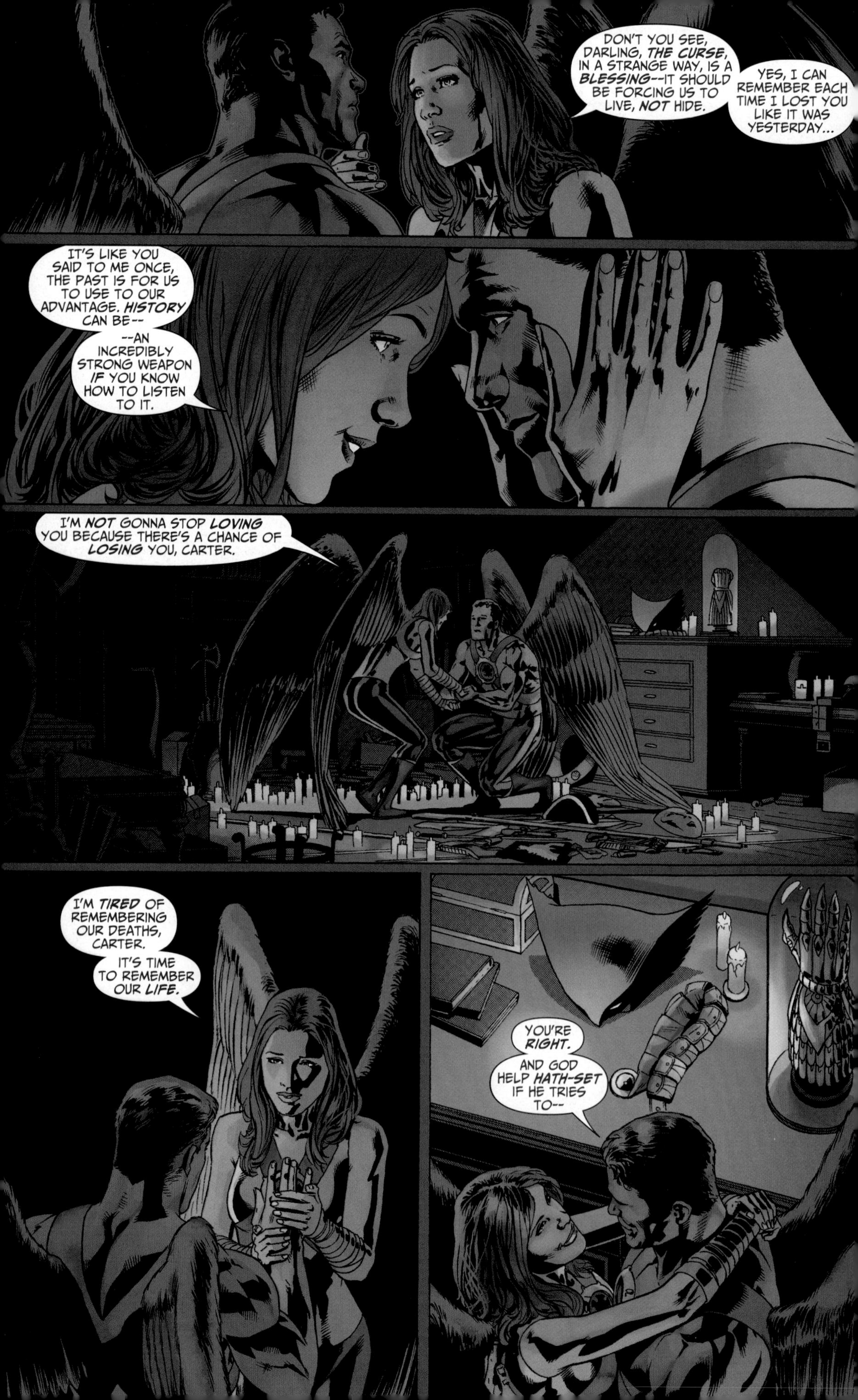
DON'T YOU SEE, DARLING, THE CURSE, IN A STRANGE WAY, IS A BLESSING--IT SHOULD BE FORCING US TO LIVE, NOT HIDE.
YES, I CAN REMEMBER EACH TIME I LOST YOU LIKE IT WAS YESTERDAY...
IT'S LIKE YOU SAID TO ME ONCE, THE PAST IS FOR US TO USE TO OUR ADVANTAGE. HISTORY CAN BE--
--AN INCREDIBLY STRONG WEAPON IF YOU KNOW HOW TO LISTEN TO IT.
I'M NOT GONNA STOP LOVING YOU BECAUSE THERE'S A CHANCE OF LOSING YOU, CARTER.
I'M TIRED OF REMEMBERING OUR DEATHS, CARTER.
IT'S TIME TO REMEMBER OUR LIFE.
YOU'RE RIGHT.
AND GOD HELP HATH-SET IF HE TRIES TO--

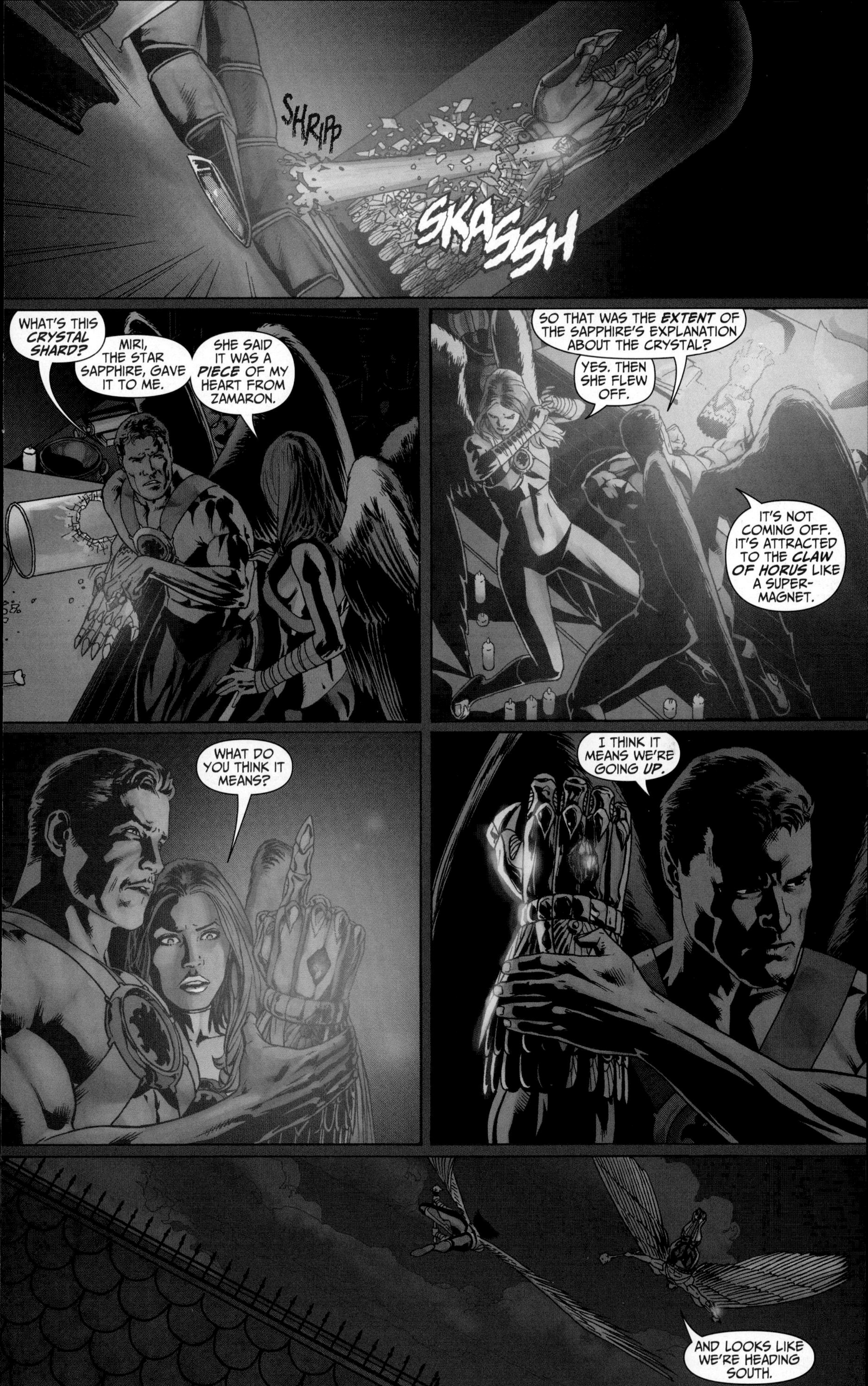
SHRIPP
SKASSH
WHAT'S THIS CRYSTAL SHARD?
MIRI, THE STAR SAPPHIRE, GAVE IT TO ME.
SHE SAID IT WAS A PIECE OF MY HEART FROM ZAMARON.
SO THAT WAS THE EXTENT OF THE SAPPHIRE'S EXPLANATION ABOUT THE CRYSTAL?
YES. THEN SHE FLEW OFF.
IT'S NOT COMING OFF. IT'S ATTRACTED TO THE CLAW OF HORUS LIKE A SUPER-MAGNET.
WHAT DO YOU THINK IT MEANS?
I THINK IT MEANS WE'RE GOING UP.
AND LOOKS LIKE WE'RE HEADING SOUTH.

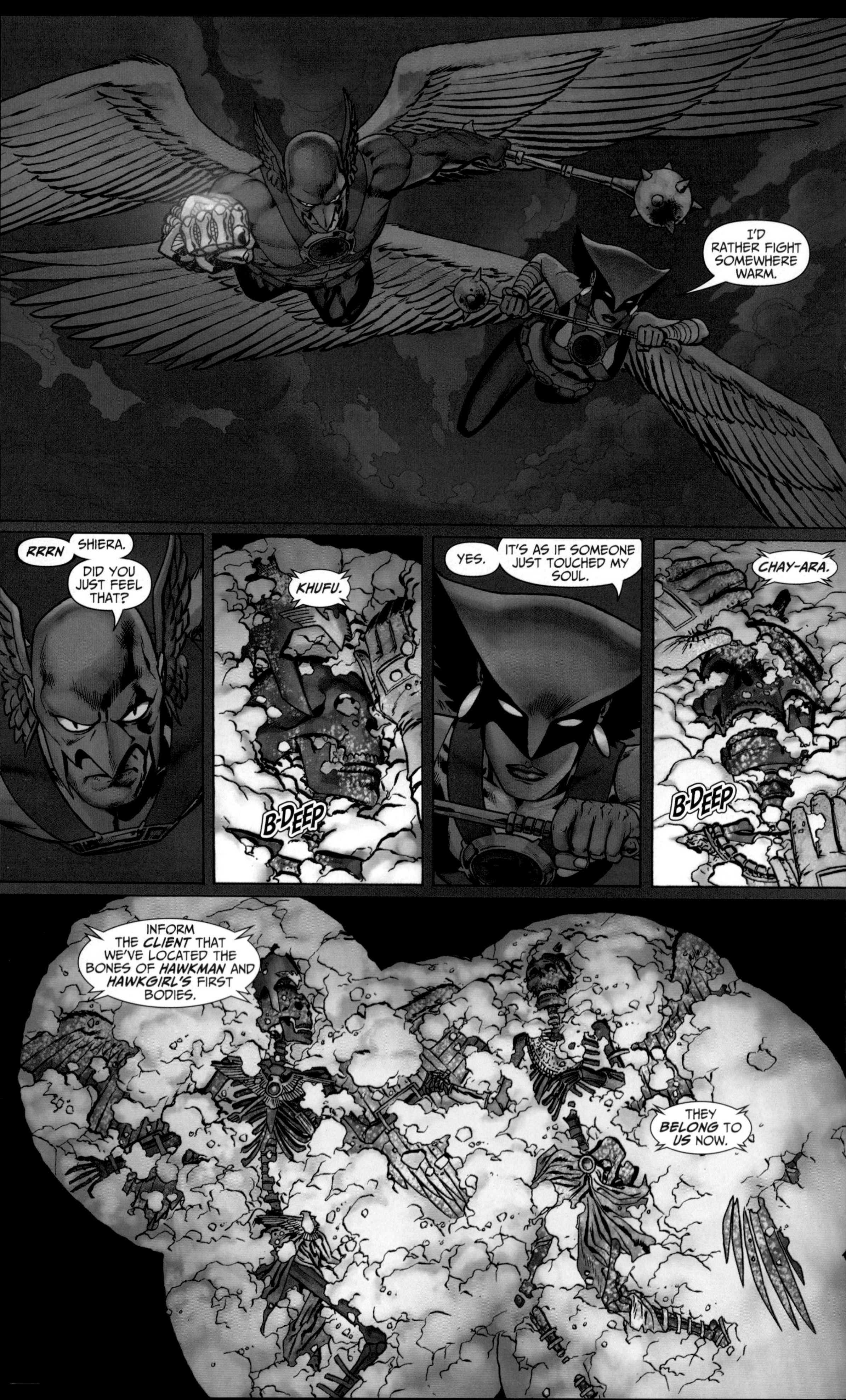
I'D RATHER FIGHT SOMEWHERE WARM.
RRRN
SHIERA.
DID YOU JUST FEEL THAT?
KHUFU.
B-DEEP
YES.
IT'S AS IF SOMEONE JUST TOUCHED MY SOUL.
CHAY-ARA.
B-DEEP
INFORM THE CLIENT THAT WE'VE LOCATED THE BONES OF HAWKMAN AND HAWKGIRL'S FIRST BODIES.
THEY BELONG TO US NOW.

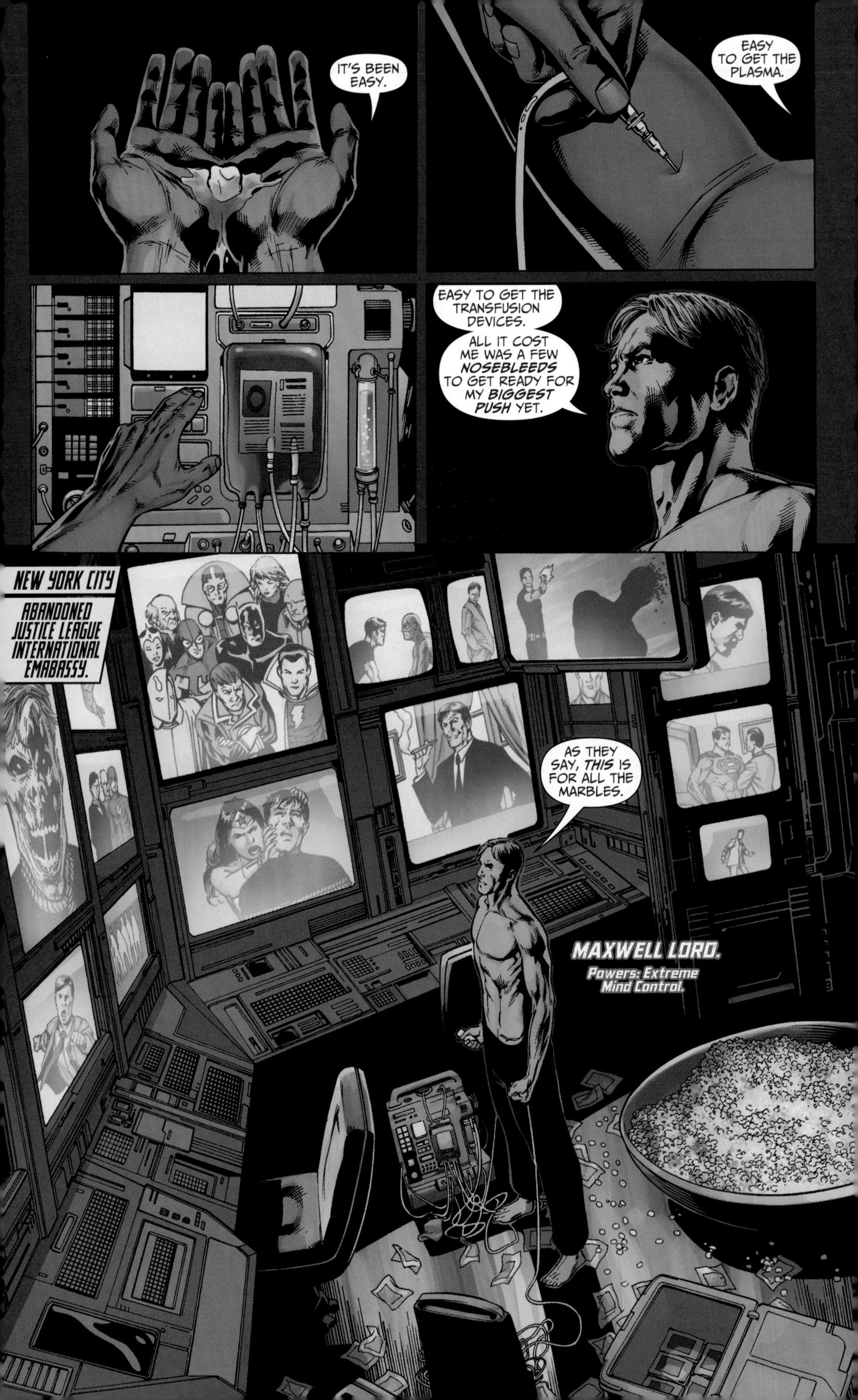
IT'S BEEN EASY.
EASY TO GET THE PLASMA.
EASY TO GET THE TRANSFUSION DEVICES.
ALL IT COST ME WAS A FEW NOSEBLEEDS TO GET READY FOR MY BIGGEST PUSH YET.
NEW YORK CITY
ABANDONED JUSTICE LEAGUE INTERNATIONAL EMABASSY.
AS THEY SAY, THIS IS FOR ALL THE MARBLES.
MAXWELL LORD.
Powers: Extreme Mind Control.

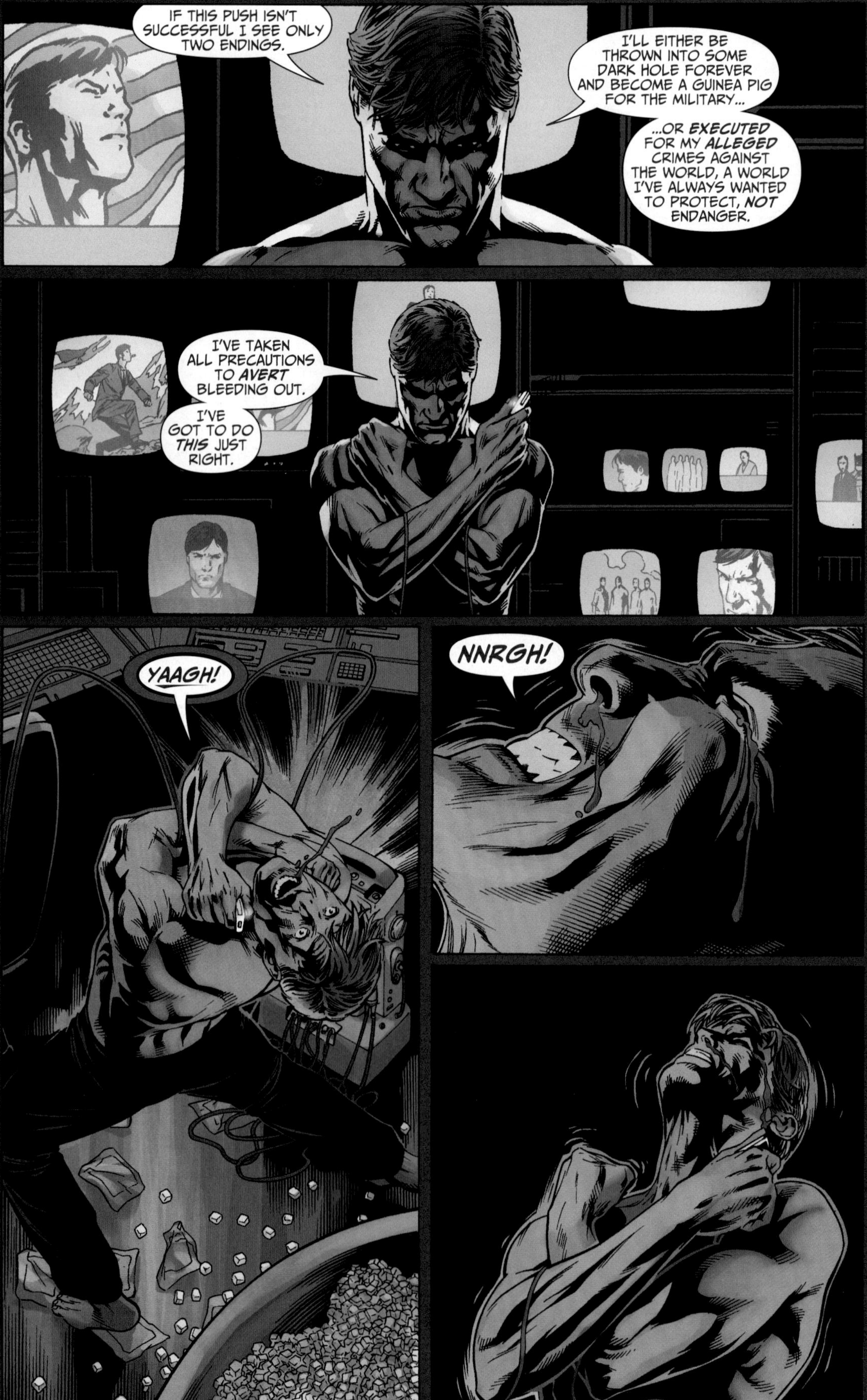
IF THIS PUSH ISN'T SUCCESSFUL I SEE ONLY TWO ENDINGS.
I'LL EITHER BE THROWN INTO SOME DARK HOLE FOREVER AND BECOME A GUINEA PIG FOR THE MILITARY...
...OR EXECUTED FOR MY ALLEGED CRIMES AGAINST THE WORLD, A WORLD I'VE ALWAYS WANTED TO PROTECT, NOT ENDANGER.
I'VE TAKEN ALL PRECAUTIONS TO AVERT BLEEDING OUT.
I'VE GOT TO DO THIS JUST RIGHT.
YAAGH!
NNRGH!

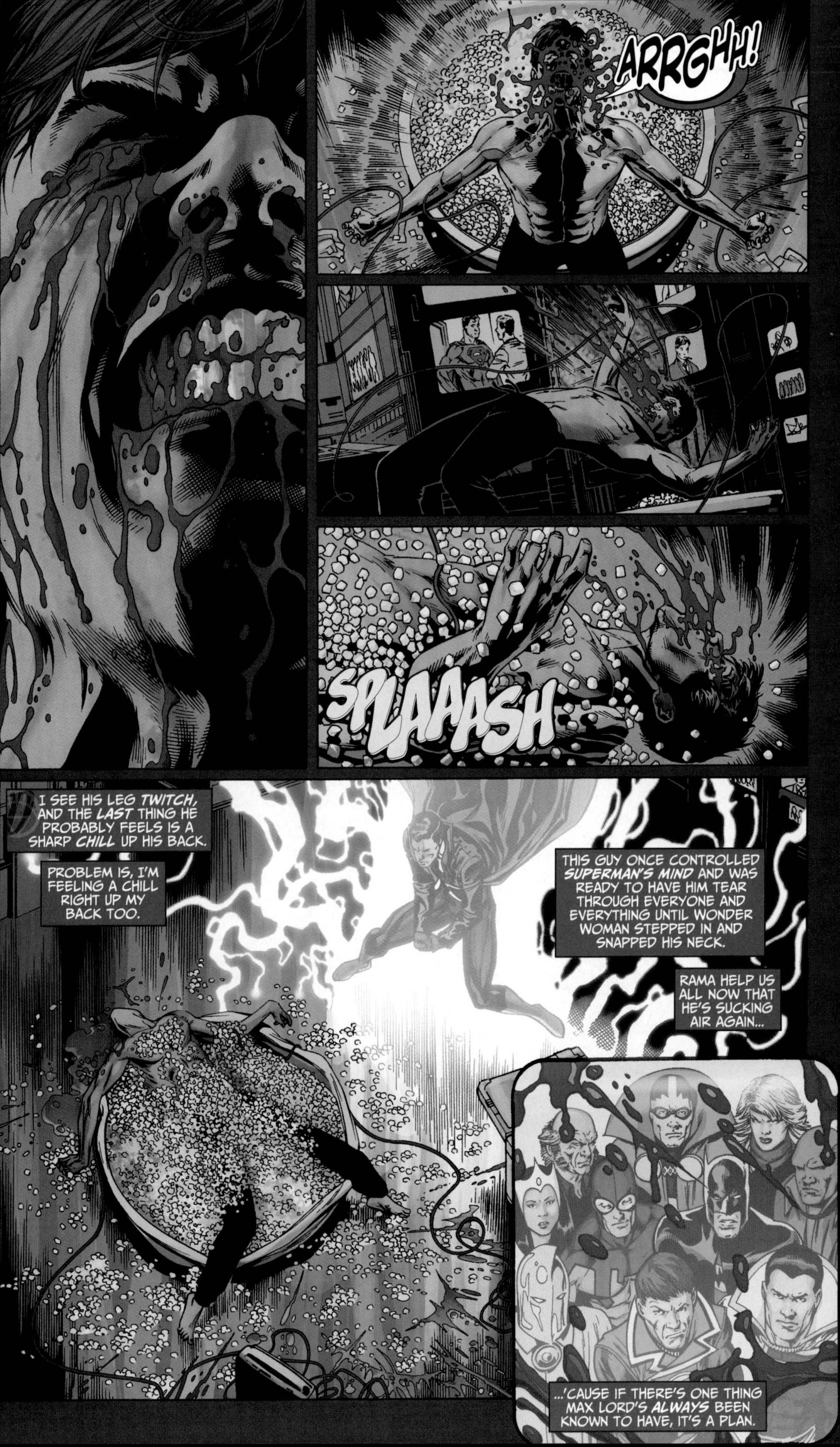
ARRGHH!
SPLAAAASH
I SEE HIS LEG TWITCH, AND THE LAST THING HE PROBABLY FEELS IS A SHARP CHILL UP HIS BACK.
PROBLEM IS, I'M FEELING A CHILL RIGHT UP MY BACK TOO.
THIS GUY ONCE CONTROLLED SUPERMAN'S MIND AND WAS READY TO HAVE HIM TEAR THROUGH EVERYONE AND EVERYTHING UNTIL WONDER WOMAN STEPPED IN AND SNAPPED HIS NECK.
RAMA HELP US ALL NOW THAT HE'S SUCKING AIR AGAIN...
...'CAUSE IF THERE'S ONE THING MAX LORD'S ALWAYS BEEN KNOWN TO HAVE, IT'S A PLAN.

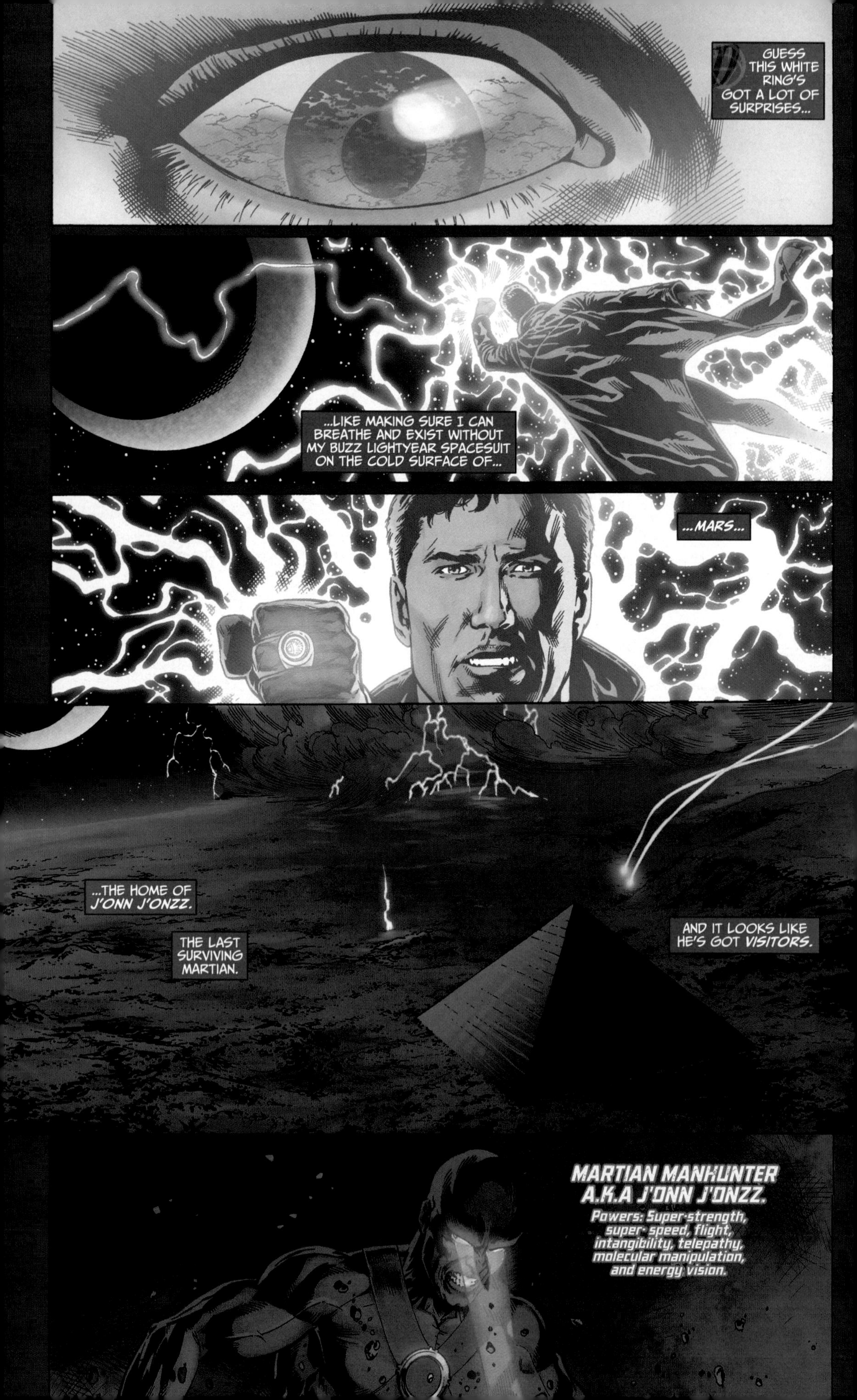
GUESS THIS WHITE RING'S GOT A LOT OF SURPRISES...
...LIKE MAKING SURE I CAN BREATHE AND EXIST WITHOUT MY BUZZ LIGHTYEAR SPACESUIT ON THE COLD SURFACE OF...
...MARS...
...THE HOME OF J'ONN J'ONZZ.
THE LAST SURVIVING MARTIAN.
AND IT LOOKS LIKE HE'S GOT VISITORS.
MARTIAN MANHUNTER A.K.A J'ONN J'ONZZ.
Powers: Super-strength, super-speed, flight, intangibility, telepathy, molecular manipulation, and energy vision.

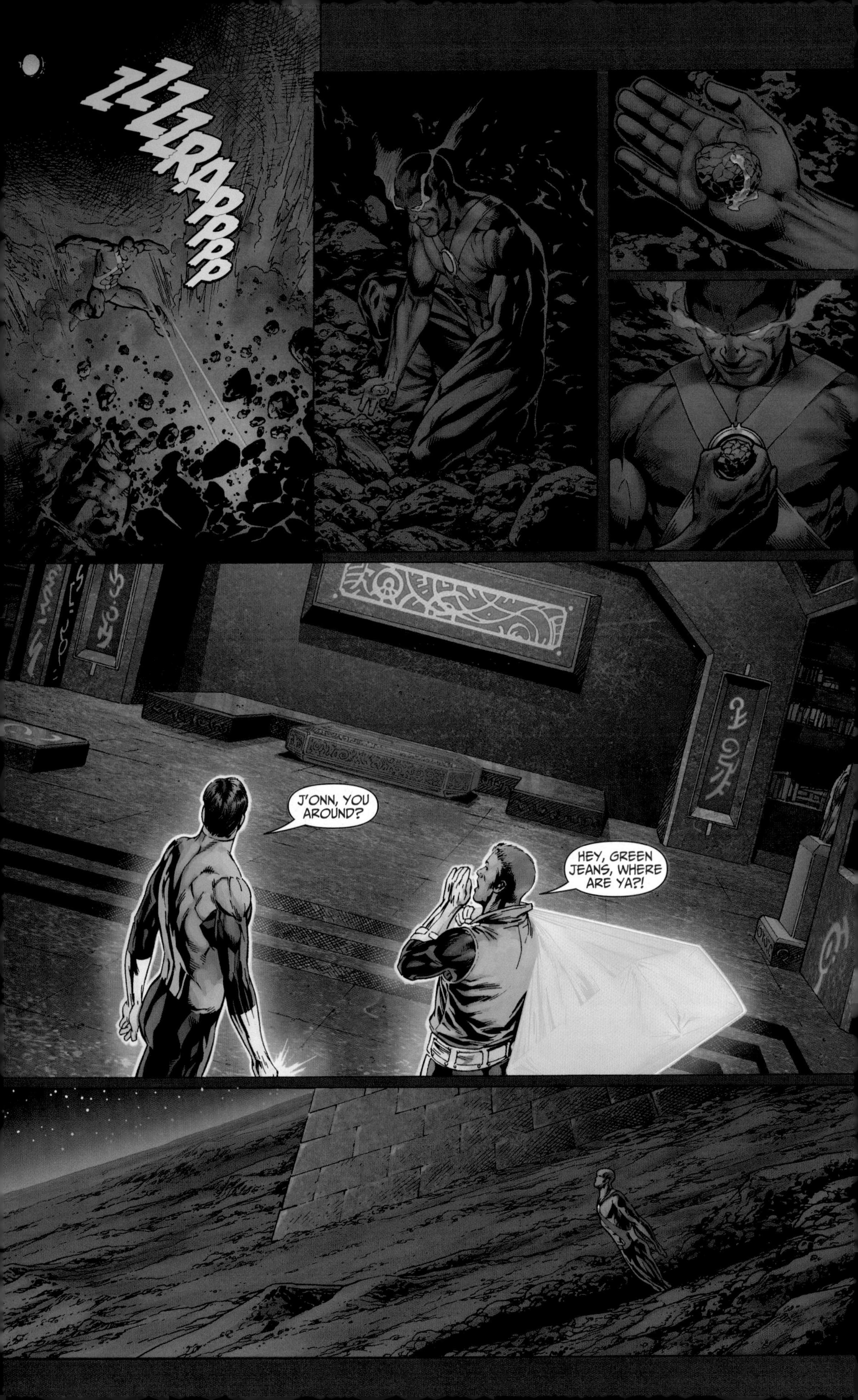
ZZZRAPPPP
J'ONN, YOU AROUND?
HEY, GREEN JEANS, WHERE ARE YA?!

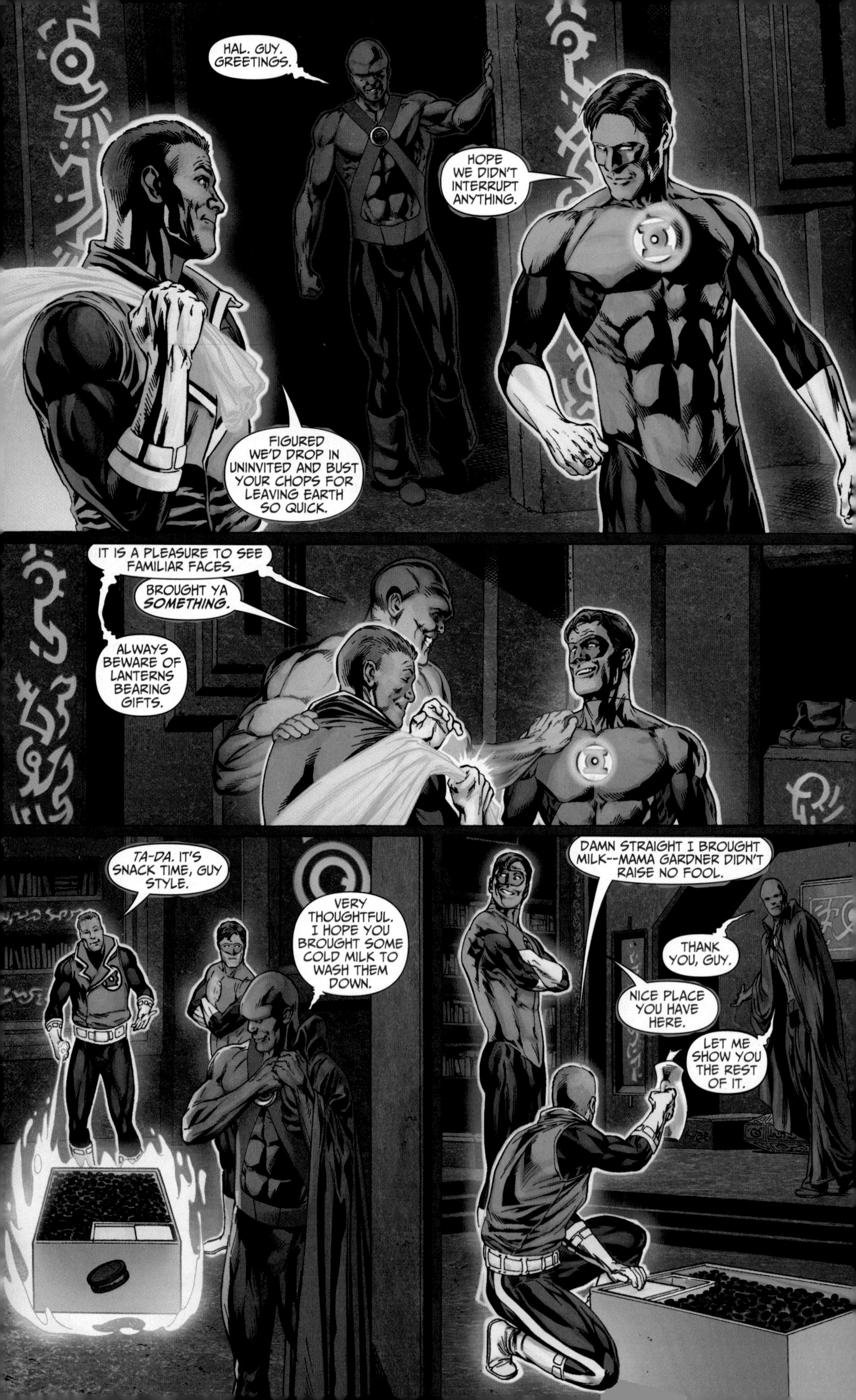
HAL. GUY. GREETINGS.
HOPE WE DIDN'T INTERRUPT ANYTHING.
FIGURED WE'D DROP IN UNINVITED AND BUST YOUR CHOPS FOR LEAVING EARTH SO QUICK.
IT IS A PLEASURE TO SEE FAMILIAR FACES.
BROUGHT YA *SOMETHING.*
ALWAYS BEWARE OF LANTERNS BEARING GIFTS.
*TA-DA.* IT'S SNACK TIME, GUY STYLE.
VERY THOUGHTFUL. I HOPE YOU BROUGHT SOME COLD MILK TO WASH THEM DOWN.
DAMN STRAIGHT I BROUGHT MILK--MAMA GARDNER DIDN'T RAISE NO FOOL.
THANK YOU, GUY.
NICE PLACE YOU HAVE HERE.
LET ME SHOW YOU THE REST OF IT.

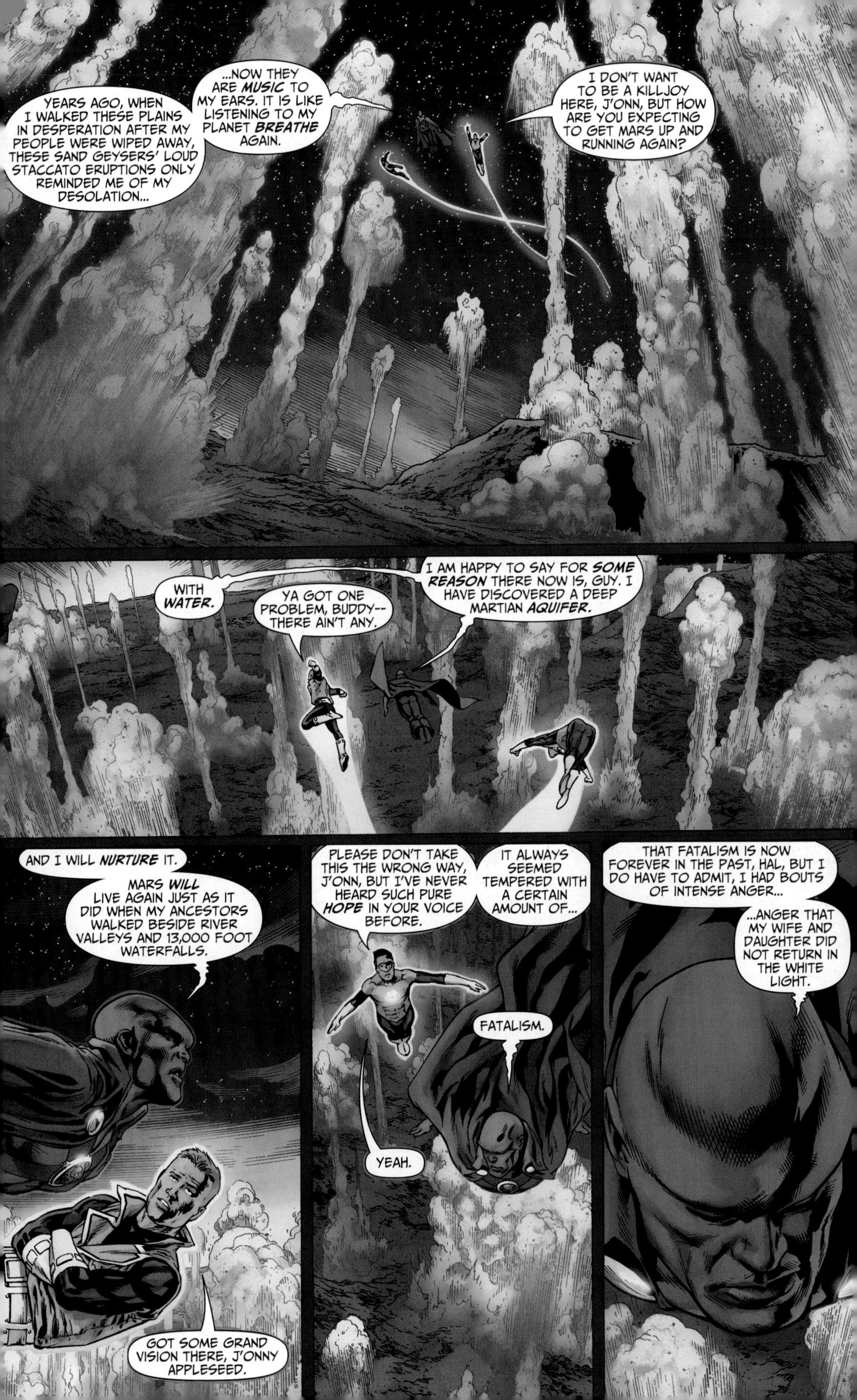

YEARS AGO, WHEN I WALKED THESE PLAINS IN DESPERATION AFTER MY PEOPLE WERE WIPED AWAY, THESE SAND GEYSERS' LOUD STACCATO ERUPTIONS ONLY REMINDED ME OF MY DESOLATION...
...NOW THEY ARE MUSIC TO MY EARS. IT IS LIKE LISTENING TO MY PLANET BREATHE AGAIN.
I DON'T WANT TO BE A KILLJOY HERE, J'ONN, BUT HOW ARE YOU EXPECTING TO GET MARS UP AND RUNNING AGAIN?
WITH WATER.
YA GOT ONE PROBLEM, BUDDY-- THERE AIN'T ANY.
I AM HAPPY TO SAY FOR SOME REASON THERE NOW IS, GUY. I HAVE DISCOVERED A DEEP MARTIAN AQUIFER.
AND I WILL NURTURE IT.
MARS WILL LIVE AGAIN JUST AS IT DID WHEN MY ANCESTORS WALKED BESIDE RIVER VALLEYS AND 13,000 FOOT WATERFALLS.
GOT SOME GRAND VISION THERE, J'ONNY APPLESEED.
PLEASE DON'T TAKE THIS THE WRONG WAY, J'ONN, BUT I'VE NEVER HEARD SUCH PURE HOPE IN YOUR VOICE BEFORE.
IT ALWAYS SEEMED TEMPERED WITH A CERTAIN AMOUNT OF...
FATALISM.
YEAH.
THAT FATALISM IS NOW FOREVER IN THE PAST, HAL, BUT I DO HAVE TO ADMIT, I HAD BOUTS OF INTENSE ANGER...
...ANGER THAT MY WIFE AND DAUGHTER DID NOT RETURN IN THE WHITE LIGHT.

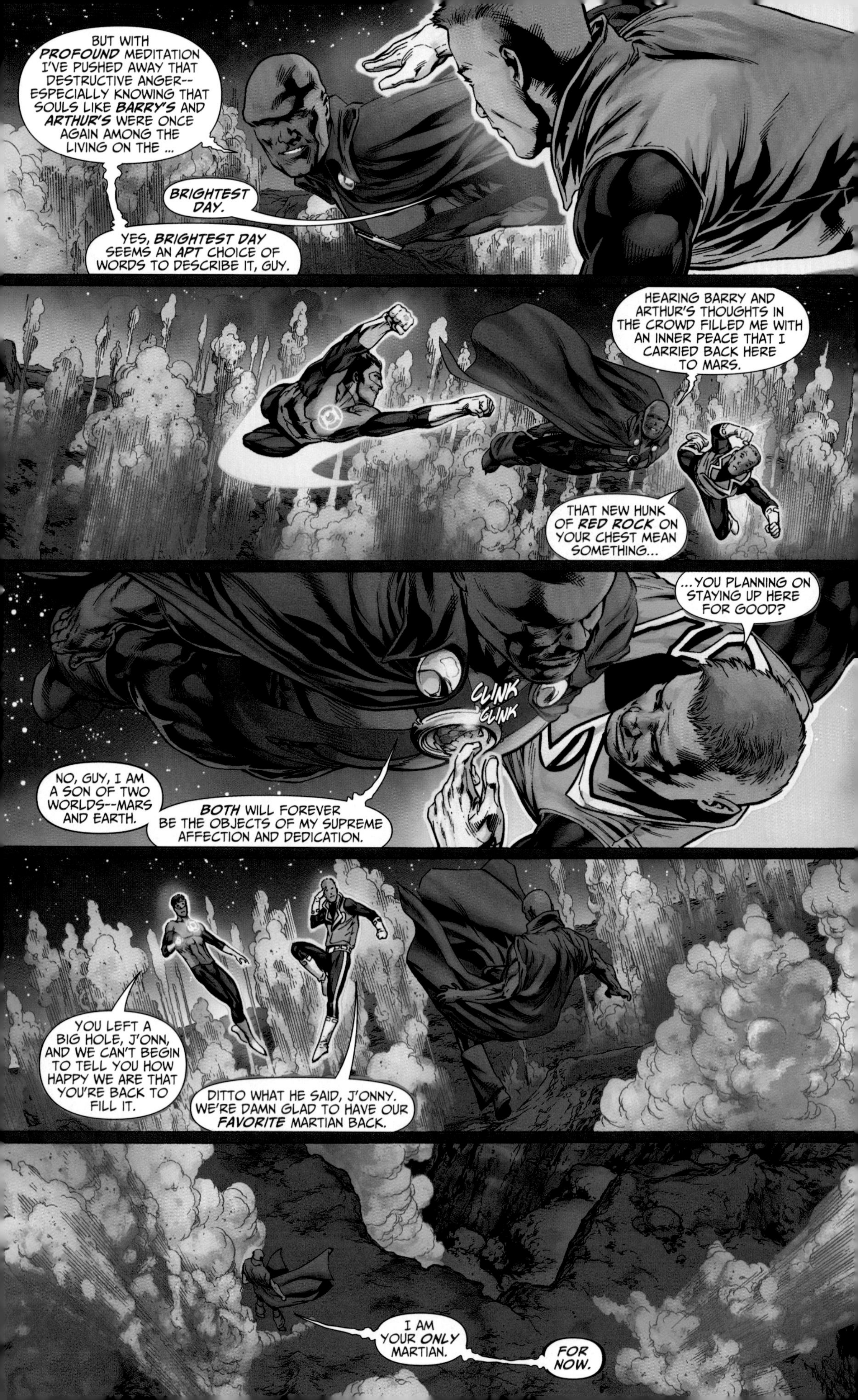
BUT WITH PROFOUND MEDITATION I'VE PUSHED AWAY THAT DESTRUCTIVE ANGER--ESPECIALLY KNOWING THAT SOULS LIKE BARRY'S AND ARTHUR'S WERE ONCE AGAIN AMONG THE LIVING ON THE ...
BRIGHTEST DAY.
YES, BRIGHTEST DAY SEEMS AN APT CHOICE OF WORDS TO DESCRIBE IT, GUY.
HEARING BARRY AND ARTHUR'S THOUGHTS IN THE CROWD FILLED ME WITH AN INNER PEACE THAT I CARRIED BACK HERE TO MARS.
THAT NEW HUNK OF RED ROCK ON YOUR CHEST MEAN SOMETHING...
...YOU PLANNING ON STAYING UP HERE FOR GOOD?
CLINK
CLINK
NO, GUY, I AM A SON OF TWO WORLDS--MARS AND EARTH.
BOTH WILL FOREVER BE THE OBJECTS OF MY SUPREME AFFECTION AND DEDICATION.
YOU LEFT A BIG HOLE, J'ONN, AND WE CAN'T BEGIN TO TELL YOU HOW HAPPY WE ARE THAT YOU'RE BACK TO FILL IT.
DITTO WHAT HE SAID, J'ONNY. WE'RE DAMN GLAD TO HAVE OUR FAVORITE MARTIAN BACK.
I AM YOUR ONLY MARTIAN.
FOR NOW.

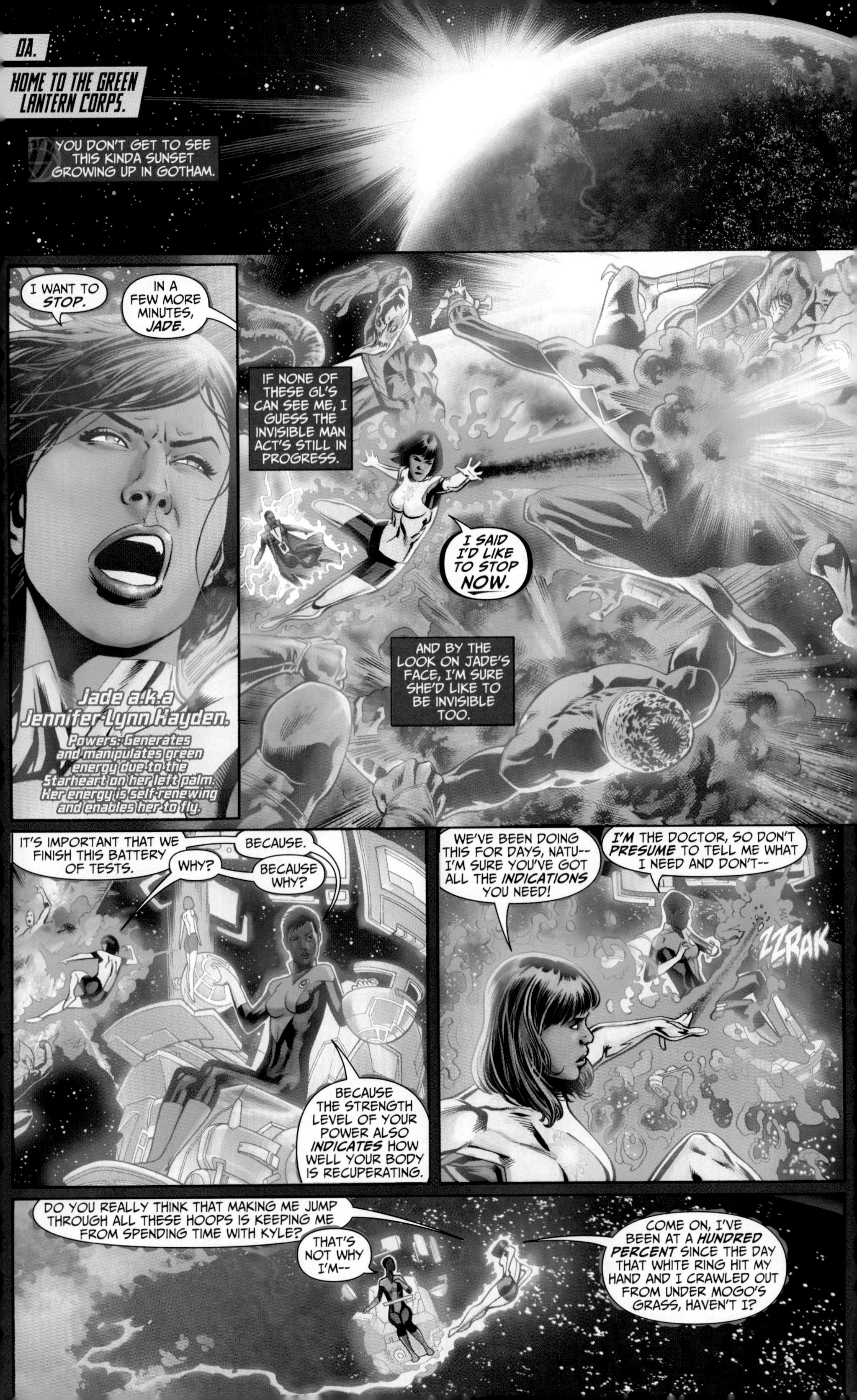
OA.
HOME TO THE GREEN LANTERN CORPS.
YOU DON'T GET TO SEE THIS KINDA SUNSET GROWING UP IN GOTHAM.
I WANT TO STOP.
IN A FEW MORE MINUTES, JADE.
Jade a.k.a Jennifer-Lynn Hayden.
Powers: Generates and manipulates green energy due to the Starheart on her left palm. Her energy is self-renewing and enables her to fly.
IF NONE OF THESE GL'S CAN SEE ME, I GUESS THE INVISIBLE MAN ACT'S STILL IN PROGRESS.
I SAID I'D LIKE TO STOP NOW.
AND BY THE LOOK ON JADE'S FACE, I'M SURE SHE'D LIKE TO BE INVISIBLE TOO.
IT'S IMPORTANT THAT WE FINISH THIS BATTERY OF TESTS.
WHY?
BECAUSE.
BECAUSE WHY?
BECAUSE THE STRENGTH LEVEL OF YOUR POWER ALSO INDICATES HOW WELL YOUR BODY IS RECUPERATING.
WE'VE BEEN DOING THIS FOR DAYS, NATU-- I'M SURE YOU'VE GOT ALL THE INDICATIONS YOU NEED!
I'M THE DOCTOR, SO DON'T PRESUME TO TELL ME WHAT I NEED AND DON'T--
ZZRAK
DO YOU REALLY THINK THAT MAKING ME JUMP THROUGH ALL THESE HOOPS IS KEEPING ME FROM SPENDING TIME WITH KYLE?
THAT'S NOT WHY I'M--
COME ON, I'VE BEEN AT A HUNDRED PERCENT SINCE THE DAY THAT WHITE RING HIT MY HAND AND I CRAWLED OUT FROM UNDER MOGO'S GRASS, HAVEN'T I?

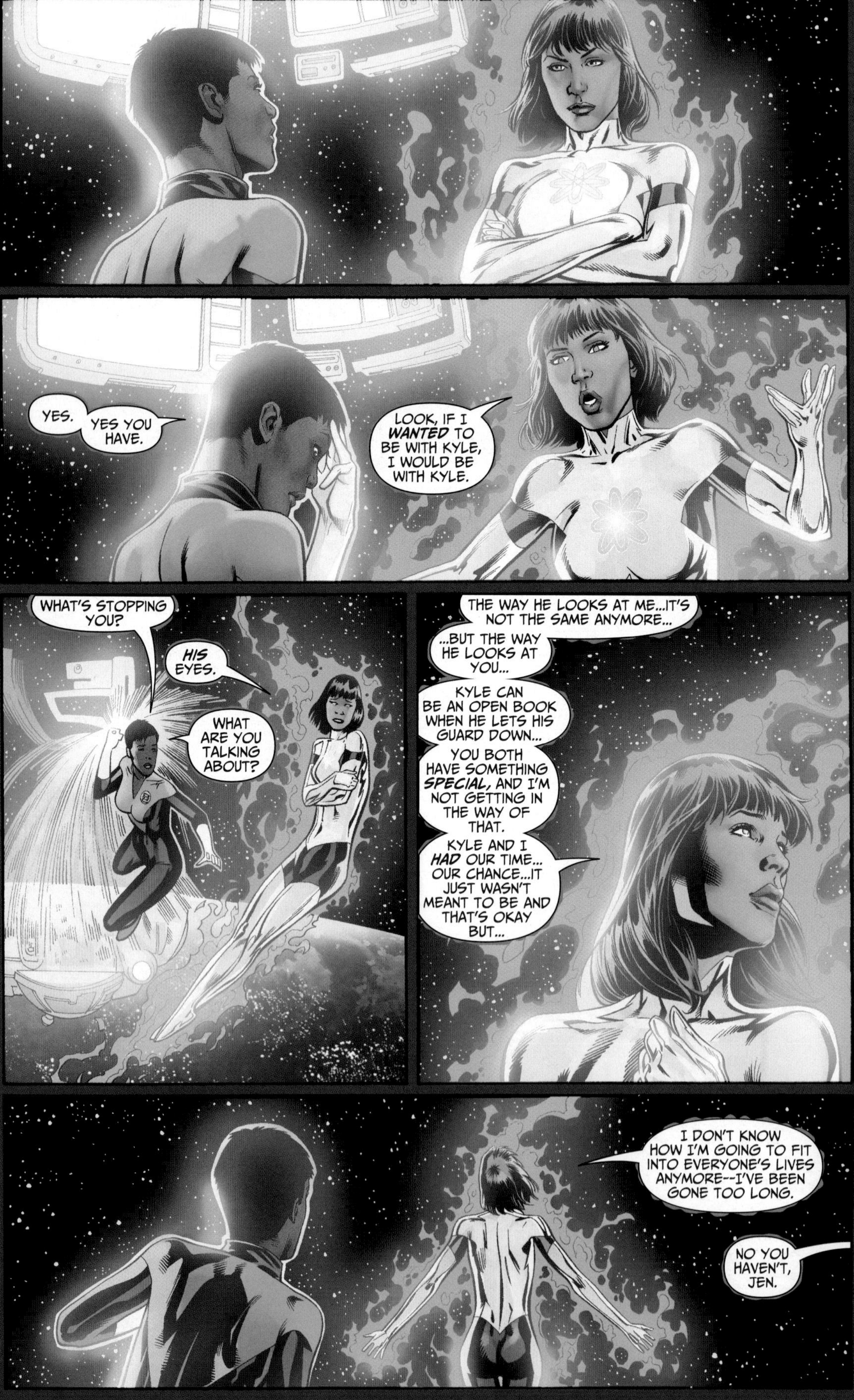
YES.
YES YOU HAVE.
LOOK, IF I **WANTED** TO BE WITH KYLE, I WOULD BE WITH KYLE.
WHAT'S STOPPING YOU?
**HIS** EYES.
WHAT ARE YOU TALKING ABOUT?
THE WAY HE LOOKS AT ME...IT'S NOT THE SAME ANYMORE...
...BUT THE WAY HE LOOKS AT YOU...
KYLE CAN BE AN OPEN BOOK WHEN HE LETS HIS GUARD DOWN...
YOU BOTH HAVE SOMETHING **SPECIAL,** AND I'M NOT GETTING IN THE WAY OF THAT.
KYLE AND I **HAD** OUR TIME... OUR CHANCE...IT JUST WASN'T MEANT TO BE AND THAT'S OKAY BUT...
I DON'T KNOW HOW I'M GOING TO FIT INTO EVERYONE'S LIVES ANYMORE--I'VE BEEN GONE TOO LONG.
NO YOU HAVEN'T, JEN.

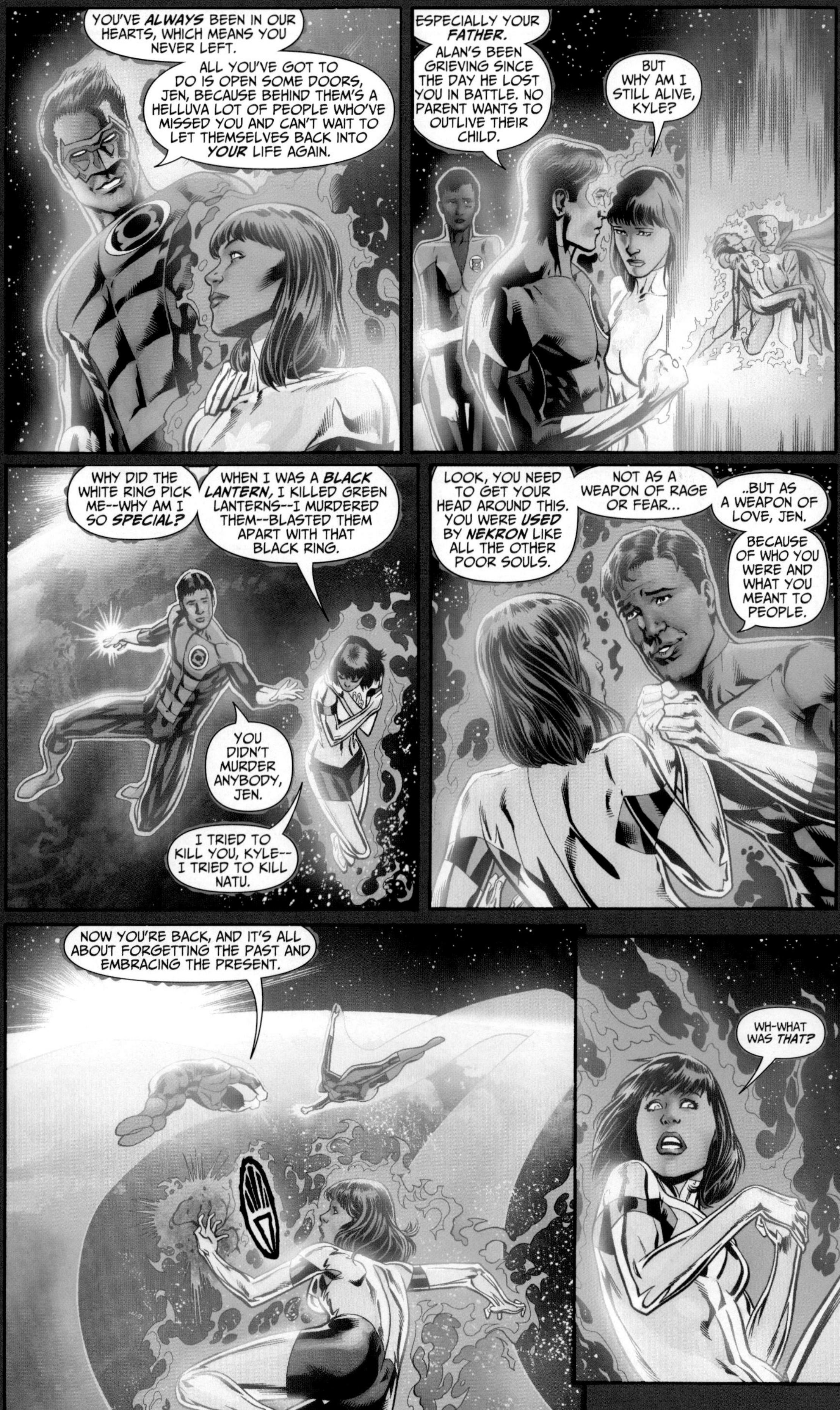
YOU'VE ALWAYS BEEN IN OUR HEARTS, WHICH MEANS YOU NEVER LEFT.
ALL YOU'VE GOT TO DO IS OPEN SOME DOORS, JEN, BECAUSE BEHIND THEM'S A HELLUVA LOT OF PEOPLE WHO'VE MISSED YOU AND CAN'T WAIT TO LET THEMSELVES BACK INTO YOUR LIFE AGAIN.
ESPECIALLY YOUR FATHER.
ALAN'S BEEN GRIEVING SINCE THE DAY HE LOST YOU IN BATTLE. NO PARENT WANTS TO OUTLIVE THEIR CHILD.
BUT WHY AM I STILL ALIVE, KYLE?
WHY DID THE WHITE RING PICK ME--WHY AM I SO SPECIAL?
WHEN I WAS A BLACK LANTERN, I KILLED GREEN LANTERNS--I MURDERED THEM--BLASTED THEM APART WITH THAT BLACK RING.
YOU DIDN'T MURDER ANYBODY, JEN.
I TRIED TO KILL YOU, KYLE-- I TRIED TO KILL NATU.
LOOK, YOU NEED TO GET YOUR HEAD AROUND THIS. YOU WERE USED BY NEKRON LIKE ALL THE OTHER POOR SOULS.
NOT AS A WEAPON OF RAGE OR FEAR...
..BUT AS A WEAPON OF LOVE, JEN.
BECAUSE OF WHO YOU WERE AND WHAT YOU MEANT TO PEOPLE.
NOW YOU'RE BACK, AND IT'S ALL ABOUT FORGETTING THE PAST AND EMBRACING THE PRESENT.
WH-WHAT WAS THAT?

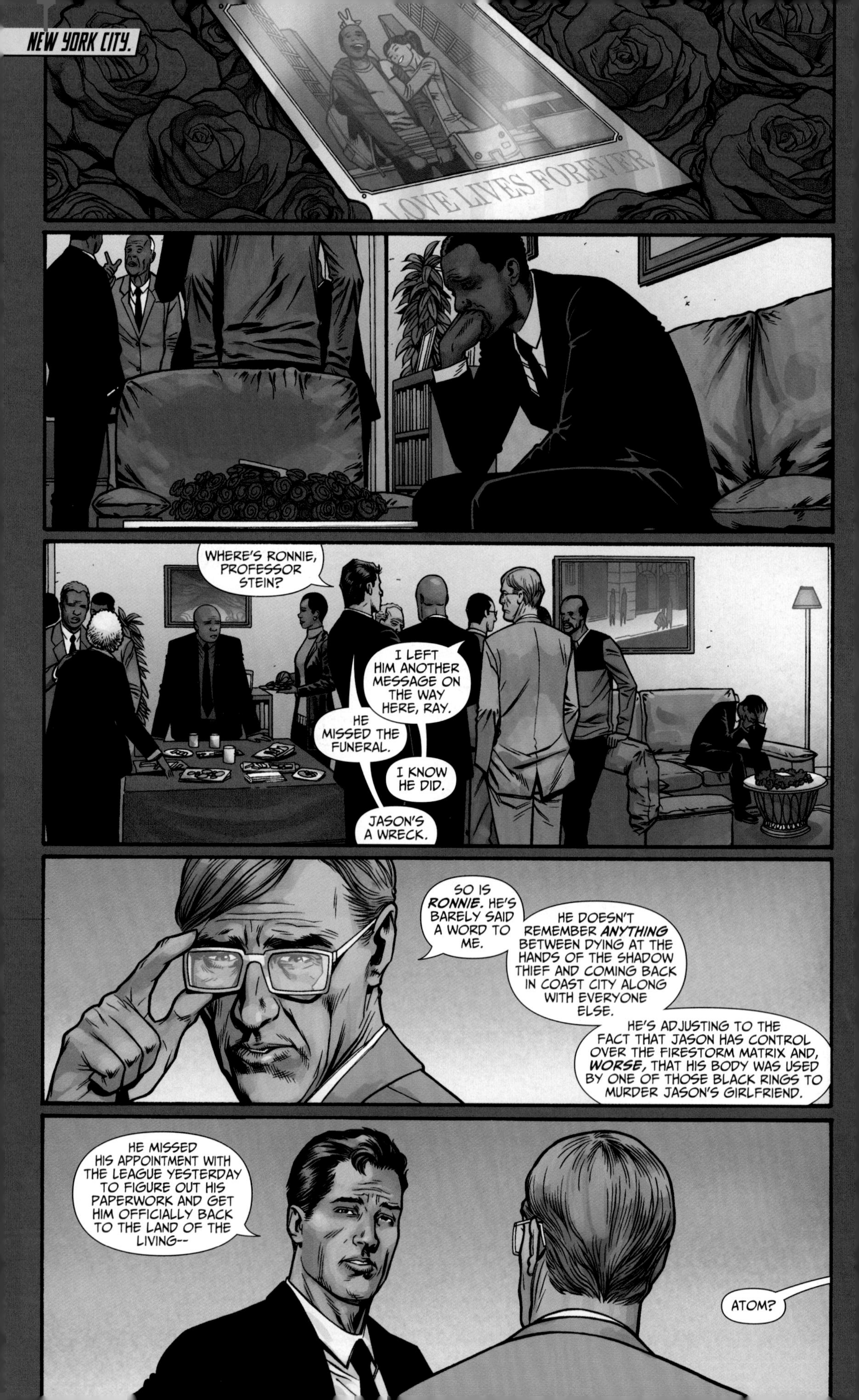
NEW YORK CITY.
LOVE LIVES FOREVER
WHERE'S RONNIE, PROFESSOR STEIN?
I LEFT HIM ANOTHER MESSAGE ON THE WAY HERE, RAY.
HE MISSED THE FUNERAL.
I KNOW HE DID.
JASON'S A WRECK.
SO IS RONNIE. HE'S BARELY SAID A WORD TO ME.
HE DOESN'T REMEMBER ANYTHING BETWEEN DYING AT THE HANDS OF THE SHADOW THIEF AND COMING BACK IN COAST CITY ALONG WITH EVERYONE ELSE.
HE'S ADJUSTING TO THE FACT THAT JASON HAS CONTROL OVER THE FIRESTORM MATRIX AND, WORSE, THAT HIS BODY WAS USED BY ONE OF THOSE BLACK RINGS TO MURDER JASON'S GIRLFRIEND.
HE MISSED HIS APPOINTMENT WITH THE LEAGUE YESTERDAY TO FIGURE OUT HIS PAPERWORK AND GET HIM OFFICIALLY BACK TO THE LAND OF THE LIVING--
ATOM?

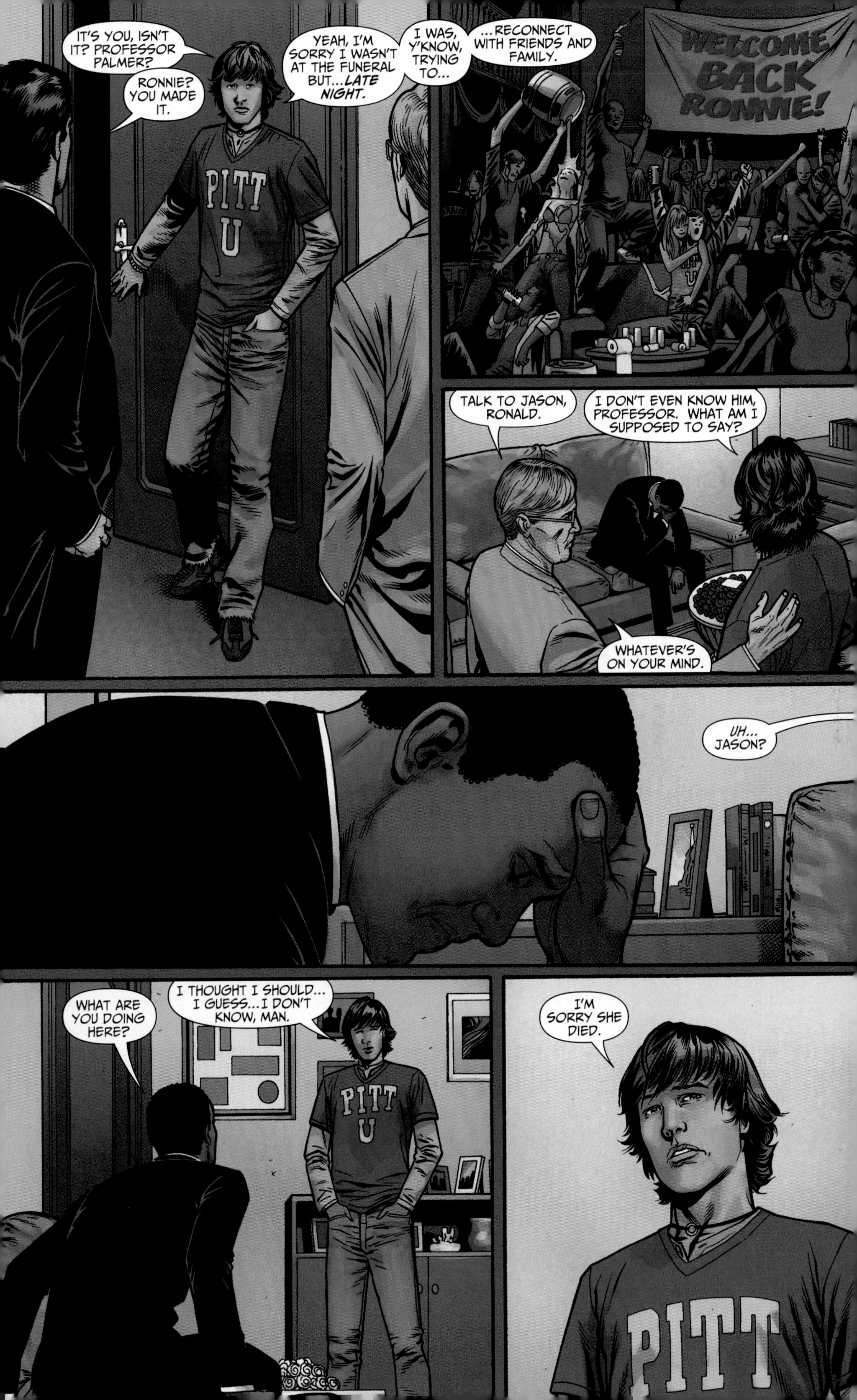
IT'S YOU, ISN'T IT? PROFESSOR PALMER?
RONNIE? YOU MADE IT.
YEAH, I'M SORRY I WASN'T AT THE FUNERAL BUT...LATE NIGHT.
I WAS, Y'KNOW, TRYING TO...
...RECONNECT WITH FRIENDS AND FAMILY.
WELCOME BACK RONNIE!
TALK TO JASON, RONALD.
I DON'T EVEN KNOW HIM, PROFESSOR. WHAT AM I SUPPOSED TO SAY?
WHATEVER'S ON YOUR MIND.
UH... JASON?
WHAT ARE YOU DOING HERE?
I THOUGHT I SHOULD... I GUESS...I DON'T KNOW, MAN.
I'M SORRY SHE DIED.

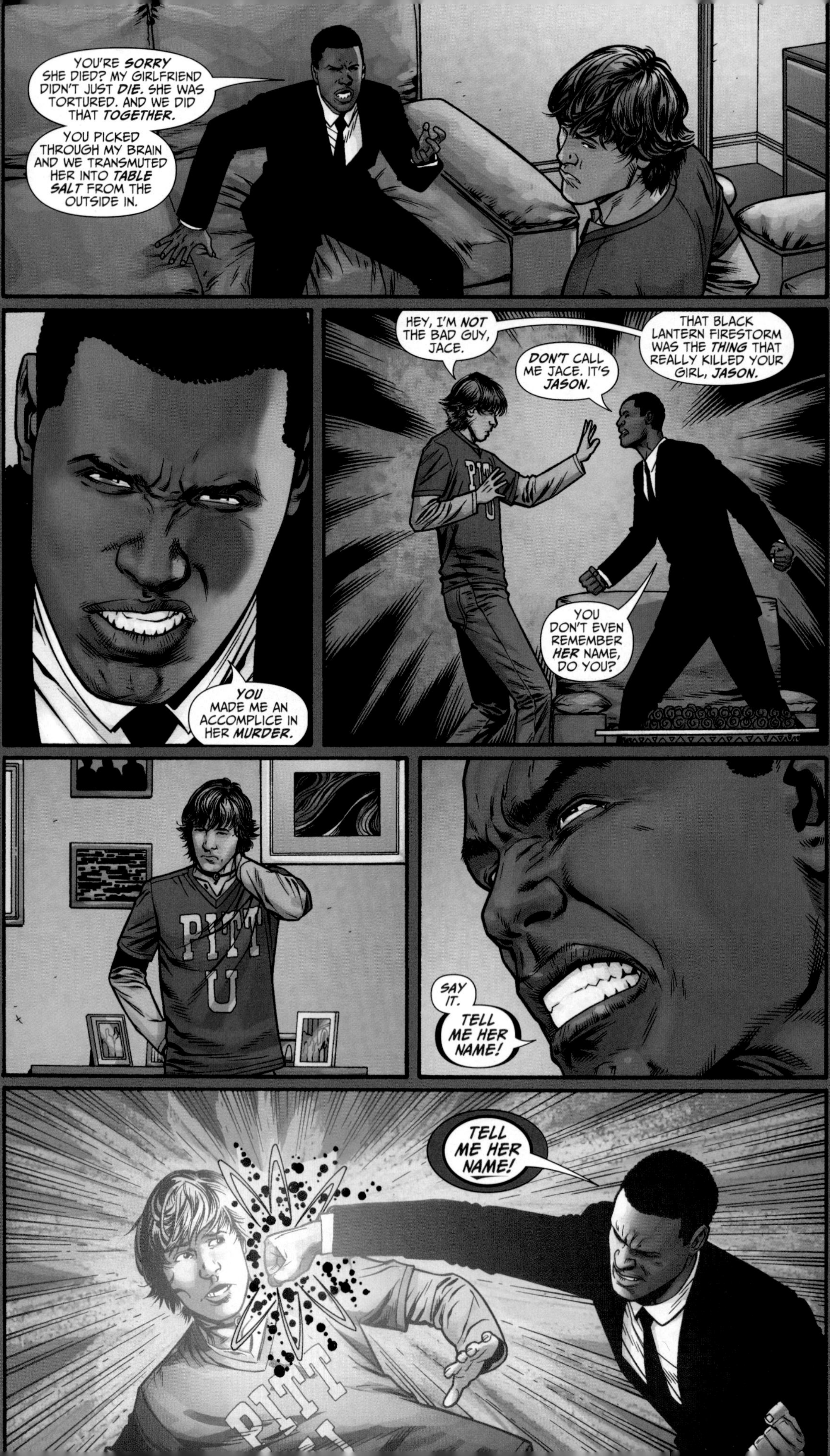
YOU'RE SORRY SHE DIED? MY GIRLFRIEND DIDN'T JUST DIE. SHE WAS TORTURED. AND WE DID THAT TOGETHER.
YOU PICKED THROUGH MY BRAIN AND WE TRANSMUTED HER INTO TABLE SALT FROM THE OUTSIDE IN.
YOU MADE ME AN ACCOMPLICE IN HER MURDER.
HEY, I'M NOT THE BAD GUY, JACE.
THAT BLACK LANTERN FIRESTORM WAS THE THING THAT REALLY KILLED YOUR GIRL, JASON.
DON'T CALL ME JACE. IT'S JASON.
YOU DON'T EVEN REMEMBER HER NAME, DO YOU?
PITT U
SAY IT.
TELL ME HER NAME!
TELL ME HER NAME!

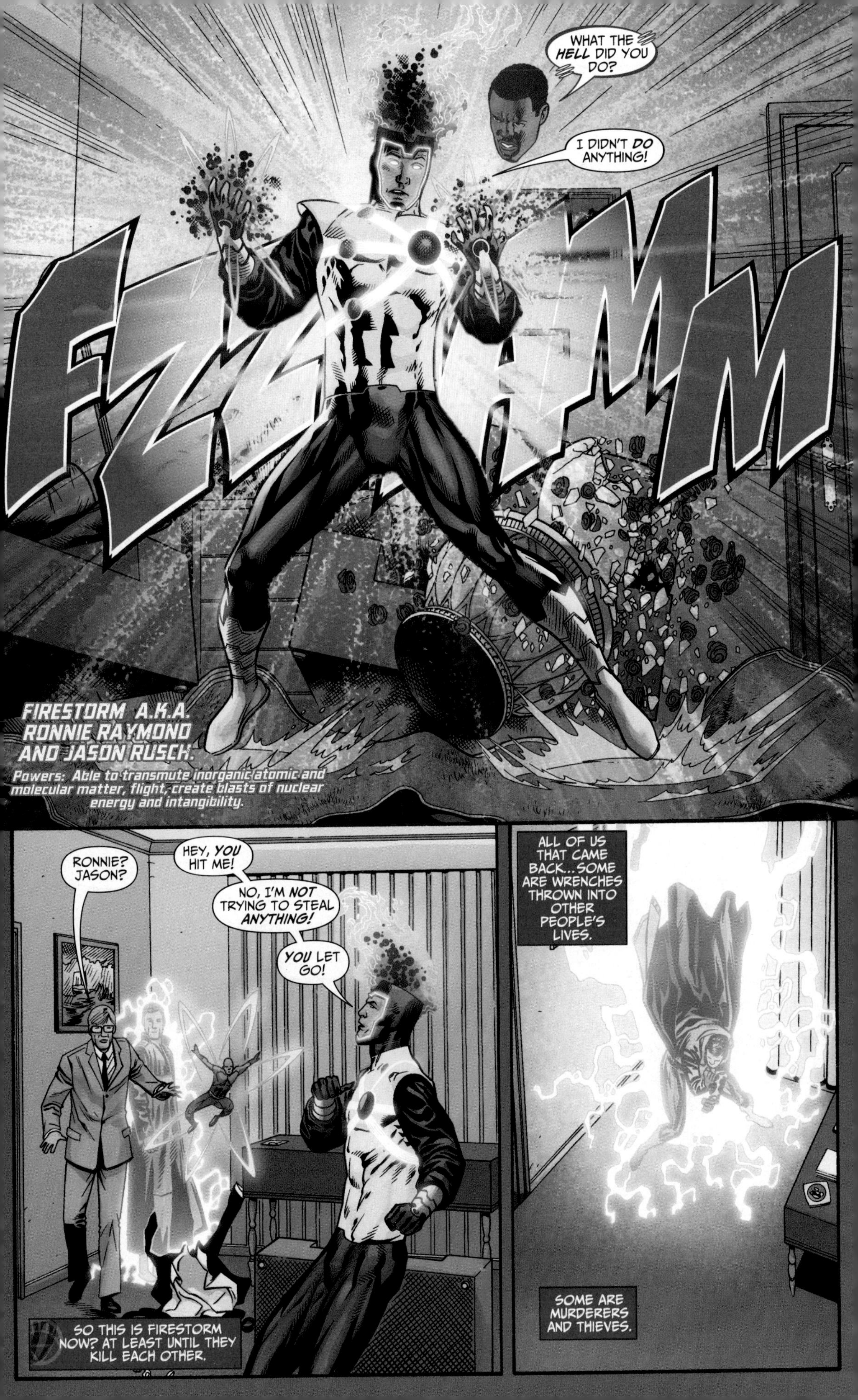
WHAT THE HELL DID YOU DO?
I DIDN'T DO ANYTHING!
FZZAMM
FIRESTORM A.K.A. RONNIE RAYMOND AND JASON RUSCH.
Powers: Able to transmute inorganic atomic and molecular matter, flight, create blasts of nuclear energy and intangibility.
RONNIE? JASON?
HEY, YOU HIT ME!
NO, I'M NOT TRYING TO STEAL ANYTHING!
YOU LET GO!
SO THIS IS FIRESTORM NOW? AT LEAST UNTIL THEY KILL EACH OTHER.
ALL OF US THAT CAME BACK...SOME ARE WRENCHES THROWN INTO OTHER PEOPLE'S LIVES.
SOME ARE MURDERERS AND THIEVES.

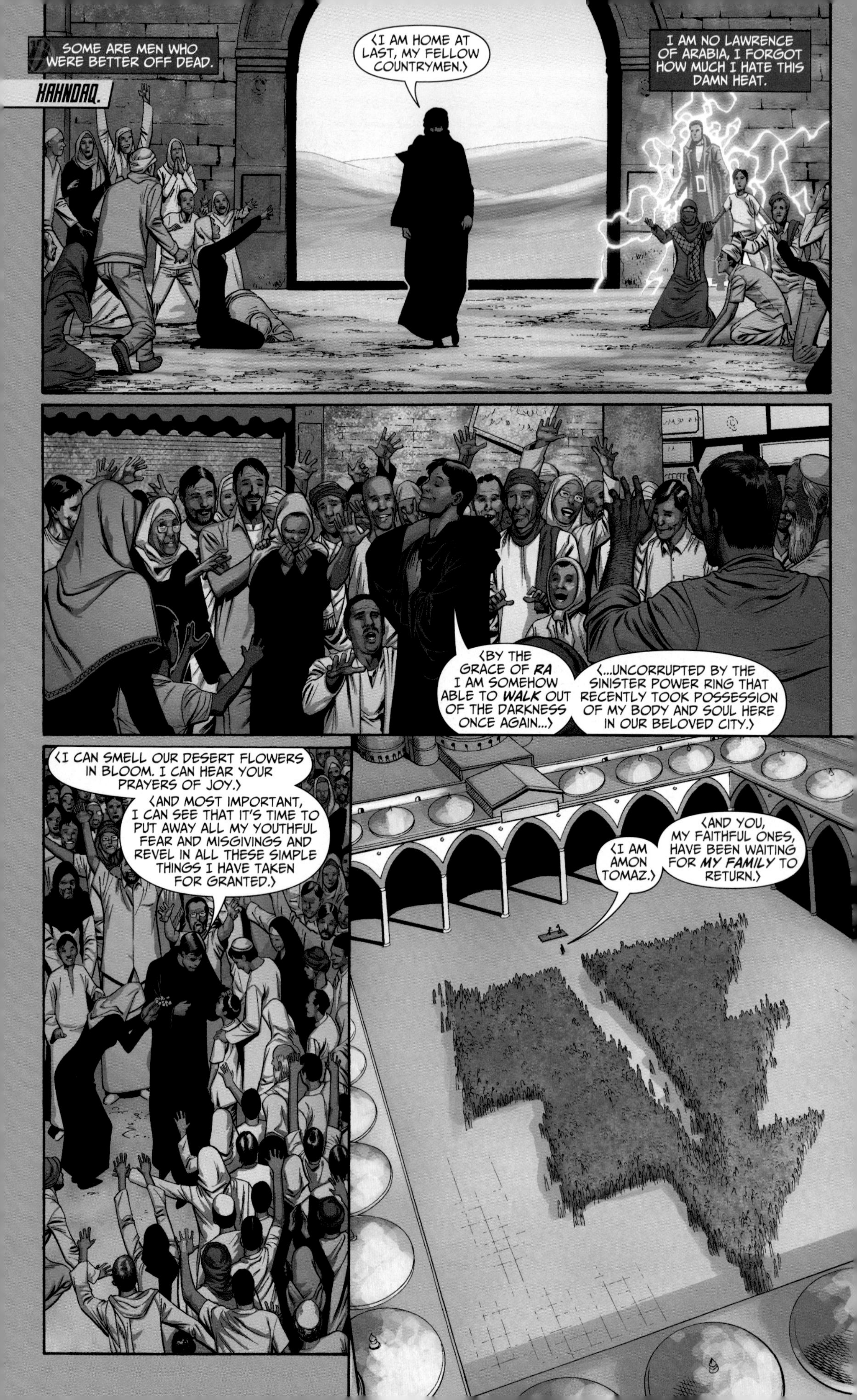
SOME ARE MEN WHO WERE BETTER OFF DEAD.
KAHNDAQ.
‹I AM HOME AT LAST, MY FELLOW COUNTRYMEN.›
I AM NO LAWRENCE OF ARABIA, I FORGOT HOW MUCH I HATE THIS DAMN HEAT.
‹BY THE GRACE OF RA I AM SOMEHOW ABLE TO WALK OUT OF THE DARKNESS ONCE AGAIN...›
‹...UNCORRUPTED BY THE SINISTER POWER RING THAT RECENTLY TOOK POSSESSION OF MY BODY AND SOUL HERE IN OUR BELOVED CITY.›
‹I CAN SMELL OUR DESERT FLOWERS IN BLOOM. I CAN HEAR YOUR PRAYERS OF JOY.›
‹AND MOST IMPORTANT, I CAN SEE THAT IT'S TIME TO PUT AWAY ALL MY YOUTHFUL FEAR AND MISGIVINGS AND REVEL IN ALL THESE SIMPLE THINGS I HAVE TAKEN FOR GRANTED.›
‹I AM AMON TOMAZ.›
‹AND YOU, MY FAITHFUL ONES, HAVE BEEN WAITING FOR MY FAMILY TO RETURN.›

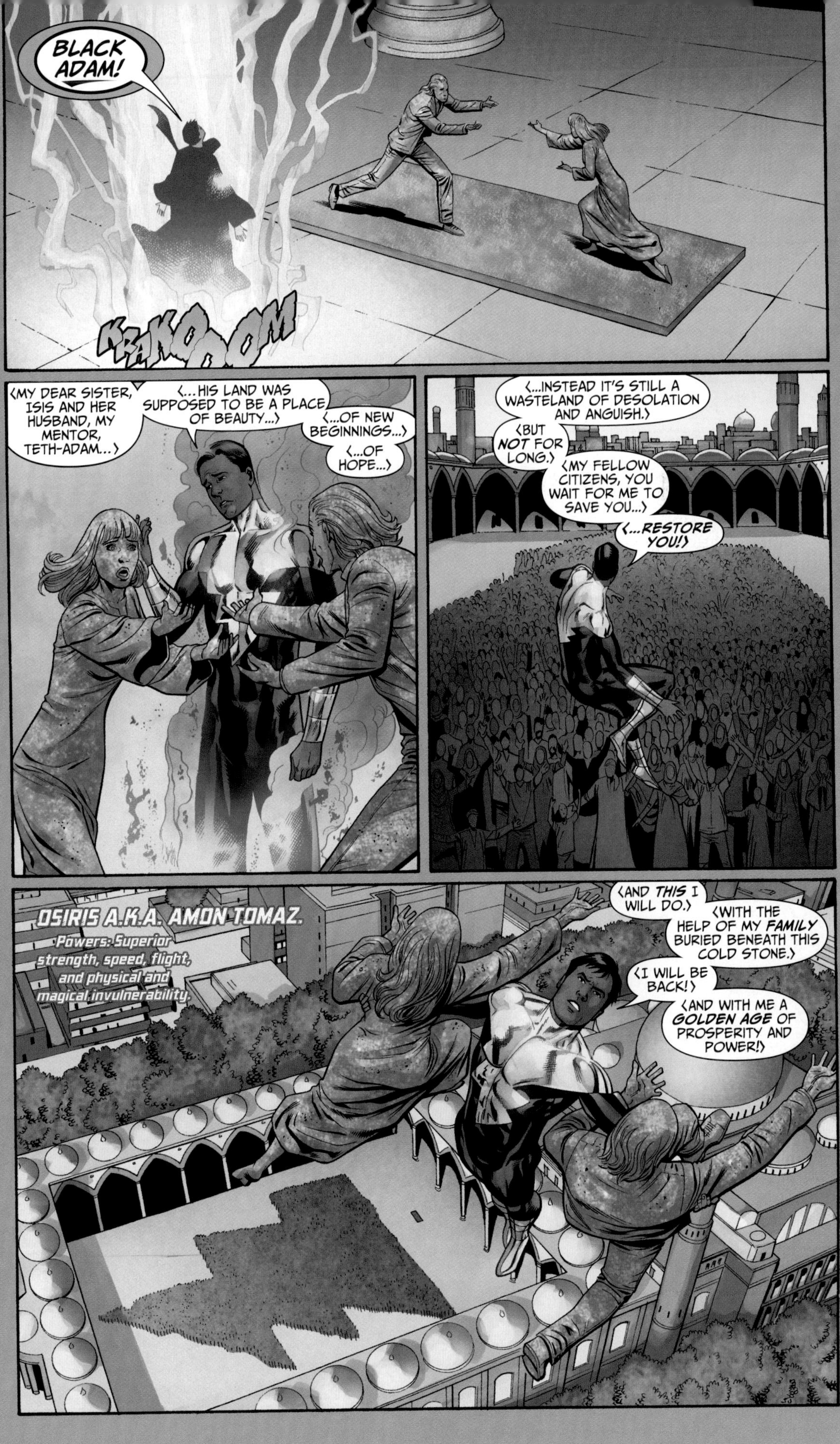
BLACK ADAM!
KRAKOOOOM
‹MY DEAR SISTER, ISIS AND HER HUSBAND, MY MENTOR, TETH-ADAM...›
‹...HIS LAND WAS SUPPOSED TO BE A PLACE OF BEAUTY...›
‹...OF NEW BEGINNINGS...›
‹...OF HOPE...›
‹...INSTEAD IT'S STILL A WASTELAND OF DESOLATION AND ANGUISH.›
‹BUT NOT FOR LONG.›
‹MY FELLOW CITIZENS, YOU WAIT FOR ME TO SAVE YOU...›
‹...RESTORE YOU!›
OSIRIS A.K.A. AMON TOMAZ.
Powers: Superior strength, speed, flight, and physical and magical invulnerability.
‹AND THIS I WILL DO.›
‹WITH THE HELP OF MY FAMILY BURIED BENEATH THIS COLD STONE.›
‹I WILL BE BACK!›
‹AND WITH ME A GOLDEN AGE OF PROSPERITY AND POWER!›

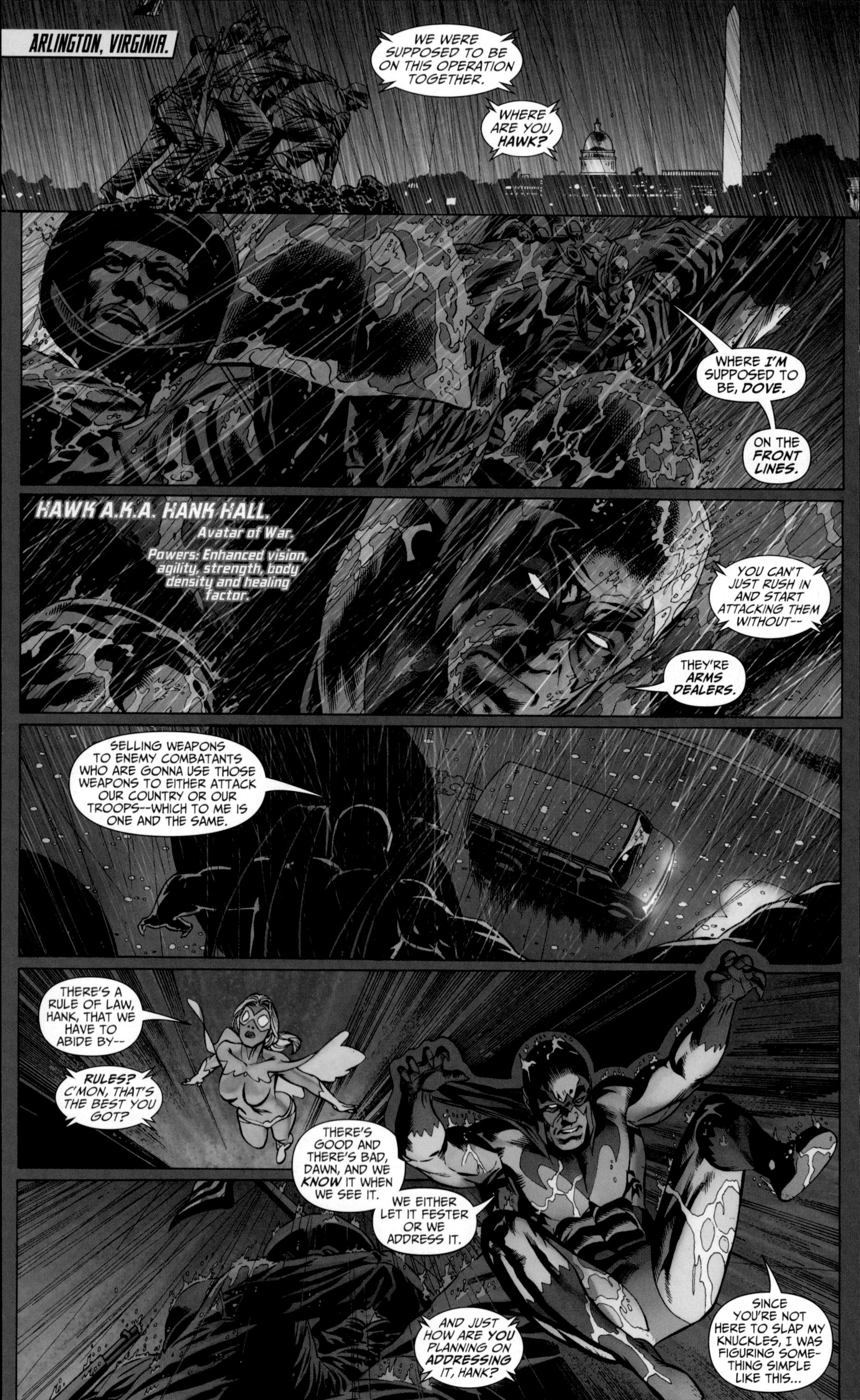
ARLINGTON, VIRGINIA.
WE WERE SUPPOSED TO BE ON THIS OPERATION TOGETHER.
WHERE ARE YOU, HAWK?
WHERE I'M SUPPOSED TO BE, DOVE.
ON THE FRONT LINES.
HAWK A.K.A. HANK HALL.
Avatar of War.
Powers: Enhanced vision, agility, strength, body density and healing factor.
YOU CAN'T JUST RUSH IN AND START ATTACKING THEM WITHOUT--
THEY'RE ARMS DEALERS.
SELLING WEAPONS TO ENEMY COMBATANTS WHO ARE GONNA USE THOSE WEAPONS TO EITHER ATTACK OUR COUNTRY OR OUR TROOPS--WHICH TO ME IS ONE AND THE SAME.
THERE'S A RULE OF LAW, HANK, THAT WE HAVE TO ABIDE BY--
RULES? C'MON, THAT'S THE BEST YOU GOT?
THERE'S GOOD AND THERE'S BAD, DAWN, AND WE KNOW IT WHEN WE SEE IT.
WE EITHER LET IT FESTER OR WE ADDRESS IT.
AND JUST HOW ARE YOU PLANNING ON ADDRESSING IT, HANK?
SINCE YOU'RE NOT HERE TO SLAP MY KNUCKLES, I WAS FIGURING SOME-THING SIMPLE LIKE THIS...

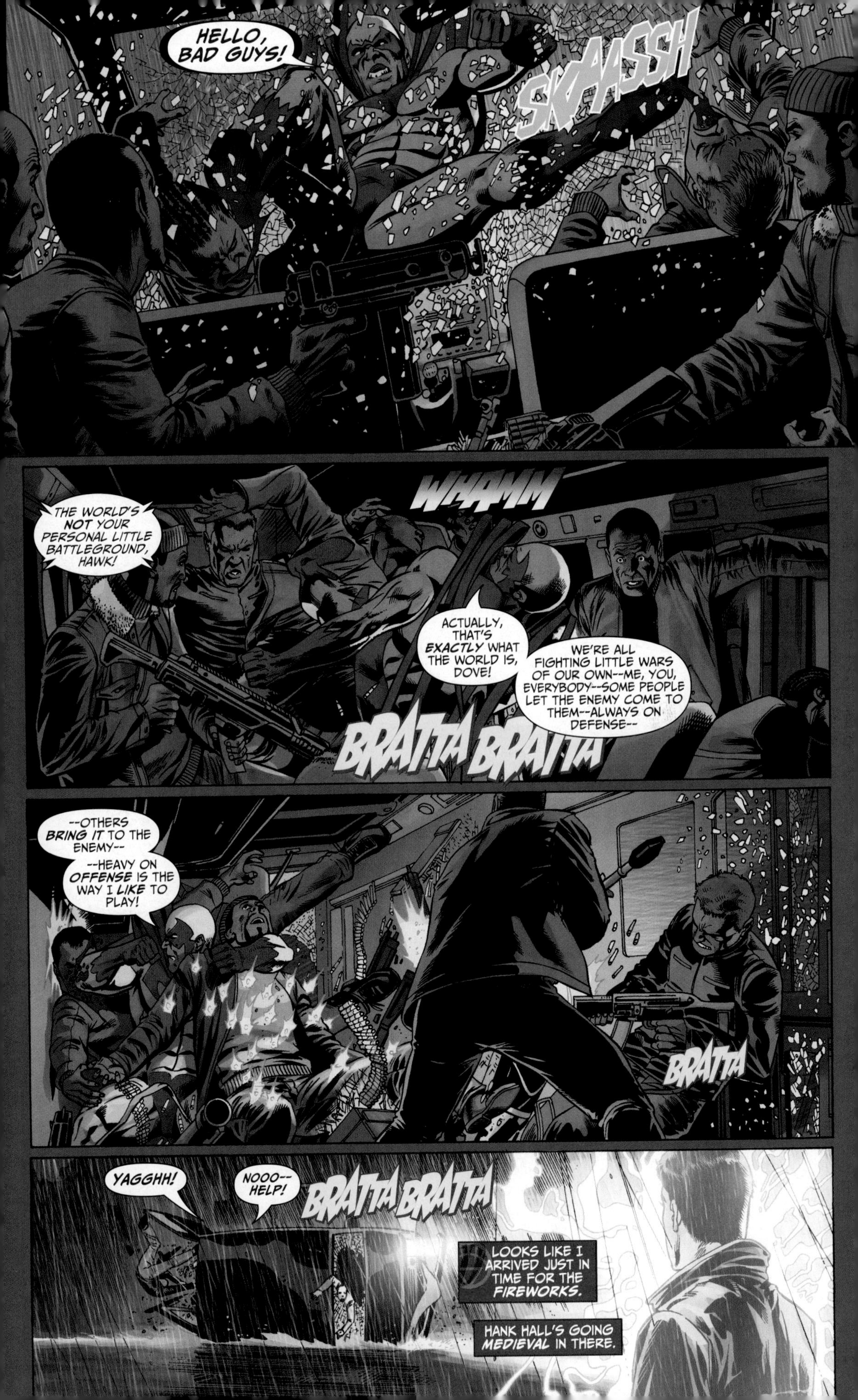
HELLO, BAD GUYS!
SKRAASSH
WHAMM
THE WORLD'S NOT YOUR PERSONAL LITTLE BATTLEGROUND, HAWK!
ACTUALLY, THAT'S EXACTLY WHAT THE WORLD IS, DOVE!
WE'RE ALL FIGHTING LITTLE WARS OF OUR OWN--ME, YOU, EVERYBODY--SOME PEOPLE LET THE ENEMY COME TO THEM--ALWAYS ON DEFENSE--
BRATTA BRATTA
--OTHERS BRING IT TO THE ENEMY--
--HEAVY ON OFFENSE IS THE WAY I LIKE TO PLAY!
BRATTA
YAGGHH!
NOOO-- HELP!
BRATTA BRATTA
LOOKS LIKE I ARRIVED JUST IN TIME FOR THE FIREWORKS.
HANK HALL'S GOING MEDIEVAL IN THERE.

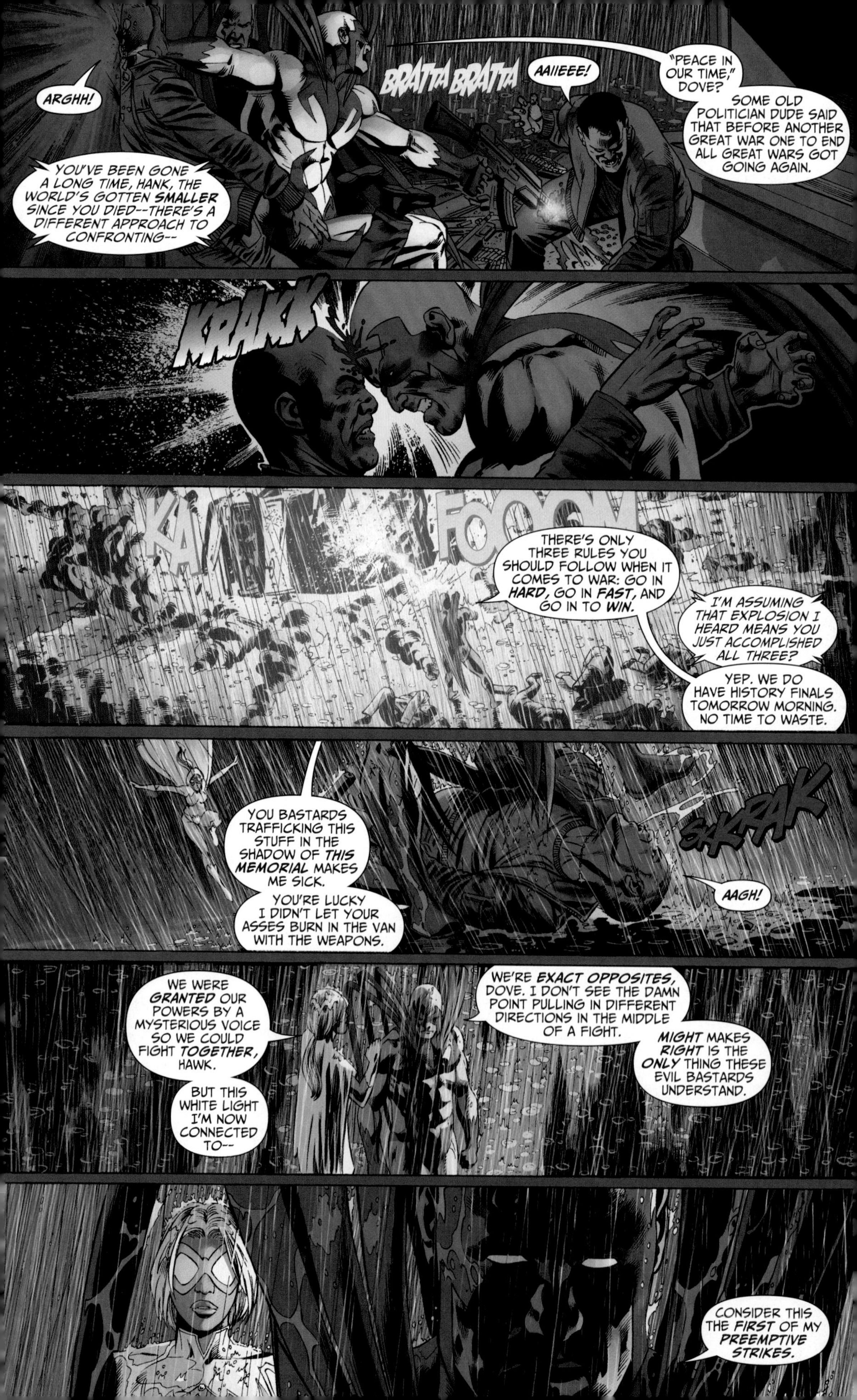
ARGHH!
YOU'VE BEEN GONE A LONG TIME, HANK, THE WORLD'S GOTTEN SMALLER SINCE YOU DIED--THERE'S A DIFFERENT APPROACH TO CONFRONTING--
BRATTA BRATTA
AAIIEEE!
"PEACE IN OUR TIME," DOVE?
SOME OLD POLITICIAN DUDE SAID THAT BEFORE ANOTHER GREAT WAR ONE TO END ALL GREAT WARS GOT GOING AGAIN.
KRAKK
FOOOM
THERE'S ONLY THREE RULES YOU SHOULD FOLLOW WHEN IT COMES TO WAR: GO IN HARD, GO IN FAST, AND GO IN TO WIN.
I'M ASSUMING THAT EXPLOSION I HEARD MEANS YOU JUST ACCOMPLISHED ALL THREE?
YEP. WE DO HAVE HISTORY FINALS TOMORROW MORNING. NO TIME TO WASTE.
YOU BASTARDS TRAFFICKING THIS STUFF IN THE SHADOW OF THIS MEMORIAL MAKES ME SICK.
YOU'RE LUCKY I DIDN'T LET YOUR ASSES BURN IN THE VAN WITH THE WEAPONS.
SKRAK
AAGH!
WE WERE GRANTED OUR POWERS BY A MYSTERIOUS VOICE SO WE COULD FIGHT TOGETHER, HAWK.
BUT THIS WHITE LIGHT I'M NOW CONNECTED TO--
WE'RE EXACT OPPOSITES, DOVE. I DON'T SEE THE DAMN POINT PULLING IN DIFFERENT DIRECTIONS IN THE MIDDLE OF A FIGHT.
MIGHT MAKES RIGHT IS THE ONLY THING THESE EVIL BASTARDS UNDERSTAND.
CONSIDER THIS THE FIRST OF MY PREEMPTIVE STRIKES.

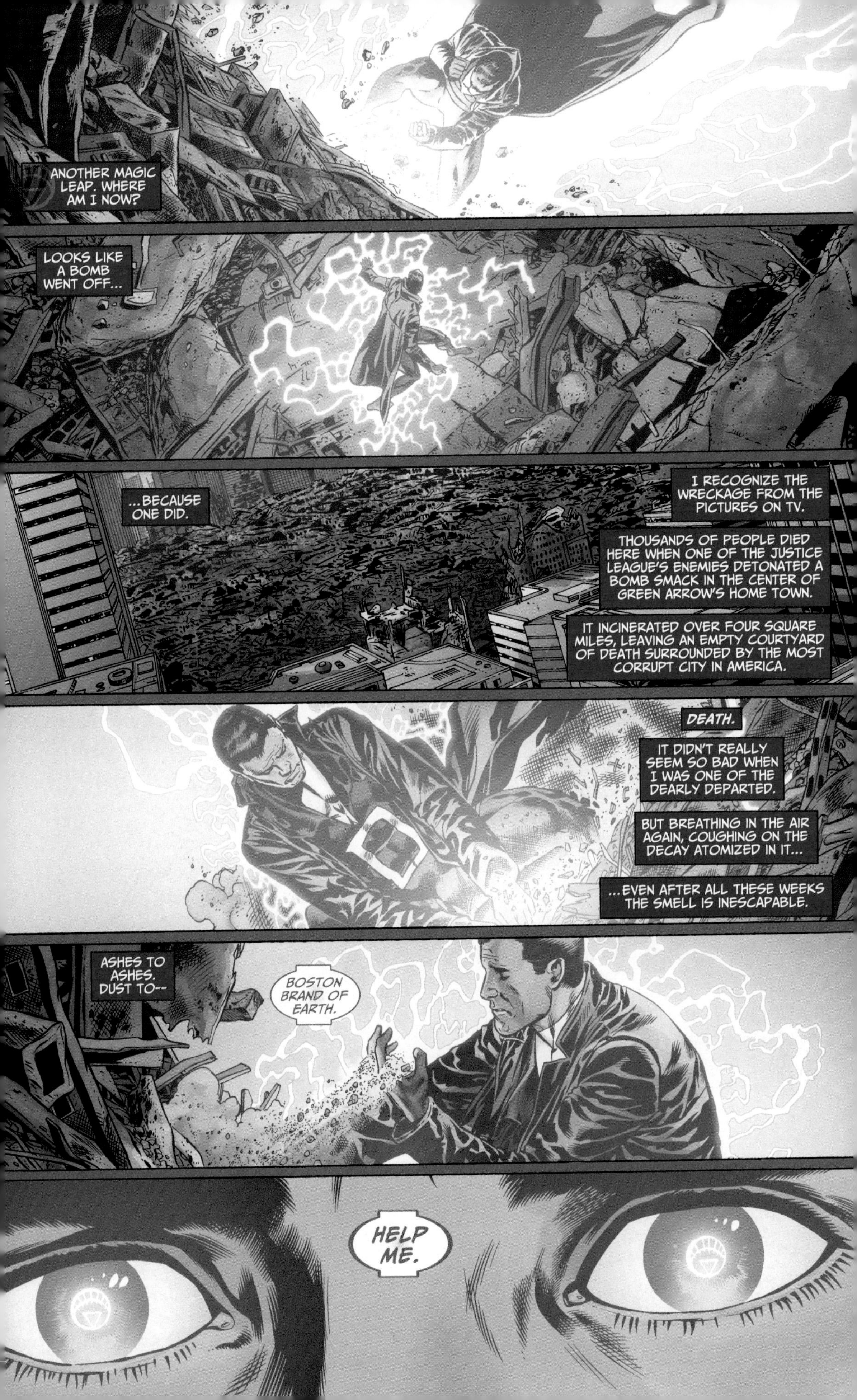
ANOTHER MAGIC LEAP. WHERE AM I NOW?
LOOKS LIKE A BOMB WENT OFF...
...BECAUSE ONE DID.
I RECOGNIZE THE WRECKAGE FROM THE PICTURES ON TV.
THOUSANDS OF PEOPLE DIED HERE WHEN ONE OF THE JUSTICE LEAGUE'S ENEMIES DETONATED A BOMB SMACK IN THE CENTER OF GREEN ARROW'S HOME TOWN.
IT INCINERATED OVER FOUR SQUARE MILES, LEAVING AN EMPTY COURTYARD OF DEATH SURROUNDED BY THE MOST CORRUPT CITY IN AMERICA.
DEATH.
IT DIDN'T REALLY SEEM SO BAD WHEN I WAS ONE OF THE DEARLY DEPARTED.
BUT BREATHING IN THE AIR AGAIN, COUGHING ON THE DECAY ATOMIZED IN IT...
...EVEN AFTER ALL THESE WEEKS THE SMELL IS INESCAPABLE.
ASHES TO ASHES. DUST TO--
BOSTON BRAND OF EARTH.
HELP ME.

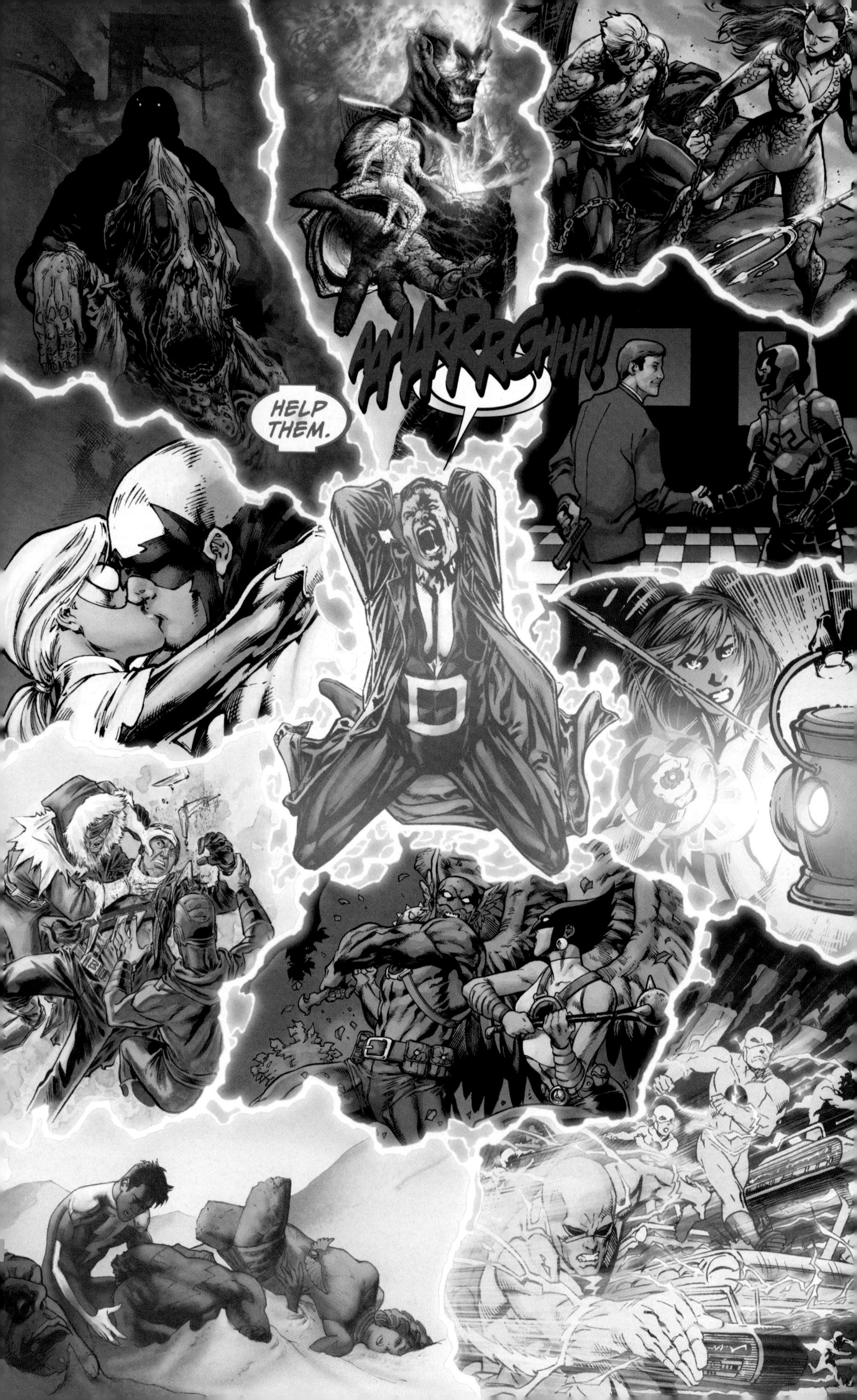
HELP THEM.
AAARRRGHHH!

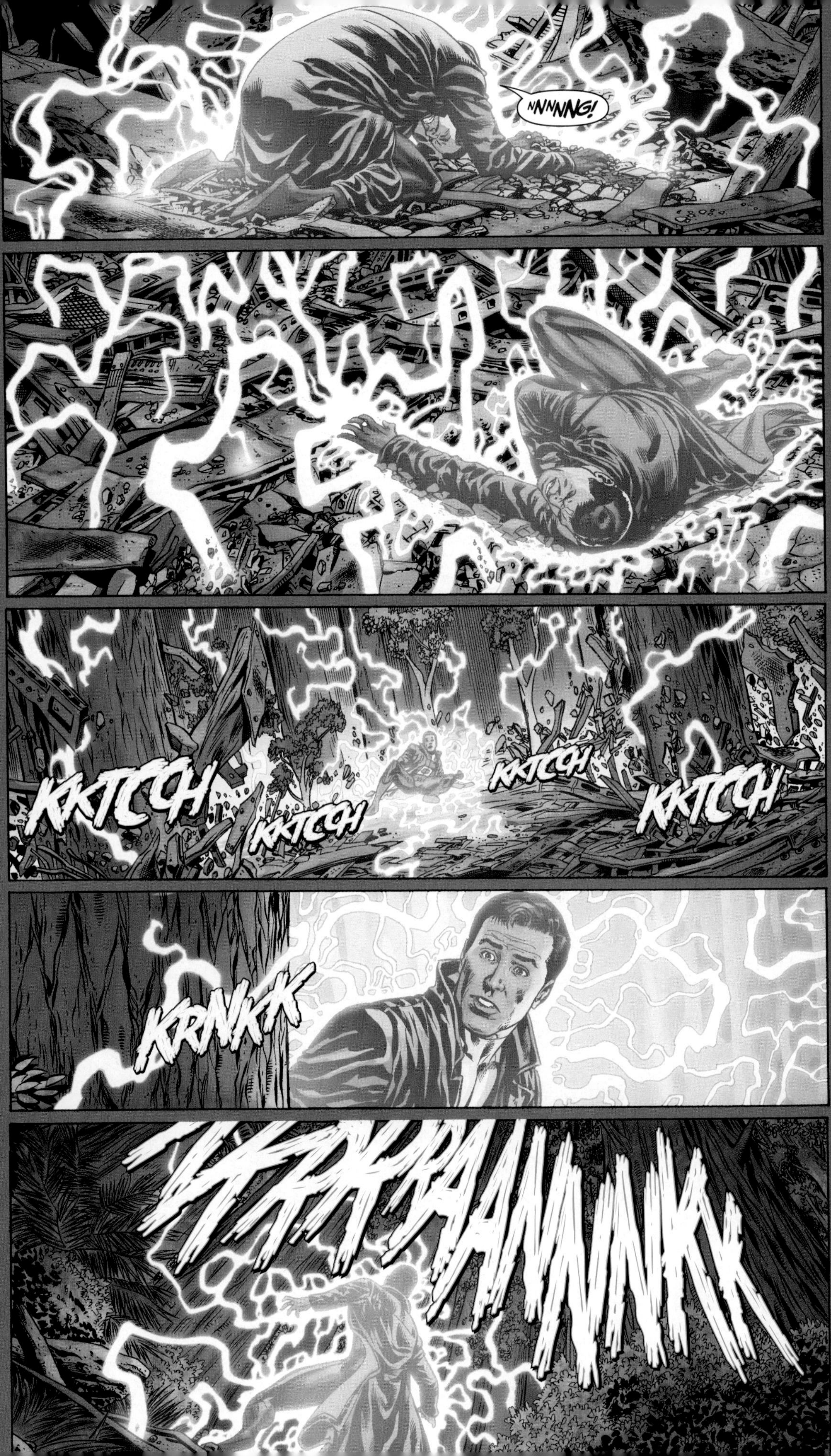
NNNNNG!
KKTCCH
KKTCCH
KKTCCH
KKTCCH
KRNKK

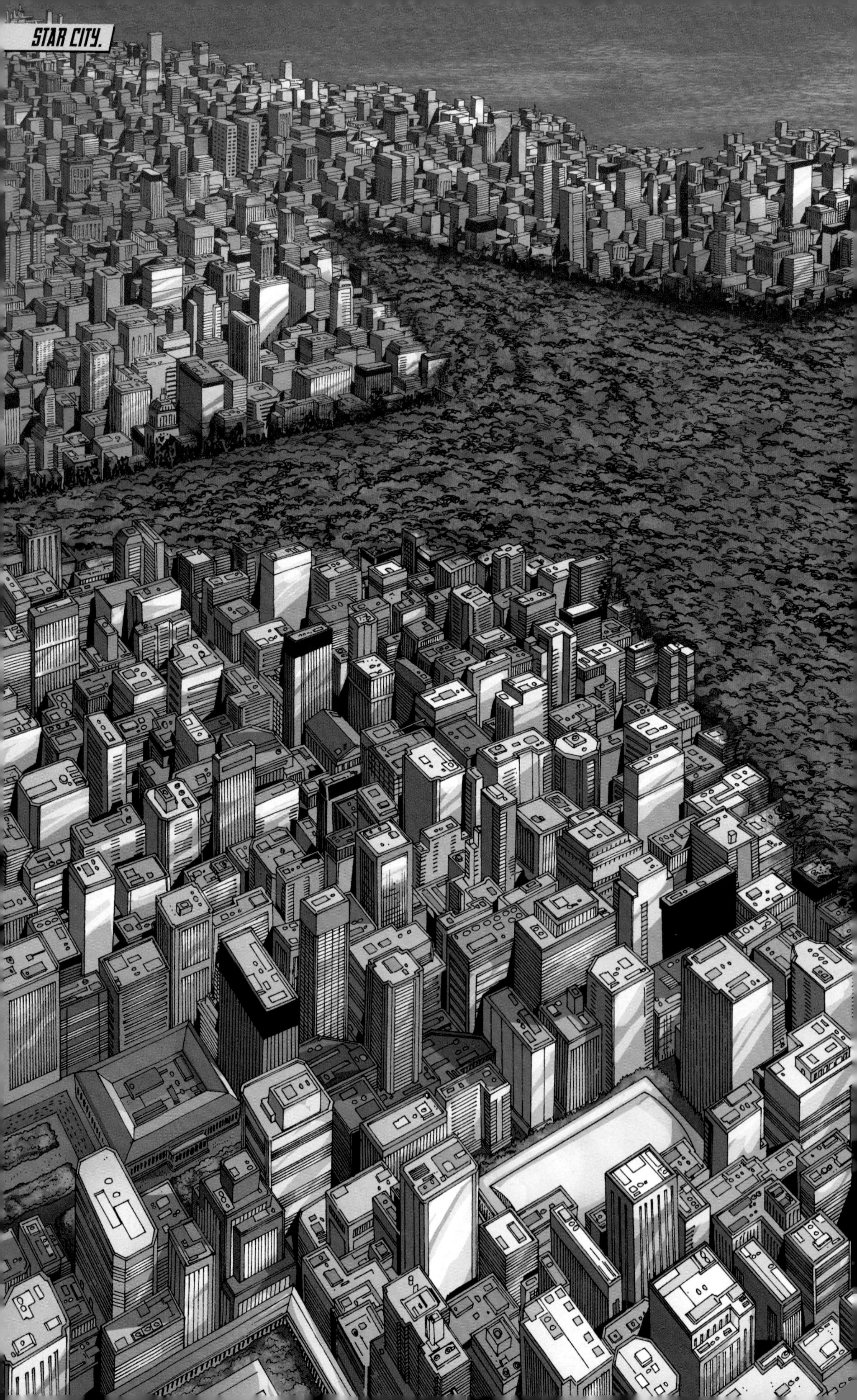
STAR CITY.

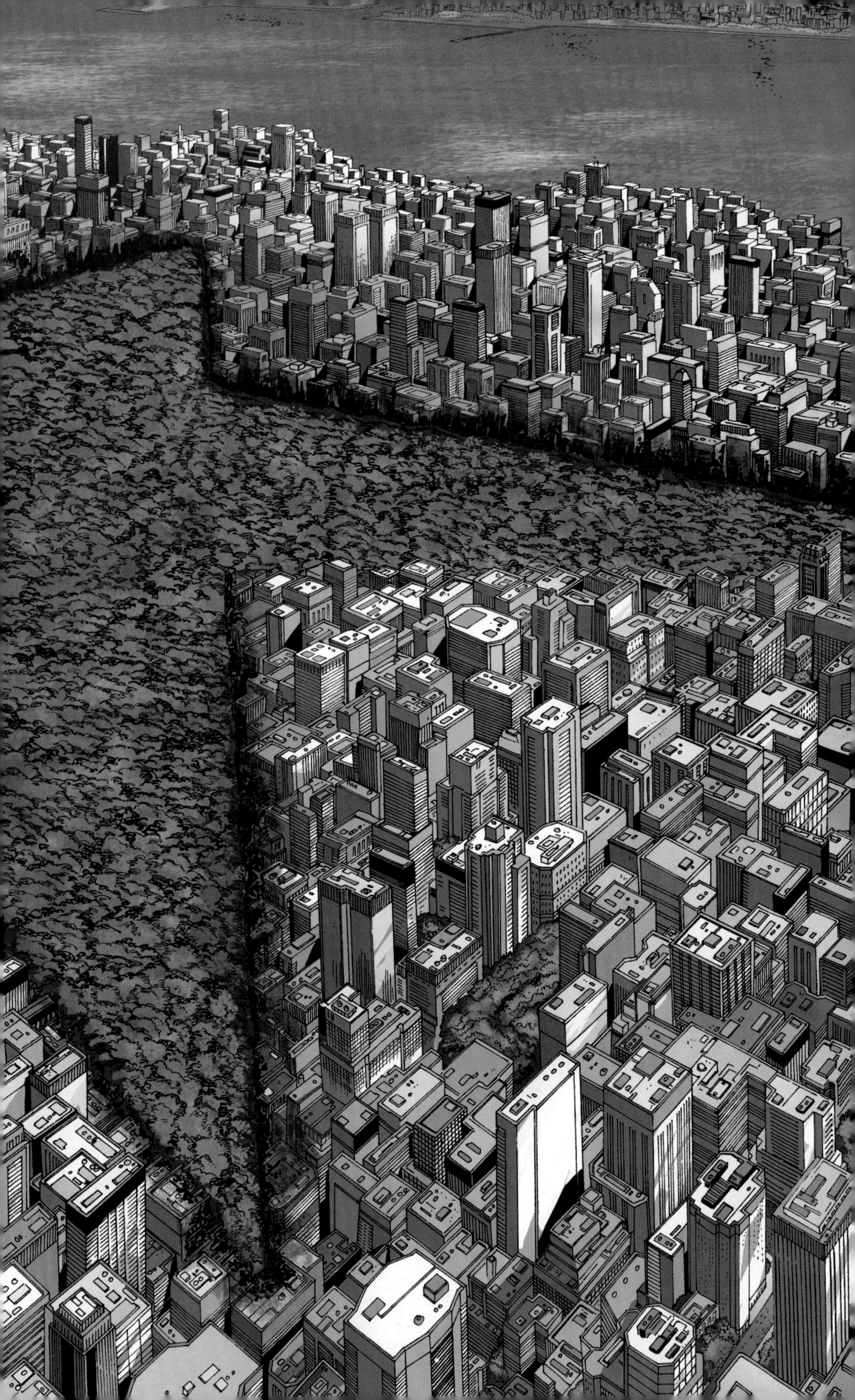

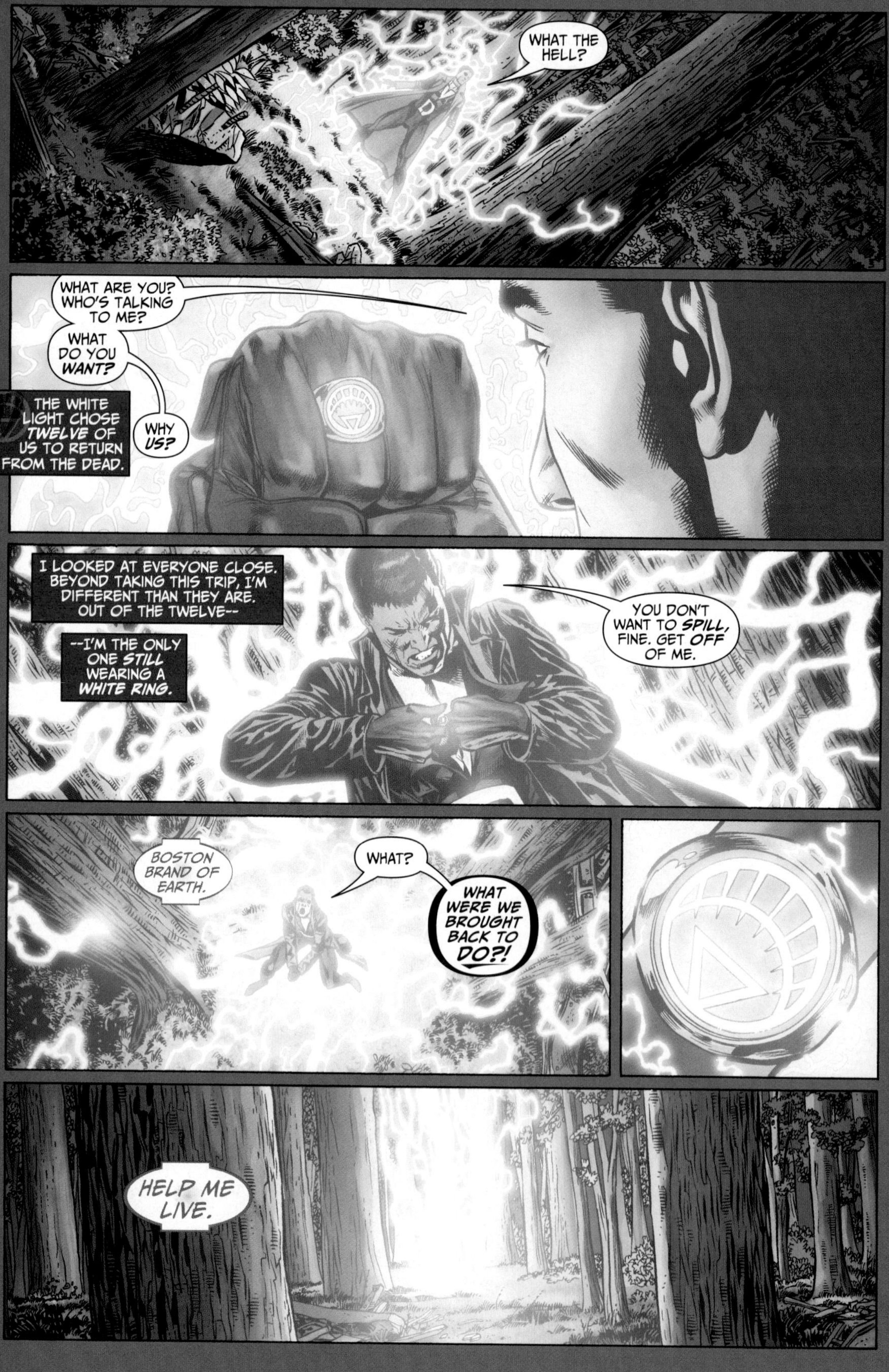
WHAT THE HELL?
WHAT ARE YOU? WHO'S TALKING TO ME?
WHAT DO YOU WANT?
THE WHITE LIGHT CHOSE TWELVE OF US TO RETURN FROM THE DEAD.
WHY US?
I LOOKED AT EVERYONE CLOSE. BEYOND TAKING THIS TRIP, I'M DIFFERENT THAN THEY ARE. OUT OF THE TWELVE--
--I'M THE ONLY ONE STILL WEARING A WHITE RING.
YOU DON'T WANT TO SPILL, FINE. GET OFF OF ME.
BOSTON BRAND OF EARTH.
WHAT?
WHAT WERE WE BROUGHT BACK TO DO?!
HELP ME LIVE.

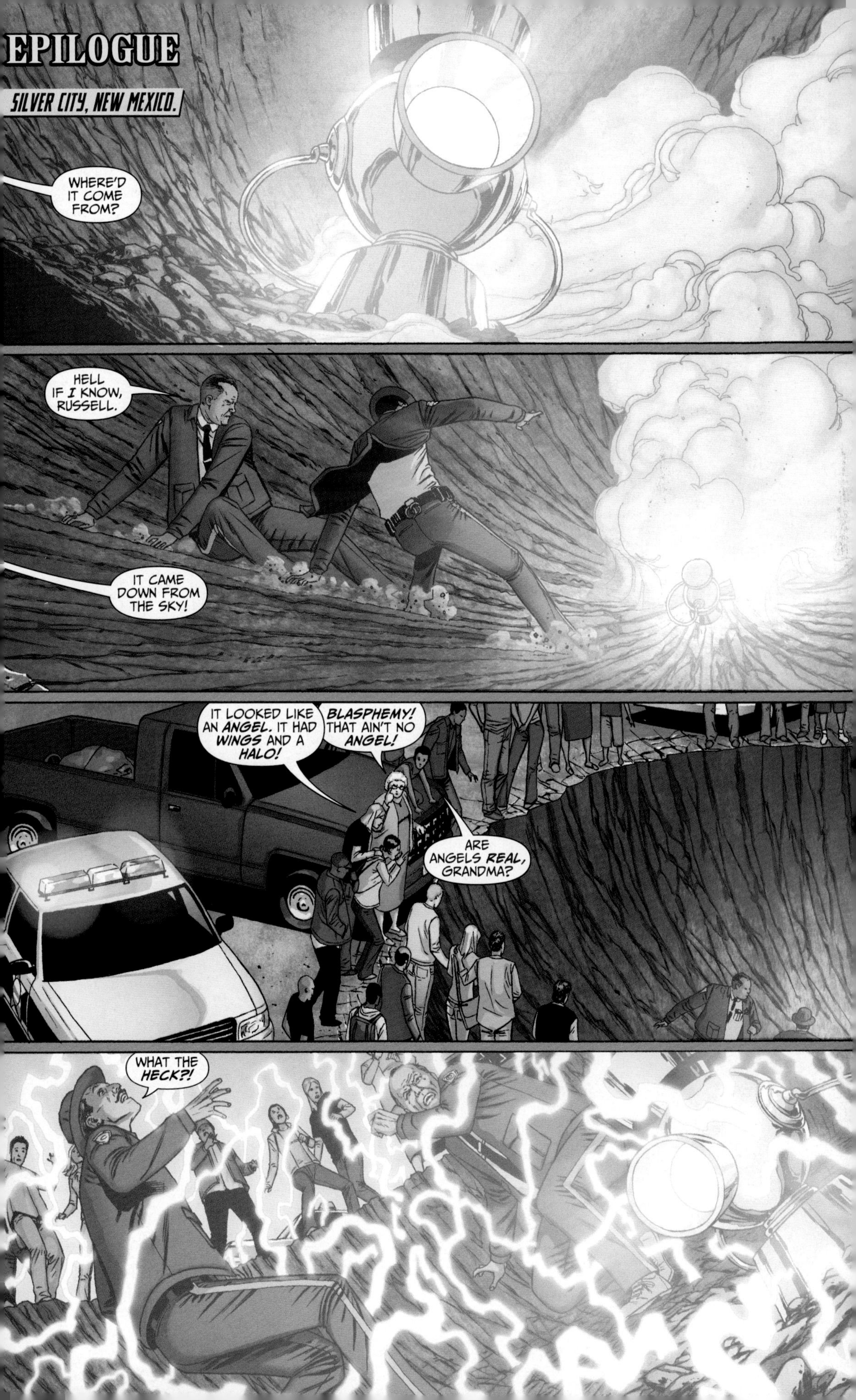
EPILOGUE
SILVER CITY, NEW MEXICO.
WHERE'D IT COME FROM?
HELL IF I KNOW, RUSSELL.
IT CAME DOWN FROM THE SKY!
IT LOOKED LIKE AN ANGEL. IT HAD WINGS AND A HALO!
BLASPHEMY! THAT AIN'T NO ANGEL!
ARE ANGELS REAL, GRANDMA?
WHAT THE HECK?!

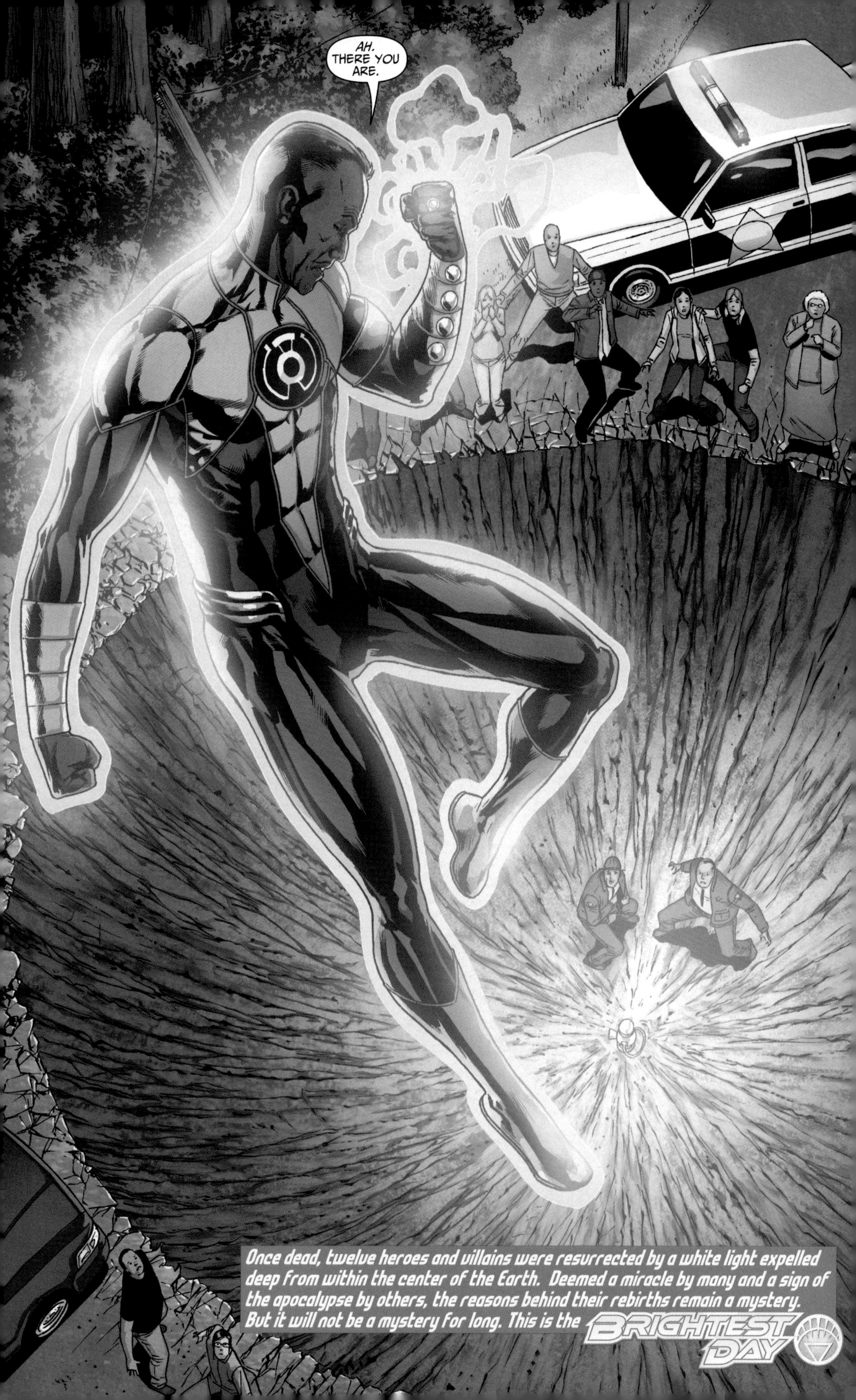
AH. THERE YOU ARE.
Once dead, twelve heroes and villains were resurrected by a white light expelled deep from within the center of the Earth. Deemed a miracle by many and a sign of the apocalypse by others, the reasons behind their rebirths remain a mystery. But it will not be a mystery for long. This is the
BRIGHTEST DAY

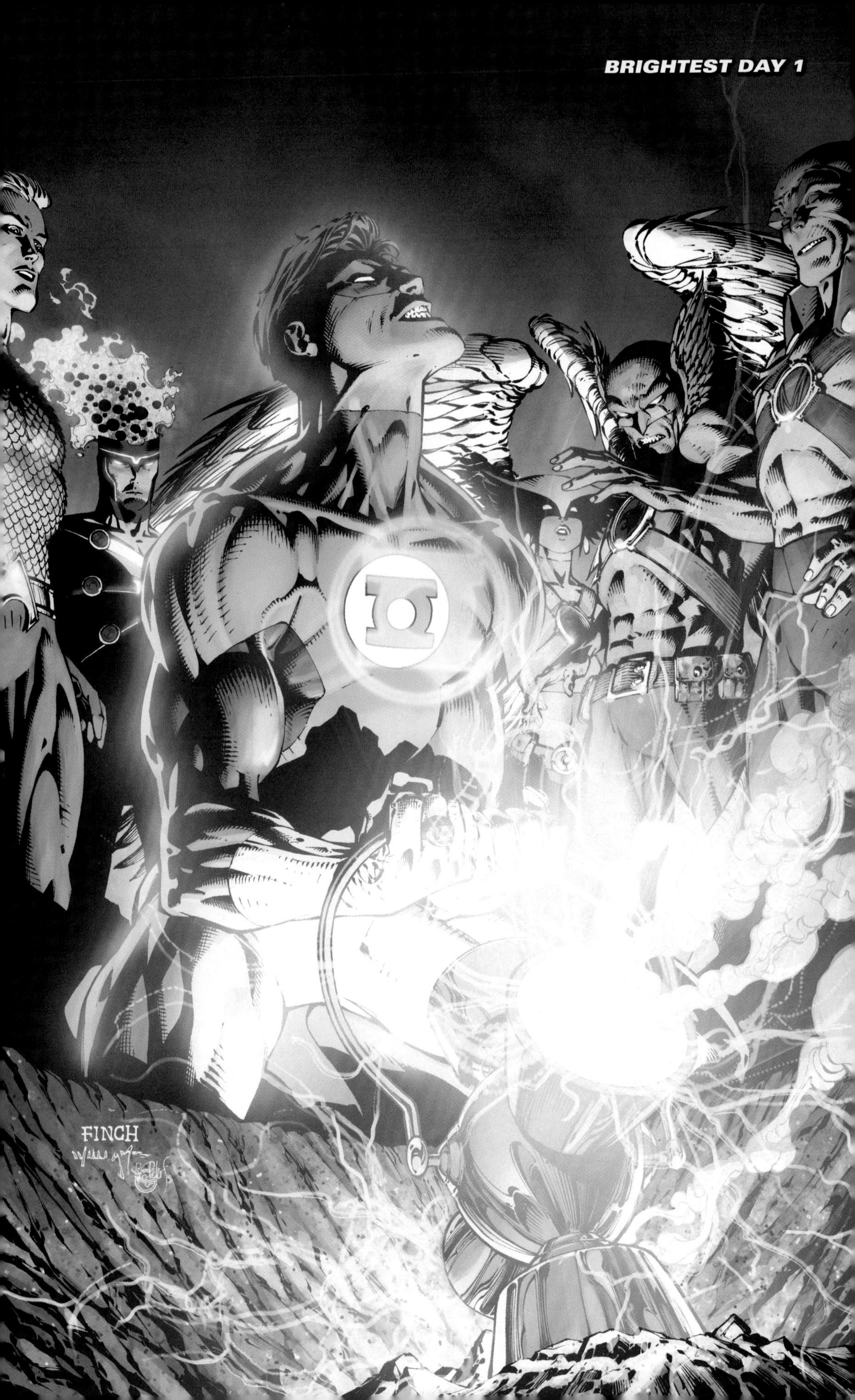
BRIGHTEST DAY 1
FINCH

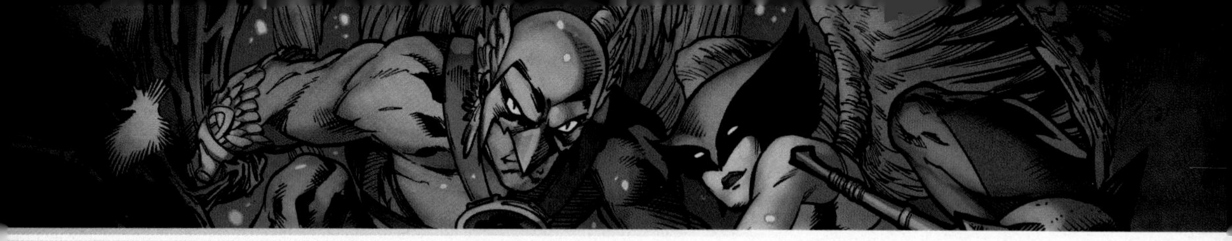

# SECOND CHANCES

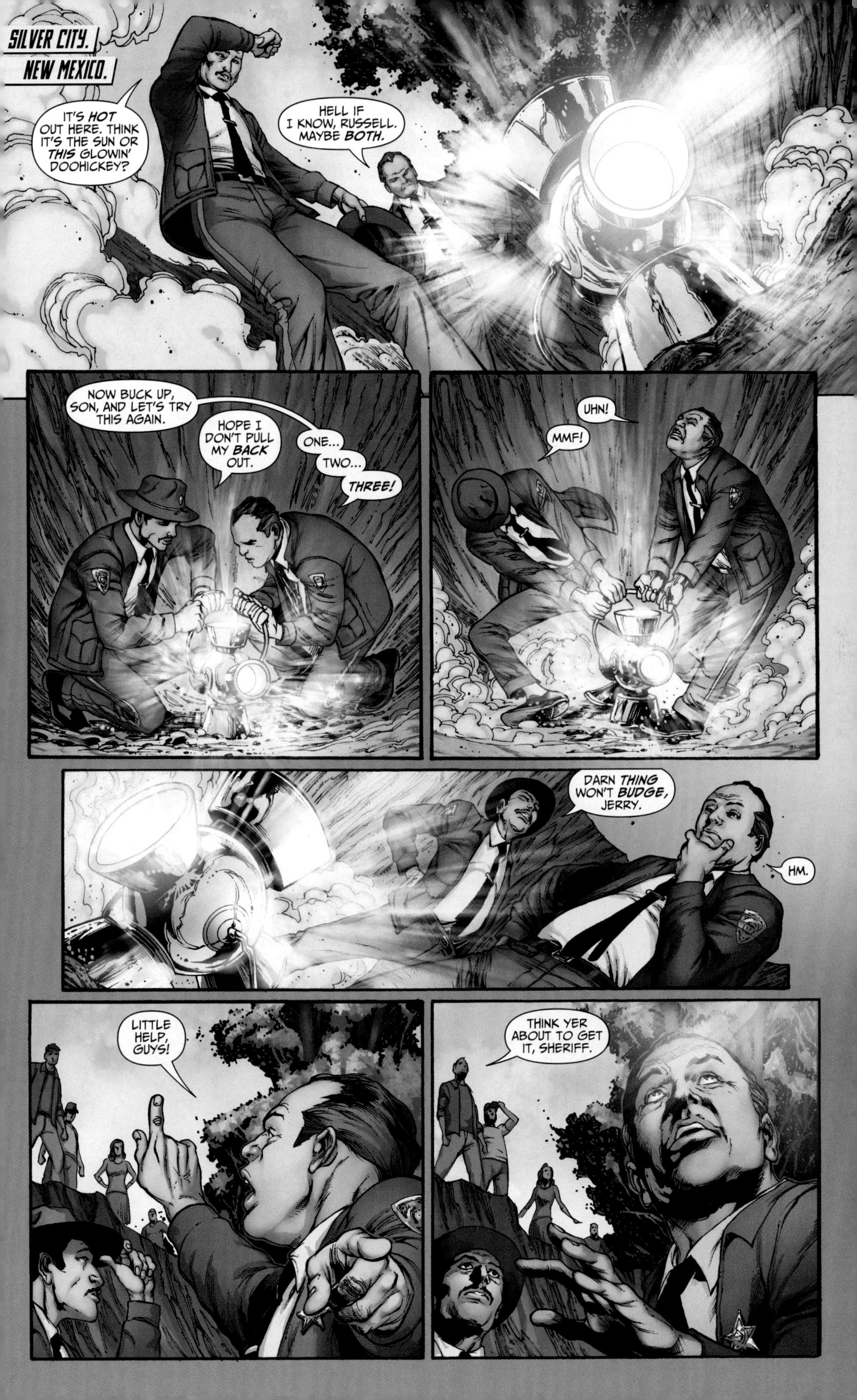
SILVER CITY.
NEW MEXICO.
IT'S HOT OUT HERE. THINK IT'S THE SUN OR THIS GLOWIN' DOOHICKEY?
HELL IF I KNOW, RUSSELL. MAYBE BOTH.
NOW BUCK UP, SON, AND LET'S TRY THIS AGAIN.
HOPE I DON'T PULL MY BACK OUT.
ONE...
TWO...
THREE!
UHN!
MMF!
DARN THING WON'T BUDGE, JERRY.
HM.
LITTLE HELP, GUYS!
THINK YER ABOUT TO GET IT, SHERIFF.

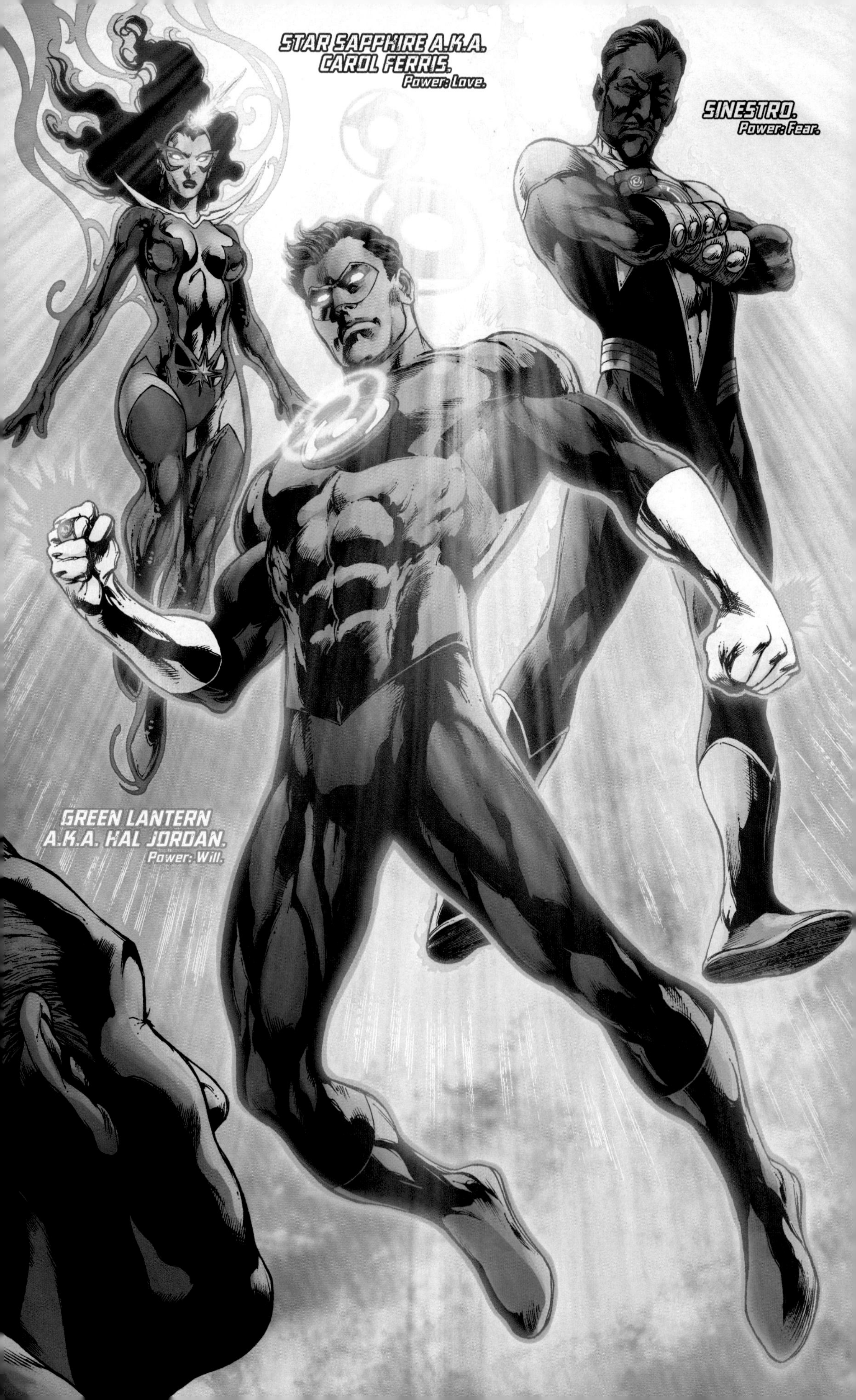
STAR SAPPHIRE A.K.A. CAROL FERRIS.
Power: Love.
SINESTRO.
Power: Fear.
GREEN LANTERN A.K.A. HAL JORDAN.
Power: Will.

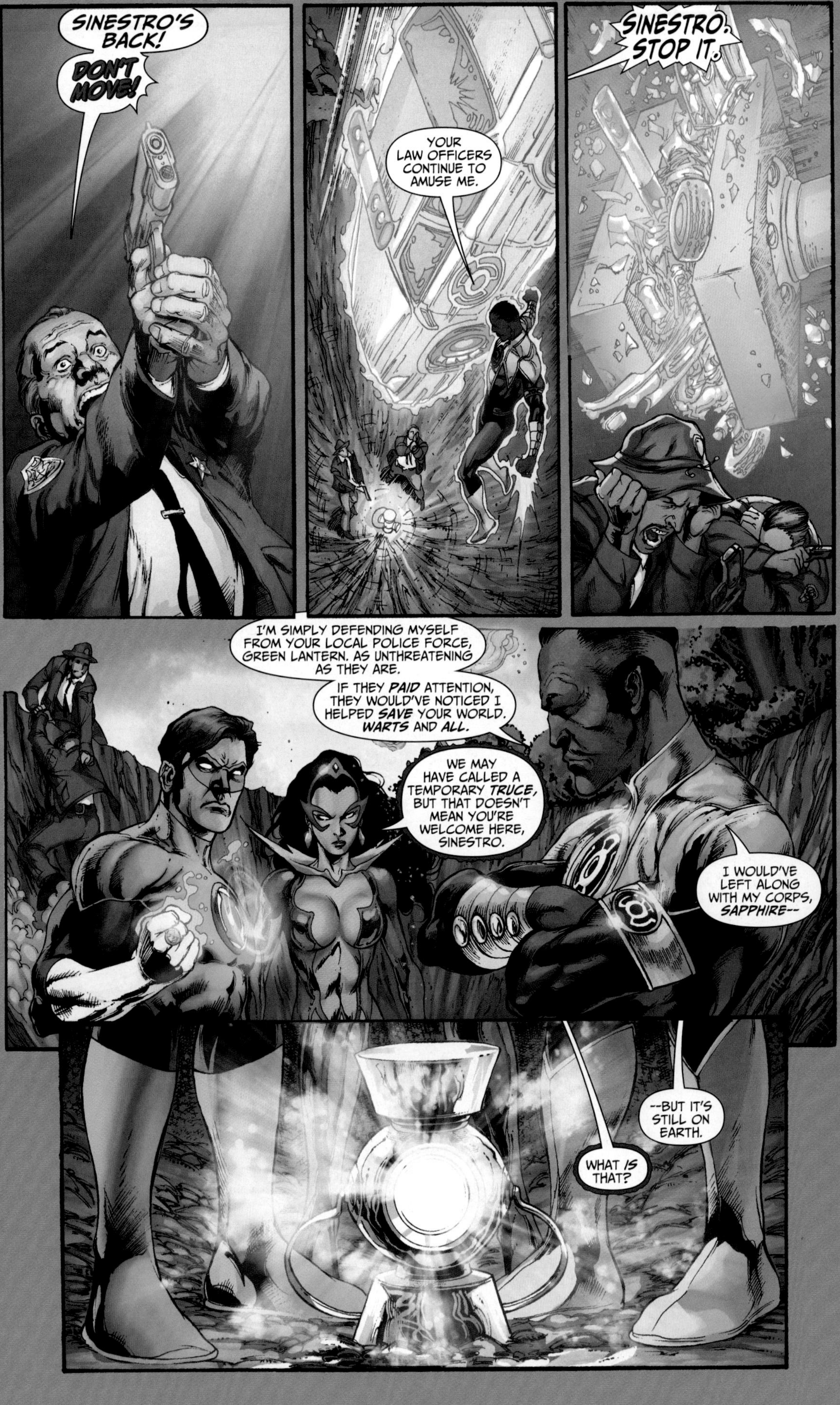

SINESTRO'S BACK!
DON'T MOVE!
YOUR LAW OFFICERS CONTINUE TO AMUSE ME.
SINESTRO. STOP IT.
I'M SIMPLY DEFENDING MYSELF FROM YOUR LOCAL POLICE FORCE, GREEN LANTERN. AS UNTHREATENING AS THEY ARE.
IF THEY PAID ATTENTION, THEY WOULD'VE NOTICED I HELPED SAVE YOUR WORLD. WARTS AND ALL.
WE MAY HAVE CALLED A TEMPORARY TRUCE, BUT THAT DOESN'T MEAN YOU'RE WELCOME HERE, SINESTRO.
I WOULD'VE LEFT ALONG WITH MY CORPS, SAPPHIRE--
--BUT IT'S STILL ON EARTH.
WHAT IS THAT?

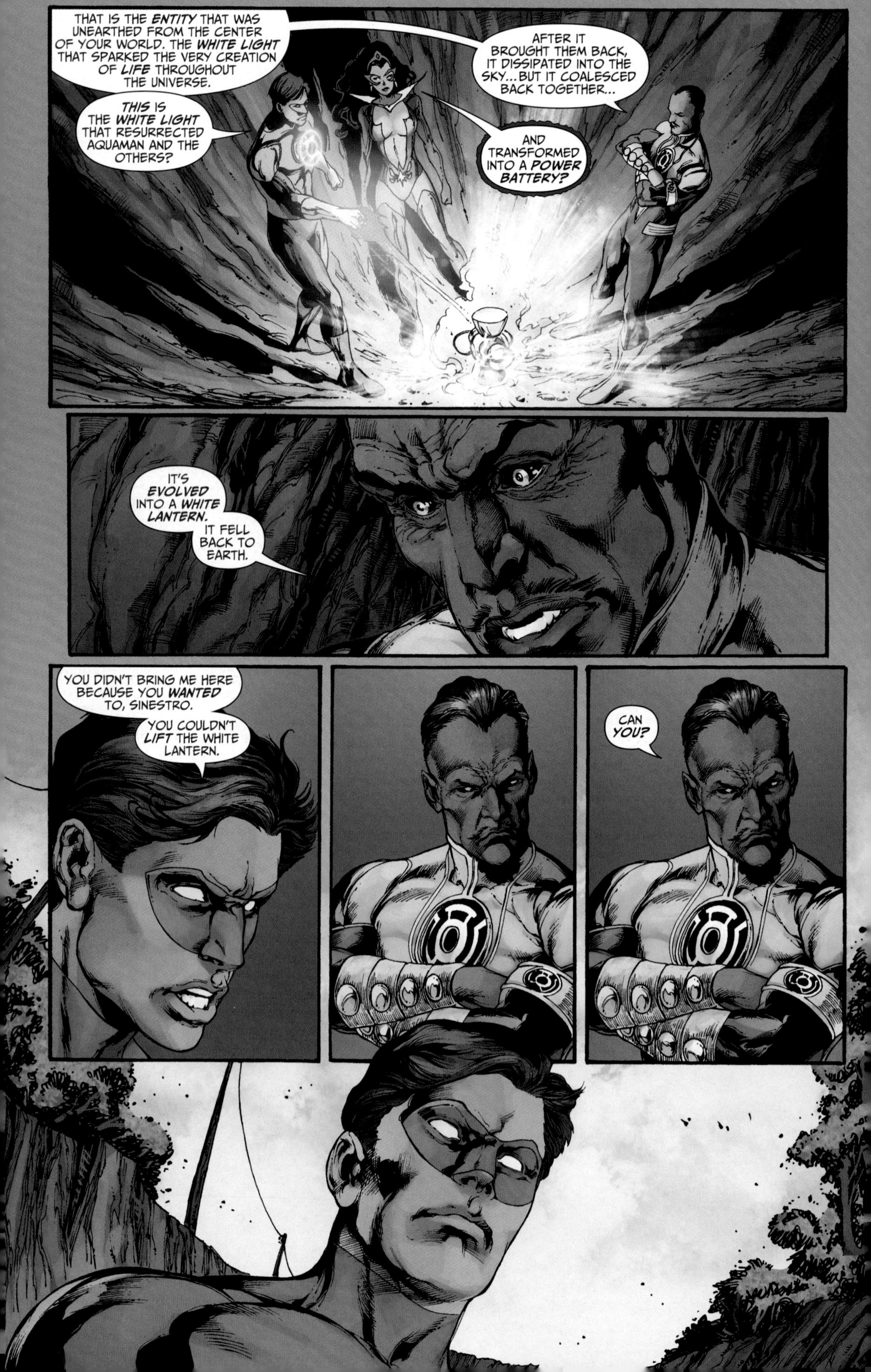
THAT IS THE ENTITY THAT WAS UNEARTHED FROM THE CENTER OF YOUR WORLD. THE WHITE LIGHT THAT SPARKED THE VERY CREATION OF LIFE THROUGHOUT THE UNIVERSE.
THIS IS THE WHITE LIGHT THAT RESURRECTED AQUAMAN AND THE OTHERS?
AFTER IT BROUGHT THEM BACK, IT DISSIPATED INTO THE SKY...BUT IT COALESCED BACK TOGETHER...
AND TRANSFORMED INTO A POWER BATTERY?
IT'S EVOLVED INTO A WHITE LANTERN.
IT FELL BACK TO EARTH.
YOU DIDN'T BRING ME HERE BECAUSE YOU WANTED TO, SINESTRO.
YOU COULDN'T LIFT THE WHITE LANTERN.
CAN YOU?

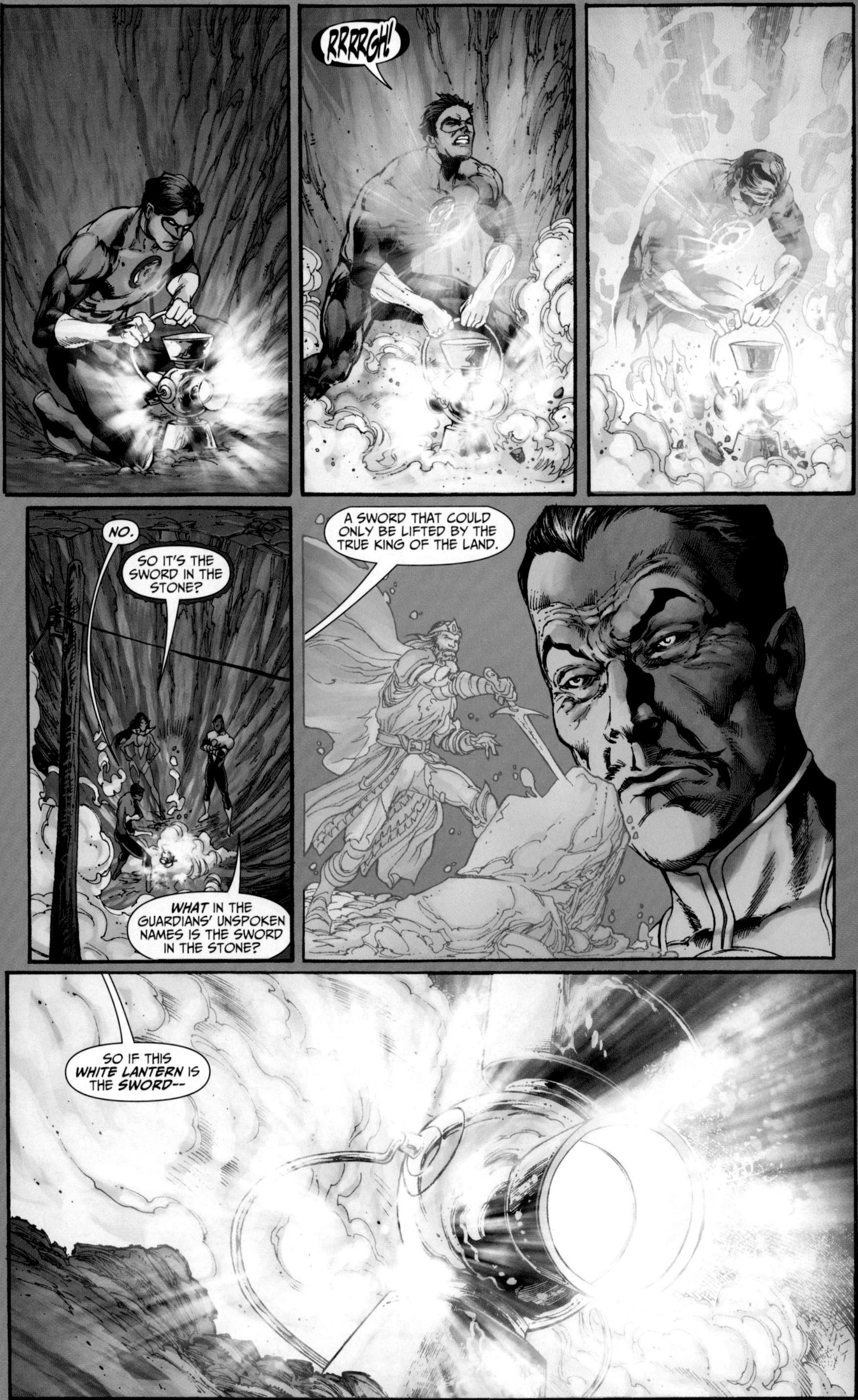
RRRRGH!
NO.
SO IT'S THE SWORD IN THE STONE?
WHAT IN THE GUARDIANS' UNSPOKEN NAMES IS THE SWORD IN THE STONE?
A SWORD THAT COULD ONLY BE LIFTED BY THE TRUE KING OF THE LAND.
SO IF THIS WHITE LANTERN IS THE SWORD--

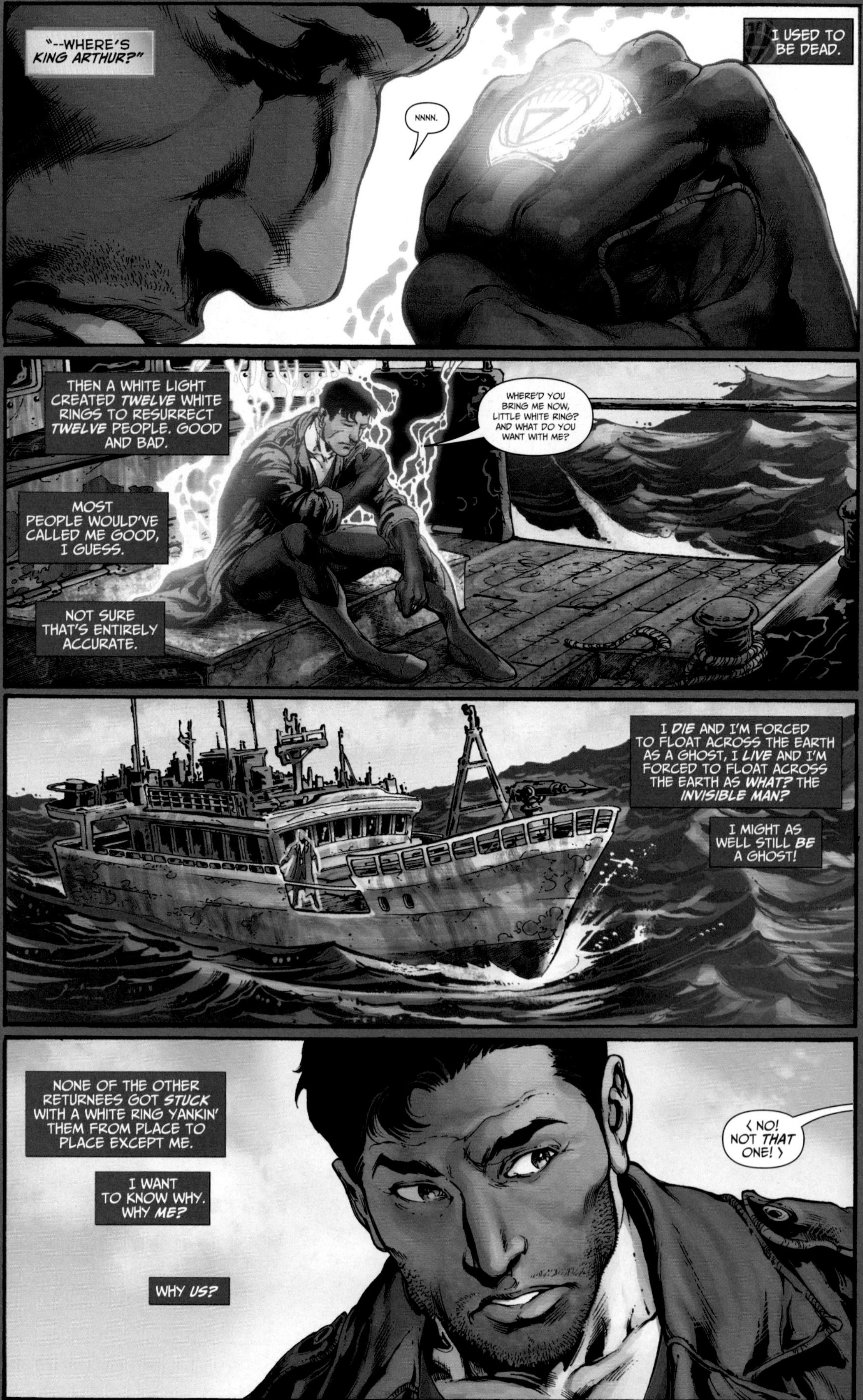
"--WHERE'S KING ARTHUR?"
I USED TO BE DEAD.
NNNN.
THEN A WHITE LIGHT CREATED TWELVE WHITE RINGS TO RESURRECT TWELVE PEOPLE. GOOD AND BAD.
WHERE'D YOU BRING ME NOW, LITTLE WHITE RING? AND WHAT DO YOU WANT WITH ME?
MOST PEOPLE WOULD'VE CALLED ME GOOD, I GUESS.
NOT SURE THAT'S ENTIRELY ACCURATE.
I DIE AND I'M FORCED TO FLOAT ACROSS THE EARTH AS A GHOST, I LIVE AND I'M FORCED TO FLOAT ACROSS THE EARTH AS WHAT? THE INVISIBLE MAN?
I MIGHT AS WELL STILL BE A GHOST!
NONE OF THE OTHER RETURNEES GOT STUCK WITH A WHITE RING YANKIN' THEM FROM PLACE TO PLACE EXCEPT ME.
I WANT TO KNOW WHY. WHY ME?
WHY US?
< NO! NOT THAT ONE! >

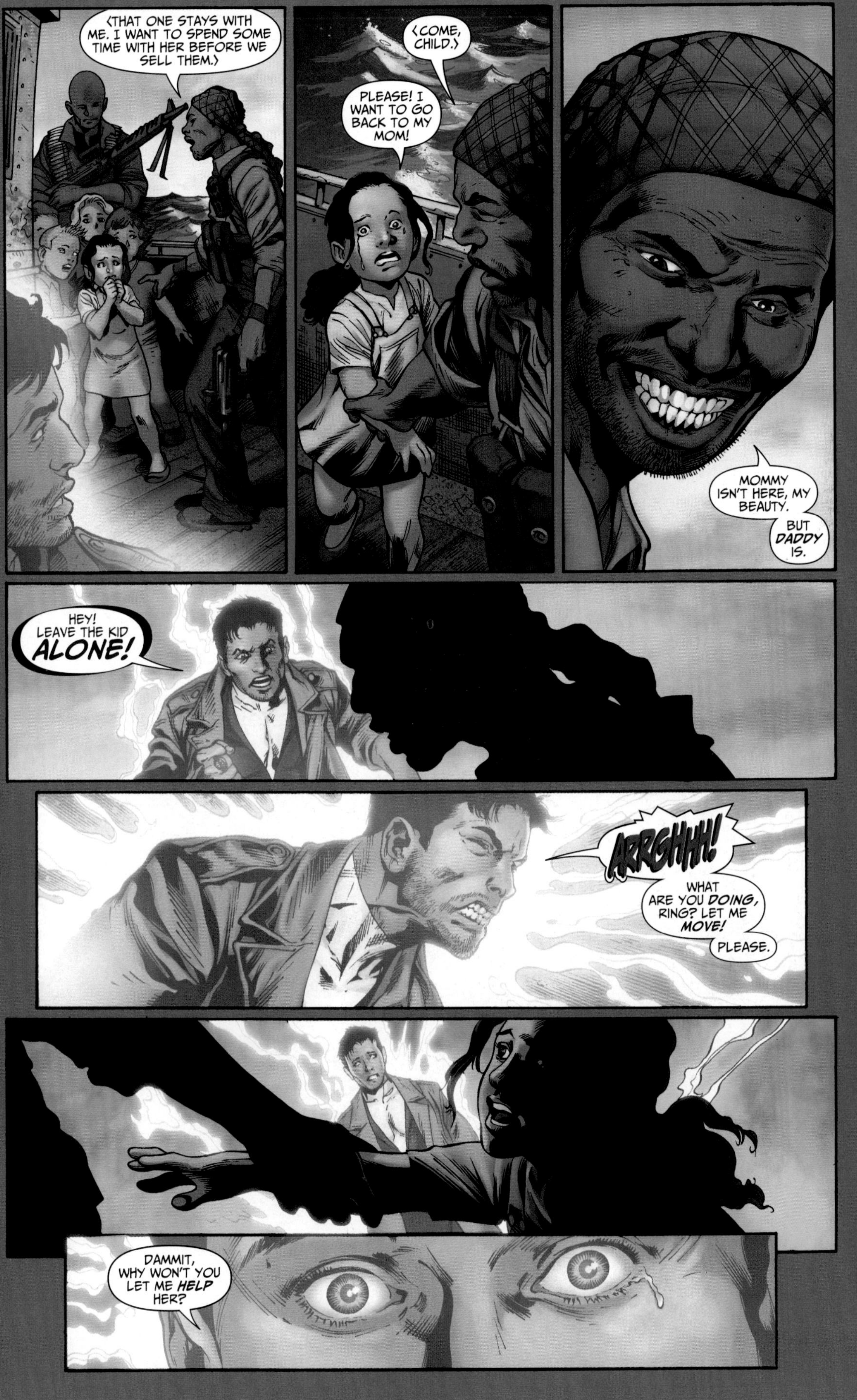
‹THAT ONE STAYS WITH ME. I WANT TO SPEND SOME TIME WITH HER BEFORE WE SELL THEM.›
‹COME, CHILD.›
PLEASE! I WANT TO GO BACK TO MY MOM!
MOMMY ISN'T HERE, MY BEAUTY.
BUT DADDY IS.
HEY! LEAVE THE KID ALONE!
ARRGHHH!
WHAT ARE YOU DOING, RING? LET ME MOVE!
PLEASE.
DAMMIT, WHY WON'T YOU LET ME HELP HER?

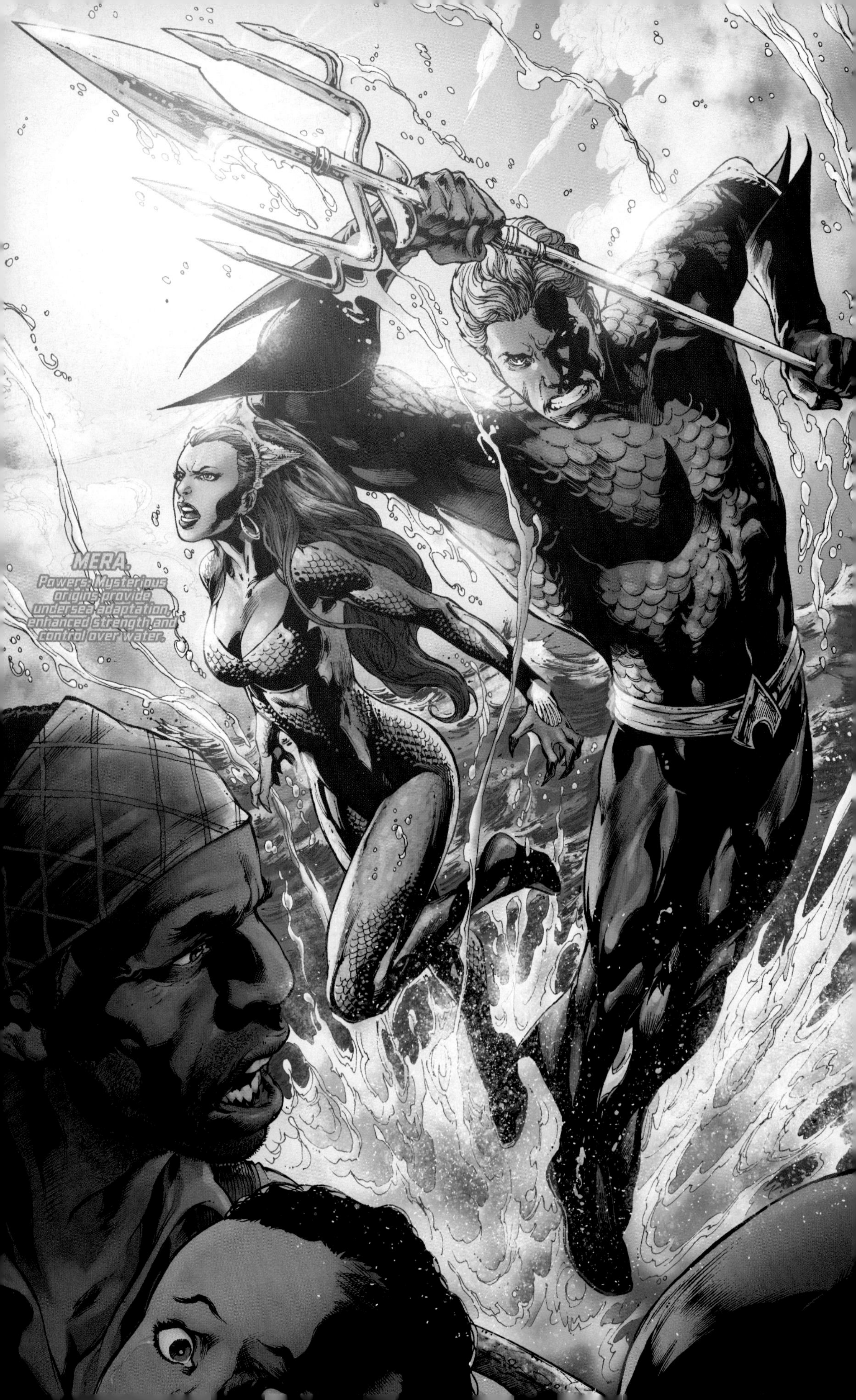
MERA.
Powers: Mysterious origins provide undersea adaptation, enhanced strength and control over water.

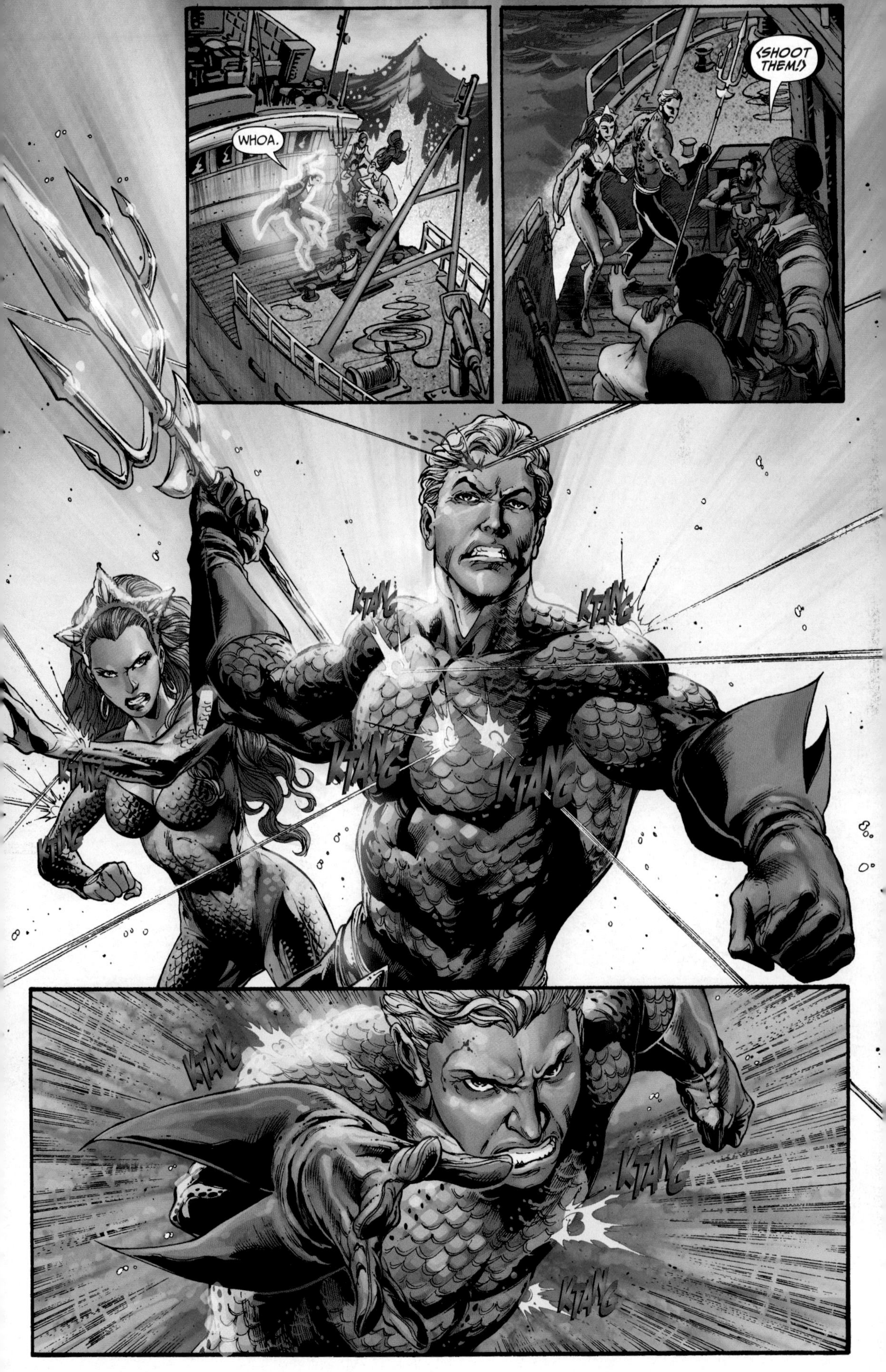
WHOA.
‹SHOOT THEM!›
KTANG
KTANG
KTANG
KTANG
KTANG
KTANG
KTANG
KTANG
KTANG
KTANG

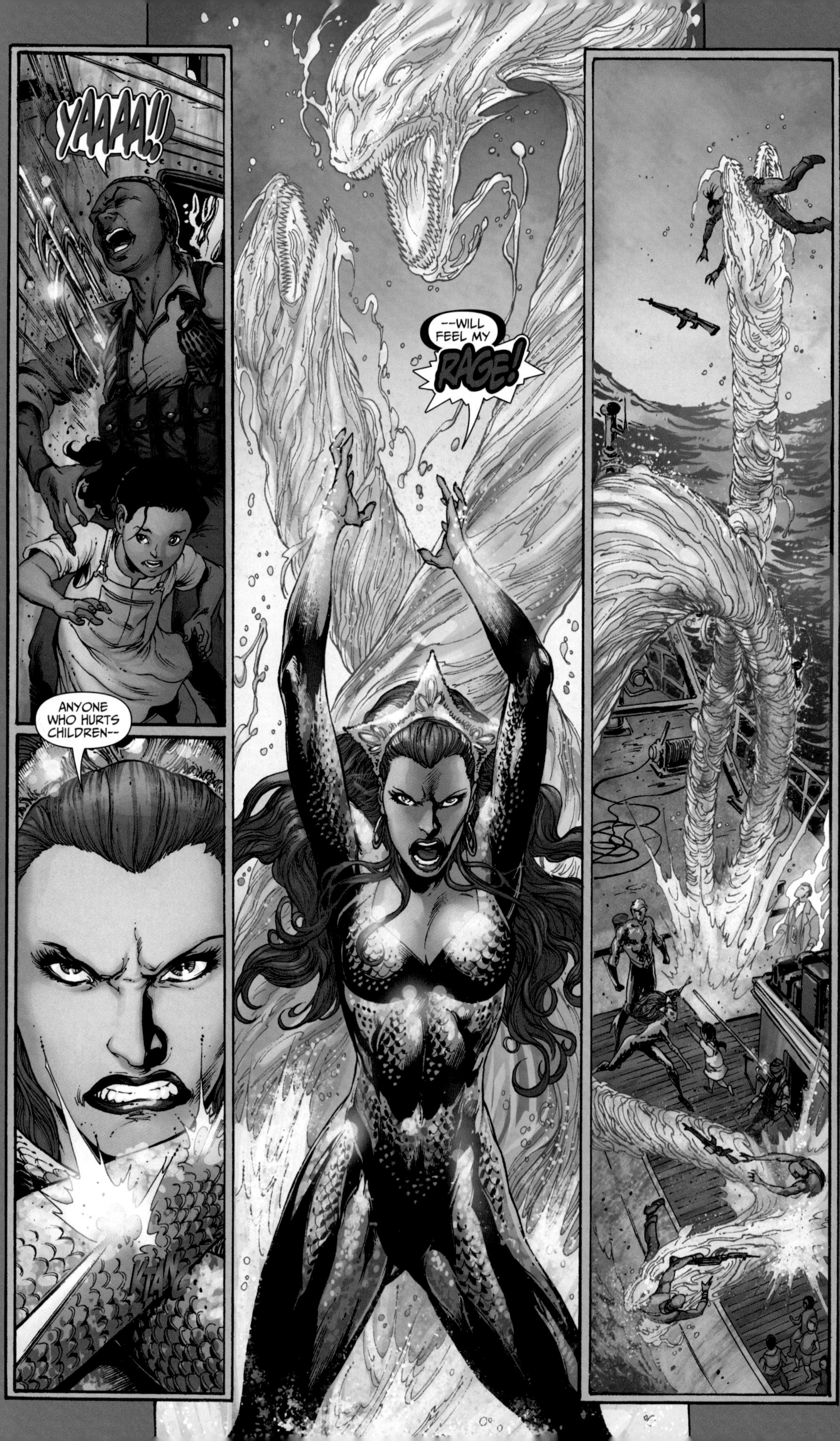
YAAAA!!
ANYONE WHO HURTS CHILDREN--
--WILL FEEL MY RAGE!

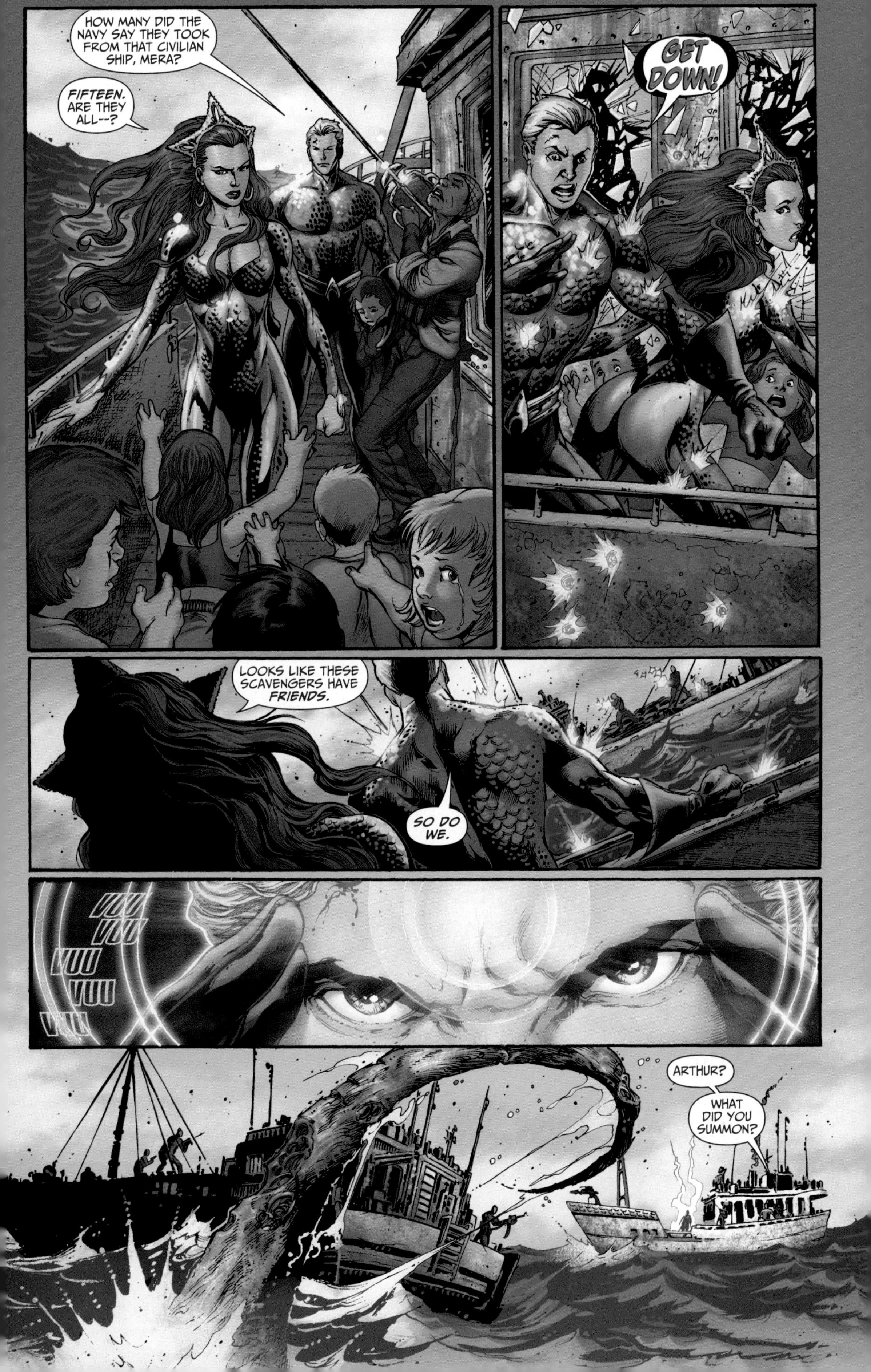
HOW MANY DID THE NAVY SAY THEY TOOK FROM THAT CIVILIAN SHIP, MERA?
FIFTEEN. ARE THEY ALL--?
GET DOWN!
LOOKS LIKE THESE SCAVENGERS HAVE FRIENDS.
SO DO WE.
VUU VUU VUU VUU VUU
ARTHUR?
WHAT DID YOU SUMMON?

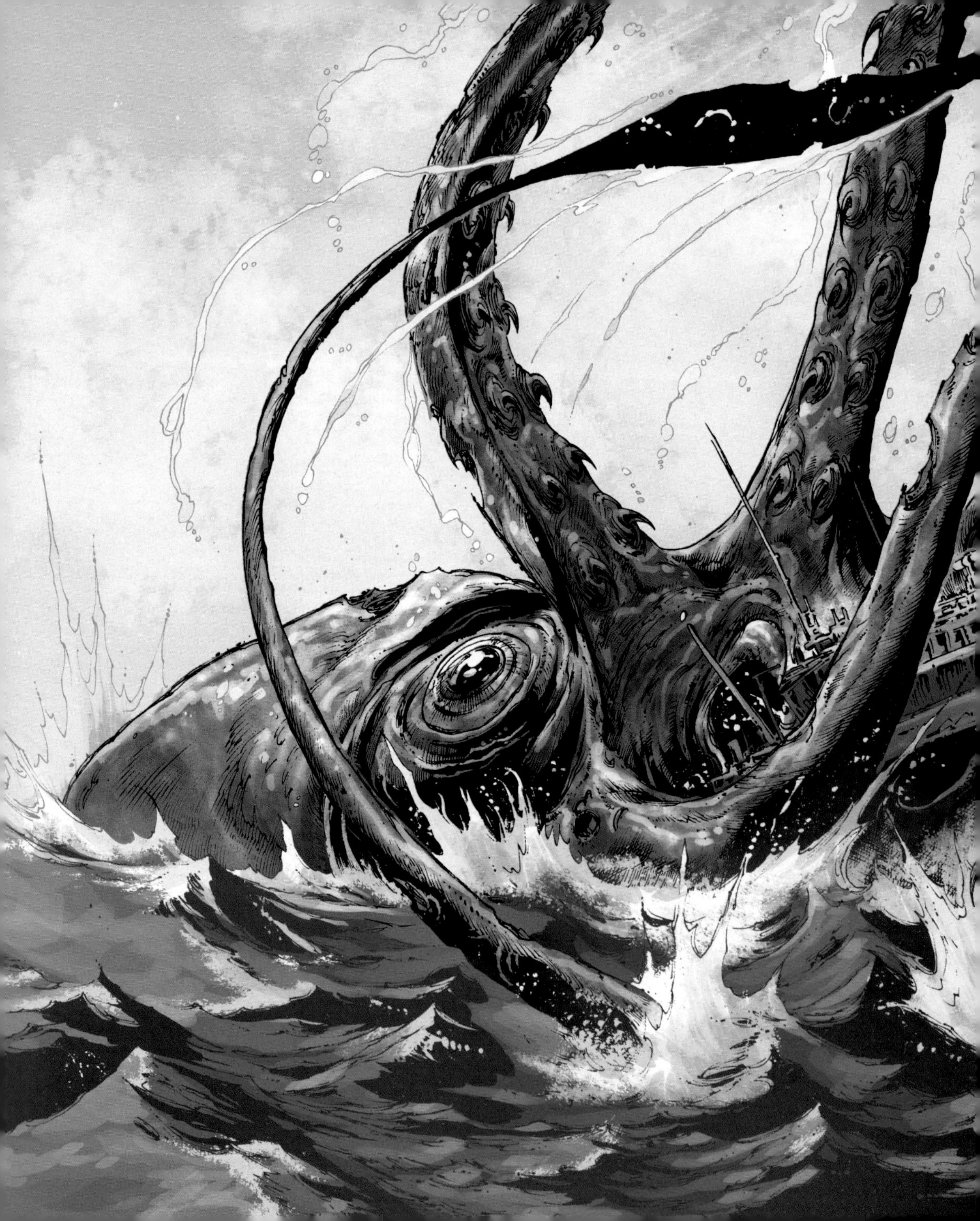

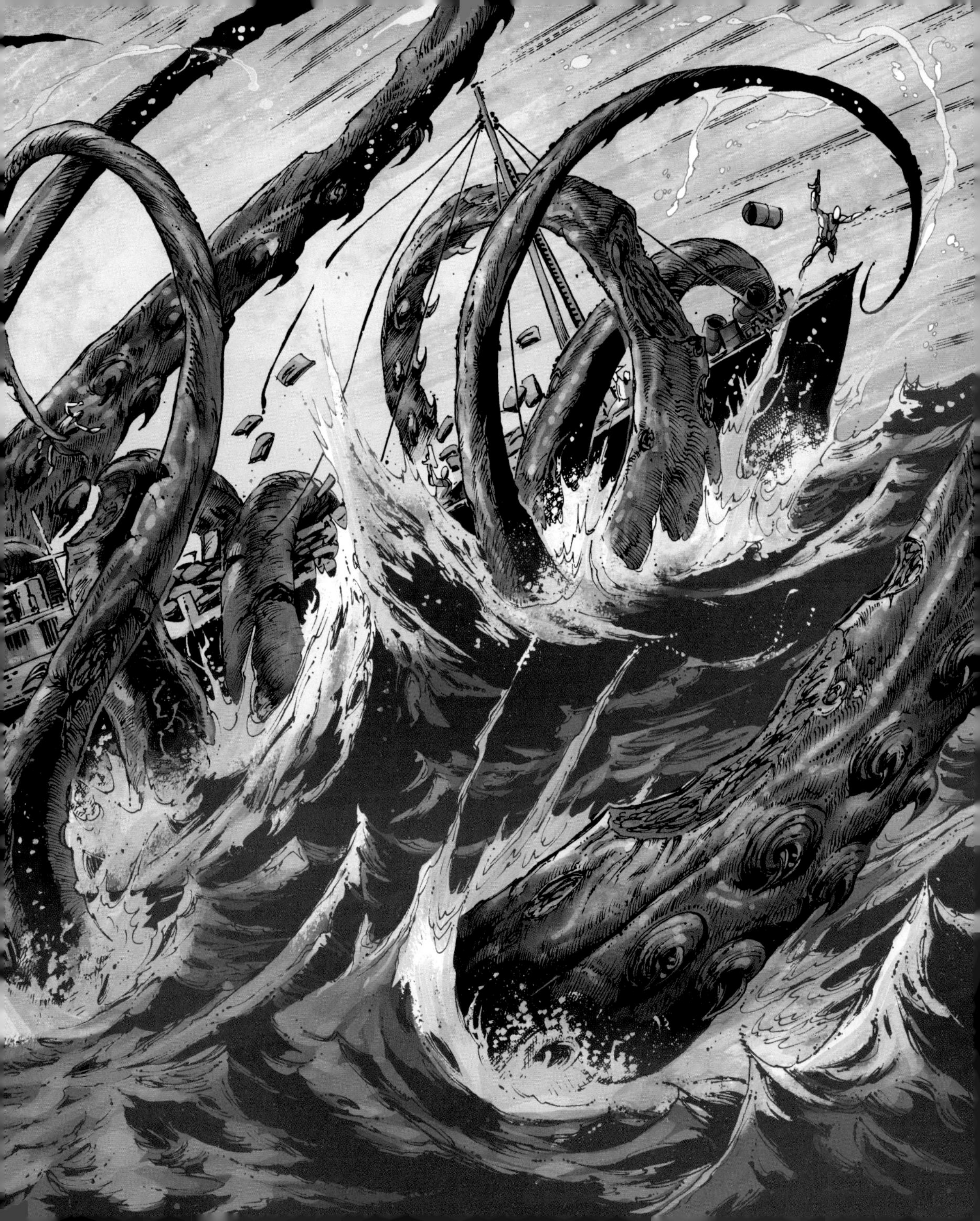

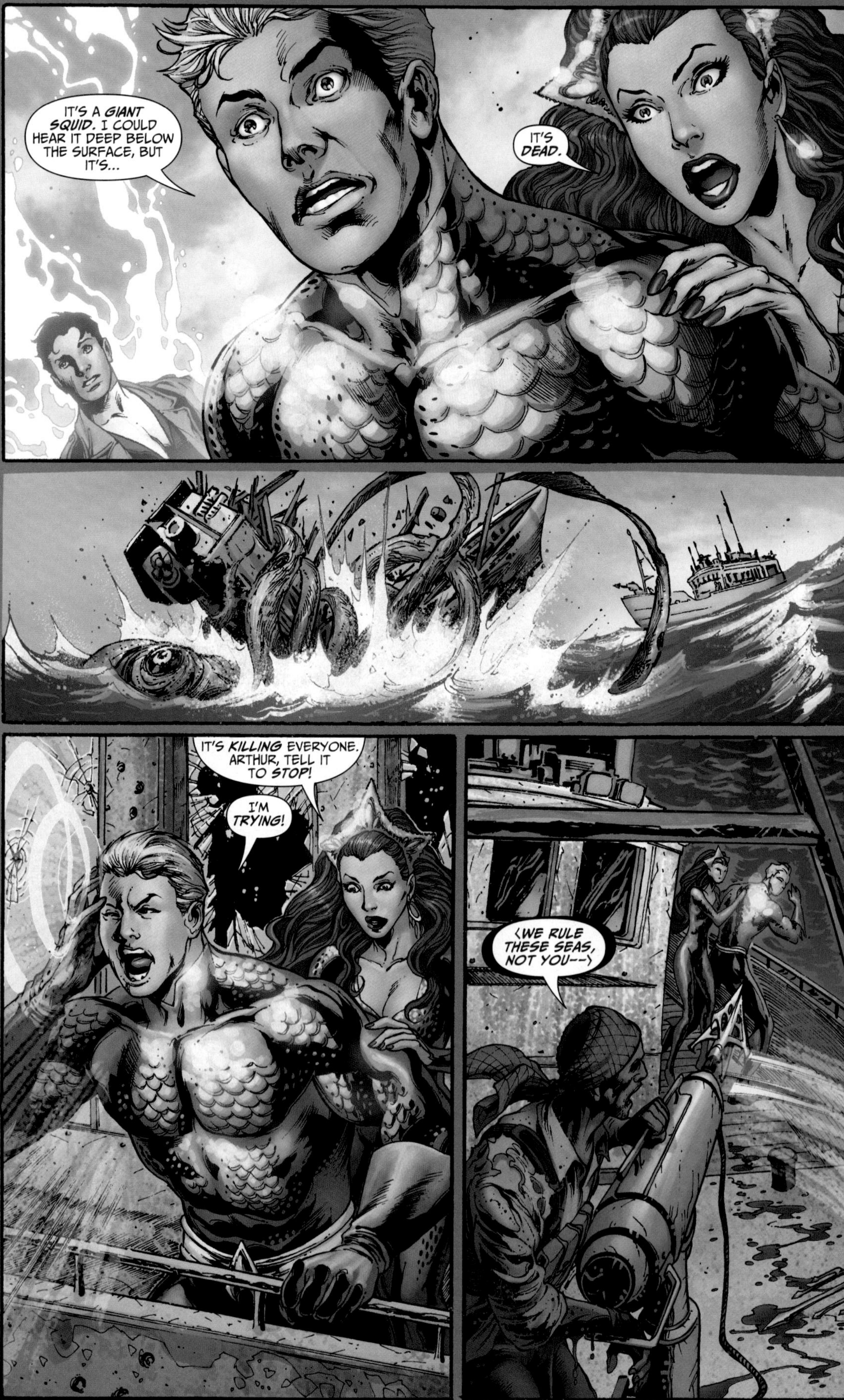
IT'S A *GIANT SQUID*. I COULD HEAR IT DEEP BELOW THE SURFACE, BUT IT'S...
IT'S *DEAD*.
IT'S *KILLING* EVERYONE. ARTHUR, TELL IT TO *STOP*!
I'M *TRYING*!
<WE RULE THESE SEAS, NOT YOU-->

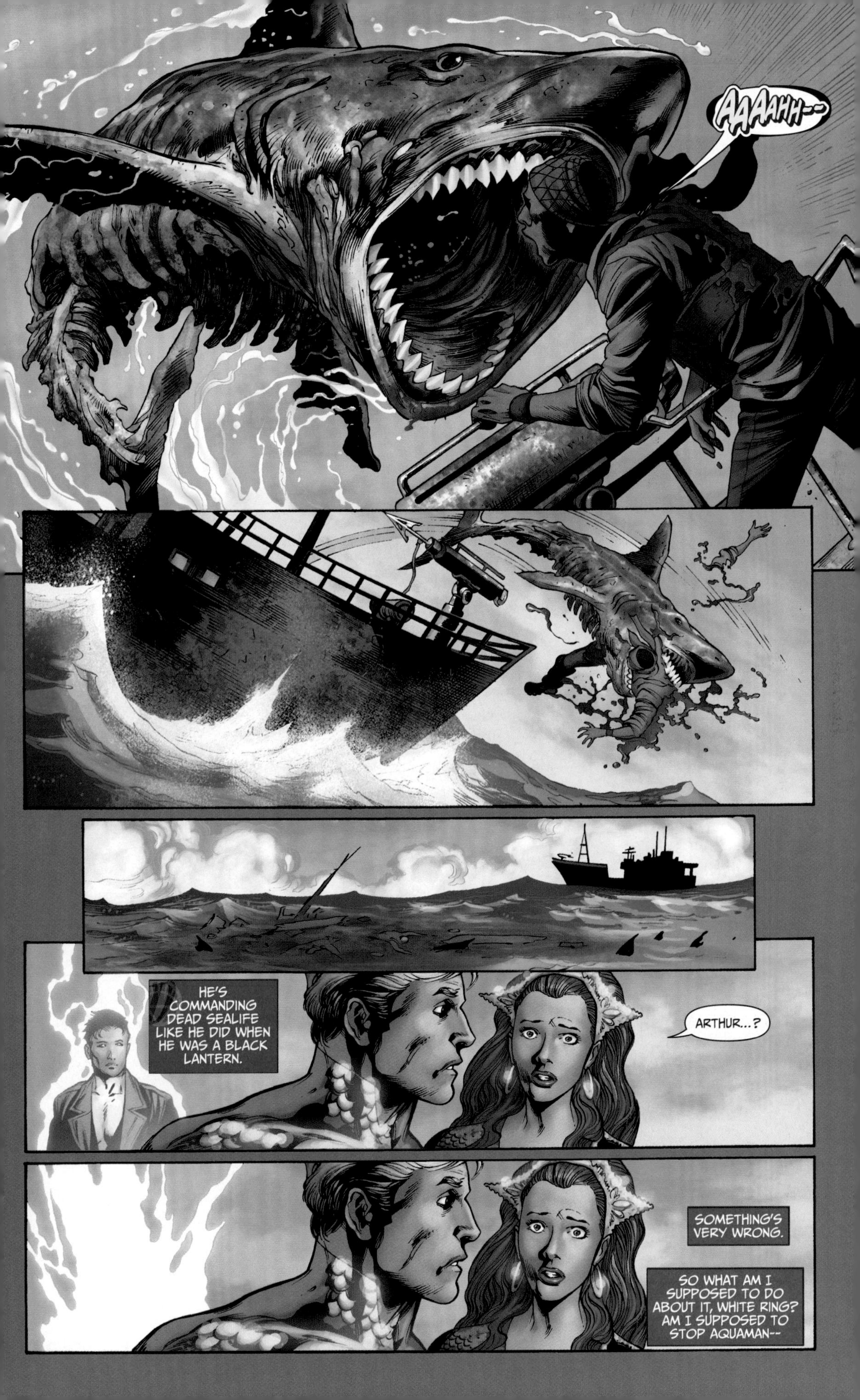
AAAAHH--
HE'S COMMANDING DEAD SEALIFE LIKE HE DID WHEN HE WAS A BLACK LANTERN.
ARTHUR...?
SOMETHING'S VERY WRONG.
SO WHAT AM I SUPPOSED TO DO ABOUT IT, WHITE RING? AM I SUPPOSED TO STOP AQUAMAN--

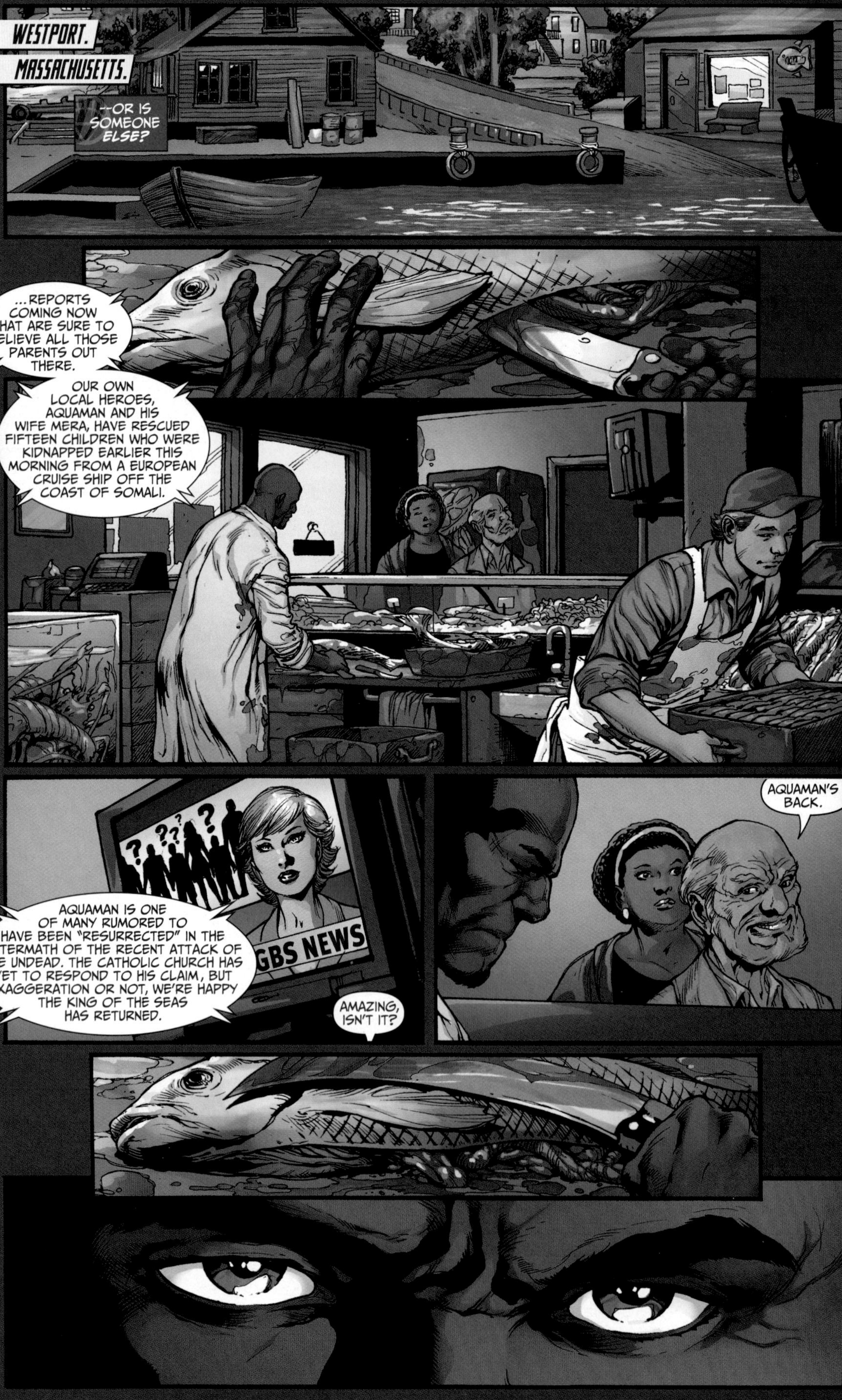
WESTPORT.
MASSACHUSETTS.
--OR IS SOMEONE ELSE?
...REPORTS COMING NOW THAT ARE SURE TO RELIEVE ALL THOSE PARENTS OUT THERE.
OUR OWN LOCAL HEROES, AQUAMAN AND HIS WIFE MERA, HAVE RESCUED FIFTEEN CHILDREN WHO WERE KIDNAPPED EARLIER THIS MORNING FROM A EUROPEAN CRUISE SHIP OFF THE COAST OF SOMALI.
GBS NEWS
AQUAMAN IS ONE OF MANY RUMORED TO HAVE BEEN "RESURRECTED" IN THE AFTERMATH OF THE RECENT ATTACK OF THE UNDEAD. THE CATHOLIC CHURCH HAS YET TO RESPOND TO HIS CLAIM, BUT EXAGGERATION OR NOT, WE'RE HAPPY THE KING OF THE SEAS HAS RETURNED.
AMAZING, ISN'T IT?
AQUAMAN'S BACK.

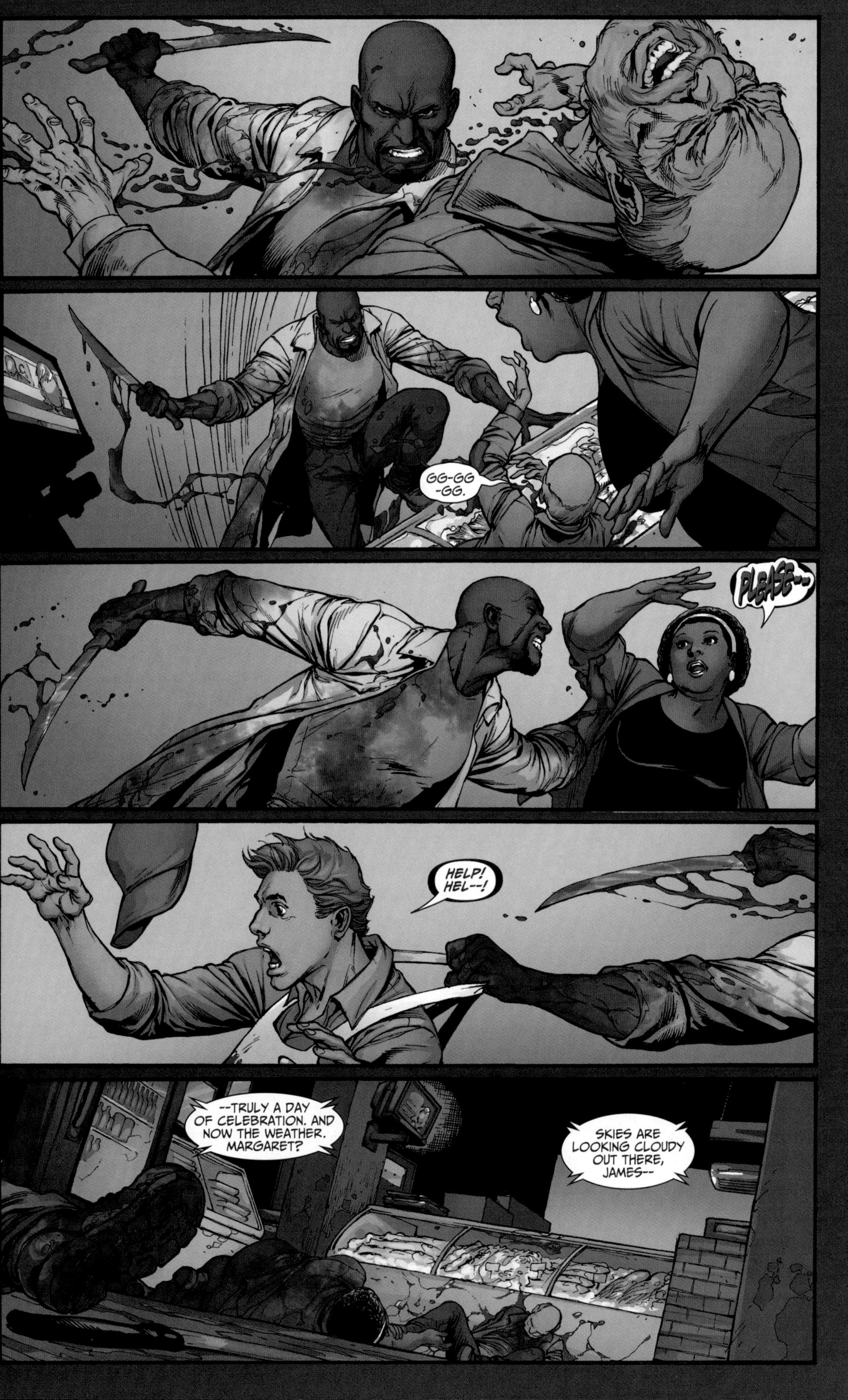
GG-GG
-GG.
PLEASE--
HELP!
HEL--!
--TRULY A DAY OF CELEBRATION. AND NOW THE WEATHER. MARGARET?
SKIES ARE LOOKING CLOUDY OUT THERE, JAMES--

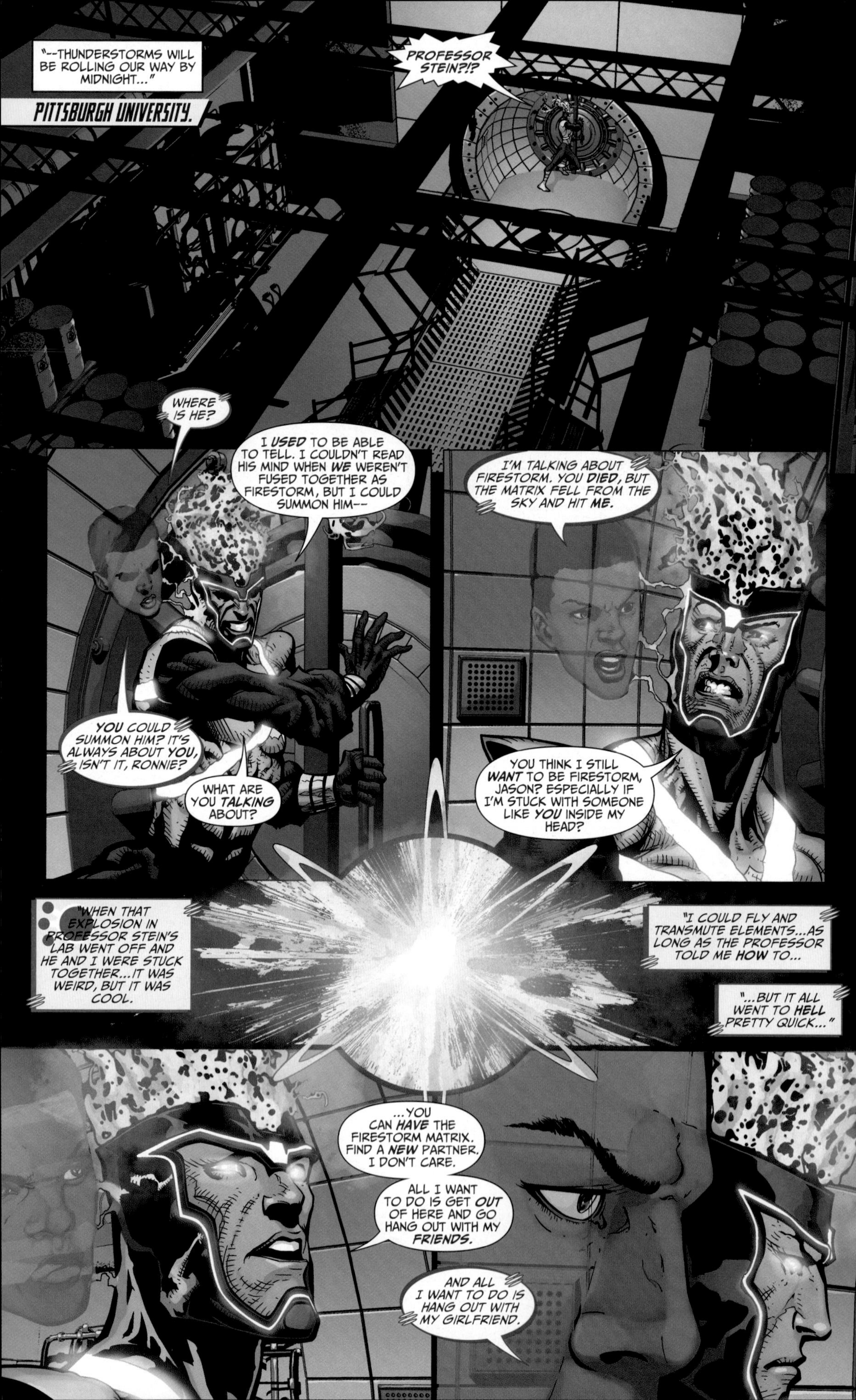
"--THUNDERSTORMS WILL BE ROLLING OUR WAY BY MIDNIGHT..."
PITTSBURGH UNIVERSITY.
PROFESSOR STEIN?!?
WHERE IS HE?
I USED TO BE ABLE TO TELL. I COULDN'T READ HIS MIND WHEN WE WEREN'T FUSED TOGETHER AS FIRESTORM, BUT I COULD SUMMON HIM--
YOU COULD SUMMON HIM? IT'S ALWAYS ABOUT YOU, ISN'T IT, RONNIE?
WHAT ARE YOU TALKING ABOUT?
I'M TALKING ABOUT FIRESTORM. YOU DIED, BUT THE MATRIX FELL FROM THE SKY AND HIT ME.
YOU THINK I STILL WANT TO BE FIRESTORM, JASON? ESPECIALLY IF I'M STUCK WITH SOMEONE LIKE YOU INSIDE MY HEAD?
"WHEN THAT EXPLOSION IN PROFESSOR STEIN'S LAB WENT OFF AND HE AND I WERE STUCK TOGETHER...IT WAS WEIRD, BUT IT WAS COOL.
"I COULD FLY AND TRANSMUTE ELEMENTS...AS LONG AS THE PROFESSOR TOLD ME HOW TO...
"...BUT IT ALL WENT TO HELL PRETTY QUICK..."
...YOU CAN HAVE THE FIRESTORM MATRIX. FIND A NEW PARTNER. I DON'T CARE.
ALL I WANT TO DO IS GET OUT OF HERE AND GO HANG OUT WITH MY FRIENDS.
AND ALL I WANT TO DO IS HANG OUT WITH MY GIRLFRIEND.

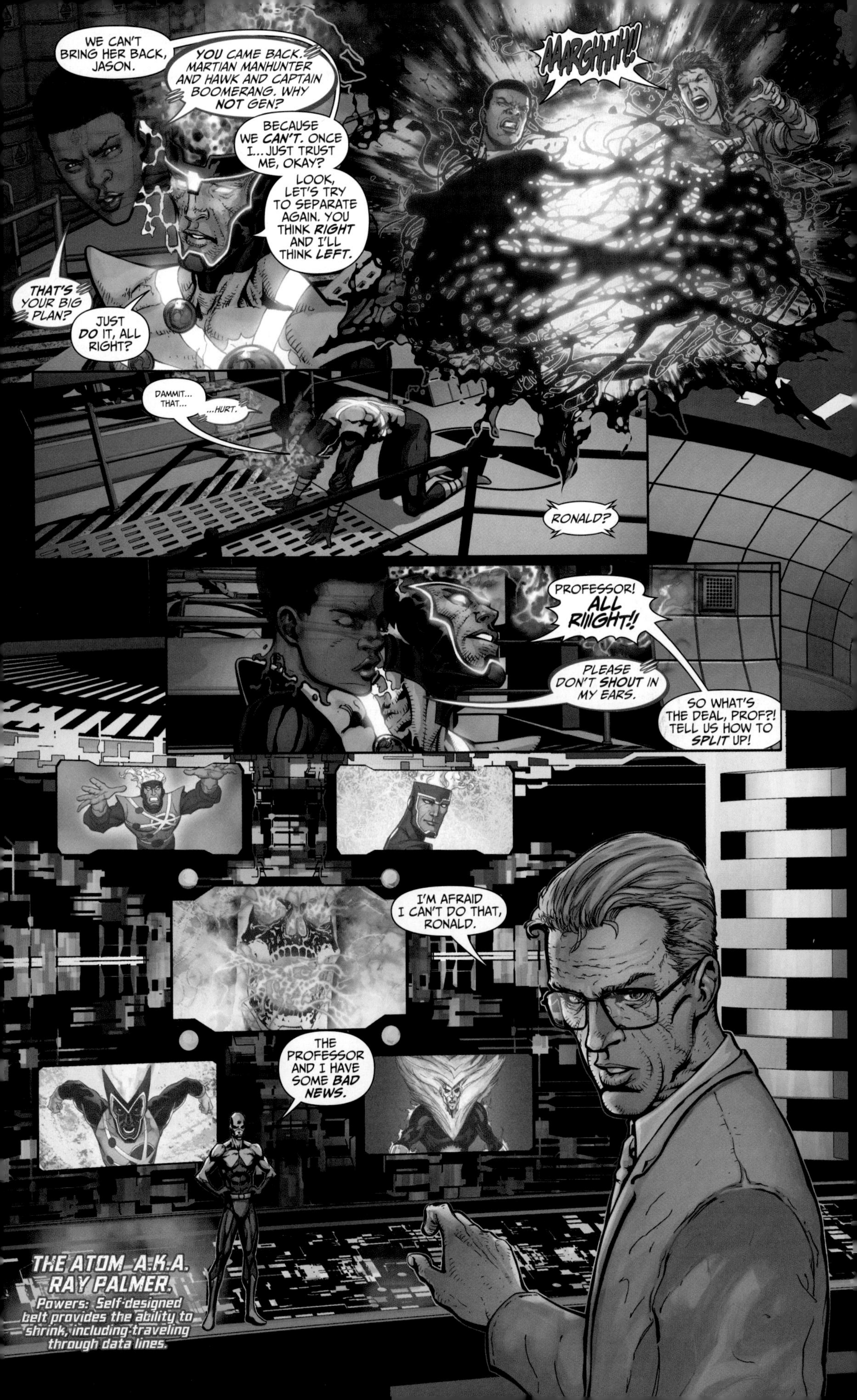

WE CAN'T BRING HER BACK, JASON.
YOU CAME BACK. MARTIAN MANHUNTER AND HAWK AND CAPTAIN BOOMERANG. WHY NOT GEN?
BECAUSE WE CAN'T. ONCE I... JUST TRUST ME, OKAY?
LOOK, LET'S TRY TO SEPARATE AGAIN. YOU THINK RIGHT AND I'LL THINK LEFT.
THAT'S YOUR BIG PLAN?
JUST DO IT, ALL RIGHT?
AAARGHHH!!
DAMMIT... THAT...
...HURT.
RONALD?
PROFESSOR! ALL RIIIGHT!!
PLEASE DON'T SHOUT IN MY EARS.
SO WHAT'S THE DEAL, PROF?! TELL US HOW TO SPLIT UP!
I'M AFRAID I CAN'T DO THAT, RONALD.
THE PROFESSOR AND I HAVE SOME BAD NEWS.
THE ATOM A.K.A. RAY PALMER.
Powers: Self-designed belt provides the ability to shrink, including traveling through data lines.

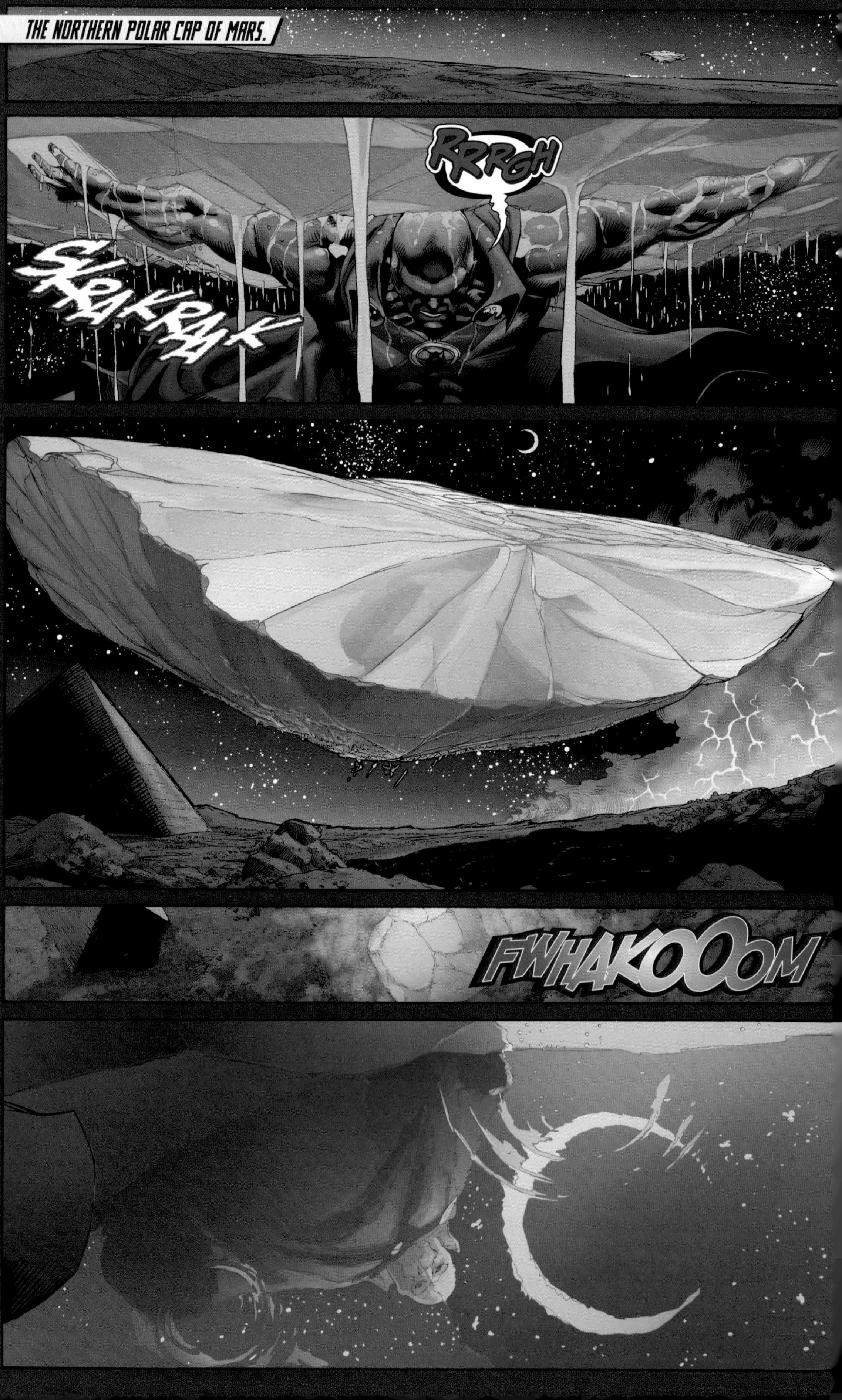
THE NORTHERN POLAR CAP OF MARS.
RRRGH
SKRAKRAK
FWHAKOOOOM

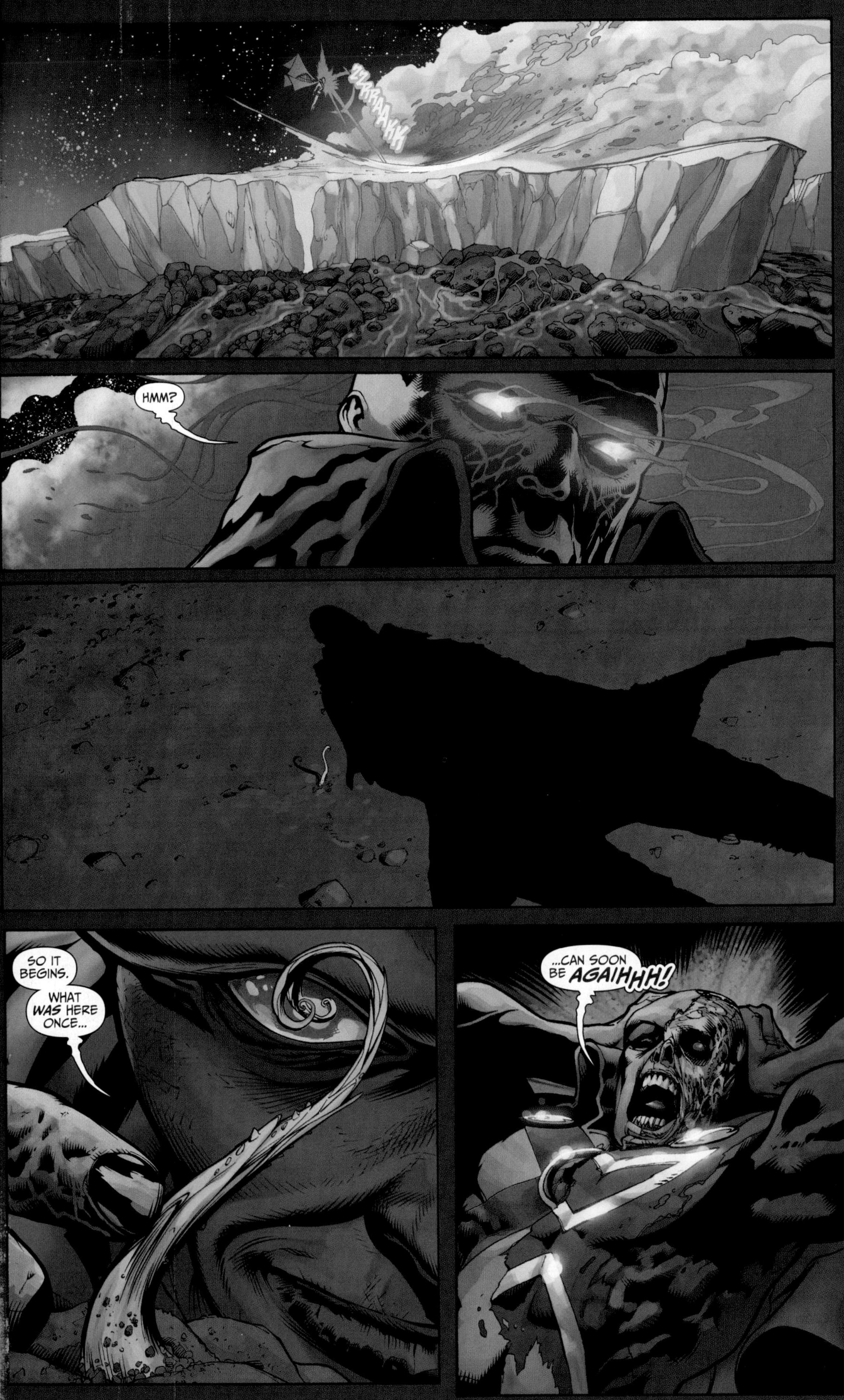
ZZRRAAKK
HMM?
SO IT BEGINS.
WHAT WAS HERE ONCE...
...CAN SOON BE AGAIHHH!

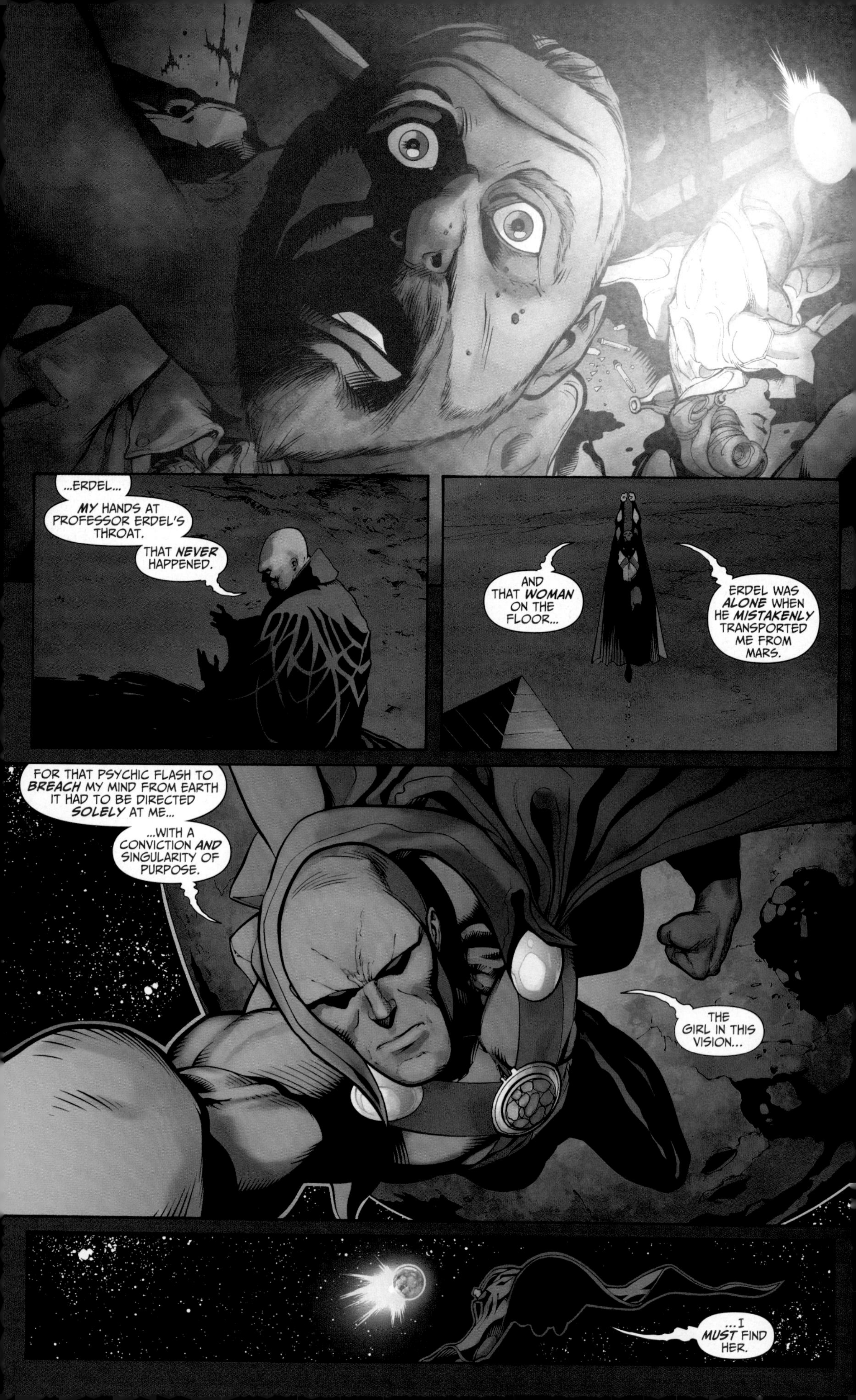
...ERDEL...
MY HANDS AT PROFESSOR ERDEL'S THROAT.
THAT NEVER HAPPENED.
AND THAT WOMAN ON THE FLOOR...
ERDEL WAS ALONE WHEN HE MISTAKENLY TRANSPORTED ME FROM MARS.
FOR THAT PSYCHIC FLASH TO BREACH MY MIND FROM EARTH IT HAD TO BE DIRECTED SOLELY AT ME...
...WITH A CONVICTION AND SINGULARITY OF PURPOSE.
THE GIRL IN THIS VISION...
...I MUST FIND HER.

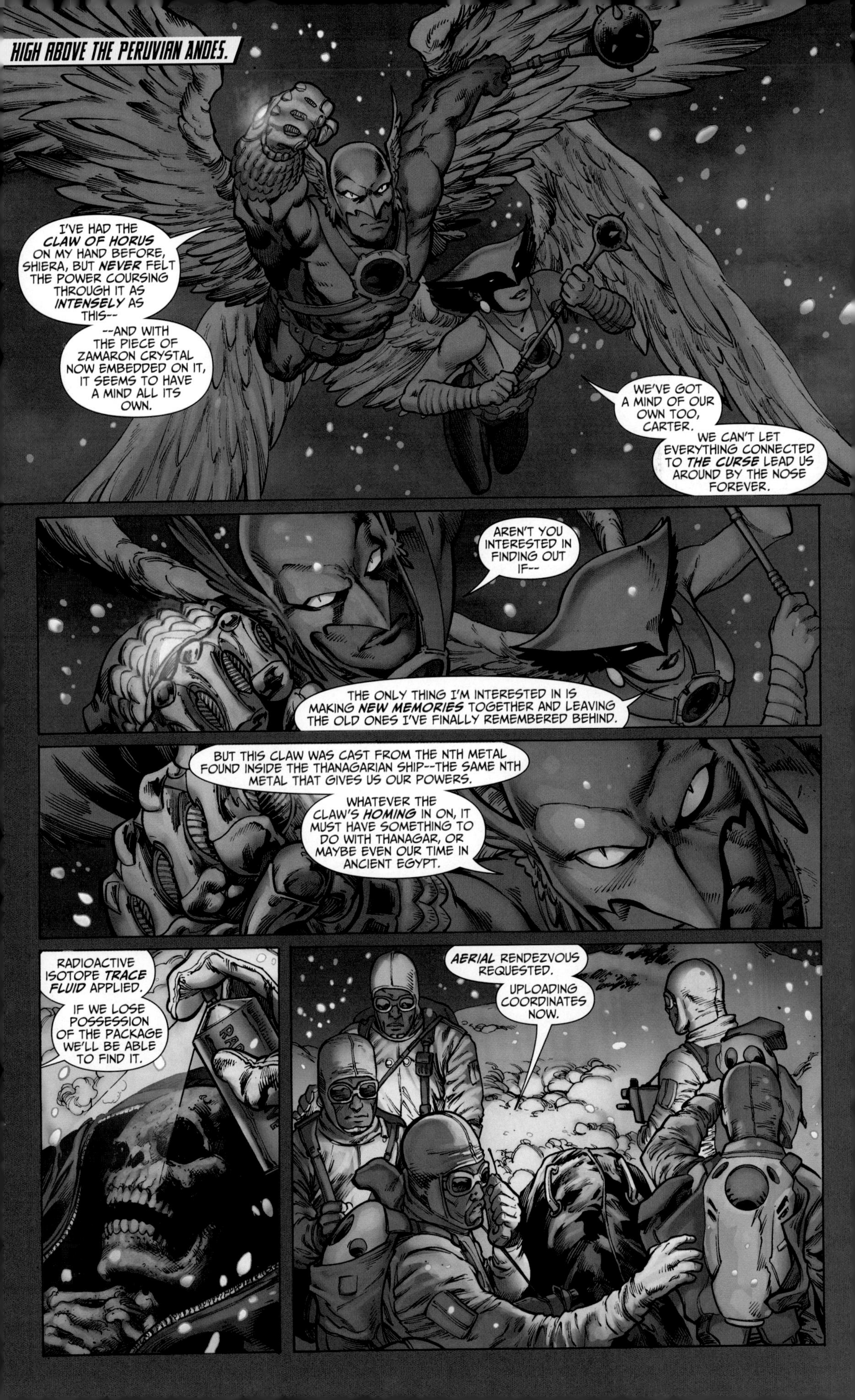
HIGH ABOVE THE PERUVIAN ANDES.
I'VE HAD THE CLAW OF HORUS ON MY HAND BEFORE, SHIERA, BUT NEVER FELT THE POWER COURSING THROUGH IT AS INTENSELY AS THIS--
--AND WITH THE PIECE OF ZAMARON CRYSTAL NOW EMBEDDED ON IT, IT SEEMS TO HAVE A MIND ALL ITS OWN.
WE'VE GOT A MIND OF OUR OWN TOO, CARTER.
WE CAN'T LET EVERYTHING CONNECTED TO THE CURSE LEAD US AROUND BY THE NOSE FOREVER.
AREN'T YOU INTERESTED IN FINDING OUT IF--
THE ONLY THING I'M INTERESTED IN IS MAKING NEW MEMORIES TOGETHER AND LEAVING THE OLD ONES I'VE FINALLY REMEMBERED BEHIND.
BUT THIS CLAW WAS CAST FROM THE NTH METAL FOUND INSIDE THE THANAGARIAN SHIP--THE SAME NTH METAL THAT GIVES US OUR POWERS.
WHATEVER THE CLAW'S HOMING IN ON, IT MUST HAVE SOMETHING TO DO WITH THANAGAR, OR MAYBE EVEN OUR TIME IN ANCIENT EGYPT.
RADIOACTIVE ISOTOPE TRACE FLUID APPLIED.
IF WE LOSE POSSESSION OF THE PACKAGE WE'LL BE ABLE TO FIND IT.
AERIAL RENDEZVOUS REQUESTED.
UPLOADING COORDINATES NOW.

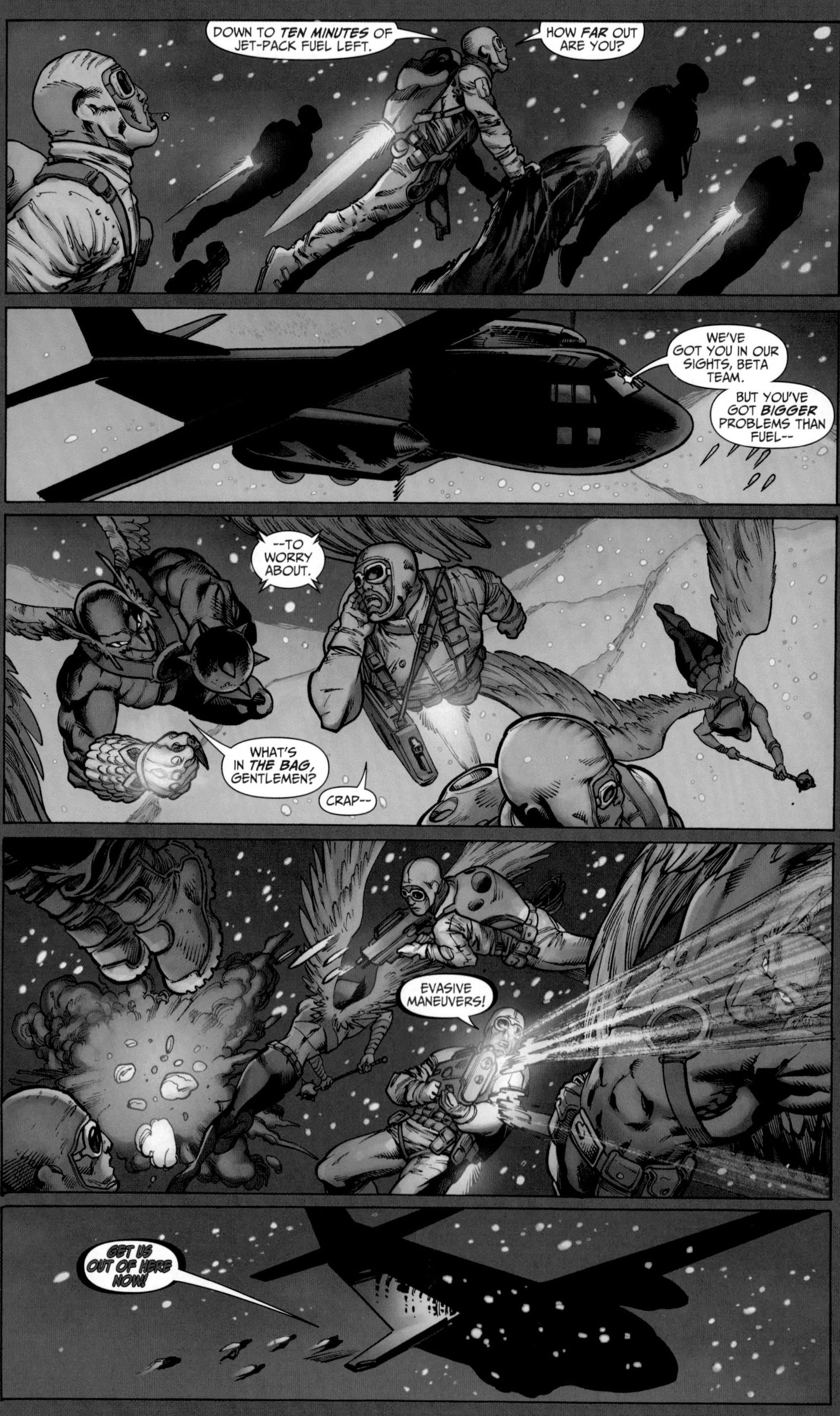
DOWN TO *TEN MINUTES* OF JET-PACK FUEL LEFT.
HOW *FAR* OUT ARE YOU?
WE'VE GOT YOU IN OUR SIGHTS, BETA TEAM.
BUT YOU'VE GOT *BIGGER* PROBLEMS THAN FUEL--
--TO WORRY ABOUT.
WHAT'S IN *THE BAG*, GENTLEMEN?
CRAP--
EVASIVE MANEUVERS!
GET US OUT OF HERE NOW!

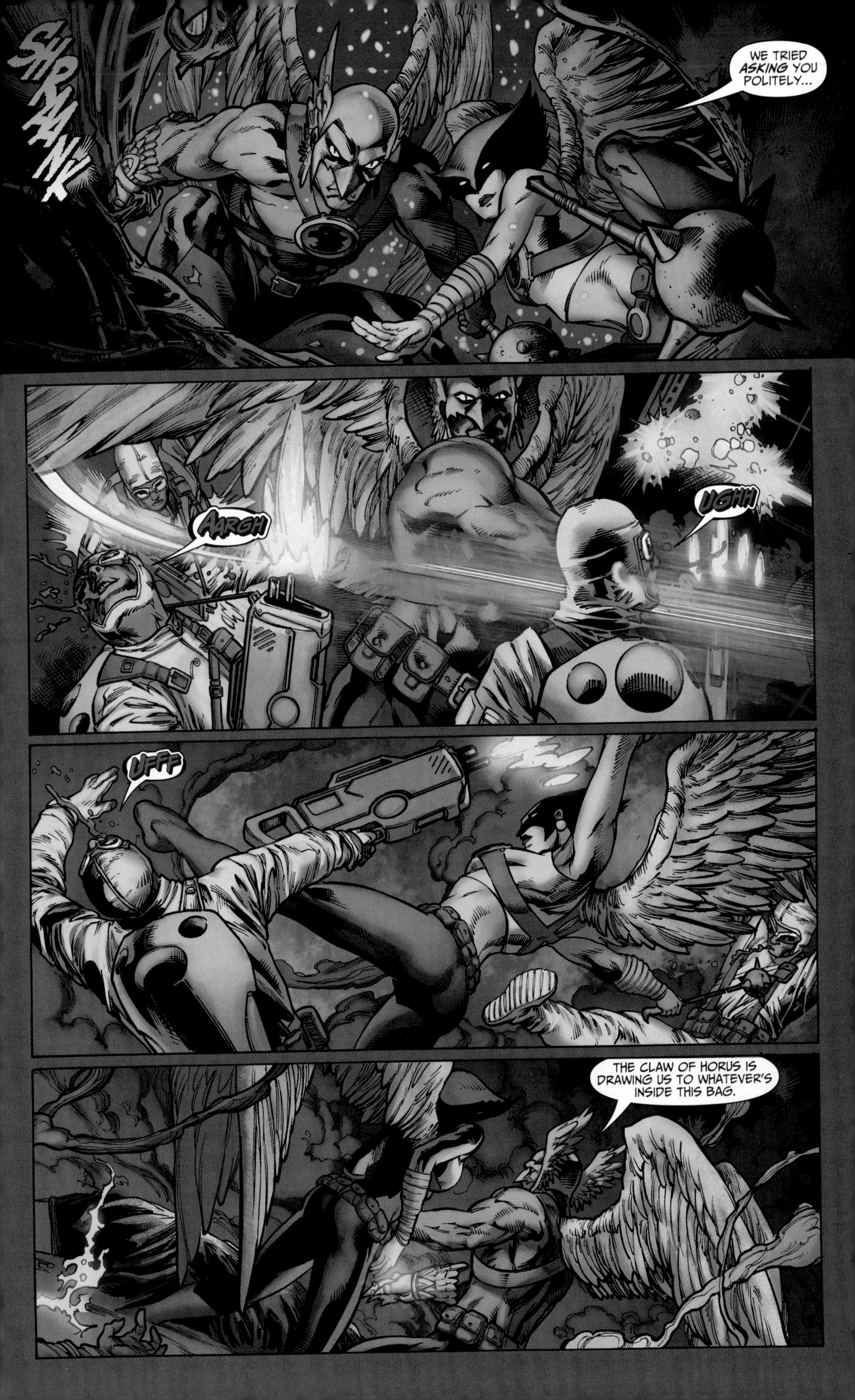
SHRAANK
WE TRIED ASKING YOU POLITELY...
AARGH
UGHH
UFFF
THE CLAW OF HORUS IS DRAWING US TO WHATEVER'S INSIDE THIS BAG.

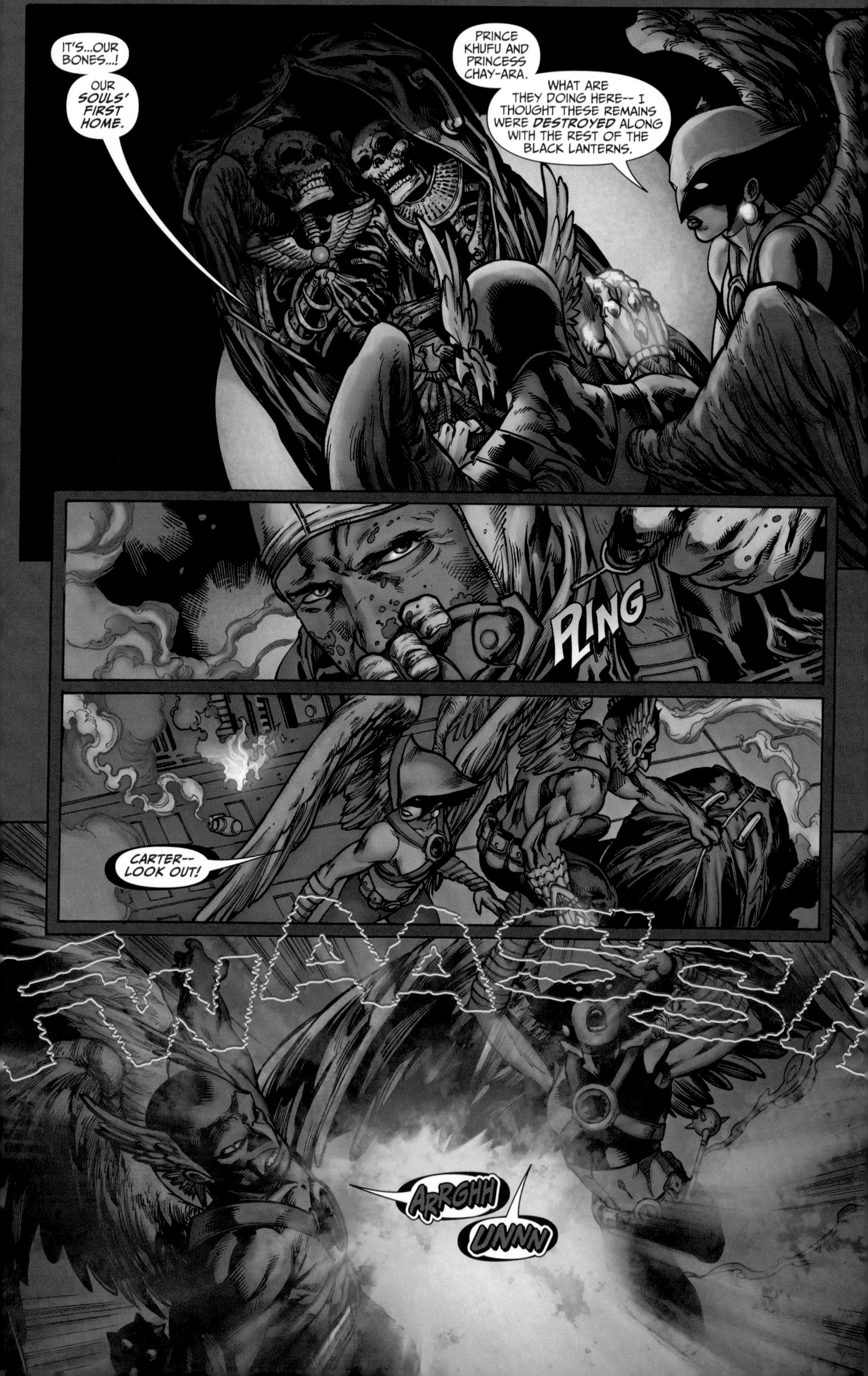
IT'S...OUR BONES...!
OUR SOULS' FIRST HOME.
PRINCE KHUFU AND PRINCESS CHAY-ARA.
WHAT ARE THEY DOING HERE-- I THOUGHT THESE REMAINS WERE DESTROYED ALONG WITH THE REST OF THE BLACK LANTERNS.
PLING
CARTER-- LOOK OUT!
ARRGHH
UNNN

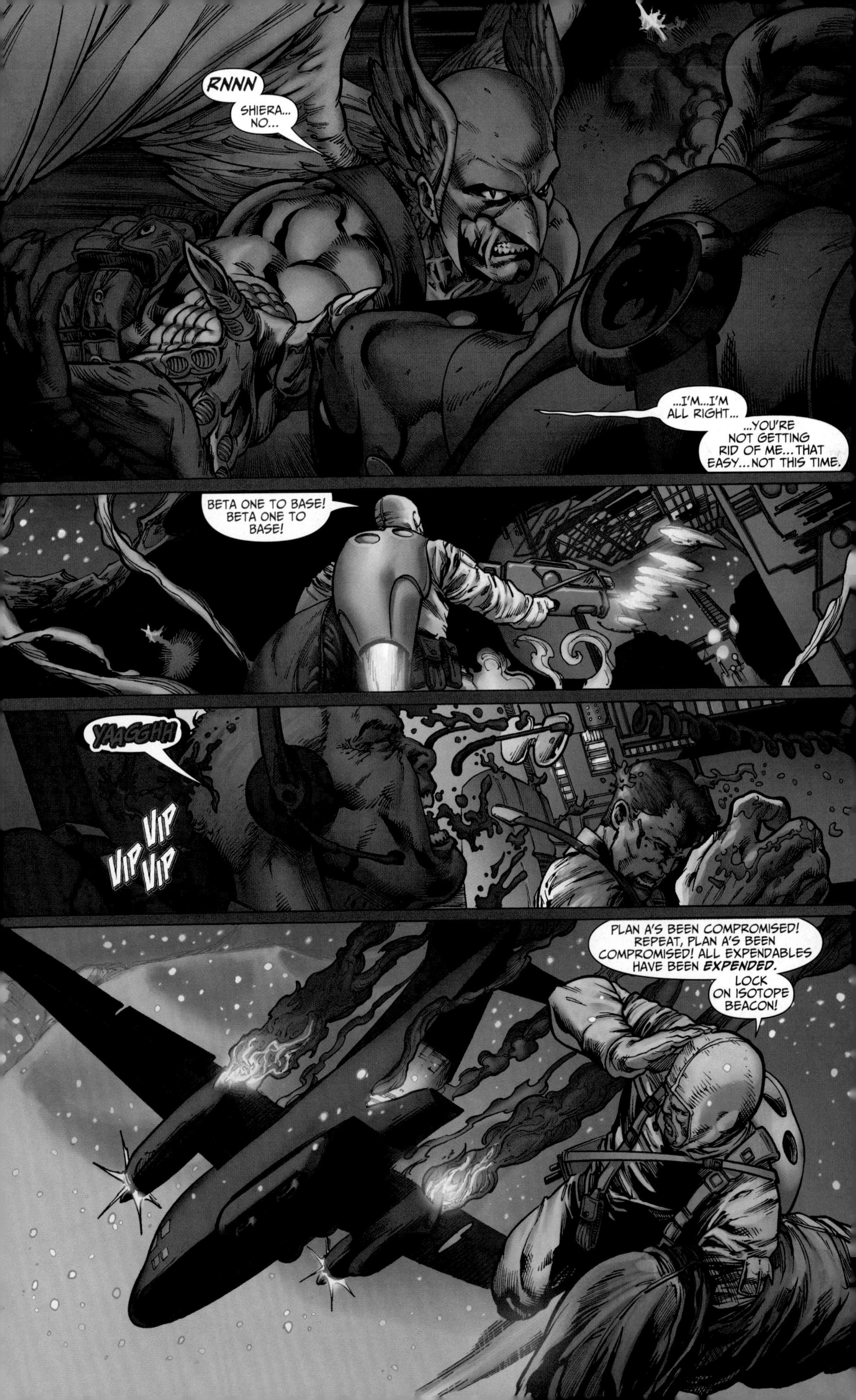
RNNN
SHIERA... NO...
...I'M...I'M ALL RIGHT...
...YOU'RE NOT GETTING RID OF ME...THAT EASY...NOT THIS TIME.
BETA ONE TO BASE! BETA ONE TO BASE!
YAAGGHH
VIP VIP VIP VIP
PLAN A'S BEEN COMPROMISED! REPEAT, PLAN A'S BEEN COMPROMISED! ALL EXPENDABLES HAVE BEEN EXPENDED.
LOCK ON ISOTOPE BEACON!

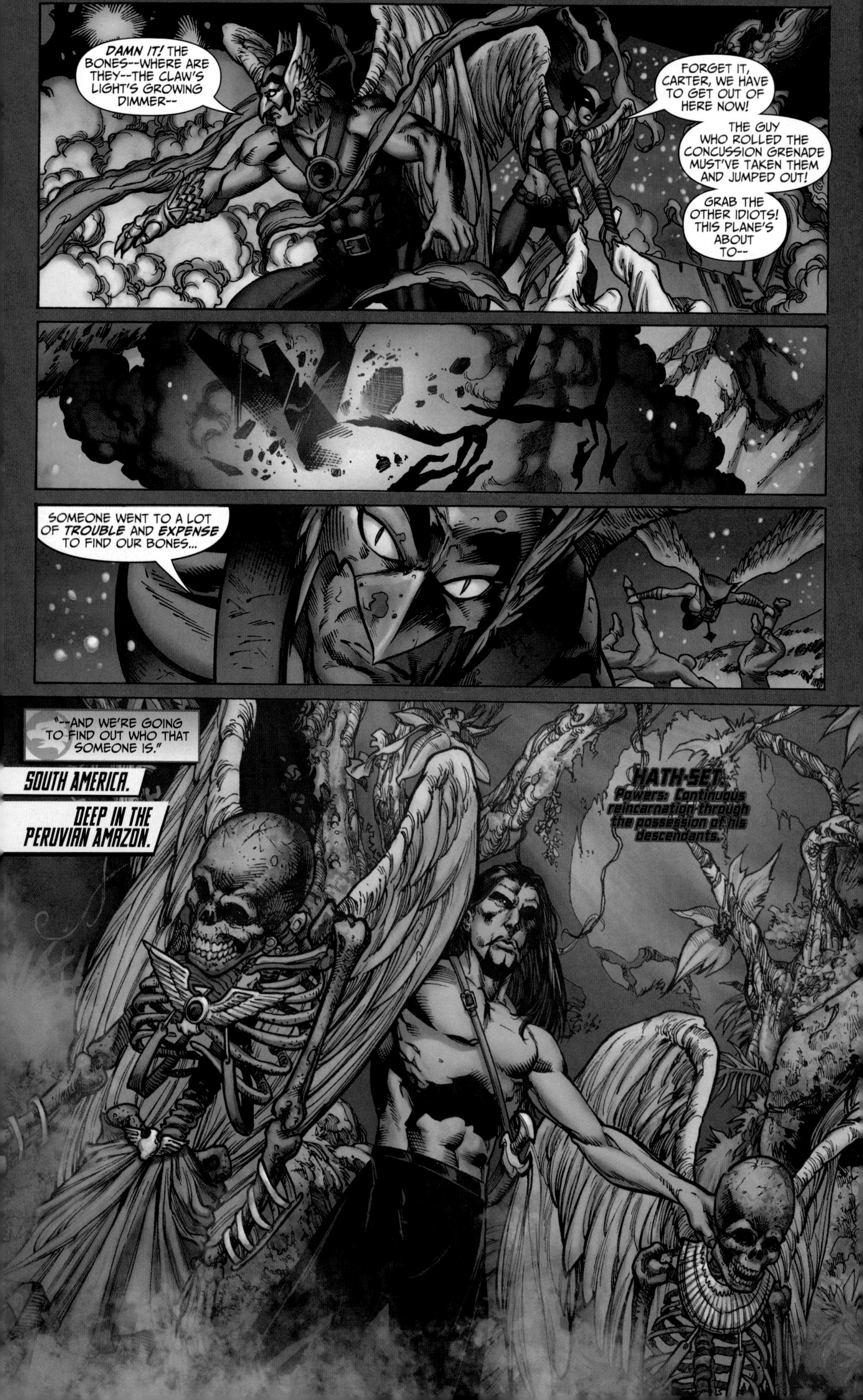
DAMN IT! THE BONES--WHERE ARE THEY--THE CLAW'S LIGHT'S GROWING DIMMER--
FORGET IT, CARTER, WE HAVE TO GET OUT OF HERE NOW!
THE GUY WHO ROLLED THE CONCUSSION GRENADE MUST'VE TAKEN THEM AND JUMPED OUT!
GRAB THE OTHER IDIOTS! THIS PLANE'S ABOUT TO--
SOMEONE WENT TO A LOT OF TROUBLE AND EXPENSE TO FIND OUR BONES...
"--AND WE'RE GOING TO FIND OUT WHO THAT SOMEONE IS."
SOUTH AMERICA.
DEEP IN THE PERUVIAN AMAZON.
HATH-SET.
Powers: Continuous reincarnation through the possession of his descendants.

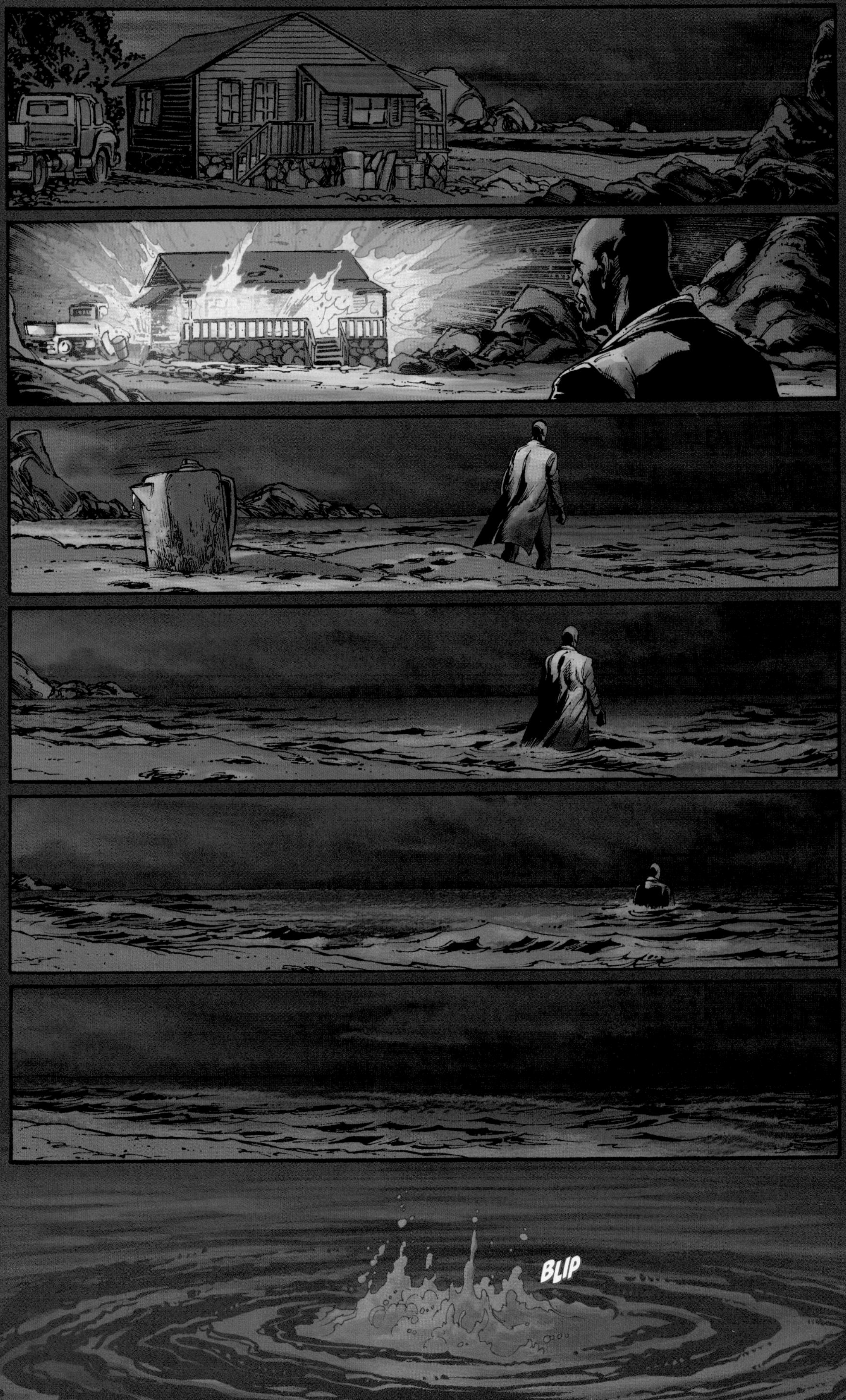
BLIP

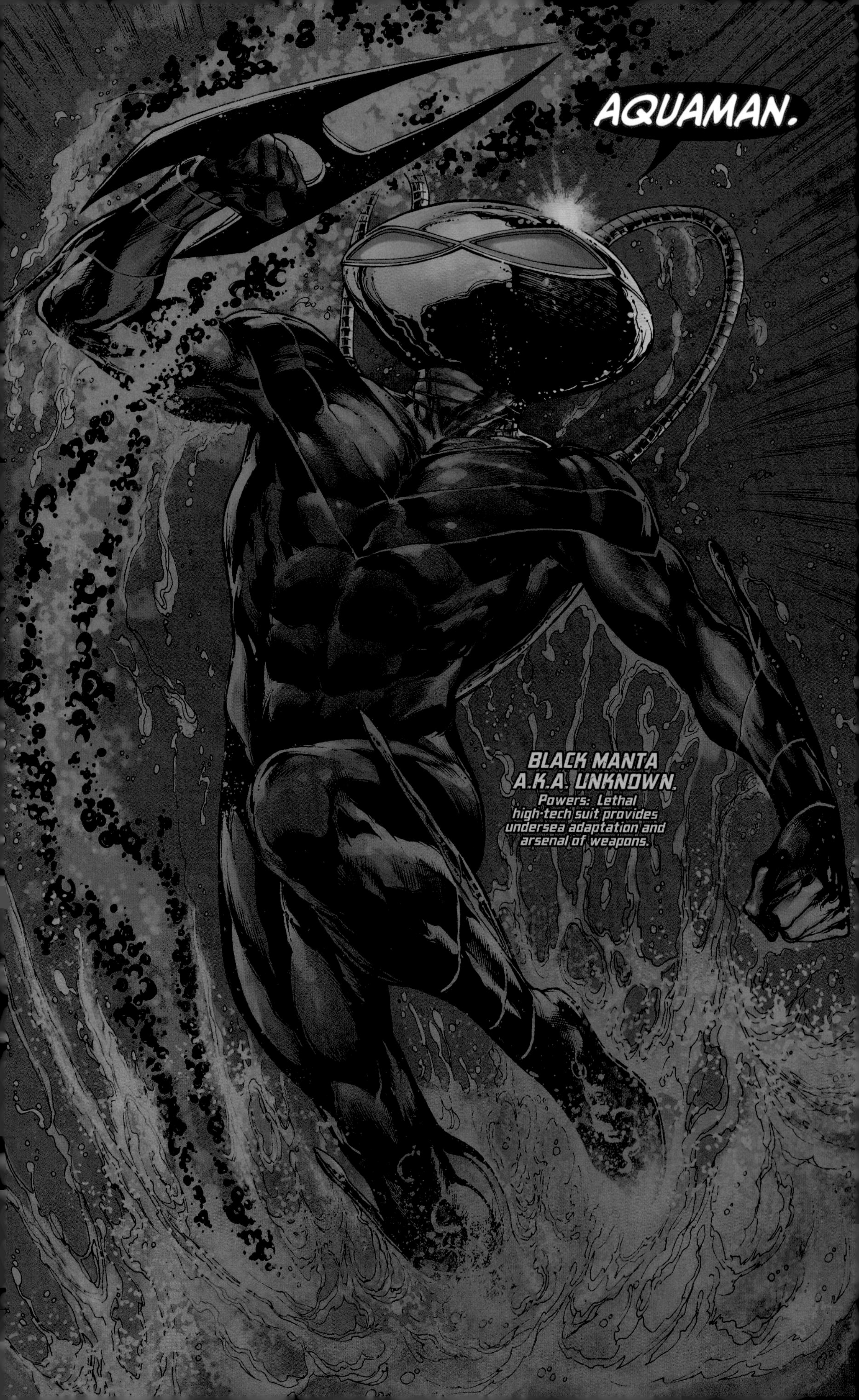
AQUAMAN.
BLACK MANTA
A.K.A. UNKNOWN.
Powers: Lethal high-tech suit provides undersea adaptation and arsenal of weapons.

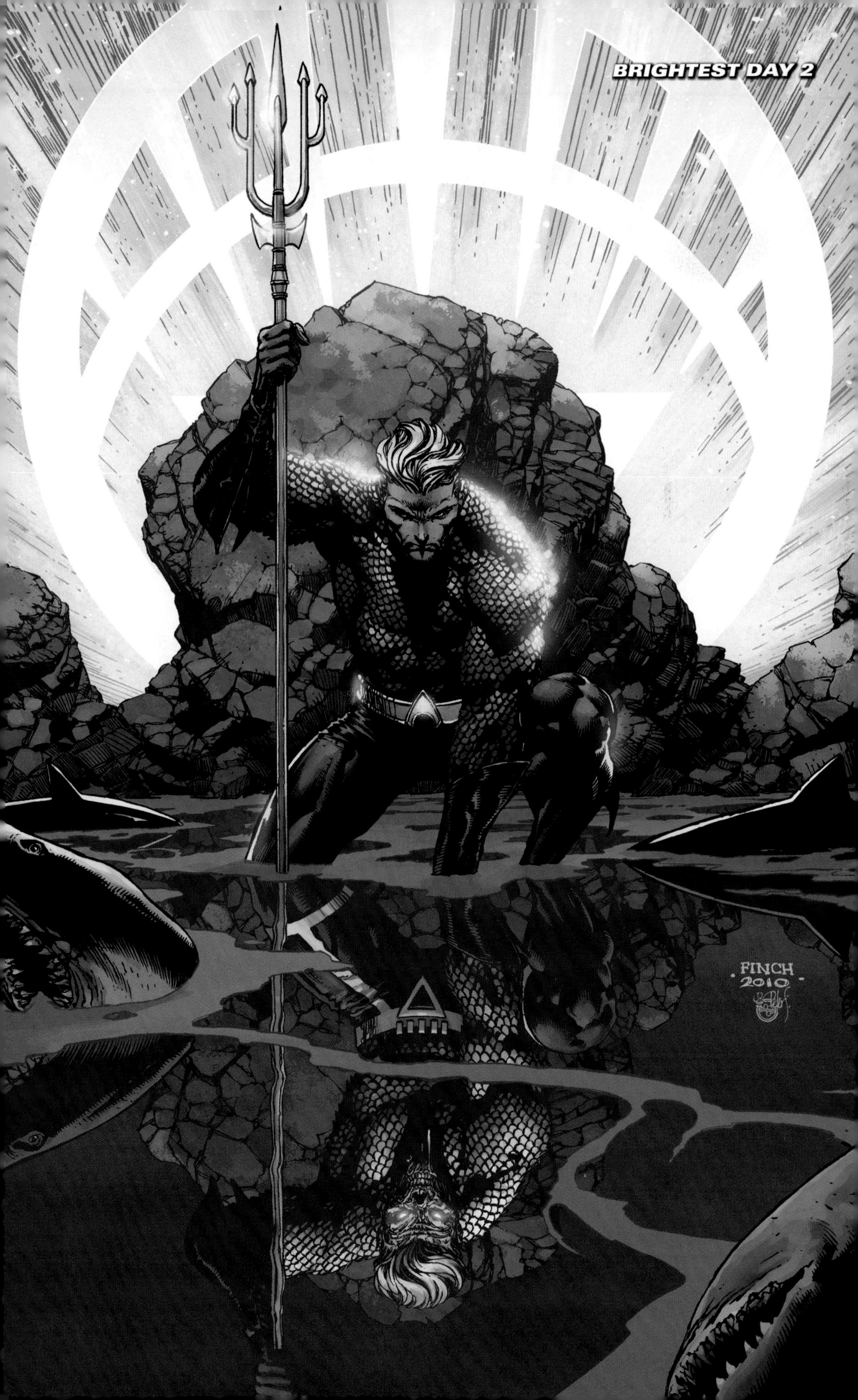
BRIGHTEST DAY 2
FINCH
2010

# NUCLEAR OPTIONS

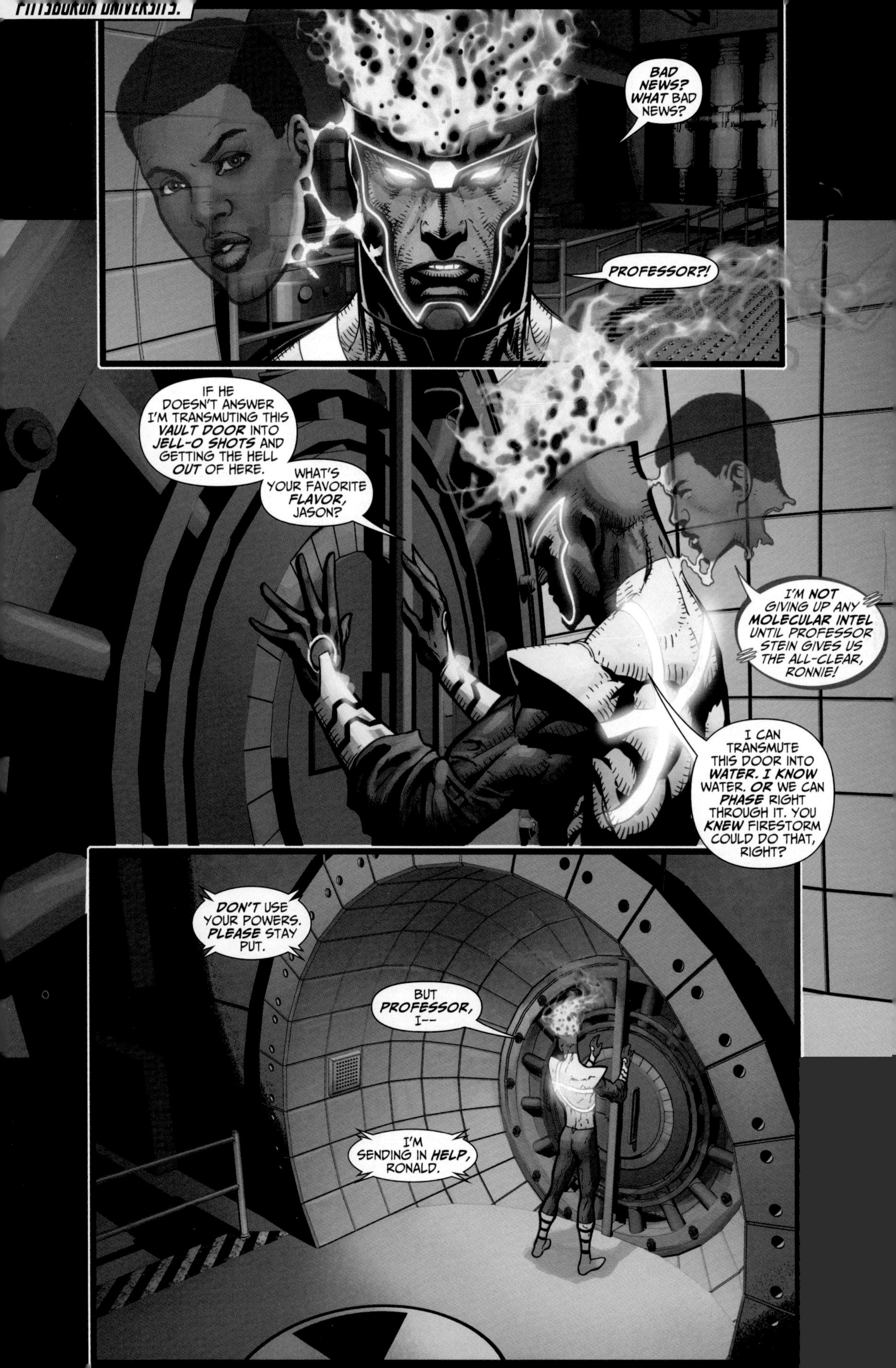
PITTSBURGH UNIVERSITY.
BAD NEWS? WHAT BAD NEWS?
PROFESSOR?!
IF HE DOESN'T ANSWER I'M TRANSMUTING THIS VAULT DOOR INTO JELL-O SHOTS AND GETTING THE HELL OUT OF HERE.
WHAT'S YOUR FAVORITE FLAVOR, JASON?
I'M NOT GIVING UP ANY MOLECULAR INTEL UNTIL PROFESSOR STEIN GIVES US THE ALL-CLEAR, RONNIE!
I CAN TRANSMUTE THIS DOOR INTO WATER. I KNOW WATER. OR WE CAN PHASE RIGHT THROUGH IT. YOU KNEW FIRESTORM COULD DO THAT, RIGHT?
DON'T USE YOUR POWERS. PLEASE STAY PUT.
BUT PROFESSOR, I--
I'M SENDING IN HELP, RONALD.

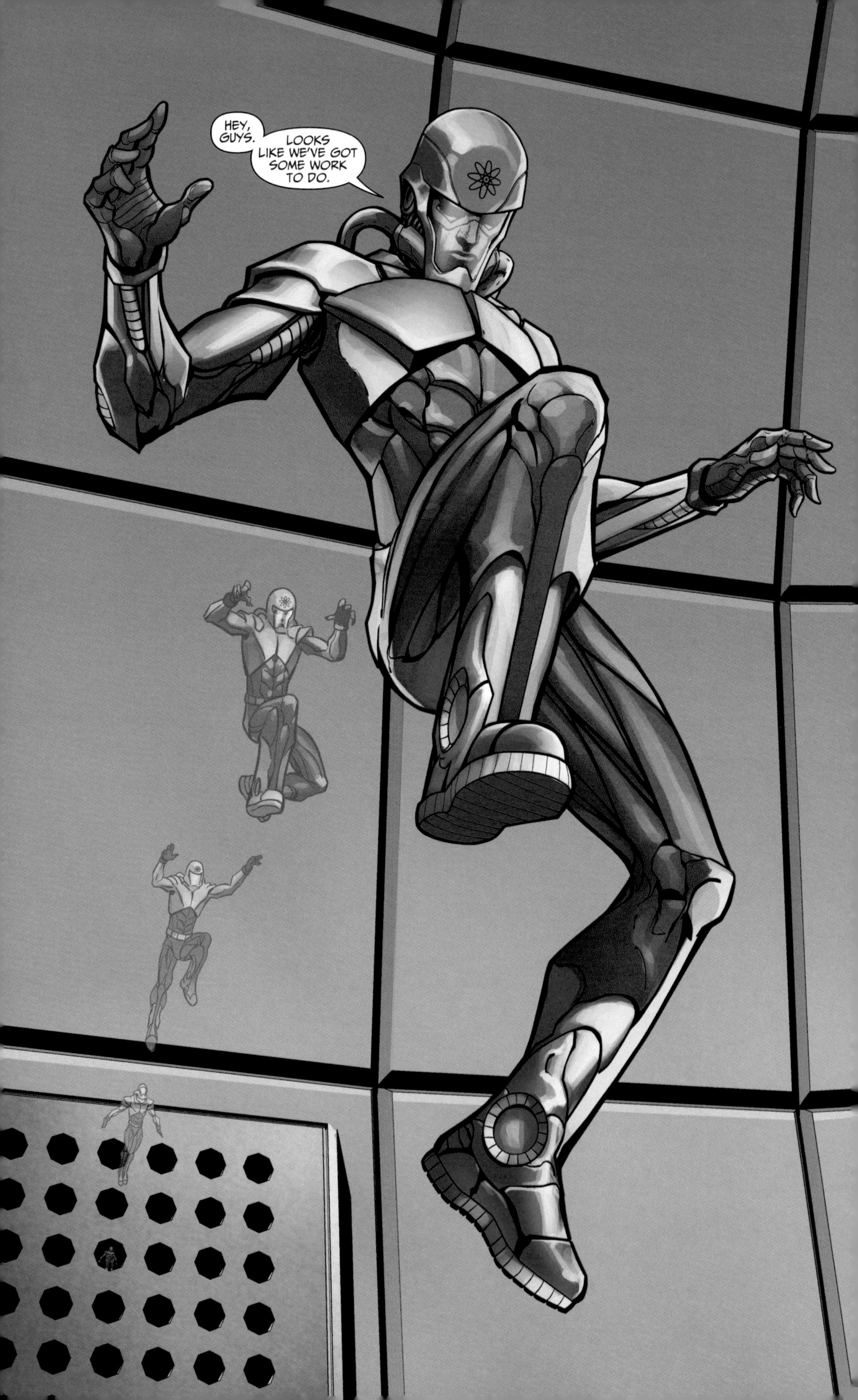
HEY, GUYS.
LOOKS LIKE WE'VE GOT SOME WORK TO DO.

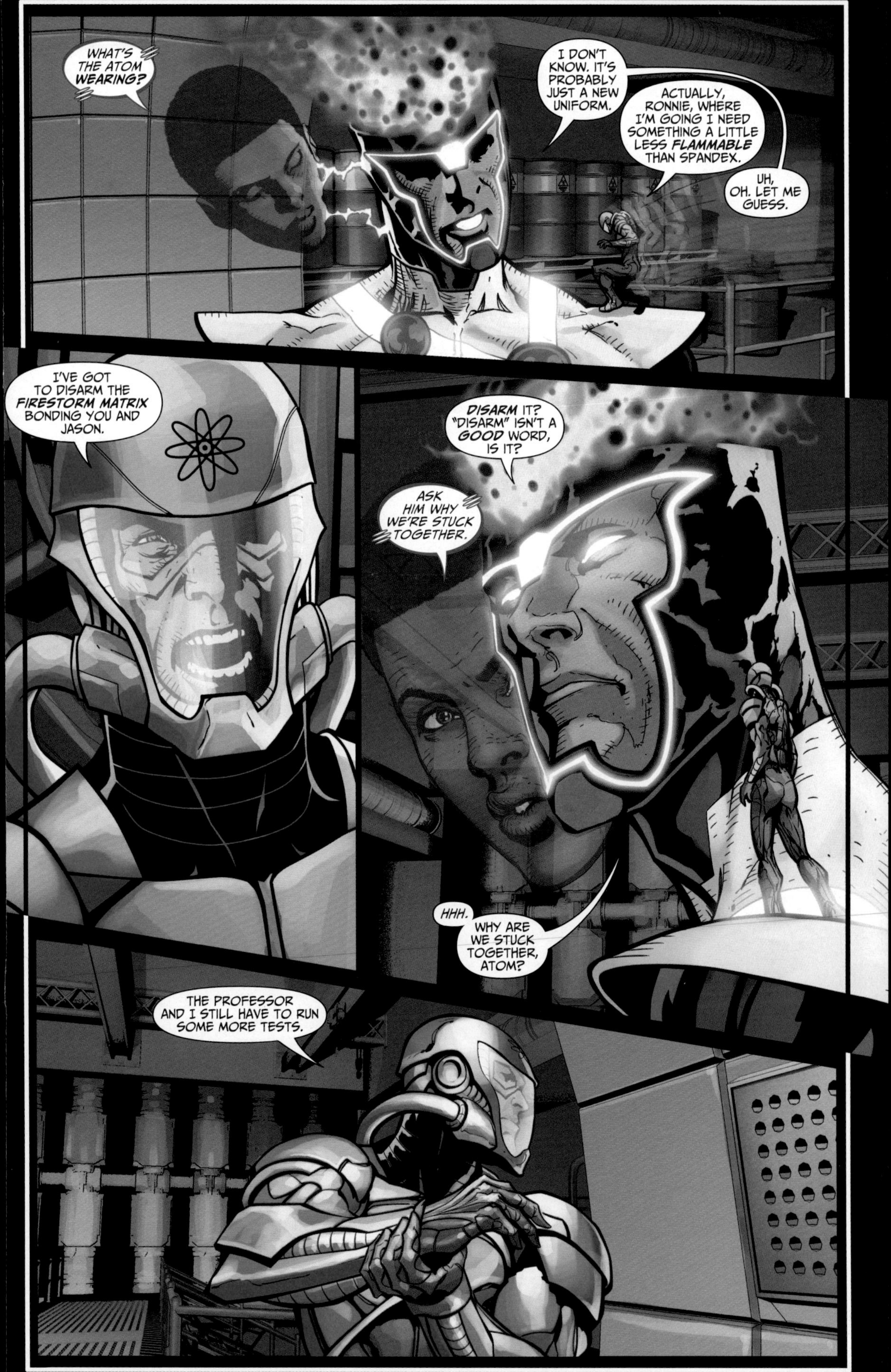
WHAT'S THE ATOM WEARING?
I DON'T KNOW. IT'S PROBABLY JUST A NEW UNIFORM.
ACTUALLY, RONNIE, WHERE I'M GOING I NEED SOMETHING A LITTLE LESS FLAMMABLE THAN SPANDEX.
UH, OH. LET ME GUESS.
I'VE GOT TO DISARM THE FIRESTORM MATRIX BONDING YOU AND JASON.
DISARM IT? "DISARM" ISN'T A GOOD WORD, IS IT?
ASK HIM WHY WE'RE STUCK TOGETHER.
HHH. WHY ARE WE STUCK TOGETHER, ATOM?
THE PROFESSOR AND I STILL HAVE TO RUN SOME MORE TESTS.

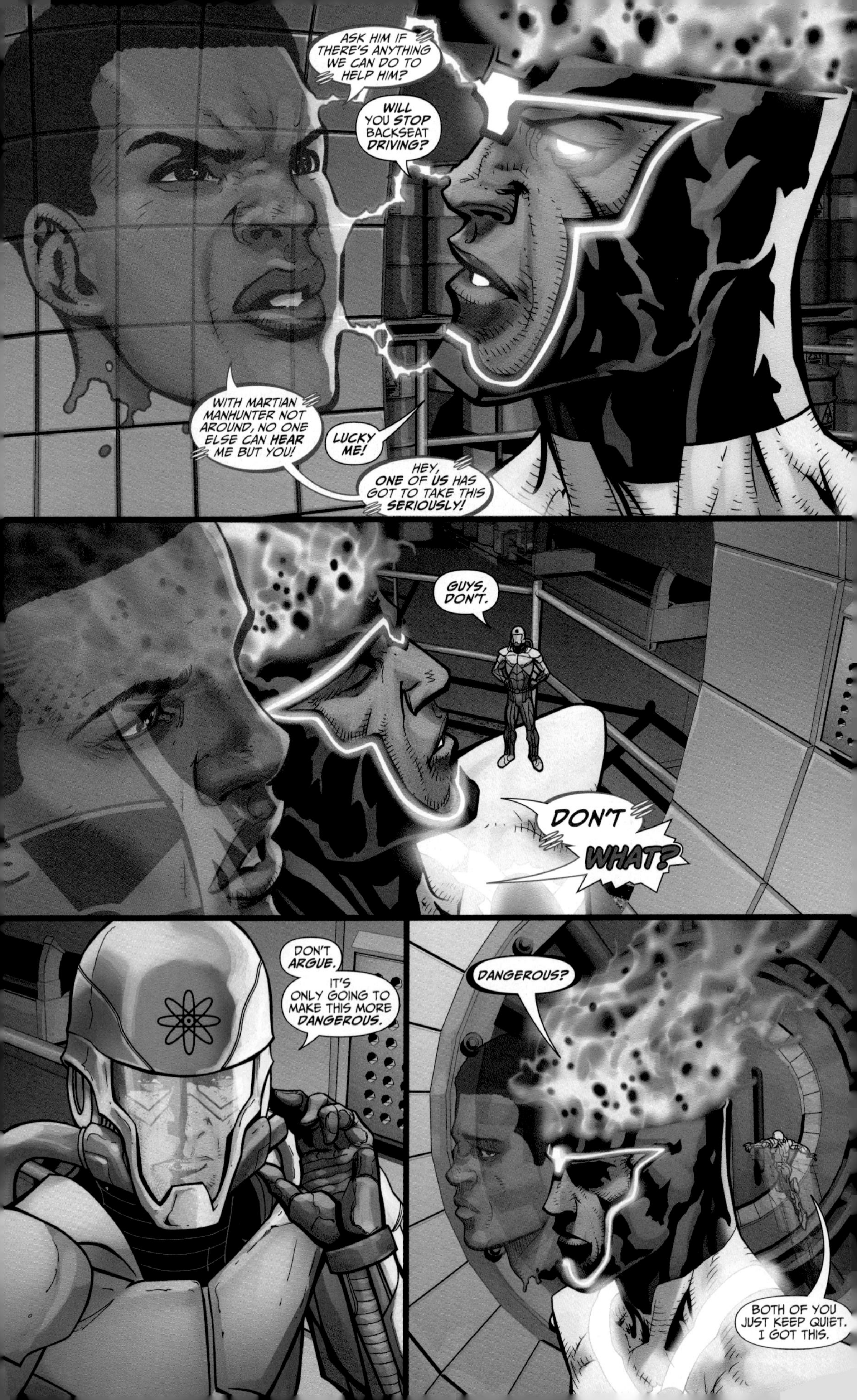
ASK HIM IF THERE'S ANYTHING WE CAN DO TO HELP HIM?
WILL YOU STOP BACKSEAT DRIVING?
WITH MARTIAN MANHUNTER NOT AROUND, NO ONE ELSE CAN HEAR ME BUT YOU!
LUCKY ME!
HEY, ONE OF US HAS GOT TO TAKE THIS SERIOUSLY!
GUYS, DON'T.
DON'T WHAT?
DON'T ARGUE.
IT'S ONLY GOING TO MAKE THIS MORE DANGEROUS.
DANGEROUS?
BOTH OF YOU JUST KEEP QUIET. I GOT THIS.

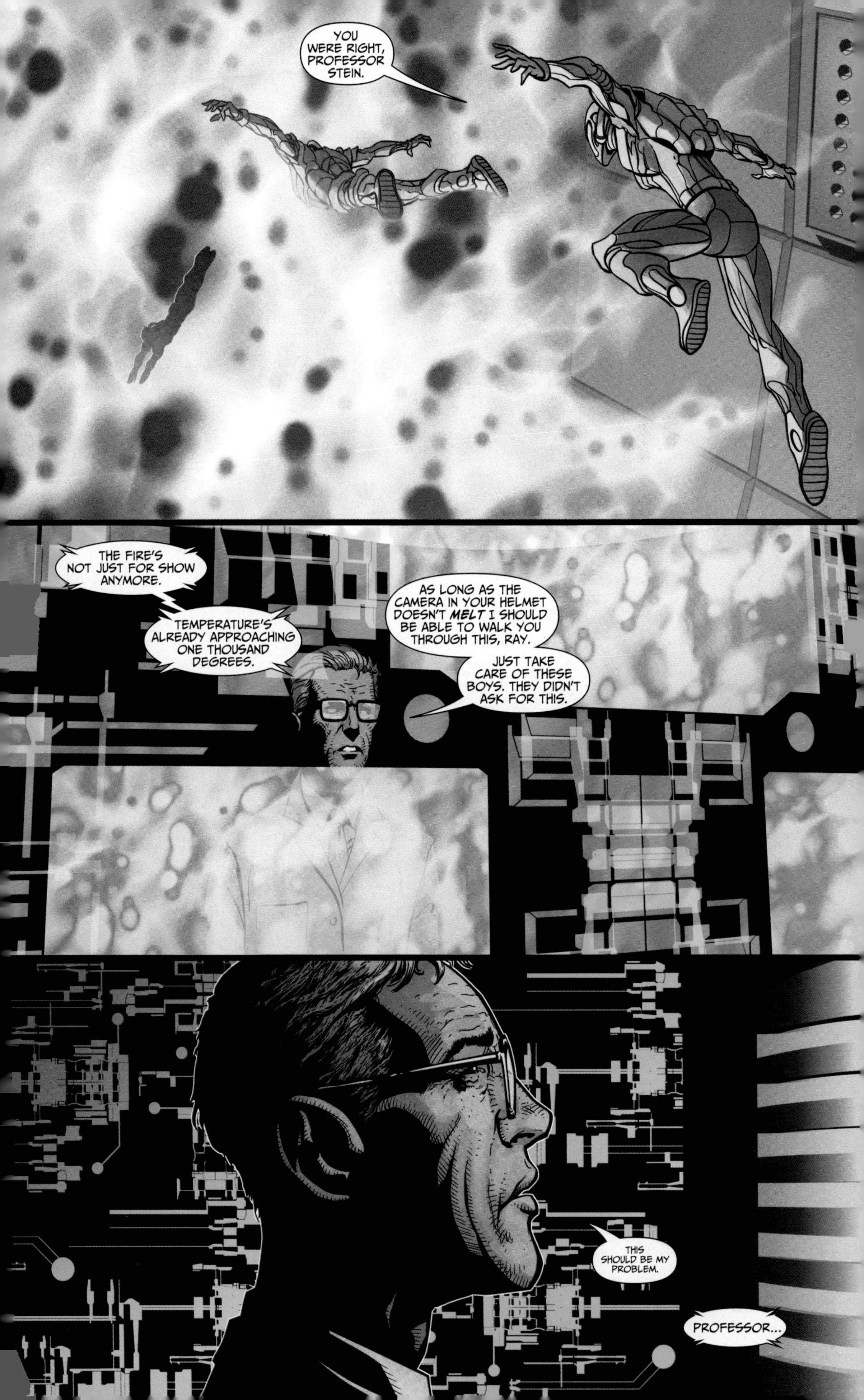
YOU WERE RIGHT, PROFESSOR STEIN.
THE FIRE'S NOT JUST FOR SHOW ANYMORE.
TEMPERATURE'S ALREADY APPROACHING ONE THOUSAND DEGREES.
AS LONG AS THE CAMERA IN YOUR HELMET DOESN'T MELT I SHOULD BE ABLE TO WALK YOU THROUGH THIS, RAY.
JUST TAKE CARE OF THESE BOYS. THEY DIDN'T ASK FOR THIS.
THIS SHOULD BE MY PROBLEM.
PROFESSOR...

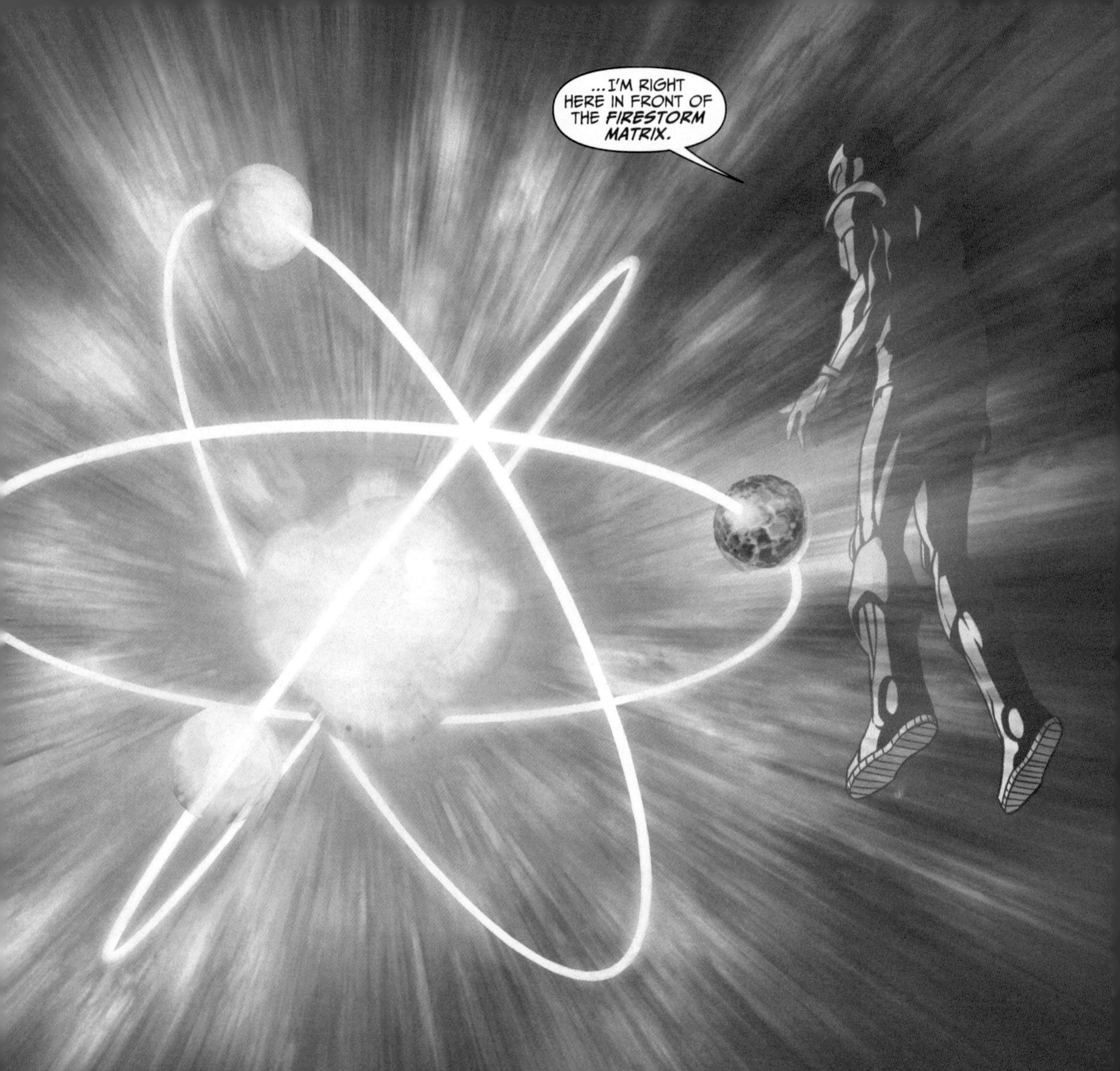
...I'M RIGHT HERE IN FRONT OF THE *FIRESTORM* *MATRIX.*

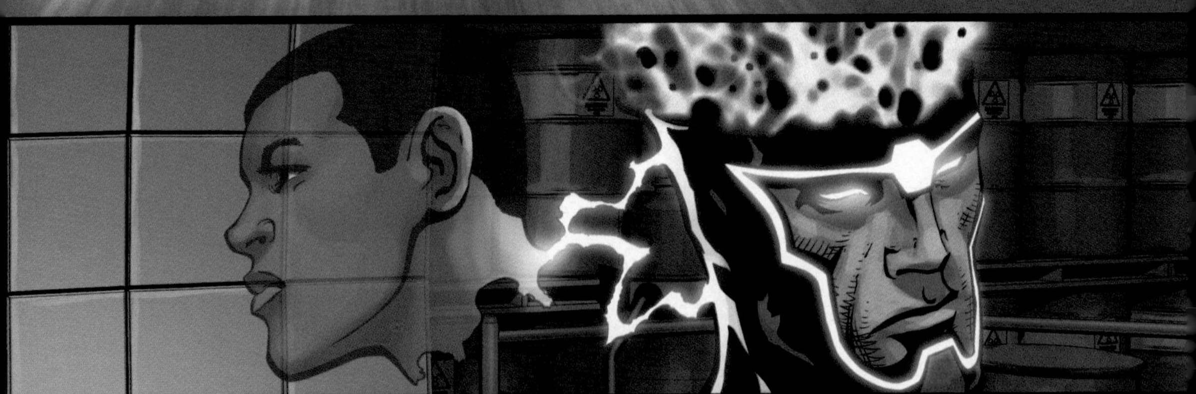

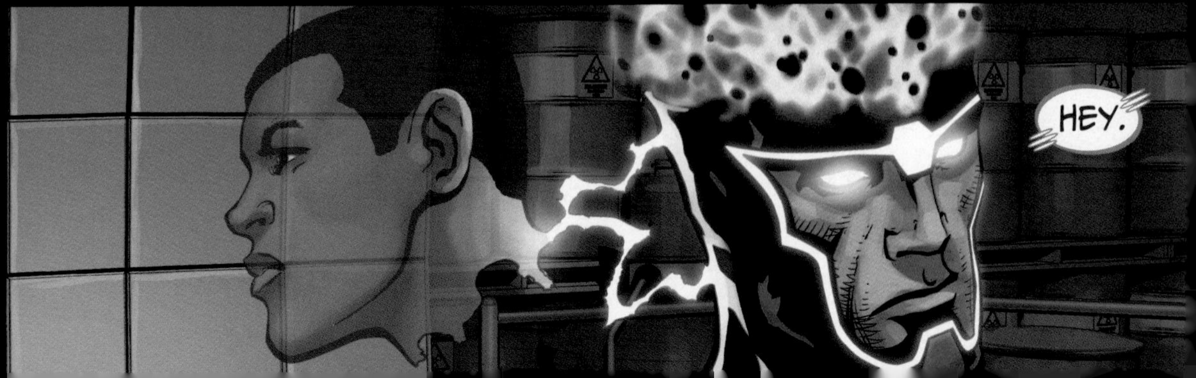
HEY.

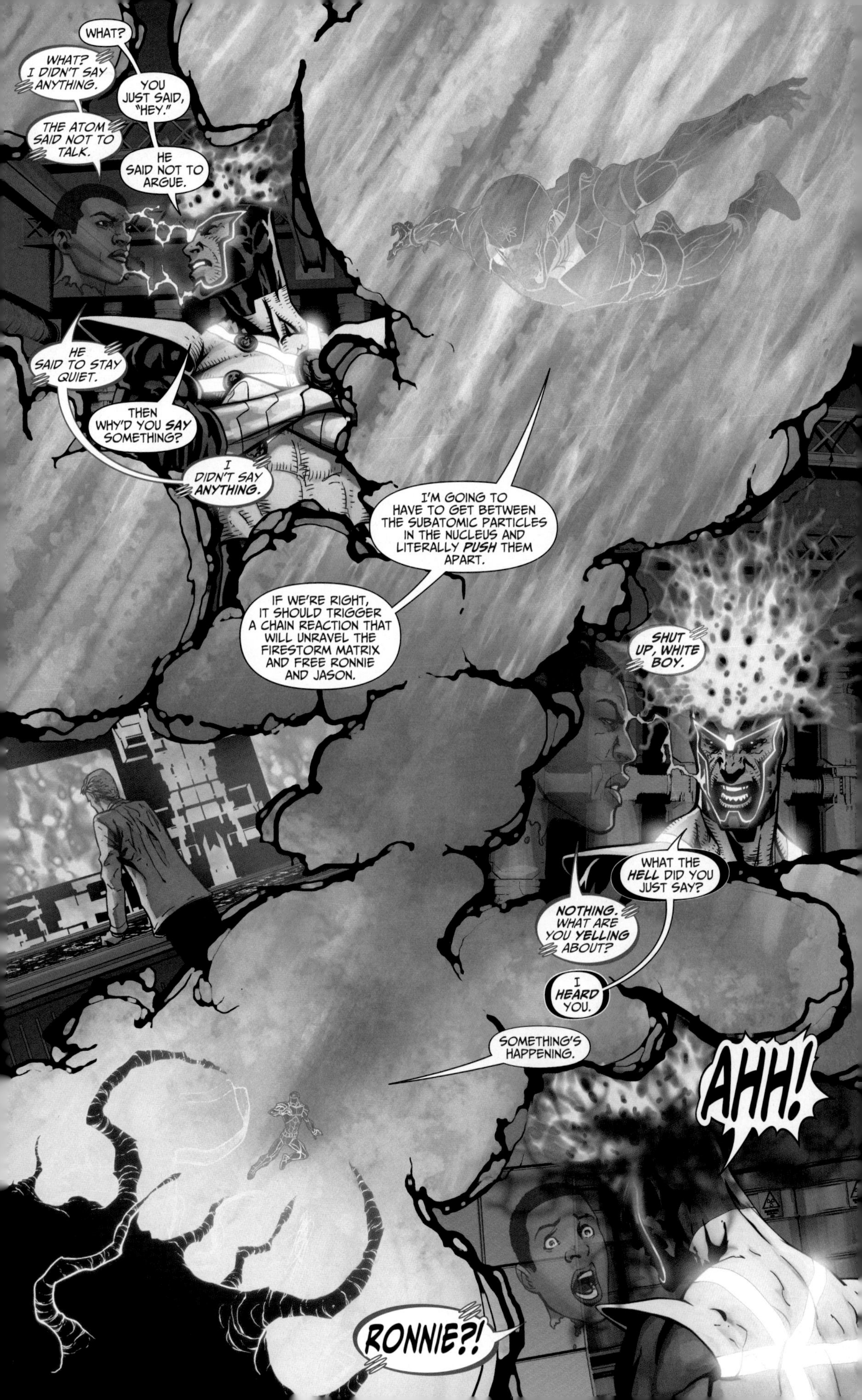
WHAT?
WHAT? I DIDN'T SAY ANYTHING.
YOU JUST SAID, "HEY."
THE ATOM SAID NOT TO TALK.
HE SAID NOT TO ARGUE.
HE SAID TO STAY QUIET.
THEN WHY'D YOU SAY SOMETHING?
I DIDN'T SAY ANYTHING.
I'M GOING TO HAVE TO GET BETWEEN THE SUBATOMIC PARTICLES IN THE NUCLEUS AND LITERALLY PUSH THEM APART.
IF WE'RE RIGHT, IT SHOULD TRIGGER A CHAIN REACTION THAT WILL UNRAVEL THE FIRESTORM MATRIX AND FREE RONNIE AND JASON.
SHUT UP, WHITE BOY.
WHAT THE HELL DID YOU JUST SAY?
NOTHING. WHAT ARE YOU YELLING ABOUT?
I HEARD YOU.
SOMETHING'S HAPPENING.
AHH!
RONNIE?!

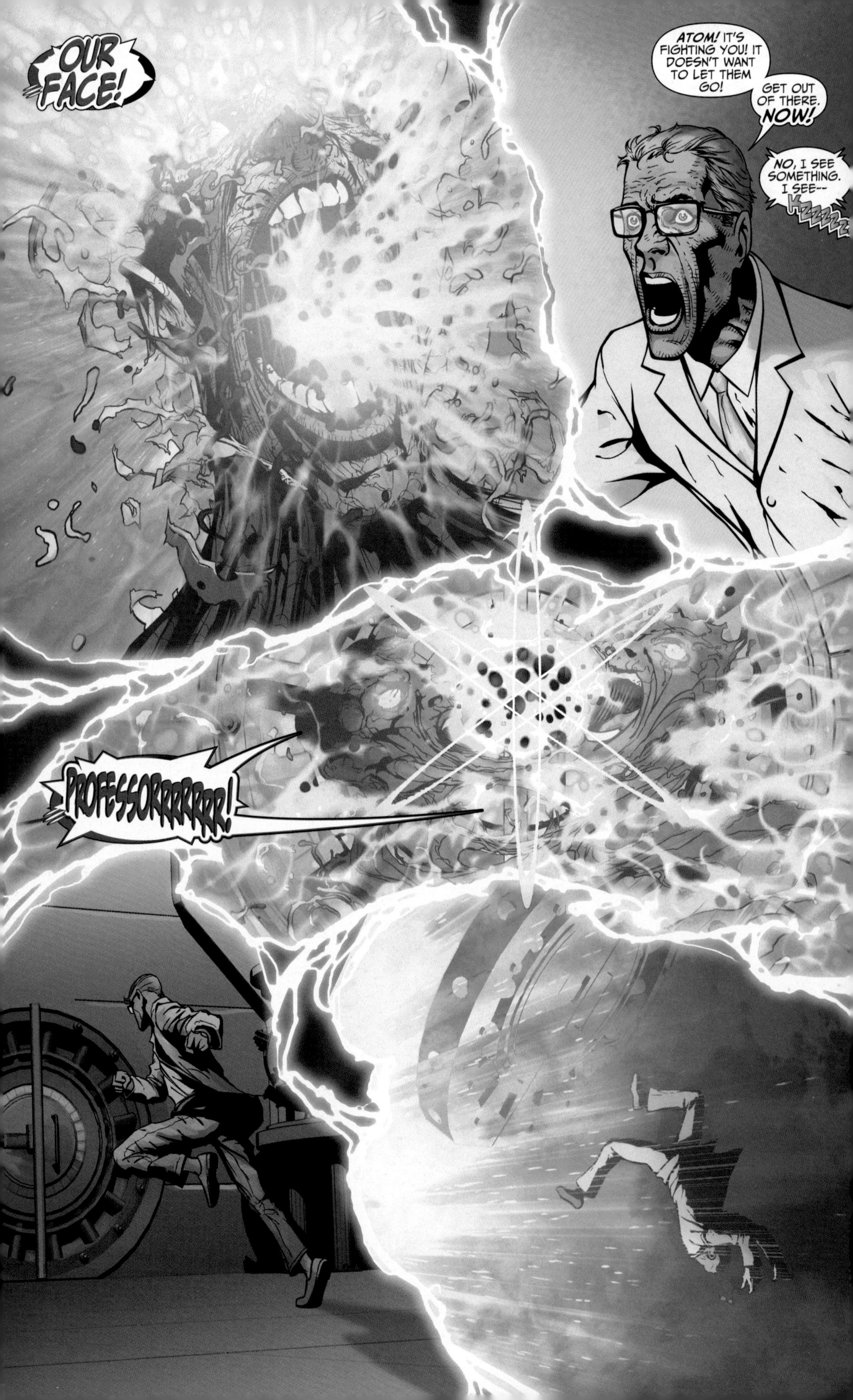
OUR FACE!
ATOM! IT'S FIGHTING YOU! IT DOESN'T WANT TO LET THEM GO!
GET OUT OF THERE. NOW!
NO, I SEE SOMETHING. I SEE--
KZZZZZZ
PROFESSORRRRRRR!

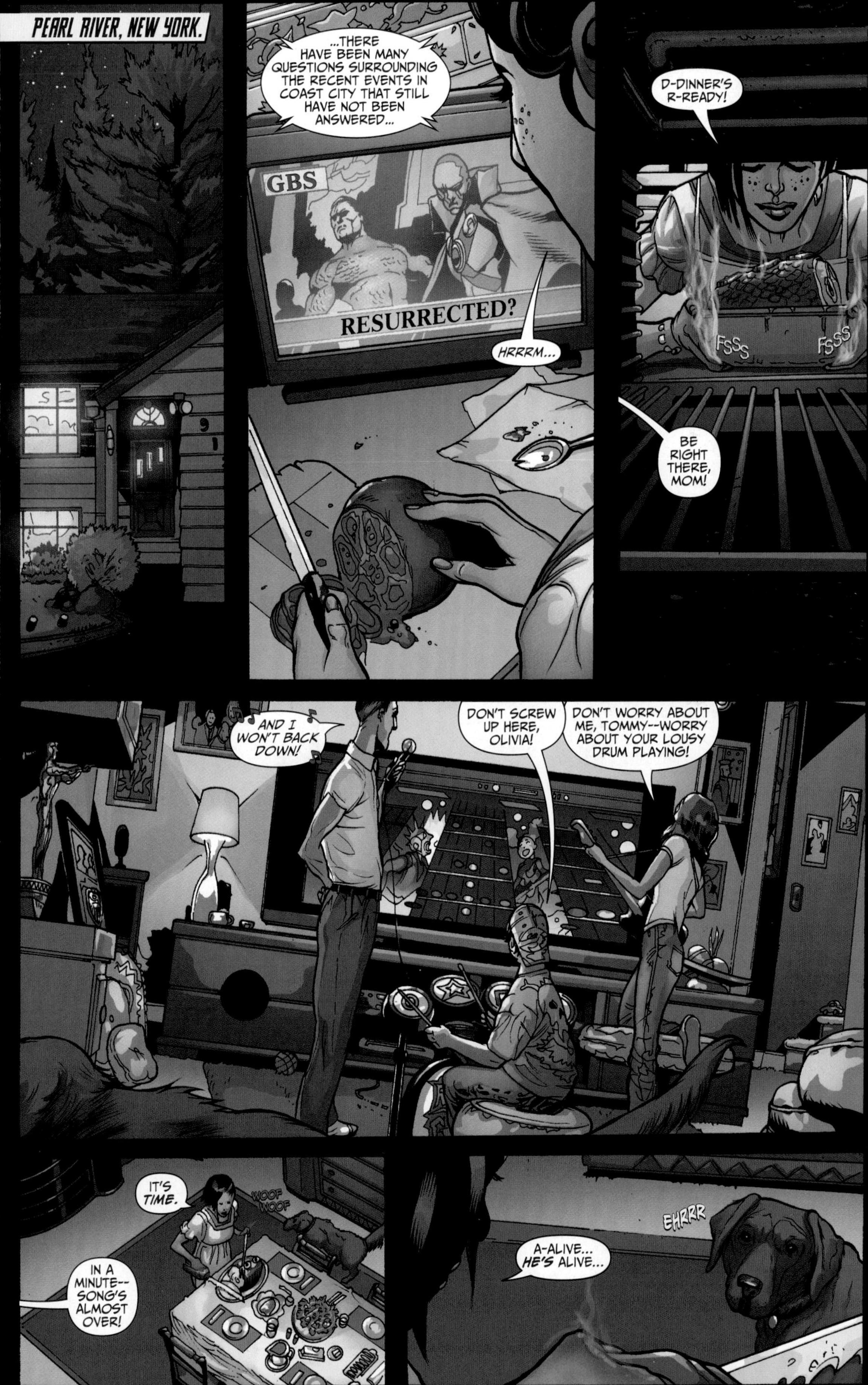
PEARL RIVER, NEW YORK.
...THERE HAVE BEEN MANY QUESTIONS SURROUNDING THE RECENT EVENTS IN COAST CITY THAT STILL HAVE NOT BEEN ANSWERED...
GBS
RESURRECTED?
HRRRM...
D-DINNER'S R-READY!
FSSS
FSSS
BE RIGHT THERE, MOM!
AND I WON'T BACK DOWN!
DON'T SCREW UP HERE, OLIVIA!
DON'T WORRY ABOUT ME, TOMMY--WORRY ABOUT YOUR LOUSY DRUM PLAYING!
IT'S TIME.
WOOF WOOF
IN A MINUTE-- SONG'S ALMOST OVER!
EHRRR
A-ALIVE... HE'S ALIVE...

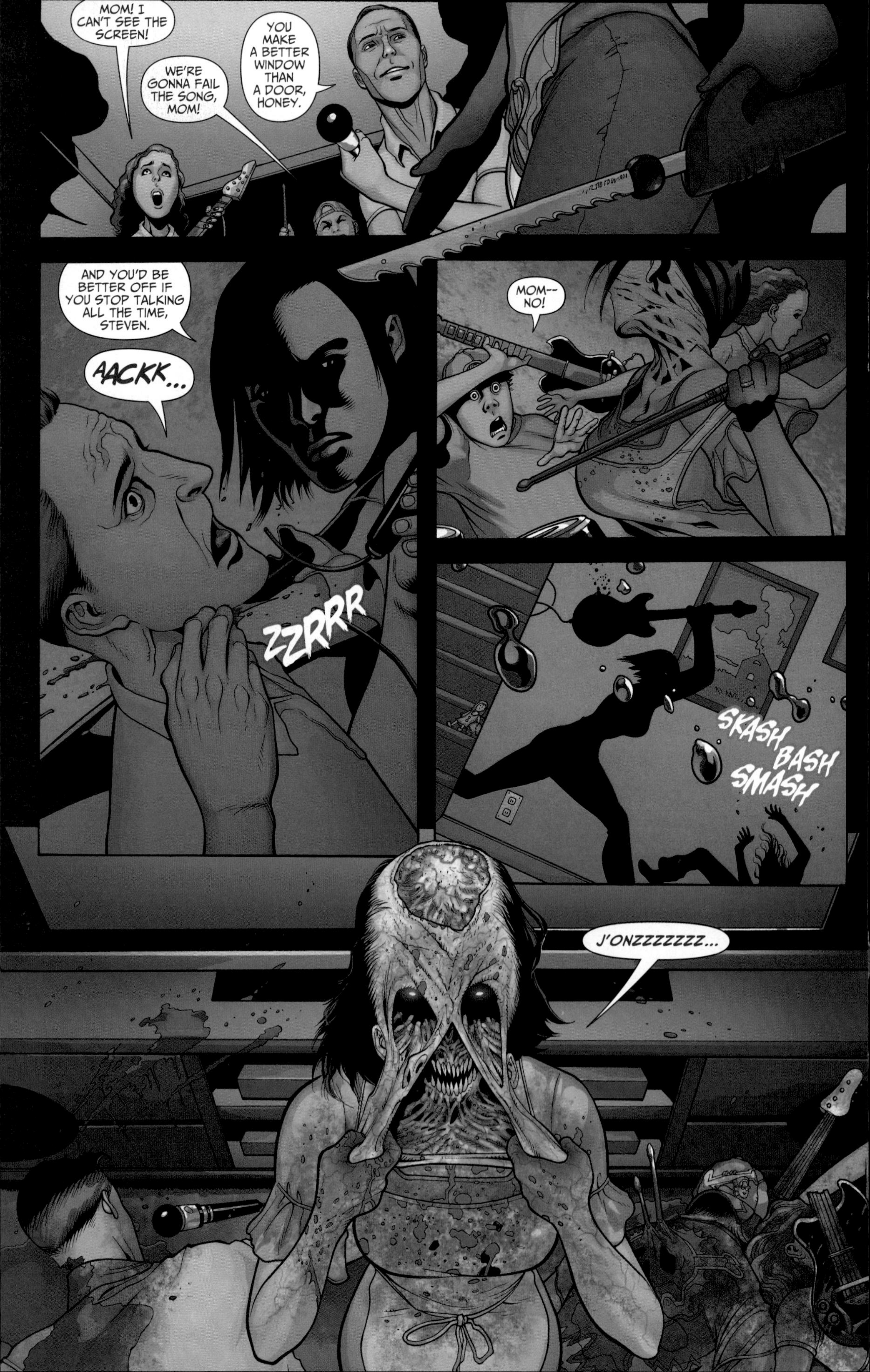
MOM! I CAN'T SEE THE SCREEN!
WE'RE GONNA FAIL THE SONG, MOM!
YOU MAKE A BETTER WINDOW THAN A DOOR, HONEY.
AND YOU'D BE BETTER OFF IF YOU STOP TALKING ALL THE TIME, STEVEN.
AACKK...
ZZRRR
MOM-- NO!
SKASH
BASH
SMASH
J'ONZZZZZZZ...

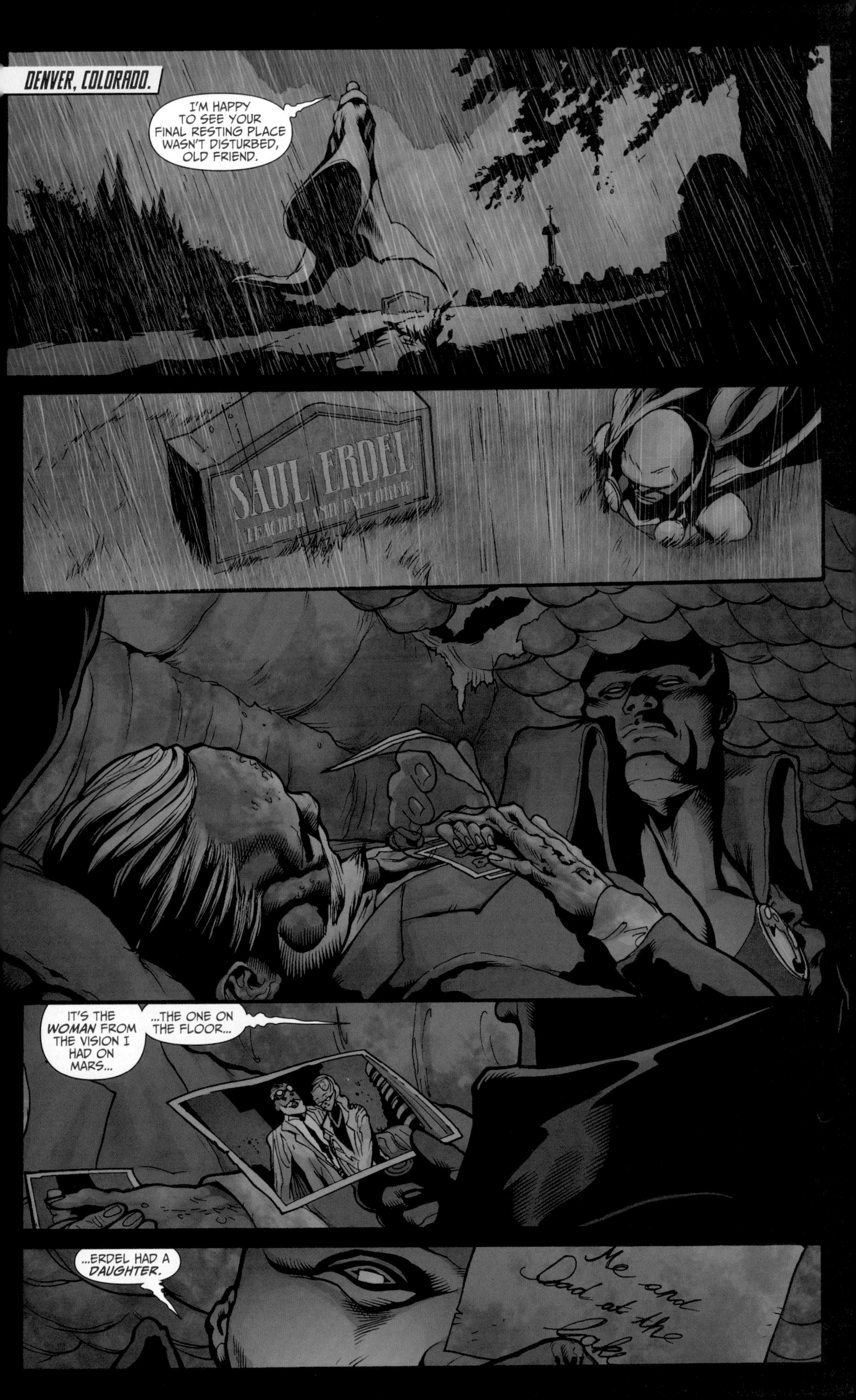
DENVER, COLORADO.
I'M HAPPY TO SEE YOUR FINAL RESTING PLACE WASN'T DISTURBED, OLD FRIEND.
SAUL ERDEL
TEACHER AND EXPLORER
IT'S THE WOMAN FROM THE VISION I HAD ON MARS...
...THE ONE ON THE FLOOR...
...ERDEL HAD A DAUGHTER.

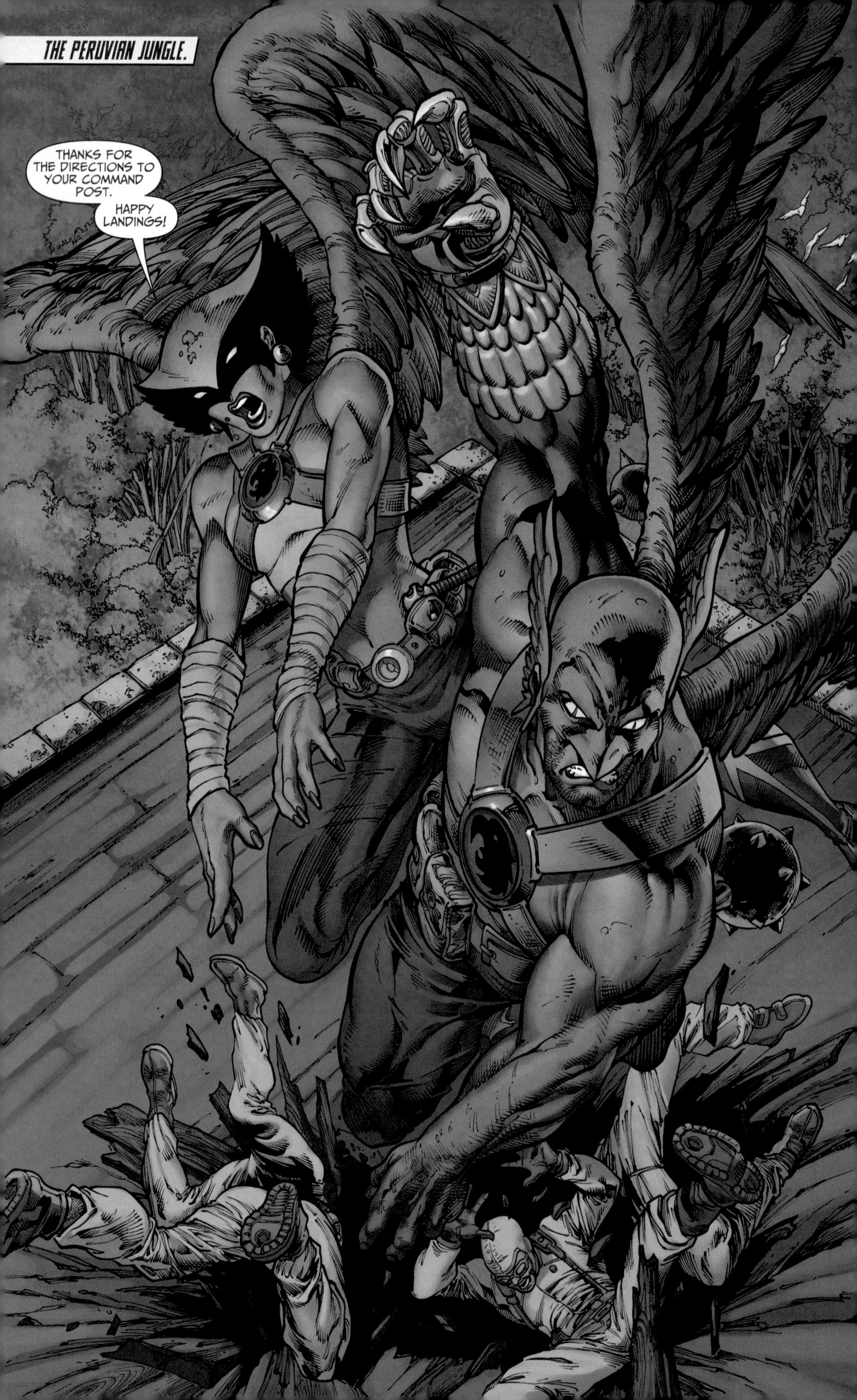
THE PERUVIAN JUNGLE.
THANKS FOR THE DIRECTIONS TO YOUR COMMAND POST.
HAPPY LANDINGS!

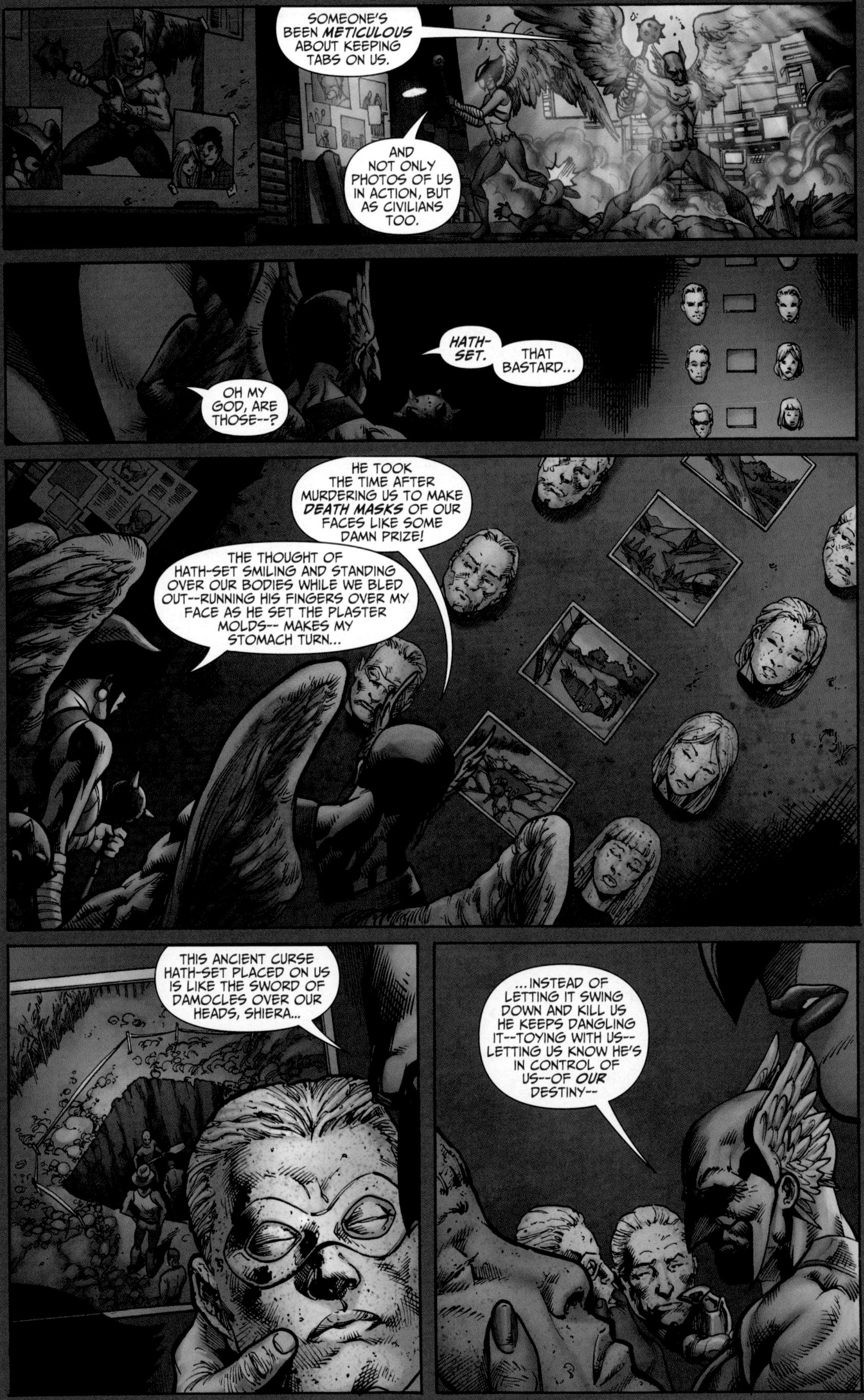
SOMEONE'S BEEN METICULOUS ABOUT KEEPING TABS ON US.
AND NOT ONLY PHOTOS OF US IN ACTION, BUT AS CIVILIANS TOO.
HATH-SET.
THAT BASTARD...
OH MY GOD, ARE THOSE--?
HE TOOK THE TIME AFTER MURDERING US TO MAKE DEATH MASKS OF OUR FACES LIKE SOME DAMN PRIZE!
THE THOUGHT OF HATH-SET SMILING AND STANDING OVER OUR BODIES WHILE WE BLED OUT--RUNNING HIS FINGERS OVER MY FACE AS HE SET THE PLASTER MOLDS-- MAKES MY STOMACH TURN...
THIS ANCIENT CURSE HATH-SET PLACED ON US IS LIKE THE SWORD OF DAMOCLES OVER OUR HEADS, SHIERA...
...INSTEAD OF LETTING IT SWING DOWN AND KILL US HE KEEPS DANGLING IT--TOYING WITH US--LETTING US KNOW HE'S IN CONTROL OF US--OF OUR DESTINY--

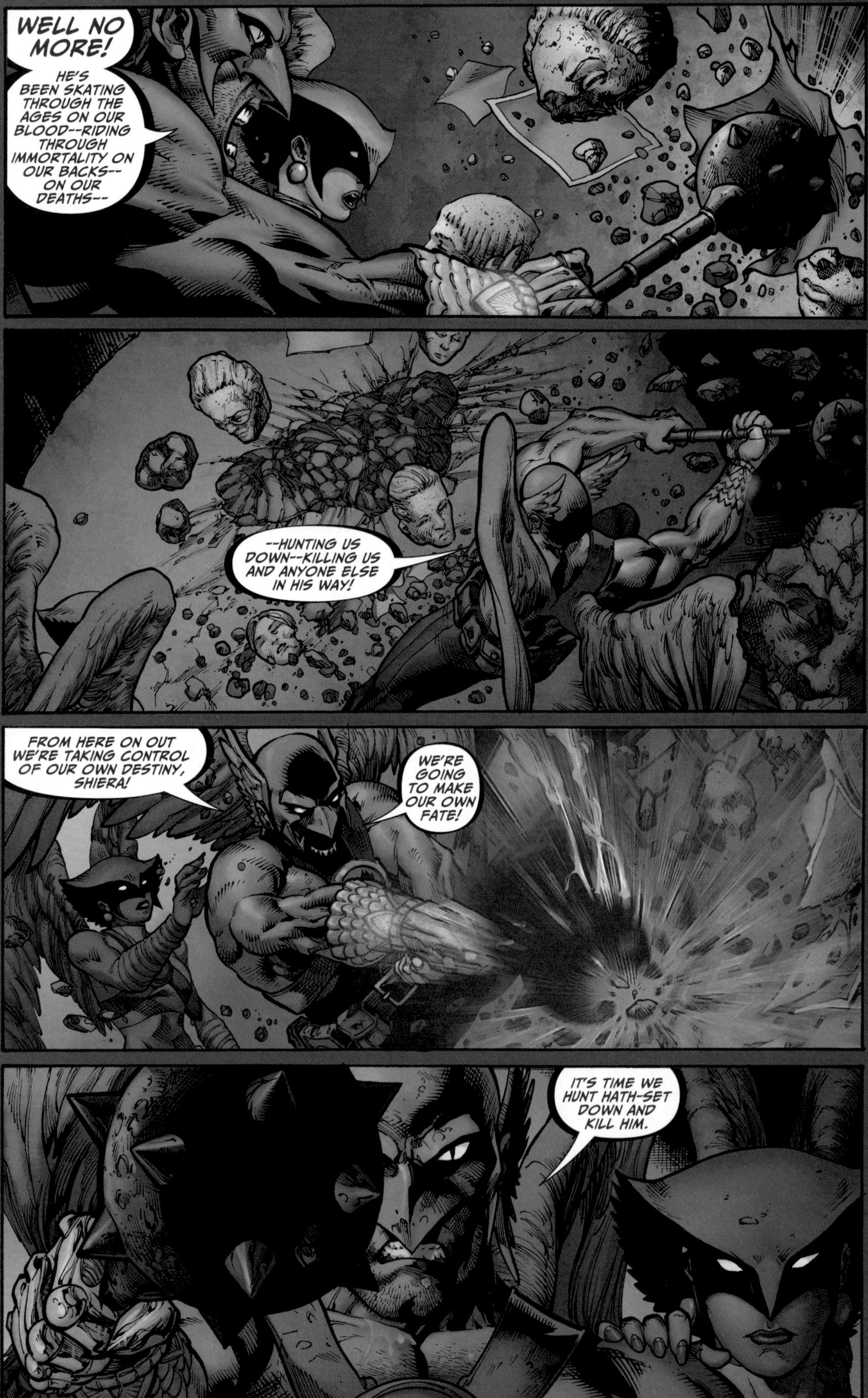
WELL NO MORE!
HE'S BEEN SKATING THROUGH THE AGES ON OUR BLOOD--RIDING THROUGH IMMORTALITY ON OUR BACKS--ON OUR DEATHS--
--HUNTING US DOWN--KILLING US AND ANYONE ELSE IN HIS WAY!
FROM HERE ON OUT WE'RE TAKING CONTROL OF OUR OWN DESTINY, SHIERA!
WE'RE GOING TO MAKE OUR OWN FATE!
IT'S TIME WE HUNT HATH-SET DOWN AND KILL HIM.

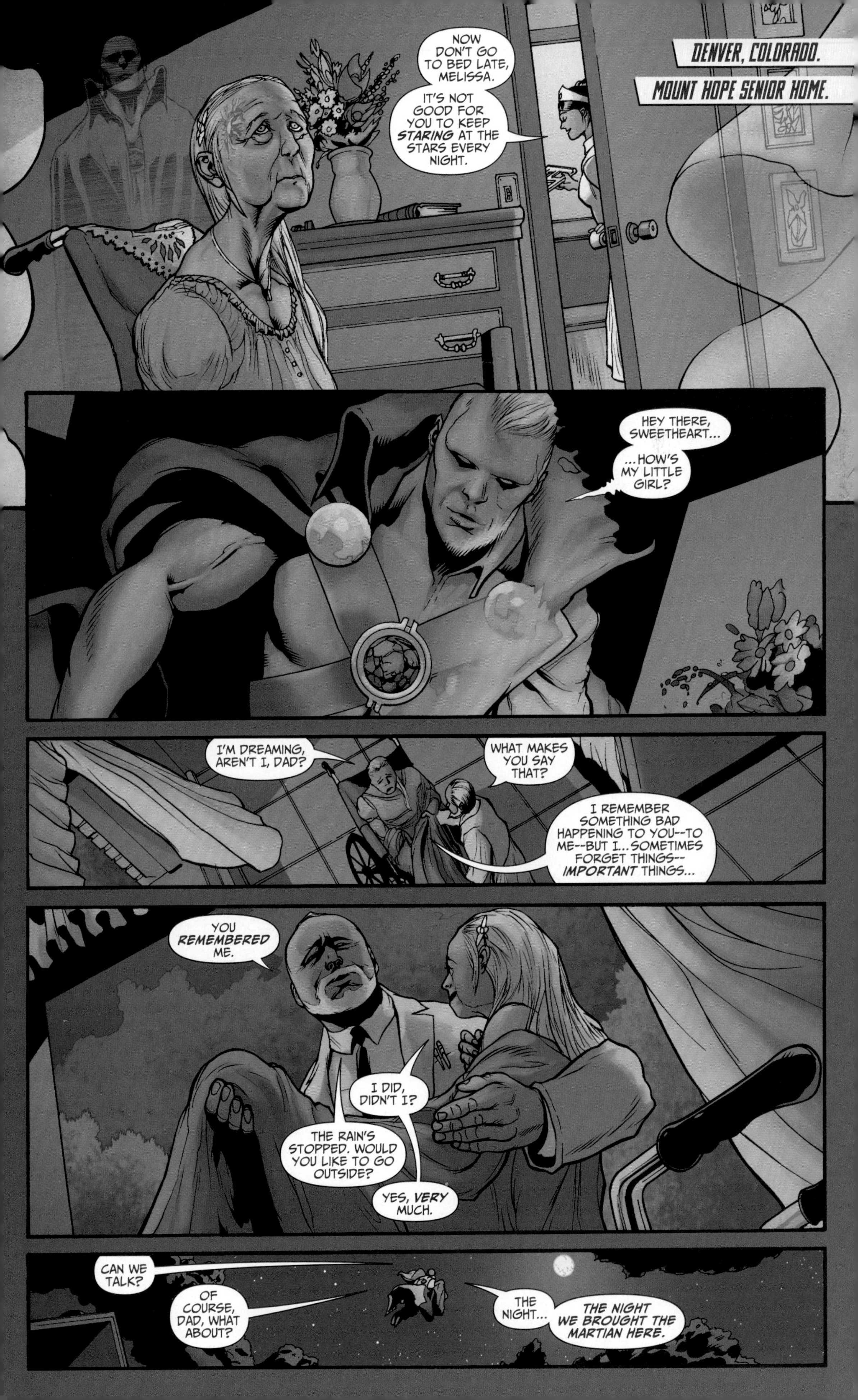
DENVER, COLORADO.
MOUNT HOPE SENIOR HOME.
NOW DON'T GO TO BED LATE, MELISSA.
IT'S NOT GOOD FOR YOU TO KEEP STARING AT THE STARS EVERY NIGHT.
HEY THERE, SWEETHEART...
...HOW'S MY LITTLE GIRL?
I'M DREAMING, AREN'T I, DAD?
WHAT MAKES YOU SAY THAT?
I REMEMBER SOMETHING BAD HAPPENING TO YOU--TO ME--BUT I...SOMETIMES FORGET THINGS-- IMPORTANT THINGS...
YOU REMEMBERED ME.
I DID, DIDN'T I?
THE RAIN'S STOPPED. WOULD YOU LIKE TO GO OUTSIDE?
YES, VERY MUCH.
CAN WE TALK?
OF COURSE, DAD, WHAT ABOUT?
THE NIGHT...
THE NIGHT WE BROUGHT THE MARTIAN HERE.

I'VE BEEN THINKING ABOUT *HIM* THE LAST FEW DAYS, DAD...

...HE'S BACK... SEEN HIM ON THE TV...BUT I CAN'T REMEMBER ANYTHING ELSE BUT HIM STANDING THERE IN THE LAB...SURROUNDED BY SMOKE... IT JUST KEEPS SLIPPING AWAY...

...PLEASE DON'T BE MAD--*DON'T MAKE ME WAKE UP*--I LIKE SPENDING TIME WITH YOU LIKE THIS...

MAD? I CAN NEVER BE MAD AT YOU. AND DON'T WORRY, YOU *DO* REMEMBER THAT NIGHT.

IT'S *ALL* IN HERE.

IT IS?

YES, WE CAN GO BACK TO THAT NIGHT *TOGETHER*, YOU AND I, BUT THERE'RE PAINFUL MEMORIES LINGERING THERE. ARE YOU SURE YOU WANT--

YES, DAD, I'M SURE.

I REMEMBER WHEN YOU FIRST SHOWED ME THE PIECE OF THE *STONE TABLET* YOU FOUND IN THE ANCIENT RUINS OF THAT AZTEC TEMPLE WHEN YOU WERE A BOY...

I CAN STILL HEAR THE WONDER IN YOUR VOICE WHEN YOU TOLD ME THE SAME BEDTIME STORY EVERY NIGHT OF HOW SPACE TRAVELERS FROM THE RED STAR ONCE VISITED OUR PLANET AND HELPED AN ANCIENT PEOPLE SURVIVE AND THRIVE.

ONCE YOU HAD IT TRANSLATED IT BECAME YOUR LIFE-- OUR LIFE--AND I WAS GLAD MOM LEFT--SHE *NEVER* UNDERSTOOD WHAT WE WERE TRYING TO DO--

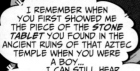

ALL SHE SAW WAS AN *OBSESSION*--

--AND ALL WE SAW WAS THE *FUTURE*...

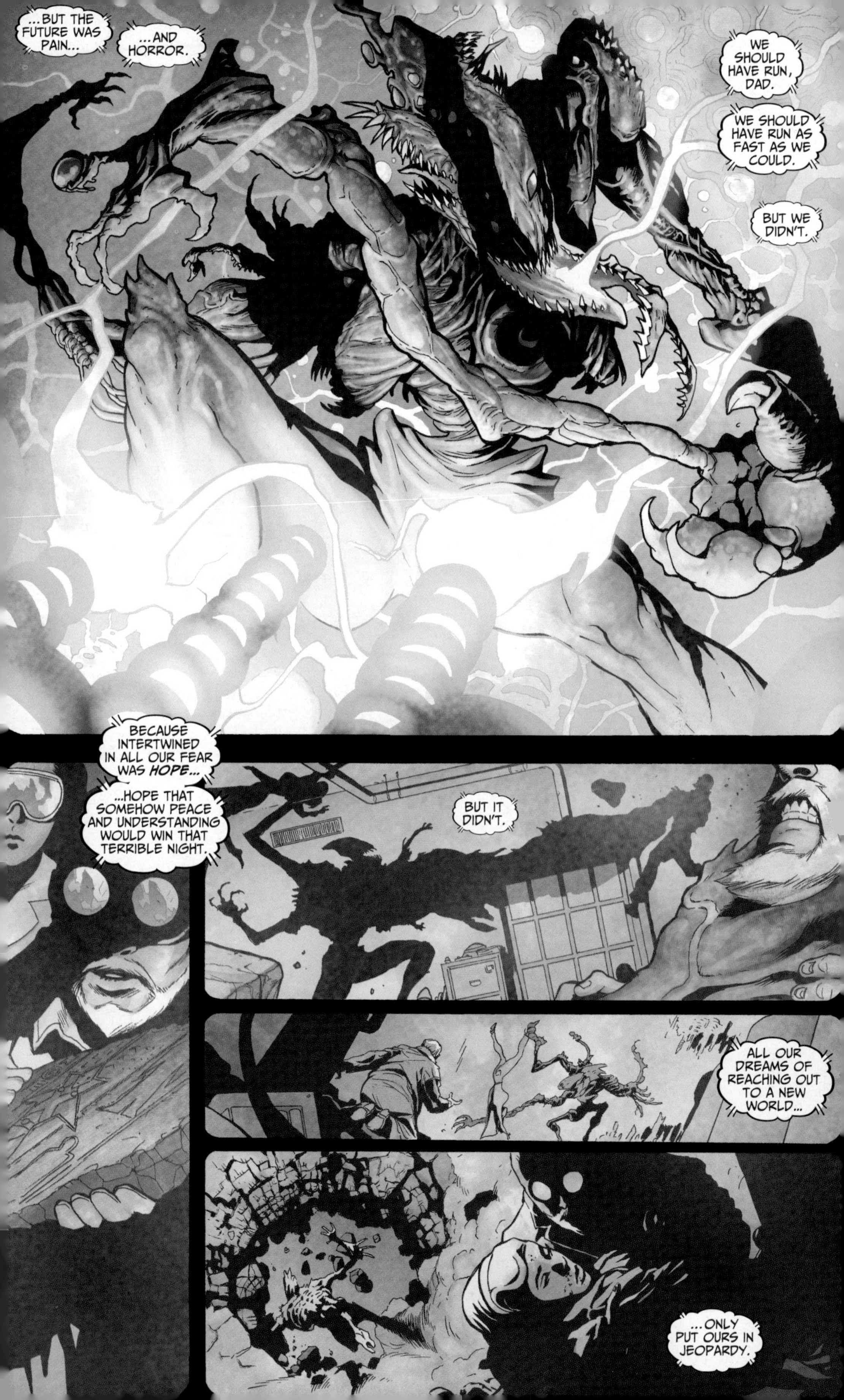
...BUT THE FUTURE WAS PAIN...
...AND HORROR.
WE SHOULD HAVE RUN, DAD.
WE SHOULD HAVE RUN AS FAST AS WE COULD.
BUT WE DIDN'T.
BECAUSE INTERTWINED IN ALL OUR FEAR WAS *HOPE*...
...HOPE THAT SOMEHOW PEACE AND UNDERSTANDING WOULD WIN THAT TERRIBLE NIGHT.
BUT IT DIDN'T.
ALL OUR DREAMS OF REACHING OUT TO A NEW WORLD...
...ONLY PUT OURS IN JEOPARDY.

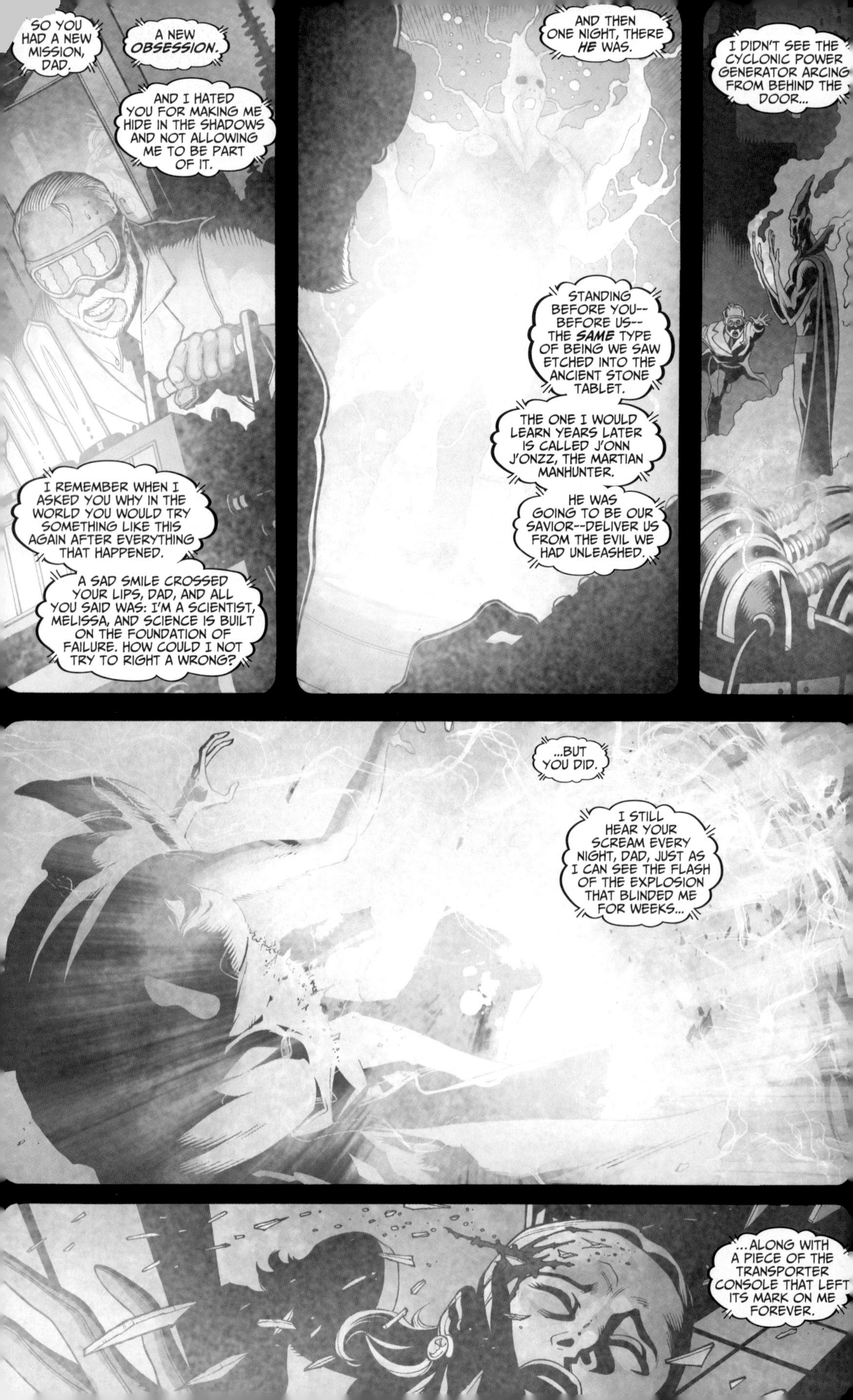

SO YOU HAD A NEW MISSION, DAD.
A NEW OBSESSION.
AND I HATED YOU FOR MAKING ME HIDE IN THE SHADOWS AND NOT ALLOWING ME TO BE PART OF IT.
I REMEMBER WHEN I ASKED YOU WHY IN THE WORLD YOU WOULD TRY SOMETHING LIKE THIS AGAIN AFTER EVERYTHING THAT HAPPENED.
A SAD SMILE CROSSED YOUR LIPS, DAD, AND ALL YOU SAID WAS: I'M A SCIENTIST, MELISSA, AND SCIENCE IS BUILT ON THE FOUNDATION OF FAILURE. HOW COULD I NOT TRY TO RIGHT A WRONG?
AND THEN ONE NIGHT, THERE HE WAS.
STANDING BEFORE YOU-- BEFORE US-- THE SAME TYPE OF BEING WE SAW ETCHED INTO THE ANCIENT STONE TABLET.
THE ONE I WOULD LEARN YEARS LATER IS CALLED J'ONN J'ONZZ, THE MARTIAN MANHUNTER.
HE WAS GOING TO BE OUR SAVIOR--DELIVER US FROM THE EVIL WE HAD UNLEASHED.
I DIDN'T SEE THE CYCLONIC POWER GENERATOR ARCING FROM BEHIND THE DOOR...
...BUT YOU DID.
I STILL HEAR YOUR SCREAM EVERY NIGHT, DAD, JUST AS I CAN SEE THE FLASH OF THE EXPLOSION THAT BLINDED ME FOR WEEKS...
...ALONG WITH A PIECE OF THE TRANSPORTER CONSOLE THAT LEFT ITS MARK ON ME FOREVER.

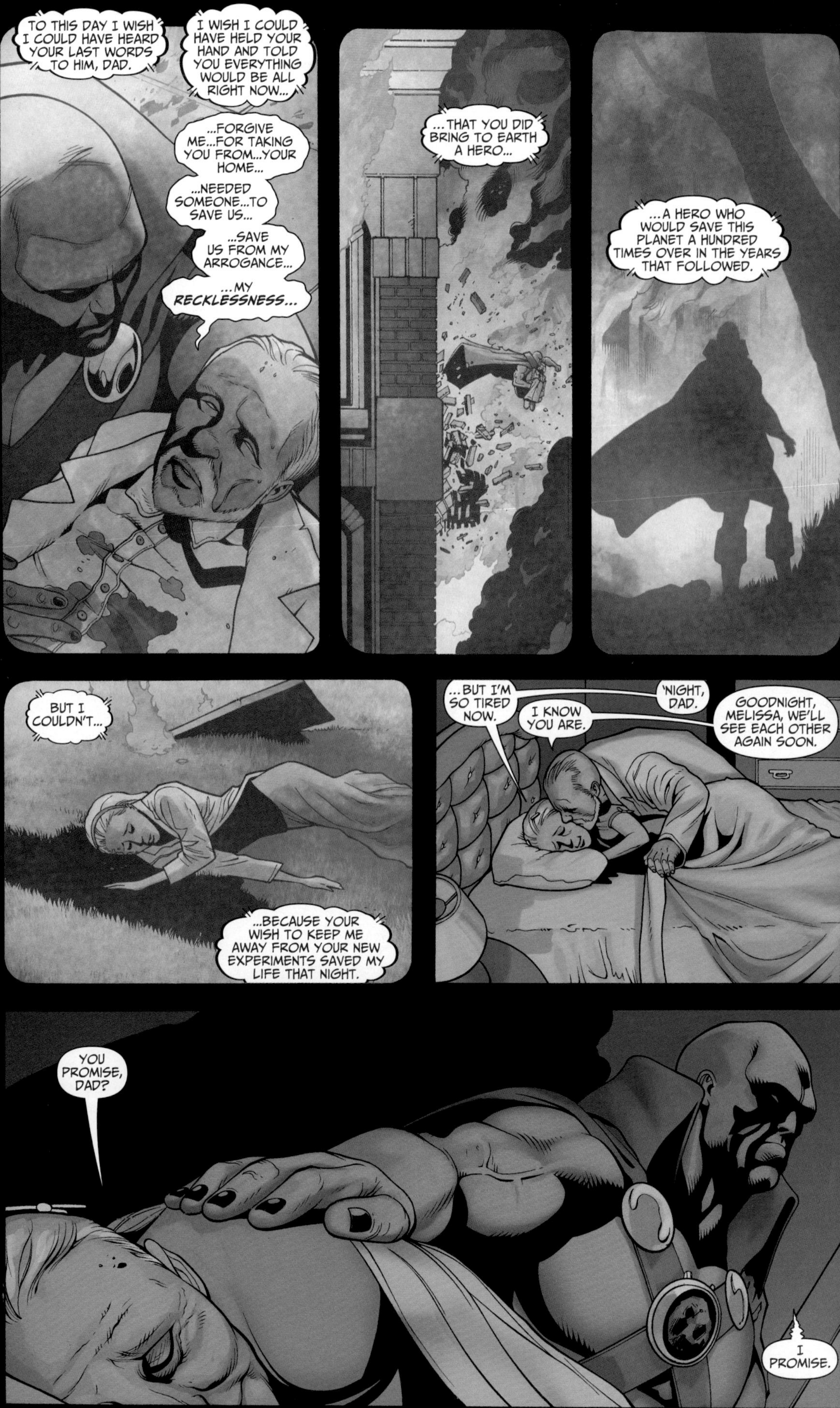
TO THIS DAY I WISH I COULD HAVE HEARD YOUR LAST WORDS TO HIM, DAD.
I WISH I COULD HAVE HELD YOUR HAND AND TOLD YOU EVERYTHING WOULD BE ALL RIGHT NOW...
...FORGIVE ME...FOR TAKING YOU FROM...YOUR HOME...
...NEEDED SOMEONE...TO SAVE US...
...SAVE US FROM MY ARROGANCE...
...MY *RECKLESSNESS...*
...THAT YOU DID BRING TO EARTH A HERO...
...A HERO WHO WOULD SAVE THIS PLANET A HUNDRED TIMES OVER IN THE YEARS THAT FOLLOWED.
BUT I COULDN'T...
...BECAUSE YOUR WISH TO KEEP ME AWAY FROM YOUR NEW EXPERIMENTS SAVED MY LIFE THAT NIGHT.
...BUT I'M SO TIRED NOW.
I KNOW YOU ARE.
'NIGHT, DAD.
GOODNIGHT, MELISSA, WE'LL SEE EACH OTHER AGAIN SOON.
YOU PROMISE, DAD?
I PROMISE.

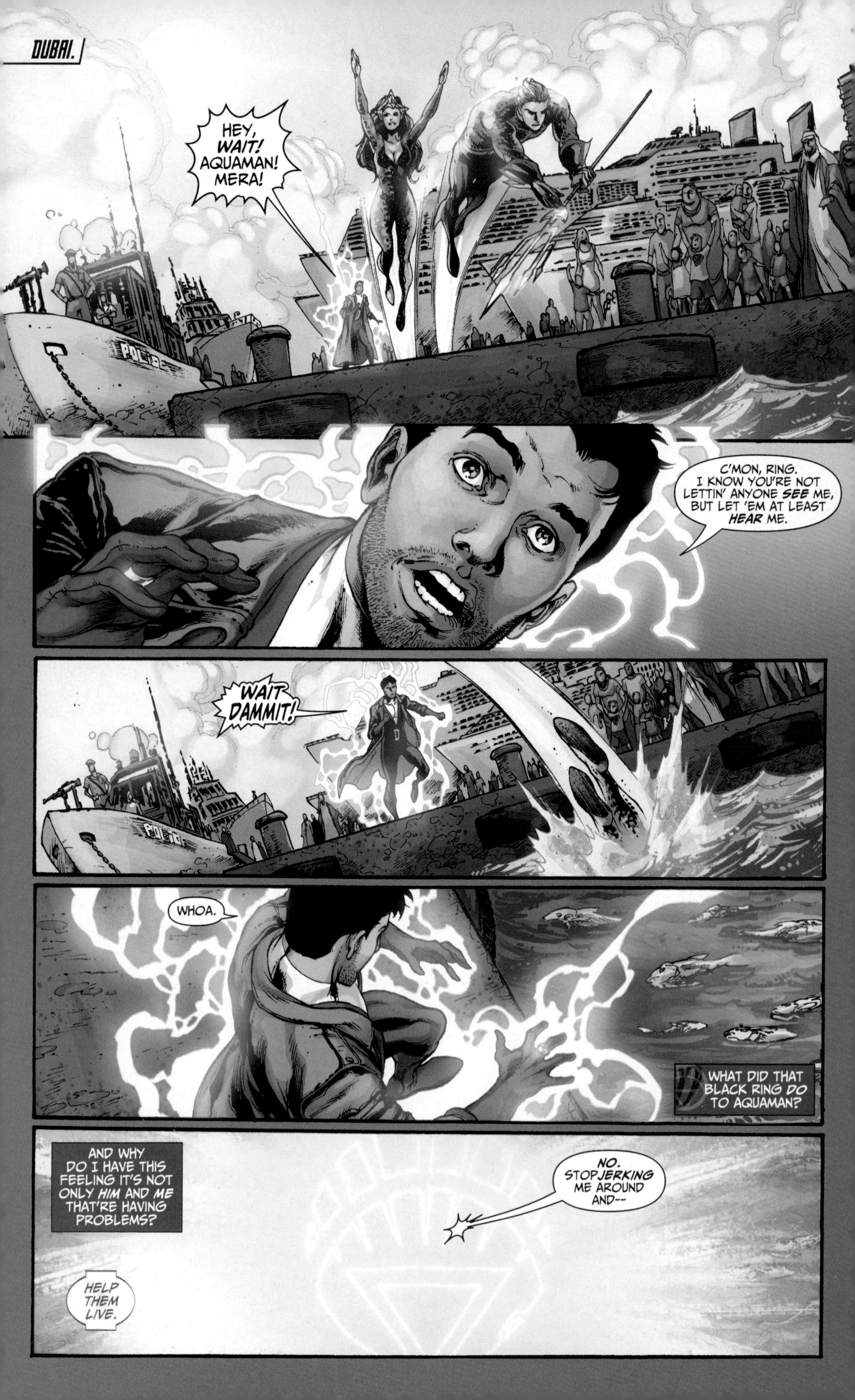
DUBAI.
HEY, WAIT! AQUAMAN! MERA!
C'MON, RING. I KNOW YOU'RE NOT LETTIN' ANYONE SEE ME, BUT LET 'EM AT LEAST HEAR ME.
WAIT DAMMIT!
WHOA.
WHAT DID THAT BLACK RING DO TO AQUAMAN?
AND WHY DO I HAVE THIS FEELING IT'S NOT ONLY HIM AND ME THAT'RE HAVING PROBLEMS?
NO. STOP JERKING ME AROUND AND--
HELP THEM LIVE.

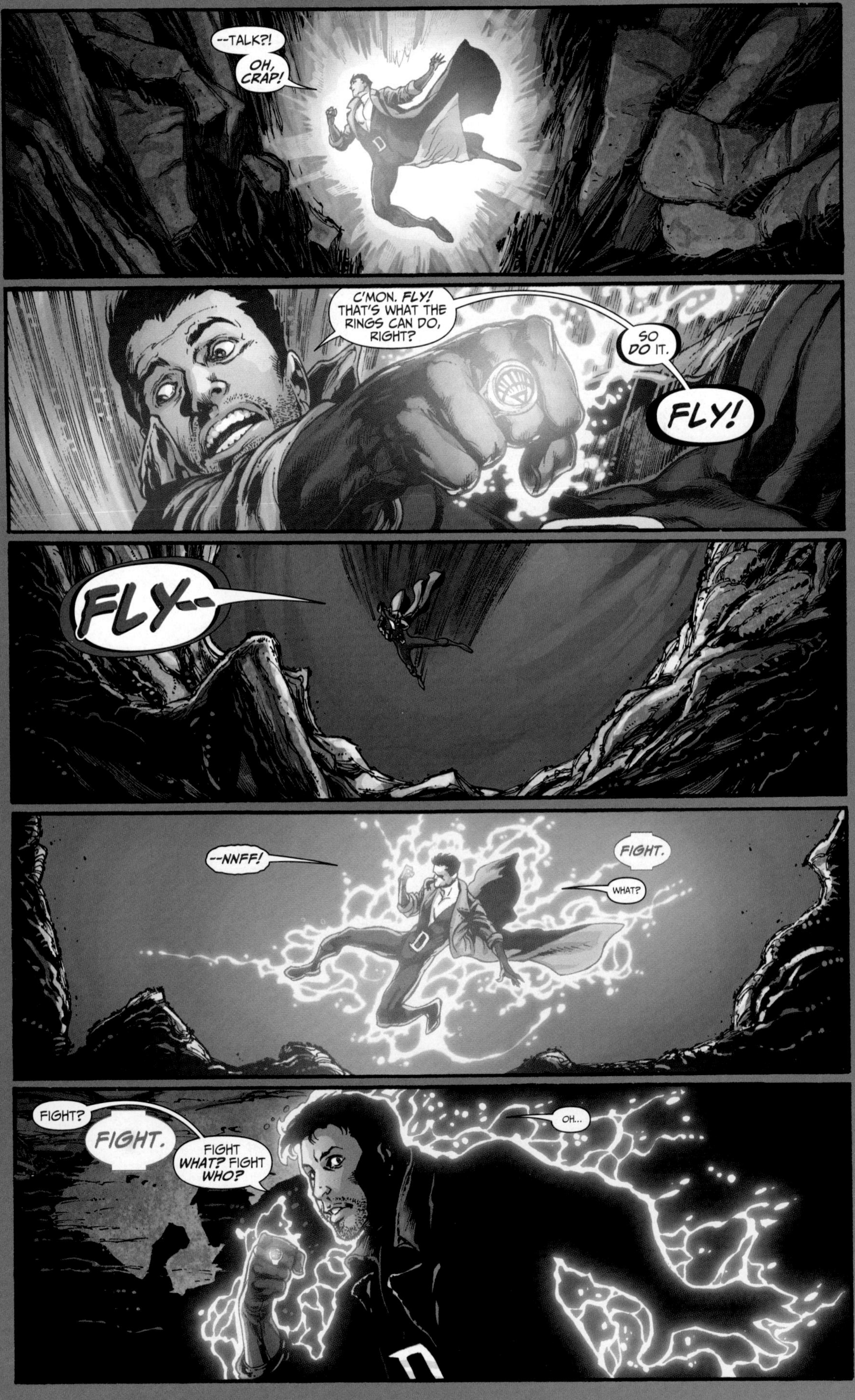
--TALK?!
OH, CRAP!
C'MON. FLY! THAT'S WHAT THE RINGS CAN DO, RIGHT?
SO DO IT.
FLY!
FLY--
--NNFF!
FIGHT.
WHAT?
FIGHT?
FIGHT.
FIGHT WHAT? FIGHT WHO?
OH...

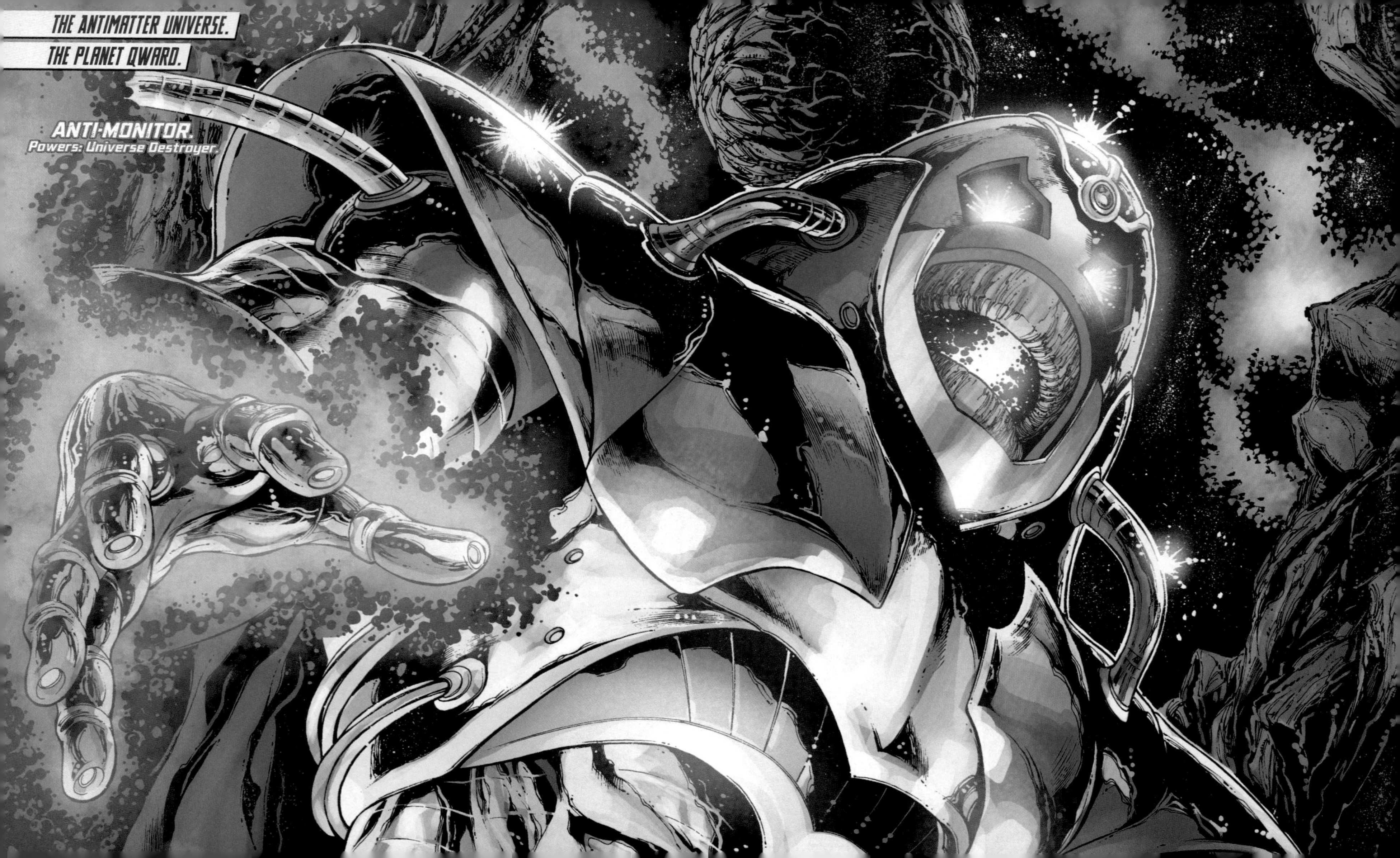
THE ANTIMATTER UNIVERSE.
THE PLANET QWARD.
ANTI-MONITOR.
Powers: Universe Destroyer.

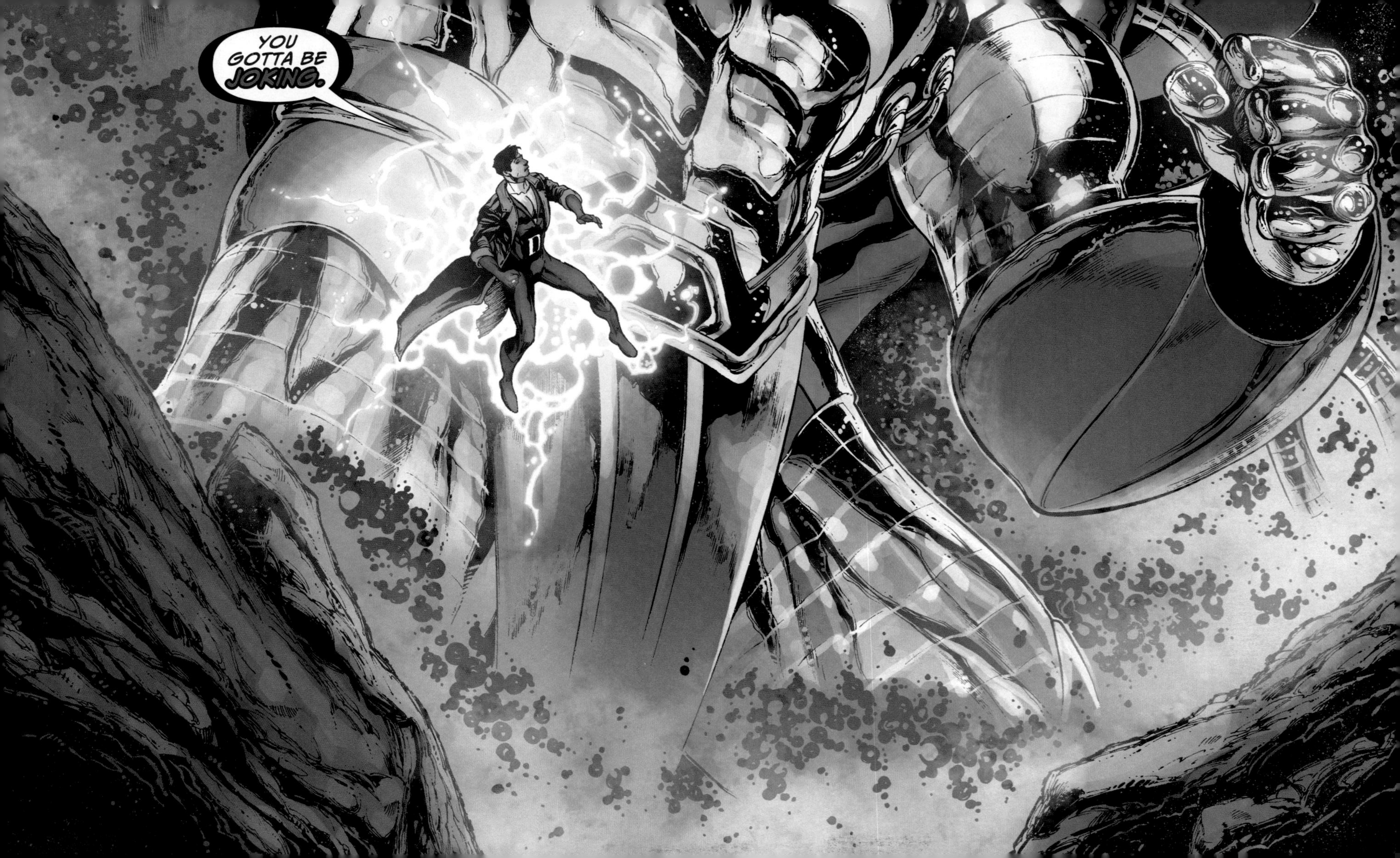
YOU GOTTA BE JOKING.

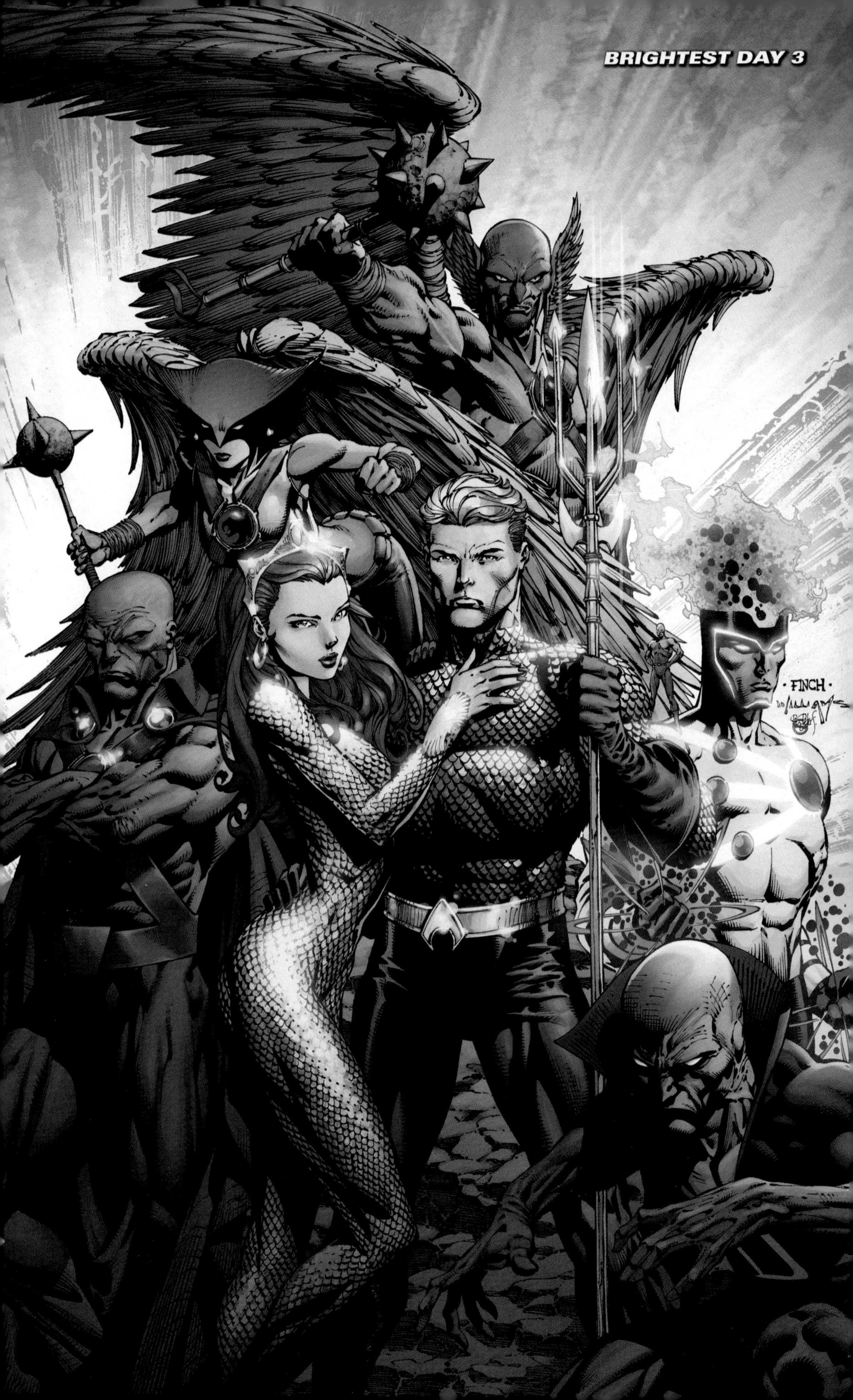
BRIGHTEST DAY 3
FINCH

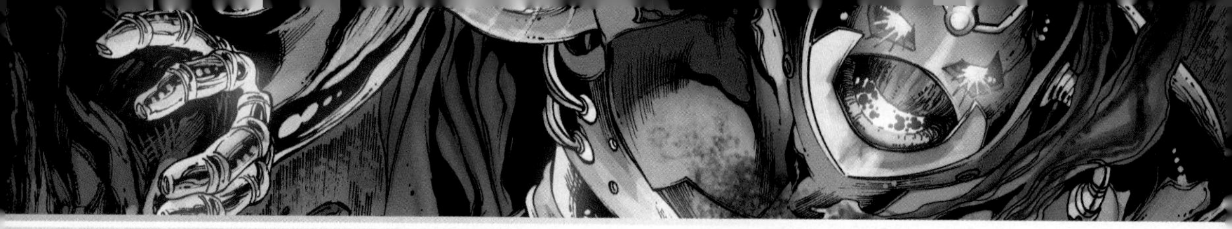

# REVELATIONS

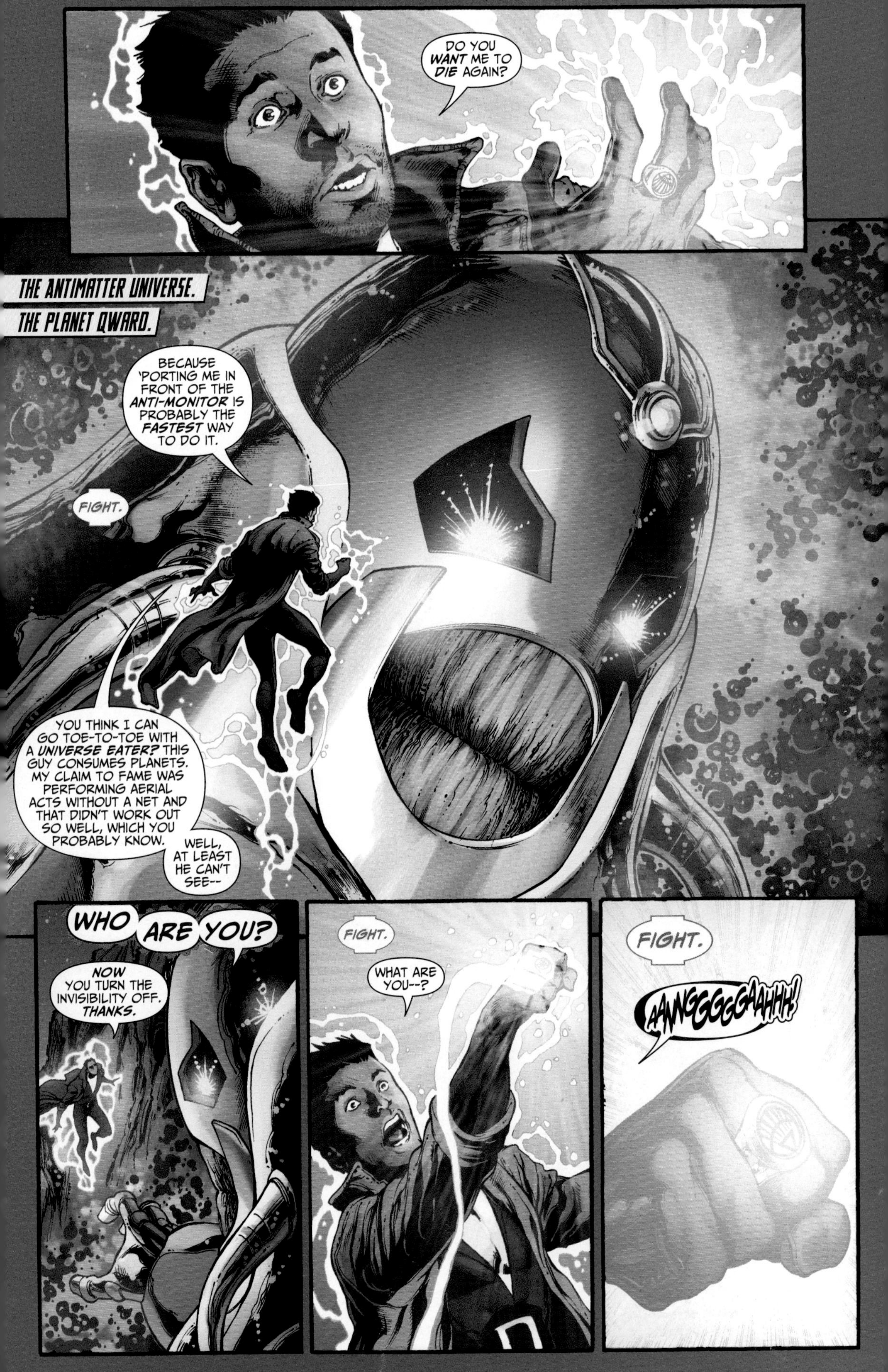

DO YOU *WANT* ME TO *DIE* AGAIN?
THE ANTIMATTER UNIVERSE.
THE PLANET QWARD.
BECAUSE 'PORTING ME IN FRONT OF THE *ANTI-MONITOR* IS PROBABLY THE *FASTEST* WAY TO DO IT.
FIGHT.
YOU THINK I CAN GO TOE-TO-TOE WITH A *UNIVERSE EATER?* THIS GUY CONSUMES PLANETS. MY CLAIM TO FAME WAS PERFORMING AERIAL ACTS WITHOUT A NET AND THAT DIDN'T WORK OUT SO WELL, WHICH YOU PROBABLY KNOW.
WELL, AT LEAST HE CAN'T SEE--
WHO ARE YOU?
*NOW* YOU TURN THE INVISIBILITY OFF. *THANKS.*
FIGHT.
WHAT ARE YOU--?
FIGHT.
AANNGGGGGAAHHH!

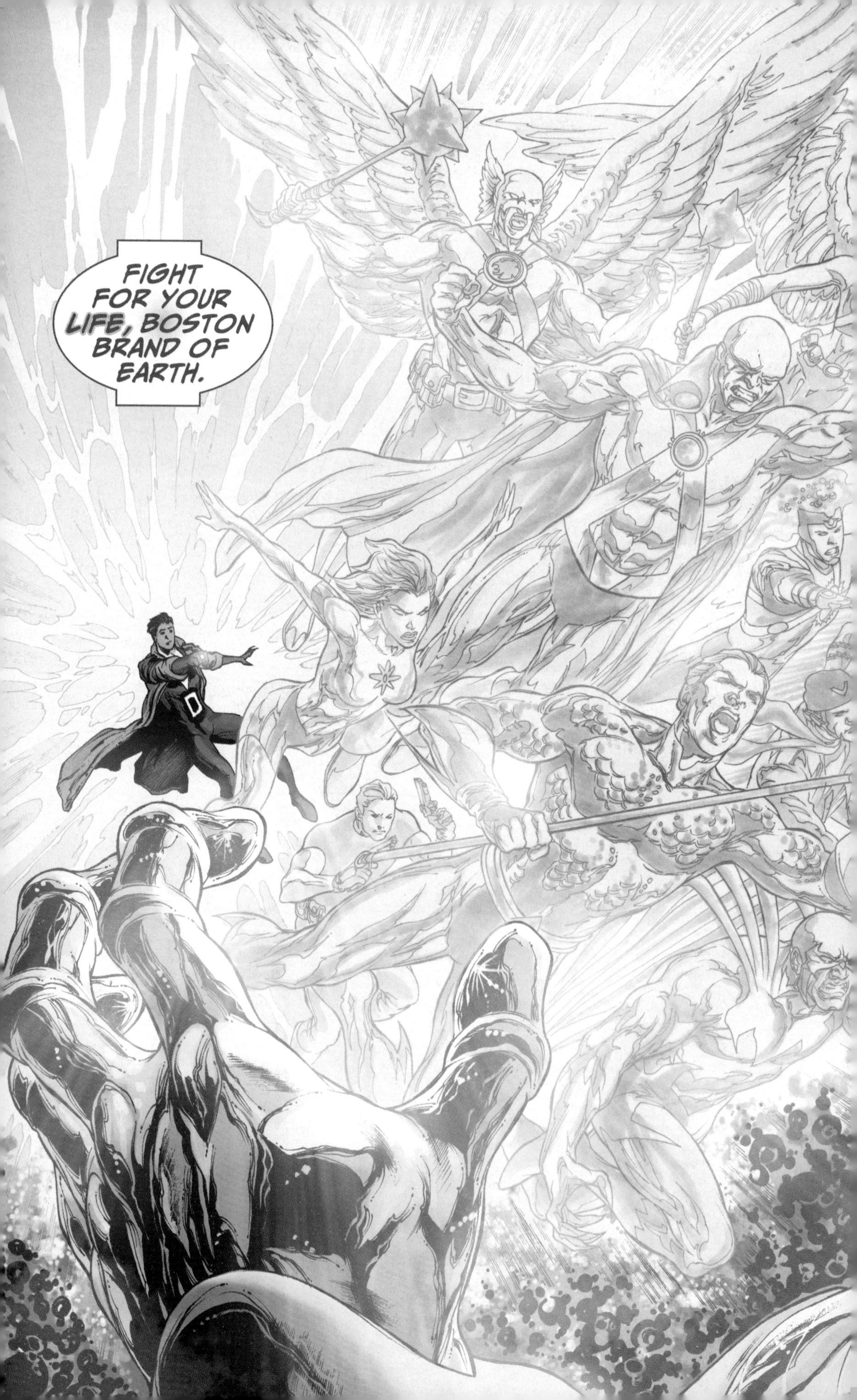
FIGHT FOR YOUR LIFE, BOSTON BRAND OF EARTH.

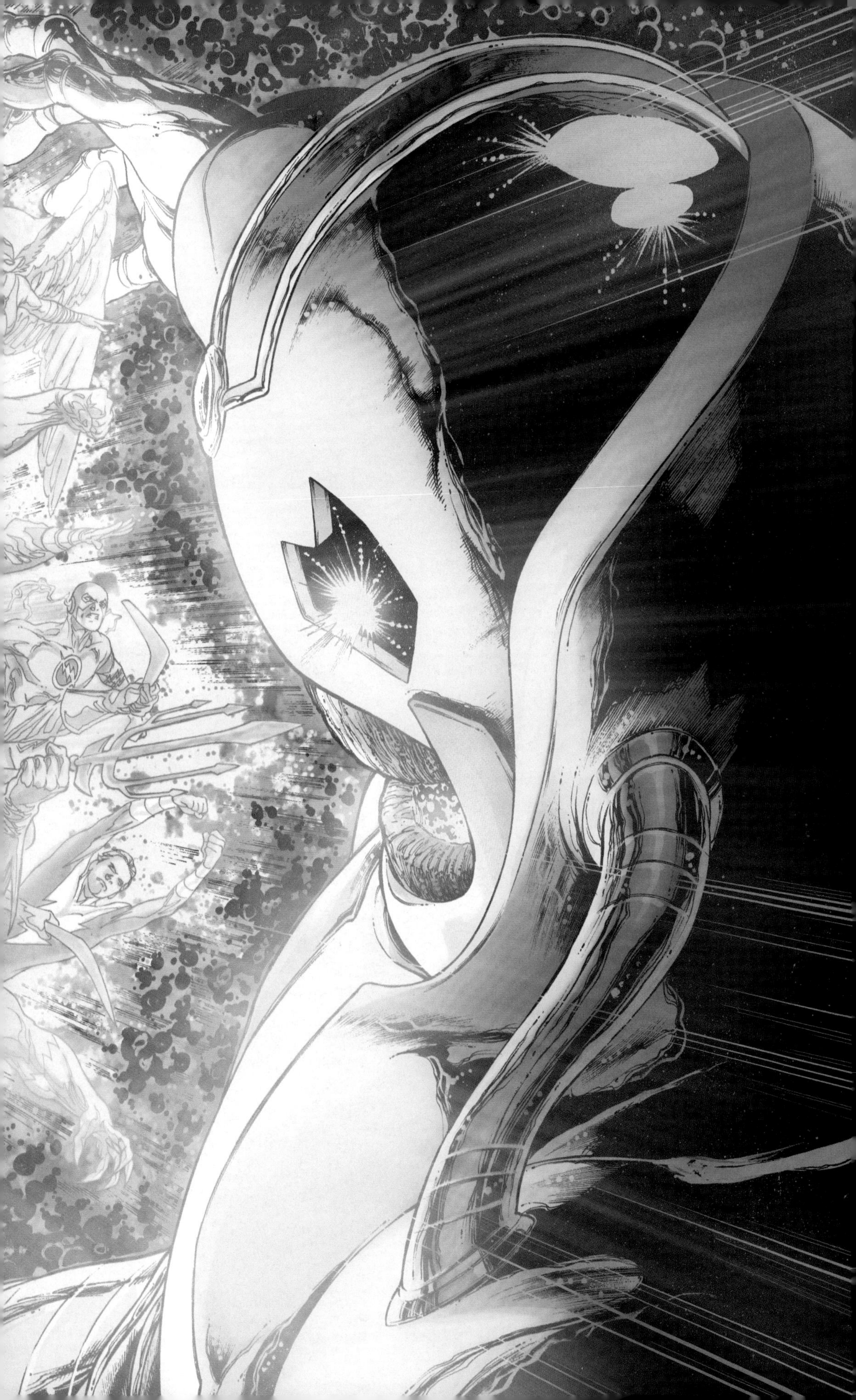

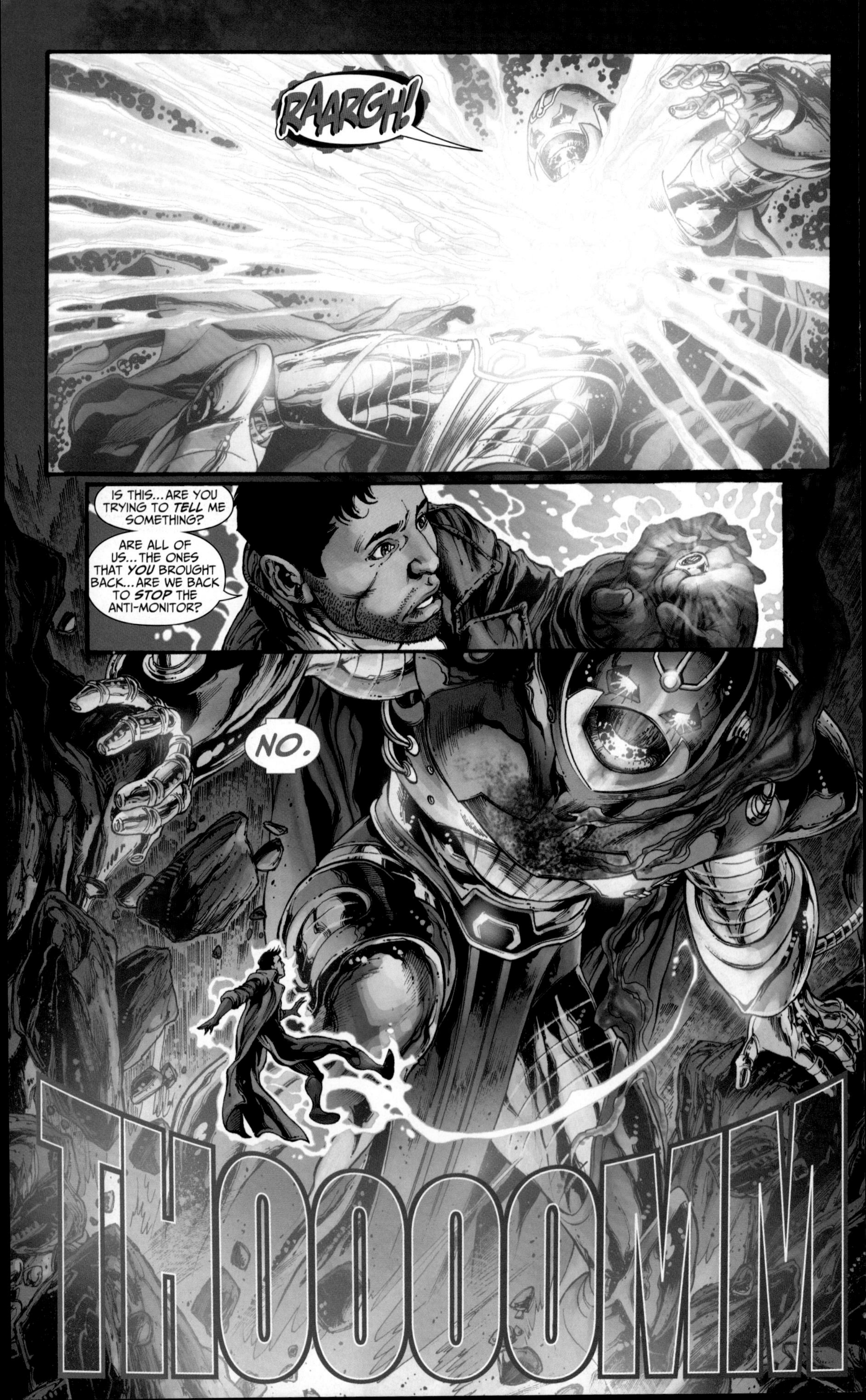
RAARGH!
IS THIS...ARE YOU TRYING TO TELL ME SOMETHING?
ARE ALL OF US...THE ONES THAT YOU BROUGHT BACK...ARE WE BACK TO STOP THE ANTI-MONITOR?
NO.
THOOOMM

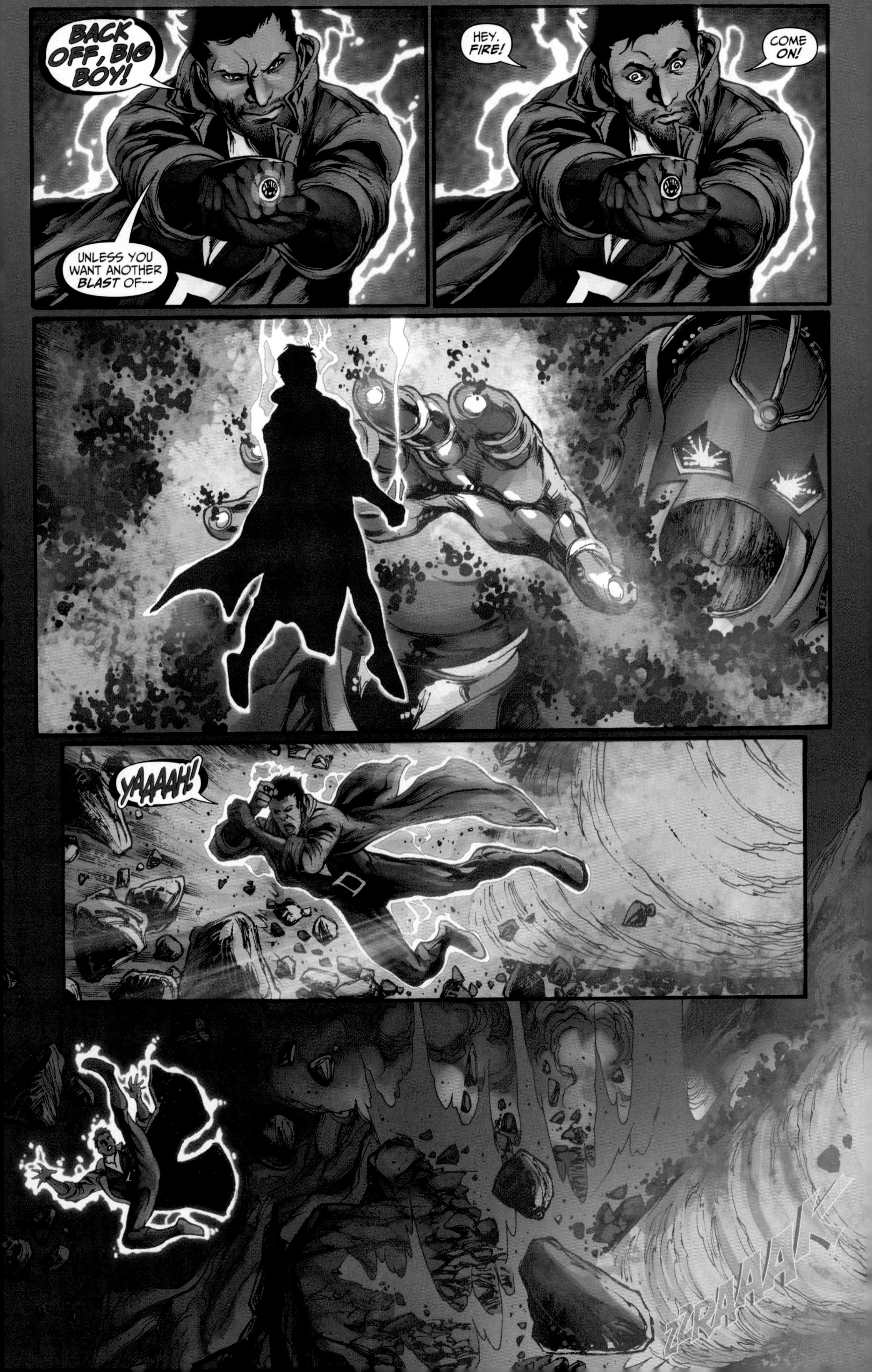
BACK OFF, BIG BOY!
UNLESS YOU WANT ANOTHER BLAST OF--
HEY. FIRE!
COME ON!
YAAAAH!
ZZRAAAK!

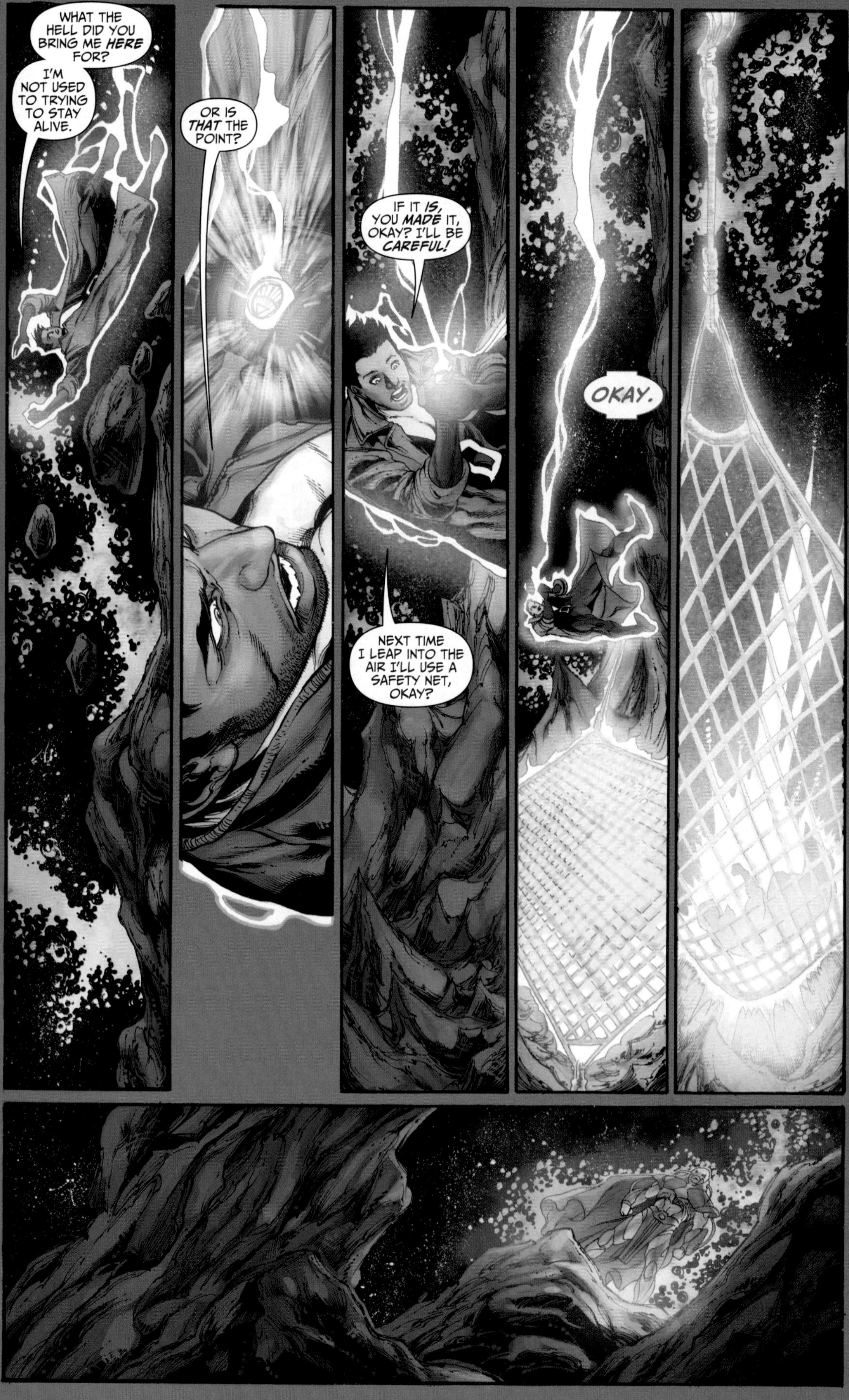
WHAT THE HELL DID YOU BRING ME *HERE* FOR?
I'M NOT USED TO TRYING TO STAY ALIVE.
OR IS *THAT* THE POINT?
IF IT *IS,* YOU *MADE* IT, OKAY? I'LL BE *CAREFUL!*
NEXT TIME I LEAP INTO THE AIR I'LL USE A SAFETY NET, OKAY?
OKAY.

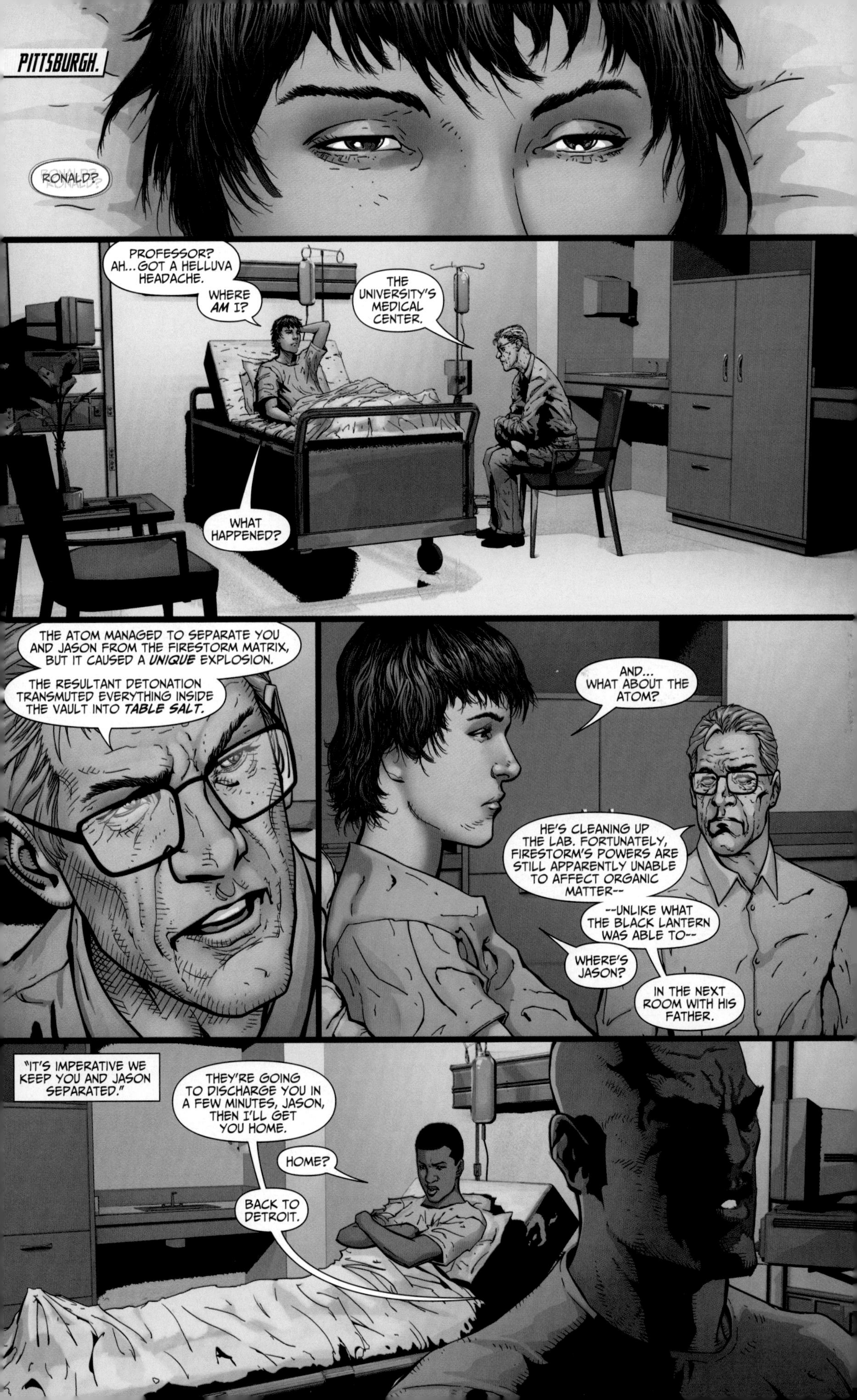
PITTSBURGH.
RONALD?
PROFESSOR? AH...GOT A HELLUVA HEADACHE.
WHERE AM I?
THE UNIVERSITY'S MEDICAL CENTER.
WHAT HAPPENED?
THE ATOM MANAGED TO SEPARATE YOU AND JASON FROM THE FIRESTORM MATRIX, BUT IT CAUSED A UNIQUE EXPLOSION.
THE RESULTANT DETONATION TRANSMUTED EVERYTHING INSIDE THE VAULT INTO TABLE SALT.
AND... WHAT ABOUT THE ATOM?
HE'S CLEANING UP THE LAB. FORTUNATELY, FIRESTORM'S POWERS ARE STILL APPARENTLY UNABLE TO AFFECT ORGANIC MATTER--
--UNLIKE WHAT THE BLACK LANTERN WAS ABLE TO--
WHERE'S JASON?
IN THE NEXT ROOM WITH HIS FATHER.
"IT'S IMPERATIVE WE KEEP YOU AND JASON SEPARATED."
THEY'RE GOING TO DISCHARGE YOU IN A FEW MINUTES, JASON, THEN I'LL GET YOU HOME.
HOME?
BACK TO DETROIT.

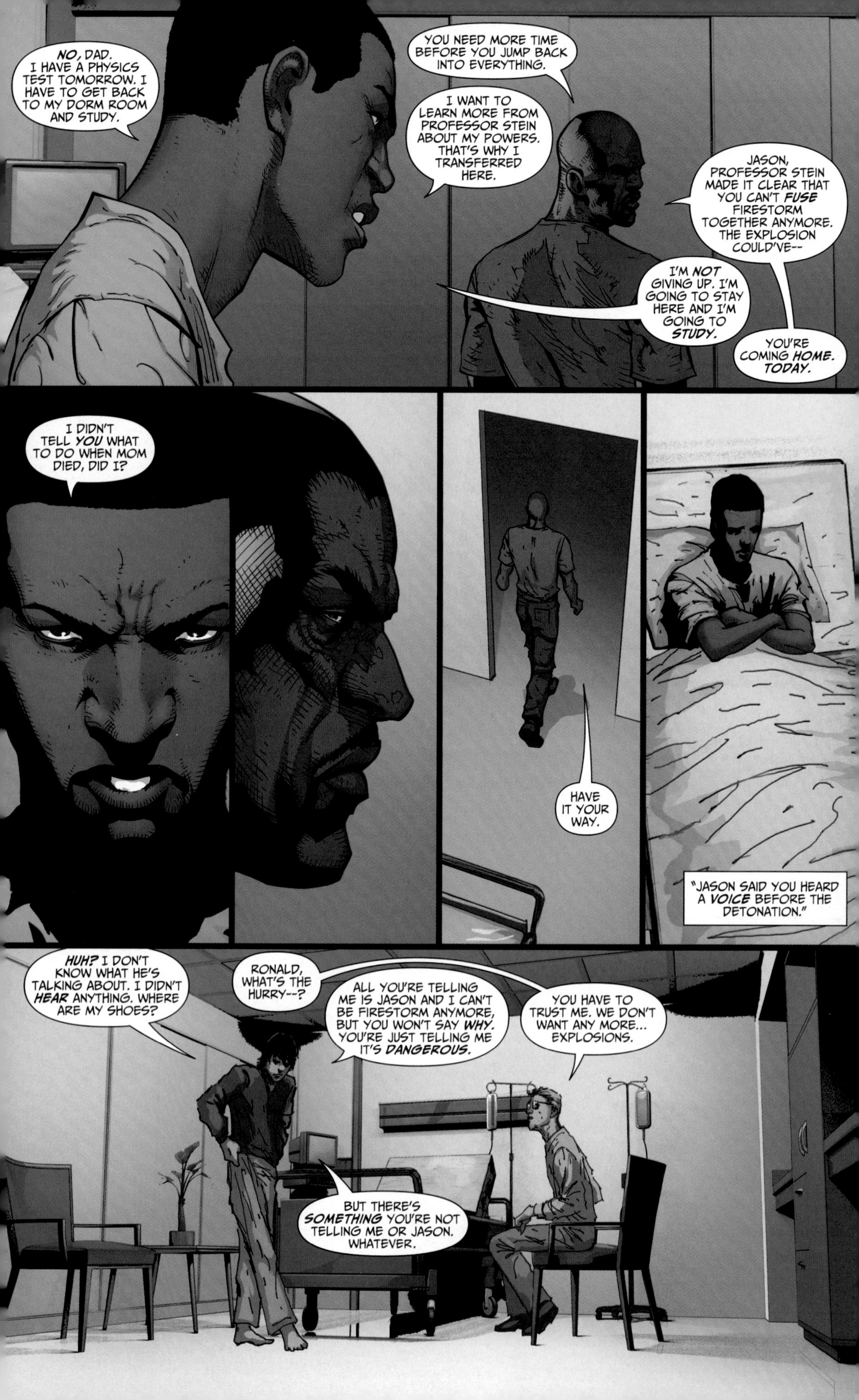
NO, DAD. I HAVE A PHYSICS TEST TOMORROW. I HAVE TO GET BACK TO MY DORM ROOM AND STUDY.
YOU NEED MORE TIME BEFORE YOU JUMP BACK INTO EVERYTHING.
I WANT TO LEARN MORE FROM PROFESSOR STEIN ABOUT MY POWERS. THAT'S WHY I TRANSFERRED HERE.
JASON, PROFESSOR STEIN MADE IT CLEAR THAT YOU CAN'T FUSE FIRESTORM TOGETHER ANYMORE. THE EXPLOSION COULD'VE--
I'M NOT GIVING UP. I'M GOING TO STAY HERE AND I'M GOING TO STUDY.
YOU'RE COMING HOME. TODAY.
I DIDN'T TELL YOU WHAT TO DO WHEN MOM DIED, DID I?
HAVE IT YOUR WAY.
"JASON SAID YOU HEARD A VOICE BEFORE THE DETONATION."
HUH? I DON'T KNOW WHAT HE'S TALKING ABOUT. I DIDN'T HEAR ANYTHING. WHERE ARE MY SHOES?
RONALD, WHAT'S THE HURRY--?
ALL YOU'RE TELLING ME IS JASON AND I CAN'T BE FIRESTORM ANYMORE, BUT YOU WON'T SAY WHY. YOU'RE JUST TELLING ME IT'S DANGEROUS.
YOU HAVE TO TRUST ME. WE DON'T WANT ANY MORE... EXPLOSIONS.
BUT THERE'S SOMETHING YOU'RE NOT TELLING ME OR JASON. WHATEVER.

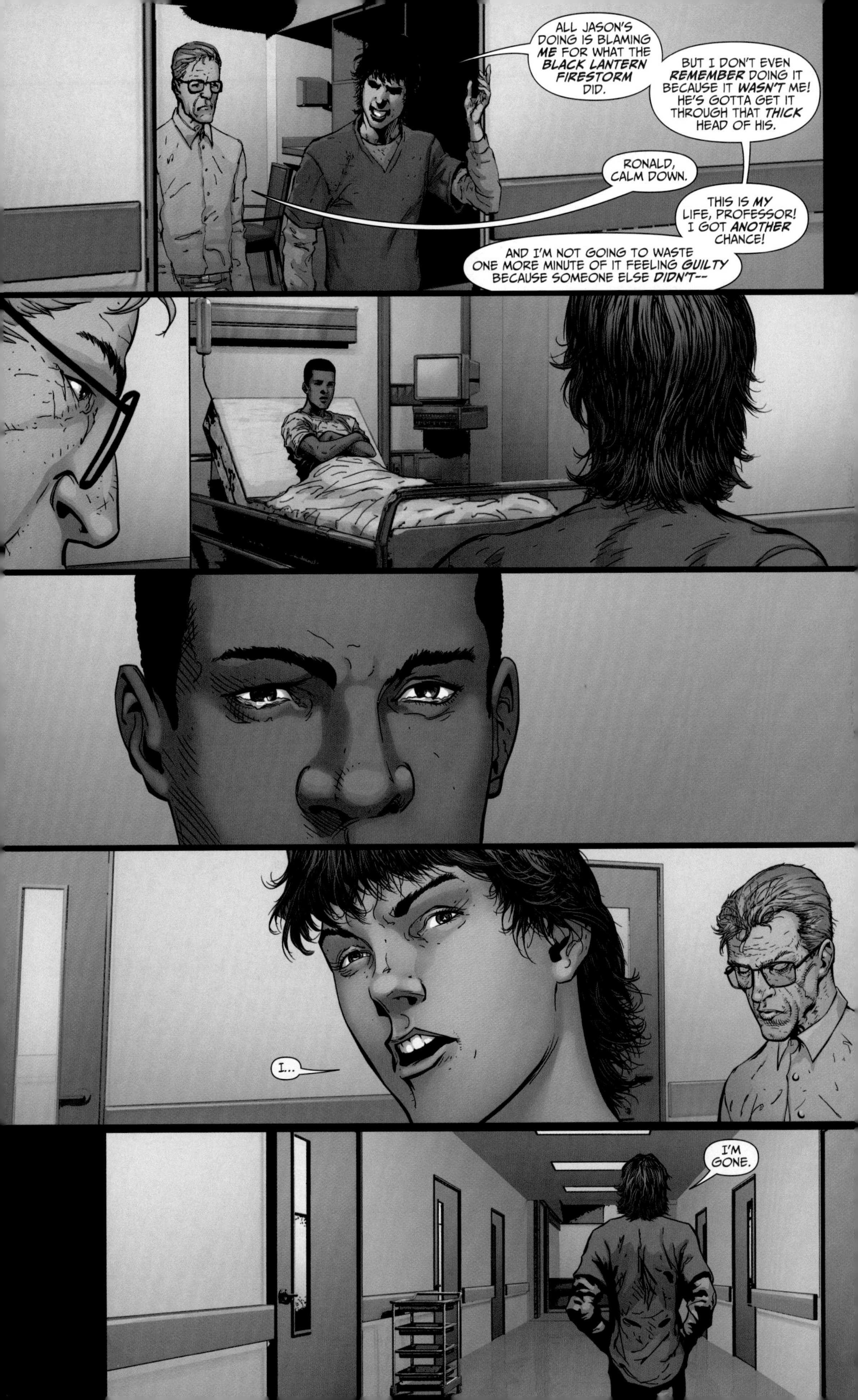
ALL JASON'S DOING IS BLAMING ME FOR WHAT THE BLACK LANTERN FIRESTORM DID.
BUT I DON'T EVEN REMEMBER DOING IT BECAUSE IT WASN'T ME! HE'S GOTTA GET IT THROUGH THAT THICK HEAD OF HIS.
RONALD, CALM DOWN.
THIS IS MY LIFE, PROFESSOR! I GOT ANOTHER CHANCE!
AND I'M NOT GOING TO WASTE ONE MORE MINUTE OF IT FEELING GUILTY BECAUSE SOMEONE ELSE DIDN'T--
I...
I'M GONE.

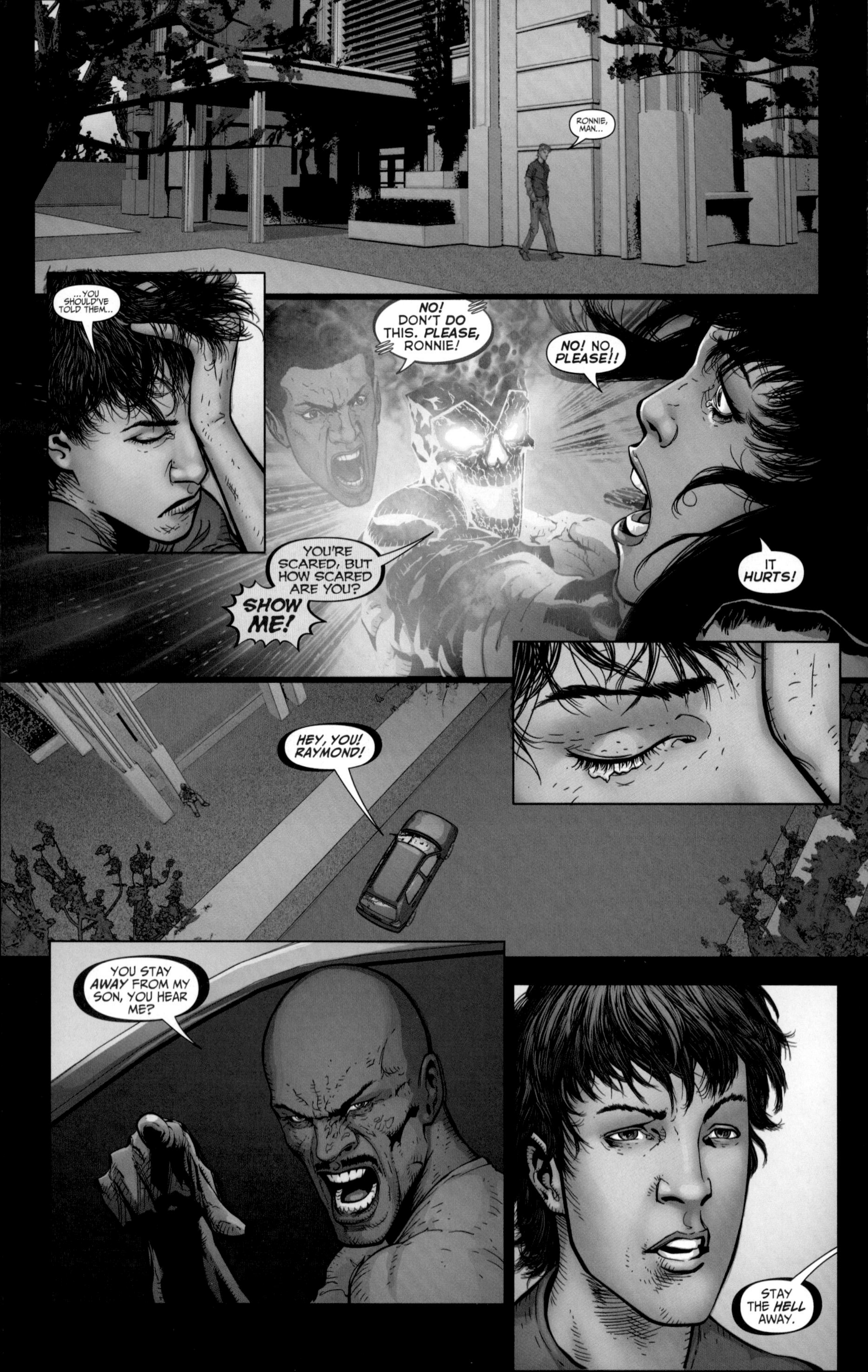
RONNIE, MAN...
...YOU SHOULD'VE TOLD THEM...
NO! DON'T DO THIS. PLEASE, RONNIE!
NO! NO, PLEASE!!
YOU'RE SCARED, BUT HOW SCARED ARE YOU?
SHOW ME!
IT HURTS!
HEY, YOU! RAYMOND!
YOU STAY AWAY FROM MY SON, YOU HEAR ME?
STAY THE HELL AWAY.

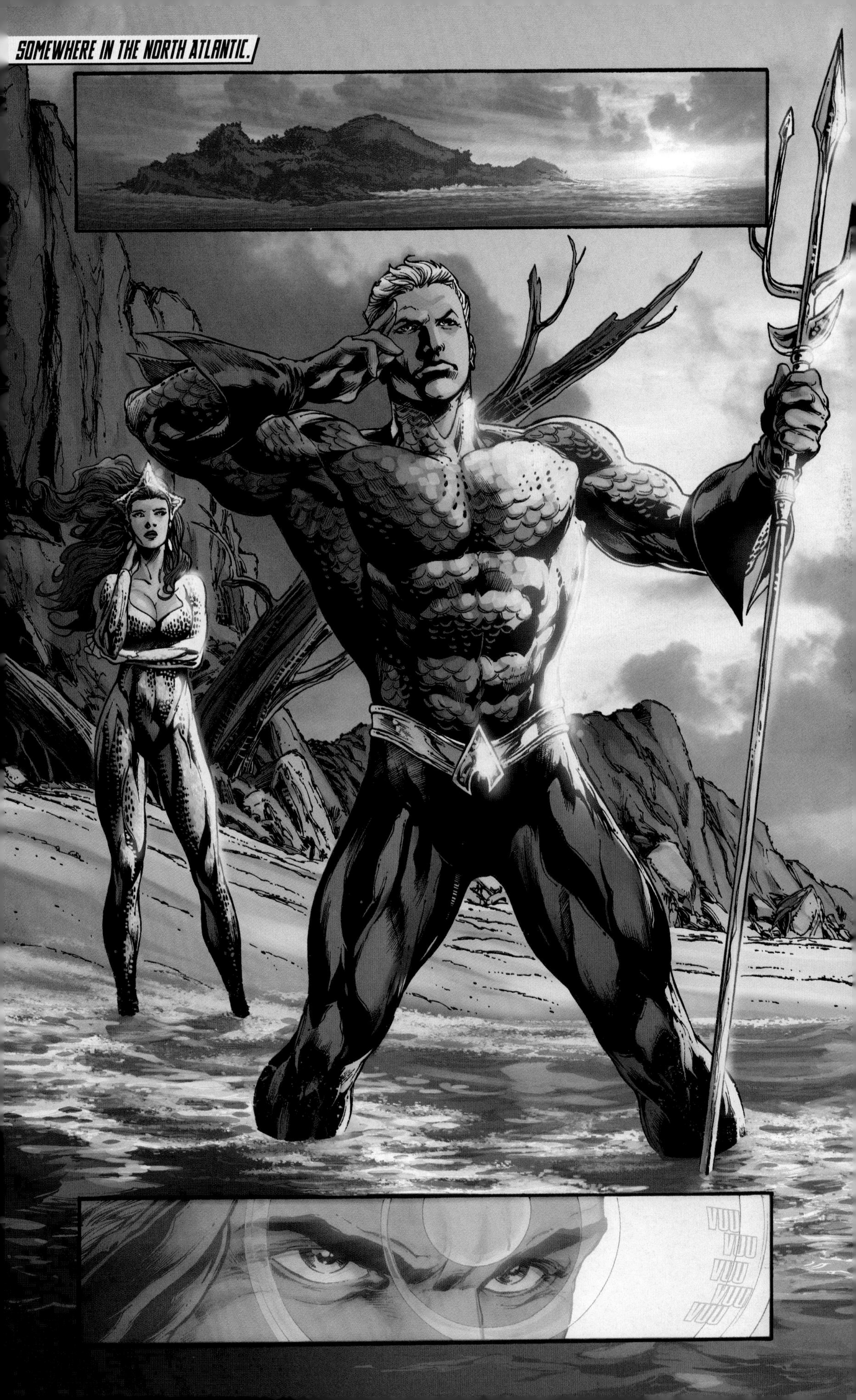
SOMEWHERE IN THE NORTH ATLANTIC.
VUU
VUU
VUU
VUU
VUU

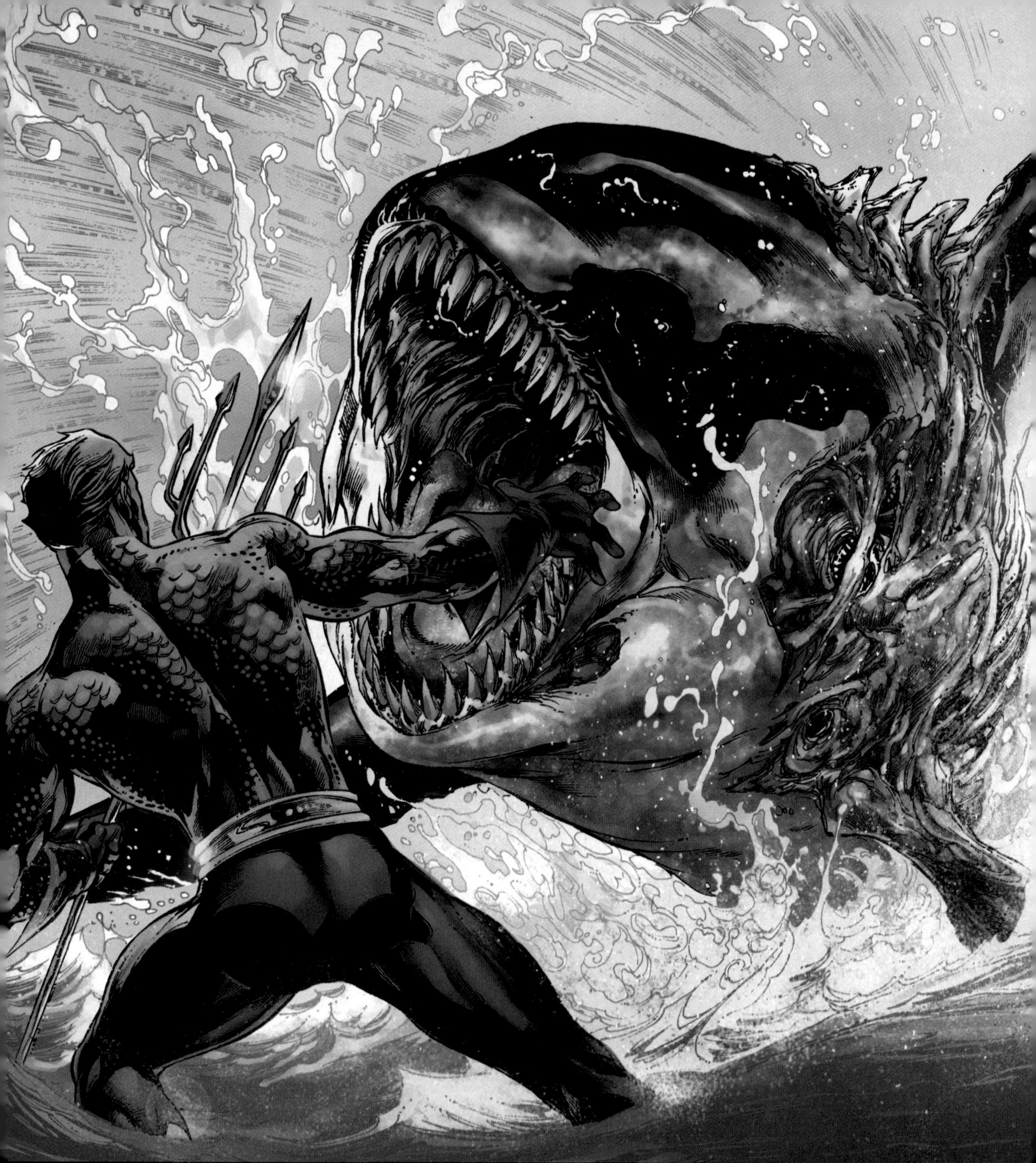

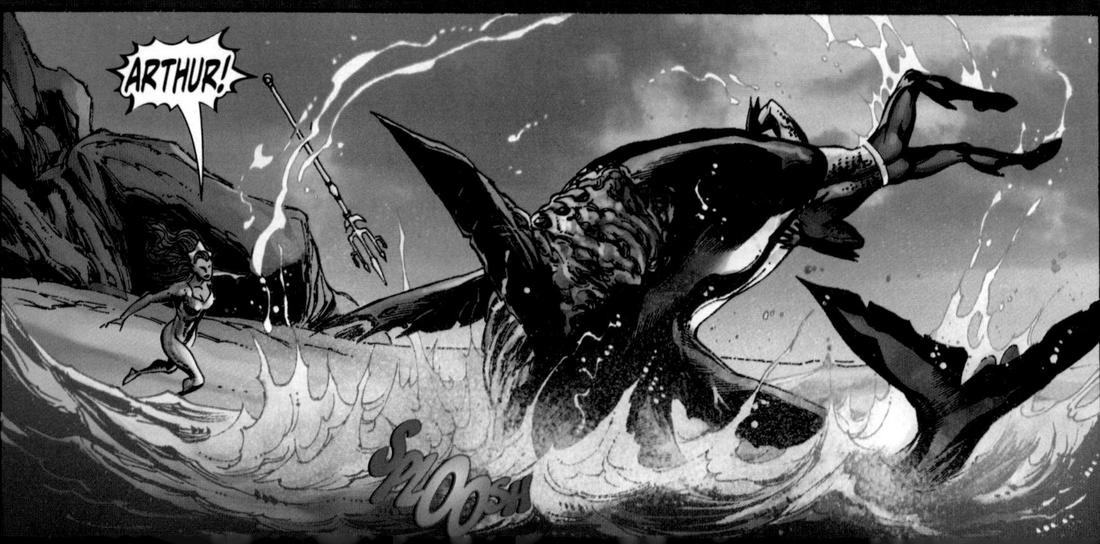
ARTHUR!
SPLOOSH

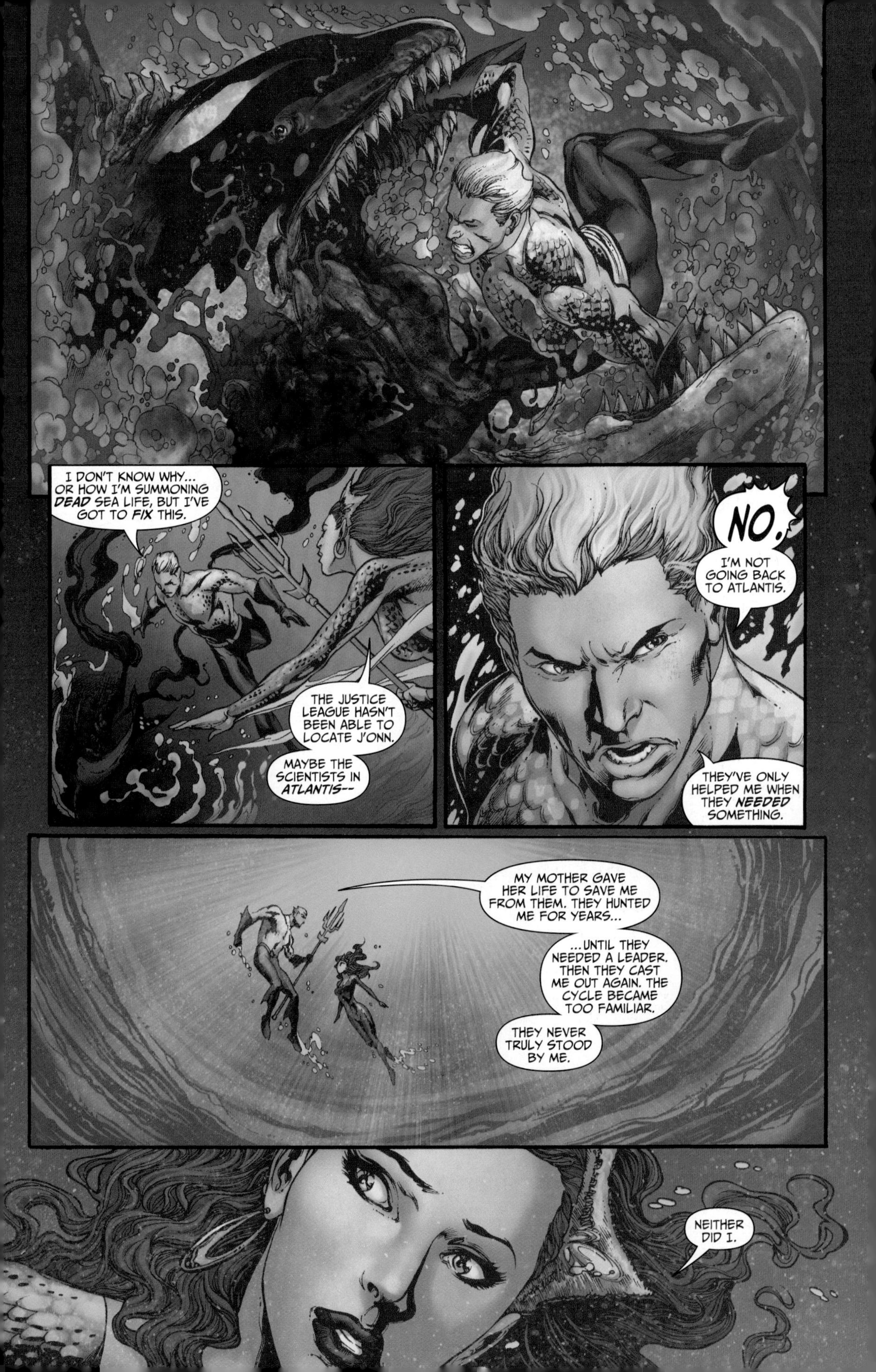
I DON'T KNOW WHY... OR HOW I'M SUMMONING DEAD SEA LIFE, BUT I'VE GOT TO FIX THIS.
THE JUSTICE LEAGUE HASN'T BEEN ABLE TO LOCATE J'ONN.
MAYBE THE SCIENTISTS IN ATLANTIS--
NO.
I'M NOT GOING BACK TO ATLANTIS.
THEY'VE ONLY HELPED ME WHEN THEY NEEDED SOMETHING.
MY MOTHER GAVE HER LIFE TO SAVE ME FROM THEM. THEY HUNTED ME FOR YEARS...
...UNTIL THEY NEEDED A LEADER. THEN THEY CAST ME OUT AGAIN. THE CYCLE BECAME TOO FAMILIAR.
THEY NEVER TRULY STOOD BY ME.
NEITHER DID I.

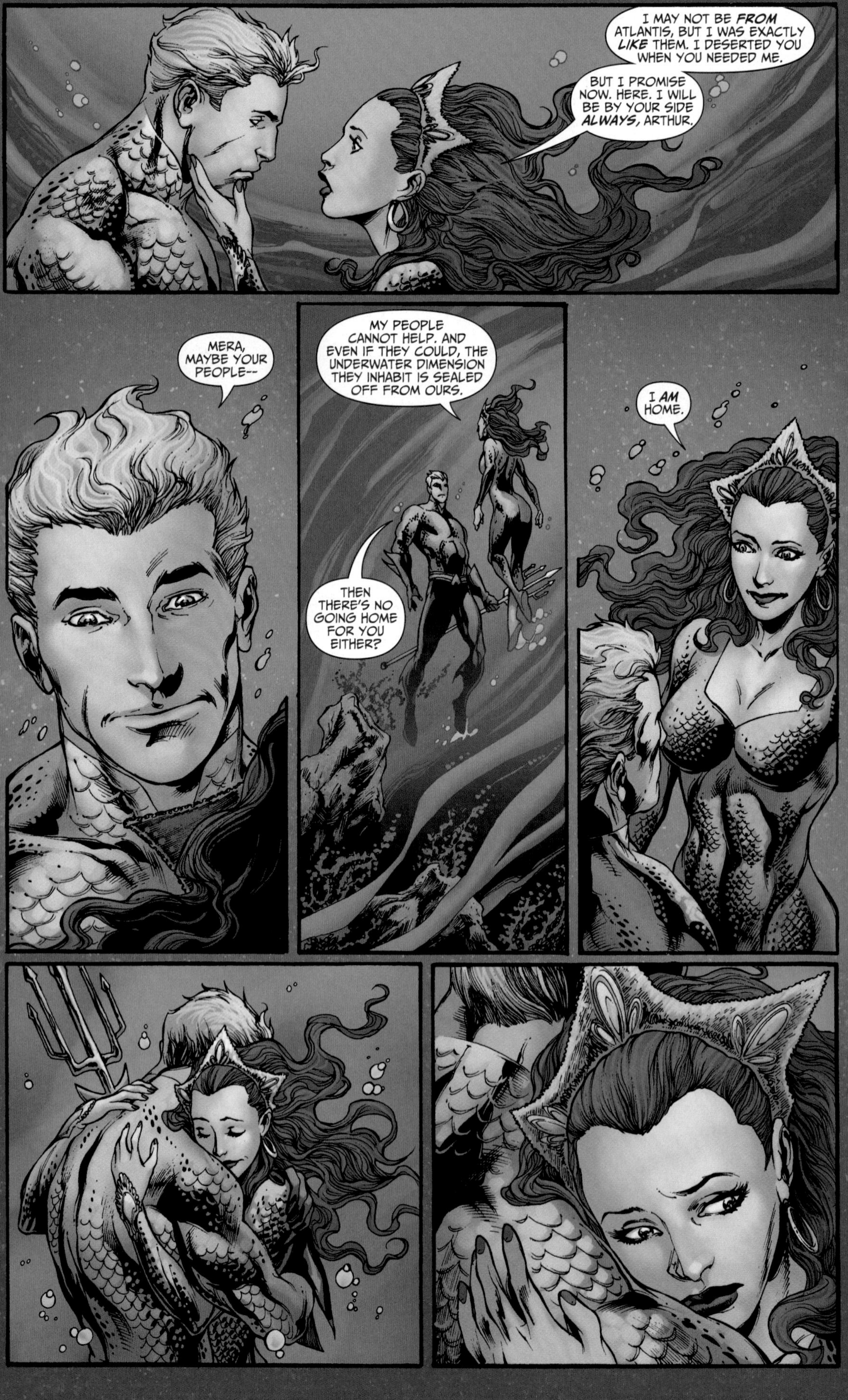
I MAY NOT BE FROM ATLANTIS, BUT I WAS EXACTLY LIKE THEM. I DESERTED YOU WHEN YOU NEEDED ME.
BUT I PROMISE NOW. HERE. I WILL BE BY YOUR SIDE ALWAYS, ARTHUR.
MERA, MAYBE YOUR PEOPLE--
MY PEOPLE CANNOT HELP. AND EVEN IF THEY COULD, THE UNDERWATER DIMENSION THEY INHABIT IS SEALED OFF FROM OURS.
THEN THERE'S NO GOING HOME FOR YOU EITHER?
I AM HOME.

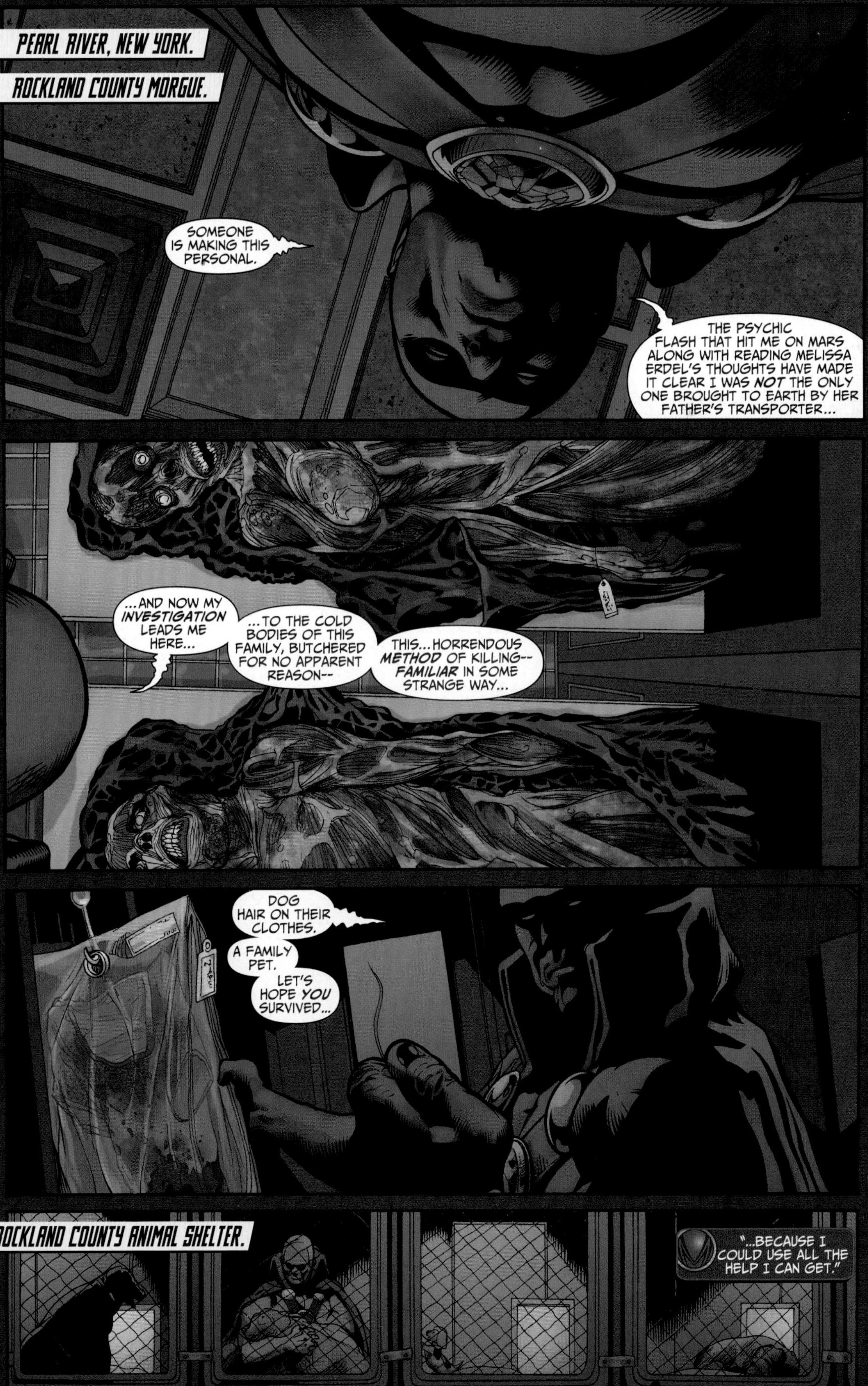
PEARL RIVER, NEW YORK.
ROCKLAND COUNTY MORGUE.
SOMEONE IS MAKING THIS PERSONAL.
THE PSYCHIC FLASH THAT HIT ME ON MARS ALONG WITH READING MELISSA ERDEL'S THOUGHTS HAVE MADE IT CLEAR I WAS NOT THE ONLY ONE BROUGHT TO EARTH BY HER FATHER'S TRANSPORTER...
...AND NOW MY INVESTIGATION LEADS ME HERE...
...TO THE COLD BODIES OF THIS FAMILY, BUTCHERED FOR NO APPARENT REASON--
THIS...HORRENDOUS METHOD OF KILLING--FAMILIAR IN SOME STRANGE WAY...
DOG HAIR ON THEIR CLOTHES.
A FAMILY PET.
LET'S HOPE YOU SURVIVED...
ROCKLAND COUNTY ANIMAL SHELTER.
"...BECAUSE I COULD USE ALL THE HELP I CAN GET."

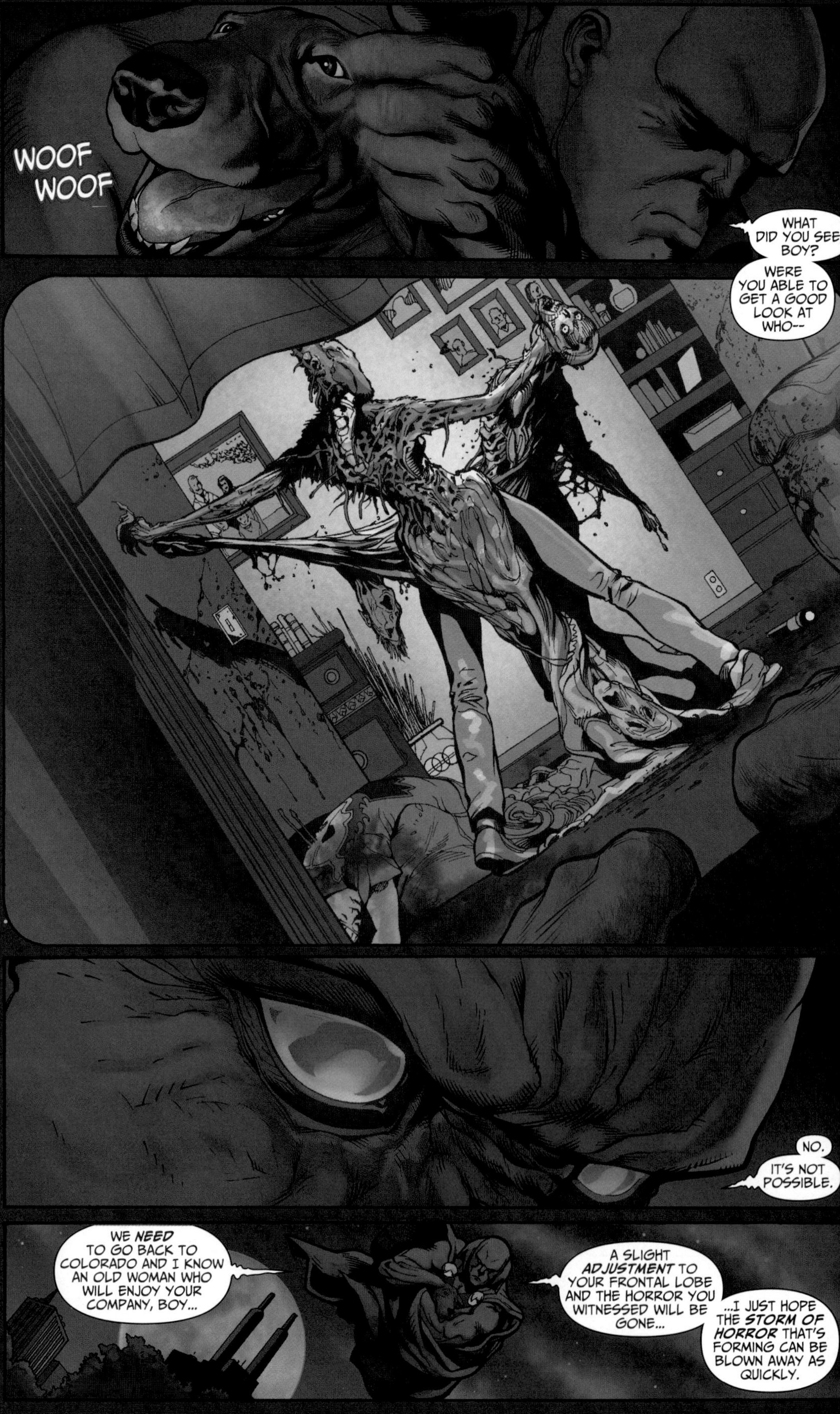
WOOF
WOOF
WHAT DID YOU SEE, BOY?
WERE YOU ABLE TO GET A GOOD LOOK AT WHO--
NO.
IT'S NOT POSSIBLE.
WE *NEED* TO GO BACK TO COLORADO AND I KNOW AN OLD WOMAN WHO WILL ENJOY YOUR COMPANY, BOY...
A SLIGHT *ADJUSTMENT* TO YOUR FRONTAL LOBE AND THE HORROR YOU WITNESSED WILL BE GONE...
...I JUST HOPE THE *STORM OF HORROR* THAT'S FORMING CAN BE BLOWN AWAY AS QUICKLY.

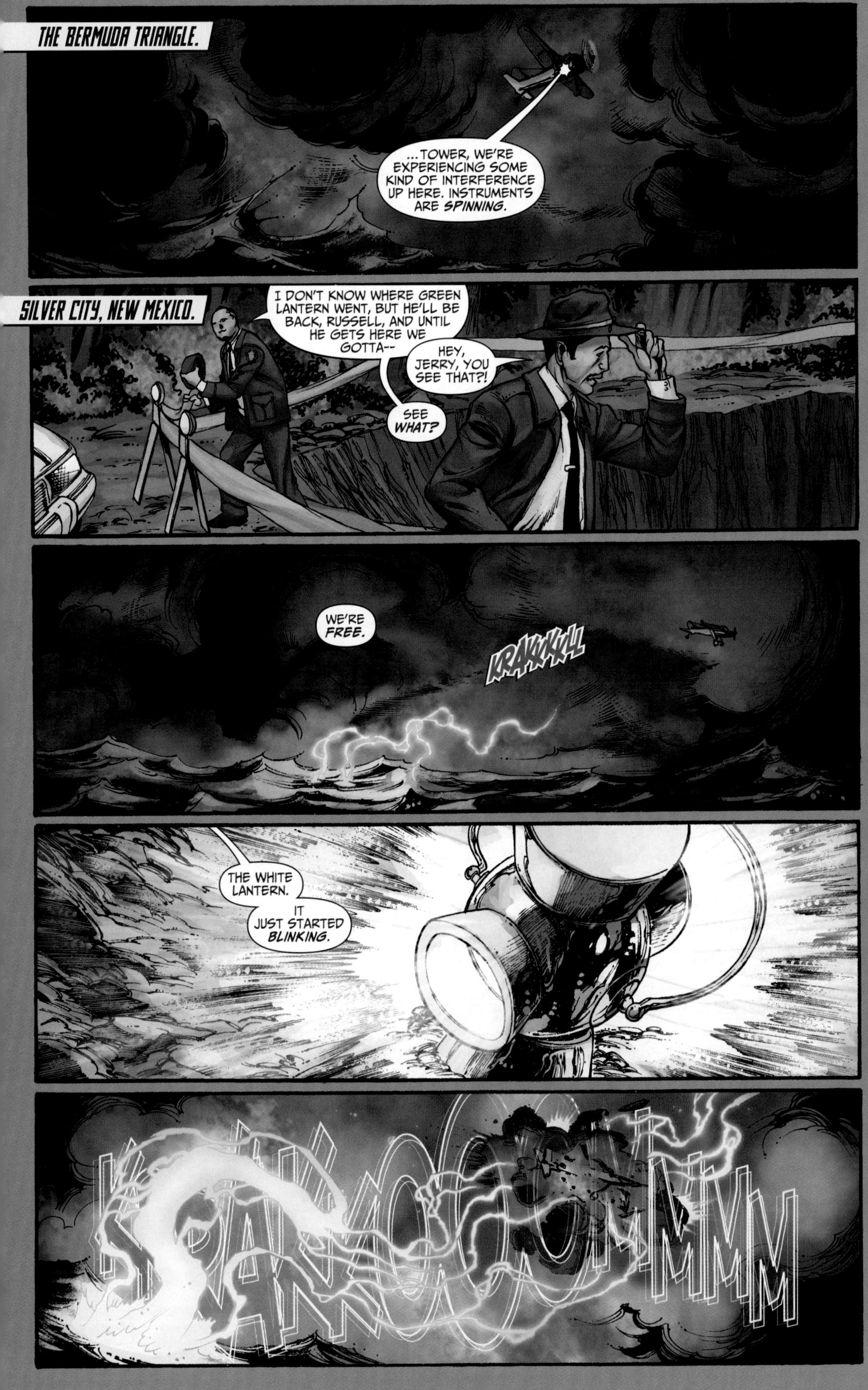

THE BERMUDA TRIANGLE.
...TOWER, WE'RE EXPERIENCING SOME KIND OF INTERFERENCE UP HERE. INSTRUMENTS ARE SPINNING.
SILVER CITY, NEW MEXICO.
I DON'T KNOW WHERE GREEN LANTERN WENT, BUT HE'LL BE BACK, RUSSELL, AND UNTIL HE GETS HERE WE GOTTA--
HEY, JERY, YOU SEE THAT?!
SEE WHAT?
WE'RE FREE.
KRAKKKLL
THE WHITE LANTERN.
IT JUST STARTED BLINKING.

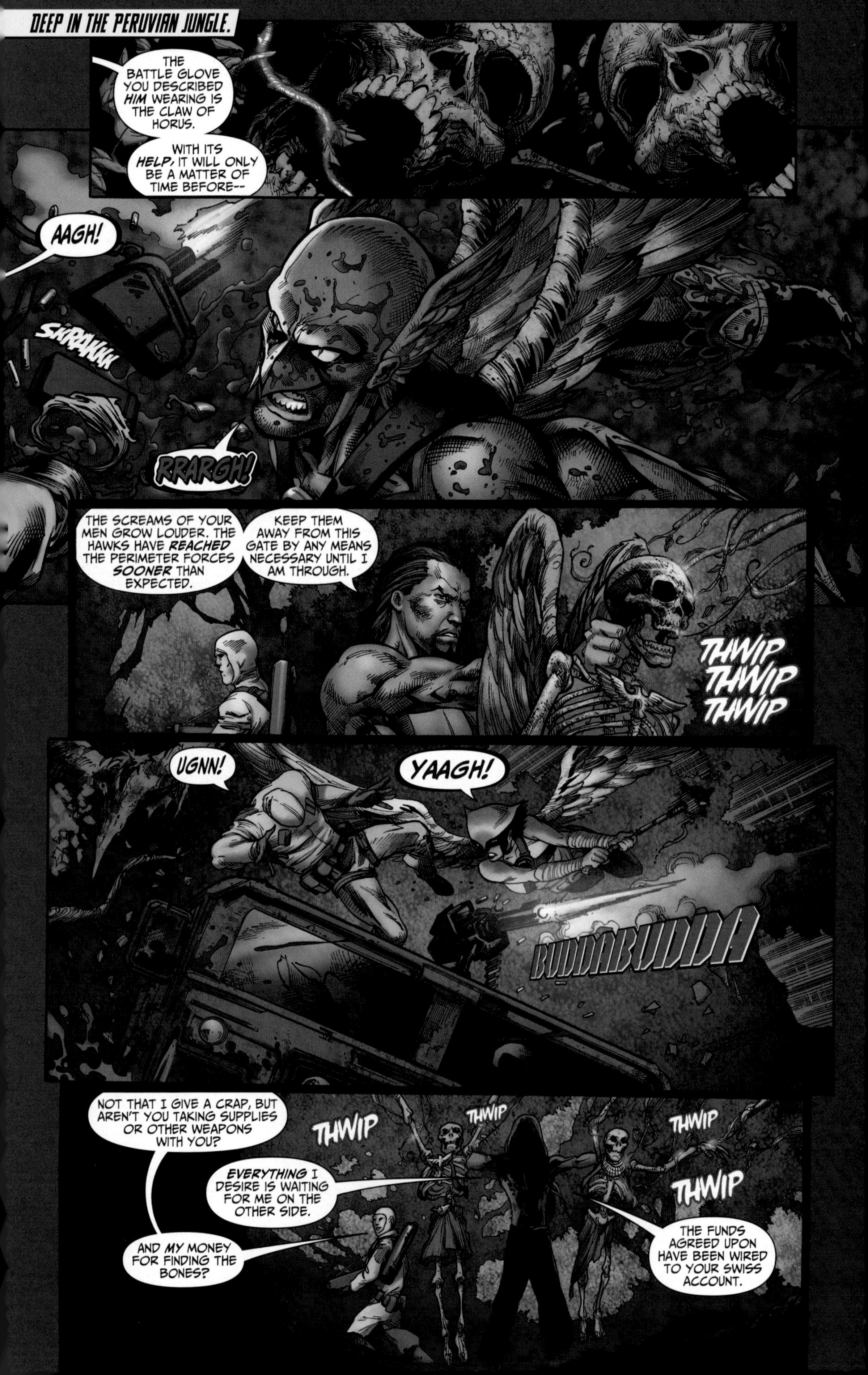
DEEP IN THE PERUVIAN JUNGLE.
THE BATTLE GLOVE YOU DESCRIBED HIM WEARING IS THE CLAW OF HORUS.
WITH ITS HELP, IT WILL ONLY BE A MATTER OF TIME BEFORE--
AAGH!
SKRAKKK
RRARGH!
THE SCREAMS OF YOUR MEN GROW LOUDER. THE HAWKS HAVE REACHED THE PERIMETER FORCES SOONER THAN EXPECTED.
KEEP THEM AWAY FROM THIS GATE BY ANY MEANS NECESSARY UNTIL I AM THROUGH.
THWIP THWIP THWIP
UGNN!
YAAGH!
BUDDABUDDA
NOT THAT I GIVE A CRAP, BUT AREN'T YOU TAKING SUPPLIES OR OTHER WEAPONS WITH YOU?
THWIP
THWIP
THWIP
EVERYTHING I DESIRE IS WAITING FOR ME ON THE OTHER SIDE.
THWIP
AND MY MONEY FOR FINDING THE BONES?
THE FUNDS AGREED UPON HAVE BEEN WIRED TO YOUR SWISS ACCOUNT.

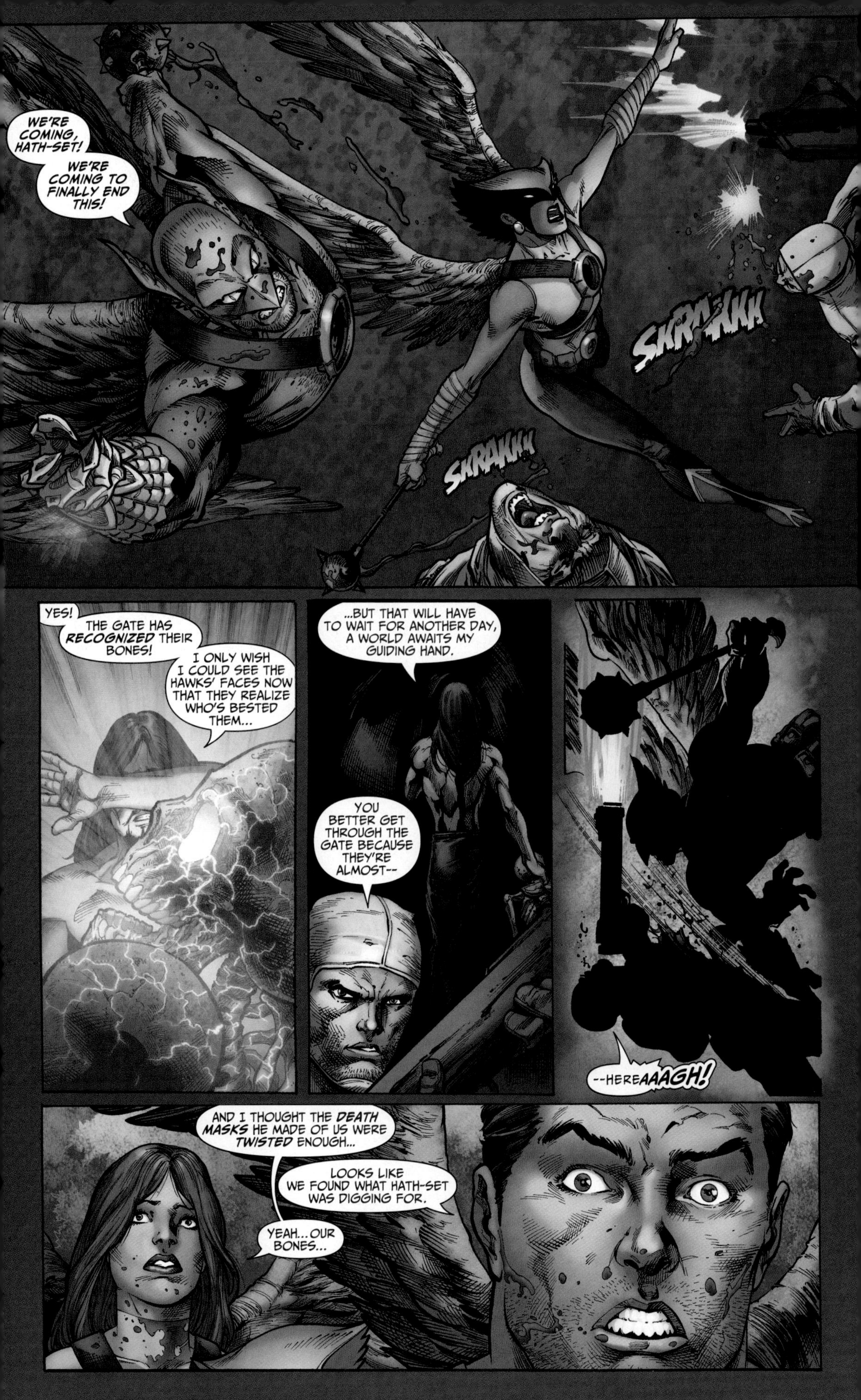
WE'RE COMING, HATH-SET!
WE'RE COMING TO FINALLY END THIS!
SKRAKKK
SKRAKKK
YES! THE GATE HAS RECOGNIZED THEIR BONES!
I ONLY WISH I COULD SEE THE HAWKS' FACES NOW THAT THEY REALIZE WHO'S BESTED THEM...
...BUT THAT WILL HAVE TO WAIT FOR ANOTHER DAY, A WORLD AWAITS MY GUIDING HAND.
YOU BETTER GET THROUGH THE GATE BECAUSE THEY'RE ALMOST--
--HEREAAAGH!
AND I THOUGHT THE DEATH MASKS HE MADE OF US WERE TWISTED ENOUGH...
LOOKS LIKE WE FOUND WHAT HATH-SET WAS DIGGING FOR.
YEAH...OUR BONES...

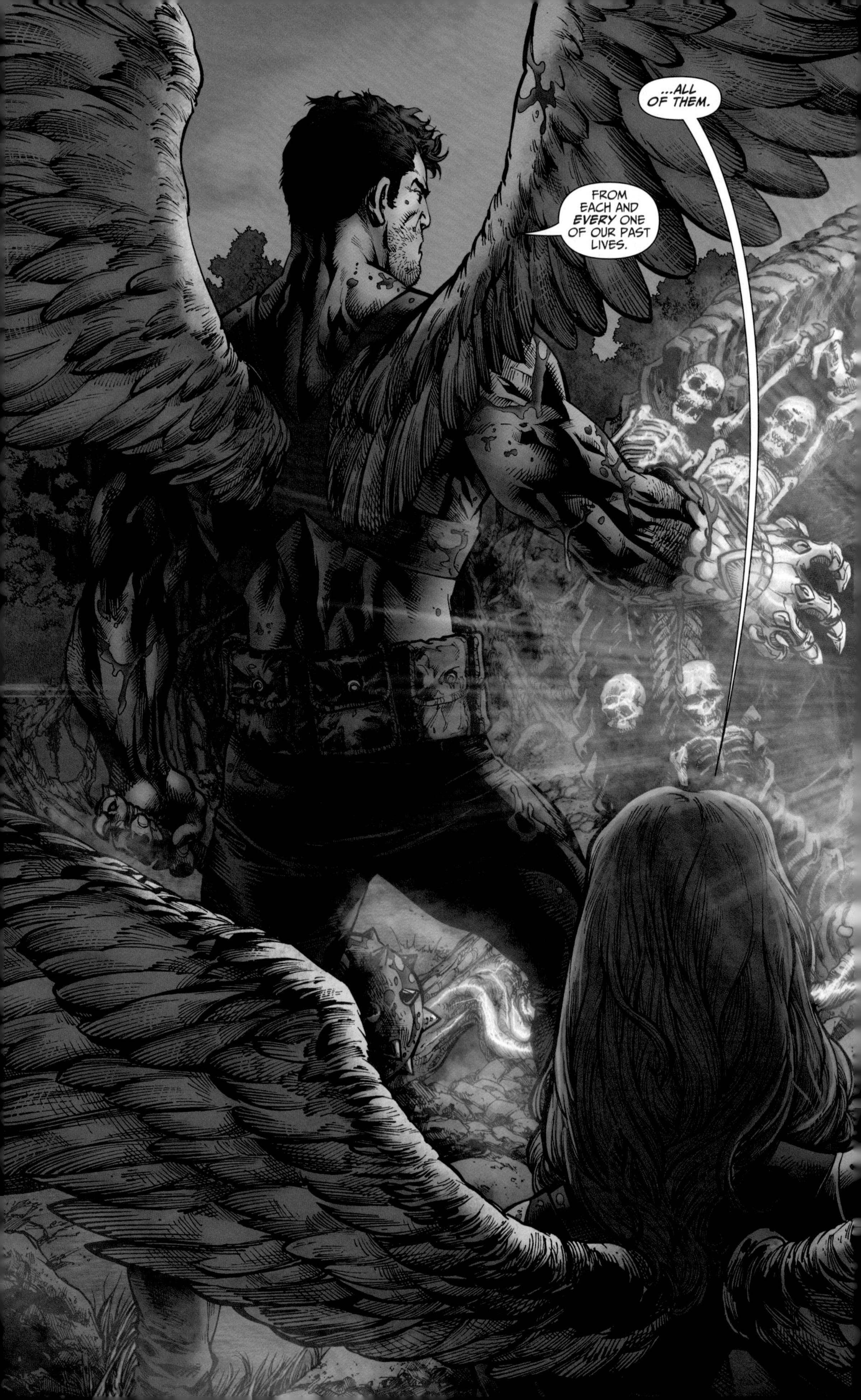
FROM EACH AND EVERY ONE OF OUR PAST LIVES.
...ALL OF THEM.

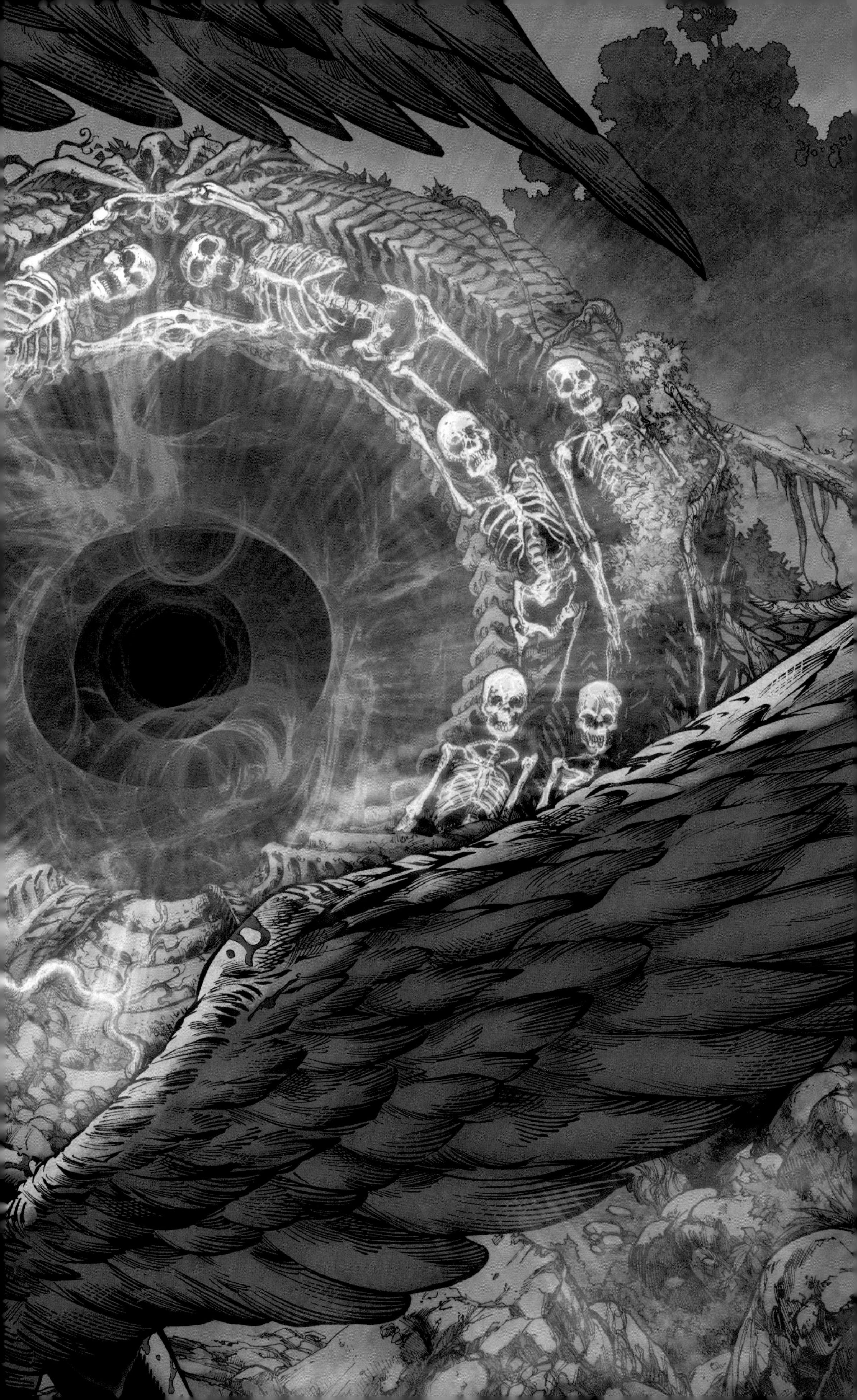

BRIGHTEST DAY 4

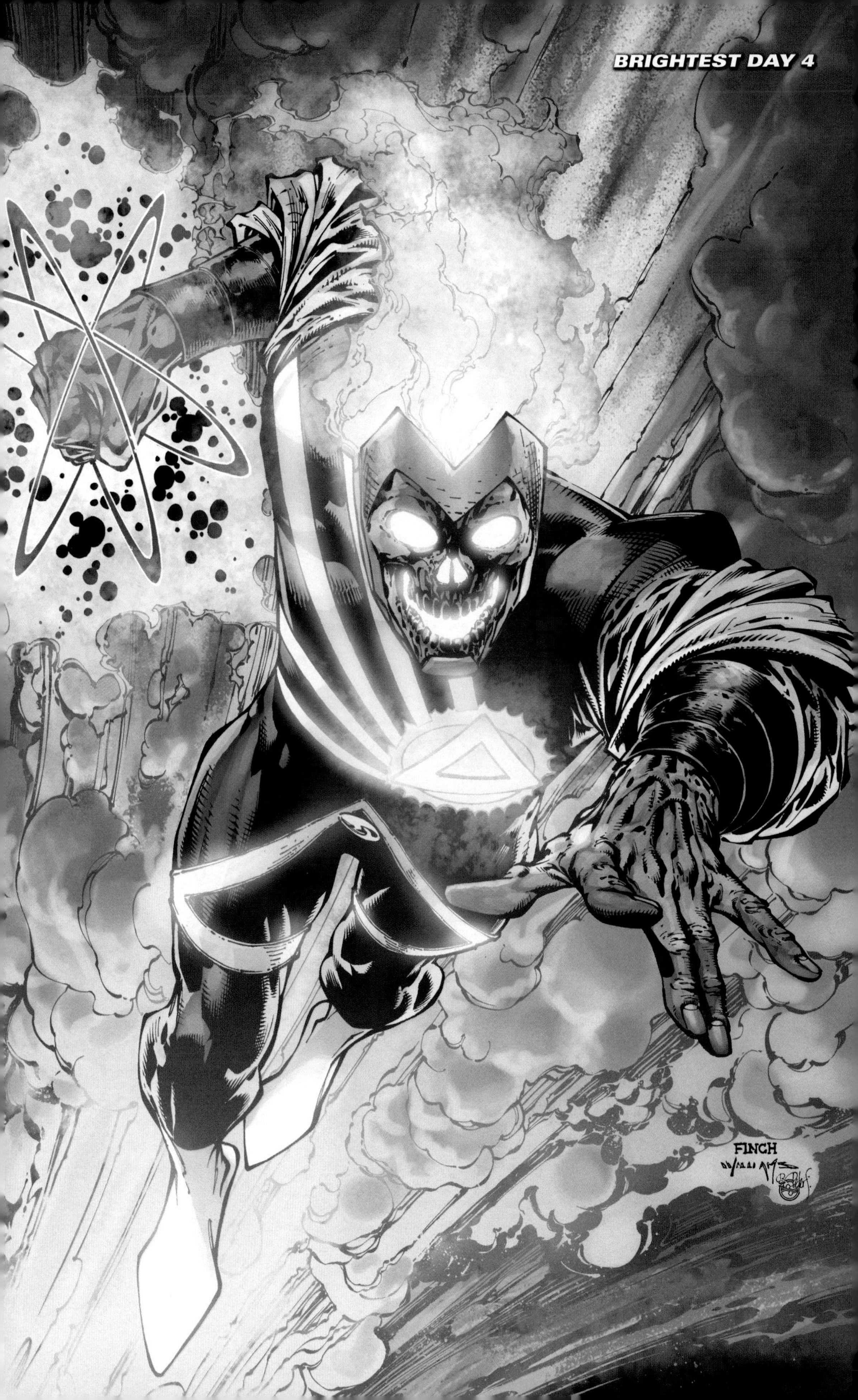

THRESHOLDS

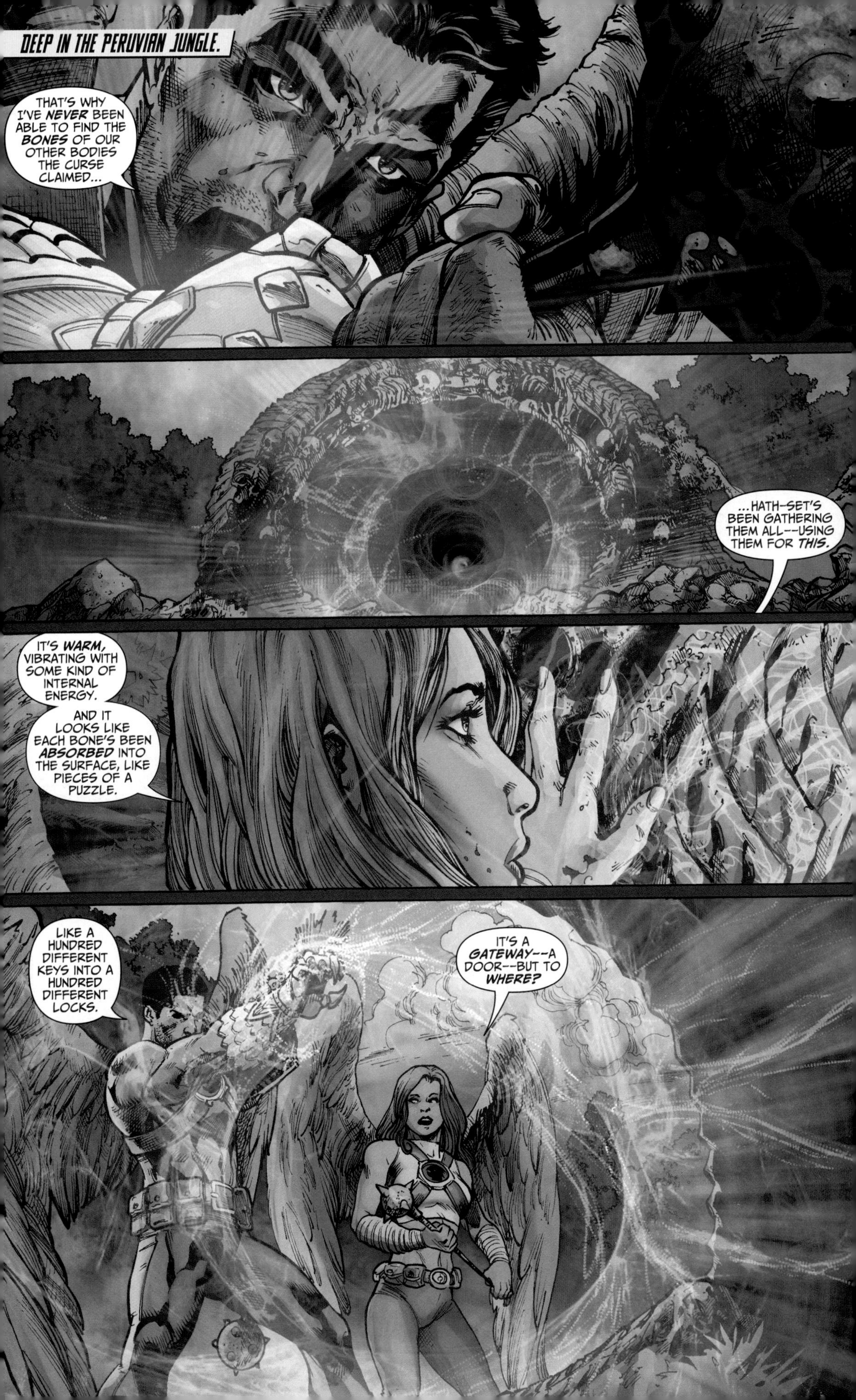
DEEP IN THE PERUVIAN JUNGLE.
THAT'S WHY I'VE NEVER BEEN ABLE TO FIND THE BONES OF OUR OTHER BODIES THE CURSE CLAIMED...
...HATH-SET'S BEEN GATHERING THEM ALL--USING THEM FOR THIS.
IT'S WARM, VIBRATING WITH SOME KIND OF INTERNAL ENERGY.
AND IT LOOKS LIKE EACH BONE'S BEEN ABSORBED INTO THE SURFACE, LIKE PIECES OF A PUZZLE.
LIKE A HUNDRED DIFFERENT KEYS INTO A HUNDRED DIFFERENT LOCKS.
IT'S A GATEWAY--A DOOR--BUT TO WHERE?

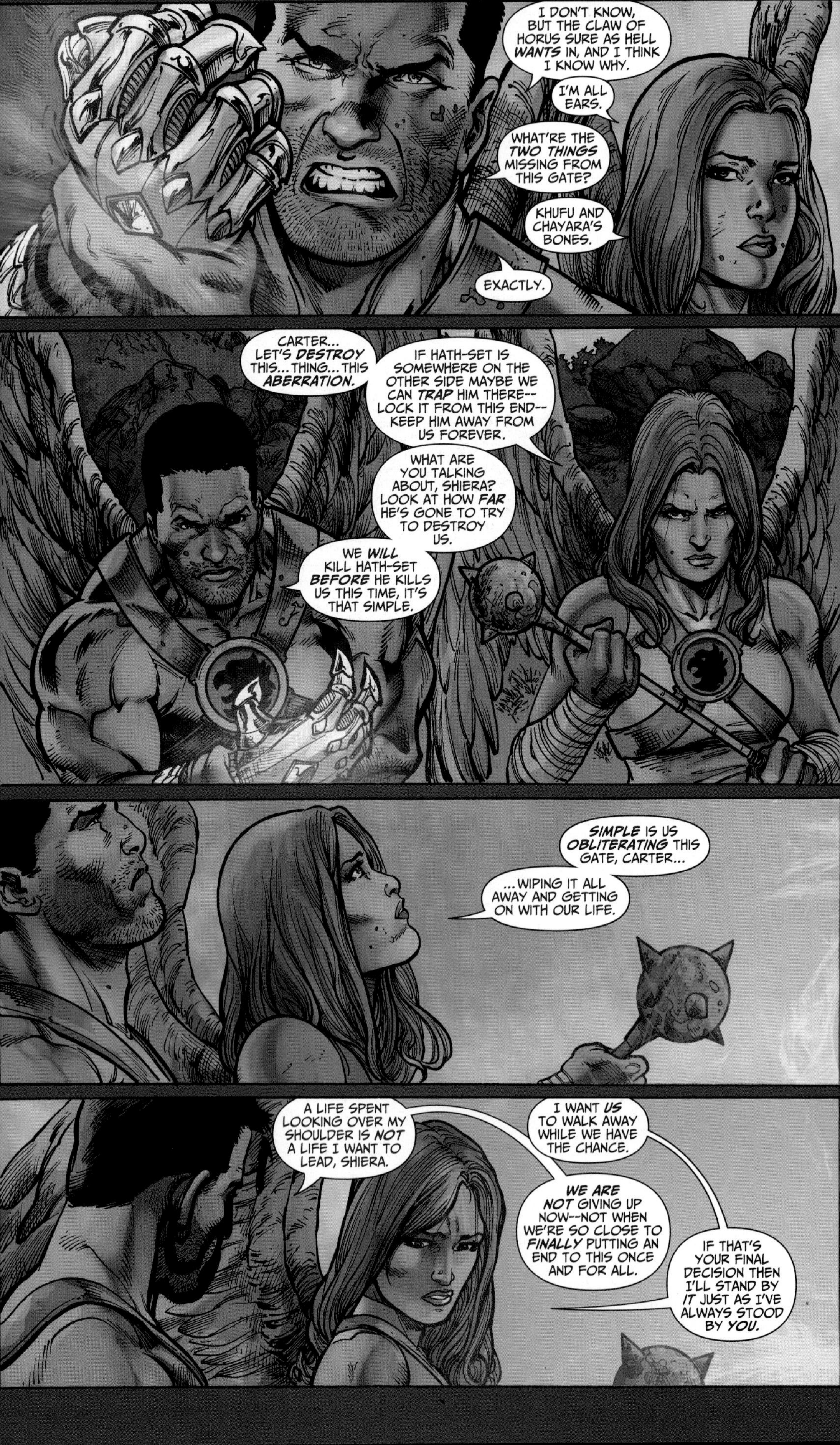

I DON'T KNOW, BUT THE CLAW OF HORUS SURE AS HELL WANTS IN, AND I THINK I KNOW WHY.
I'M ALL EARS.
WHAT'RE THE TWO THINGS MISSING FROM THIS GATE?
KHUFU AND CHAYARA'S BONES.
EXACTLY.
CARTER... LET'S DESTROY THIS... THING... THIS ABERRATION.
IF HATH-SET IS SOMEWHERE ON THE OTHER SIDE MAYBE WE CAN TRAP HIM THERE-- LOCK IT FROM THIS END-- KEEP HIM AWAY FROM US FOREVER.
WHAT ARE YOU TALKING ABOUT, SHIERA? LOOK AT HOW FAR HE'S GONE TO TRY TO DESTROY US.
WE WILL KILL HATH-SET BEFORE HE KILLS US THIS TIME, IT'S THAT SIMPLE.
SIMPLE IS US OBLITERATING THIS GATE, CARTER...
...WIPING IT ALL AWAY AND GETTING ON WITH OUR LIFE.
A LIFE SPENT LOOKING OVER MY SHOULDER IS NOT A LIFE I WANT TO LEAD, SHIERA.
I WANT US TO WALK AWAY WHILE WE HAVE THE CHANCE.
WE ARE NOT GIVING UP NOW--NOT WHEN WE'RE SO CLOSE TO FINALLY PUTTING AN END TO THIS ONCE AND FOR ALL.
IF THAT'S YOUR FINAL DECISION THEN I'LL STAND BY IT JUST AS I'VE ALWAYS STOOD BY YOU.

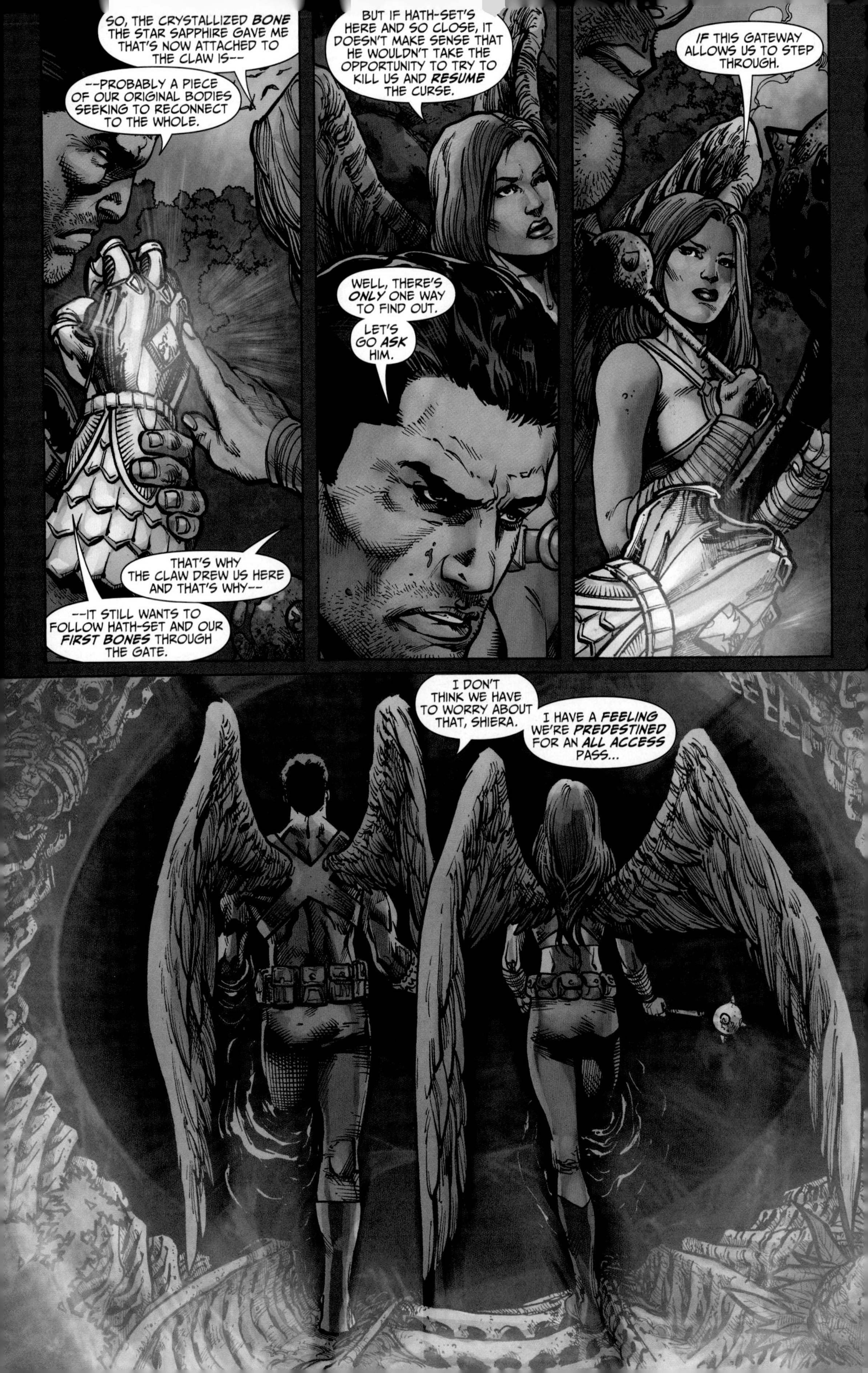
SO, THE CRYSTALLIZED BONE THE STAR SAPPHIRE GAVE ME THAT'S NOW ATTACHED TO THE CLAW IS--
--PROBABLY A PIECE OF OUR ORIGINAL BODIES SEEKING TO RECONNECT TO THE WHOLE.
THAT'S WHY THE CLAW DREW US HERE AND THAT'S WHY--
--IT STILL WANTS TO FOLLOW HATH-SET AND OUR FIRST BONES THROUGH THE GATE.
BUT IF HATH-SET'S HERE AND SO CLOSE, IT DOESN'T MAKE SENSE THAT HE WOULDN'T TAKE THE OPPORTUNITY TO TRY TO KILL US AND RESUME THE CURSE.
WELL, THERE'S ONLY ONE WAY TO FIND OUT.
LET'S GO ASK HIM.
IF THIS GATEWAY ALLOWS US TO STEP THROUGH.
I DON'T THINK WE HAVE TO WORRY ABOUT THAT, SHIERA.
I HAVE A FEELING WE'RE PREDESTINED FOR AN ALL ACCESS PASS...

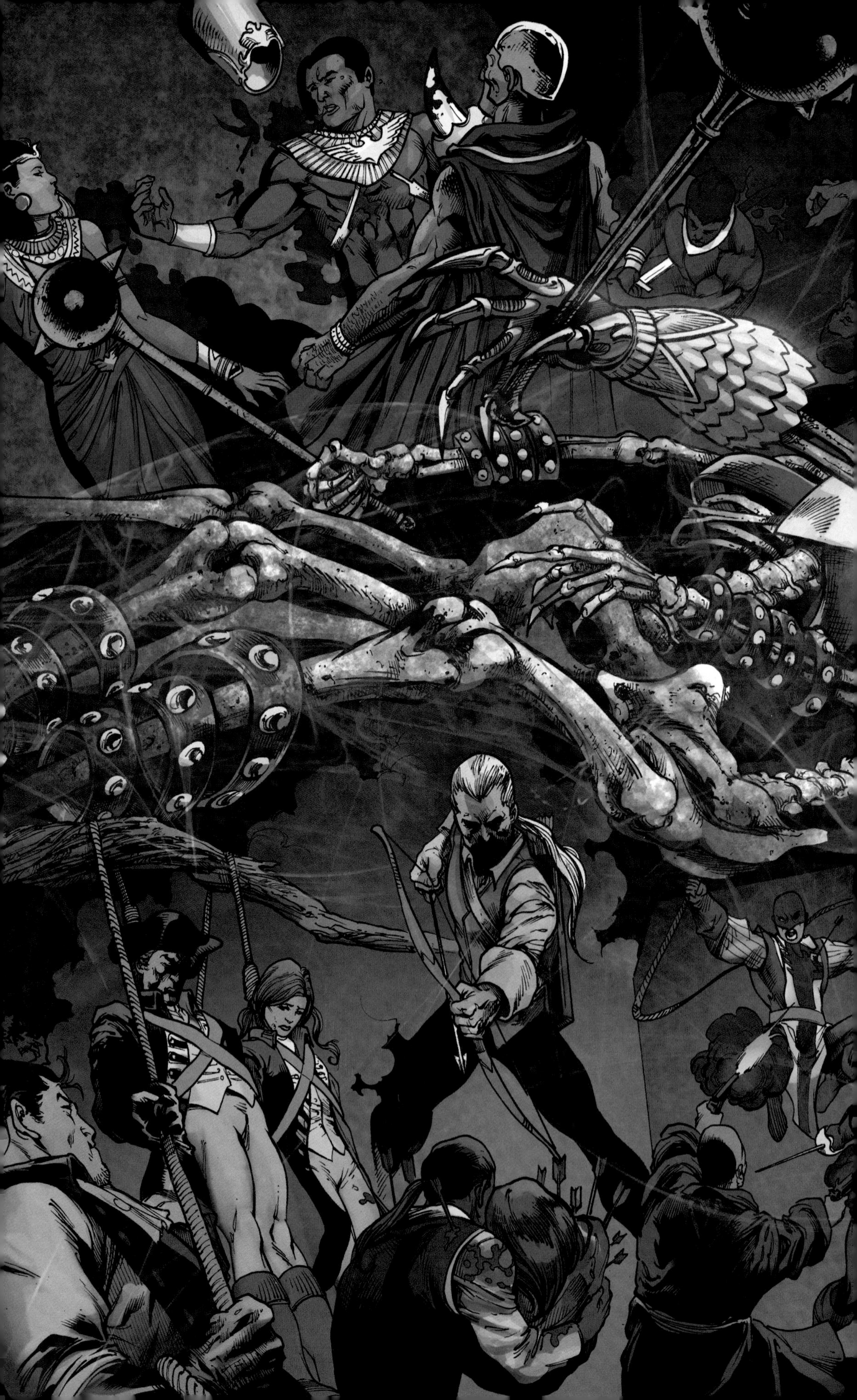

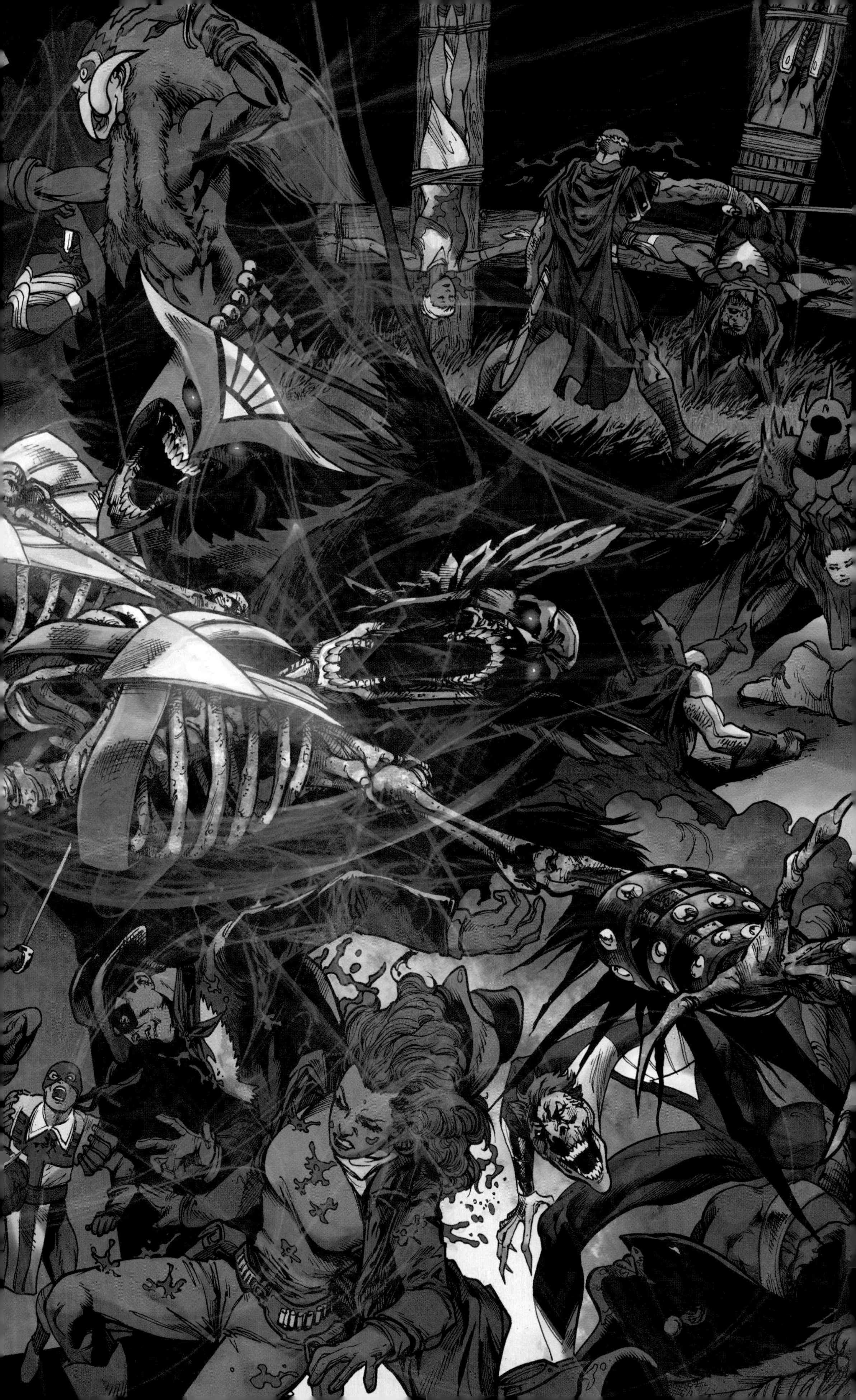

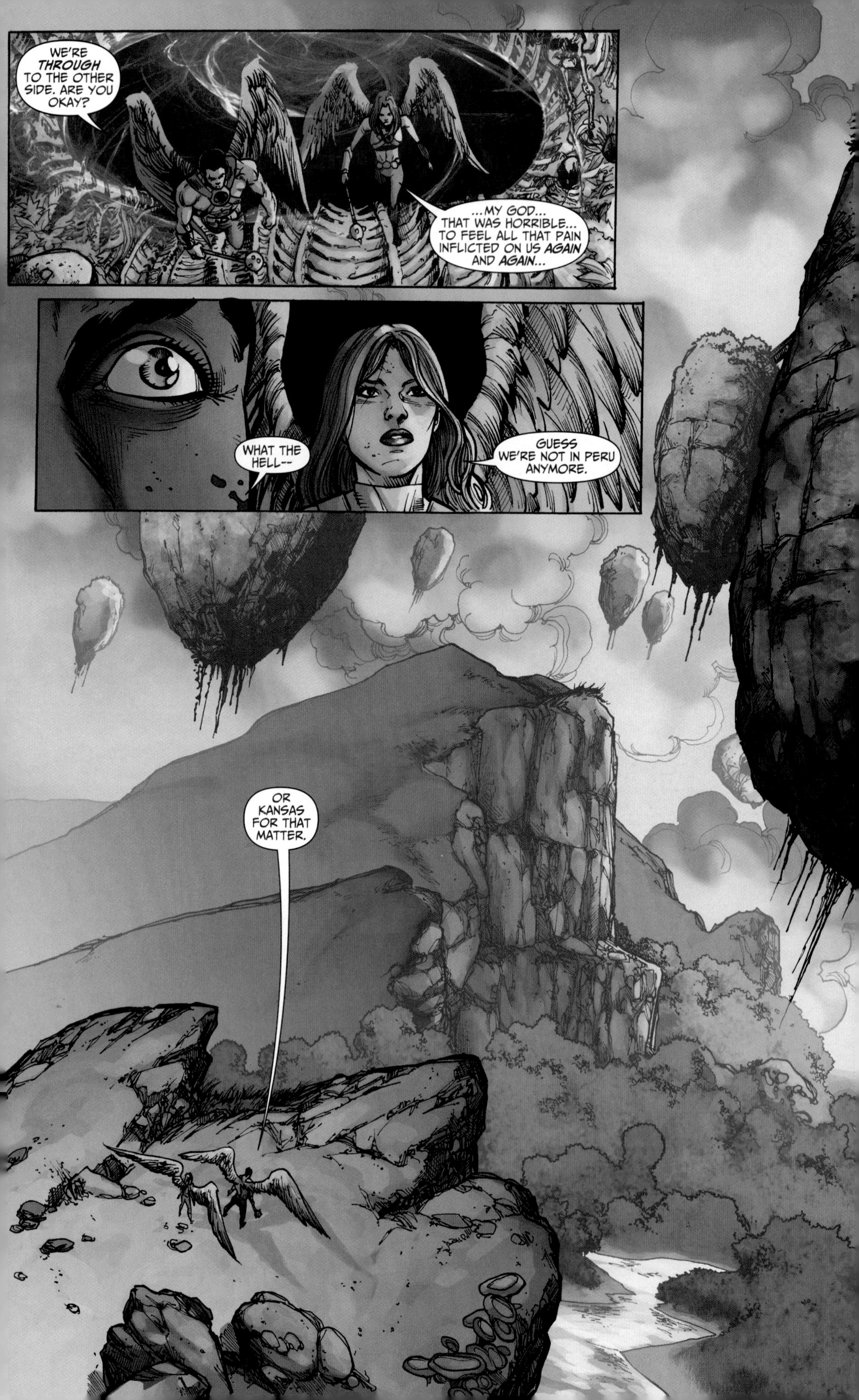
WE'RE *THROUGH* TO THE OTHER SIDE. ARE YOU OKAY?
...MY GOD... THAT WAS HORRIBLE... TO FEEL ALL THAT PAIN INFLICTED ON US *AGAIN* AND *AGAIN*...
WHAT THE HELL--
GUESS WE'RE NOT IN PERU ANYMORE.
OR KANSAS FOR THAT MATTER.

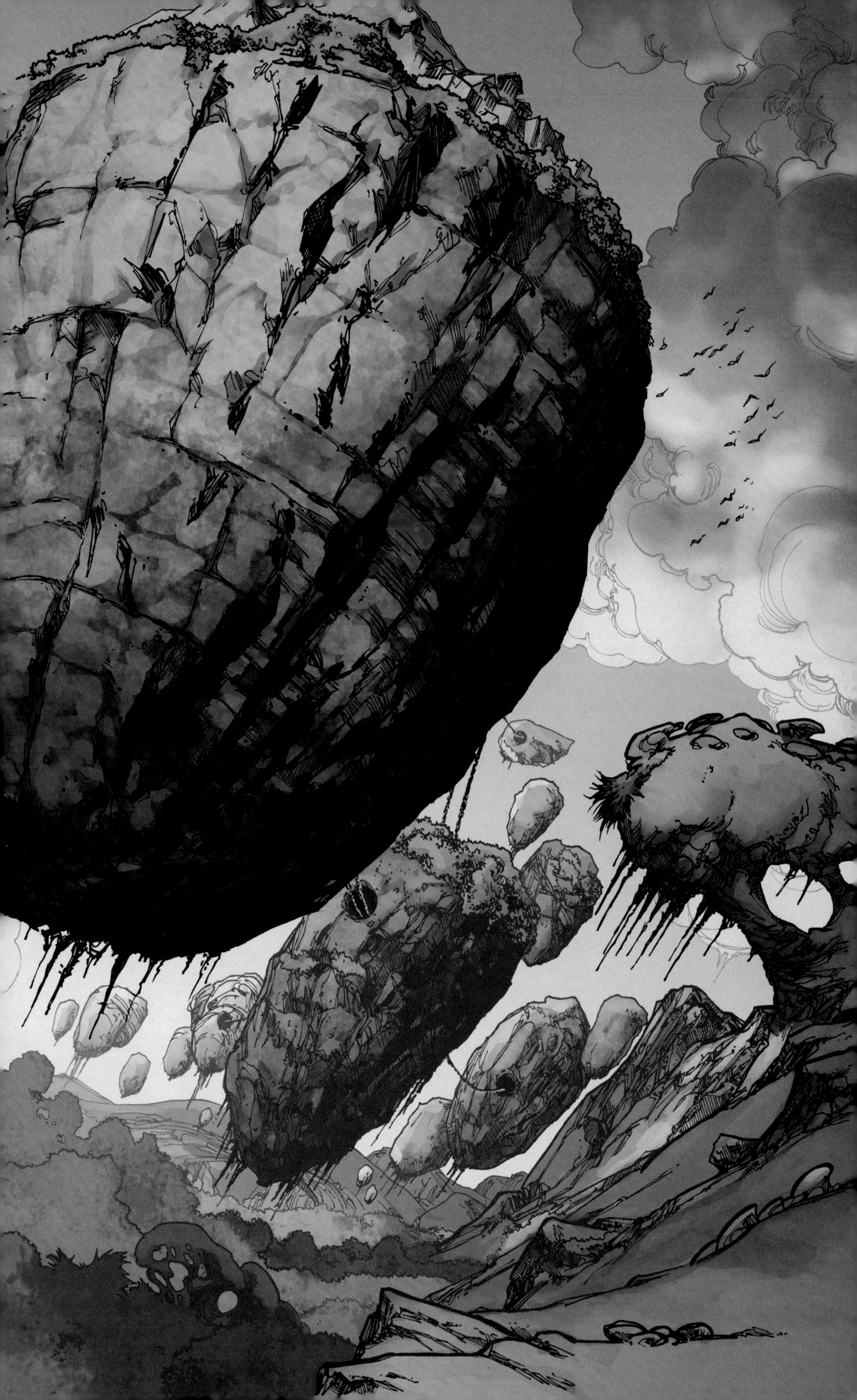

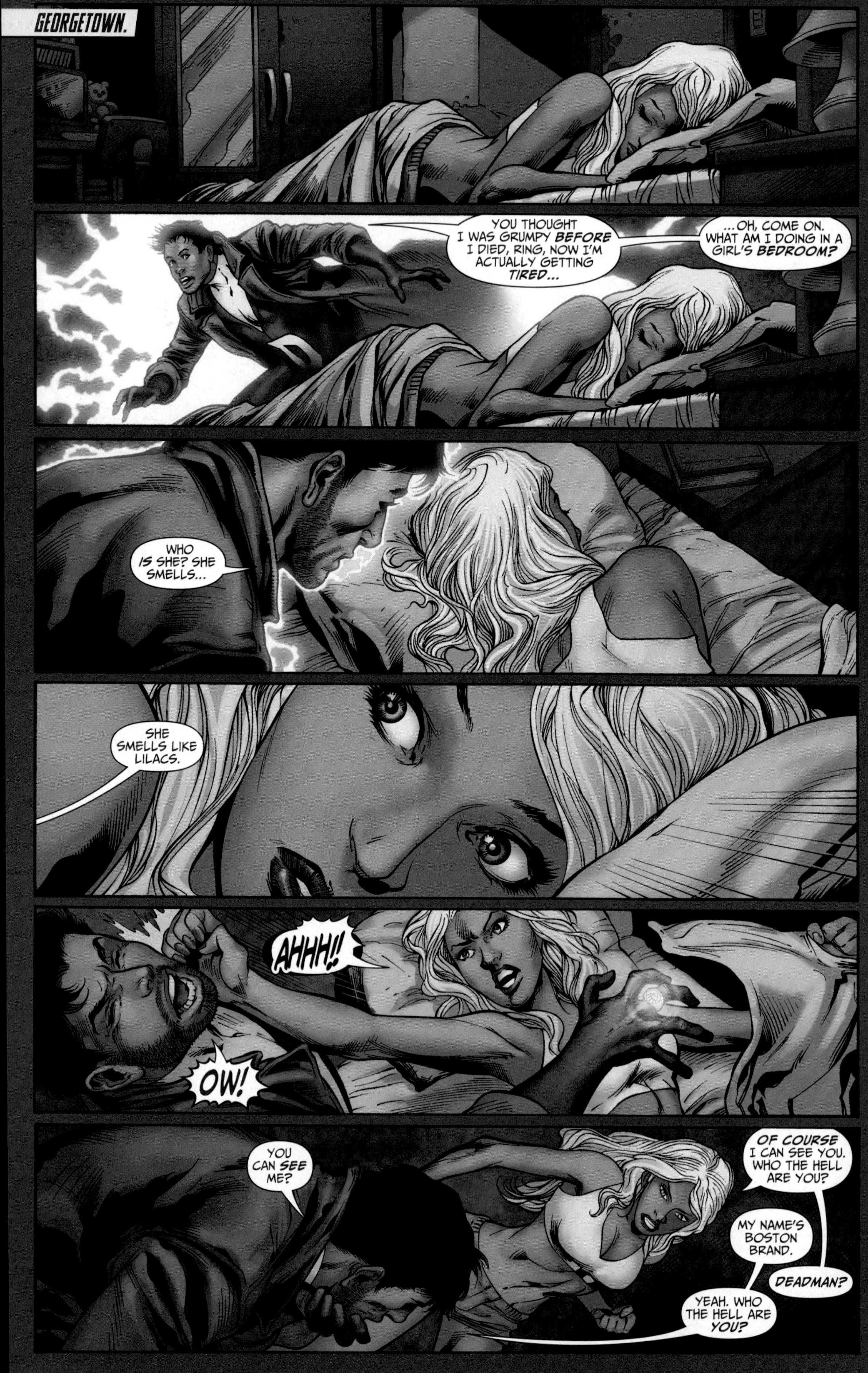
GEORGETOWN.
YOU THOUGHT I WAS GRUMPY BEFORE I DIED, RING, NOW I'M ACTUALLY GETTING TIRED...
...OH, COME ON. WHAT AM I DOING IN A GIRL'S BEDROOM?
WHO IS SHE? SHE SMELLS...
SHE SMELLS LIKE LILACS.
AHHH!!
OW!
YOU CAN SEE ME?
OF COURSE I CAN SEE YOU. WHO THE HELL ARE YOU?
MY NAME'S BOSTON BRAND.
DEADMAN?
YEAH. WHO THE HELL ARE YOU?

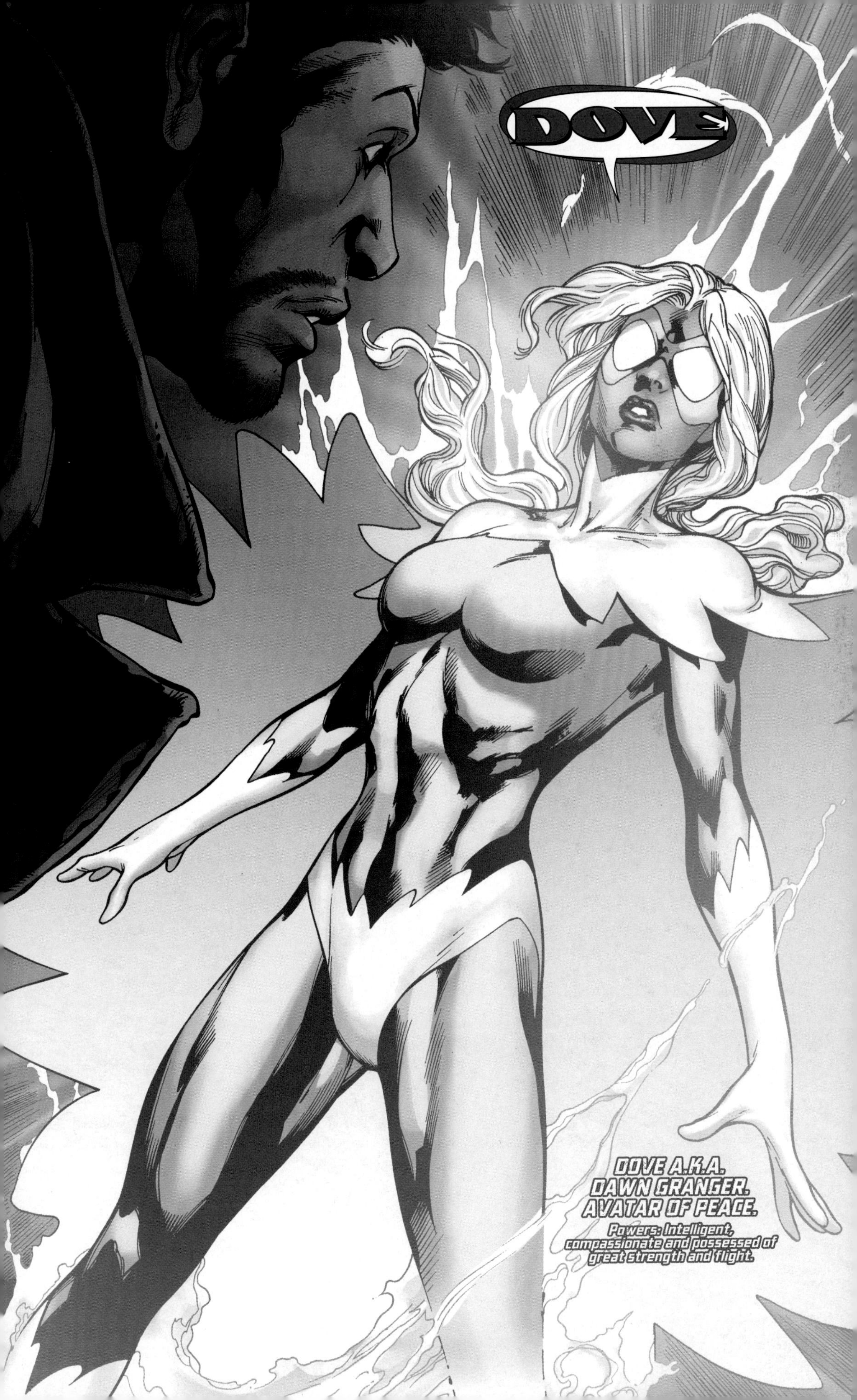
DOVE
DOVE A.K.A.
DAWN GRANGER.
AVATAR OF PEACE.
Powers: Intelligent, compassionate and possessed of great strength and flight.

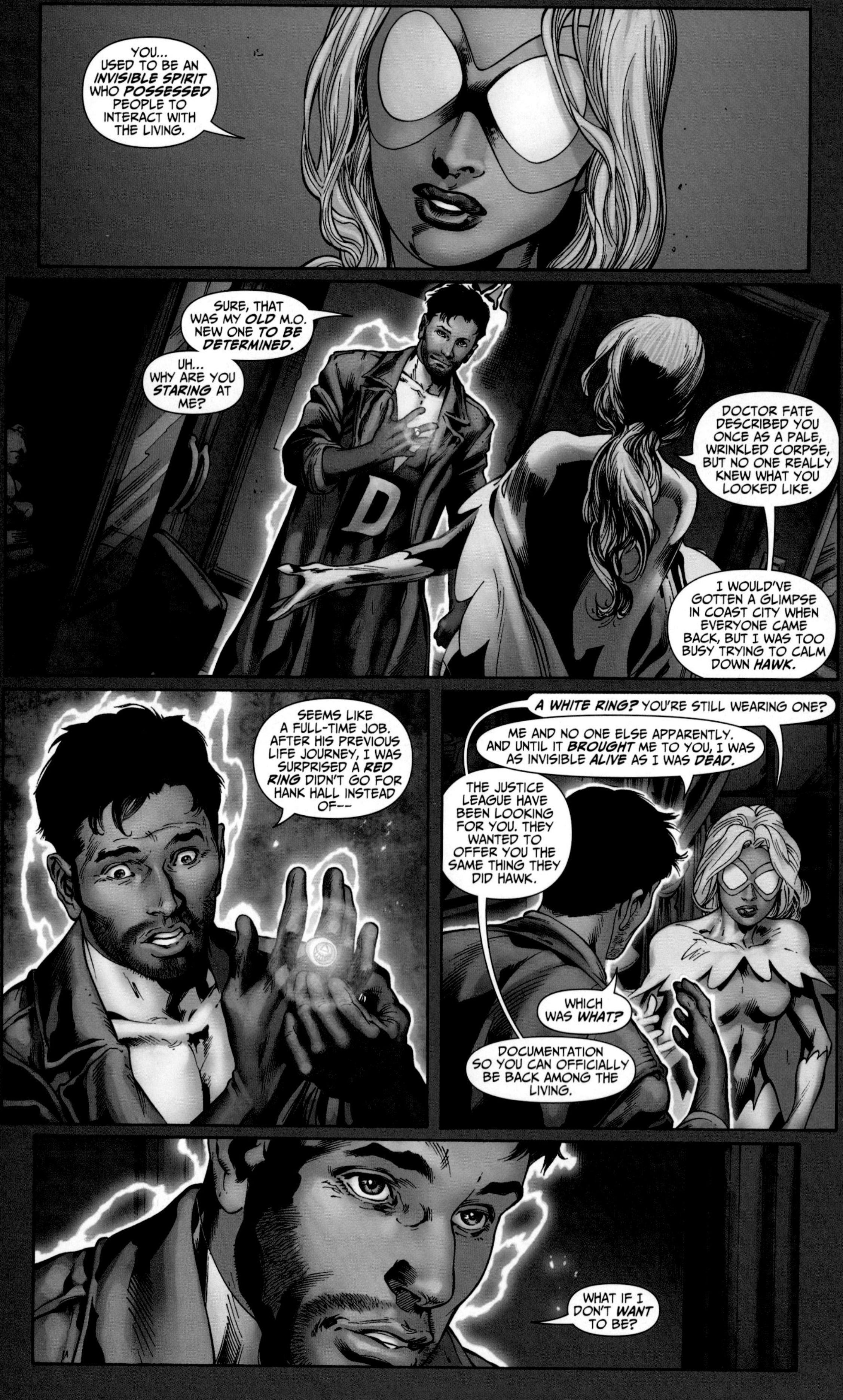
YOU... USED TO BE AN INVISIBLE SPIRIT WHO POSSESSED PEOPLE TO INTERACT WITH THE LIVING.
SURE, THAT WAS MY OLD M.O. NEW ONE TO BE DETERMINED.
UH... WHY ARE YOU STARING AT ME?
DOCTOR FATE DESCRIBED YOU ONCE AS A PALE, WRINKLED CORPSE, BUT NO ONE REALLY KNEW WHAT YOU LOOKED LIKE.
I WOULD'VE GOTTEN A GLIMPSE IN COAST CITY WHEN EVERYONE CAME BACK, BUT I WAS TOO BUSY TRYING TO CALM DOWN HAWK.
SEEMS LIKE A FULL-TIME JOB. AFTER HIS PREVIOUS LIFE JOURNEY, I WAS SURPRISED A RED RING DIDN'T GO FOR HANK HALL INSTEAD OF--
A WHITE RING? YOU'RE STILL WEARING ONE?
ME AND NO ONE ELSE APPARENTLY. AND UNTIL IT BROUGHT ME TO YOU, I WAS AS INVISIBLE ALIVE AS I WAS DEAD.
THE JUSTICE LEAGUE HAVE BEEN LOOKING FOR YOU. THEY WANTED TO OFFER YOU THE SAME THING THEY DID HAWK.
WHICH WAS WHAT?
DOCUMENTATION SO YOU CAN OFFICIALLY BE BACK AMONG THE LIVING.
WHAT IF I DON'T WANT TO BE?

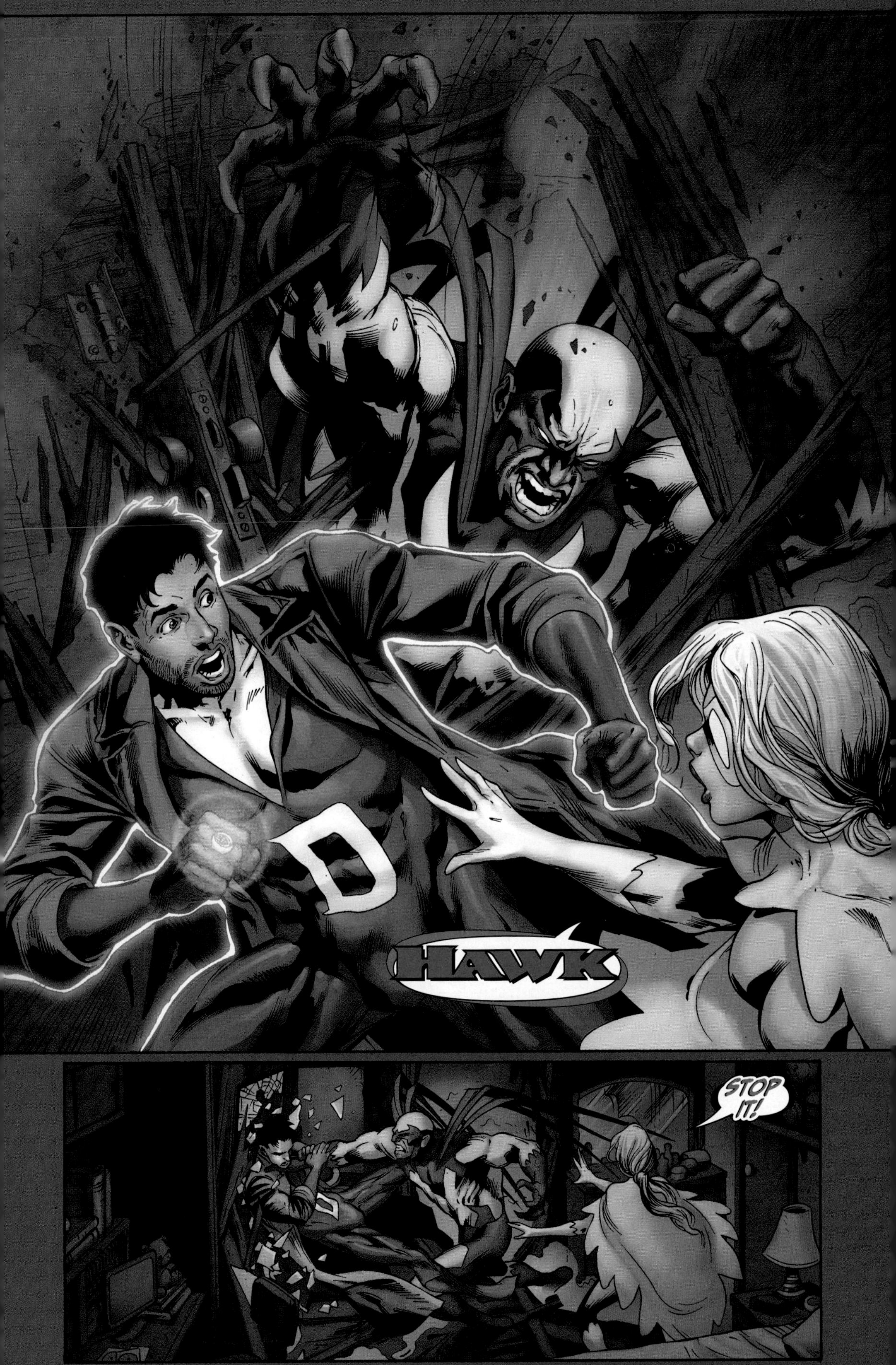
HAWK
STOP IT!

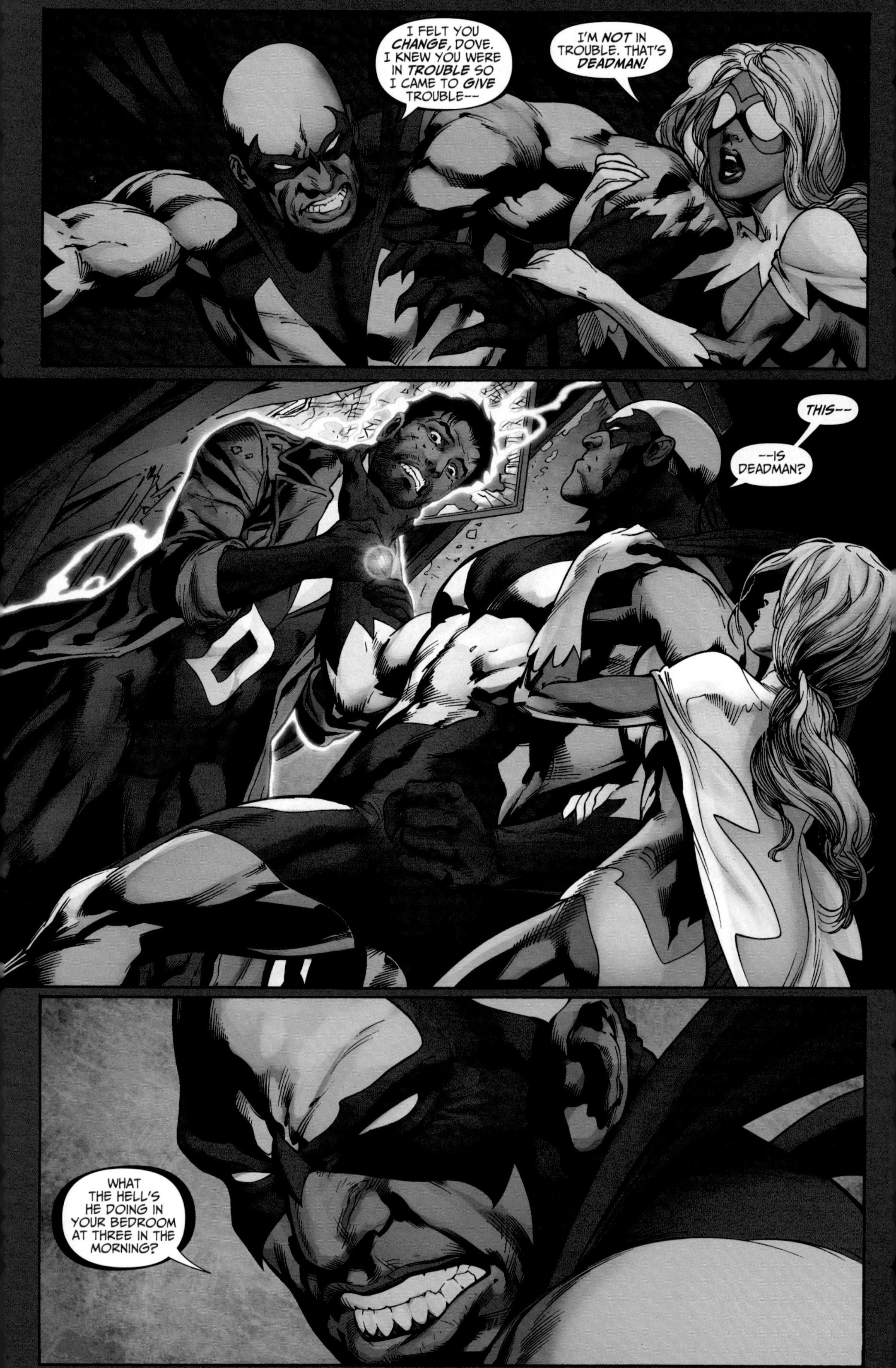
I FELT YOU *CHANGE,* DOVE. I KNEW YOU WERE IN *TROUBLE* SO I CAME TO *GIVE* TROUBLE--
I'M *NOT* IN TROUBLE. THAT'S *DEADMAN!*
*THIS--*
--IS DEADMAN?
WHAT THE HELL'S HE DOING IN YOUR BEDROOM AT THREE IN THE MORNING?

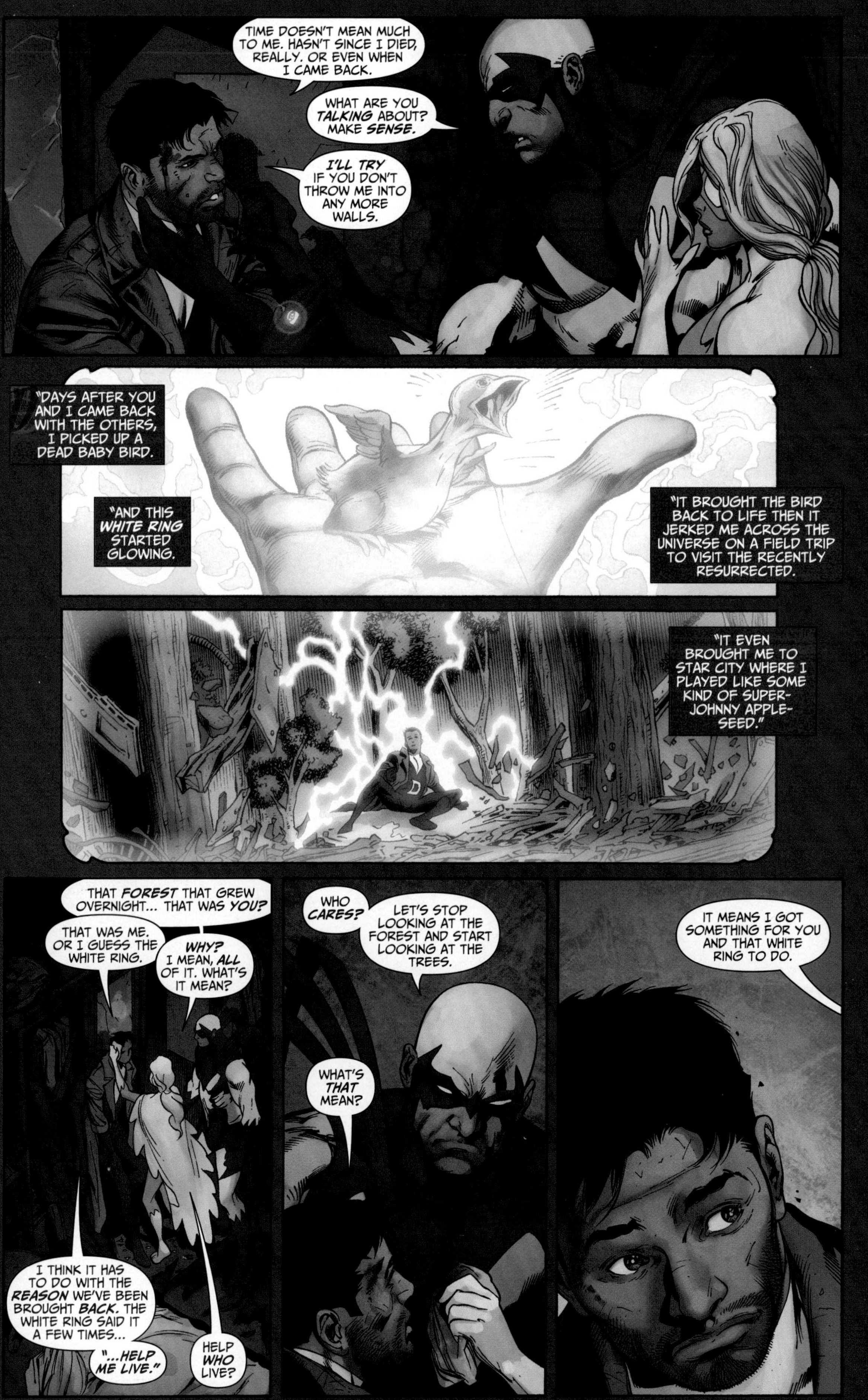
TIME DOESN'T MEAN MUCH TO ME. HASN'T SINCE I DIED, REALLY. OR EVEN WHEN I CAME BACK.
WHAT ARE YOU TALKING ABOUT? MAKE SENSE.
I'LL TRY IF YOU DON'T THROW ME INTO ANY MORE WALLS.
"DAYS AFTER YOU AND I CAME BACK WITH THE OTHERS, I PICKED UP A DEAD BABY BIRD.
"AND THIS WHITE RING STARTED GLOWING.
"IT BROUGHT THE BIRD BACK TO LIFE THEN IT JERKED ME ACROSS THE UNIVERSE ON A FIELD TRIP TO VISIT THE RECENTLY RESURRECTED.
"IT EVEN BROUGHT ME TO STAR CITY WHERE I PLAYED LIKE SOME KIND OF SUPER-JOHNNY APPLE-SEED."
THAT FOREST THAT GREW OVERNIGHT... THAT WAS YOU?
THAT WAS ME. OR I GUESS THE WHITE RING.
WHY? I MEAN, ALL OF IT. WHAT'S IT MEAN?
I THINK IT HAS TO DO WITH THE REASON WE'VE BEEN BROUGHT BACK. THE WHITE RING SAID IT A FEW TIMES...
"...HELP ME LIVE."
HELP WHO LIVE?
WHO CARES?
LET'S STOP LOOKING AT THE FOREST AND START LOOKING AT THE TREES.
WHAT'S THAT MEAN?
IT MEANS I GOT SOMETHING FOR YOU AND THAT WHITE RING TO DO.

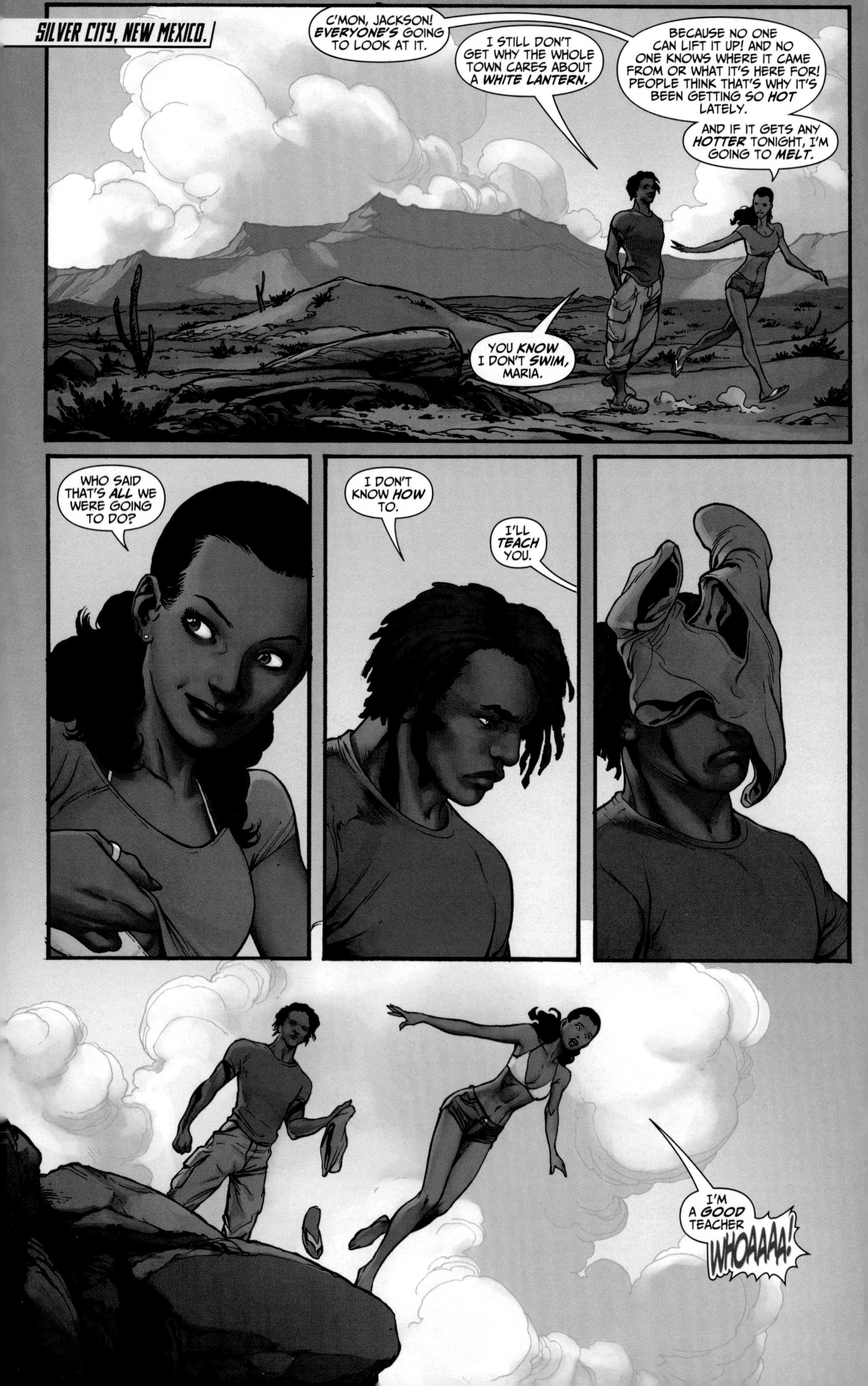
SILVER CITY, NEW MEXICO.
C'MON, JACKSON! EVERYONE'S GOING TO LOOK AT IT.
I STILL DON'T GET WHY THE WHOLE TOWN CARES ABOUT A WHITE LANTERN.
BECAUSE NO ONE CAN LIFT IT UP! AND NO ONE KNOWS WHERE IT CAME FROM OR WHAT IT'S HERE FOR! PEOPLE THINK THAT'S WHY IT'S BEEN GETTING SO HOT LATELY.
AND IF IT GETS ANY HOTTER TONIGHT, I'M GOING TO MELT.
YOU KNOW I DON'T SWIM, MARIA.
WHO SAID THAT'S ALL WE WERE GOING TO DO?
I DON'T KNOW HOW TO.
I'LL TEACH YOU.
I'M A GOOD TEACHER
WHOAAAA!

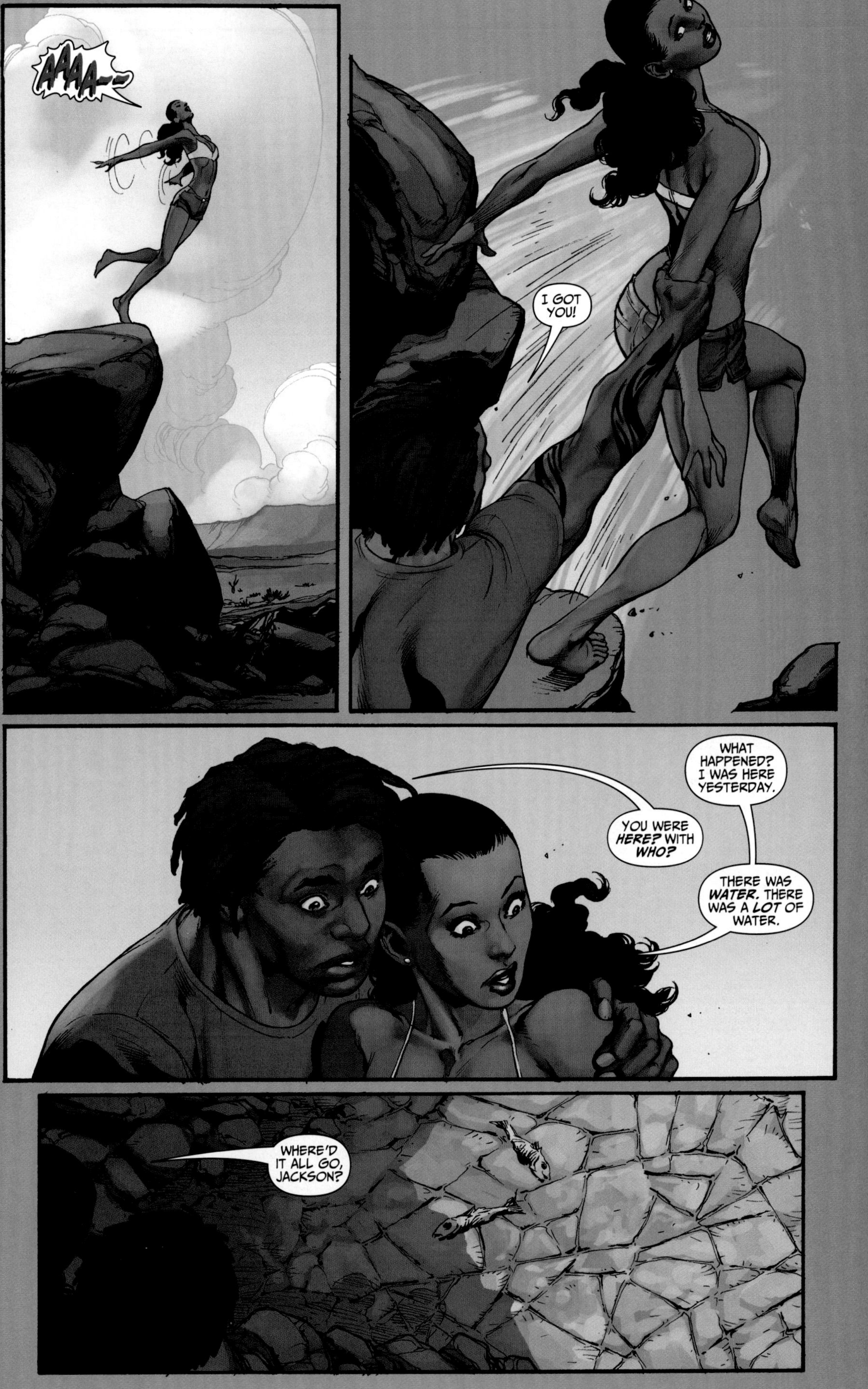
AAAA--
I GOT YOU!
WHAT HAPPENED? I WAS HERE YESTERDAY.
YOU WERE *HERE?* WITH *WHO?*
THERE WAS *WATER.* THERE WAS A *LOT* OF WATER.
WHERE'D IT ALL GO, JACKSON?

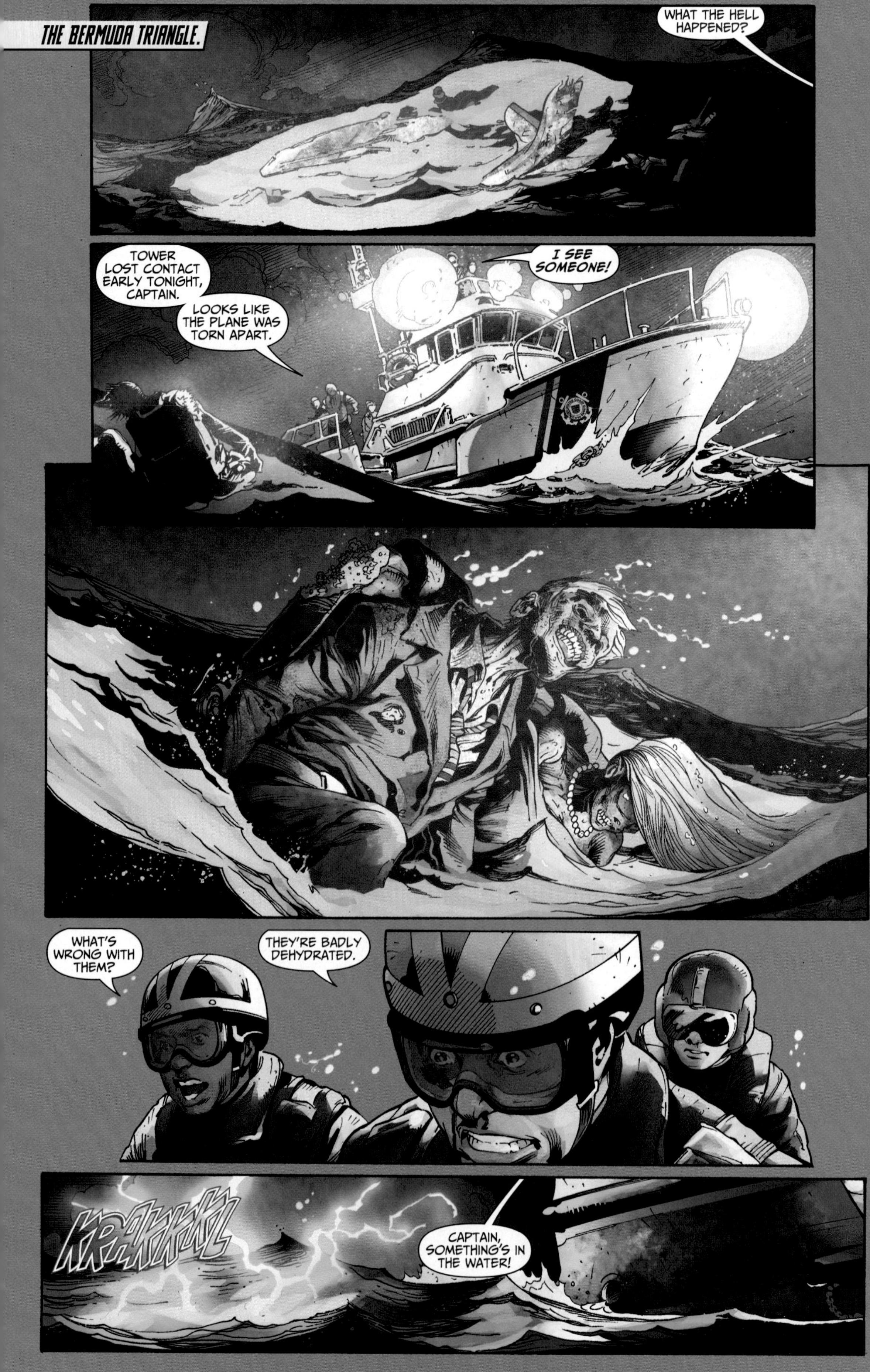
THE BERMUDA TRIANGLE.
WHAT THE HELL HAPPENED?
TOWER LOST CONTACT EARLY TONIGHT, CAPTAIN.
LOOKS LIKE THE PLANE WAS TORN APART.
I SEE SOMEONE!
WHAT'S WRONG WITH THEM?
THEY'RE BADLY DEHYDRATED.
KRAKKKL
CAPTAIN, SOMETHING'S IN THE WATER!

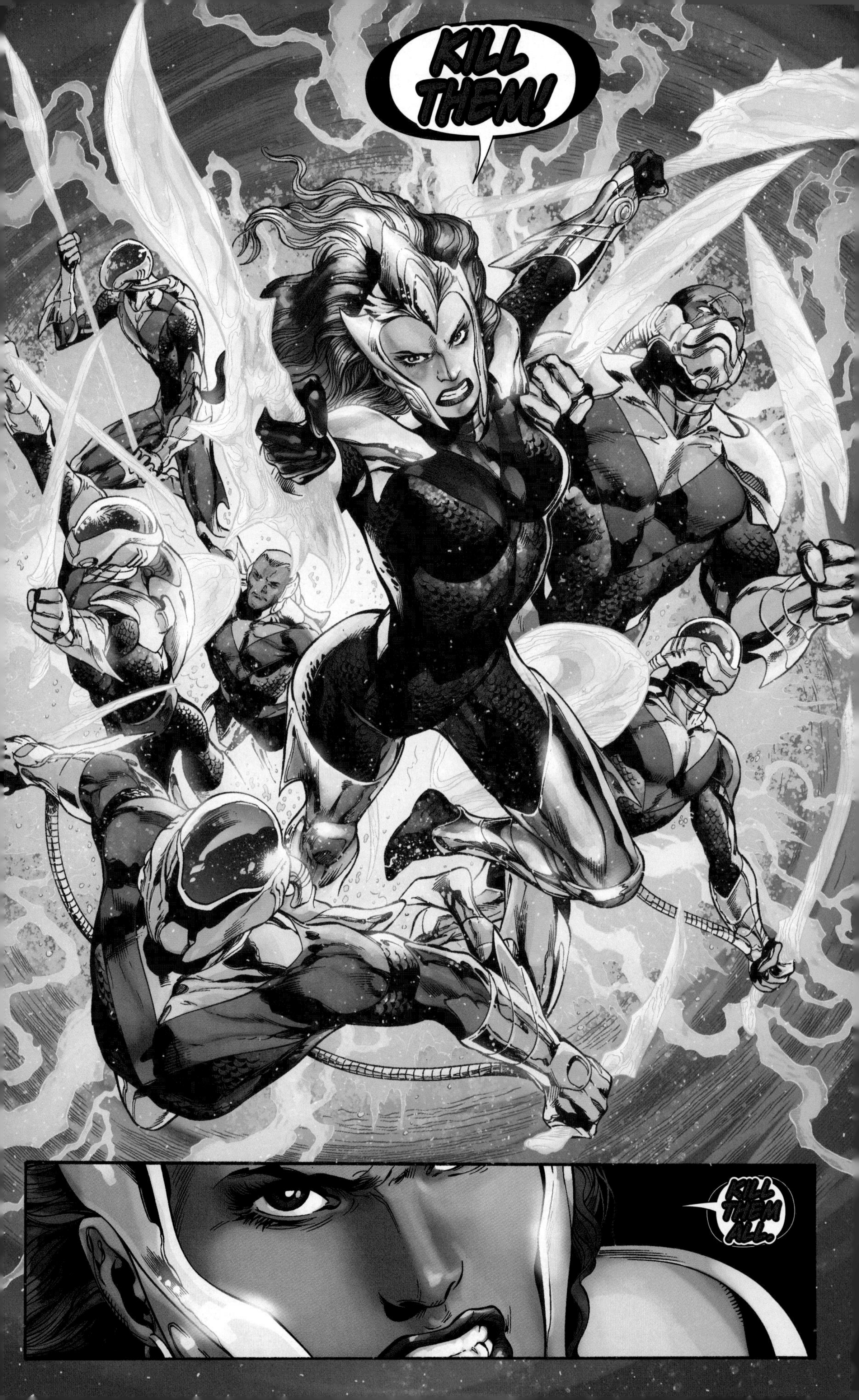
KILL THEM!
KILL THEM ALL.

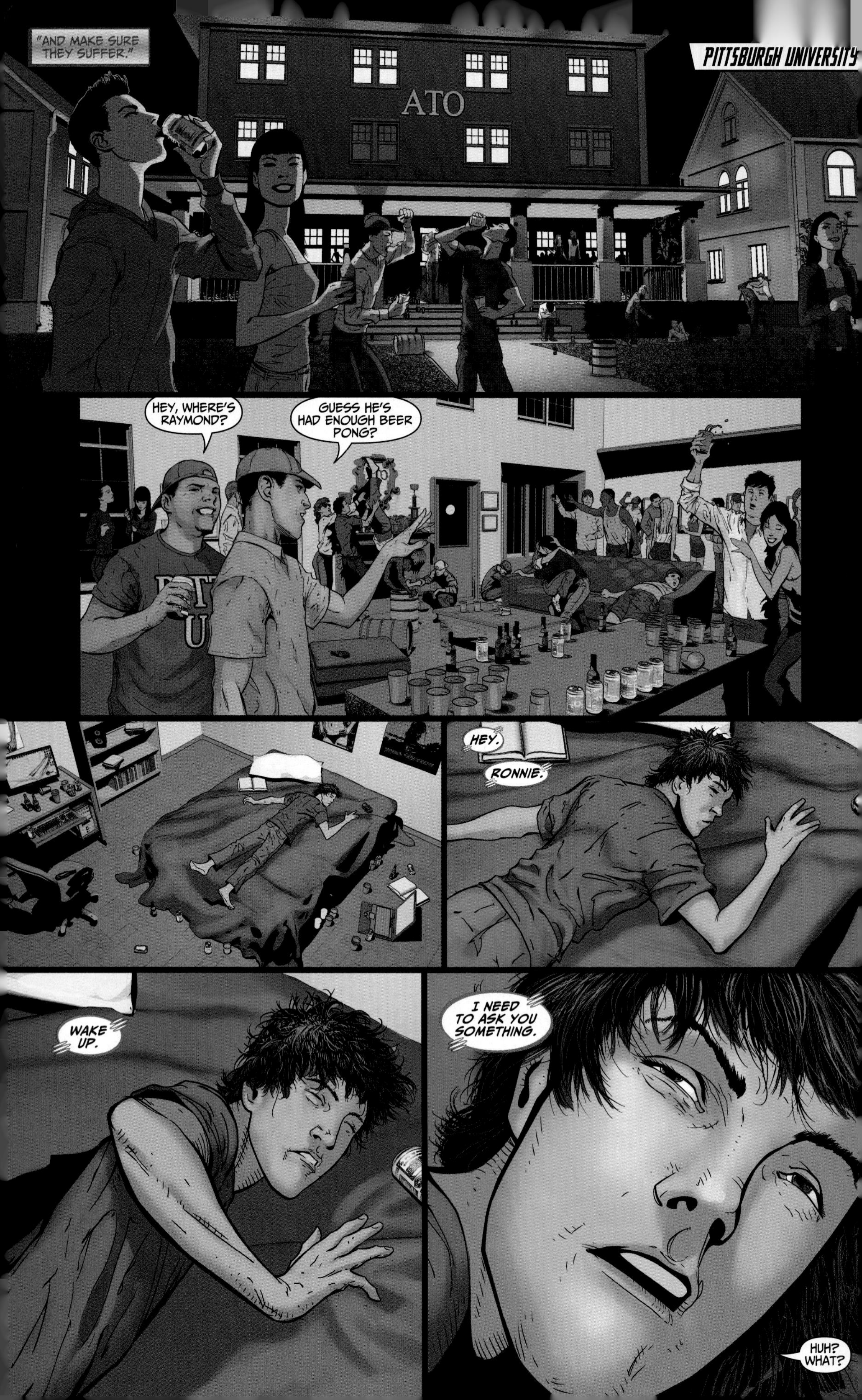
"AND MAKE SURE THEY SUFFER."
PITTSBURGH UNIVERSITY
ATO
HEY, WHERE'S RAYMOND?
GUESS HE'S HAD ENOUGH BEER PONG?
HEY.
RONNIE.
WAKE UP.
I NEED TO ASK YOU SOMETHING.
HUH? WHAT?

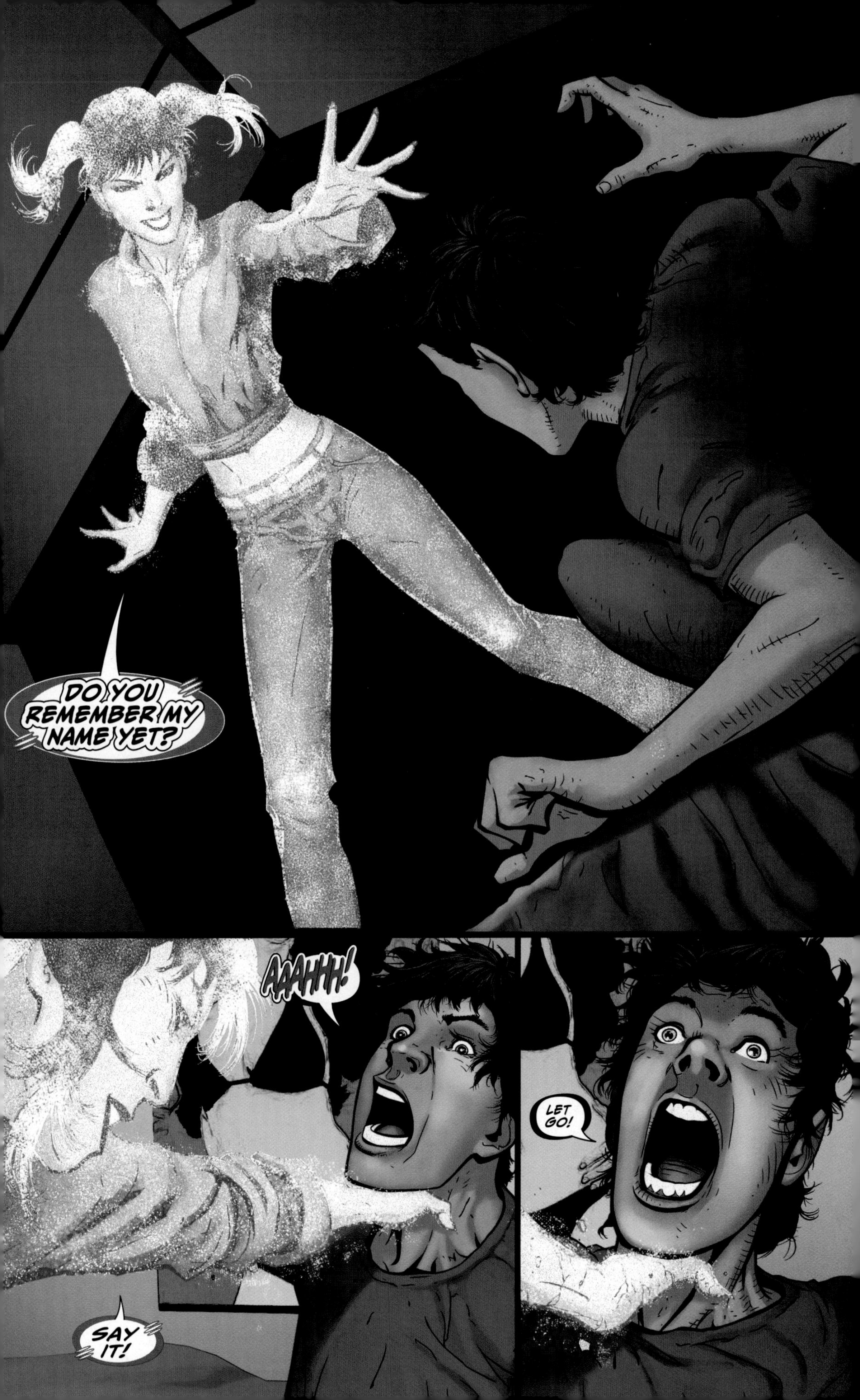
DO YOU REMEMBER MY NAME YET?
AAAHHH!
SAY IT!
LET GO!

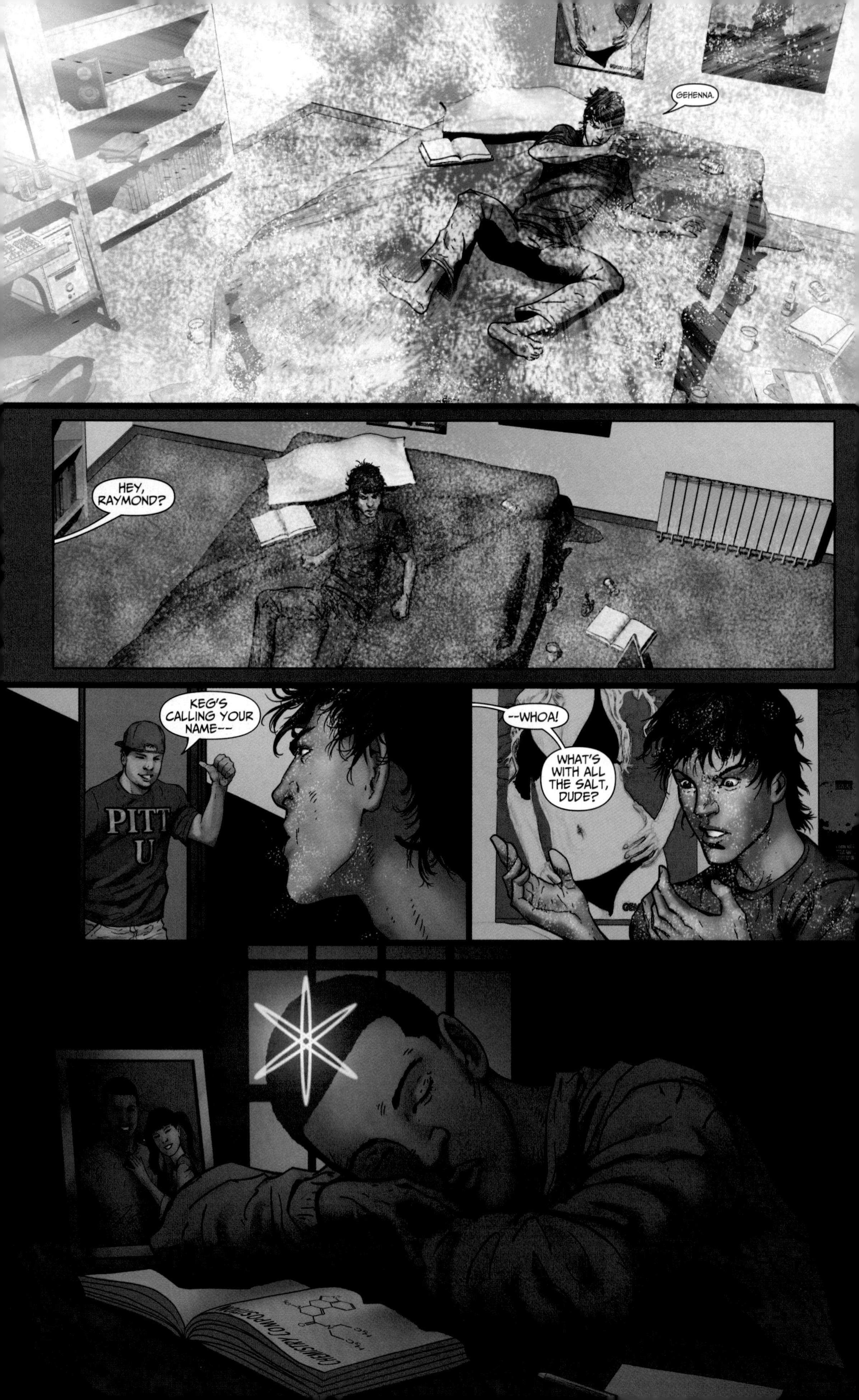
GEHENNA.
HEY, RAYMOND?
KEG'S CALLING YOUR NAME--
PITT U
--WHOA!
WHAT'S WITH ALL THE SALT, DUDE?
CHEMISTRY COMPOSITION

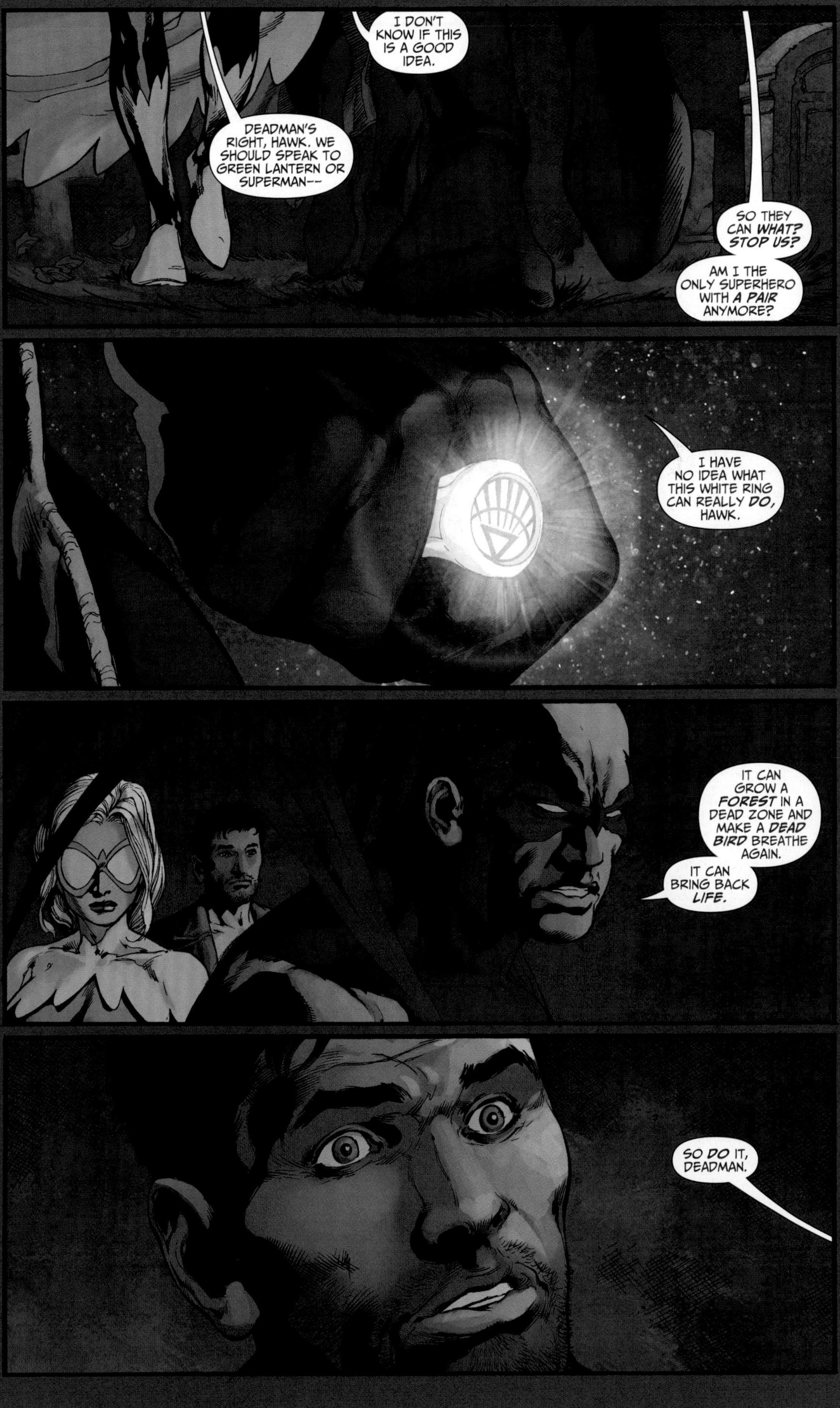
I DON'T KNOW IF THIS IS A GOOD IDEA.
DEADMAN'S RIGHT, HAWK. WE SHOULD SPEAK TO GREEN LANTERN OR SUPERMAN--
SO THEY CAN *WHAT? STOP US?*
AM I THE ONLY SUPERHERO WITH *A PAIR* ANYMORE?
I HAVE NO IDEA WHAT THIS WHITE RING CAN REALLY *DO,* HAWK.
IT CAN GROW A *FOREST* IN A DEAD ZONE AND MAKE A *DEAD BIRD* BREATHE AGAIN.
IT CAN BRING BACK *LIFE.*
SO *DO* IT, DEADMAN.

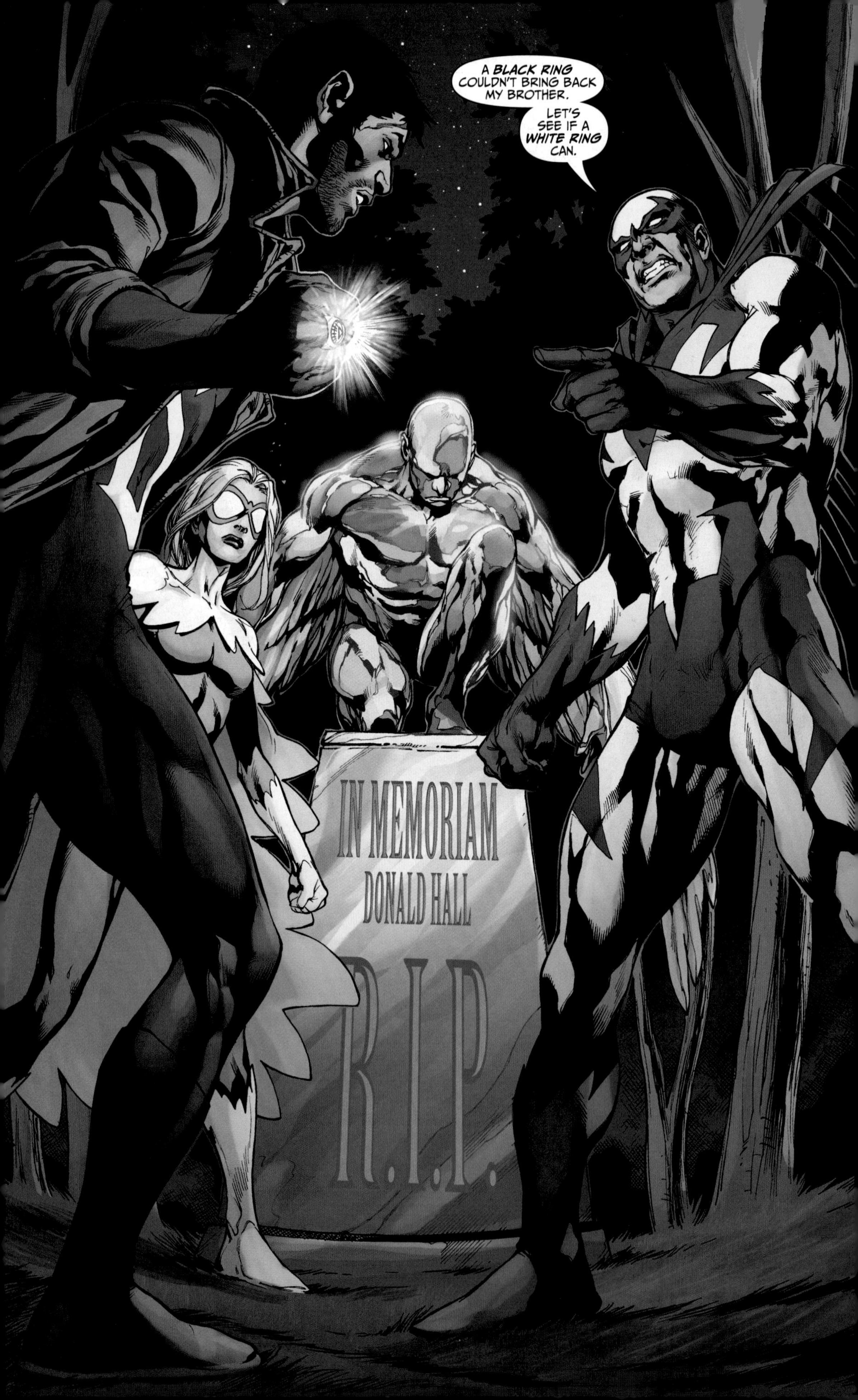
A BLACK RING COULDN'T BRING BACK MY BROTHER.
LET'S SEE IF A WHITE RING CAN.
IN MEMORIAM
DONALD HALL
R.I.P.

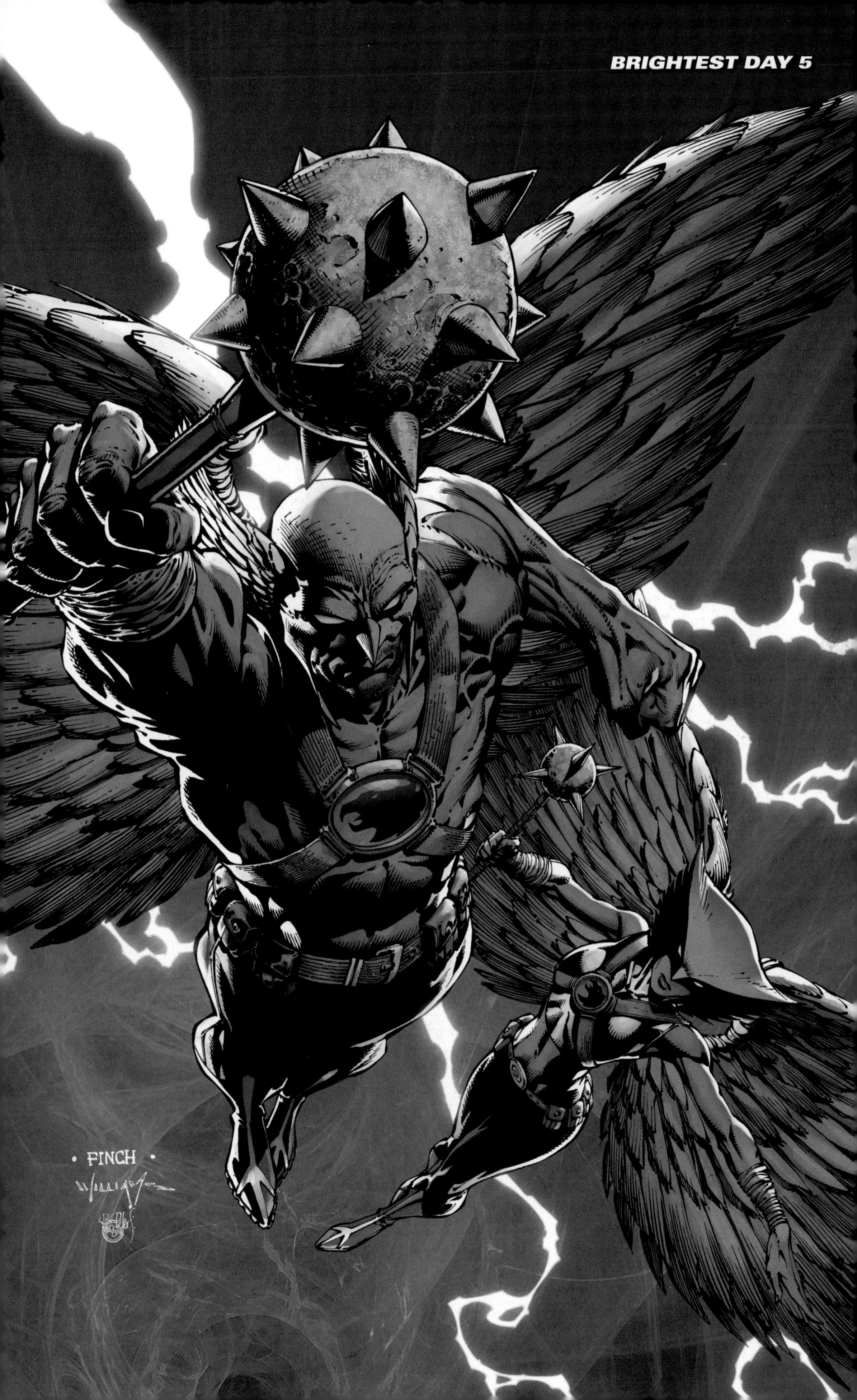
FINCH

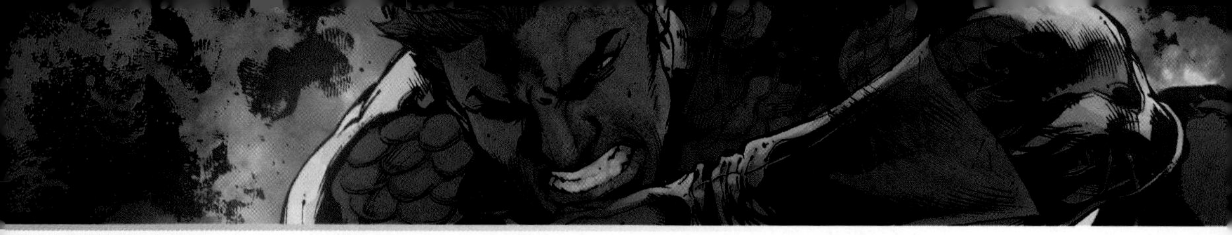

# UNDER PRESSURE

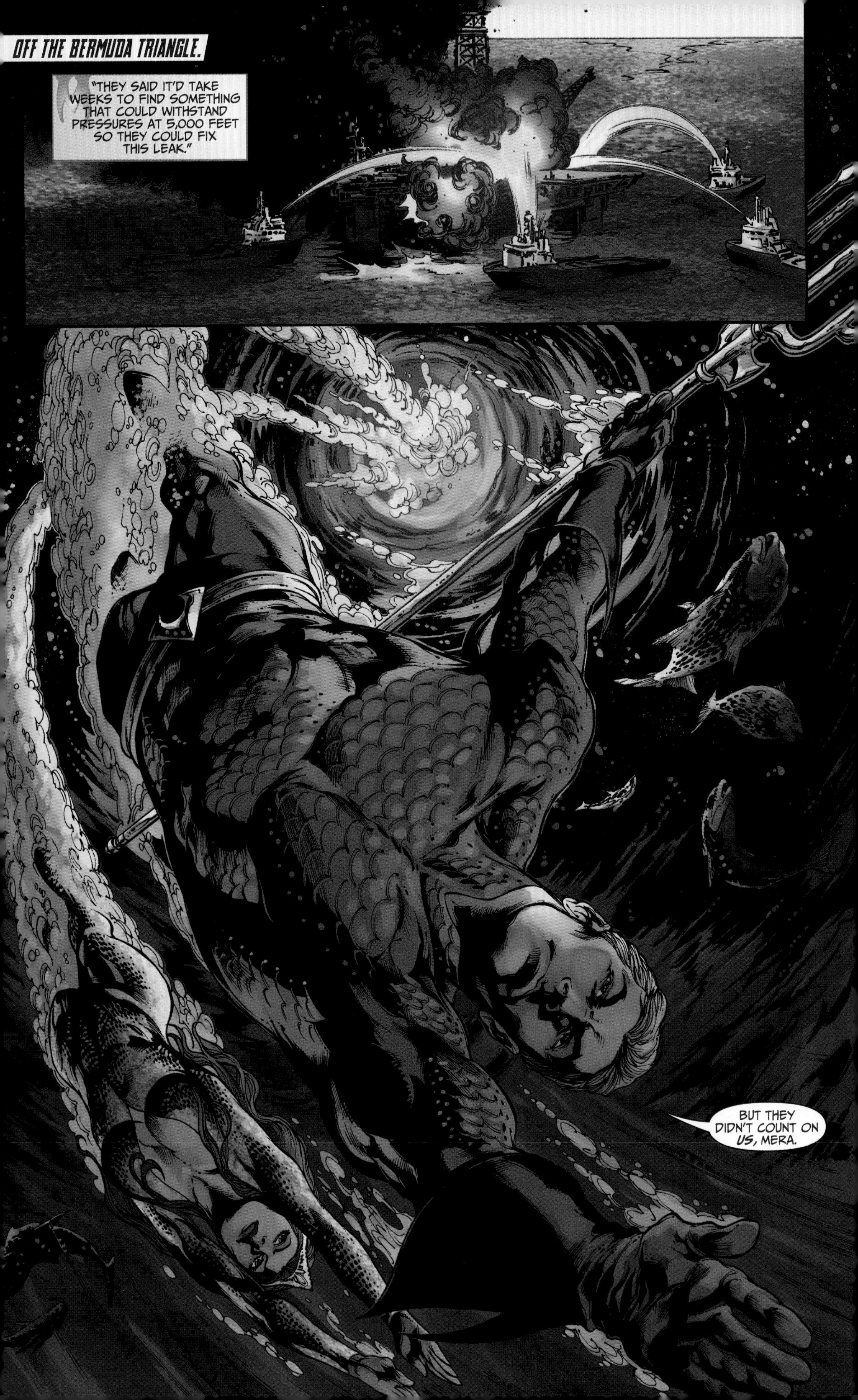
OFF THE BERMUDA TRIANGLE.
"THEY SAID IT'D TAKE WEEKS TO FIND SOMETHING THAT COULD WITHSTAND PRESSURES AT 5,000 FEET SO THEY COULD FIX THIS LEAK."
BUT THEY DIDN'T COUNT ON US, MERA.

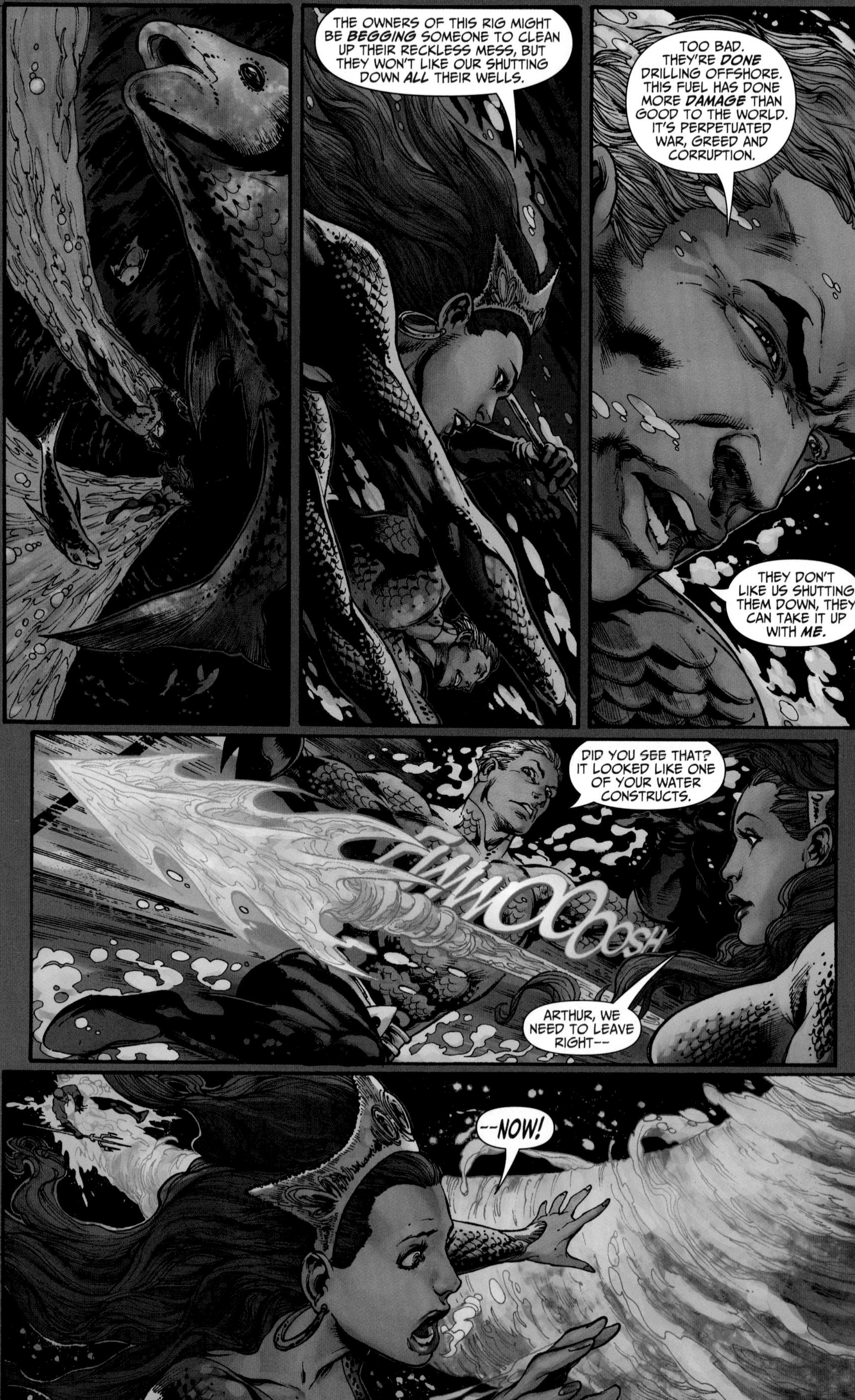

THE OWNERS OF THIS RIG MIGHT BE BEGGING SOMEONE TO CLEAN UP THEIR RECKLESS MESS, BUT THEY WON'T LIKE OUR SHUTTING DOWN ALL THEIR WELLS.
TOO BAD. THEY'RE DONE DRILLING OFFSHORE. THIS FUEL HAS DONE MORE DAMAGE THAN GOOD TO THE WORLD. IT'S PERPETUATED WAR, GREED AND CORRUPTION.
THEY DON'T LIKE US SHUTTING THEM DOWN, THEY CAN TAKE IT UP WITH ME.
DID YOU SEE THAT? IT LOOKED LIKE ONE OF YOUR WATER CONSTRUCTS.
WHOOOOOSH
ARTHUR, WE NEED TO LEAVE RIGHT--
--NOW!

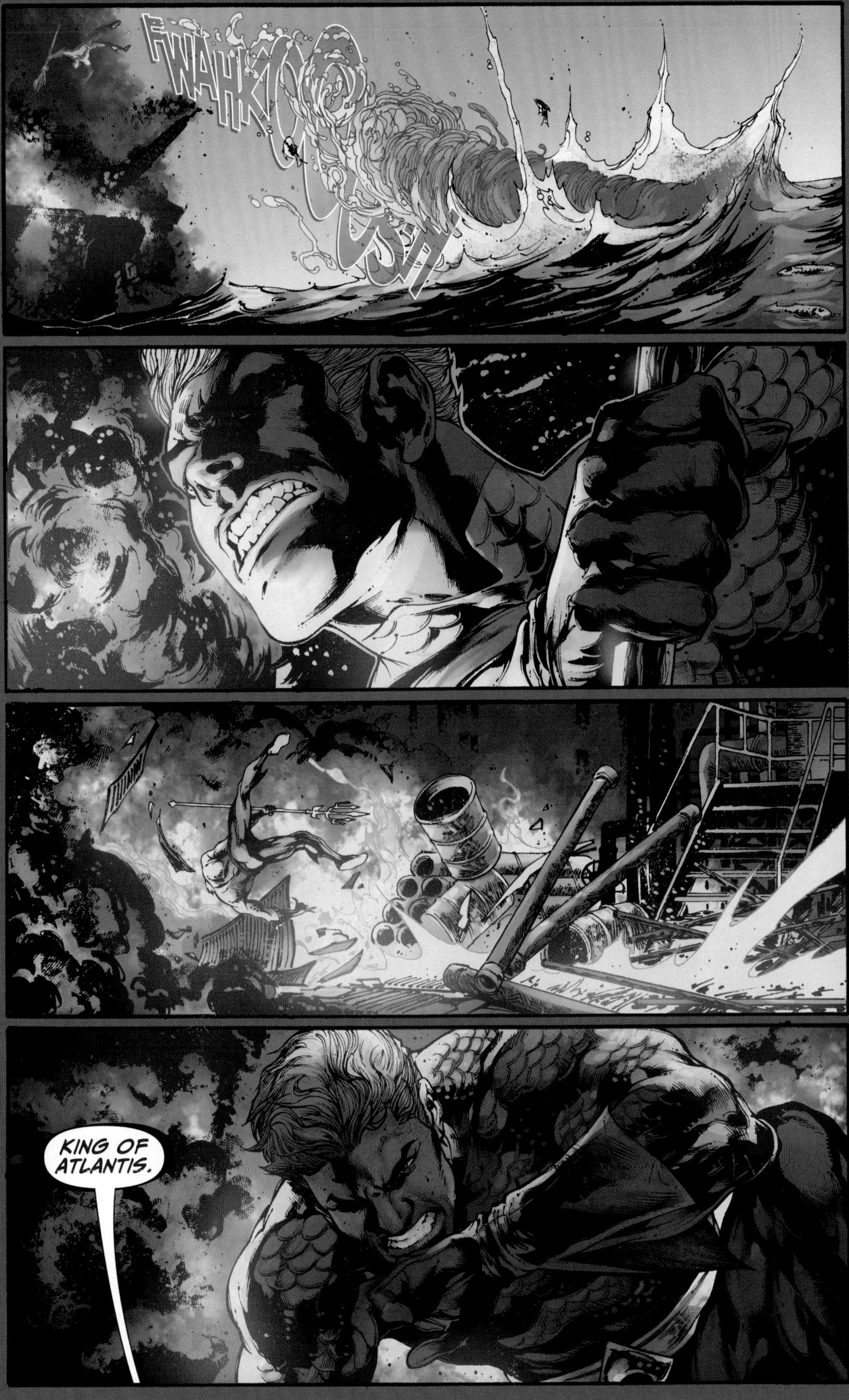
FWAHK
KING OF ATLANTIS.

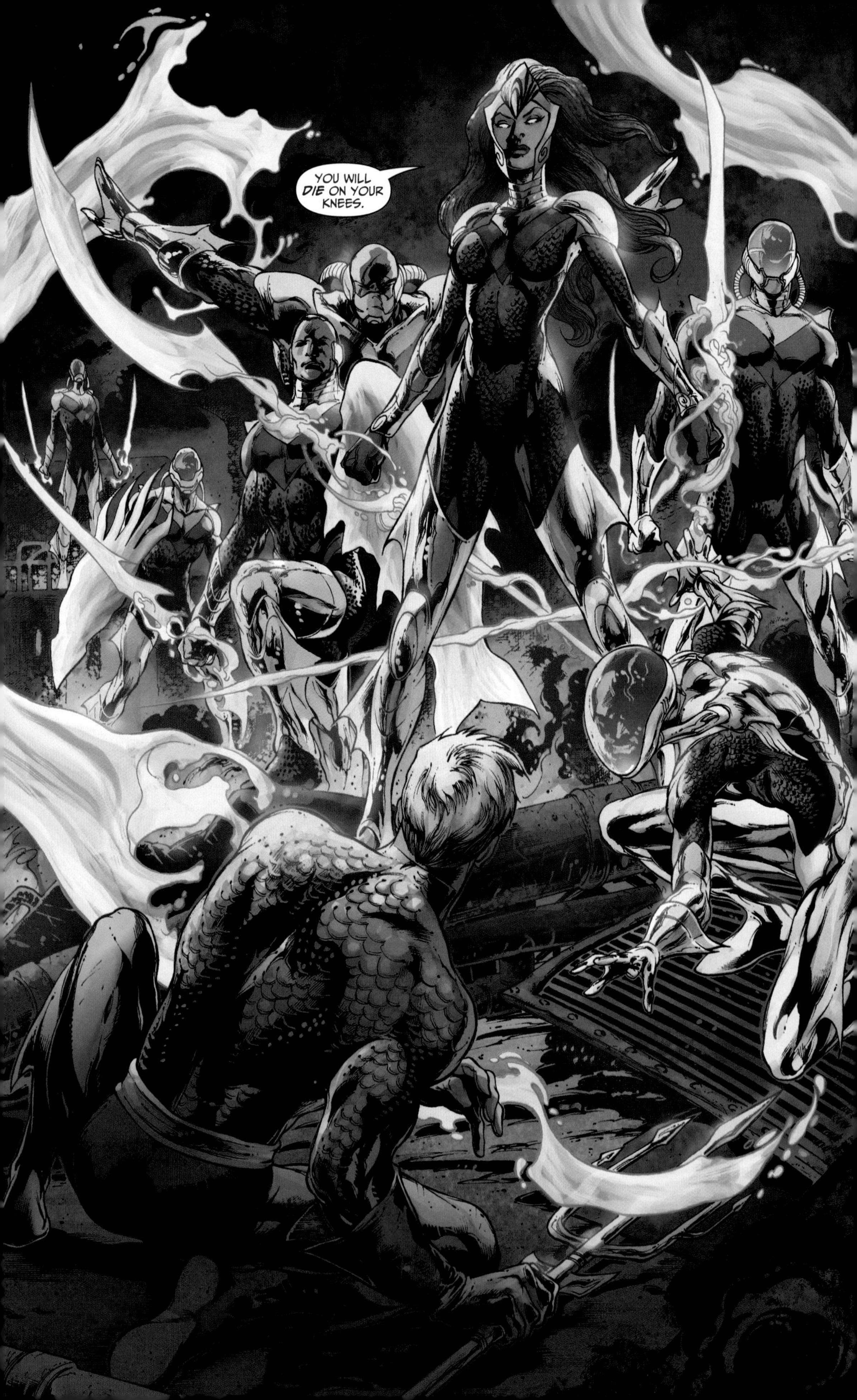
YOU WILL DIE ON YOUR KNEES.

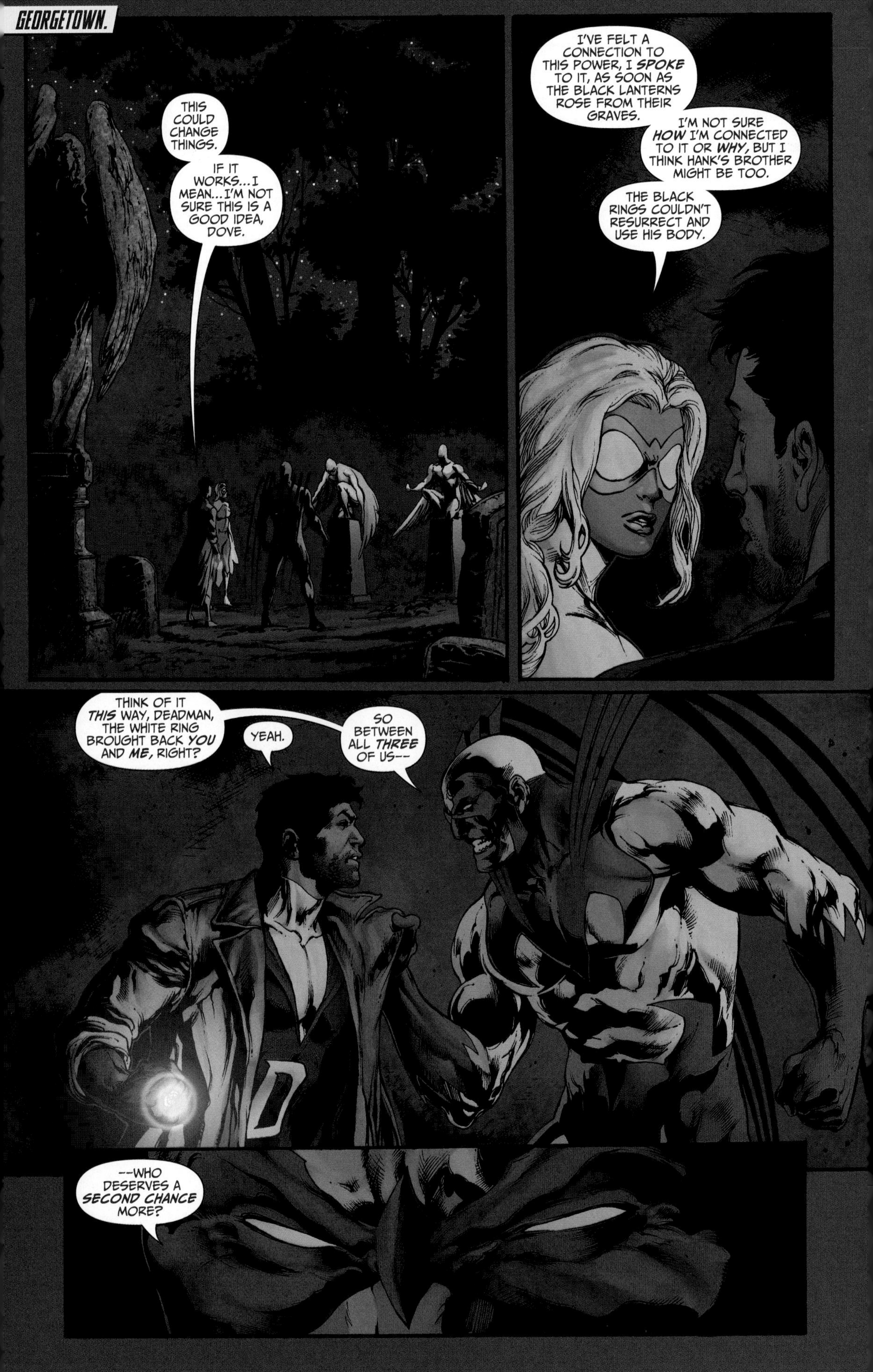
GEORGETOWN.
THIS COULD CHANGE THINGS.
IF IT WORKS...I MEAN...I'M NOT SURE THIS IS A GOOD IDEA, DOVE.
I'VE FELT A CONNECTION TO THIS POWER, I SPOKE TO IT, AS SOON AS THE BLACK LANTERNS ROSE FROM THEIR GRAVES.
I'M NOT SURE HOW I'M CONNECTED TO IT OR WHY, BUT I THINK HANK'S BROTHER MIGHT BE TOO.
THE BLACK RINGS COULDN'T RESURRECT AND USE HIS BODY.
THINK OF IT THIS WAY, DEADMAN, THE WHITE RING BROUGHT BACK YOU AND ME, RIGHT?
YEAH.
SO BETWEEN ALL THREE OF US--
--WHO DESERVES A SECOND CHANCE MORE?

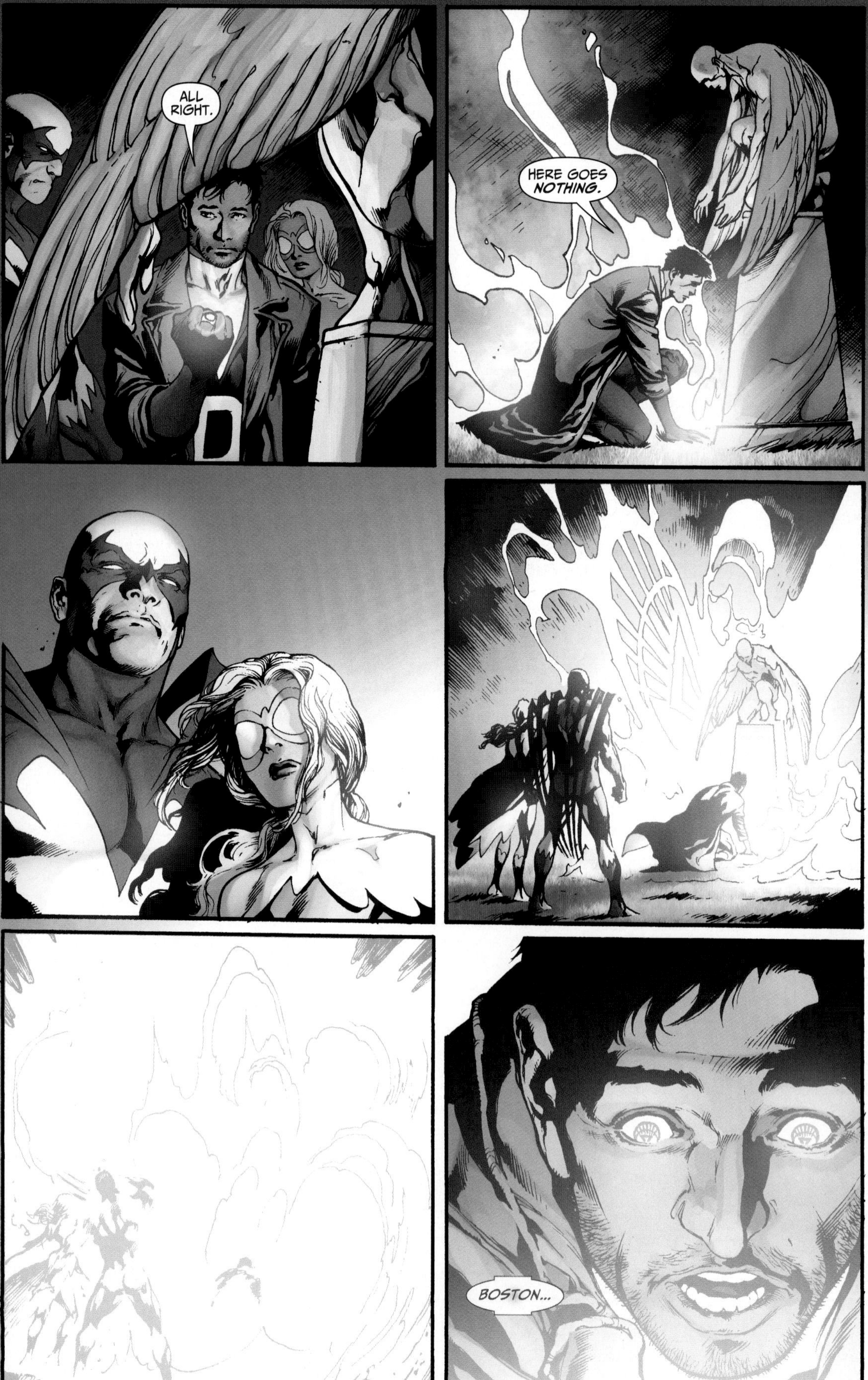
ALL RIGHT.
HERE GOES NOTHING.
BOSTON...

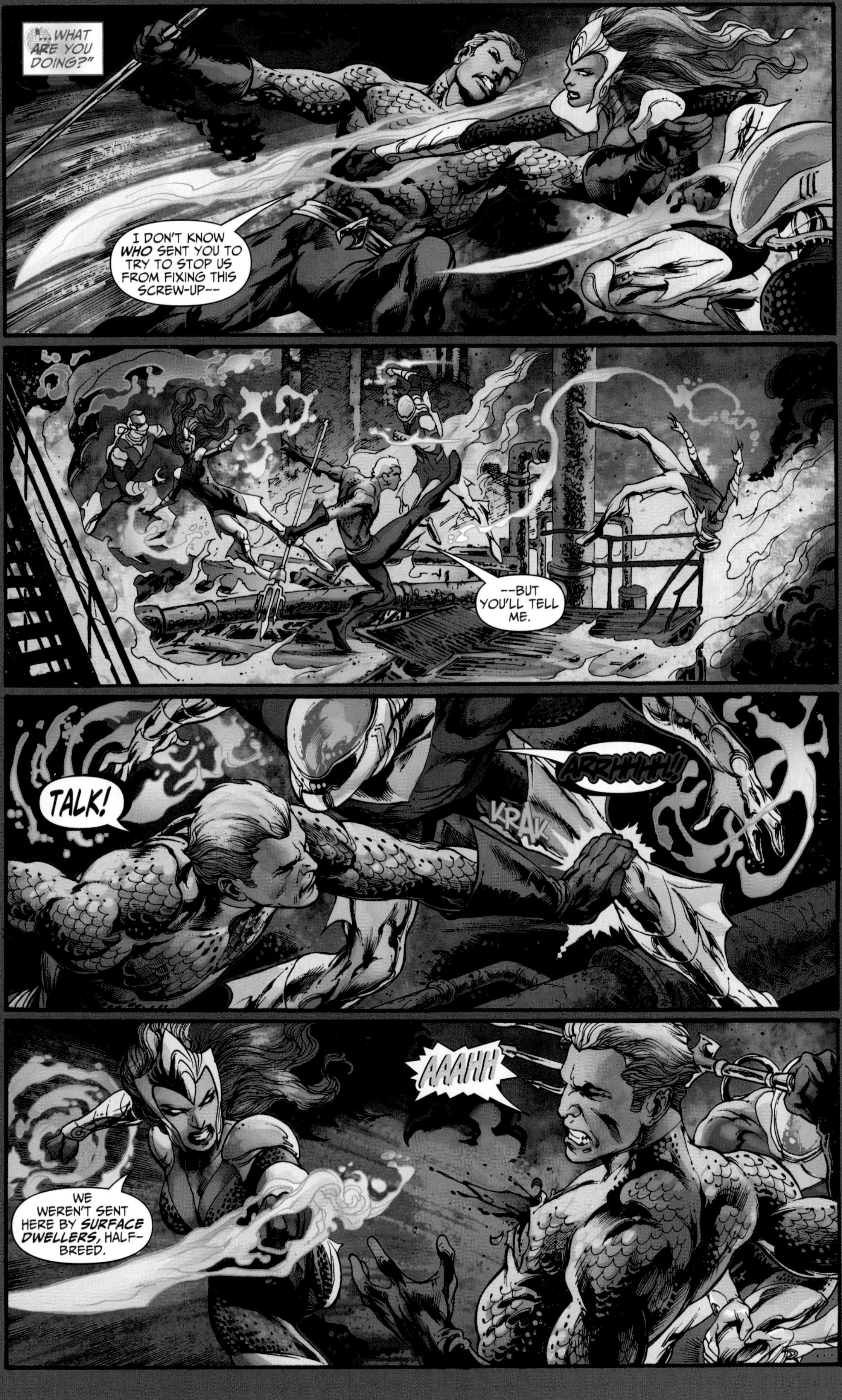
"...WHAT ARE YOU DOING?"
I DON'T KNOW WHO SENT YOU TO TRY TO STOP US FROM FIXING THIS SCREW-UP--
--BUT YOU'LL TELL ME.
TALK!
ARRHHHH!!
KRAK
AAAHH
WE WEREN'T SENT HERE BY SURFACE DWELLERS, HALF-BREED.

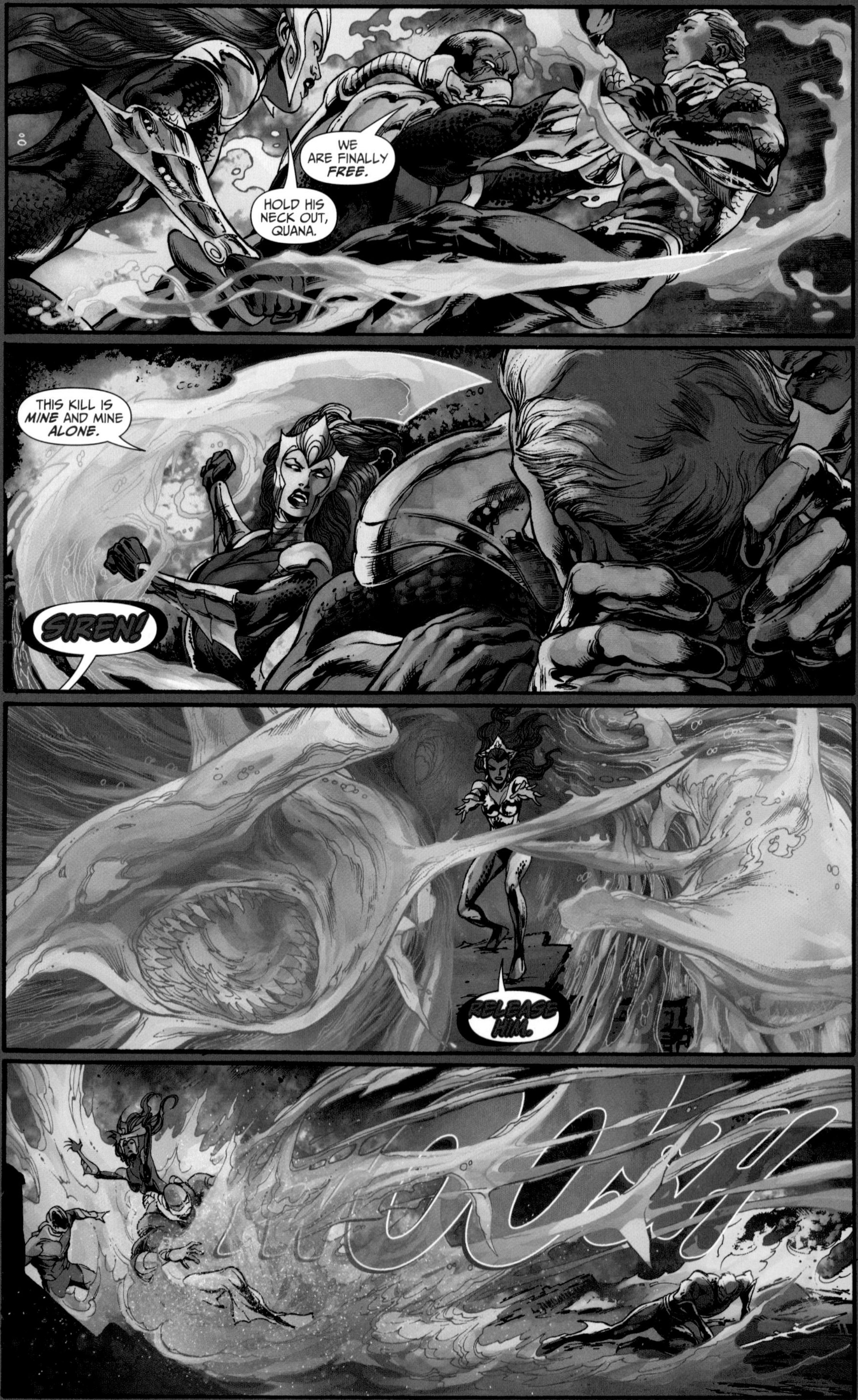
WE ARE FINALLY FREE.
HOLD HIS NECK OUT, QUANA.
THIS KILL IS MINE AND MINE ALONE.
SIREN!
RELEASE HIM.

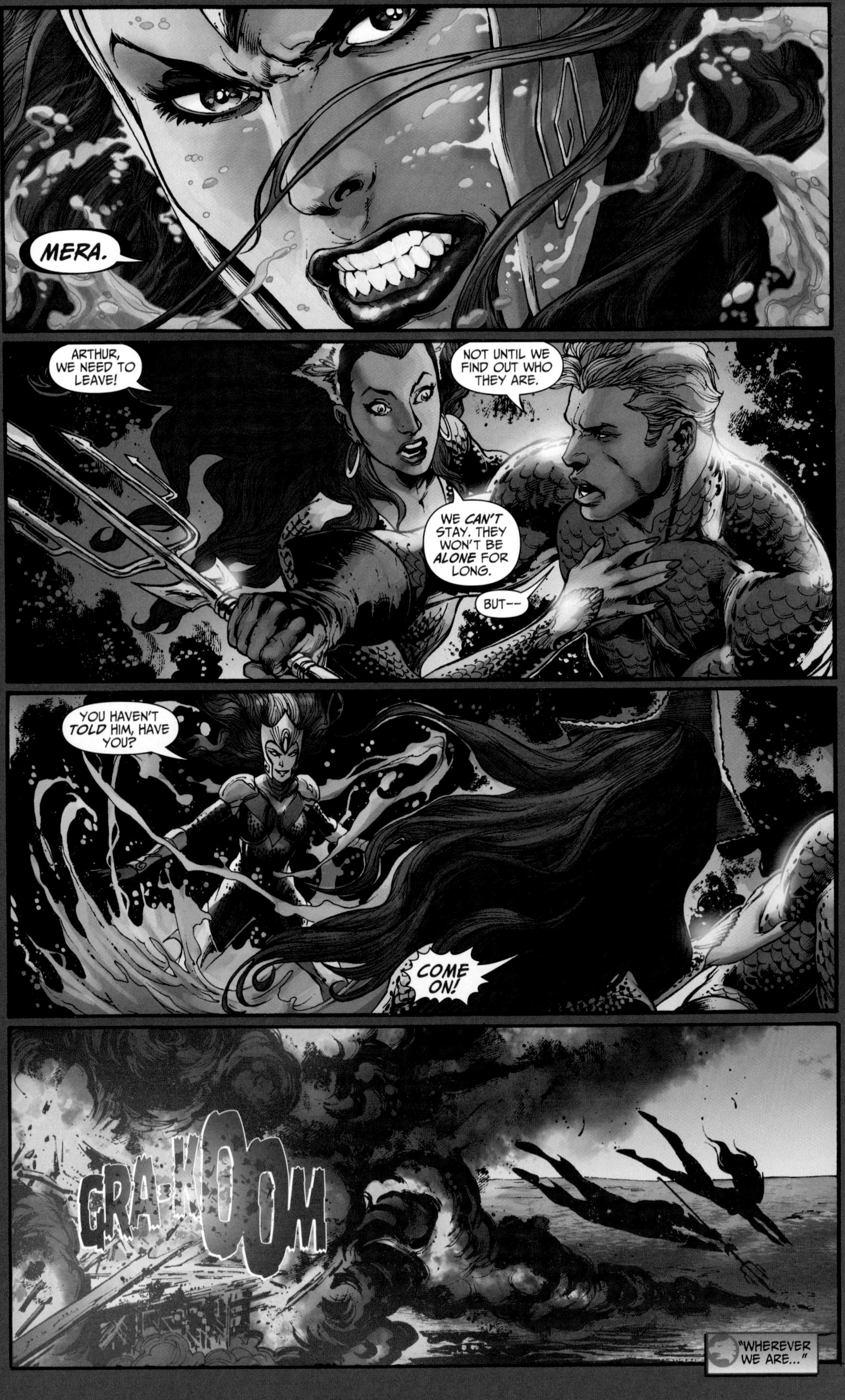
MERA.
ARTHUR, WE NEED TO LEAVE!
NOT UNTIL WE FIND OUT WHO THEY ARE.
WE CAN'T STAY. THEY WON'T BE ALONE FOR LONG.
BUT--
YOU HAVEN'T TOLD HIM, HAVE YOU?
COME ON!
GRA-KOOM
"WHEREVER WE ARE..."

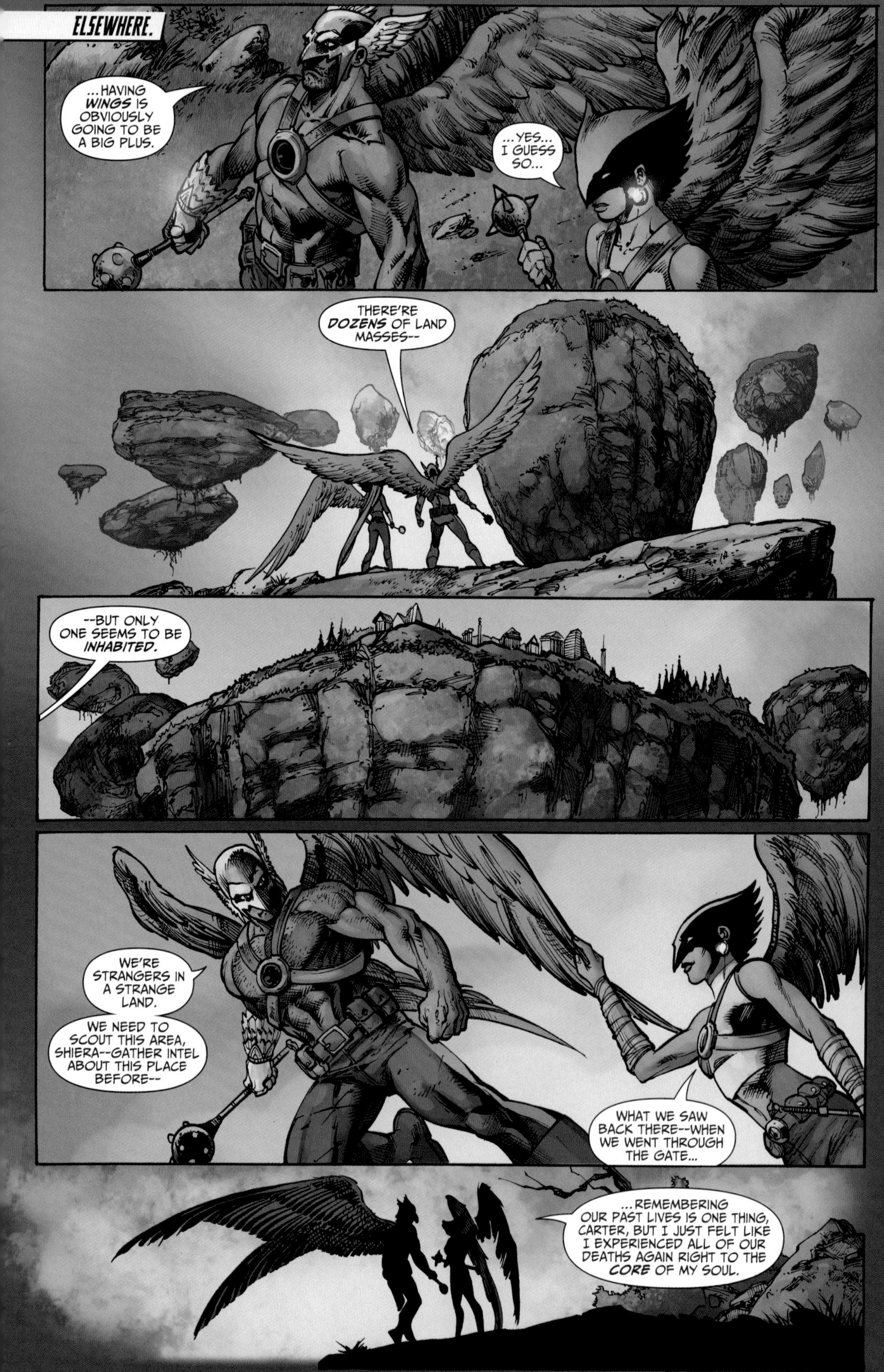
ELSEWHERE.
...HAVING WINGS IS OBVIOUSLY GOING TO BE A BIG PLUS.
...YES... I GUESS SO...
THERE'RE DOZENS OF LAND MASSES--
--BUT ONLY ONE SEEMS TO BE INHABITED.
WE'RE STRANGERS IN A STRANGE LAND.
WE NEED TO SCOUT THIS AREA, SHIERA--GATHER INTEL ABOUT THIS PLACE BEFORE--
WHAT WE SAW BACK THERE--WHEN WE WENT THROUGH THE GATE...
...REMEMBERING OUR PAST LIVES IS ONE THING, CARTER, BUT I JUST FELT LIKE I EXPERIENCED ALL OF OUR DEATHS AGAIN RIGHT TO THE CORE OF MY SOUL.

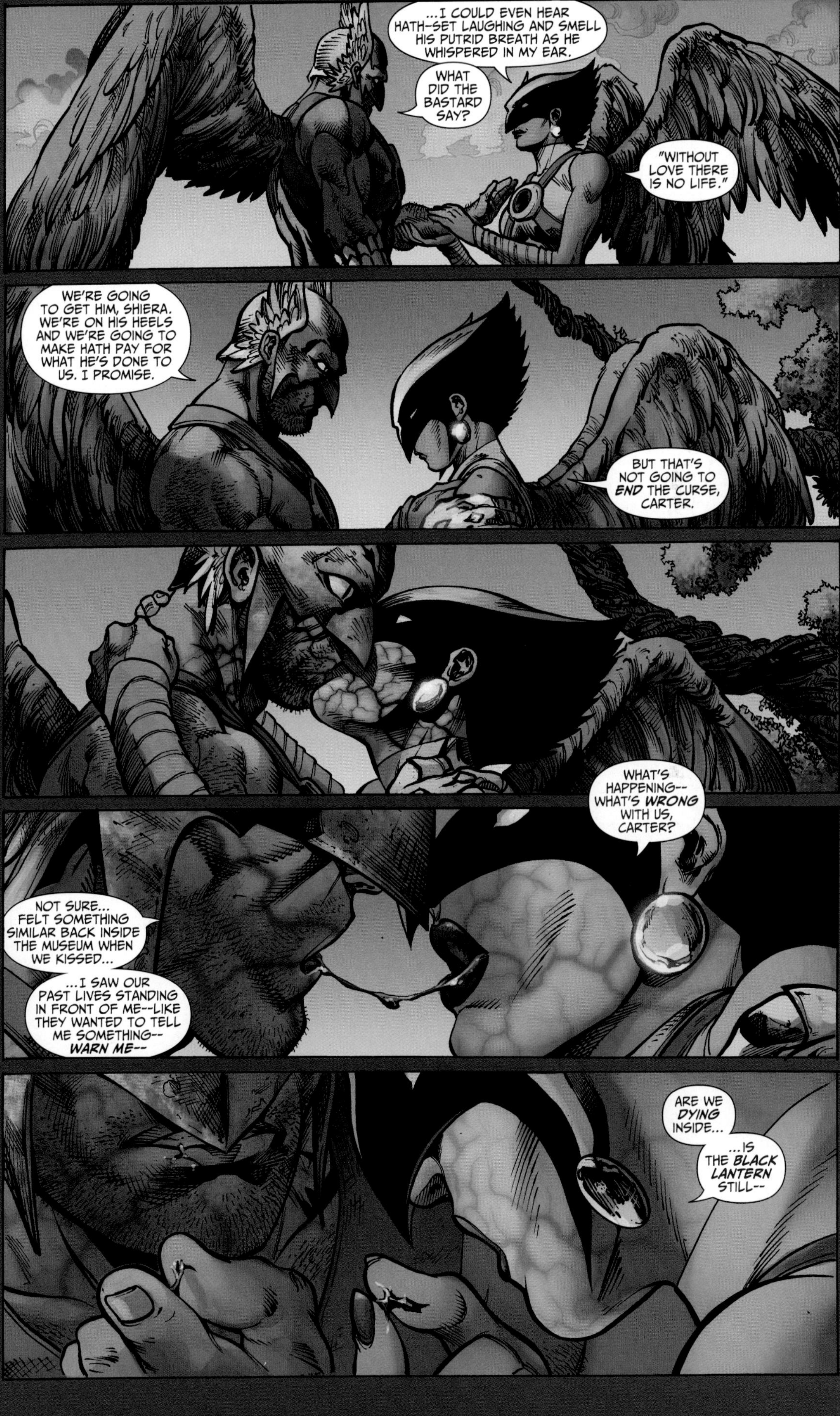
...I COULD EVEN HEAR HATH-SET LAUGHING AND SMELL HIS PUTRID BREATH AS HE WHISPERED IN MY EAR.
WHAT DID THE BASTARD SAY?
"WITHOUT LOVE THERE IS NO LIFE."
WE'RE GOING TO GET HIM, SHIERA. WE'RE ON HIS HEELS AND WE'RE GOING TO MAKE HATH PAY FOR WHAT HE'S DONE TO US. I PROMISE.
BUT THAT'S NOT GOING TO END THE CURSE, CARTER.
WHAT'S HAPPENING--WHAT'S WRONG WITH US, CARTER?
NOT SURE... FELT SOMETHING SIMILAR BACK INSIDE THE MUSEUM WHEN WE KISSED...
...I SAW OUR PAST LIVES STANDING IN FRONT OF ME--LIKE THEY WANTED TO TELL ME SOMETHING--WARN ME--
ARE WE DYING INSIDE...
...IS THE BLACK LANTERN STILL--

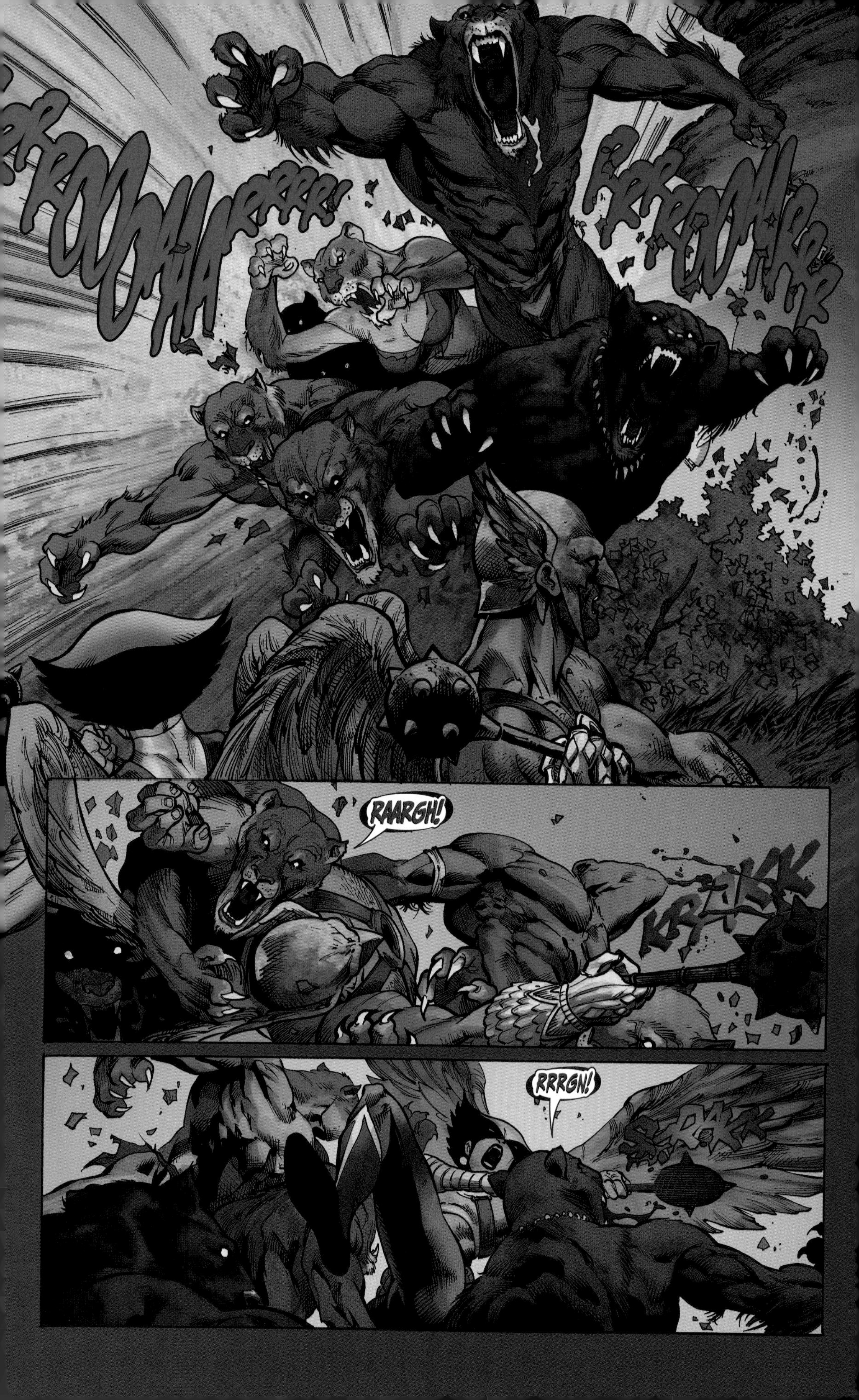
RAARGH!
KRAKK
RRRGN!

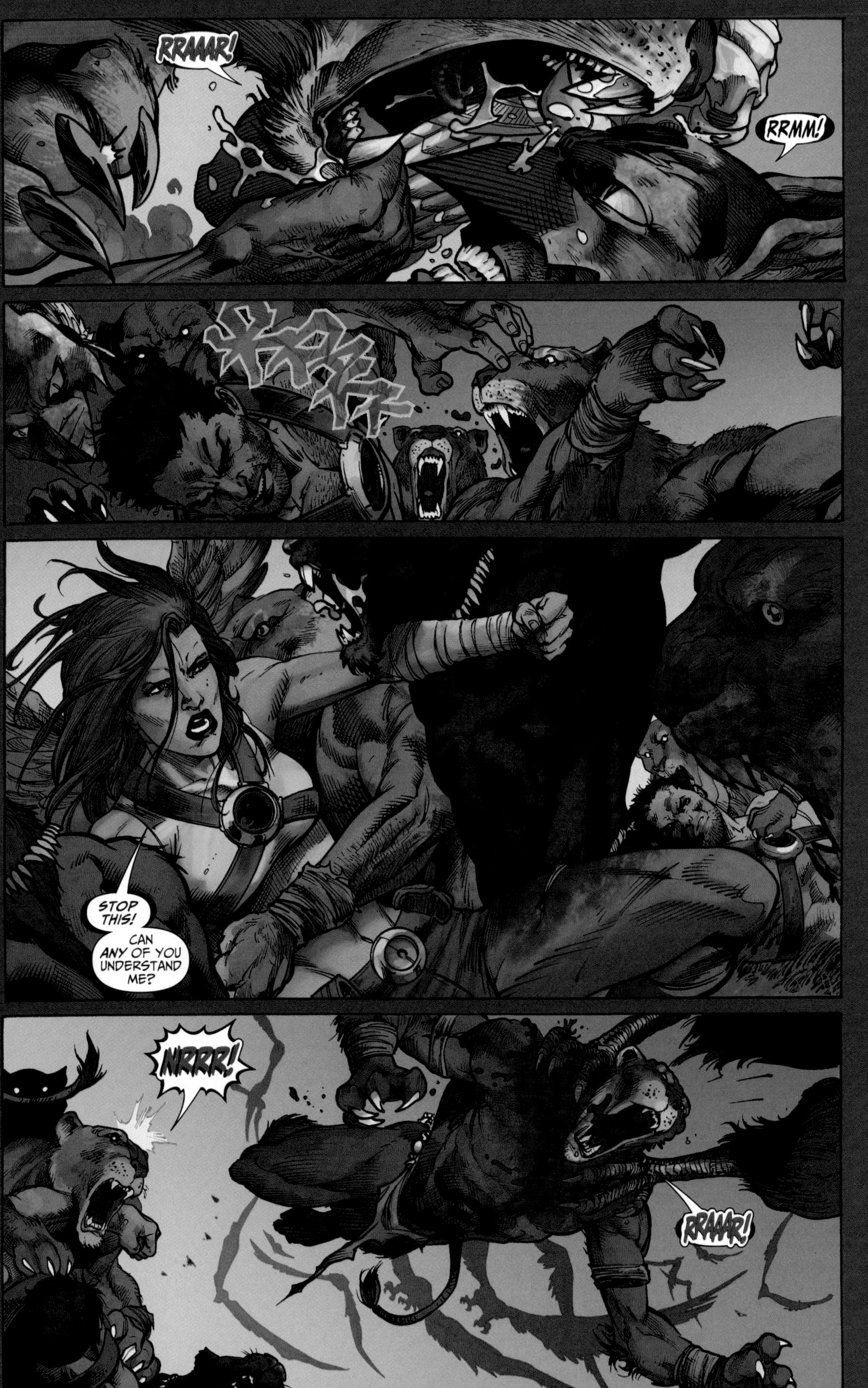
RRAAAR!
RRMM!
STOP THIS!
CAN ANY OF YOU UNDERSTAND ME?
NRRR!
RRAAAR!

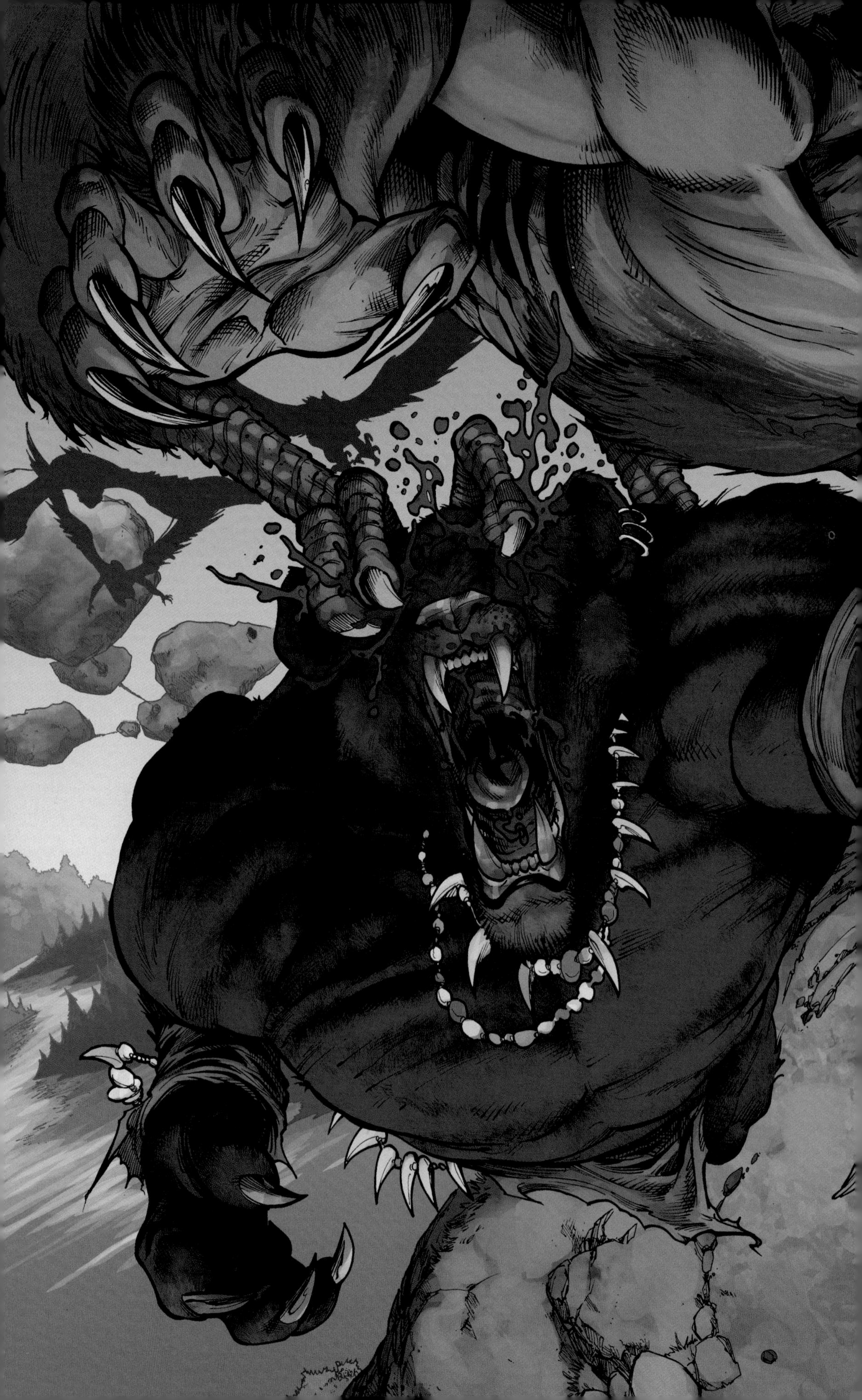

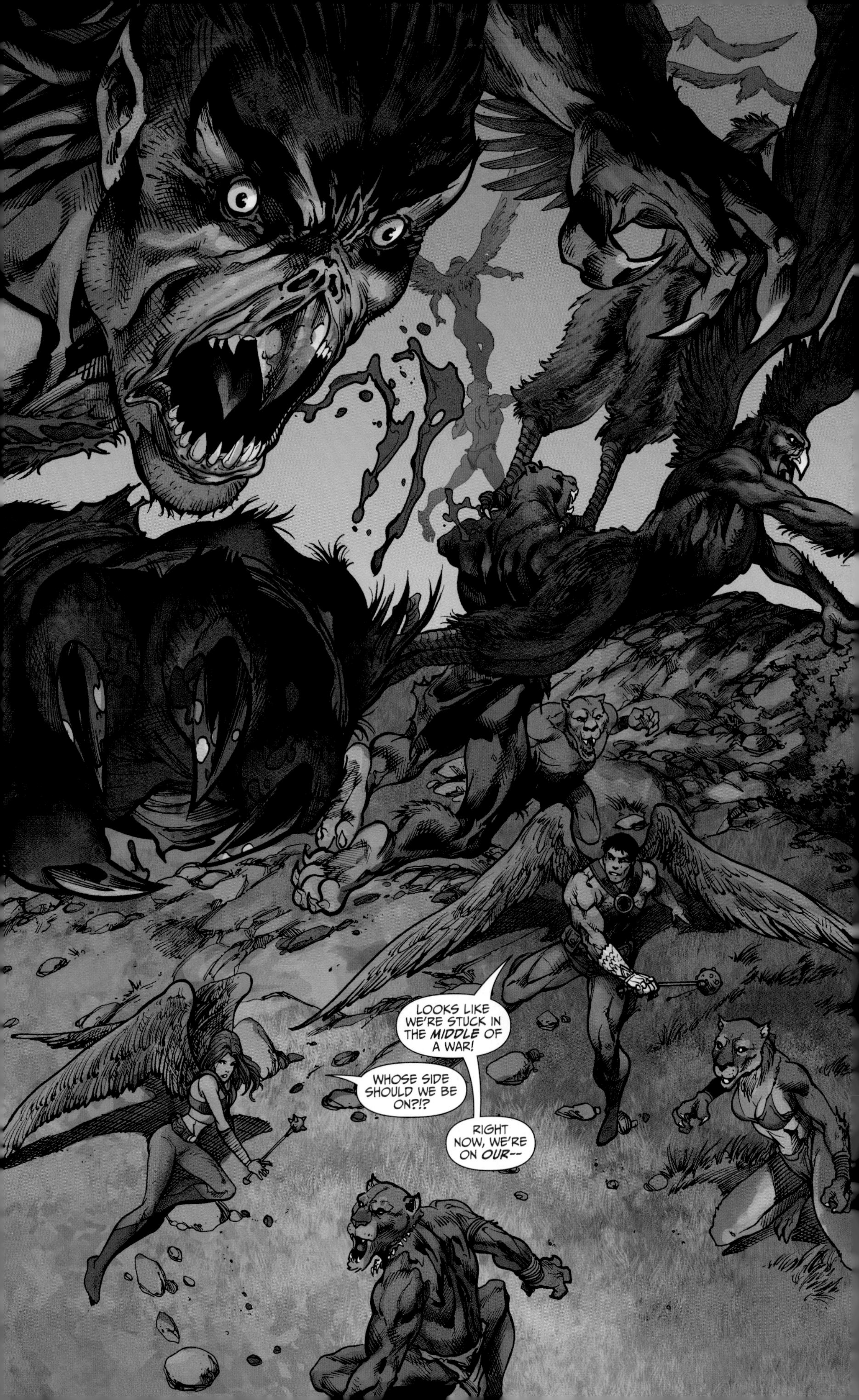
LOOKS LIKE WE'RE STUCK IN THE *MIDDLE* OF A WAR!
WHOSE SIDE SHOULD WE BE ON?!?
RIGHT NOW, WE'RE ON *OUR*--

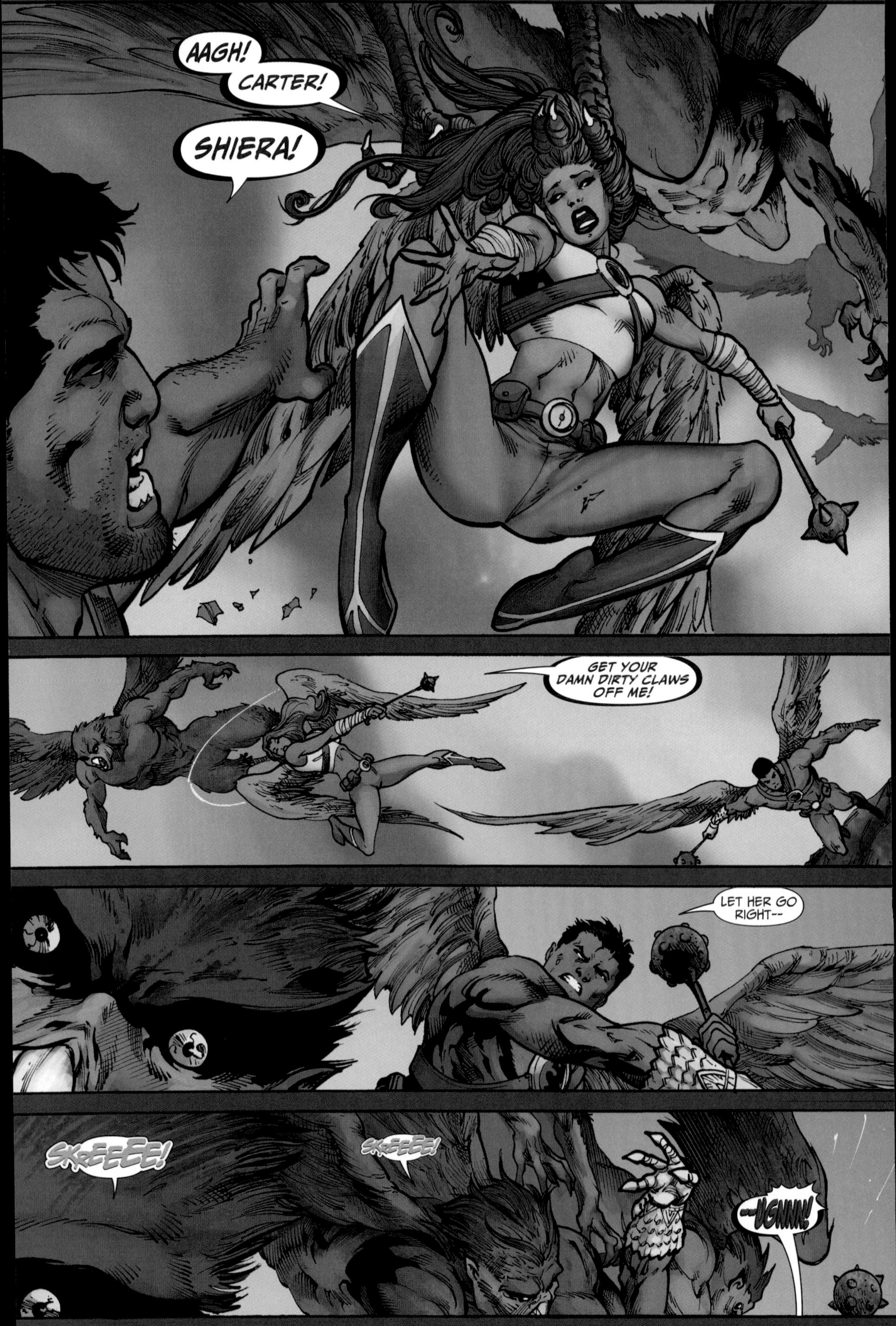
AAGH!
CARTER!
SHIERA!
GET YOUR DAMN DIRTY CLAWS OFF ME!
LET HER GO RIGHT--
SKREEEEE!
SKREEEEE!
--UGNNN!

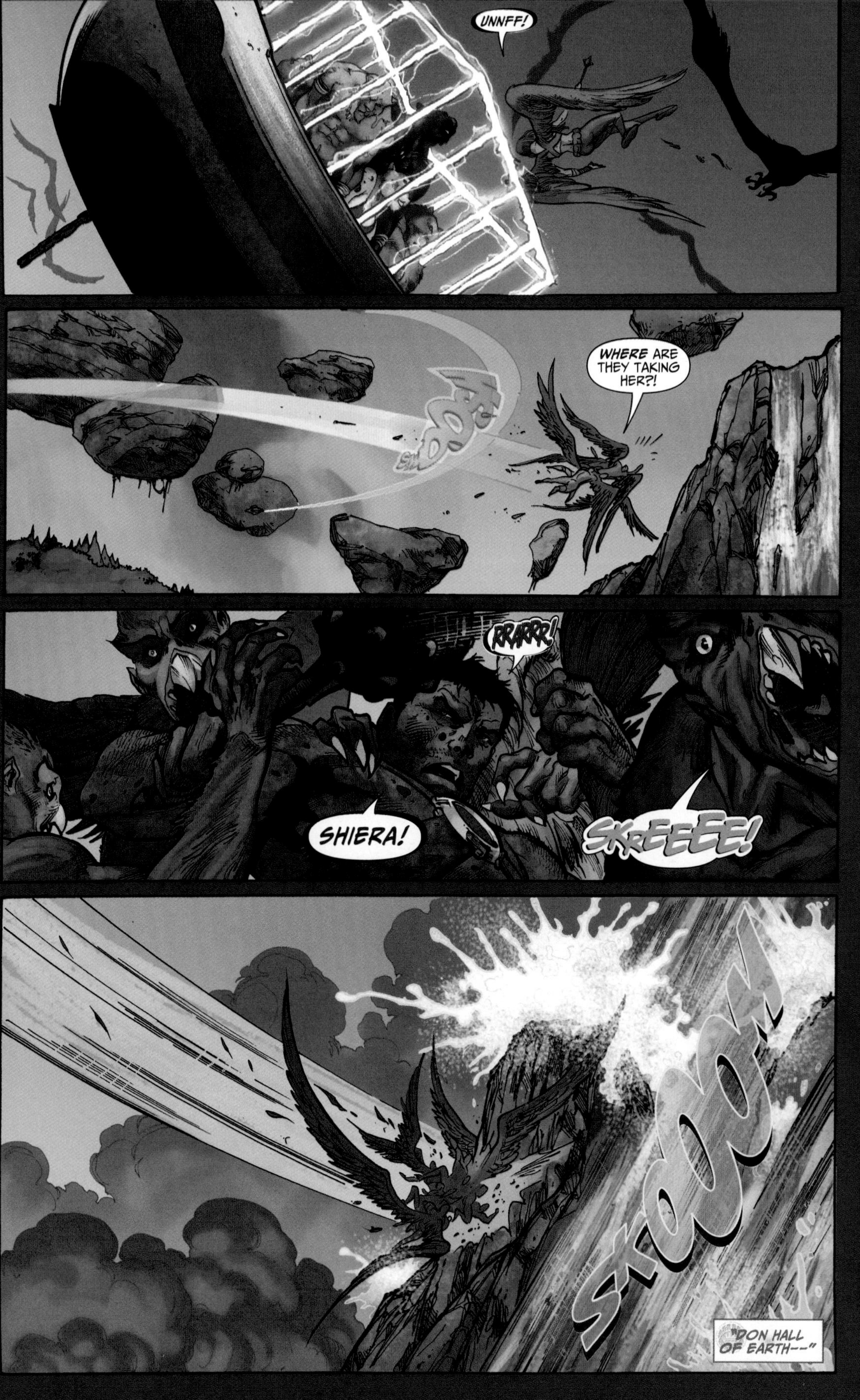
UNNFF!
WHERE ARE THEY TAKING HER?!
RRARRR!
SHIERA!
SKREEEEE!
"DON HALL OF EARTH--"

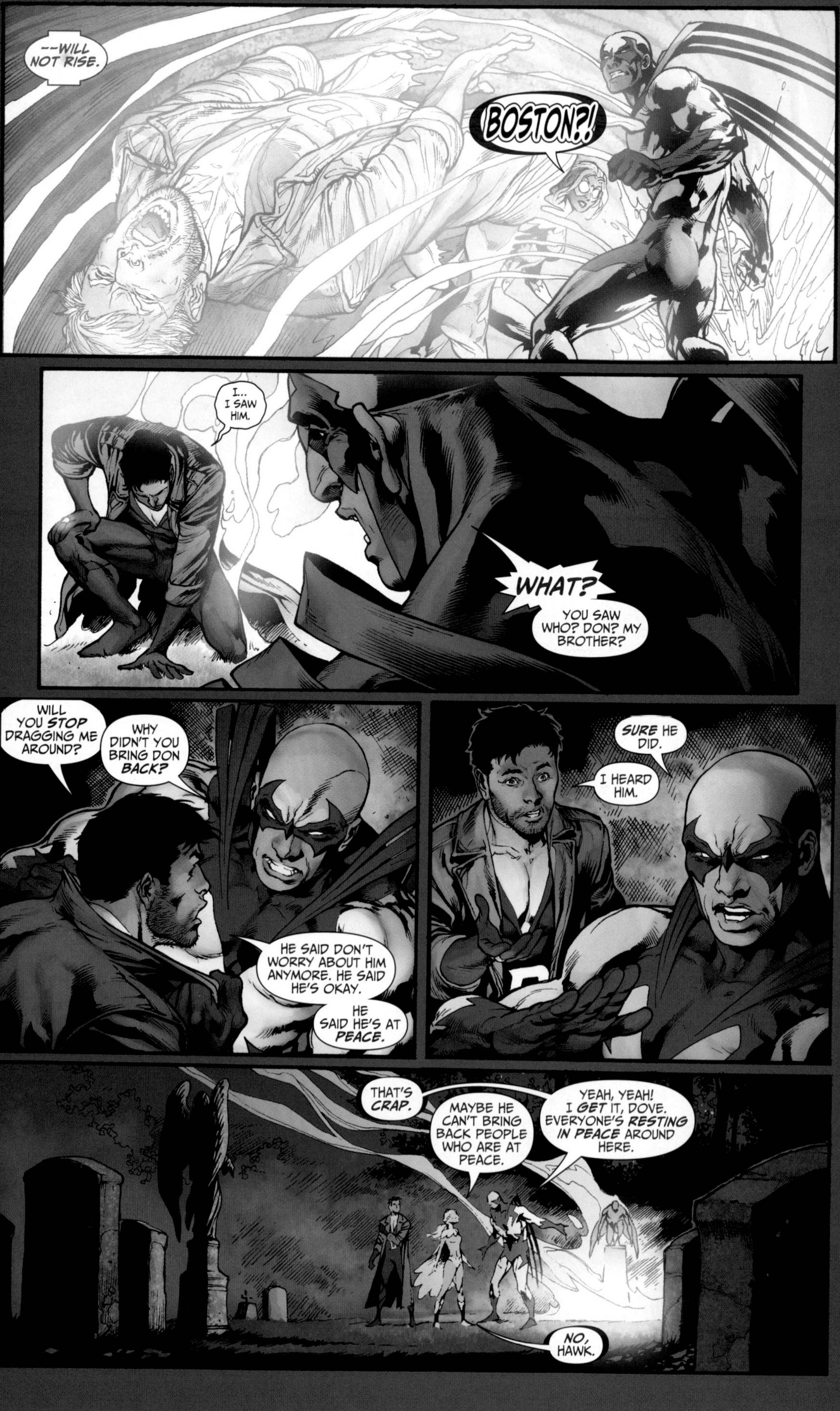
--WILL NOT RISE.
BOSTON?!
I... I SAW HIM.
WHAT?
YOU SAW WHO? DON? MY BROTHER?
WILL YOU STOP DRAGGING ME AROUND?
WHY DIDN'T YOU BRING DON BACK?
HE SAID DON'T WORRY ABOUT HIM ANYMORE. HE SAID HE'S OKAY.
HE SAID HE'S AT PEACE.
SURE HE DID.
I HEARD HIM.
THAT'S CRAP.
MAYBE HE CAN'T BRING BACK PEOPLE WHO ARE AT PEACE.
YEAH, YEAH! I GET IT, DOVE. EVERYONE'S RESTING IN PEACE AROUND HERE.
NO, HAWK.

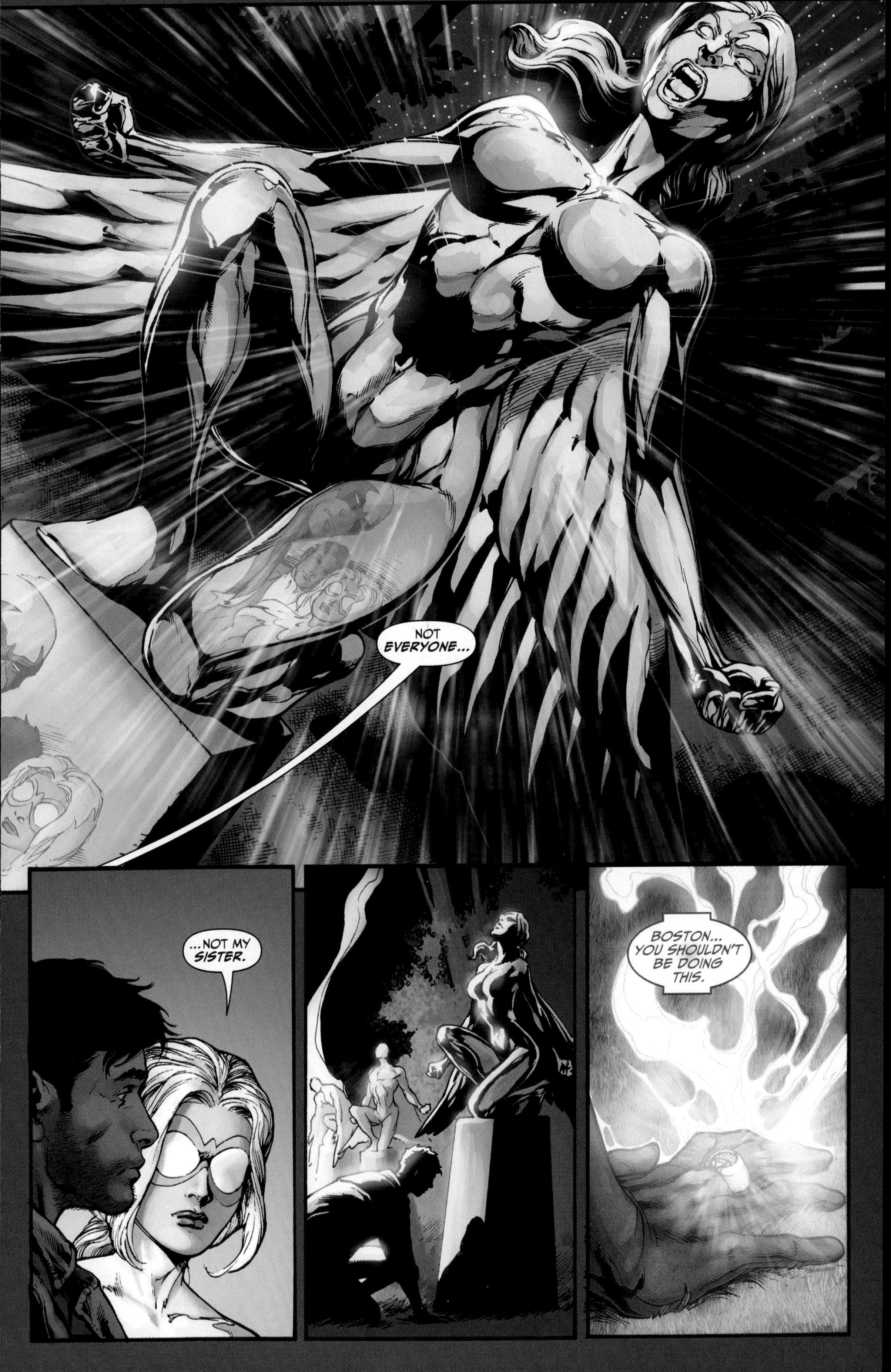
NOT EVERYONE...
...NOT MY SISTER.
BOSTON... YOU SHOULDN'T BE DOING THIS.

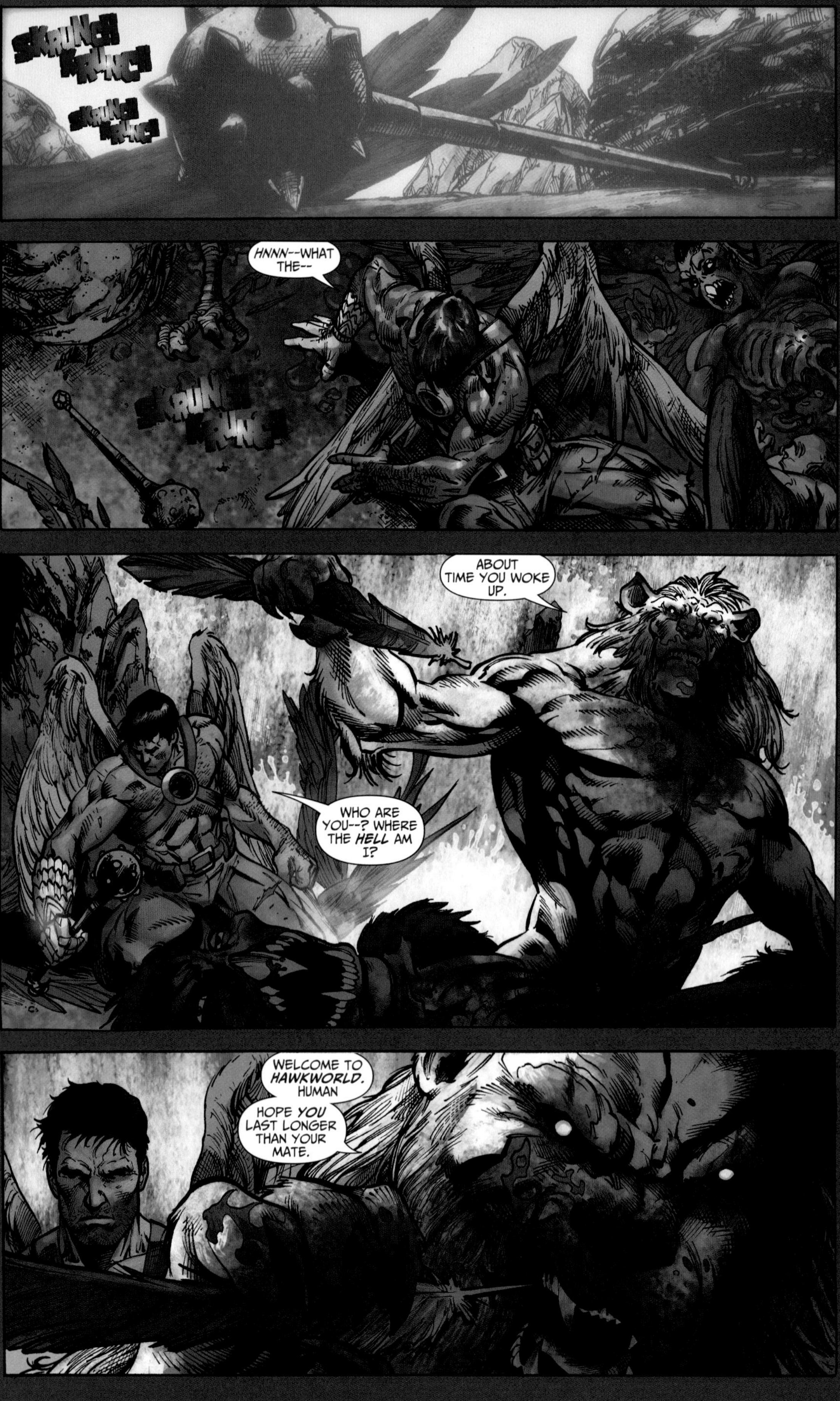
SKRUNCH KRUNCH
SKRUNCH KRUNCH
HNNN--WHAT THE--
SKRUNCH KRUNCH
ABOUT TIME YOU WOKE UP.
WHO ARE YOU--? WHERE THE HELL AM I?
WELCOME TO HAWKWORLD. HUMAN
HOPE YOU LAST LONGER THAN YOUR MATE.

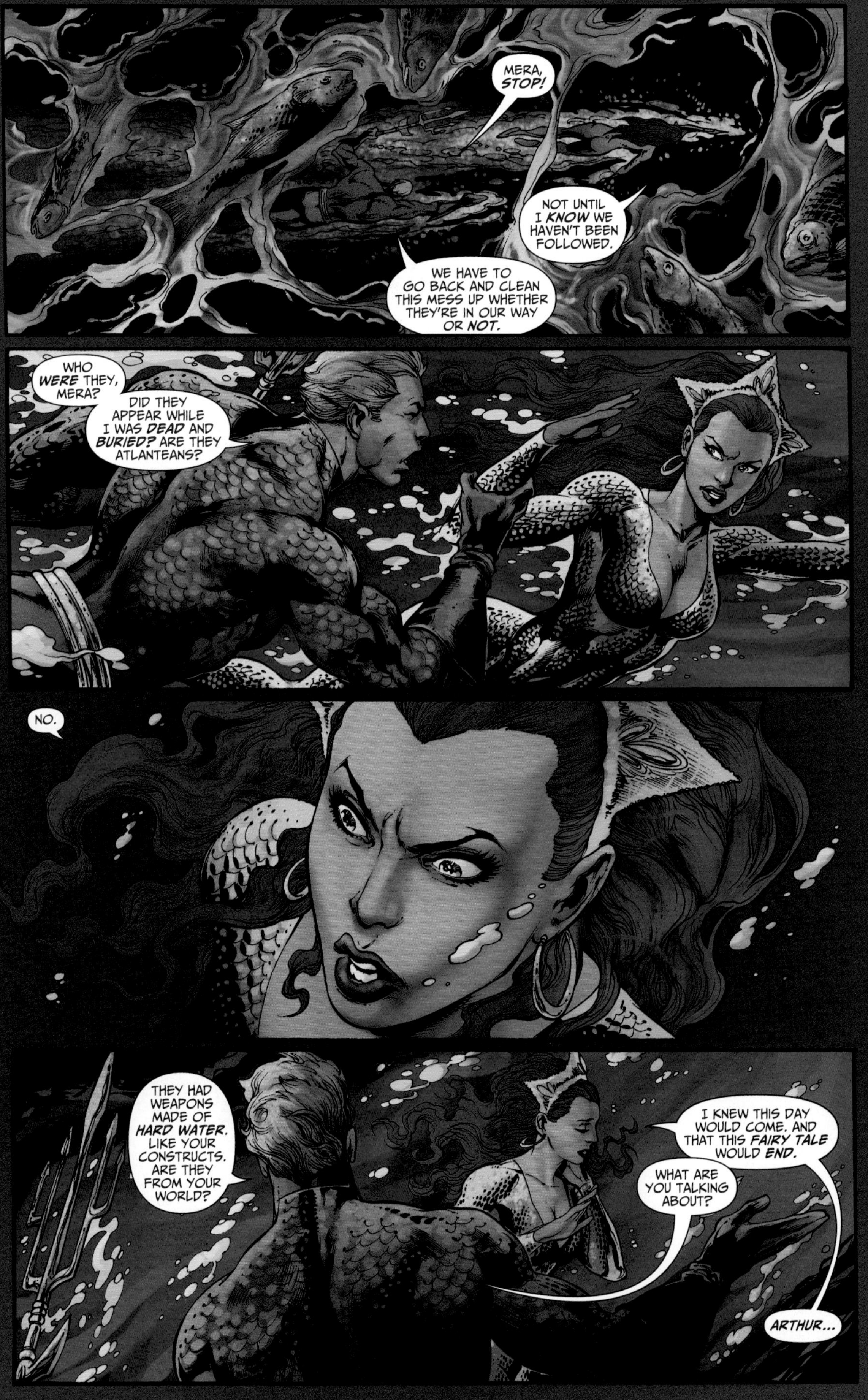
MERA, STOP!
NOT UNTIL I KNOW WE HAVEN'T BEEN FOLLOWED.
WE HAVE TO GO BACK AND CLEAN THIS MESS UP WHETHER THEY'RE IN OUR WAY OR NOT.
WHO WERE THEY, MERA?
DID THEY APPEAR WHILE I WAS DEAD AND BURIED? ARE THEY ATLANTEANS?
NO.
THEY HAD WEAPONS MADE OF HARD WATER. LIKE YOUR CONSTRUCTS. ARE THEY FROM YOUR WORLD?
I KNEW THIS DAY WOULD COME. AND THAT THIS FAIRY TALE WOULD END.
WHAT ARE YOU TALKING ABOUT?
ARTHUR...

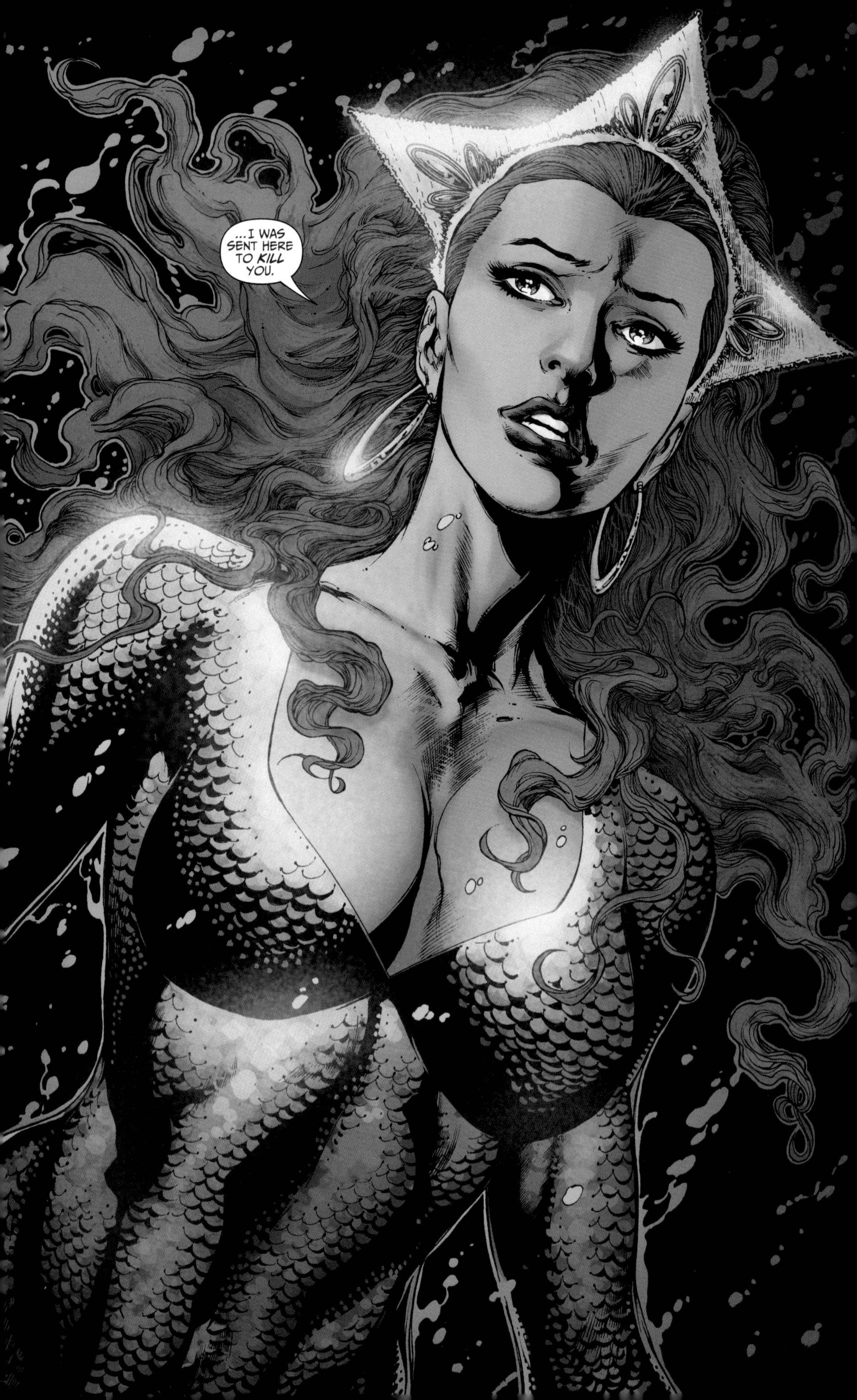
...I WAS SENT HERE TO KILL YOU.

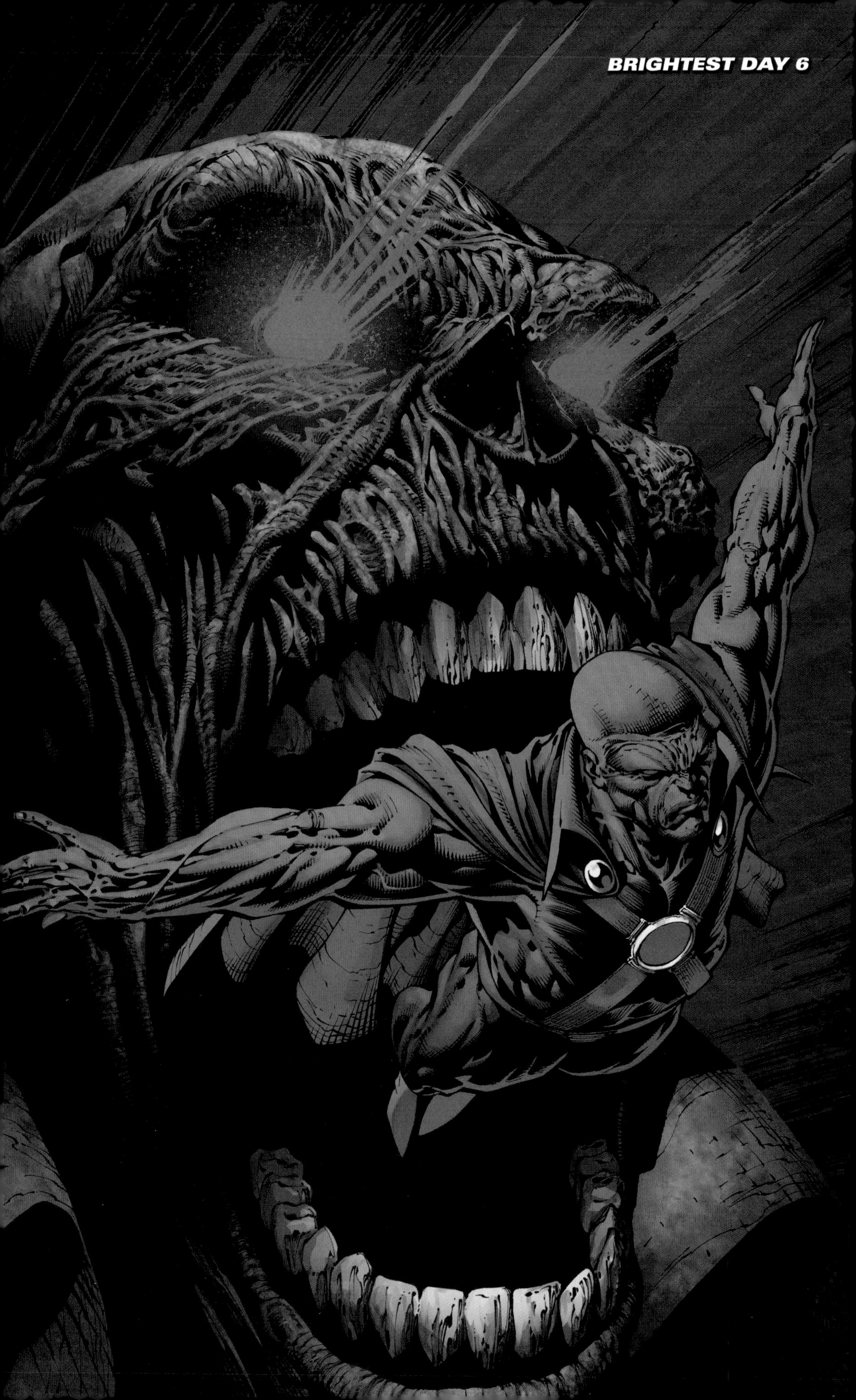
BRIGHTEST DAY 6

DEAD ZONE

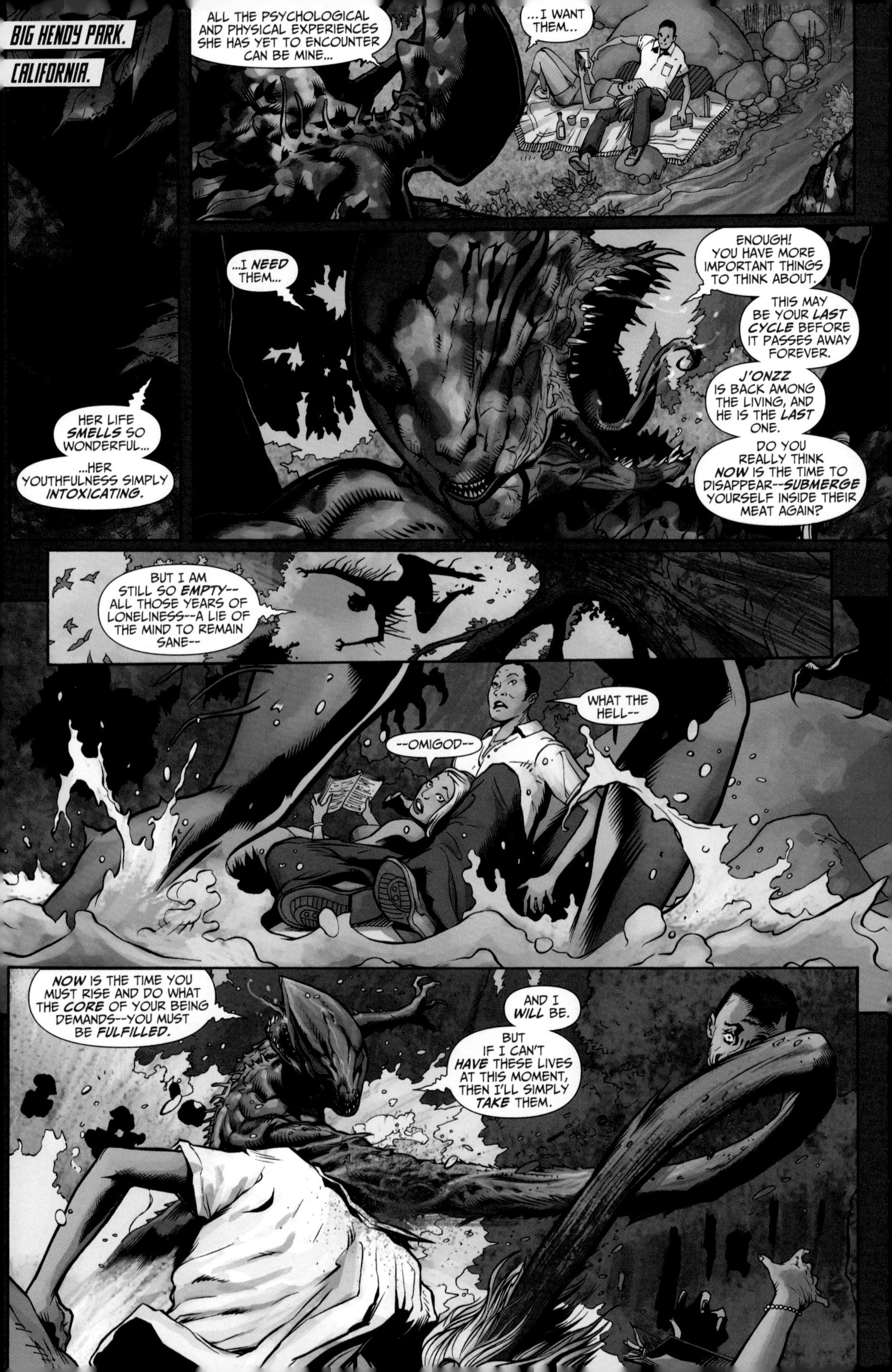
BIG HENDY PARK.
CALIFORNIA.
ALL THE PSYCHOLOGICAL AND PHYSICAL EXPERIENCES SHE HAS YET TO ENCOUNTER CAN BE MINE...
...I WANT THEM...
...I NEED THEM...
HER LIFE SMELLS SO WONDERFUL...
...HER YOUTHFULNESS SIMPLY INTOXICATING.
ENOUGH! YOU HAVE MORE IMPORTANT THINGS TO THINK ABOUT.
THIS MAY BE YOUR LAST CYCLE BEFORE IT PASSES AWAY FOREVER.
J'ONZZ IS BACK AMONG THE LIVING, AND HE IS THE LAST ONE.
DO YOU REALLY THINK NOW IS THE TIME TO DISAPPEAR--SUBMERGE YOURSELF INSIDE THEIR MEAT AGAIN?
BUT I AM STILL SO EMPTY--ALL THOSE YEARS OF LONELINESS--A LIE OF THE MIND TO REMAIN SANE--
WHAT THE HELL--
--OMIGOD--
NOW IS THE TIME YOU MUST RISE AND DO WHAT THE CORE OF YOUR BEING DEMANDS--YOU MUST BE FULFILLED.
AND I WILL BE.
BUT IF I CAN'T HAVE THESE LIVES AT THIS MOMENT, THEN I'LL SIMPLY TAKE THEM.

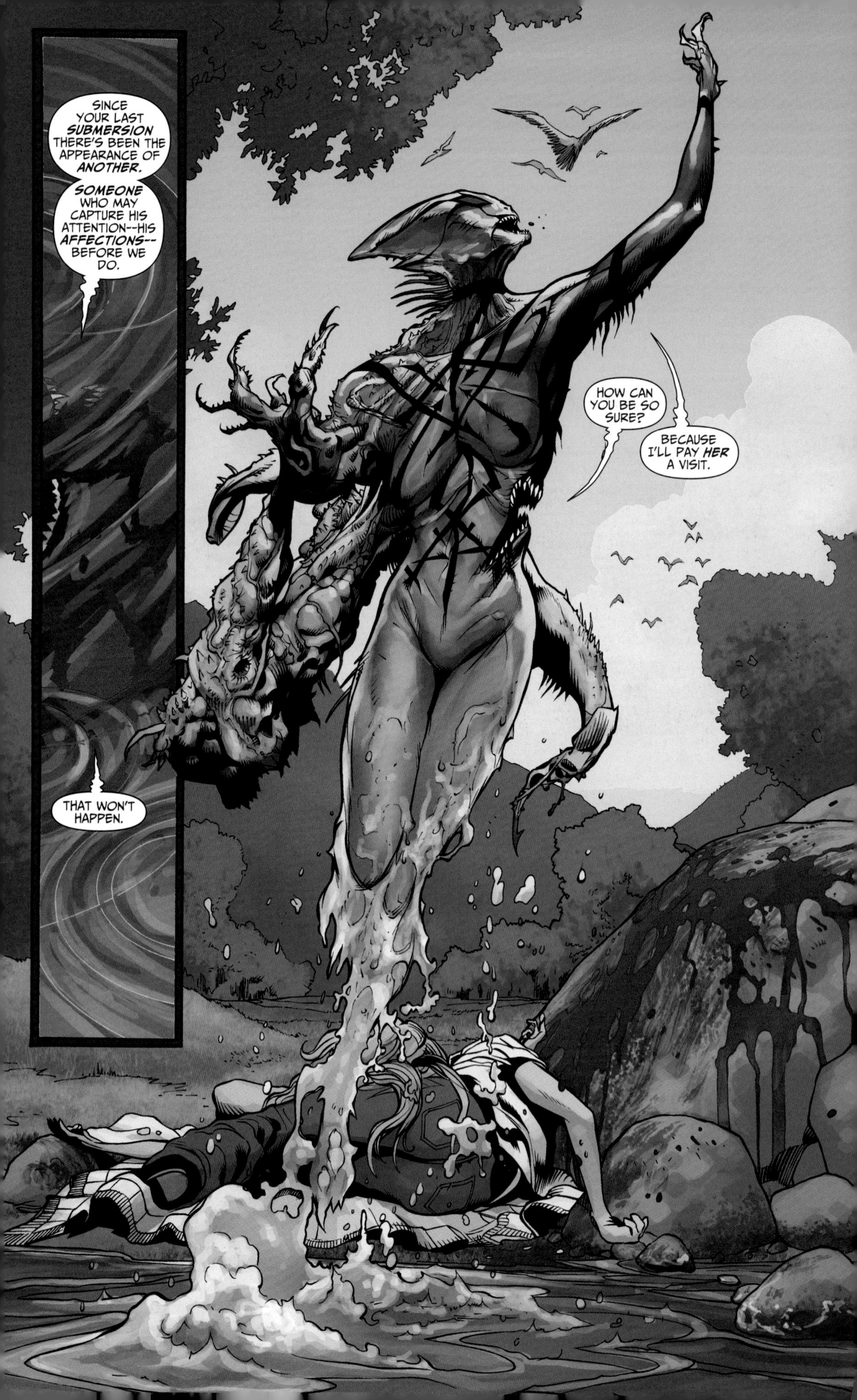
SINCE YOUR LAST SUBMERSION THERE'S BEEN THE APPEARANCE OF ANOTHER.
SOMEONE WHO MAY CAPTURE HIS ATTENTION--HIS AFFECTIONS--BEFORE WE DO.
THAT WON'T HAPPEN.
HOW CAN YOU BE SO SURE?
BECAUSE I'LL PAY HER A VISIT.

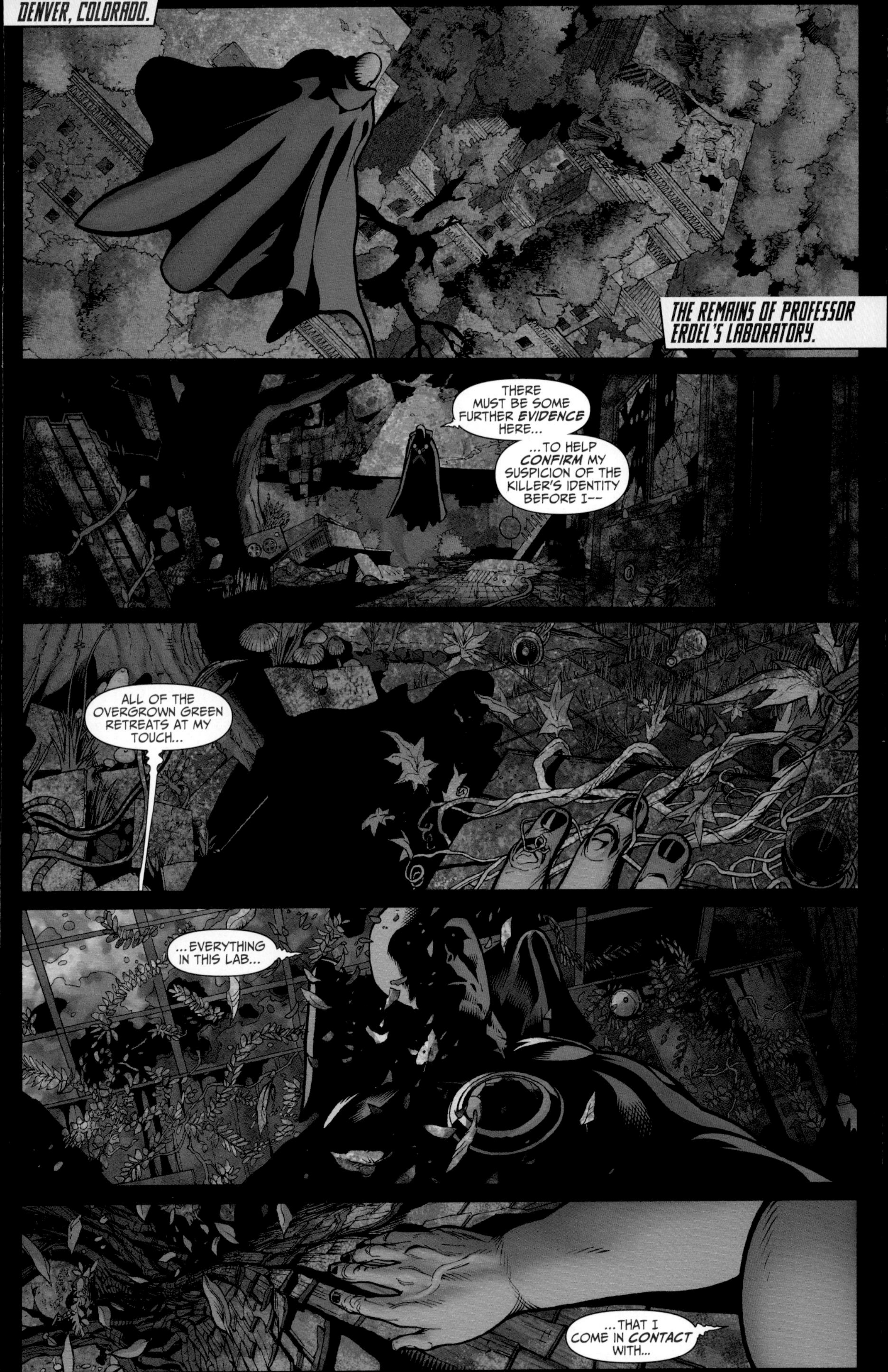
DENVER, COLORADO.
THE REMAINS OF PROFESSOR ERDEL'S LABORATORY.
THERE MUST BE SOME FURTHER EVIDENCE HERE...
...TO HELP CONFIRM MY SUSPICION OF THE KILLER'S IDENTITY BEFORE I--
ALL OF THE OVERGROWN GREEN RETREATS AT MY TOUCH...
...EVERYTHING IN THIS LAB...
...THAT I COME IN CONTACT WITH...

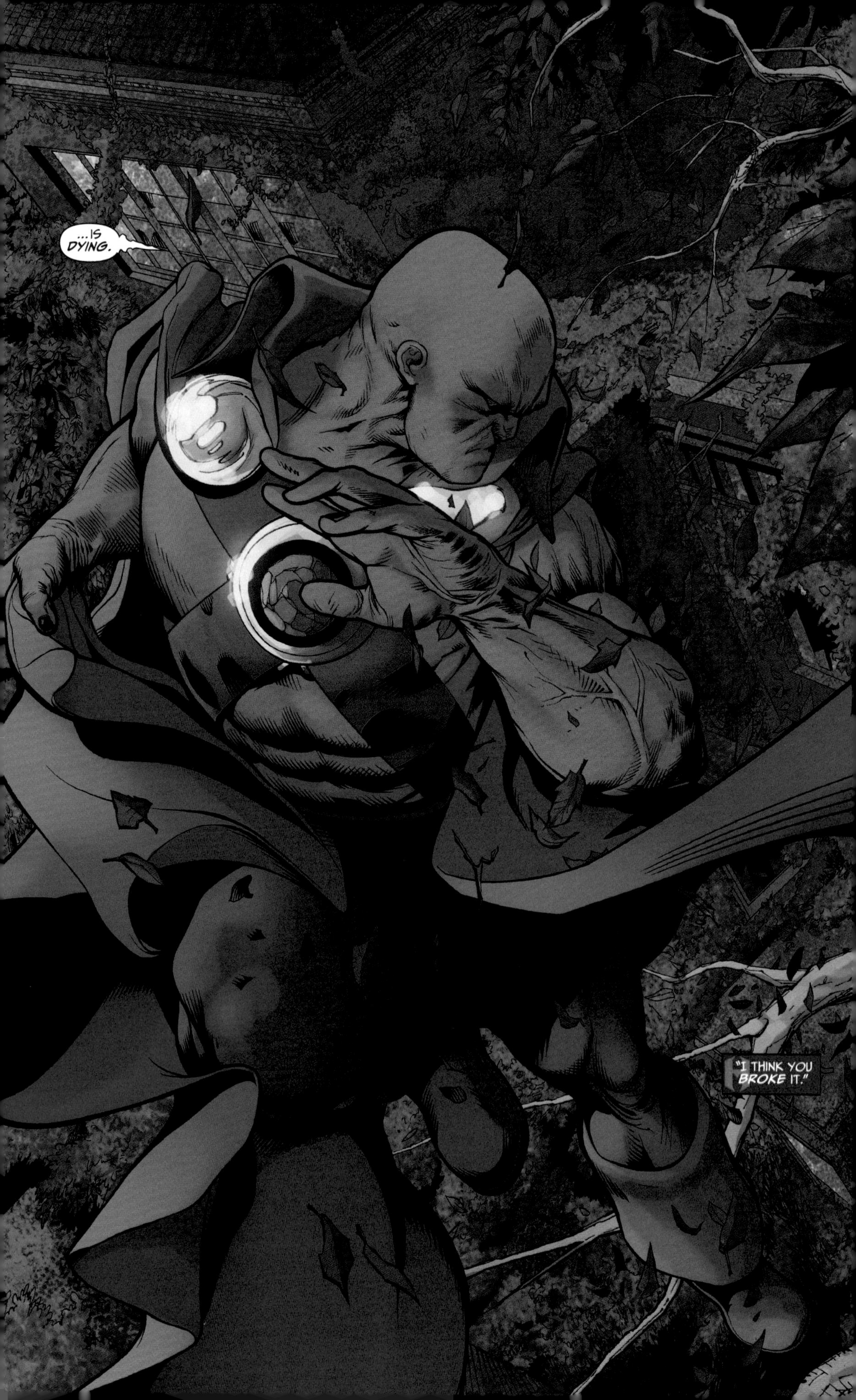
...IS DYING.
"I THINK YOU BROKE IT."

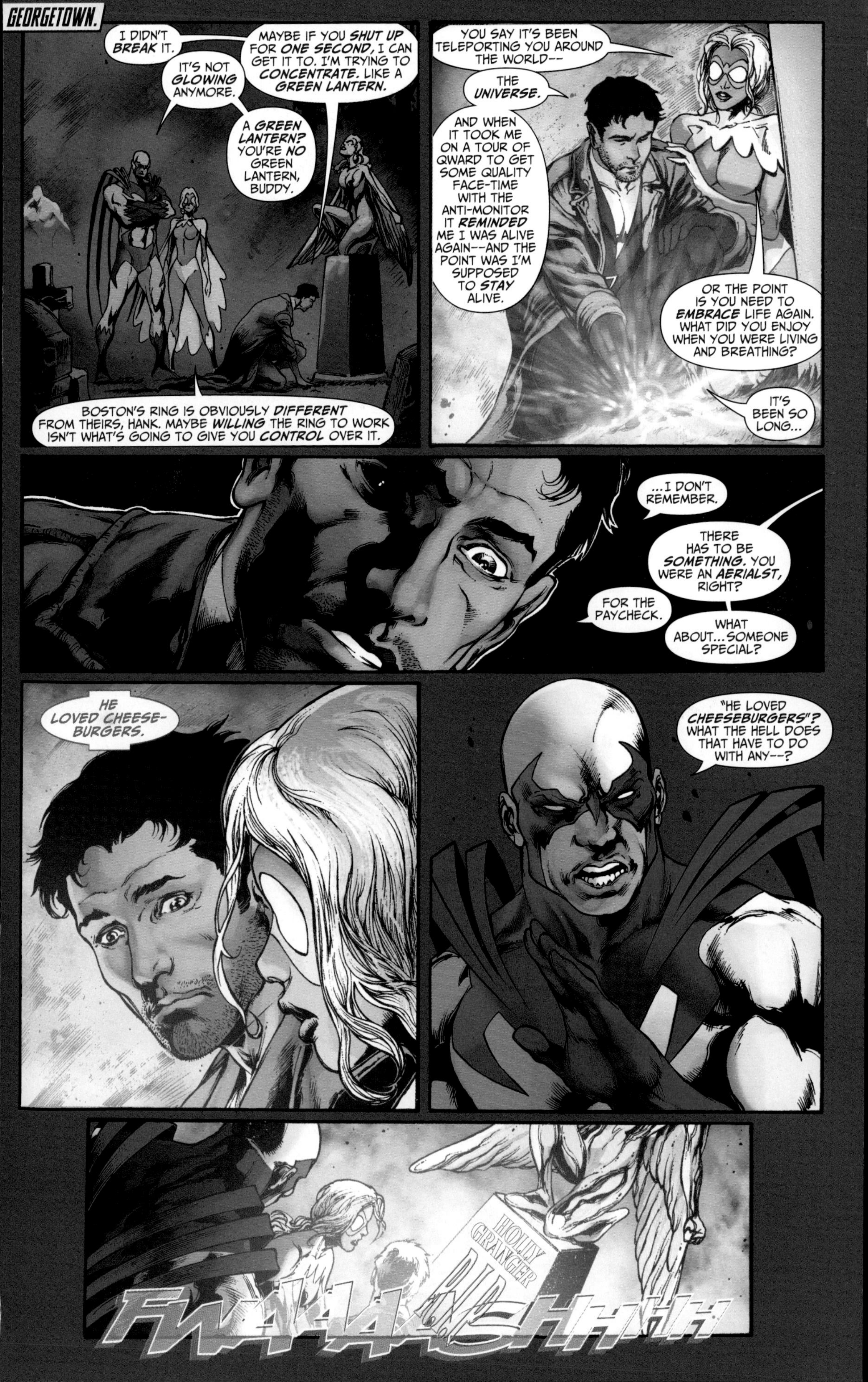
GEORGETOWN.
I DIDN'T BREAK IT.
IT'S NOT GLOWING ANYMORE.
MAYBE IF YOU SHUT UP FOR ONE SECOND, I CAN GET IT TO. I'M TRYING TO CONCENTRATE. LIKE A GREEN LANTERN.
A GREEN LANTERN? YOU'RE NO GREEN LANTERN, BUDDY.
BOSTON'S RING IS OBVIOUSLY DIFFERENT FROM THEIRS, HANK. MAYBE WILLING THE RING TO WORK ISN'T WHAT'S GOING TO GIVE YOU CONTROL OVER IT.
YOU SAY IT'S BEEN TELEPORTING YOU AROUND THE WORLD--
THE UNIVERSE.
AND WHEN IT TOOK ME ON A TOUR OF QWARD TO GET SOME QUALITY FACE-TIME WITH THE ANTI-MONITOR IT REMINDED ME I WAS ALIVE AGAIN--AND THE POINT WAS I'M SUPPOSED TO STAY ALIVE.
OR THE POINT IS YOU NEED TO EMBRACE LIFE AGAIN. WHAT DID YOU ENJOY WHEN YOU WERE LIVING AND BREATHING?
IT'S BEEN SO LONG...
...I DON'T REMEMBER.
THERE HAS TO BE SOMETHING. YOU WERE AN AERIALST, RIGHT?
FOR THE PAYCHECK.
WHAT ABOUT...SOMEONE SPECIAL?
HE LOVED CHEESE-BURGERS.
"HE LOVED CHEESEBURGERS"? WHAT THE HELL DOES THAT HAVE TO DO WITH ANY--?
HOLLY GRANGER
FWAAAASHHHH

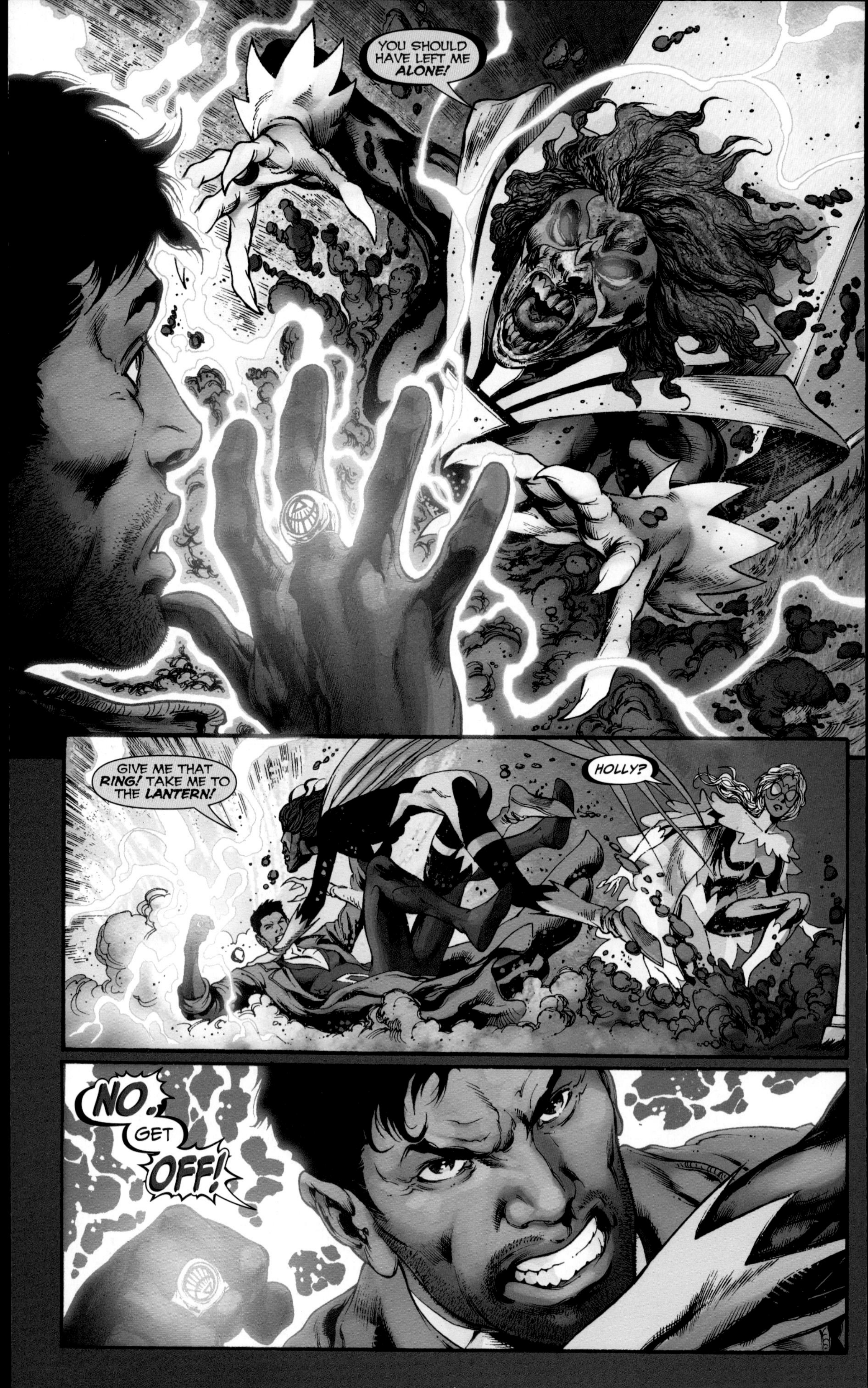
YOU SHOULD HAVE LEFT ME ALONE!
GIVE ME THAT RING! TAKE ME TO THE LANTERN!
HOLLY?
NO. GET OFF!

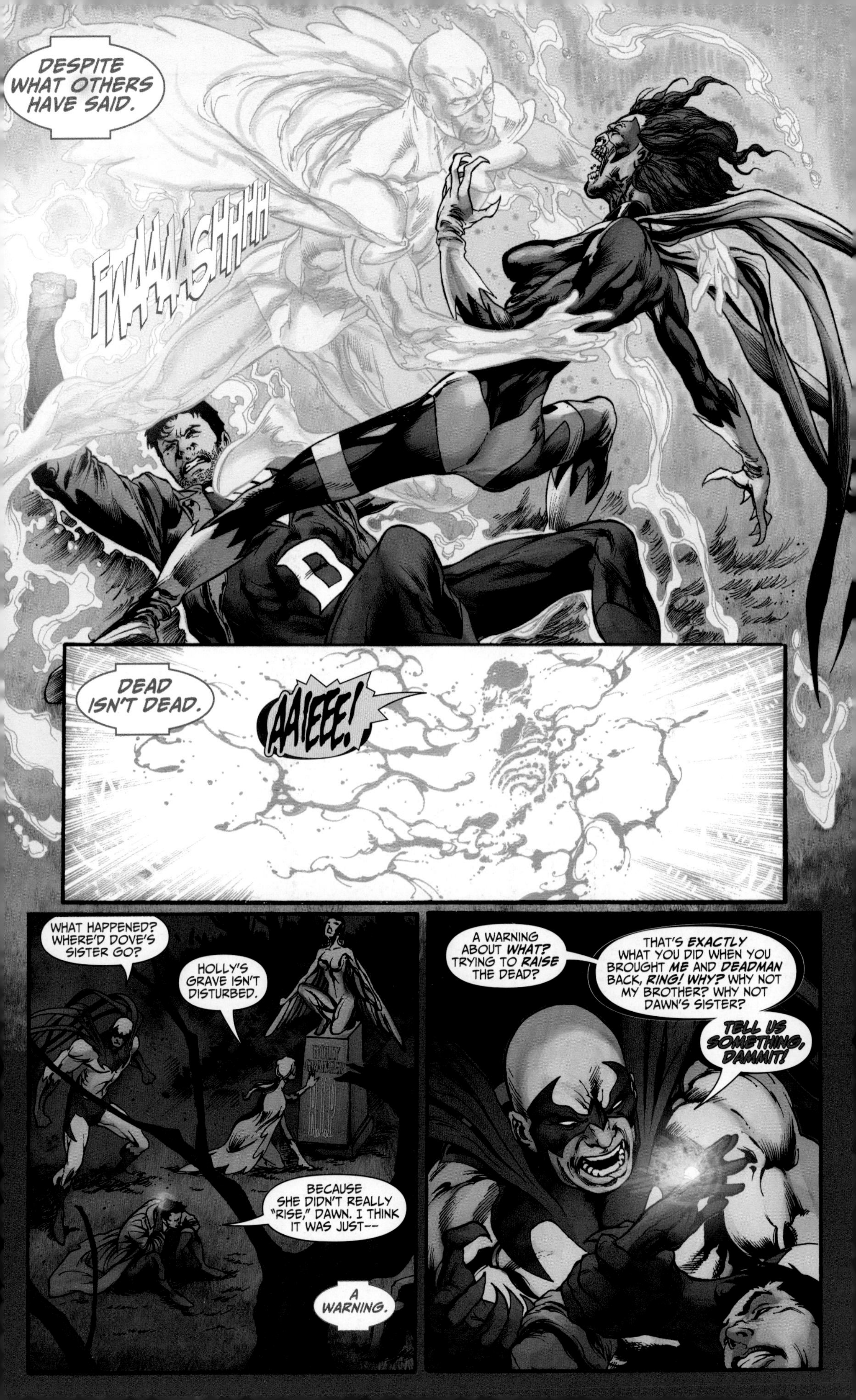
DESPITE WHAT OTHERS HAVE SAID.
FWAAAASHHHH
DEAD ISN'T DEAD.
AAIEEE!
WHAT HAPPENED? WHERE'D DOVE'S SISTER GO?
HOLLY'S GRAVE ISN'T DISTURBED.
BECAUSE SHE DIDN'T REALLY "RISE," DAWN. I THINK IT WAS JUST--
A WARNING.
A WARNING ABOUT WHAT? TRYING TO RAISE THE DEAD?
THAT'S EXACTLY WHAT YOU DID WHEN YOU BROUGHT ME AND DEADMAN BACK, RING! WHY? WHY NOT MY BROTHER? WHY NOT DAWN'S SISTER?
TELL US SOMETHING, DAMMIT!

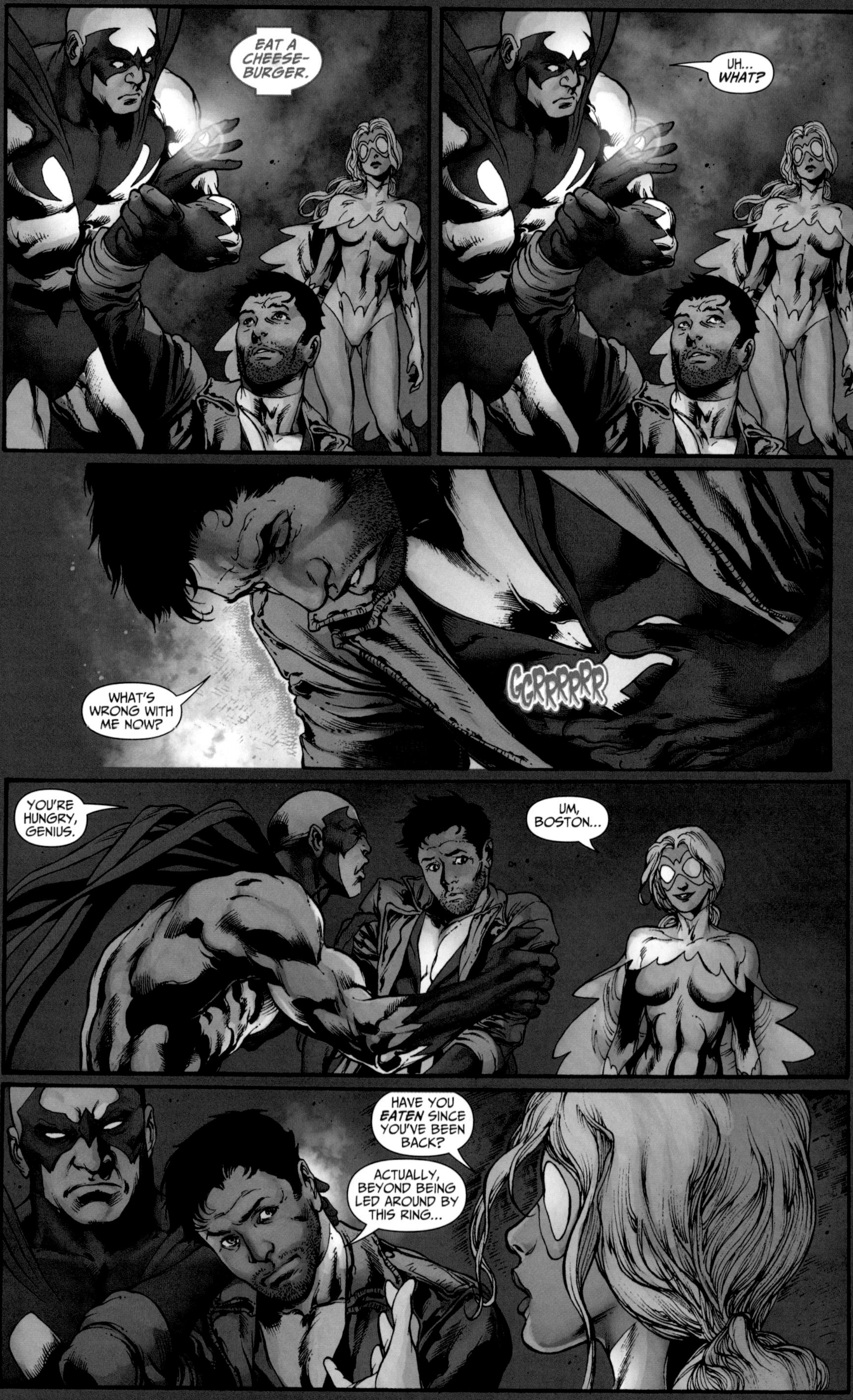
EAT A CHEESE-BURGER.
UH... WHAT?
WHAT'S WRONG WITH ME NOW?
GGRRRRRR
YOU'RE HUNGRY, GENIUS.
UM, BOSTON...
HAVE YOU EATEN SINCE YOU'VE BEEN BACK?
ACTUALLY, BEYOND BEING LED AROUND BY THIS RING...

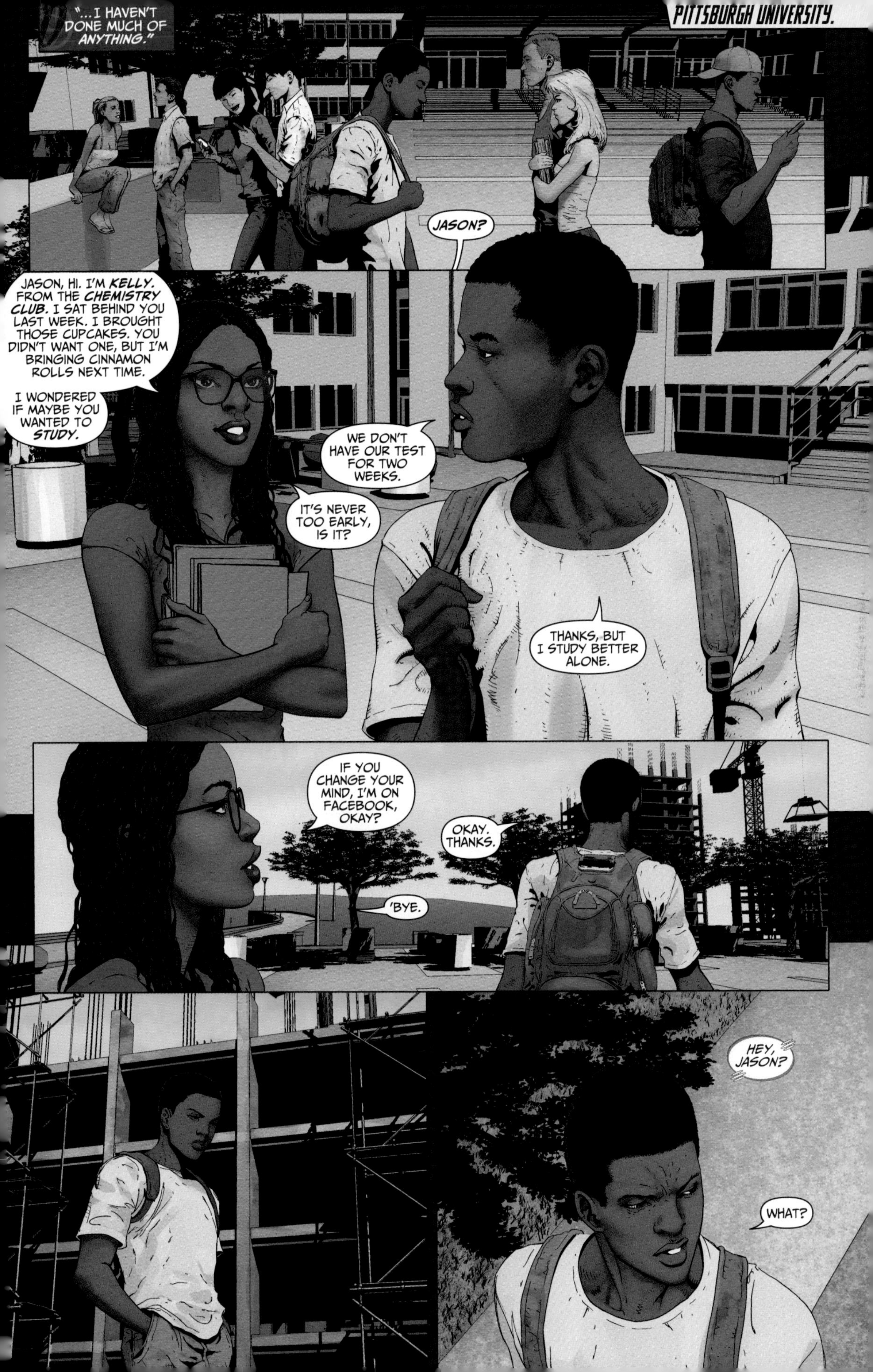
"...I HAVEN'T DONE MUCH OF ANYTHING."
PITTSBURGH UNIVERSITY.
JASON?
JASON, HI. I'M KELLY. FROM THE CHEMISTRY CLUB. I SAT BEHIND YOU LAST WEEK. I BROUGHT THOSE CUPCAKES. YOU DIDN'T WANT ONE, BUT I'M BRINGING CINNAMON ROLLS NEXT TIME.
I WONDERED IF MAYBE YOU WANTED TO STUDY.
WE DON'T HAVE OUR TEST FOR TWO WEEKS.
IT'S NEVER TOO EARLY, IS IT?
THANKS, BUT I STUDY BETTER ALONE.
IF YOU CHANGE YOUR MIND, I'M ON FACEBOOK, OKAY?
OKAY. THANKS.
'BYE.
HEY, JASON?
WHAT?

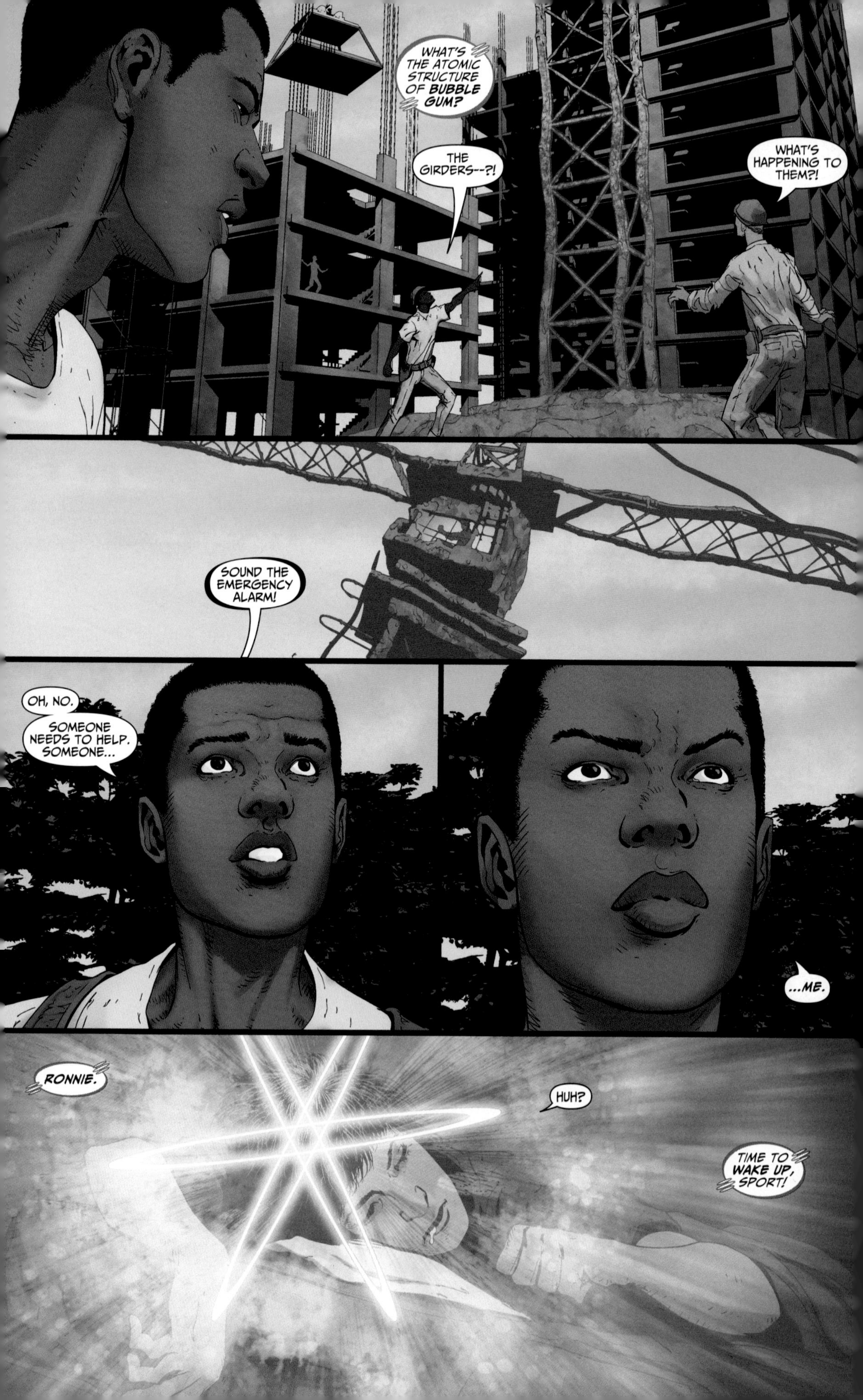
WHAT'S THE ATOMIC STRUCTURE OF BUBBLE GUM?
THE GIRDERS--?!
WHAT'S HAPPENING TO THEM?!
SOUND THE EMERGENCY ALARM!
OH, NO.
SOMEONE NEEDS TO HELP. SOMEONE...
...ME.
RONNIE.
HUH?
TIME TO WAKE UP, SPORT!

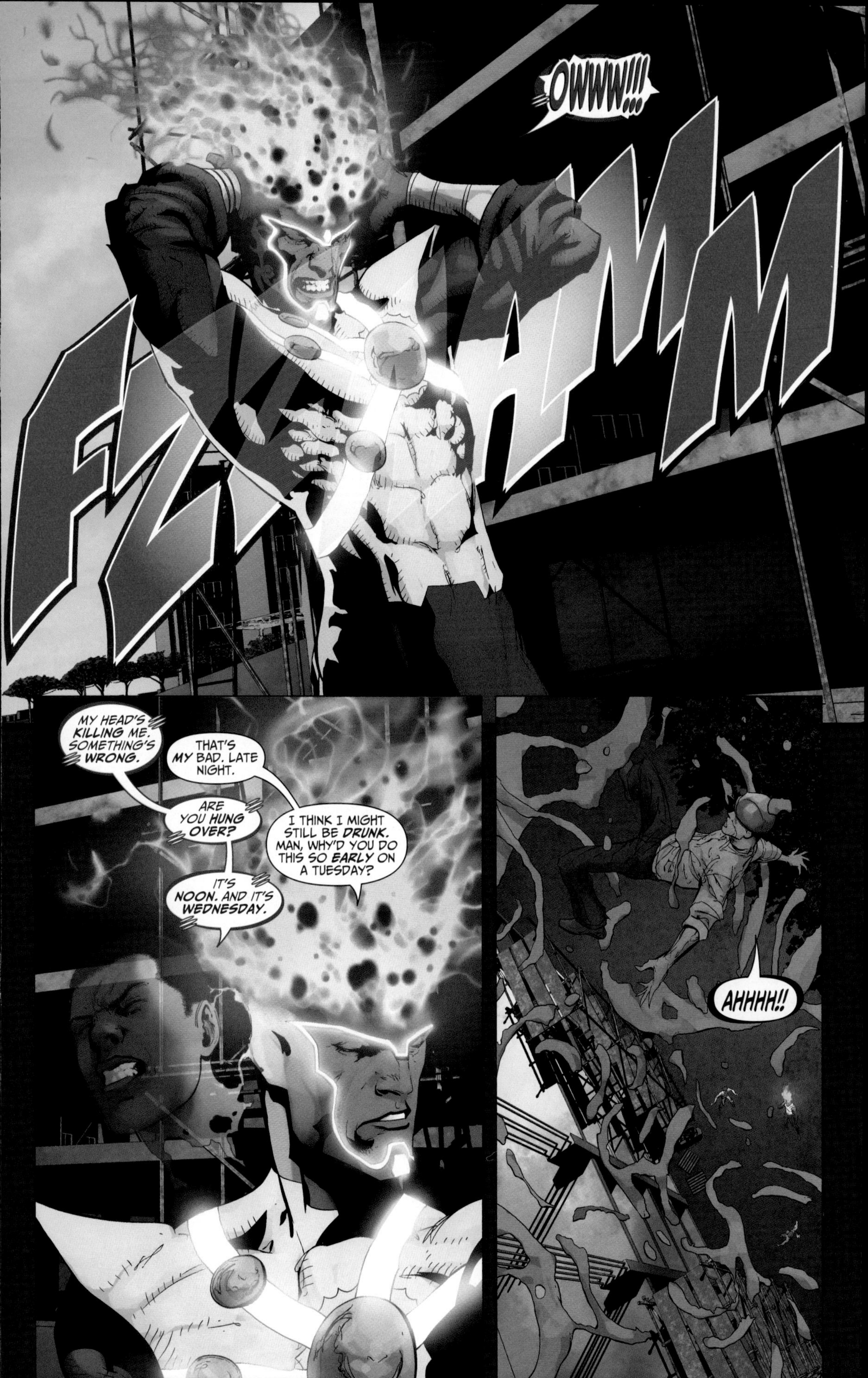
OWWW!!!
FZZAMM
MY HEAD'S KILLING ME. SOMETHING'S WRONG.
THAT'S MY BAD. LATE NIGHT.
ARE YOU HUNG OVER?
I THINK I MIGHT STILL BE DRUNK. MAN, WHY'D YOU DO THIS SO EARLY ON A TUESDAY?
IT'S NOON. AND IT'S WEDNESDAY.
AHHHH!!

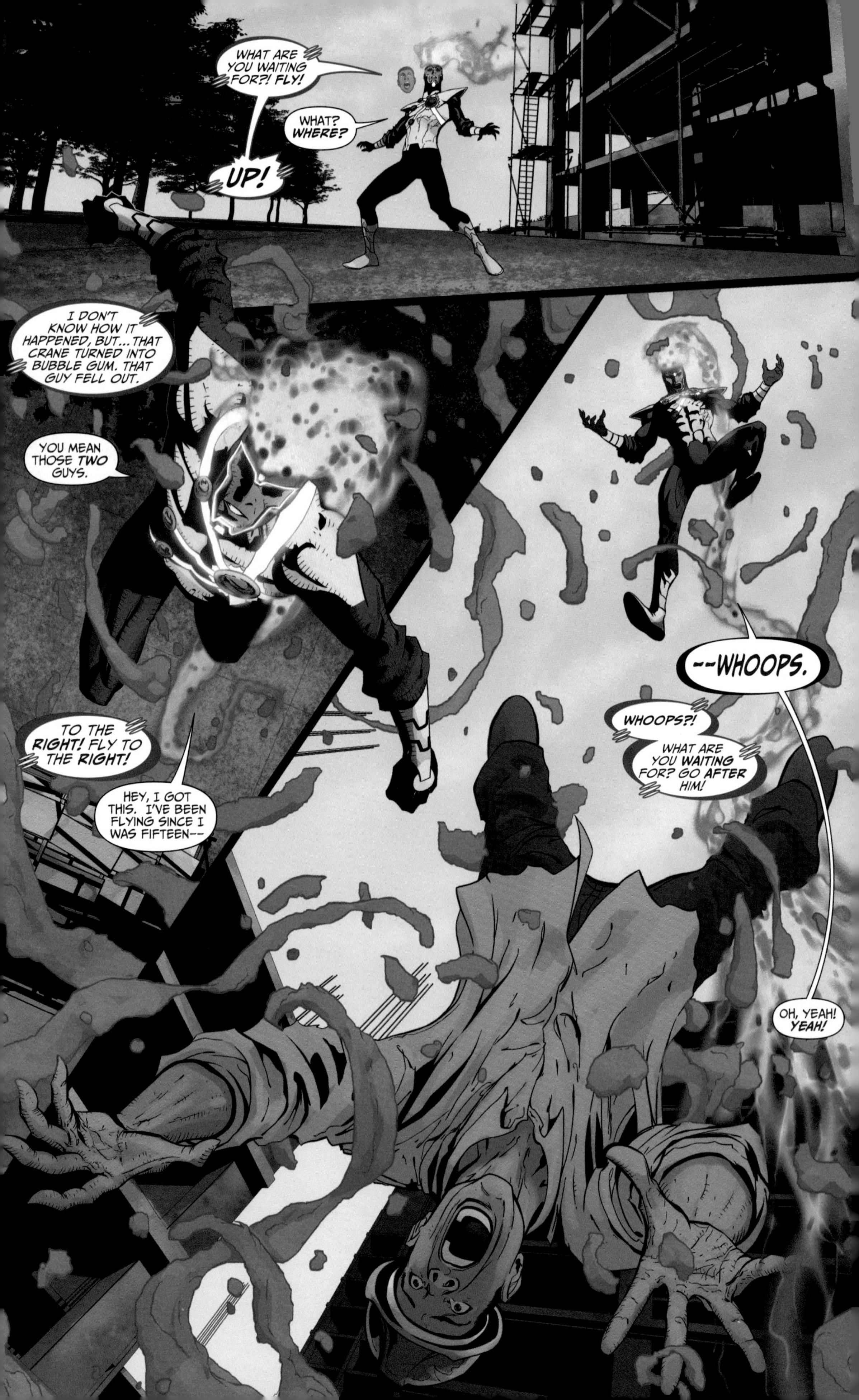
WHAT ARE YOU WAITING FOR?! FLY!
WHAT? WHERE?
UP!
I DON'T KNOW HOW IT HAPPENED, BUT... THAT CRANE TURNED INTO BUBBLE GUM. THAT GUY FELL OUT.
YOU MEAN THOSE TWO GUYS.
TO THE RIGHT! FLY TO THE RIGHT!
HEY, I GOT THIS. I'VE BEEN FLYING SINCE I WAS FIFTEEN--
--WHOOPS.
WHOOPS?!
WHAT ARE YOU WAITING FOR? GO AFTER HIM!
OH, YEAH! YEAH!

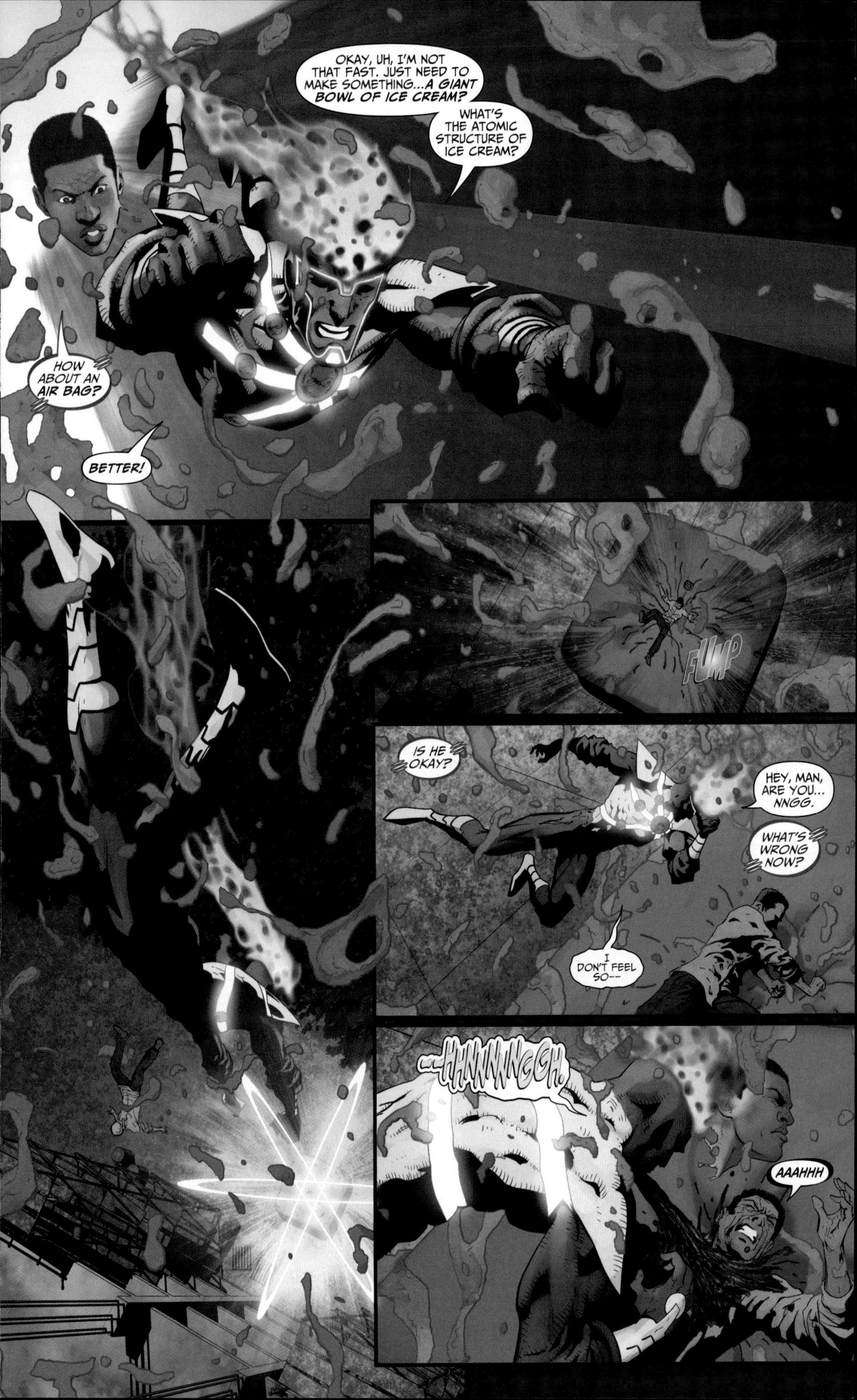
OKAY, UH, I'M NOT THAT FAST. JUST NEED TO MAKE SOMETHING...A GIANT BOWL OF ICE CREAM?
WHAT'S THE ATOMIC STRUCTURE OF ICE CREAM?
HOW ABOUT AN AIR BAG?
BETTER!
FUMP
IS HE OKAY?
HEY, MAN, ARE YOU... NNGG.
WHAT'S WRONG NOW?
I DON'T FEEL SO--
--HHNNNNGGH.
AAAHHH

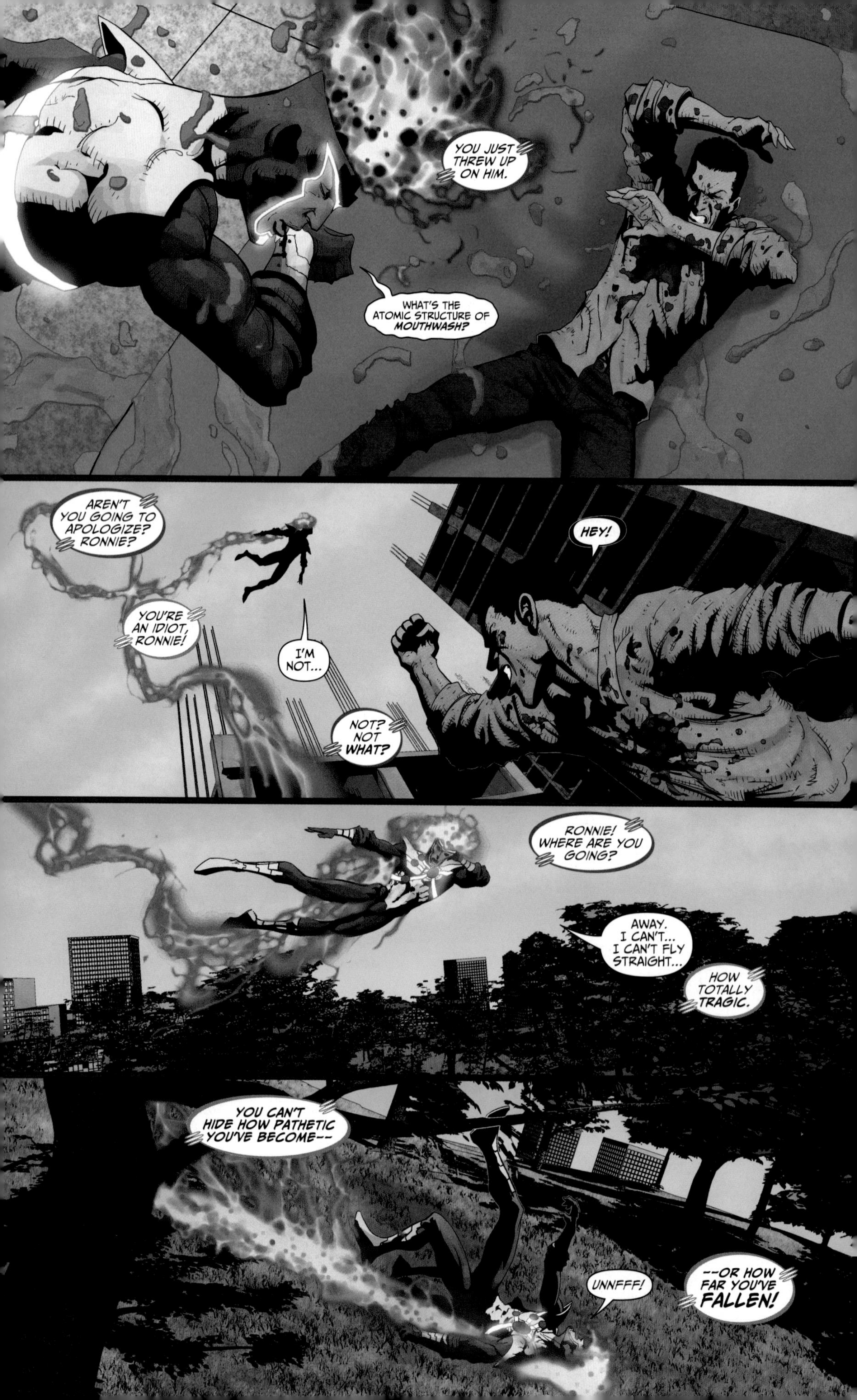
YOU JUST THREW UP ON HIM.
WHAT'S THE ATOMIC STRUCTURE OF MOUTHWASH?
AREN'T YOU GOING TO APOLOGIZE? RONNIE?
HEY!
YOU'RE AN IDIOT, RONNIE!
I'M NOT...
NOT? NOT WHAT?
RONNIE! WHERE ARE YOU GOING?
AWAY. I CAN'T... I CAN'T FLY STRAIGHT...
HOW TOTALLY TRAGIC.
YOU CAN'T HIDE HOW PATHETIC YOU'VE BECOME--
UNNFFF!
--OR HOW FAR YOU'VE FALLEN!

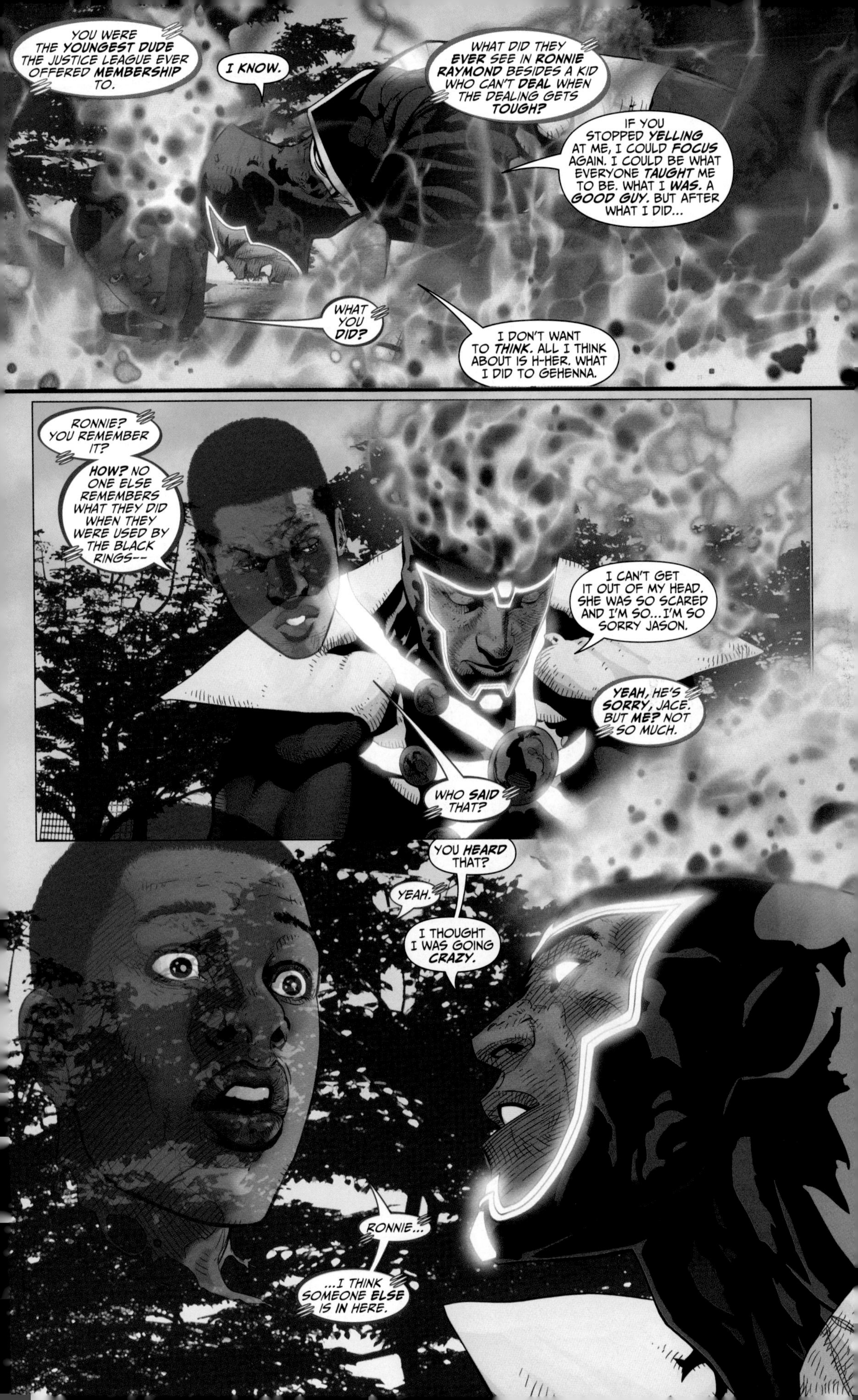
YOU WERE THE YOUNGEST DUDE THE JUSTICE LEAGUE EVER OFFERED MEMBERSHIP TO.
I KNOW.
WHAT DID THEY EVER SEE IN RONNIE RAYMOND BESIDES A KID WHO CAN'T DEAL WHEN THE DEALING GETS TOUGH?
IF YOU STOPPED YELLING AT ME, I COULD FOCUS AGAIN. I COULD BE WHAT EVERYONE TAUGHT ME TO BE. WHAT I WAS. A GOOD GUY. BUT AFTER WHAT I DID...
WHAT YOU DID?
I DON'T WANT TO THINK. ALL I THINK ABOUT IS H-HER. WHAT I DID TO GEHENNA.
RONNIE? YOU REMEMBER IT?
HOW? NO ONE ELSE REMEMBERS WHAT THEY DID WHEN THEY WERE USED BY THE BLACK RINGS--
I CAN'T GET IT OUT OF MY HEAD. SHE WAS SO SCARED AND I'M SO...I'M SO SORRY JASON.
YEAH, HE'S SORRY, JACE. BUT ME? NOT SO MUCH.
WHO SAID THAT?
YOU HEARD THAT?
YEAH.
I THOUGHT I WAS GOING CRAZY.
RONNIE...
...I THINK SOMEONE ELSE IS IN HERE.

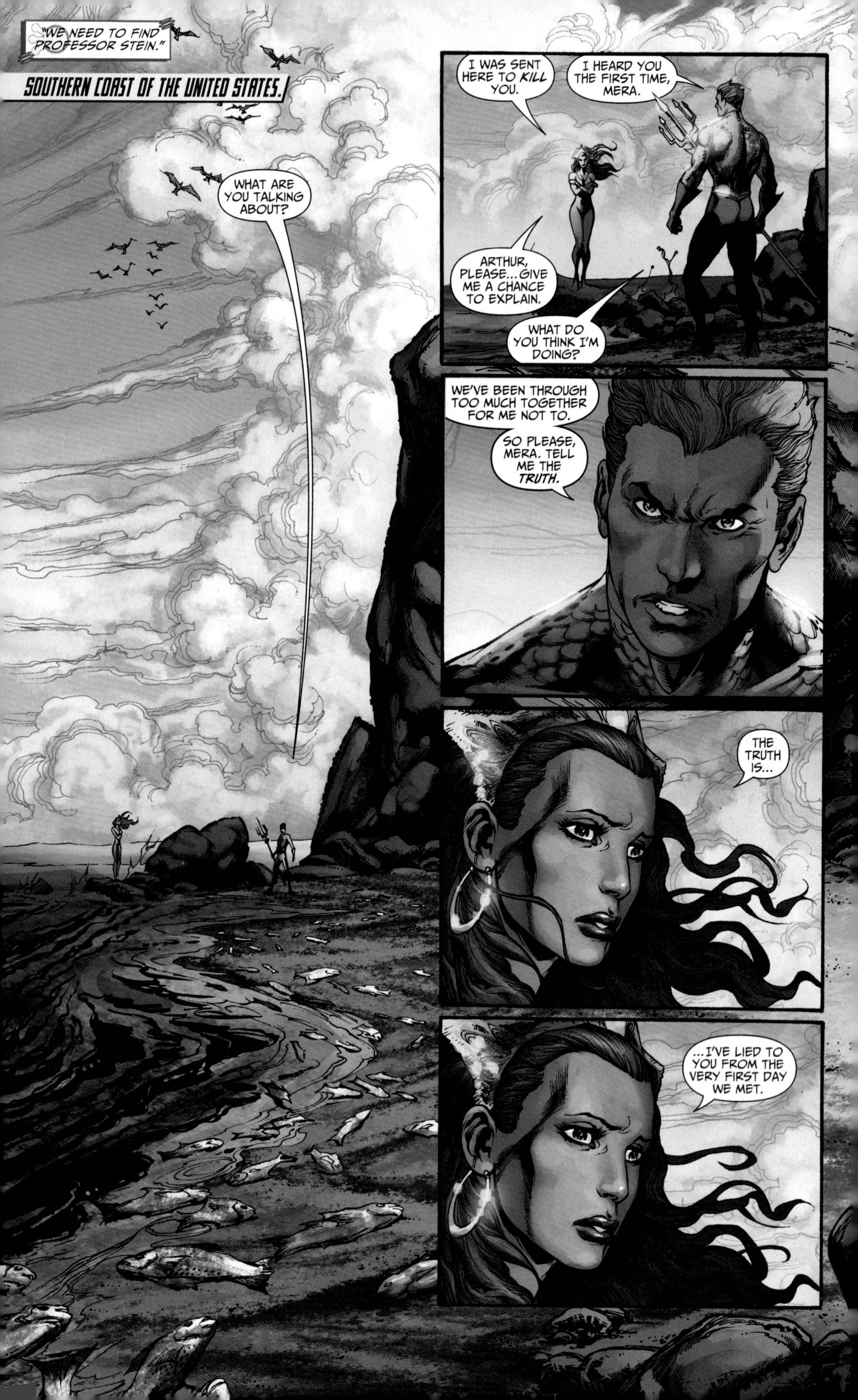
"WE NEED TO FIND PROFESSOR STEIN."
SOUTHERN COAST OF THE UNITED STATES.
WHAT ARE YOU TALKING ABOUT?
I WAS SENT HERE TO KILL YOU.
I HEARD YOU THE FIRST TIME, MERA.
ARTHUR, PLEASE...GIVE ME A CHANCE TO EXPLAIN.
WHAT DO YOU THINK I'M DOING?
WE'VE BEEN THROUGH TOO MUCH TOGETHER FOR ME NOT TO.
SO PLEASE, MERA. TELL ME THE TRUTH.
THE TRUTH IS...
...I'VE LIED TO YOU FROM THE VERY FIRST DAY WE MET.

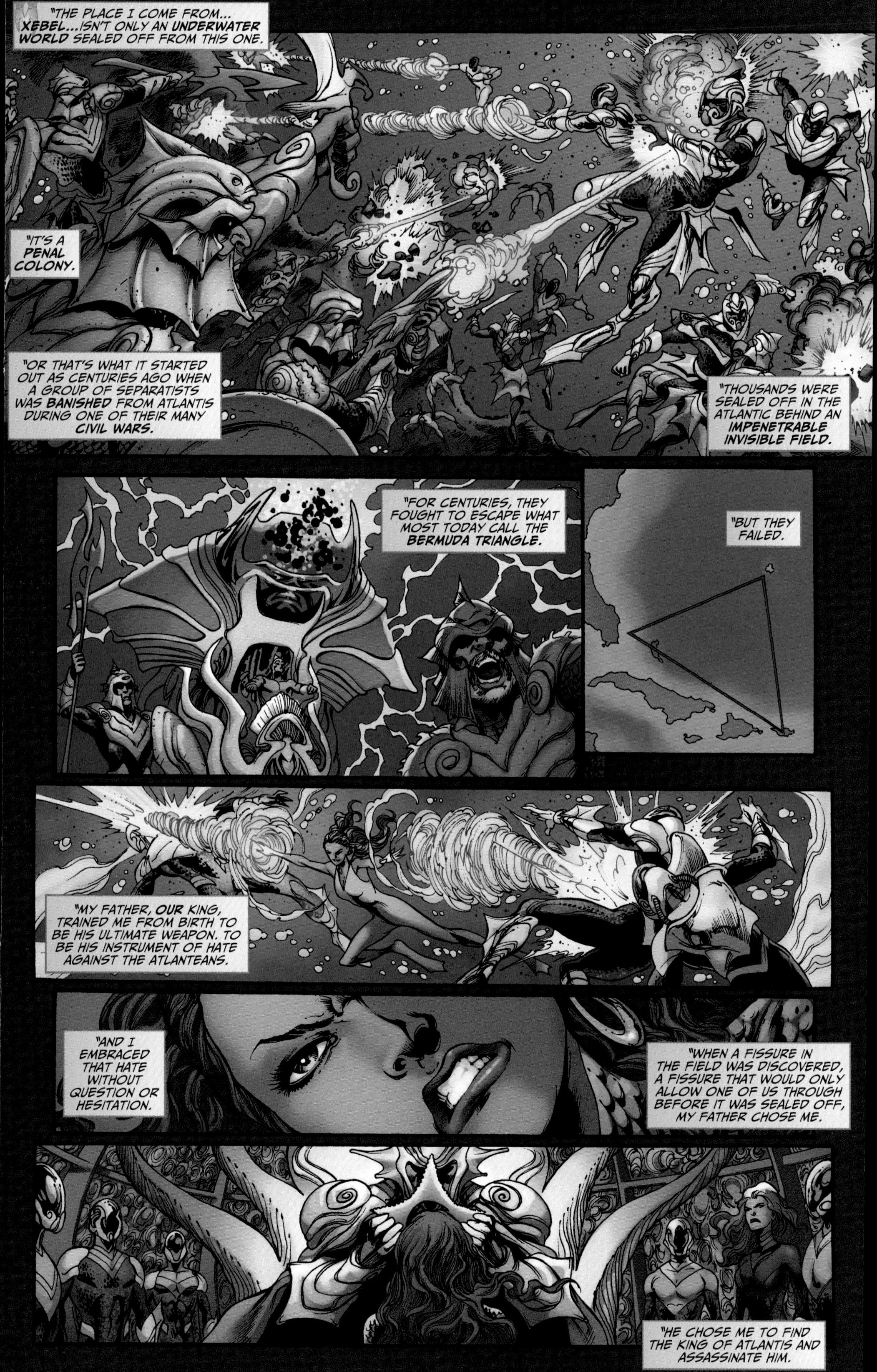

"THE PLACE I COME FROM... **XEBEL**...ISN'T ONLY AN **UNDERWATER WORLD** SEALED OFF FROM THIS ONE.
"IT'S A **PENAL COLONY**.
"OR THAT'S WHAT IT STARTED OUT AS CENTURIES AGO WHEN A GROUP OF SEPARATISTS WAS **BANISHED** FROM ATLANTIS DURING ONE OF THEIR MANY **CIVIL WARS**.
"THOUSANDS WERE SEALED OFF IN THE ATLANTIC BEHIND AN **IMPENETRABLE INVISIBLE FIELD**.
"FOR CENTURIES, THEY FOUGHT TO ESCAPE WHAT MOST TODAY CALL THE **BERMUDA TRIANGLE**.
"BUT THEY FAILED.
"MY FATHER, **OUR** KING, TRAINED ME FROM BIRTH TO BE HIS ULTIMATE WEAPON. TO BE HIS INSTRUMENT OF HATE AGAINST THE ATLANTEANS.
"AND I EMBRACED THAT HATE WITHOUT QUESTION OR HESITATION.
"WHEN A FISSURE IN THE FIELD WAS DISCOVERED, A FISSURE THAT WOULD ONLY ALLOW ONE OF US THROUGH BEFORE IT WAS SEALED OFF, MY FATHER CHOSE ME.
"HE CHOSE ME TO FIND THE KING OF ATLANTIS AND ASSASSINATE HIM.

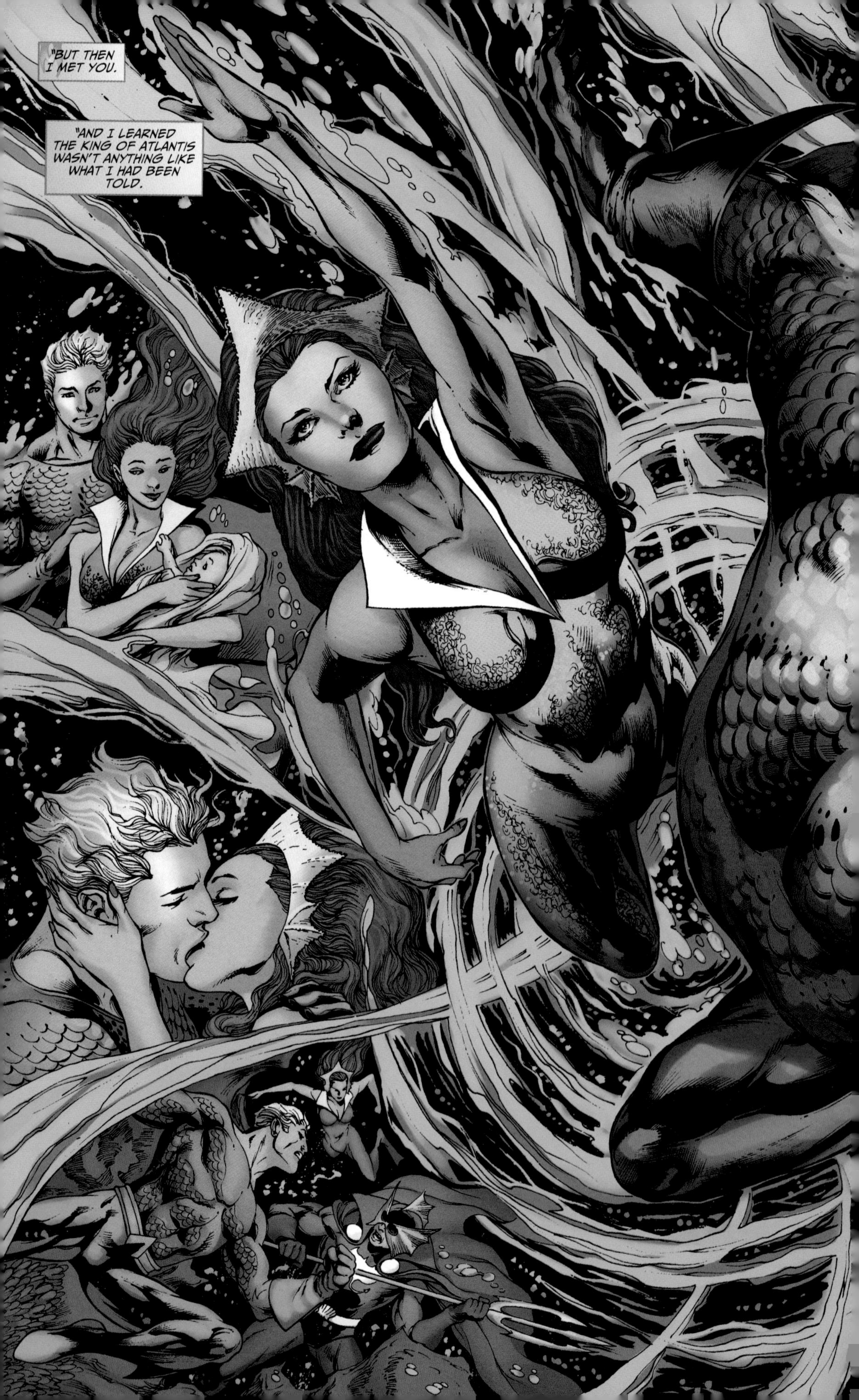
"BUT THEN I MET YOU.
"AND I LEARNED THE KING OF ATLANTIS WASN'T ANYTHING LIKE WHAT I HAD BEEN TOLD.

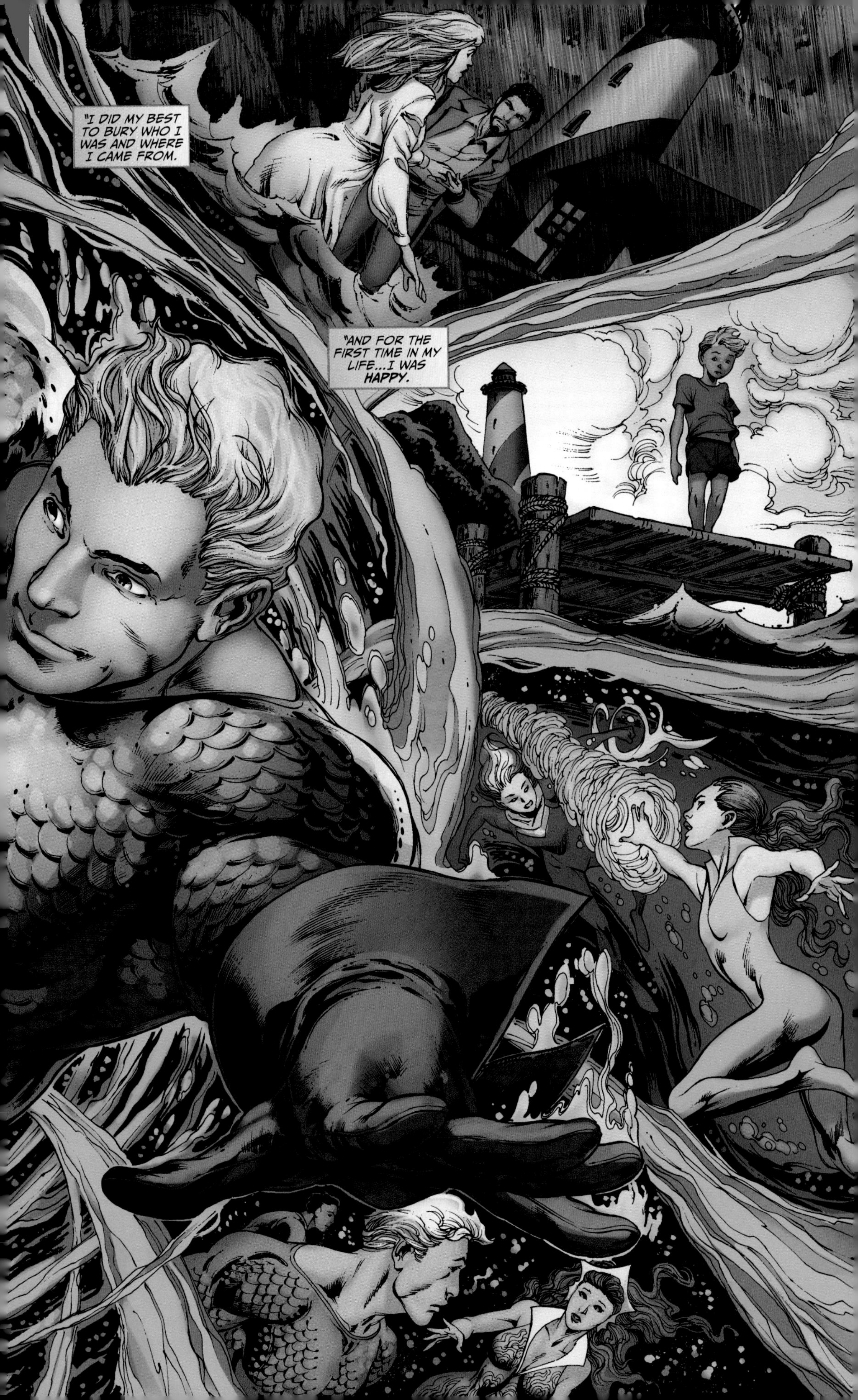
"I DID MY BEST TO BURY WHO I WAS AND WHERE I CAME FROM.
"AND FOR THE FIRST TIME IN MY LIFE...I WAS HAPPY.

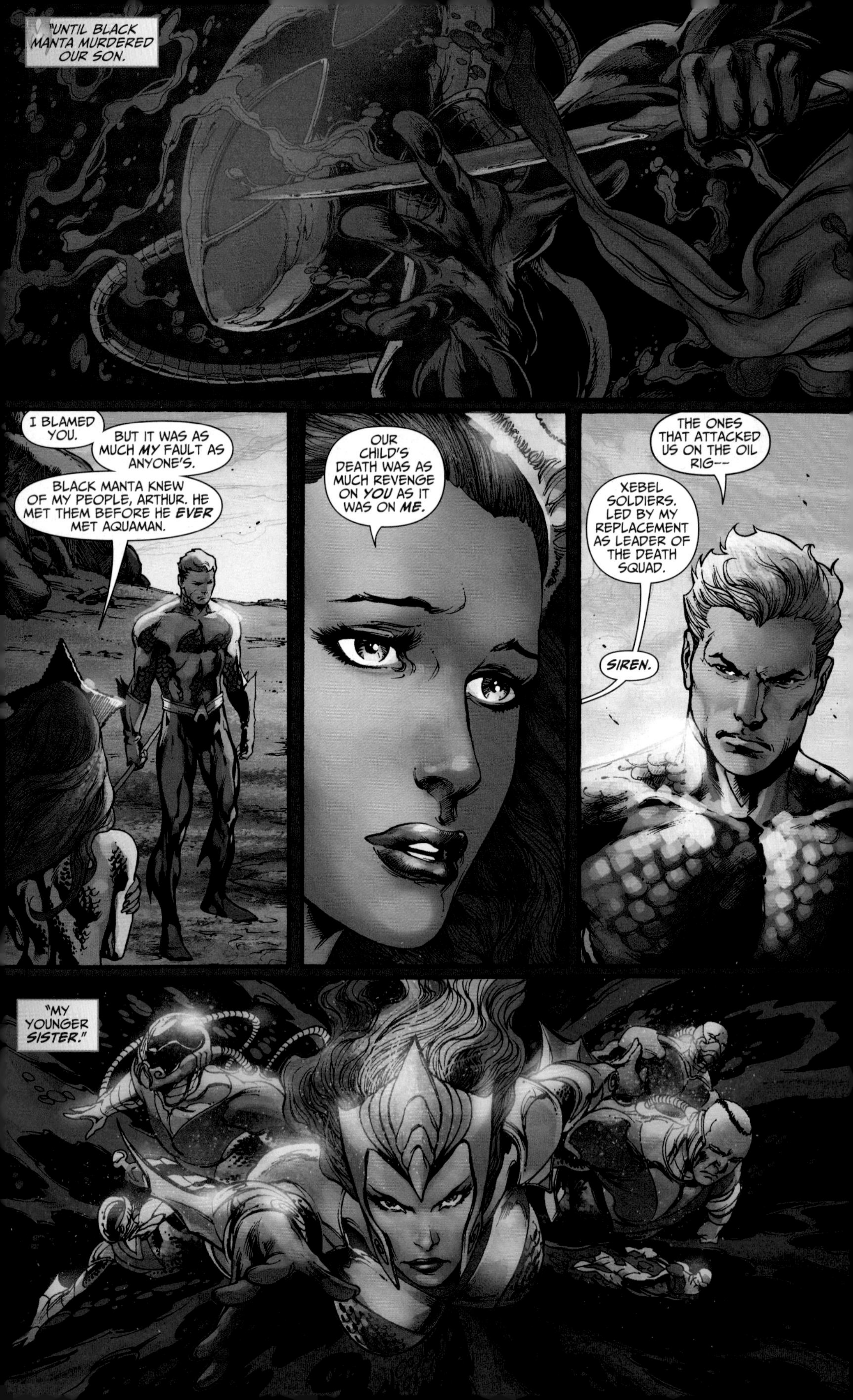
"UNTIL BLACK MANTA MURDERED OUR SON.
I BLAMED YOU.
BUT IT WAS AS MUCH MY FAULT AS ANYONE'S.
BLACK MANTA KNEW OF MY PEOPLE, ARTHUR. HE MET THEM BEFORE HE EVER MET AQUAMAN.
OUR CHILD'S DEATH WAS AS MUCH REVENGE ON YOU AS IT WAS ON ME.
THE ONES THAT ATTACKED US ON THE OIL RIG--
XEBEL SOLDIERS. LED BY MY REPLACEMENT AS LEADER OF THE DEATH SQUAD.
SIREN.
"MY YOUNGER SISTER."

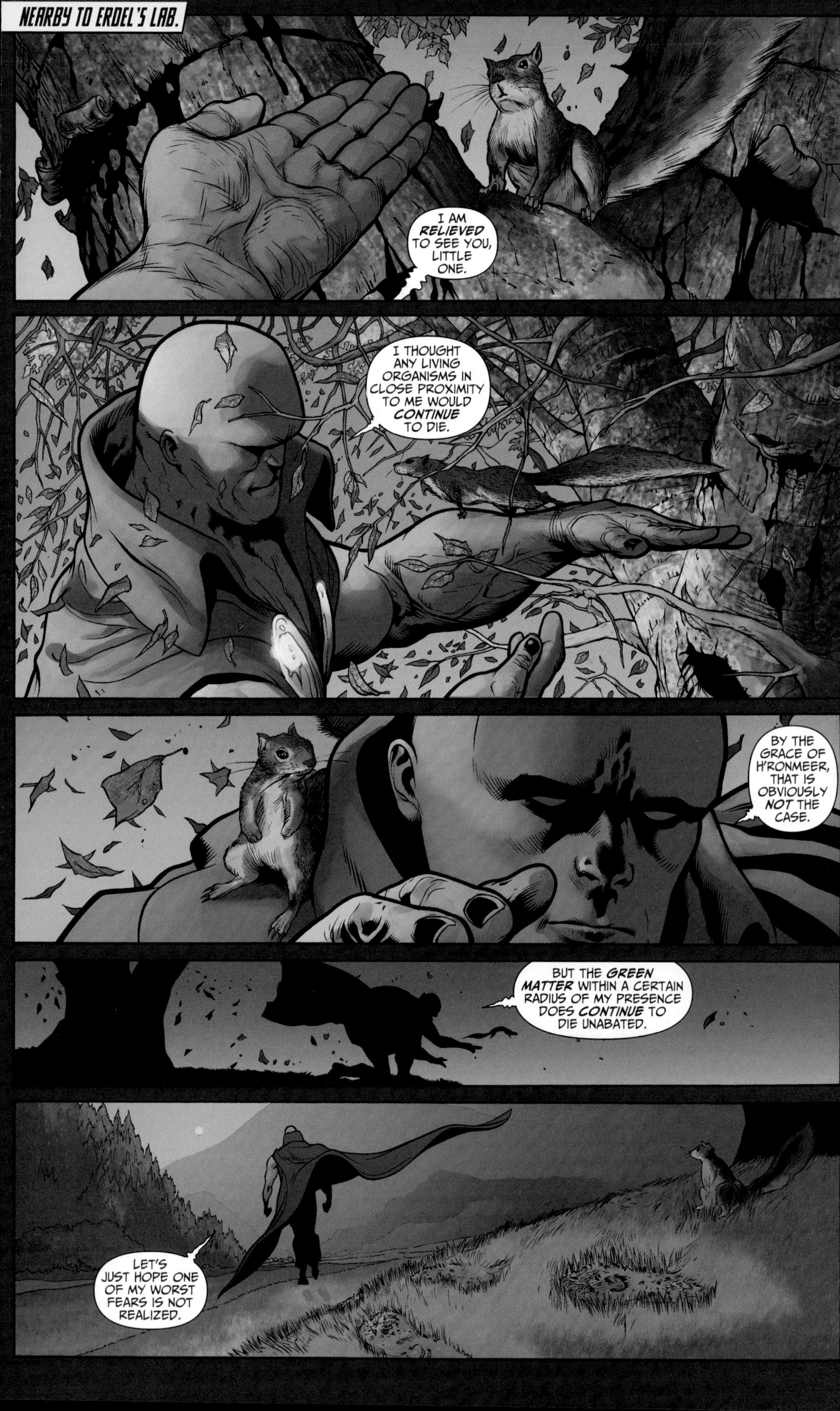
NEARBY TO ERDEL'S LAB.
I AM RELIEVED TO SEE YOU, LITTLE ONE.
I THOUGHT ANY LIVING ORGANISMS IN CLOSE PROXIMITY TO ME WOULD CONTINUE TO DIE.
BY THE GRACE OF H'RONMEER, THAT IS OBVIOUSLY NOT THE CASE.
BUT THE GREEN MATTER WITHIN A CERTAIN RADIUS OF MY PRESENCE DOES CONTINUE TO DIE UNABATED.
LET'S JUST HOPE ONE OF MY WORST FEARS IS NOT REALIZED.

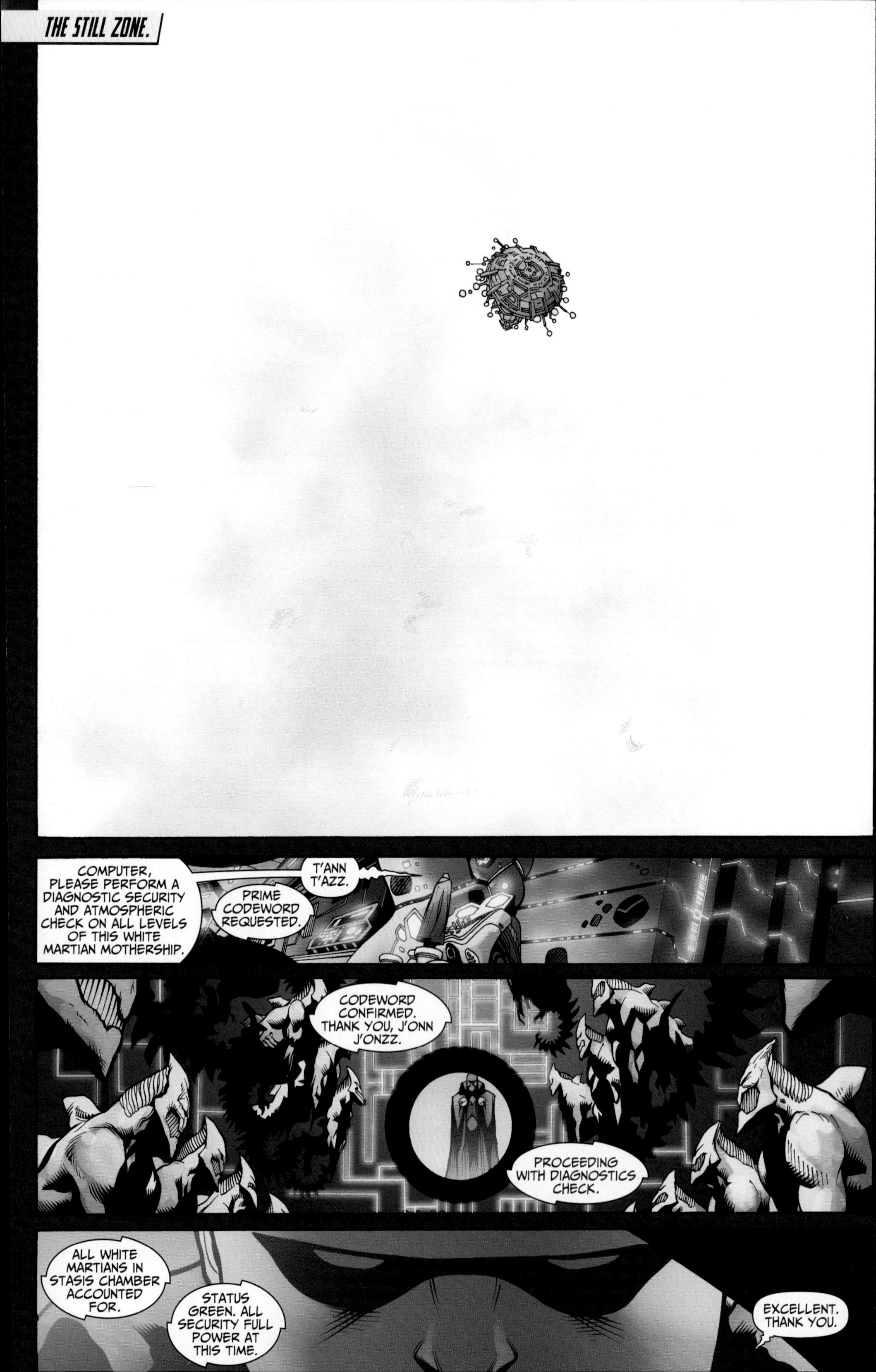
THE STILL ZONE.
COMPUTER, PLEASE PERFORM A DIAGNOSTIC SECURITY AND ATMOSPHERIC CHECK ON ALL LEVELS OF THIS WHITE MARTIAN MOTHERSHIP.
PRIME CODEWORD REQUESTED.
T'ANN T'AZZ.
CODEWORD CONFIRMED. THANK YOU, J'ONN J'ONZZ.
PROCEEDING WITH DIAGNOSTICS CHECK.
ALL WHITE MARTIANS IN STASIS CHAMBER ACCOUNTED FOR.
STATUS GREEN. ALL SECURITY FULL POWER AT THIS TIME.
EXCELLENT. THANK YOU.

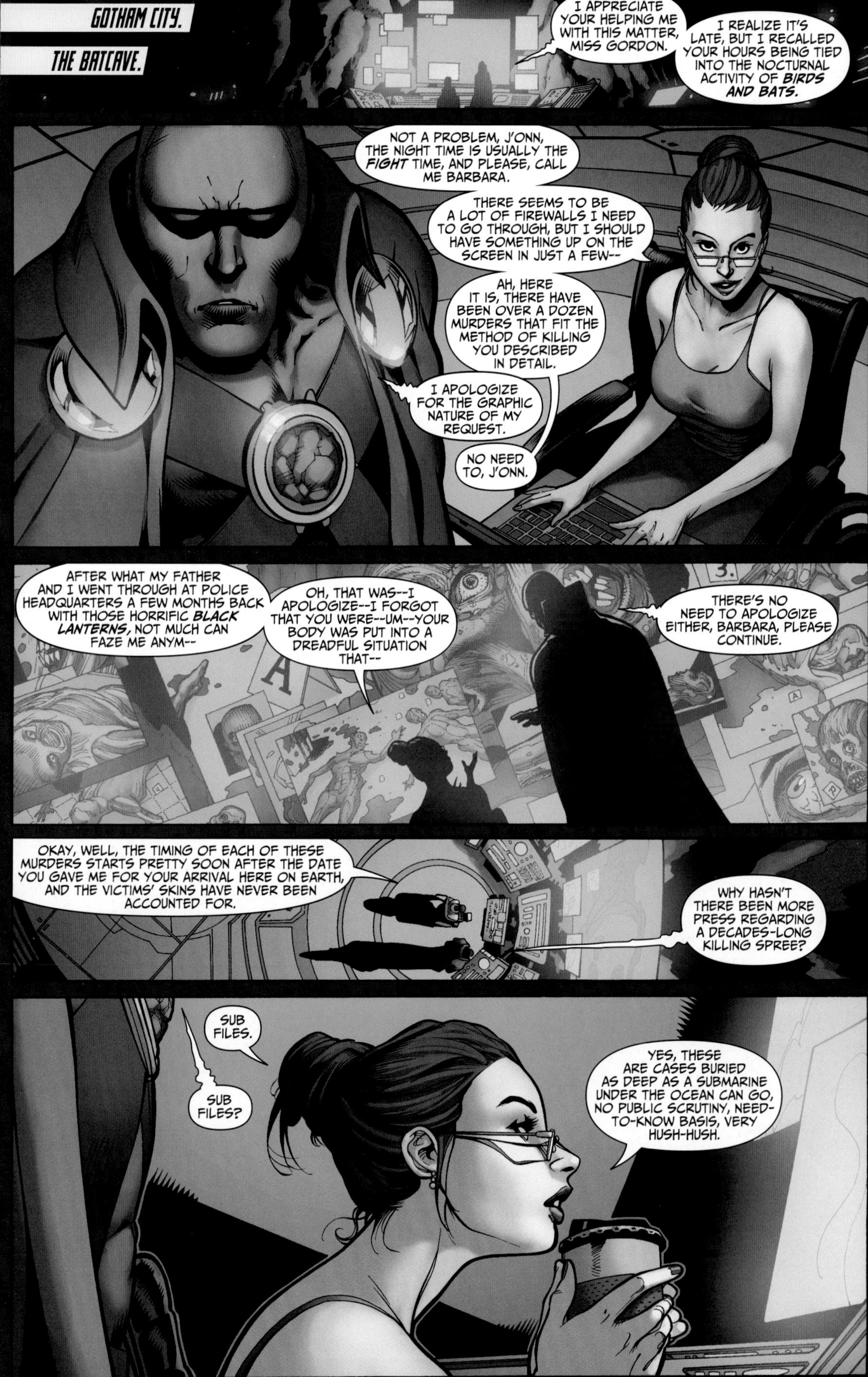
GOTHAM CITY.
THE BATCAVE.
I APPRECIATE YOUR HELPING ME WITH THIS MATTER, MISS GORDON.
I REALIZE IT'S LATE, BUT I RECALLED YOUR HOURS BEING TIED INTO THE NOCTURNAL ACTIVITY OF BIRDS AND BATS.
NOT A PROBLEM, J'ONN, THE NIGHT TIME IS USUALLY THE FIGHT TIME, AND PLEASE, CALL ME BARBARA.
THERE SEEMS TO BE A LOT OF FIREWALLS I NEED TO GO THROUGH, BUT I SHOULD HAVE SOMETHING UP ON THE SCREEN IN JUST A FEW--
AH, HERE IT IS, THERE HAVE BEEN OVER A DOZEN MURDERS THAT FIT THE METHOD OF KILLING YOU DESCRIBED IN DETAIL.
I APOLOGIZE FOR THE GRAPHIC NATURE OF MY REQUEST.
NO NEED TO, J'ONN.
AFTER WHAT MY FATHER AND I WENT THROUGH AT POLICE HEADQUARTERS A FEW MONTHS BACK WITH THOSE HORRIFIC BLACK LANTERNS, NOT MUCH CAN FAZE ME ANYM--
OH, THAT WAS--I APOLOGIZE--I FORGOT THAT YOU WERE--UM--YOUR BODY WAS PUT INTO A DREADFUL SITUATION THAT--
THERE'S NO NEED TO APOLOGIZE EITHER, BARBARA, PLEASE CONTINUE.
OKAY, WELL, THE TIMING OF EACH OF THESE MURDERS STARTS PRETTY SOON AFTER THE DATE YOU GAVE ME FOR YOUR ARRIVAL HERE ON EARTH, AND THE VICTIMS' SKINS HAVE NEVER BEEN ACCOUNTED FOR.
WHY HASN'T THERE BEEN MORE PRESS REGARDING A DECADES-LONG KILLING SPREE?
SUB FILES.
SUB FILES?
YES, THESE ARE CASES BURIED AS DEEP AS A SUBMARINE UNDER THE OCEAN CAN GO, NO PUBLIC SCRUTINY, NEED-TO-KNOW BASIS, VERY HUSH-HUSH.

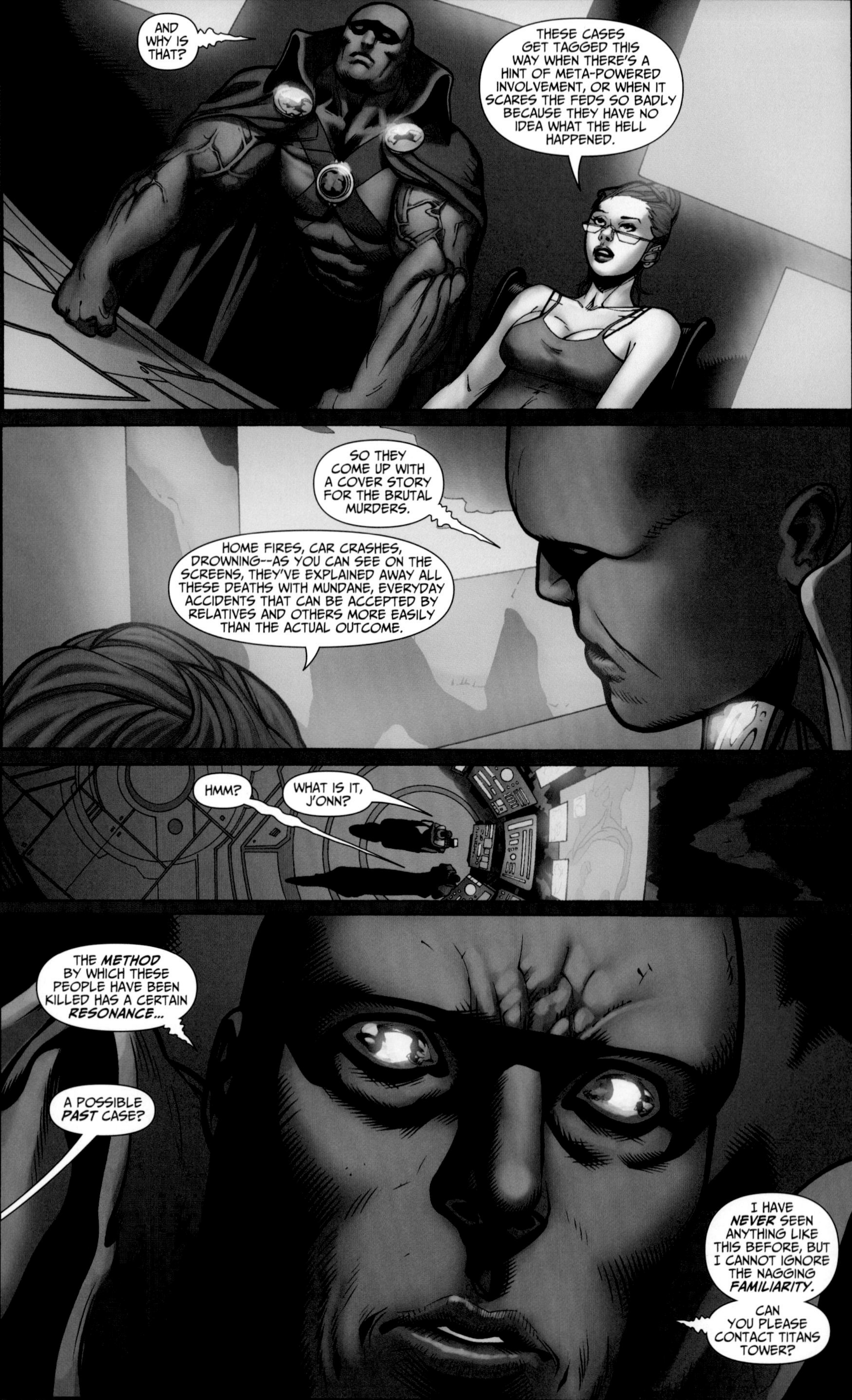

AND WHY IS THAT?
THESE CASES GET TAGGED THIS WAY WHEN THERE'S A HINT OF META-POWERED INVOLVEMENT, OR WHEN IT SCARES THE FEDS SO BADLY BECAUSE THEY HAVE NO IDEA WHAT THE HELL HAPPENED.
SO THEY COME UP WITH A COVER STORY FOR THE BRUTAL MURDERS.
HOME FIRES, CAR CRASHES, DROWNING--AS YOU CAN SEE ON THE SCREENS, THEY'VE EXPLAINED AWAY ALL THESE DEATHS WITH MUNDANE, EVERYDAY ACCIDENTS THAT CAN BE ACCEPTED BY RELATIVES AND OTHERS MORE EASILY THAN THE ACTUAL OUTCOME.
HMM?
WHAT IS IT, J'ONN?
THE *METHOD* BY WHICH THESE PEOPLE HAVE BEEN KILLED HAS A CERTAIN *RESONANCE*...
A POSSIBLE *PAST* CASE?
I HAVE *NEVER* SEEN ANYTHING LIKE THIS BEFORE, BUT I CANNOT IGNORE THE NAGGING *FAMILIARITY.*
CAN YOU PLEASE CONTACT TITANS TOWER?

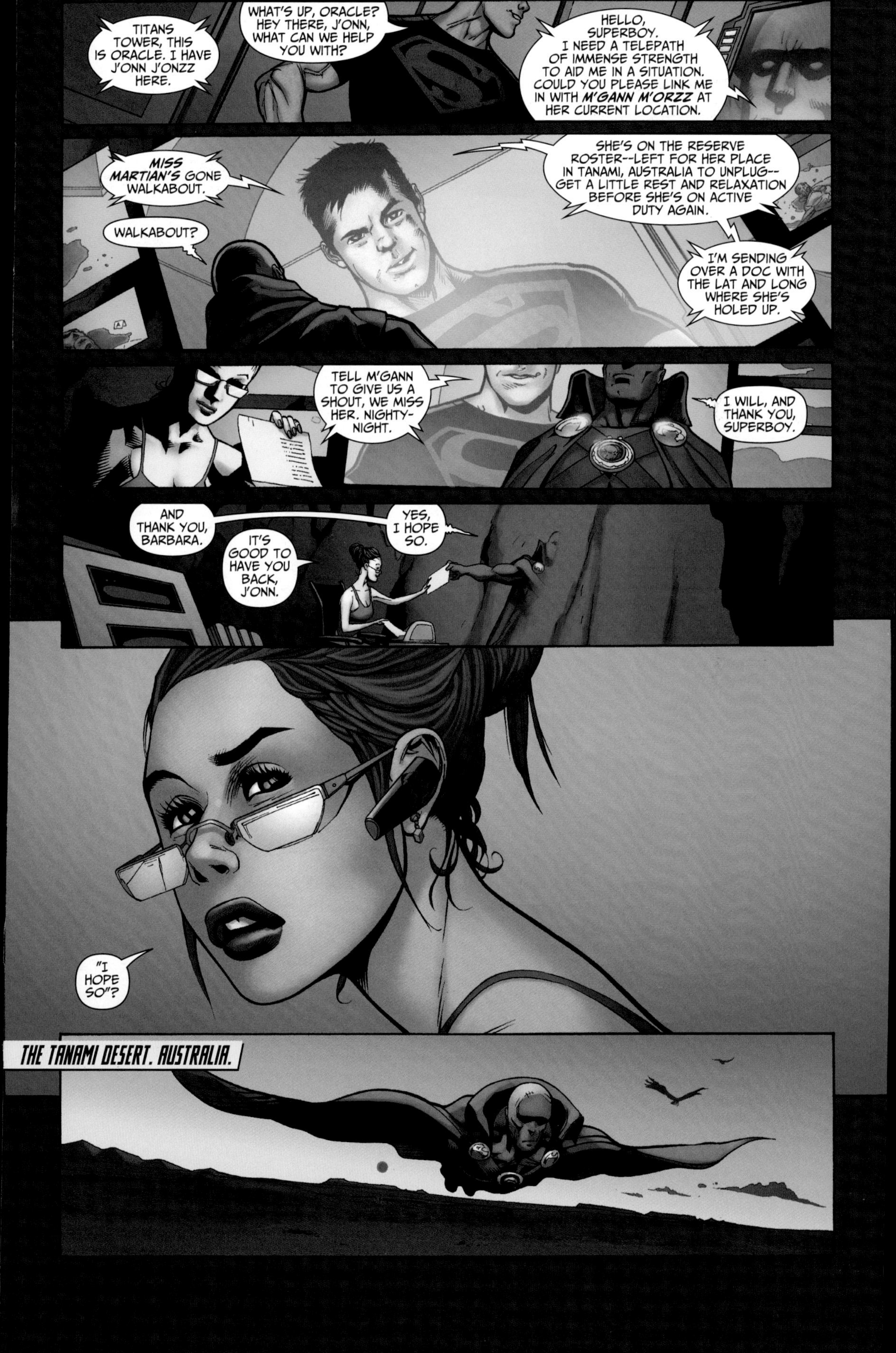
TITANS TOWER, THIS IS ORACLE. I HAVE J'ONN J'ONZZ HERE.
WHAT'S UP, ORACLE? HEY THERE, J'ONN, WHAT CAN WE HELP YOU WITH?
HELLO, SUPERBOY. I NEED A TELEPATH OF IMMENSE STRENGTH TO AID ME IN A SITUATION. COULD YOU PLEASE LINK ME IN WITH M'GANN M'ORZZ AT HER CURRENT LOCATION.
MISS MARTIAN'S GONE WALKABOUT.
WALKABOUT?
SHE'S ON THE RESERVE ROSTER--LEFT FOR HER PLACE IN TANAMI, AUSTRALIA TO UNPLUG--GET A LITTLE REST AND RELAXATION BEFORE SHE'S ON ACTIVE DUTY AGAIN.
I'M SENDING OVER A DOC WITH THE LAT AND LONG WHERE SHE'S HOLED UP.
TELL M'GANN TO GIVE US A SHOUT, WE MISS HER. NIGHTY-NIGHT.
I WILL, AND THANK YOU, SUPERBOY.
AND THANK YOU, BARBARA.
IT'S GOOD TO HAVE YOU BACK, J'ONN.
YES, I HOPE SO.
"I HOPE SO"?
THE TANAMI DESERT. AUSTRALIA.

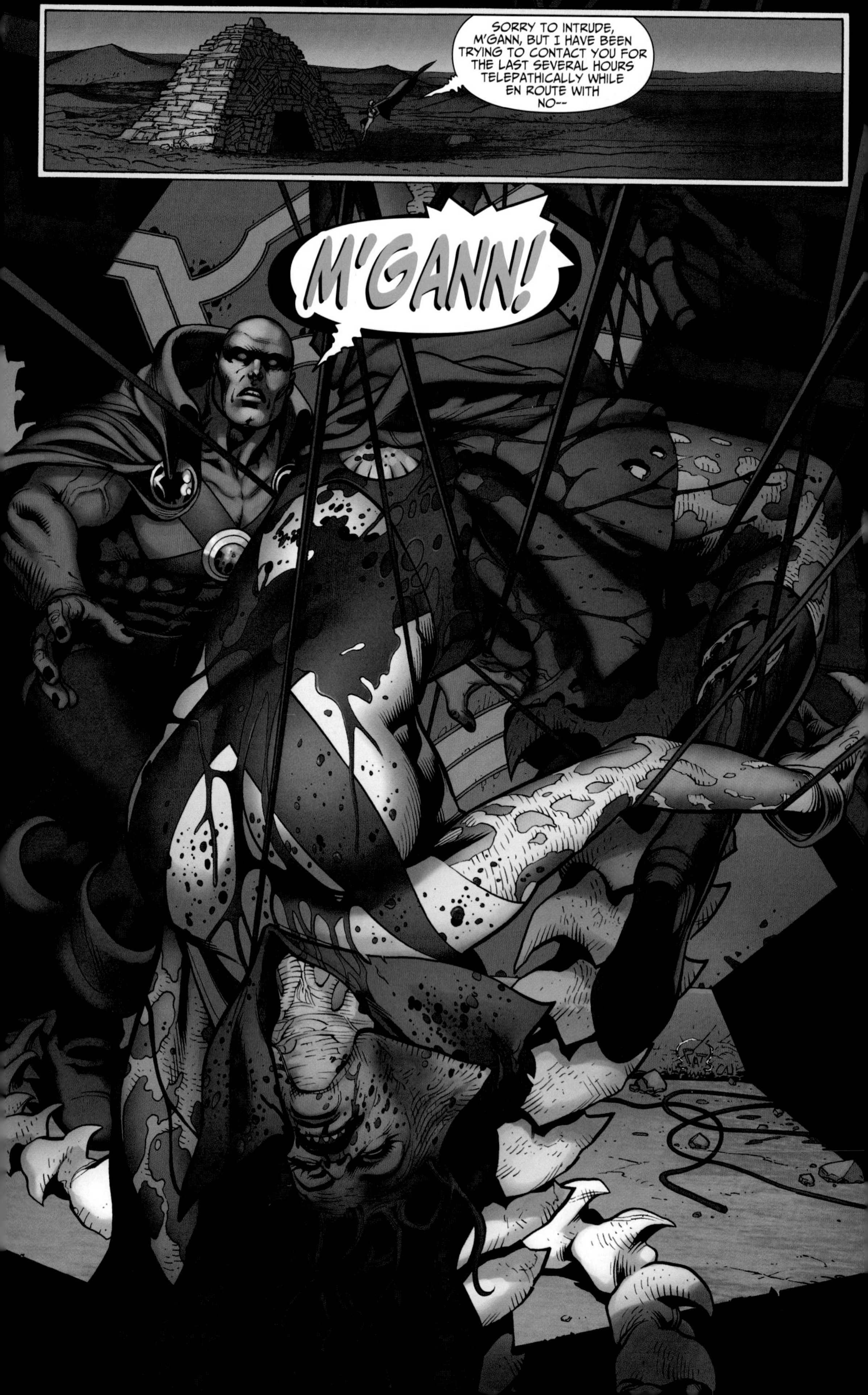
SORRY TO INTRUDE, M'GANN, BUT I HAVE BEEN TRYING TO CONTACT YOU FOR THE LAST SEVERAL HOURS TELEPATHICALLY WHILE EN ROUTE WITH NO--
M'GANN!

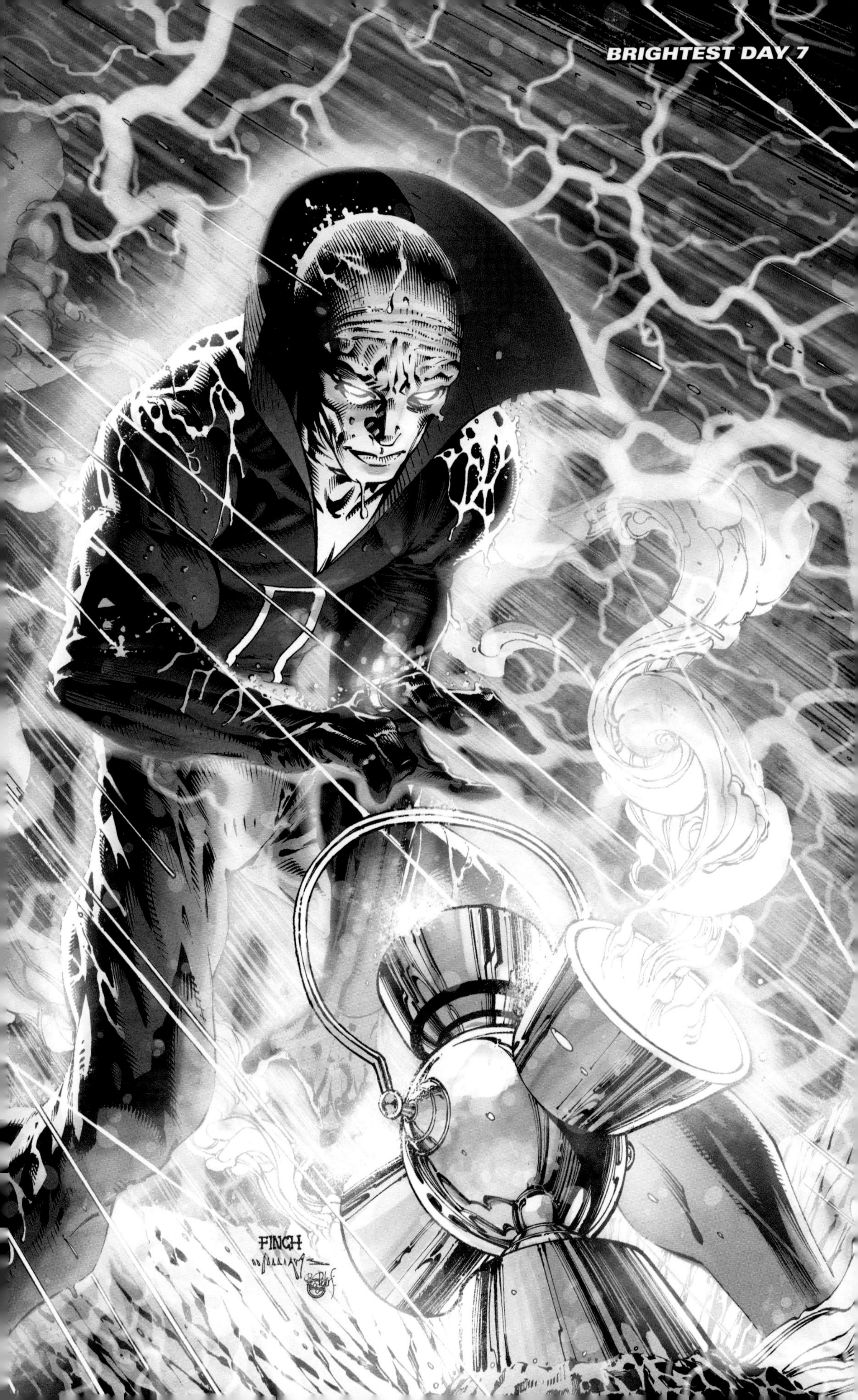
BRIGHTEST DAY 7
FINCH

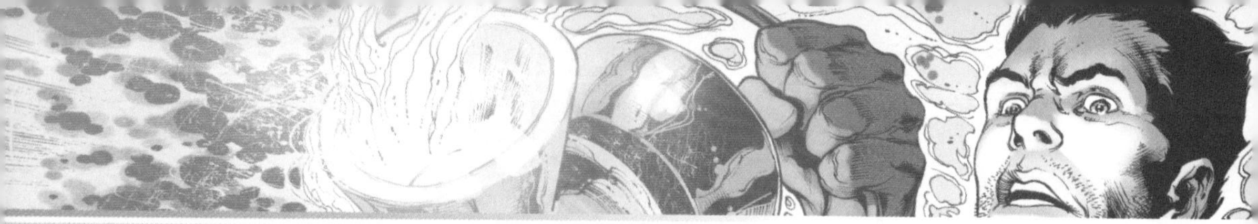

# THE SECRET OF LIFE

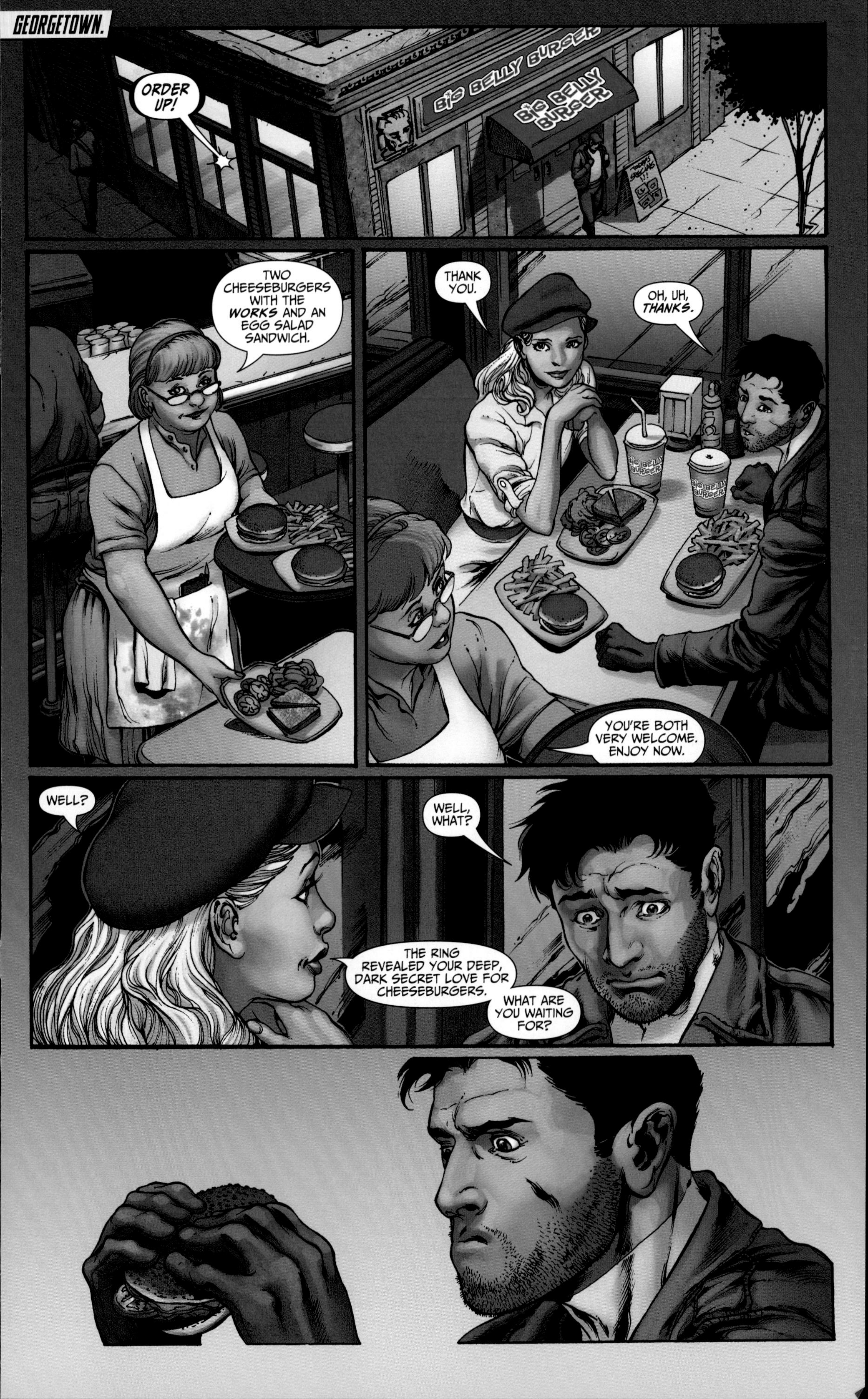
GEORGETOWN.
ORDER UP!
BIG BELLY BURGER
TWO CHEESEBURGERS WITH THE **WORKS** AND AN EGG SALAD SANDWICH.
THANK YOU.
OH, UH, *THANKS.*
YOU'RE BOTH VERY WELCOME. ENJOY NOW.
WELL?
WELL, WHAT?
THE RING REVEALED YOUR DEEP, DARK SECRET LOVE FOR CHEESEBURGERS.
WHAT ARE YOU WAITING FOR?

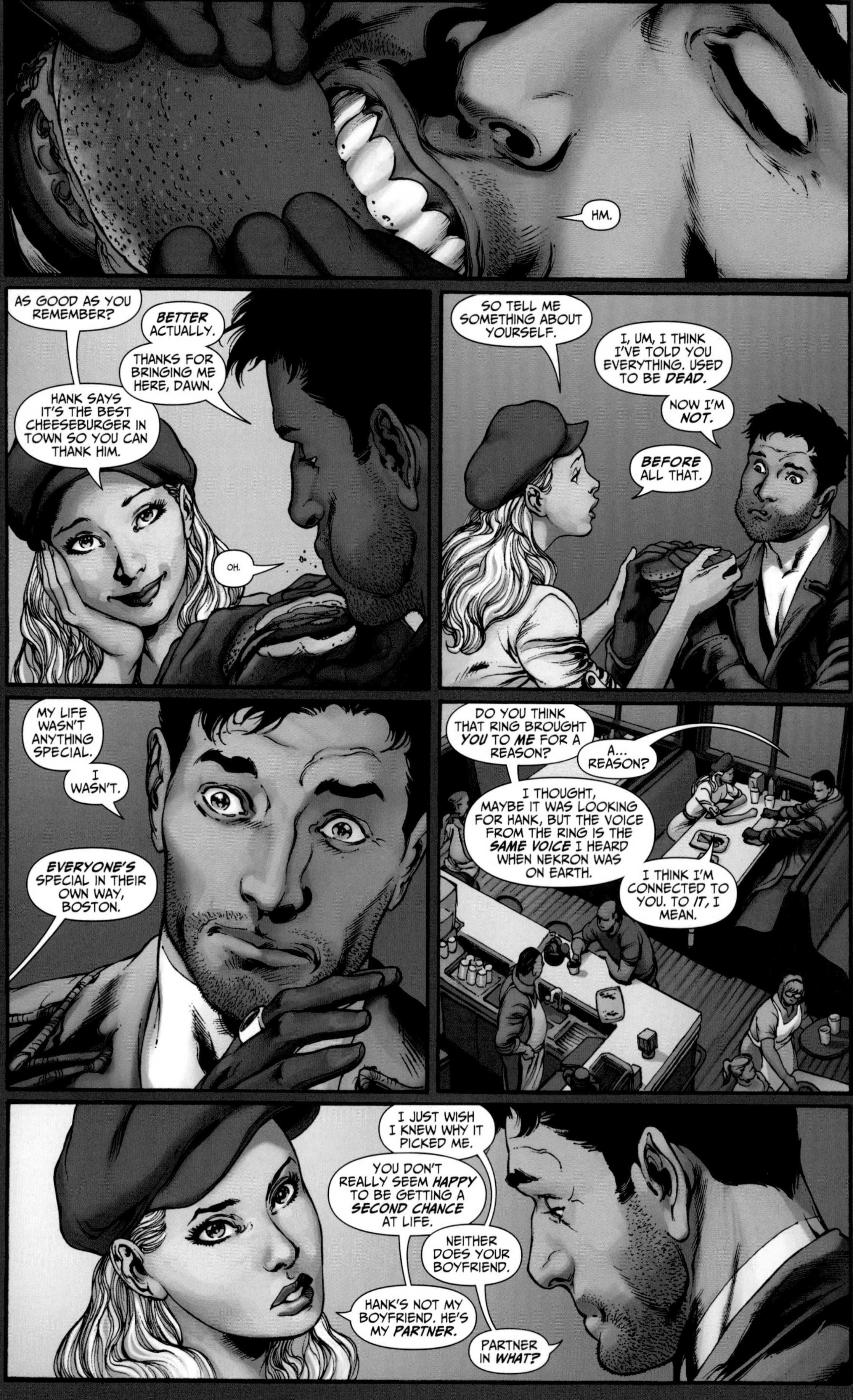
HM.
AS GOOD AS YOU REMEMBER?
BETTER ACTUALLY.
THANKS FOR BRINGING ME HERE, DAWN.
HANK SAYS IT'S THE BEST CHEESEBURGER IN TOWN SO YOU CAN THANK HIM.
OH.
SO TELL ME SOMETHING ABOUT YOURSELF.
I, UM, I THINK I'VE TOLD YOU EVERYTHING. USED TO BE DEAD.
NOW I'M NOT.
BEFORE ALL THAT.
MY LIFE WASN'T ANYTHING SPECIAL.
I WASN'T.
EVERYONE'S SPECIAL IN THEIR OWN WAY, BOSTON.
DO YOU THINK THAT RING BROUGHT YOU TO ME FOR A REASON?
A... REASON?
I THOUGHT, MAYBE IT WAS LOOKING FOR HANK, BUT THE VOICE FROM THE RING IS THE SAME VOICE I HEARD WHEN NEKRON WAS ON EARTH.
I THINK I'M CONNECTED TO YOU. TO IT, I MEAN.
I JUST WISH I KNEW WHY IT PICKED ME.
YOU DON'T REALLY SEEM HAPPY TO BE GETTING A SECOND CHANCE AT LIFE.
NEITHER DOES YOUR BOYFRIEND.
HANK'S NOT MY BOYFRIEND. HE'S MY PARTNER.
PARTNER IN WHAT?

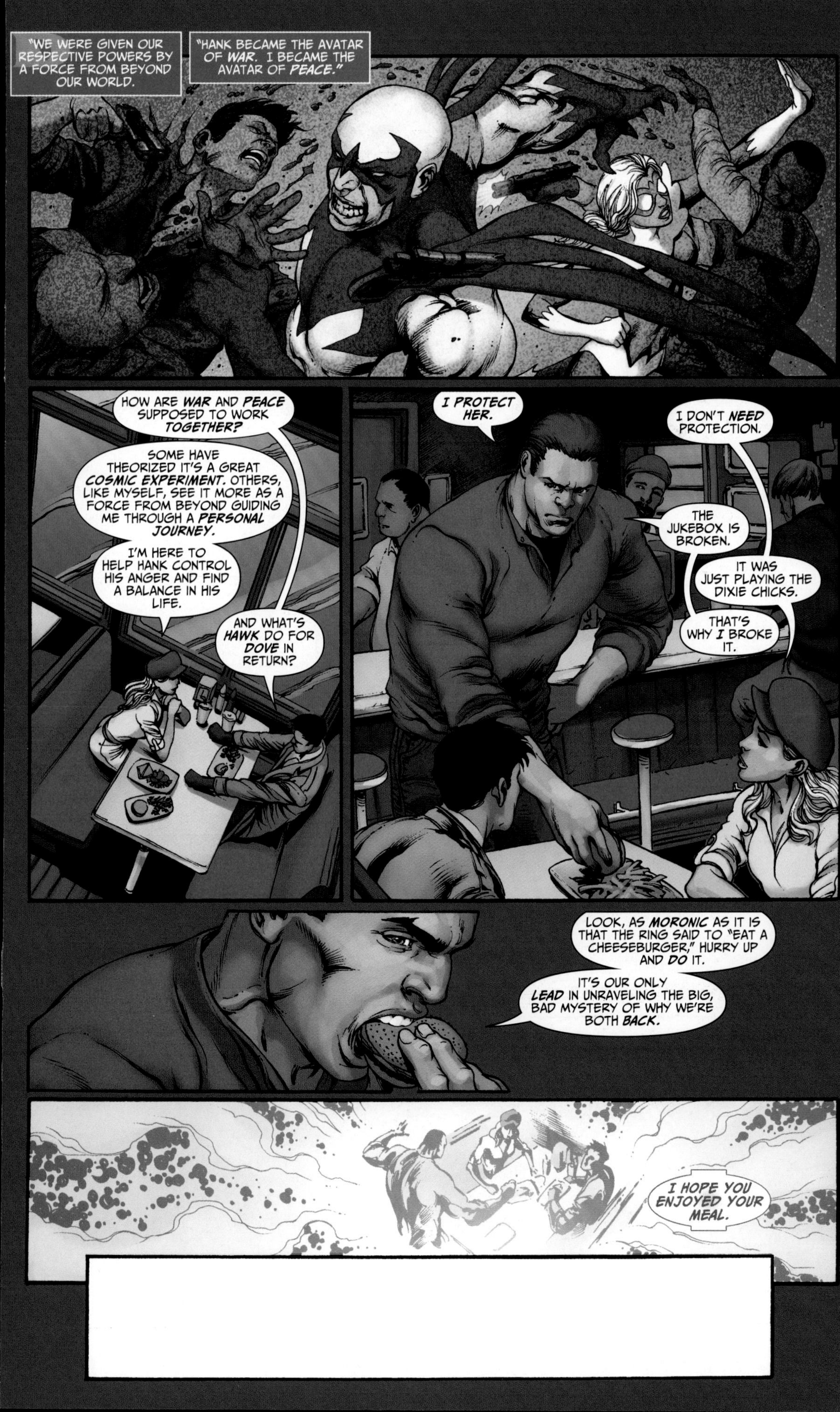

"WE WERE GIVEN OUR RESPECTIVE POWERS BY A FORCE FROM BEYOND OUR WORLD.
"HANK BECAME THE AVATAR OF WAR. I BECAME THE AVATAR OF PEACE."
HOW ARE WAR AND PEACE SUPPOSED TO WORK TOGETHER?
SOME HAVE THEORIZED IT'S A GREAT COSMIC EXPERIMENT. OTHERS, LIKE MYSELF, SEE IT MORE AS A FORCE FROM BEYOND GUIDING ME THROUGH A PERSONAL JOURNEY.
I'M HERE TO HELP HANK CONTROL HIS ANGER AND FIND A BALANCE IN HIS LIFE.
AND WHAT'S HAWK DO FOR DOVE IN RETURN?
I PROTECT HER.
I DON'T NEED PROTECTION.
THE JUKEBOX IS BROKEN.
IT WAS JUST PLAYING THE DIXIE CHICKS.
THAT'S WHY I BROKE IT.
LOOK, AS MORONIC AS IT IS THAT THE RING SAID TO "EAT A CHEESEBURGER," HURRY UP AND DO IT.
IT'S OUR ONLY LEAD IN UNRAVELING THE BIG, BAD MYSTERY OF WHY WE'RE BOTH BACK.
I HOPE YOU ENJOYED YOUR MEAL.

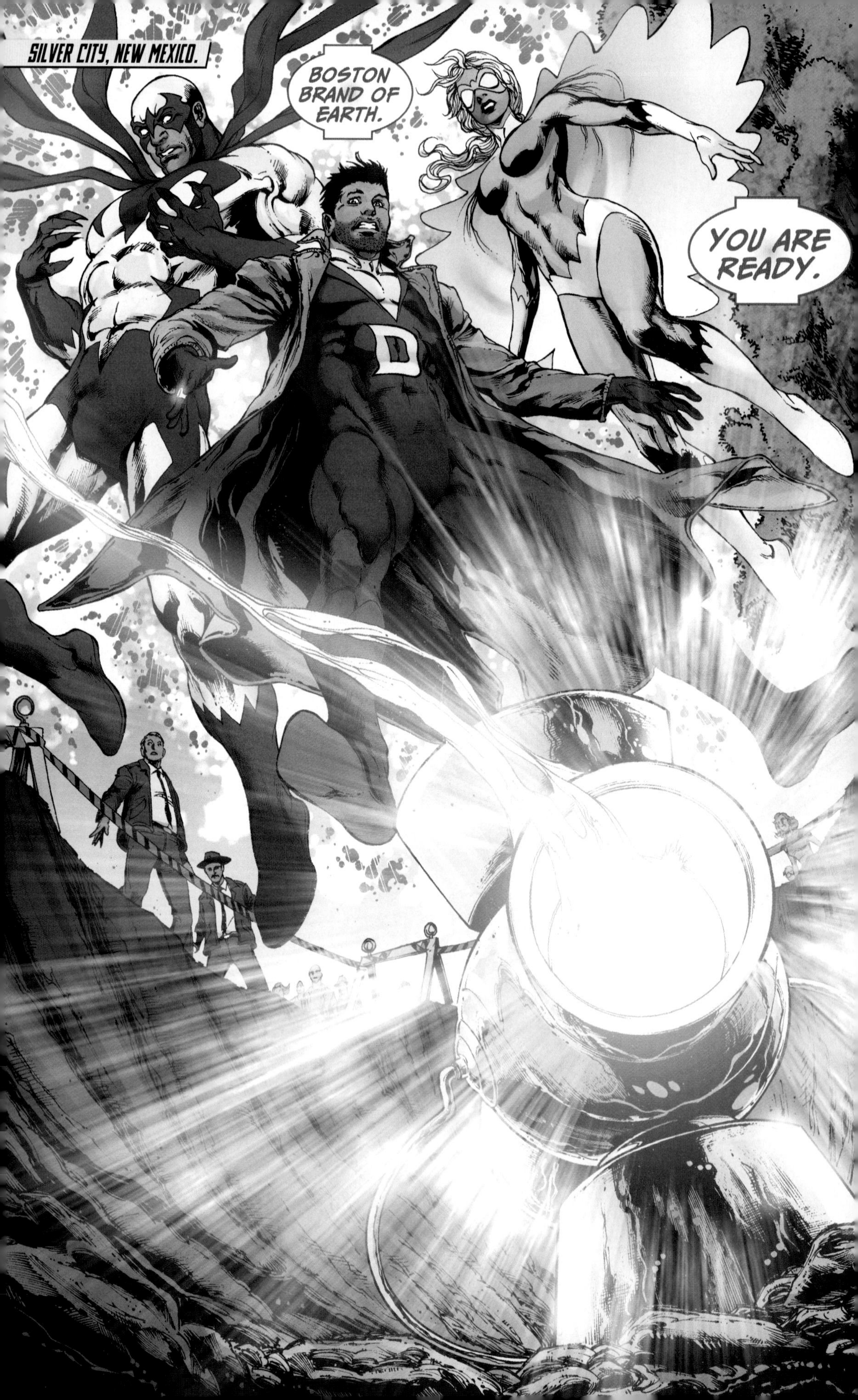
SILVER CITY, NEW MEXICO.
BOSTON BRAND OF EARTH.
YOU ARE READY.

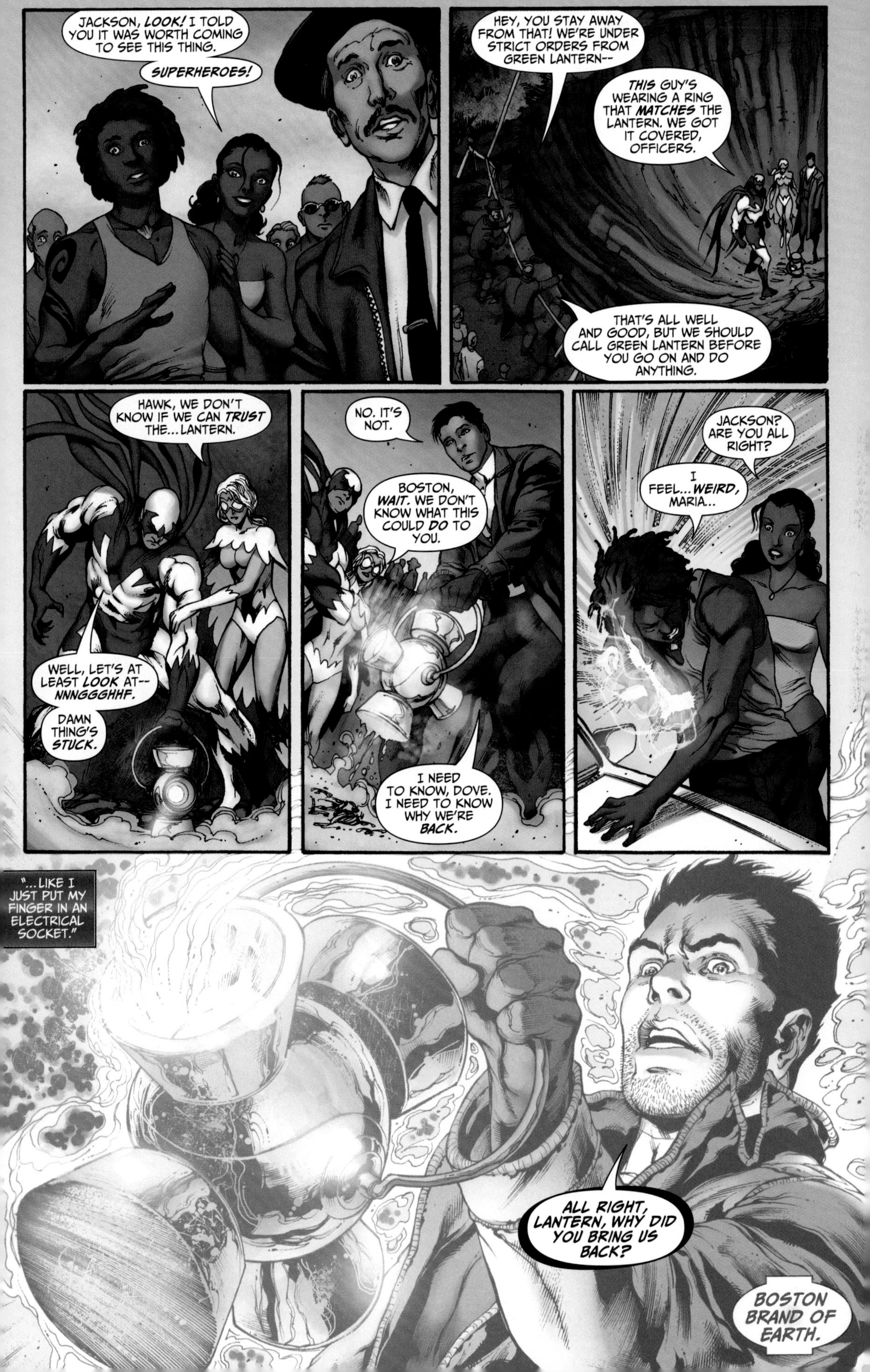
JACKSON, LOOK! I TOLD YOU IT WAS WORTH COMING TO SEE THIS THING.
SUPERHEROES!
HEY, YOU STAY AWAY FROM THAT! WE'RE UNDER STRICT ORDERS FROM GREEN LANTERN--
THIS GUY'S WEARING A RING THAT MATCHES THE LANTERN. WE GOT IT COVERED, OFFICERS.
THAT'S ALL WELL AND GOOD, BUT WE SHOULD CALL GREEN LANTERN BEFORE YOU GO ON AND DO ANYTHING.
HAWK, WE DON'T KNOW IF WE CAN TRUST THE... LANTERN.
WELL, LET'S AT LEAST LOOK AT-- NNNGGGHHF.
DAMN THING'S STUCK.
NO. IT'S NOT.
BOSTON, WAIT. WE DON'T KNOW WHAT THIS COULD DO TO YOU.
I NEED TO KNOW, DOVE. I NEED TO KNOW WHY WE'RE BACK.
JACKSON? ARE YOU ALL RIGHT?
I FEEL... WEIRD, MARIA...
"...LIKE I JUST PUT MY FINGER IN AN ELECTRICAL SOCKET."
ALL RIGHT, LANTERN, WHY DID YOU BRING US BACK?
BOSTON BRAND OF EARTH.

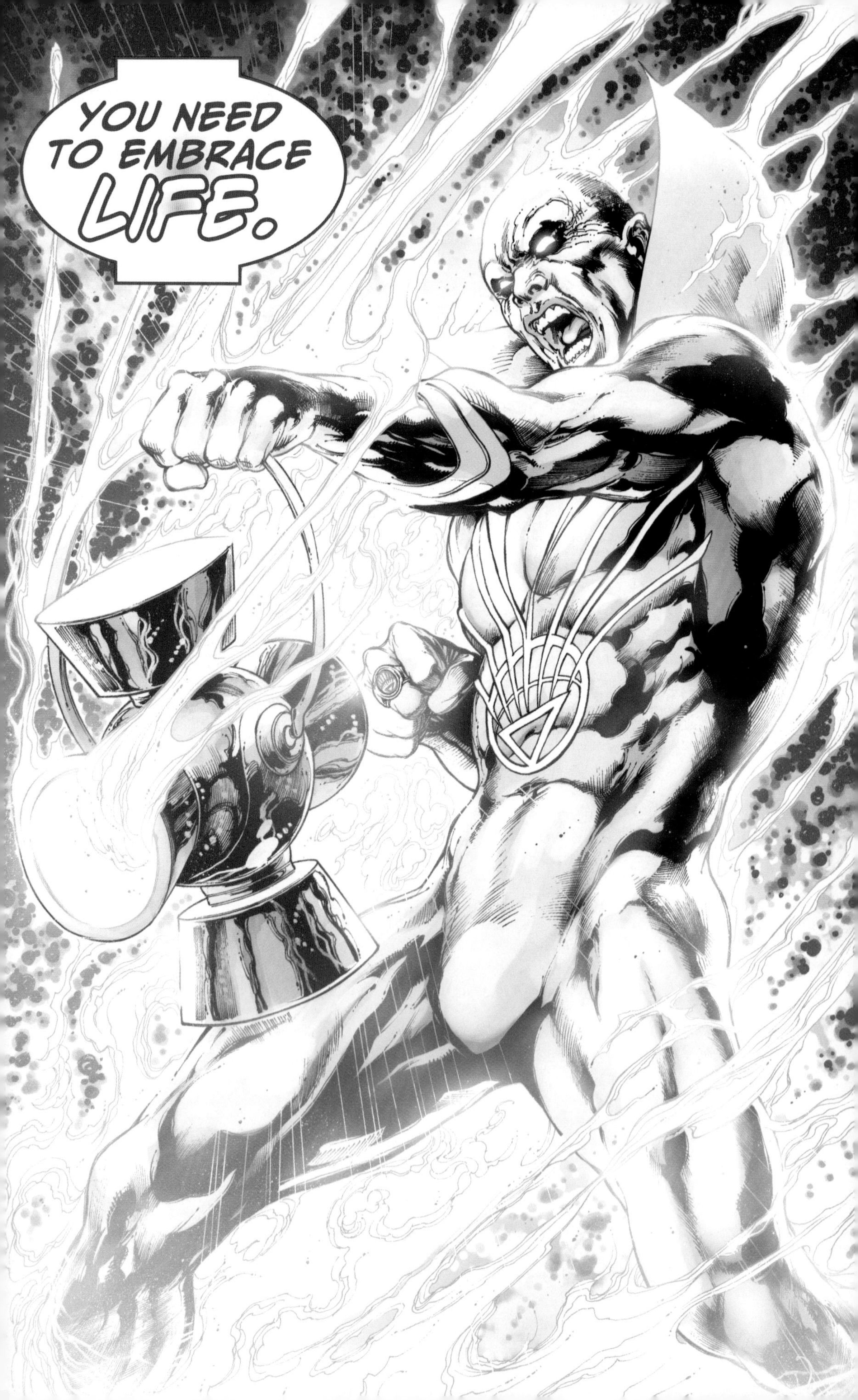
YOU NEED TO EMBRACE LIFE.

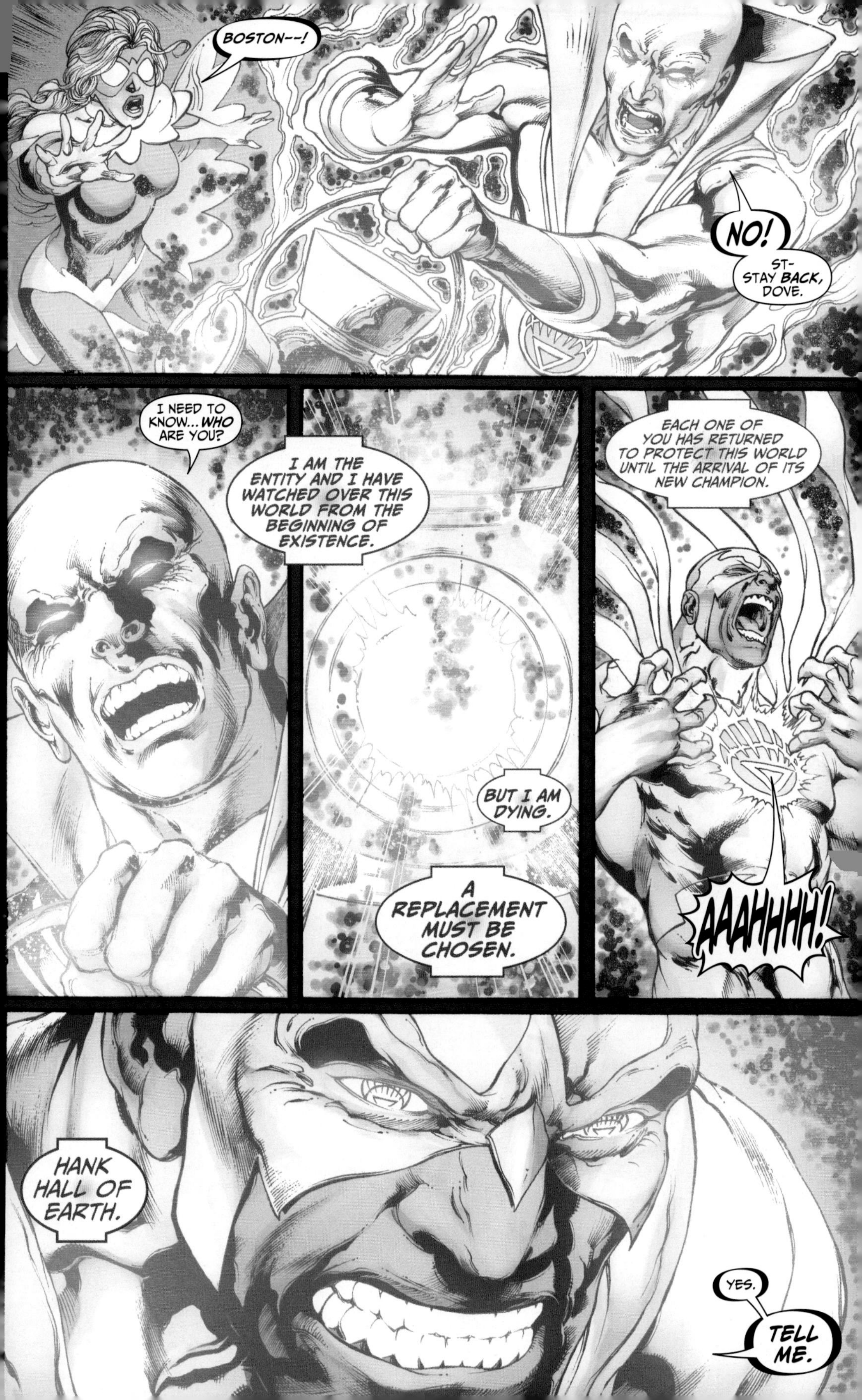
BOSTON--!
NO!
ST- STAY BACK, DOVE.
I NEED TO KNOW... WHO ARE YOU?
I AM THE ENTITY AND I HAVE WATCHED OVER THIS WORLD FROM THE BEGINNING OF EXISTENCE.
BUT I AM DYING.
A REPLACEMENT MUST BE CHOSEN.
EACH ONE OF YOU HAS RETURNED TO PROTECT THIS WORLD UNTIL THE ARRIVAL OF ITS NEW CHAMPION.
AAAHHHH!
HANK HALL OF EARTH.
YES.
TELL ME.

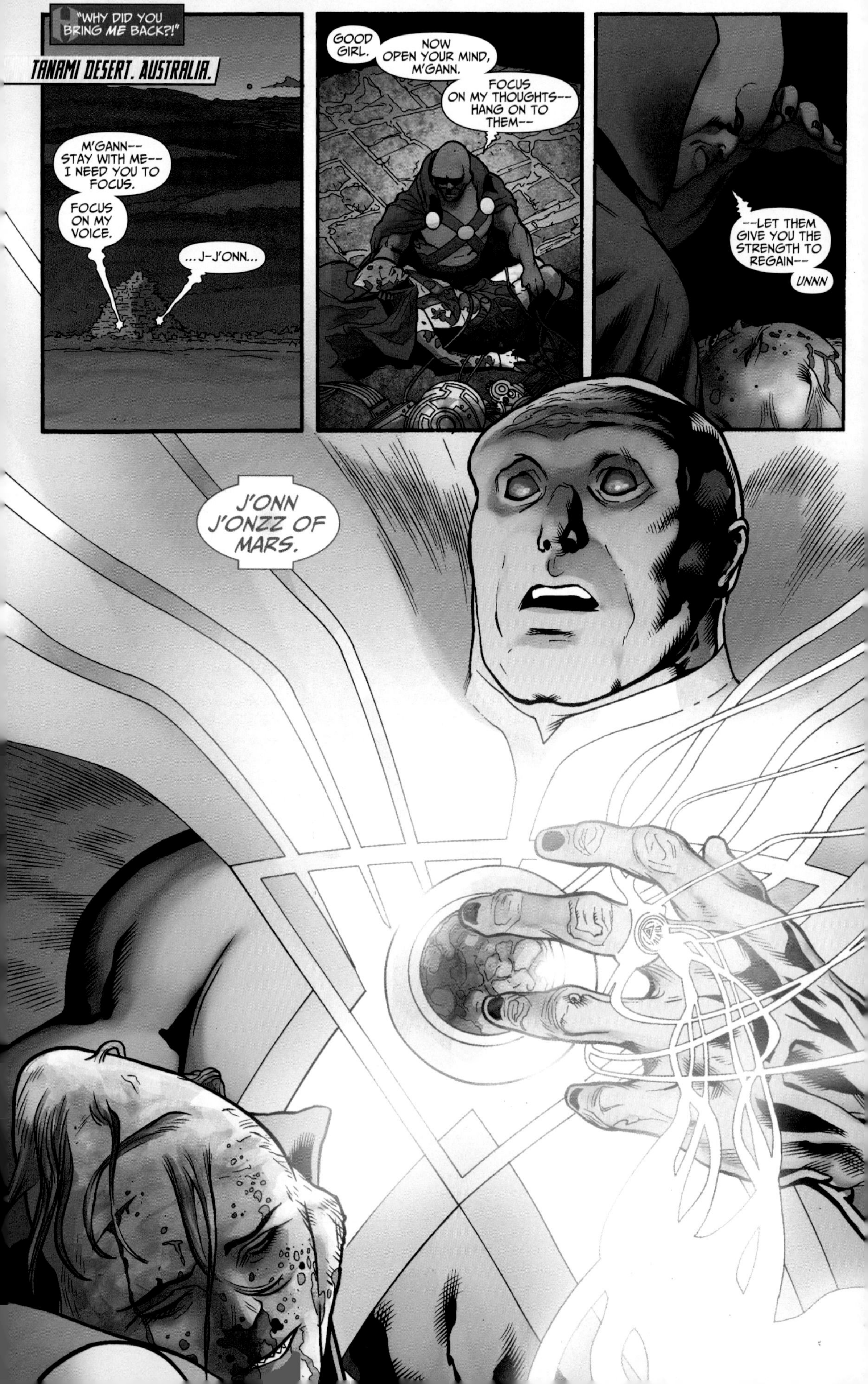
"WHY DID YOU BRING ME BACK?!"
TANAMI DESERT. AUSTRALIA.
M'GANN-- STAY WITH ME-- I NEED YOU TO FOCUS.
FOCUS ON MY VOICE.
...J-J'ONN...
GOOD GIRL.
NOW OPEN YOUR MIND, M'GANN.
FOCUS ON MY THOUGHTS-- HANG ON TO THEM--
--LET THEM GIVE YOU THE STRENGTH TO REGAIN--
UNNN
J'ONN J'ONZZ OF MARS.

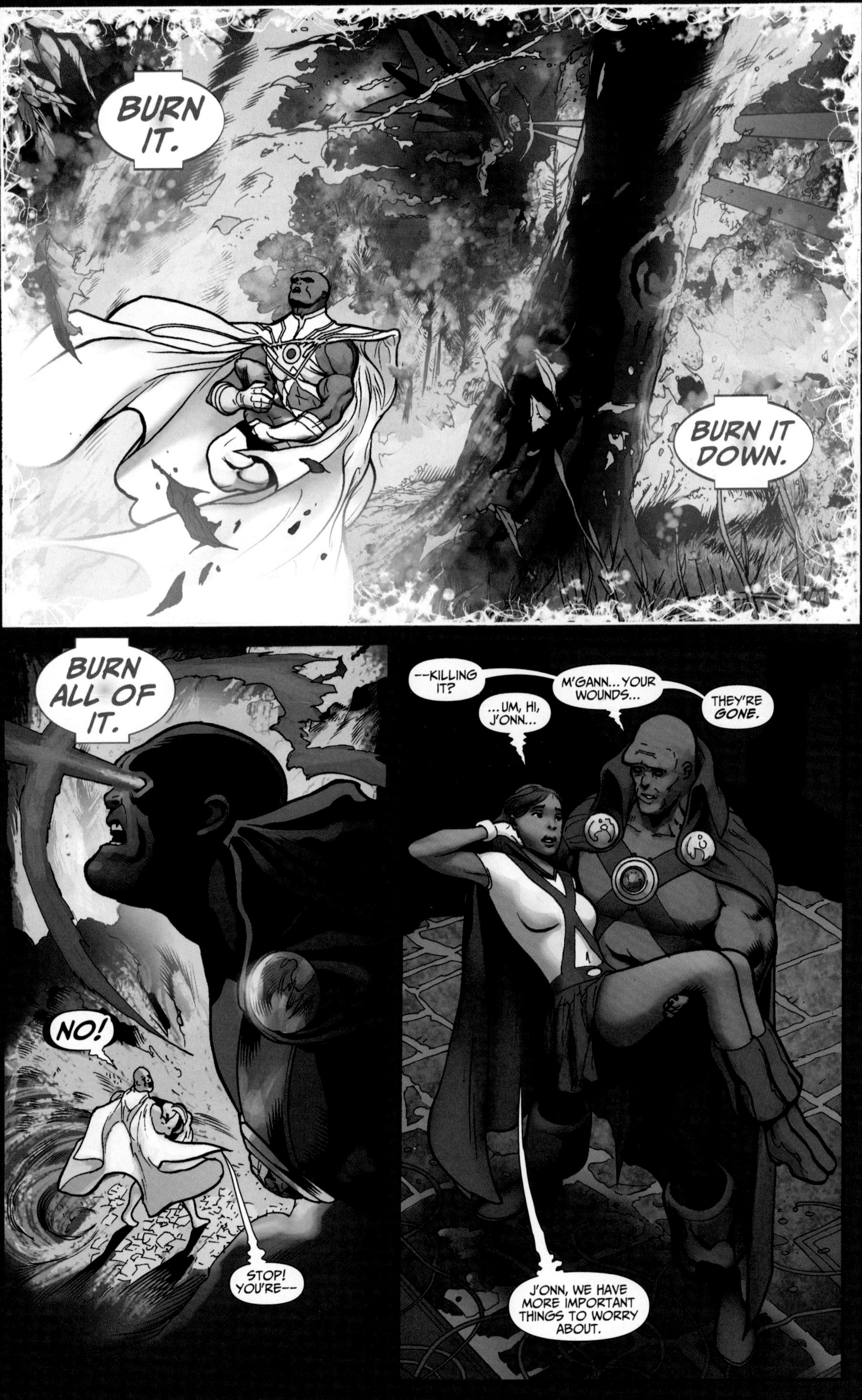
BURN IT.
BURN IT DOWN.
BURN ALL OF IT.
NO!
STOP! YOU'RE--
--KILLING IT?
...UM, HI, J'ONN...
M'GANN... YOUR WOUNDS...
THEY'RE GONE.
J'ONN, WE HAVE MORE IMPORTANT THINGS TO WORRY ABOUT.

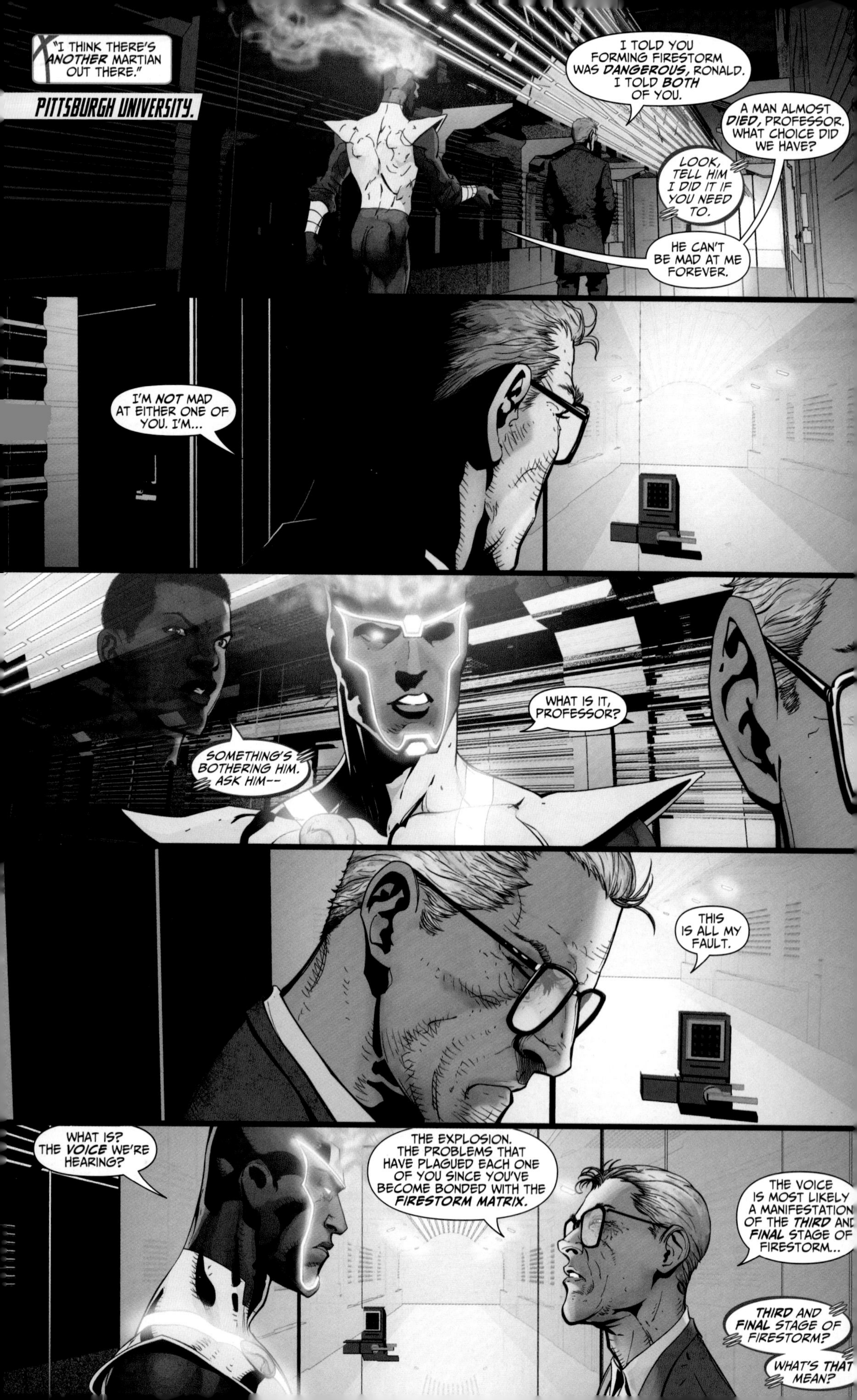
"I THINK THERE'S ANOTHER MARTIAN OUT THERE."
PITTSBURGH UNIVERSITY.
I TOLD YOU FORMING FIRESTORM WAS DANGEROUS, RONALD. I TOLD BOTH OF YOU.
A MAN ALMOST DIED, PROFESSOR. WHAT CHOICE DID WE HAVE?
LOOK, TELL HIM I DID IT IF YOU NEED TO.
HE CAN'T BE MAD AT ME FOREVER.
I'M NOT MAD AT EITHER ONE OF YOU. I'M...
WHAT IS IT, PROFESSOR?
SOMETHING'S BOTHERING HIM. ASK HIM--
THIS IS ALL MY FAULT.
WHAT IS? THE VOICE WE'RE HEARING?
THE EXPLOSION. THE PROBLEMS THAT HAVE PLAGUED EACH ONE OF YOU SINCE YOU'VE BECOME BONDED WITH THE FIRESTORM MATRIX.
THE VOICE IS MOST LIKELY A MANIFESTATION OF THE THIRD AND FINAL STAGE OF FIRESTORM...
THIRD AND FINAL STAGE OF FIRESTORM?
WHAT'S THAT MEAN?

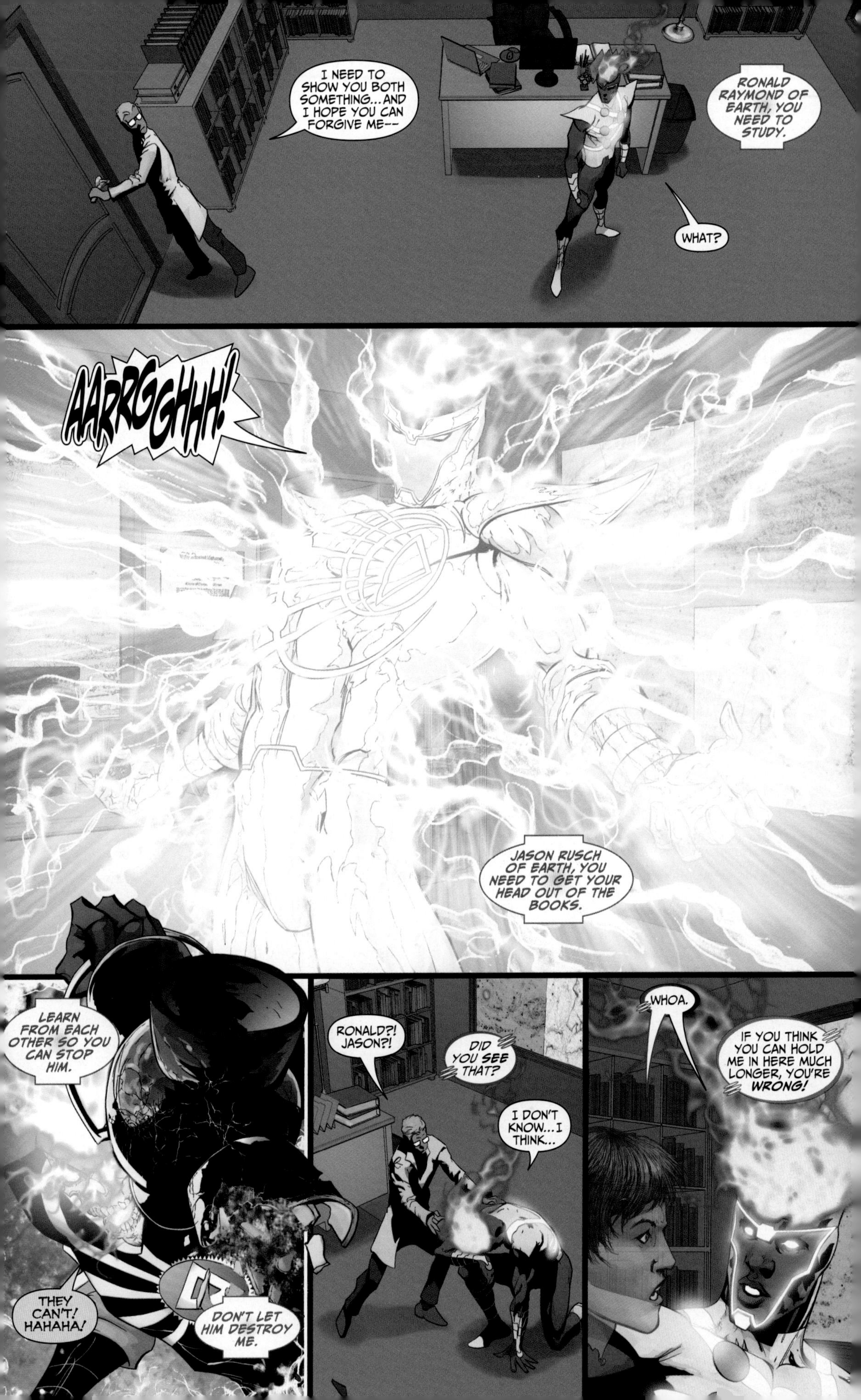
I NEED TO SHOW YOU BOTH SOMETHING...AND I HOPE YOU CAN FORGIVE ME--
RONALD RAYMOND OF EARTH, YOU NEED TO STUDY.
WHAT?
AARRGGHHH!
JASON RUSCH OF EARTH, YOU NEED TO GET YOUR HEAD OUT OF THE BOOKS.
LEARN FROM EACH OTHER SO YOU CAN STOP HIM.
THEY CAN'T! HAHAHA!
DON'T LET HIM DESTROY ME.
RONALD?! JASON?!
DID YOU SEE THAT?
I DON'T KNOW...I THINK...
WHOA.
IF YOU THINK YOU CAN HOLD ME IN HERE MUCH LONGER, YOU'RE WRONG!

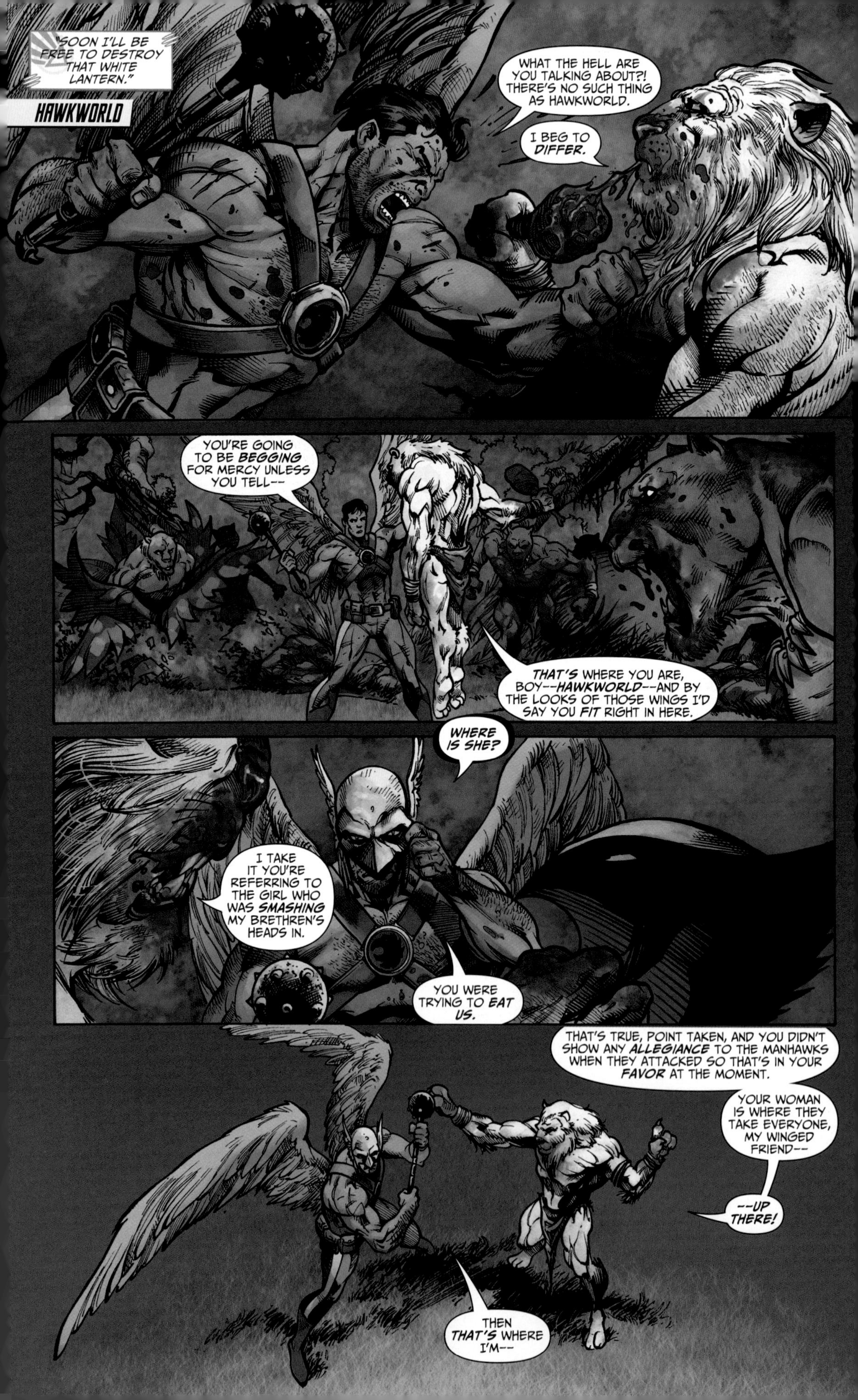

"SOON I'LL BE FREE TO DESTROY THAT WHITE LANTERN."
HAWKWORLD
WHAT THE HELL ARE YOU TALKING ABOUT?! THERE'S NO SUCH THING AS HAWKWORLD.
I BEG TO DIFFER.
YOU'RE GOING TO BE BEGGING FOR MERCY UNLESS YOU TELL--
THAT'S WHERE YOU ARE, BOY--HAWKWORLD--AND BY THE LOOKS OF THOSE WINGS I'D SAY YOU FIT RIGHT IN HERE.
WHERE IS SHE?
I TAKE IT YOU'RE REFERRING TO THE GIRL WHO WAS SMASHING MY BRETHREN'S HEADS IN.
YOU WERE TRYING TO EAT US.
THAT'S TRUE, POINT TAKEN, AND YOU DIDN'T SHOW ANY ALLEGIANCE TO THE MANHAWKS WHEN THEY ATTACKED SO THAT'S IN YOUR FAVOR AT THE MOMENT.
YOUR WOMAN IS WHERE THEY TAKE EVERYONE, MY WINGED FRIEND--
--UP THERE!
THEN THAT'S WHERE I'M--

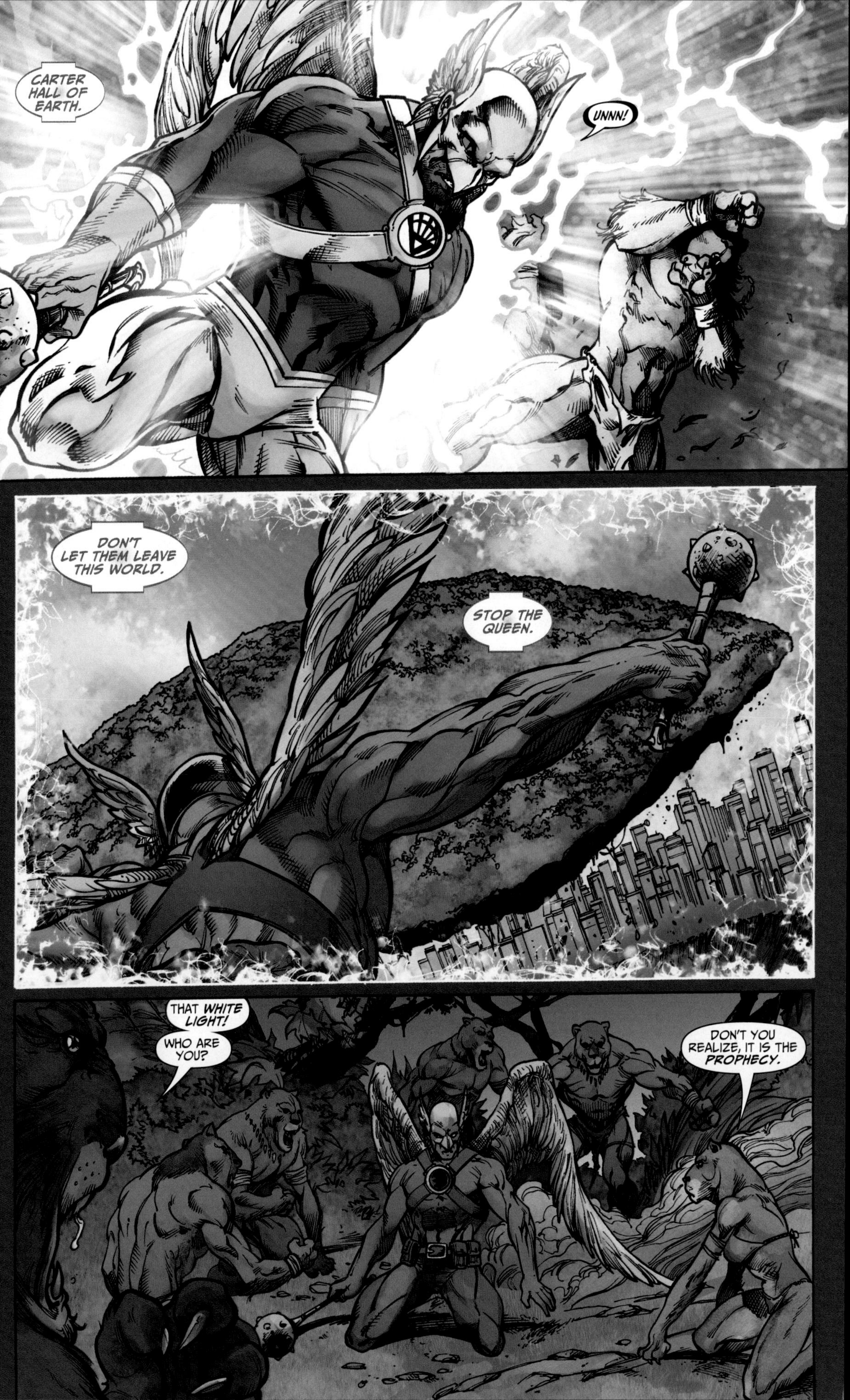
CARTER HALL OF EARTH.
UNNN!
DON'T LET THEM LEAVE THIS WORLD.
STOP THE QUEEN.
THAT WHITE LIGHT!
WHO ARE YOU?
DON'T YOU REALIZE, IT IS THE PROPHECY.

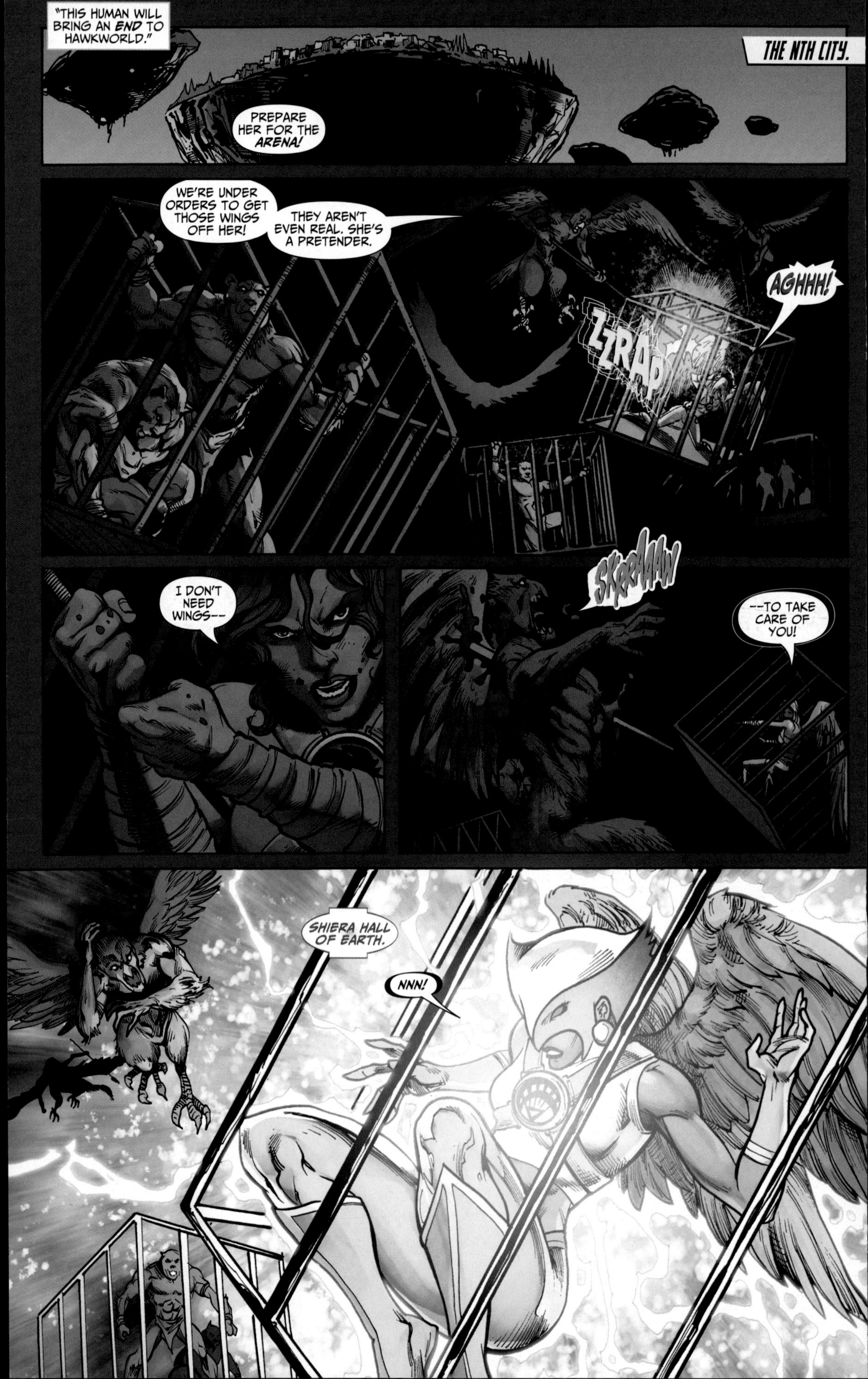
"THIS HUMAN WILL BRING AN *END* TO HAWKWORLD."
THE NTH CITY.
PREPARE HER FOR THE *ARENA!*
WE'RE UNDER ORDERS TO GET THOSE WINGS OFF HER!
THEY AREN'T EVEN REAL. SHE'S A PRETENDER.
ZZRAP
AGHHH!
I DON'T NEED WINGS--
SKRRAAAW
--TO TAKE CARE OF YOU!
SHIERA HALL OF EARTH.
NNN!

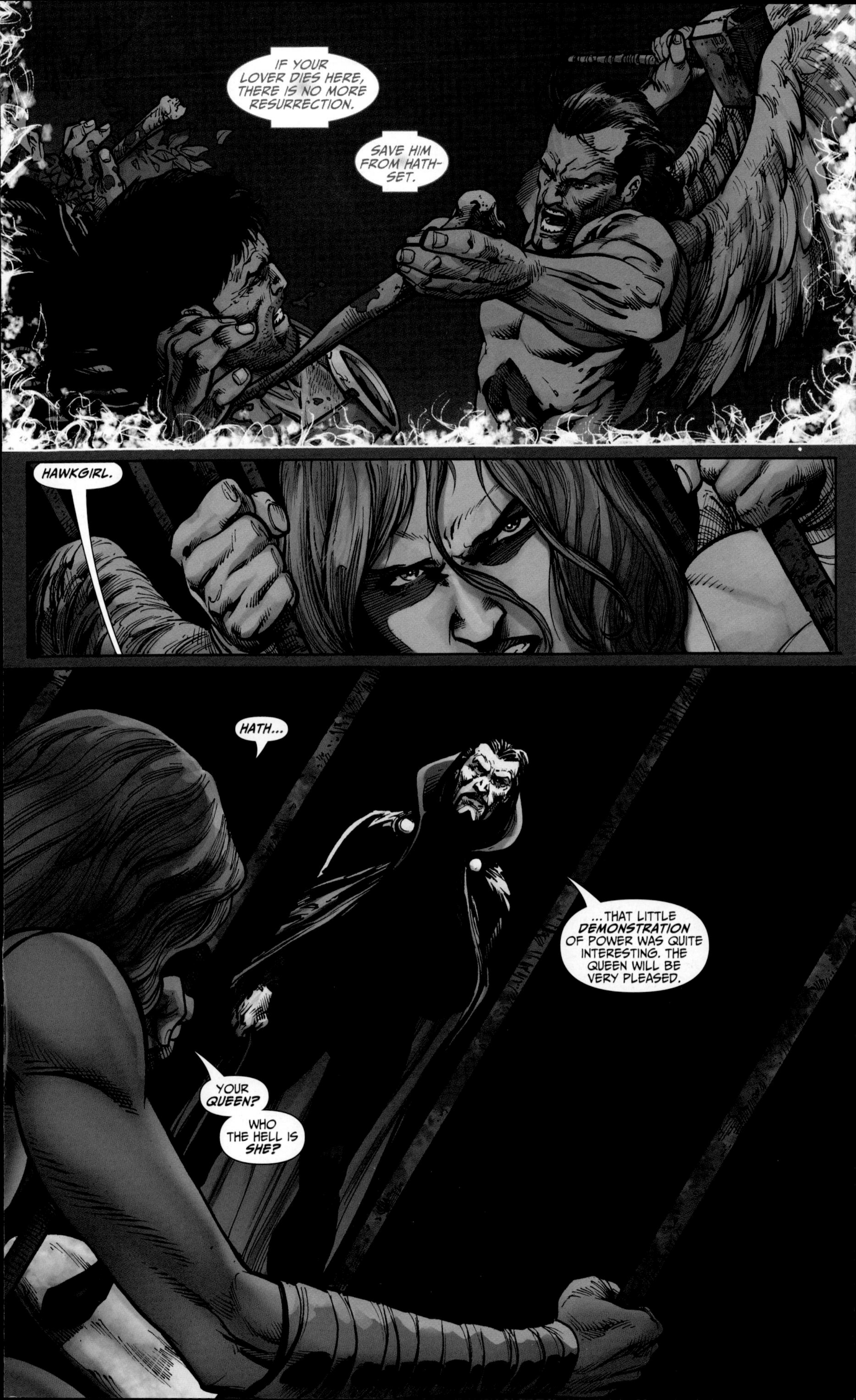
IF YOUR LOVER DIES HERE, THERE IS NO MORE RESURRECTION.
SAVE HIM FROM HATH-SET.
HAWKGIRL.
HATH...
...THAT LITTLE DEMONSTRATION OF POWER WAS QUITE INTERESTING. THE QUEEN WILL BE VERY PLEASED.
YOUR QUEEN?
WHO THE HELL IS SHE?

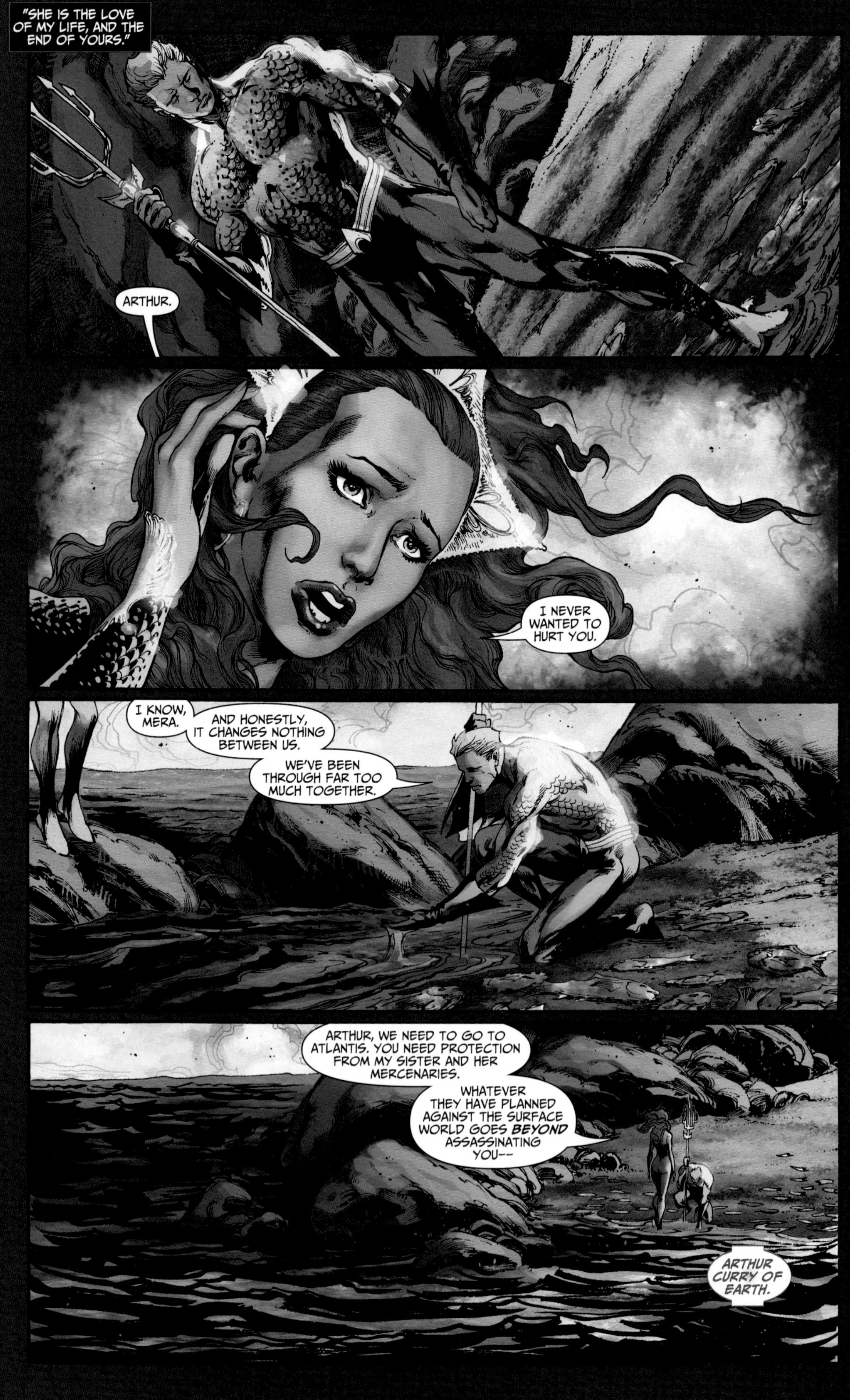
"SHE IS THE LOVE OF MY LIFE, AND THE END OF YOURS."
ARTHUR.
I NEVER WANTED TO HURT YOU.
I KNOW, MERA.
AND HONESTLY, IT CHANGES NOTHING BETWEEN US.
WE'VE BEEN THROUGH FAR TOO MUCH TOGETHER.
ARTHUR, WE NEED TO GO TO ATLANTIS. YOU NEED PROTECTION FROM MY SISTER AND HER MERCENARIES.
WHATEVER THEY HAVE PLANNED AGAINST THE SURFACE WORLD GOES **BEYOND** ASSASSINATING YOU--
ARTHUR CURRY OF EARTH.

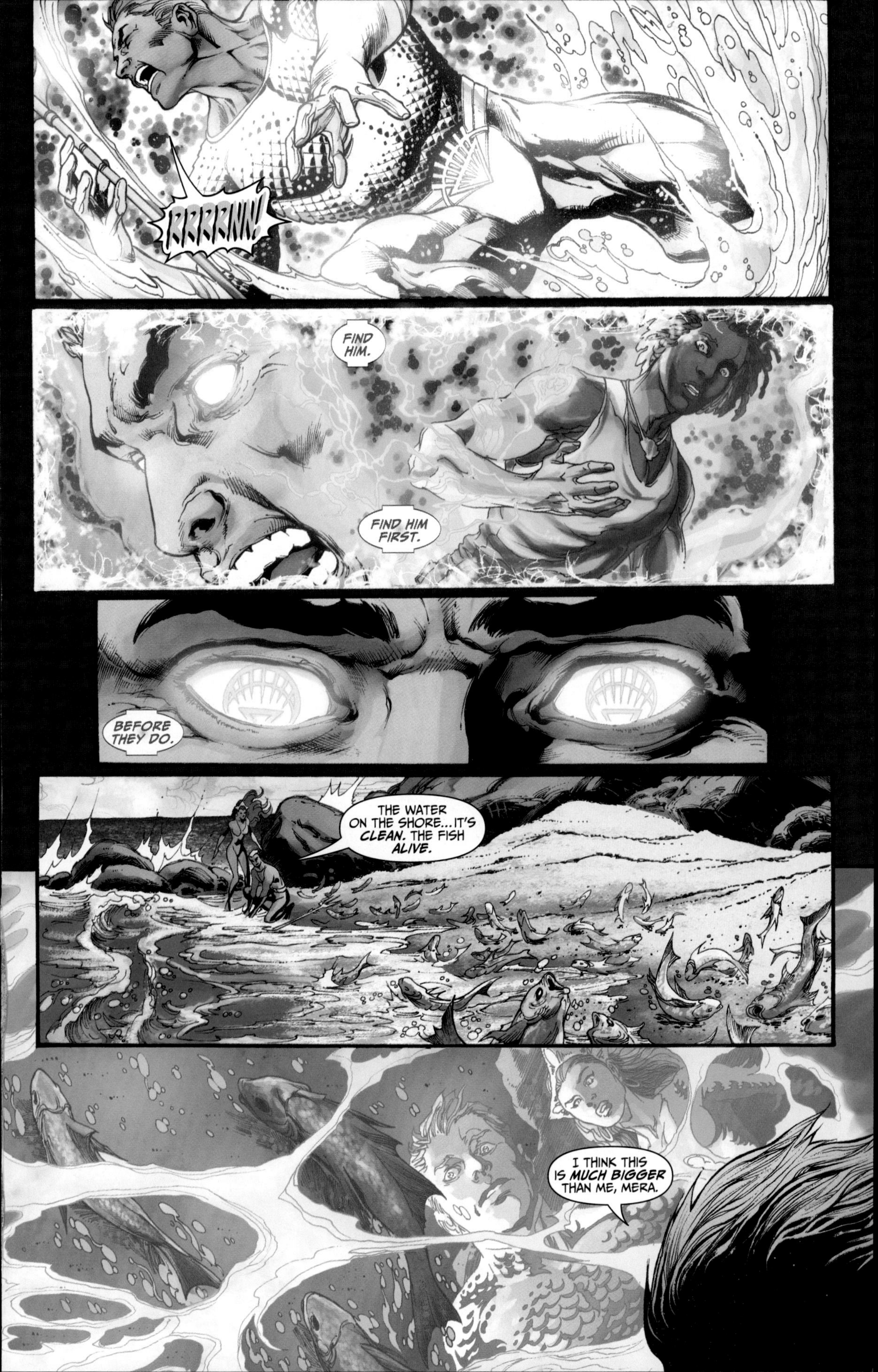
RRRRNN!
FIND HIM.
FIND HIM FIRST.
BEFORE THEY DO.
THE WATER ON THE SHORE...IT'S CLEAN. THE FISH ALIVE.
I THINK THIS IS MUCH BIGGER THAN ME, MERA.

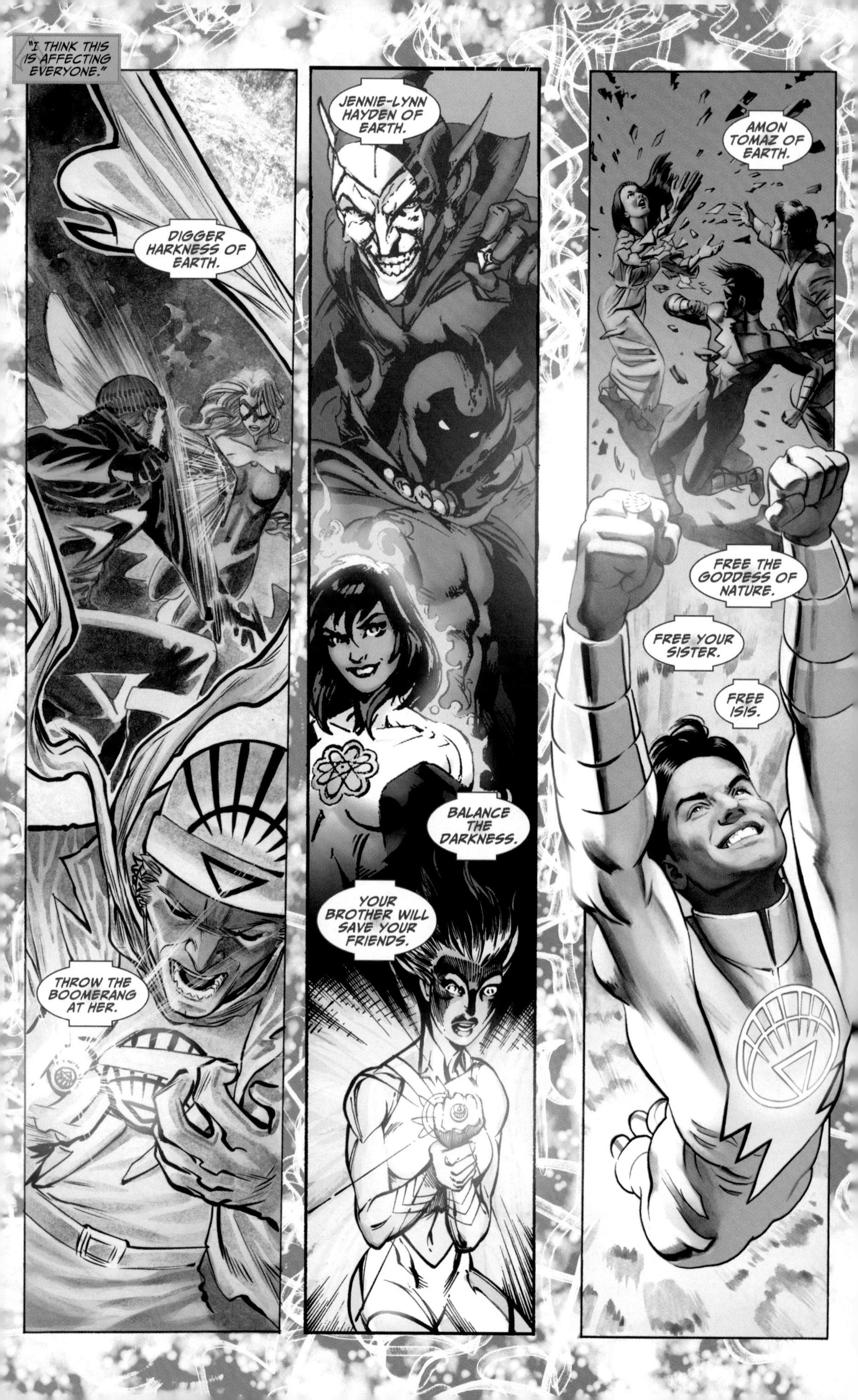
"I THINK THIS IS AFFECTING EVERYONE."
DIGGER HARKNESS OF EARTH.
THROW THE BOOMERANG AT HER.
JENNIE-LYNN HAYDEN OF EARTH.
BALANCE THE DARKNESS.
YOUR BROTHER WILL SAVE YOUR FRIENDS.
AMON TOMAZ OF EARTH.
FREE THE GODDESS OF NATURE.
FREE YOUR SISTER.
FREE ISIS.

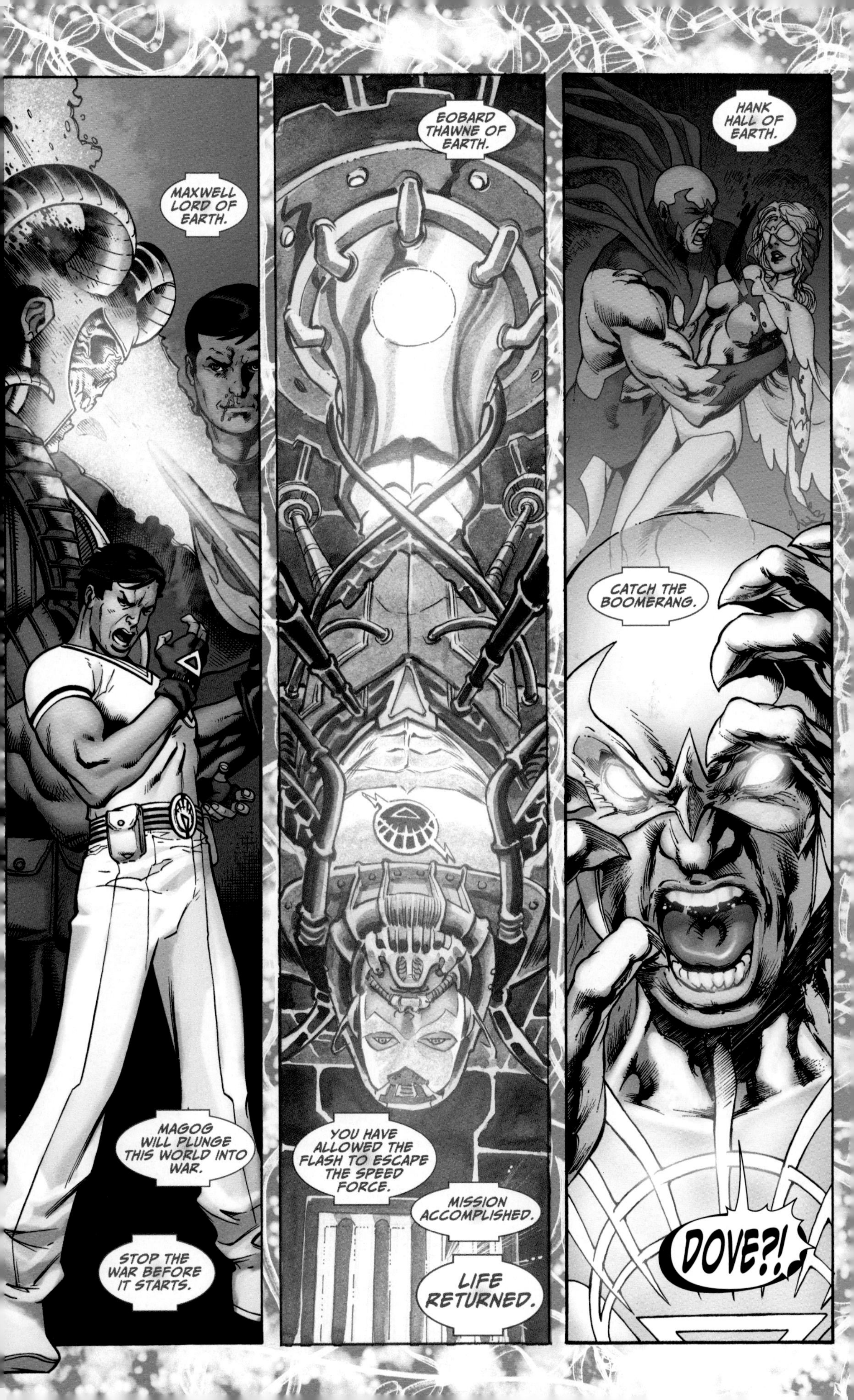
MAXWELL LORD OF EARTH.
MAGOG WILL PLUNGE THIS WORLD INTO WAR.
STOP THE WAR BEFORE IT STARTS.
EOBARD THAWNE OF EARTH.
YOU HAVE ALLOWED THE FLASH TO ESCAPE THE SPEED FORCE.
MISSION ACCOMPLISHED.
LIFE RETURNED.
HANK HALL OF EARTH.
CATCH THE BOOMERANG.
DOVE?!

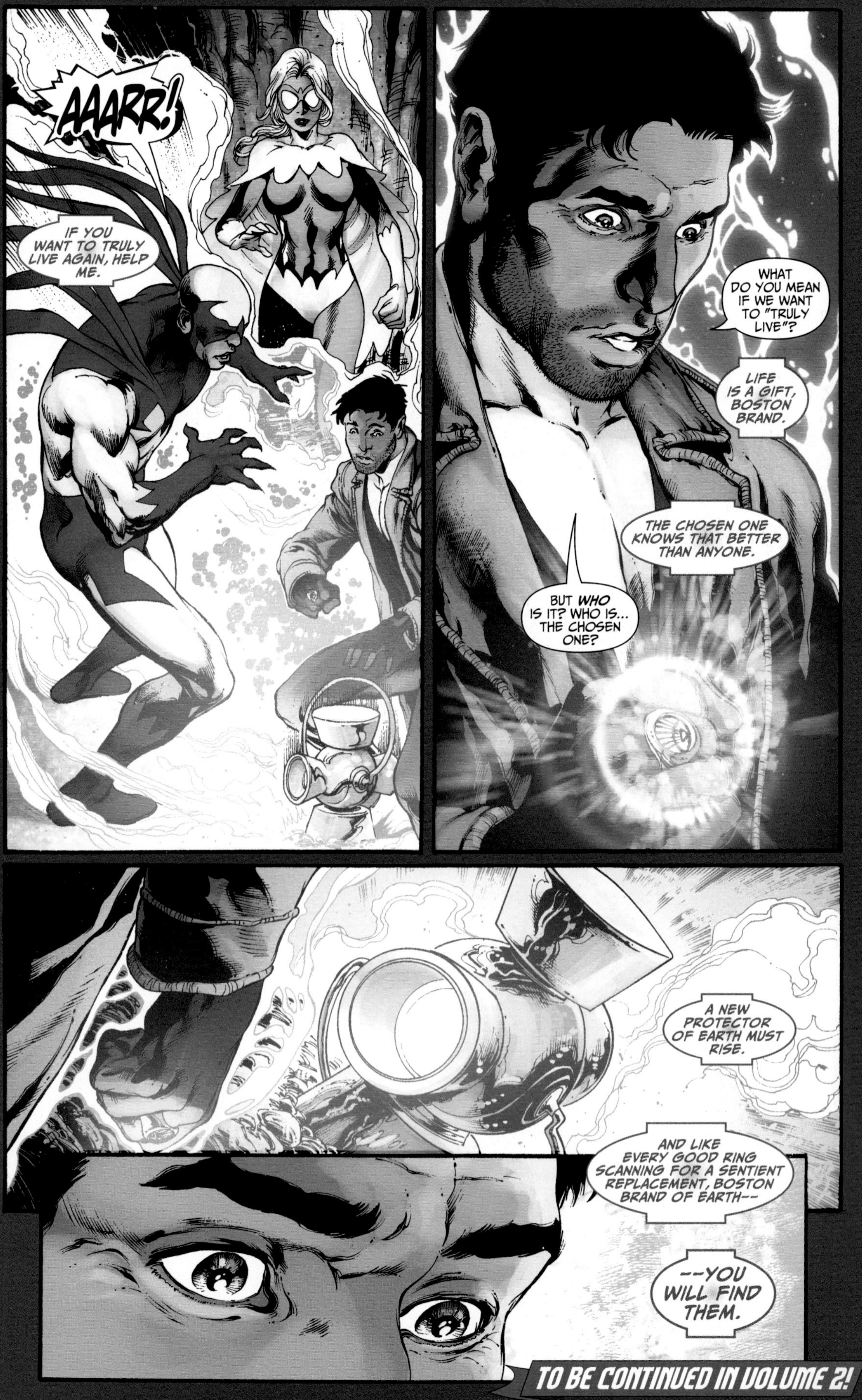
AAARR!
IF YOU WANT TO TRULY LIVE AGAIN, HELP ME.
WHAT DO YOU MEAN IF WE WANT TO "TRULY LIVE"?
LIFE IS A GIFT, BOSTON BRAND.
THE CHOSEN ONE KNOWS THAT BETTER THAN ANYONE.
BUT WHO IS IT? WHO IS... THE CHOSEN ONE?
A NEW PROTECTOR OF EARTH MUST RISE.
AND LIKE EVERY GOOD RING SCANNING FOR A SENTIENT REPLACEMENT, BOSTON BRAND OF EARTH--
--YOU WILL FIND THEM.
TO BE CONTINUED IN VOLUME 2!

**BRIGHTEST DAY 0**
*Variant cover by Ivan Reis with Chuck Pires*

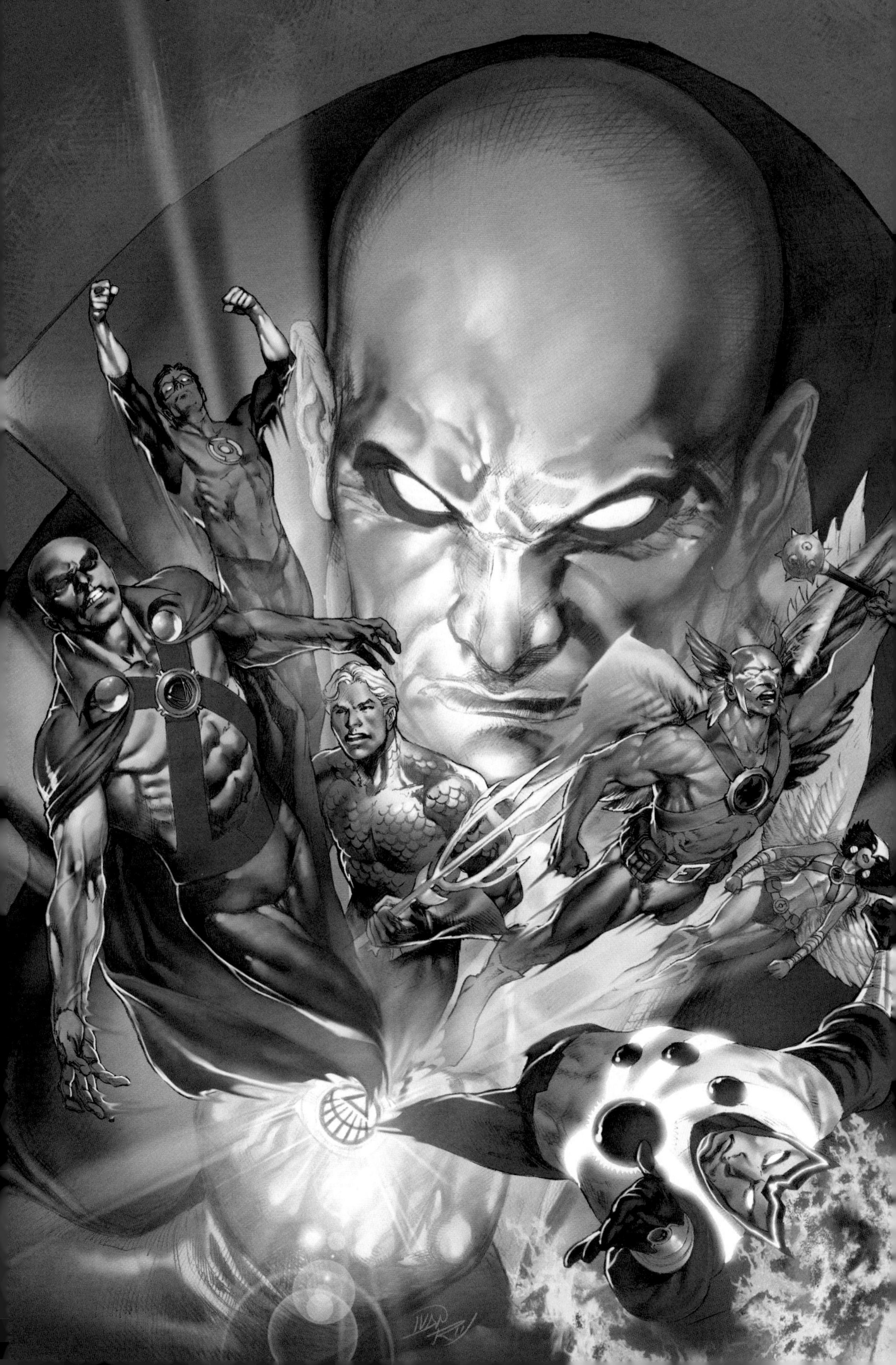

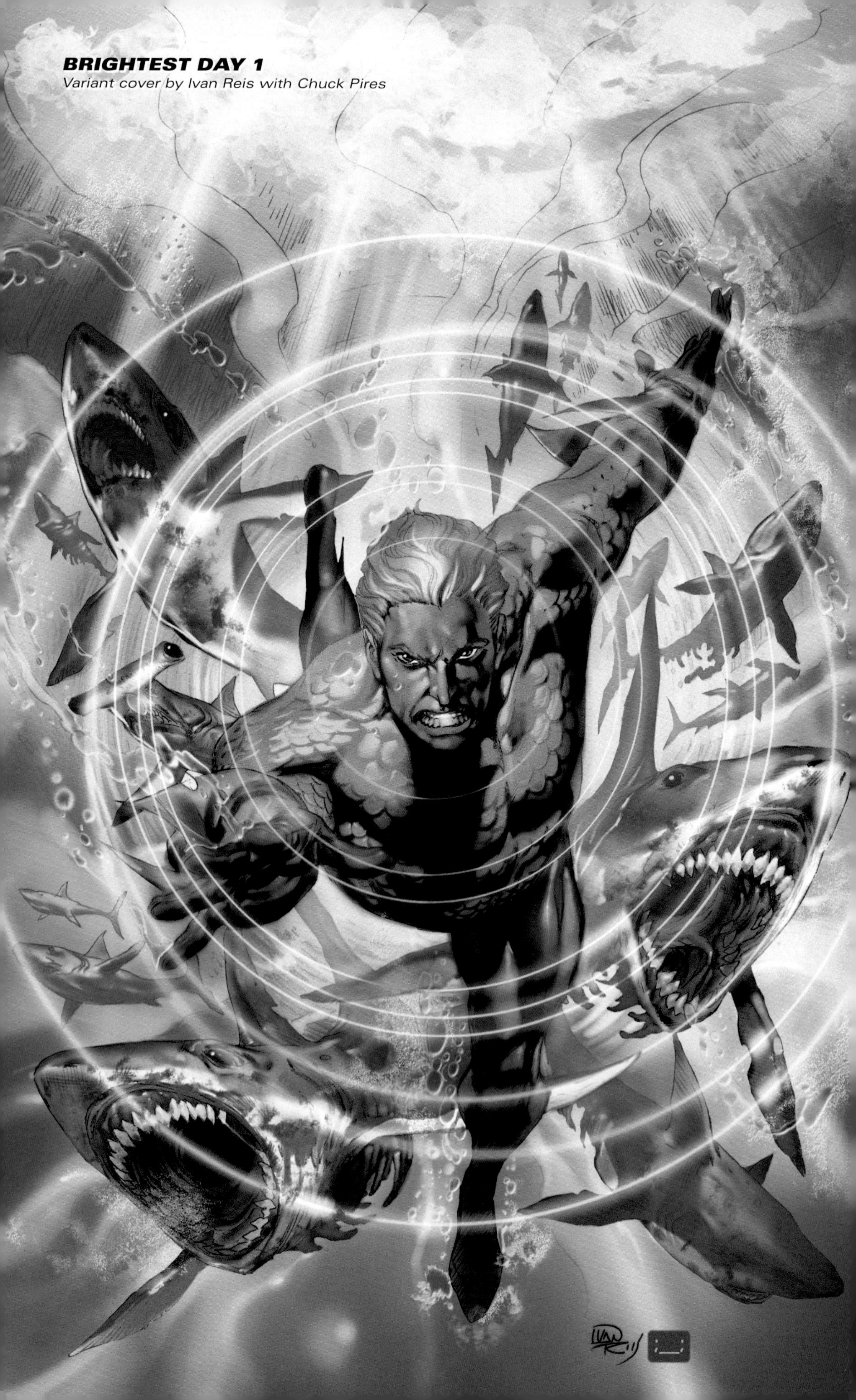

**BRIGHTEST DAY 1**
*Variant cover by Ivan Reis with Chuck Pires*

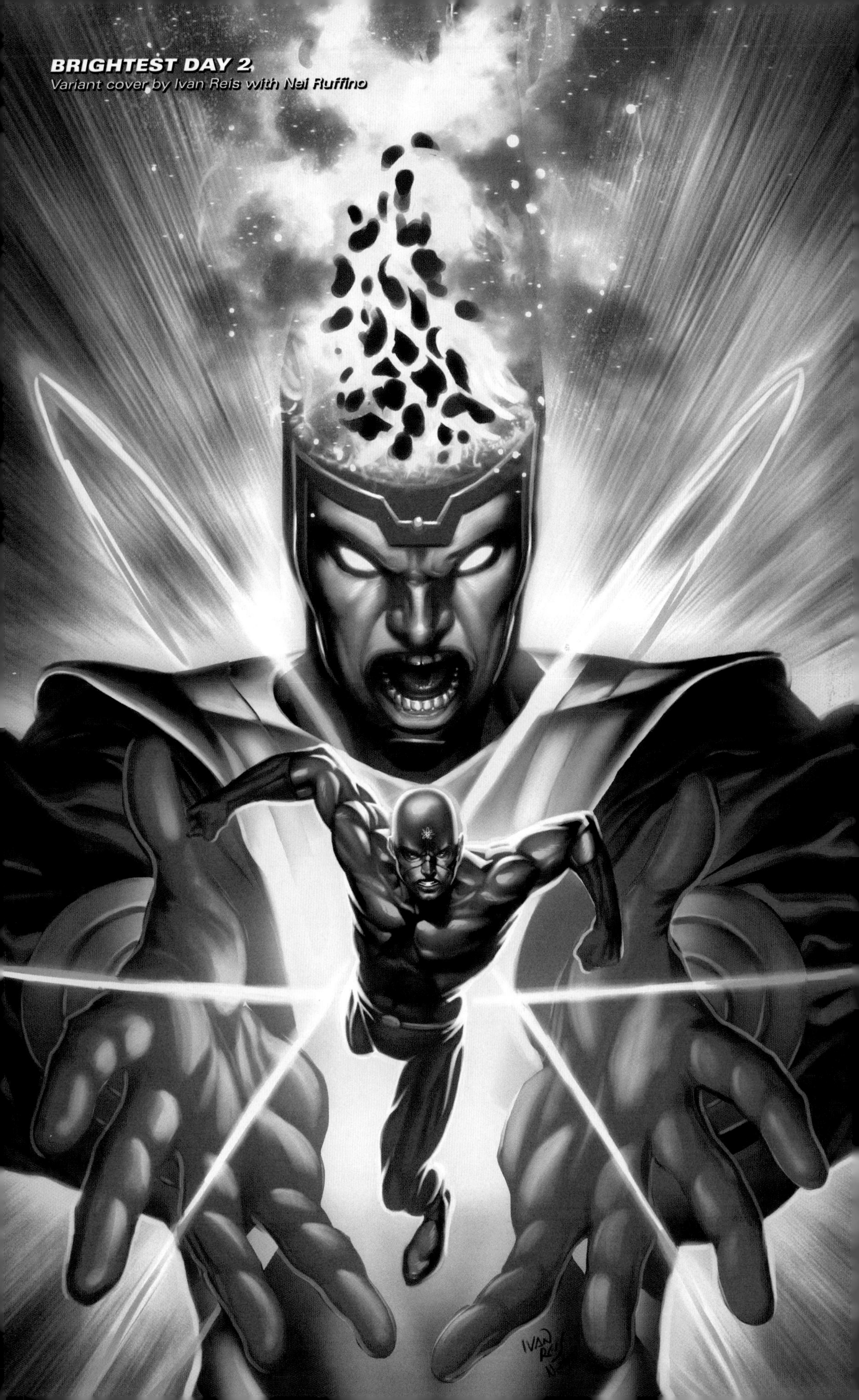

**BRIGHTEST DAY 2**
*Variant cover by Ivan Reis with Nei Ruffino*

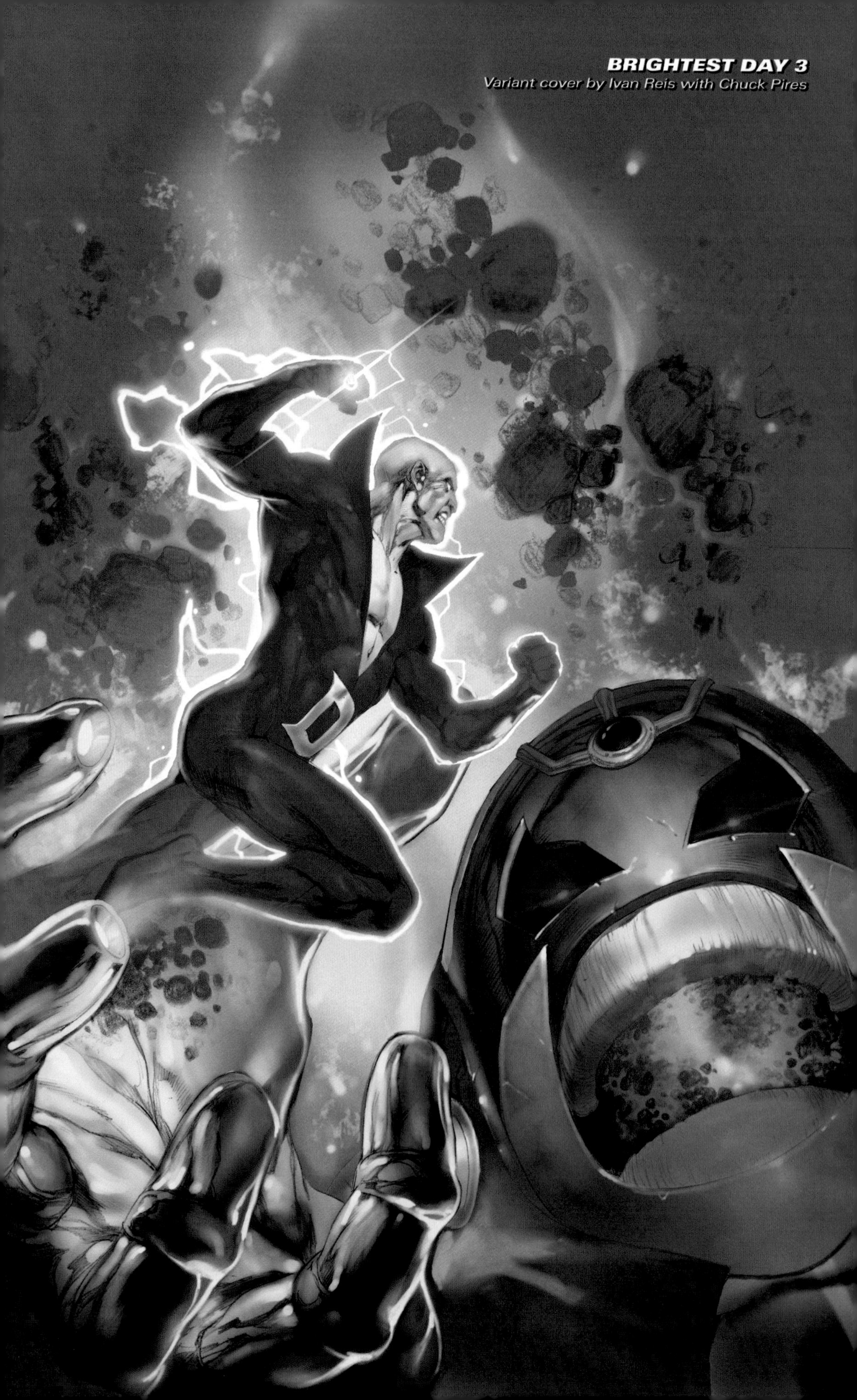

**BRIGHTEST DAY 3**
*Variant cover by Ivan Reis with Chuck Pires*

**BRIGHTEST DAY 4**

*Variant cover by Ivan Reis with Chuck Pires*

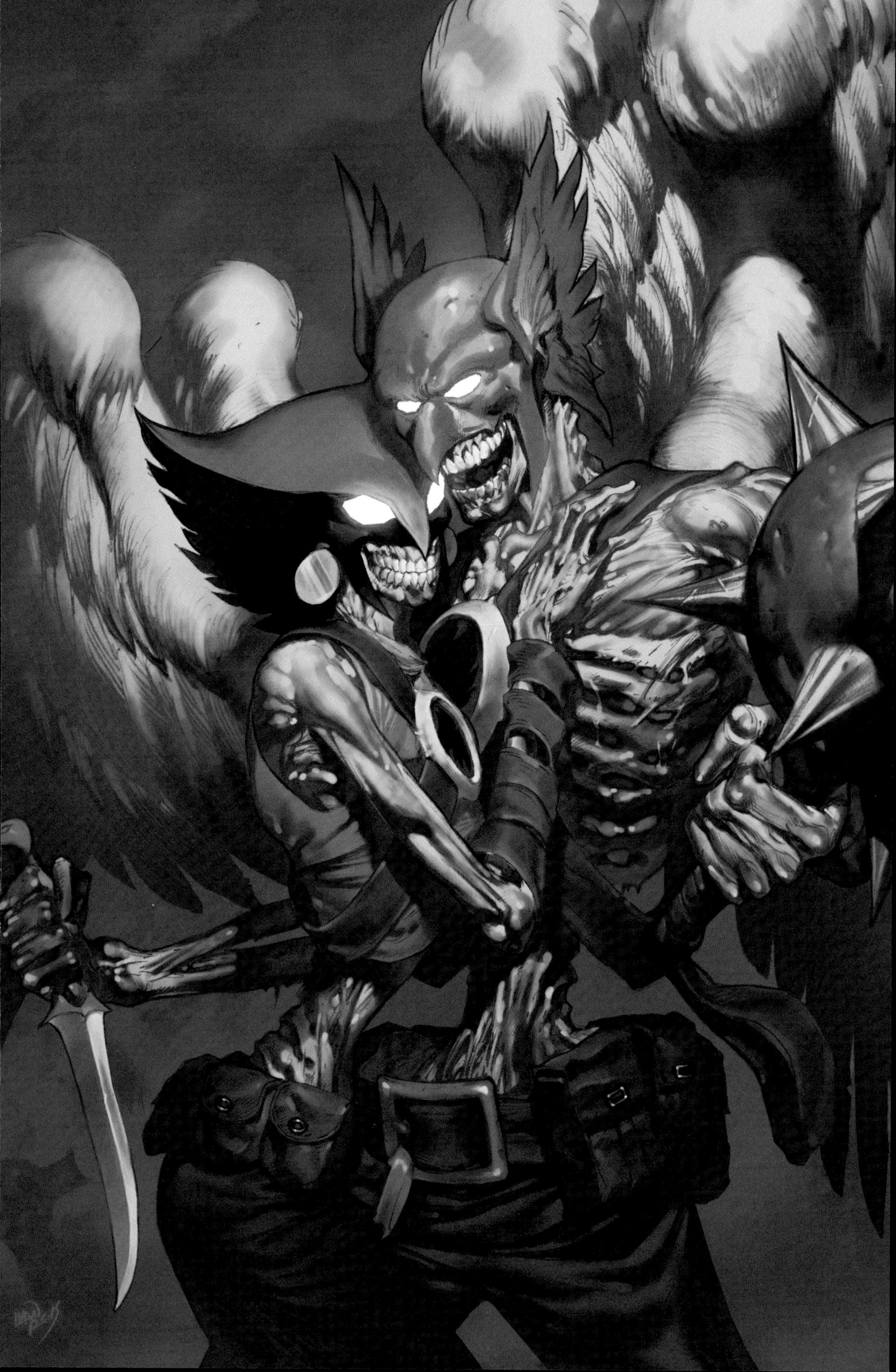

**BRIGHTEST DAY 5**
*Variant cover by Ivan Reis with Chuck Pires*

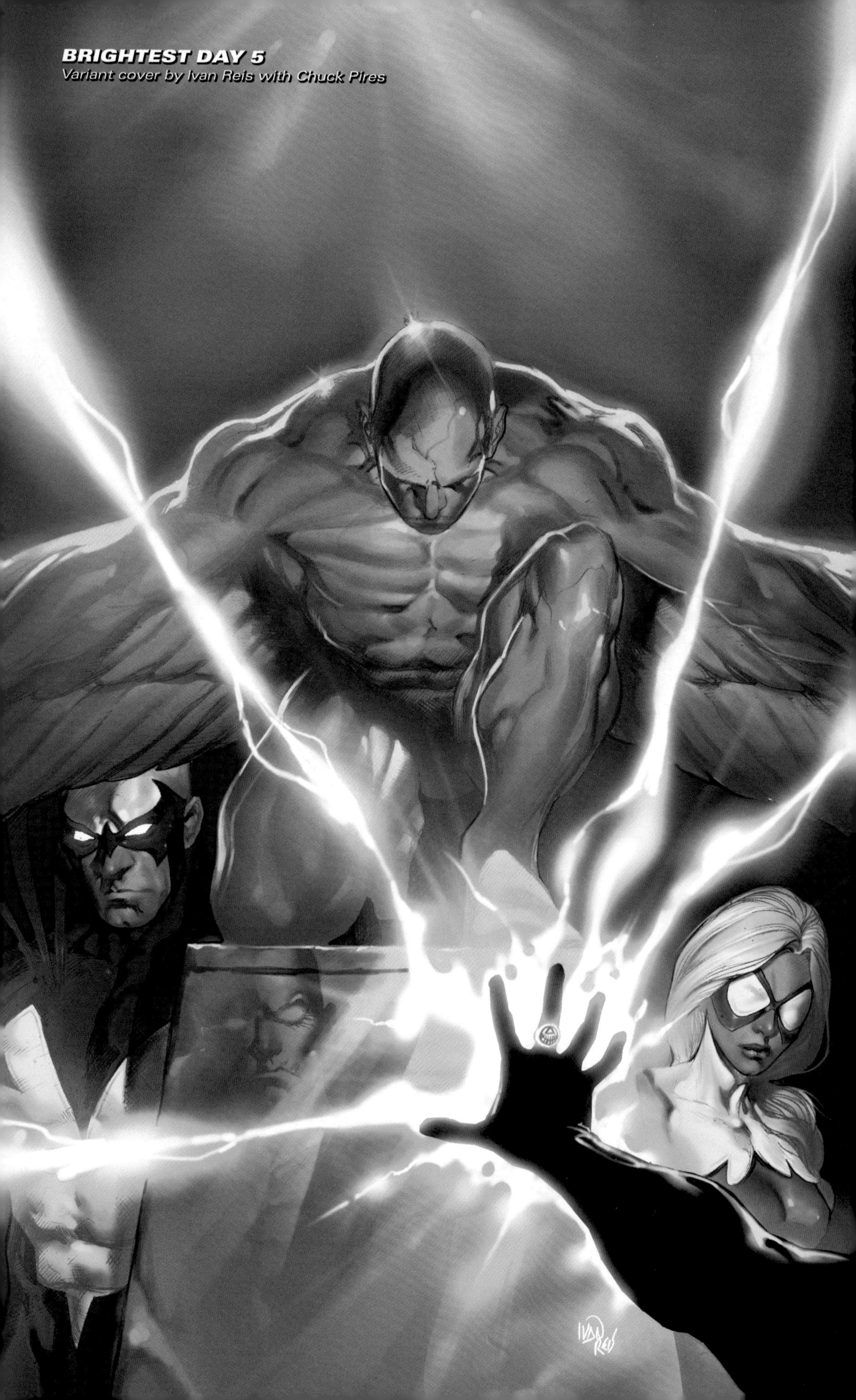

**BRIGHTEST DAY 6**
*Variant cover by Ivan Reis with Dave McCaig*

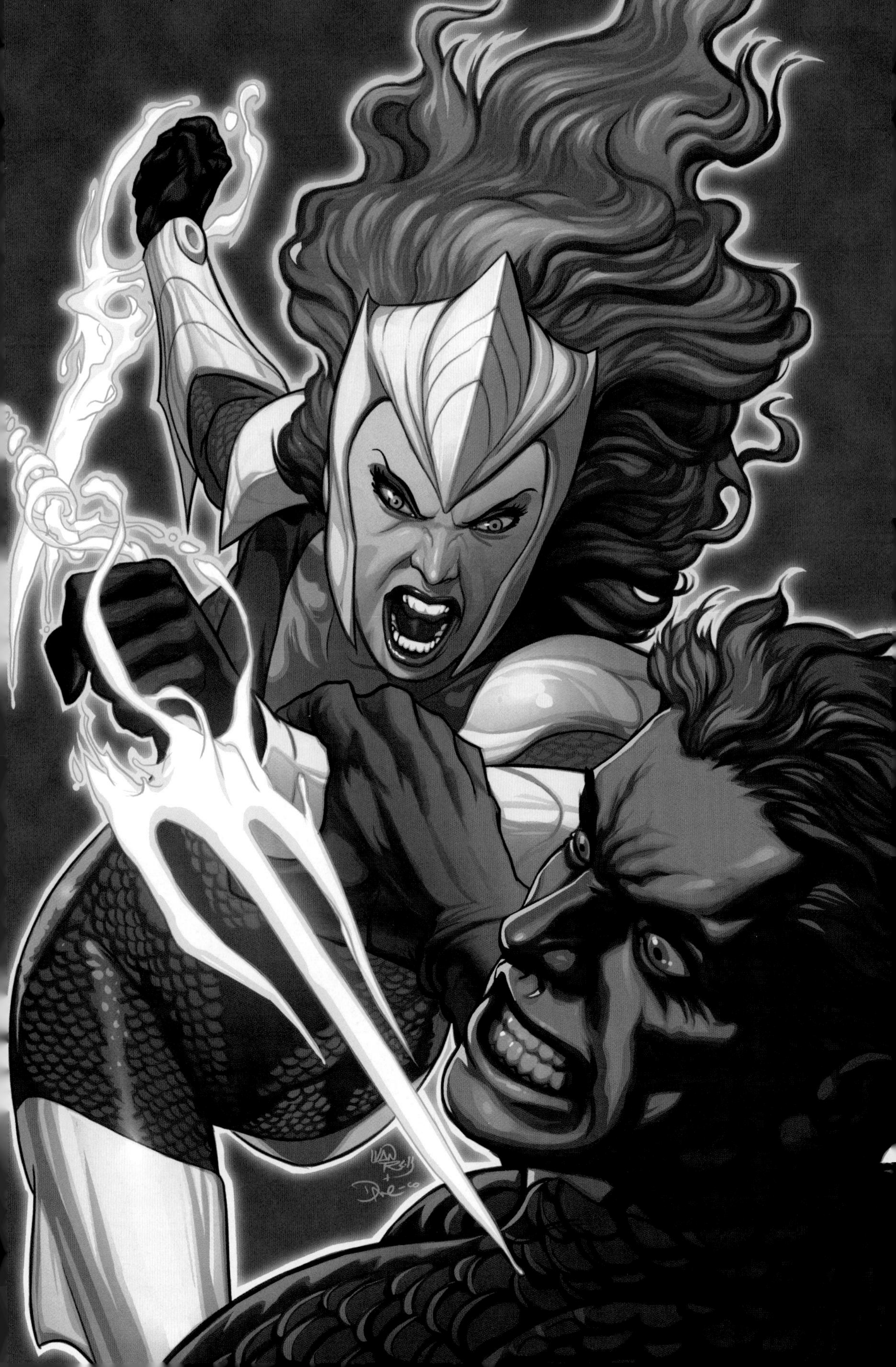

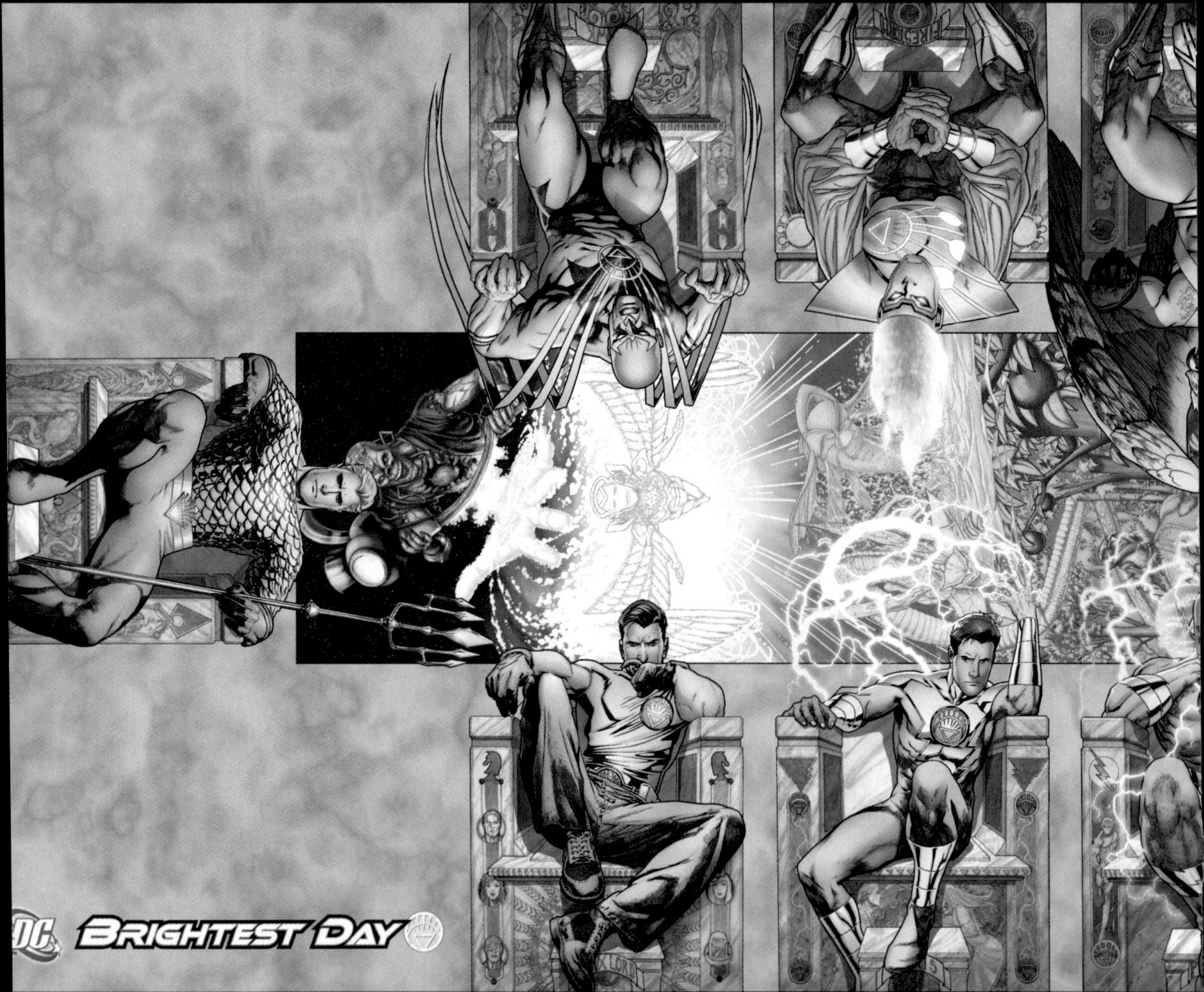
BRIGHTEST DAY

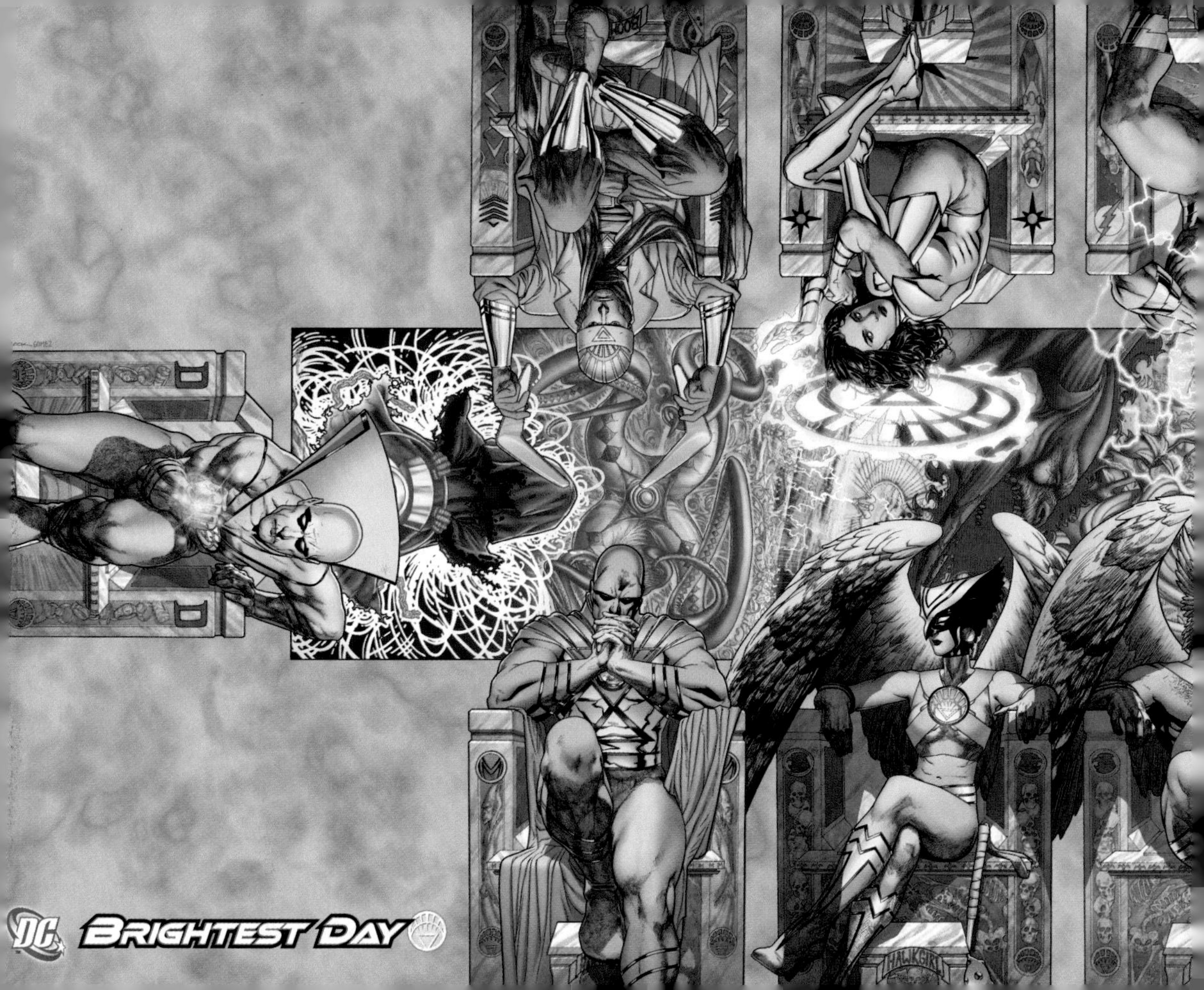
HAWKGIRL

BRIGHTEST DAY 7

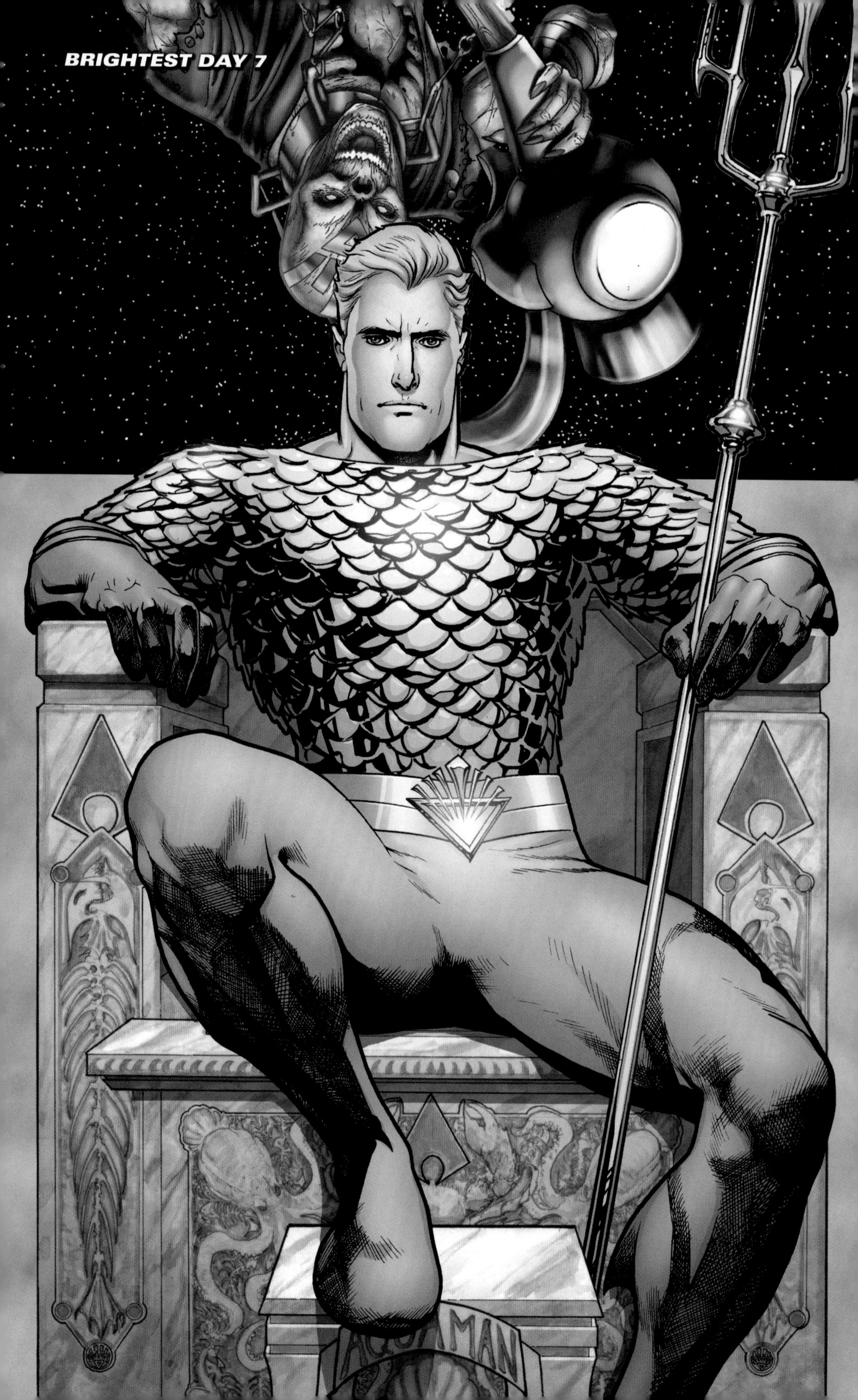
AQUAMAN

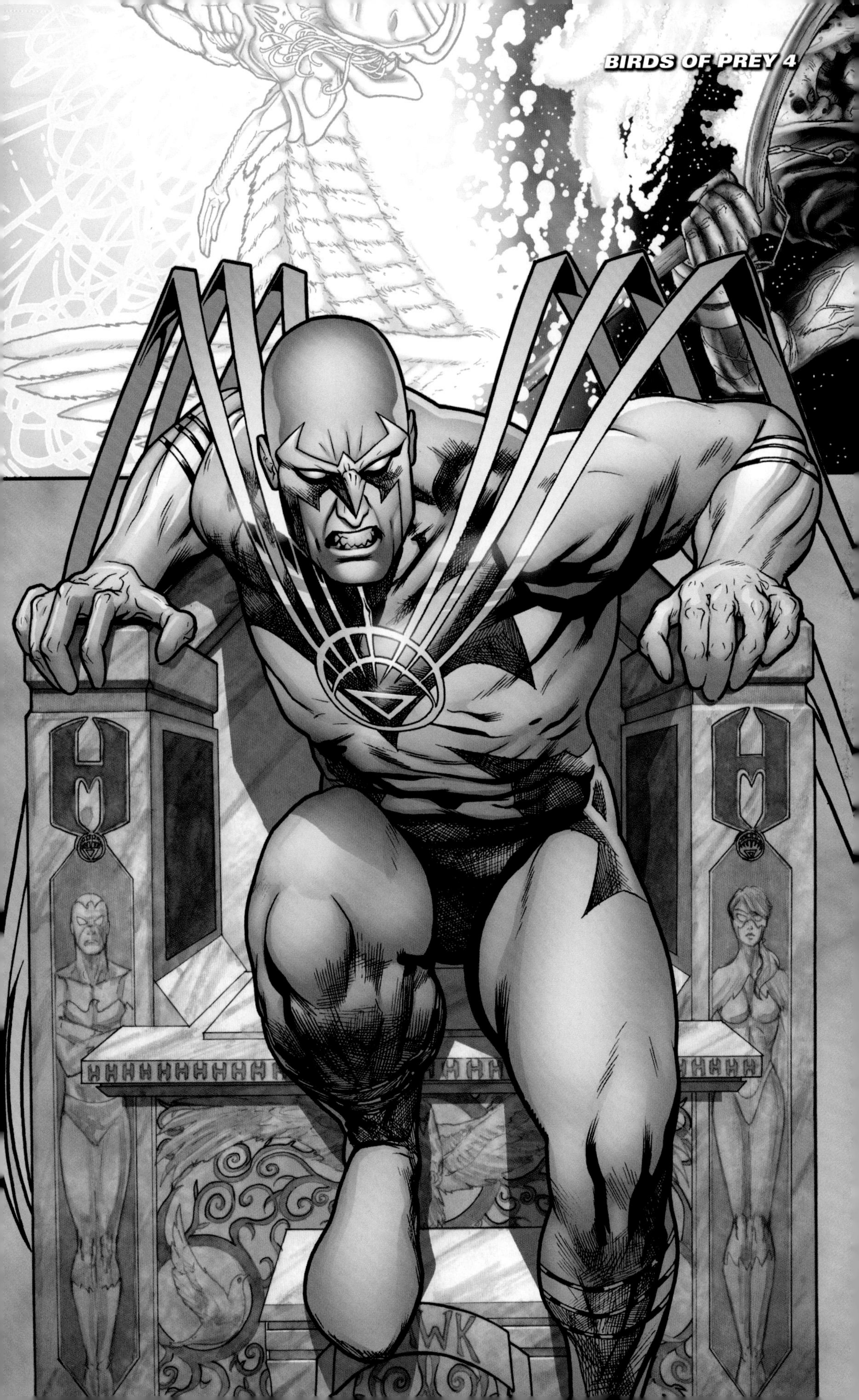

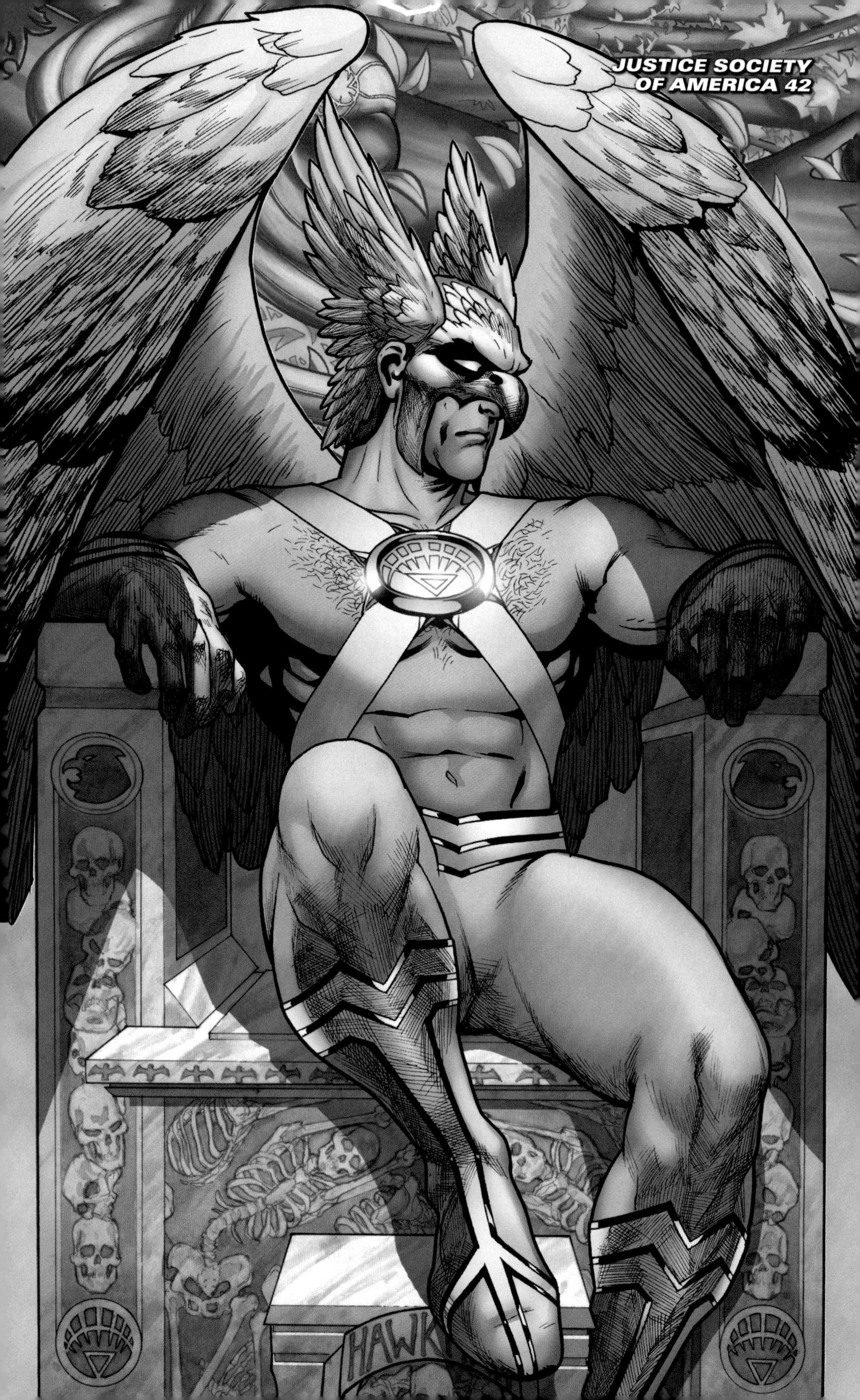
JUSTICE SOCIETY
OF AMERICA 42
HAWK

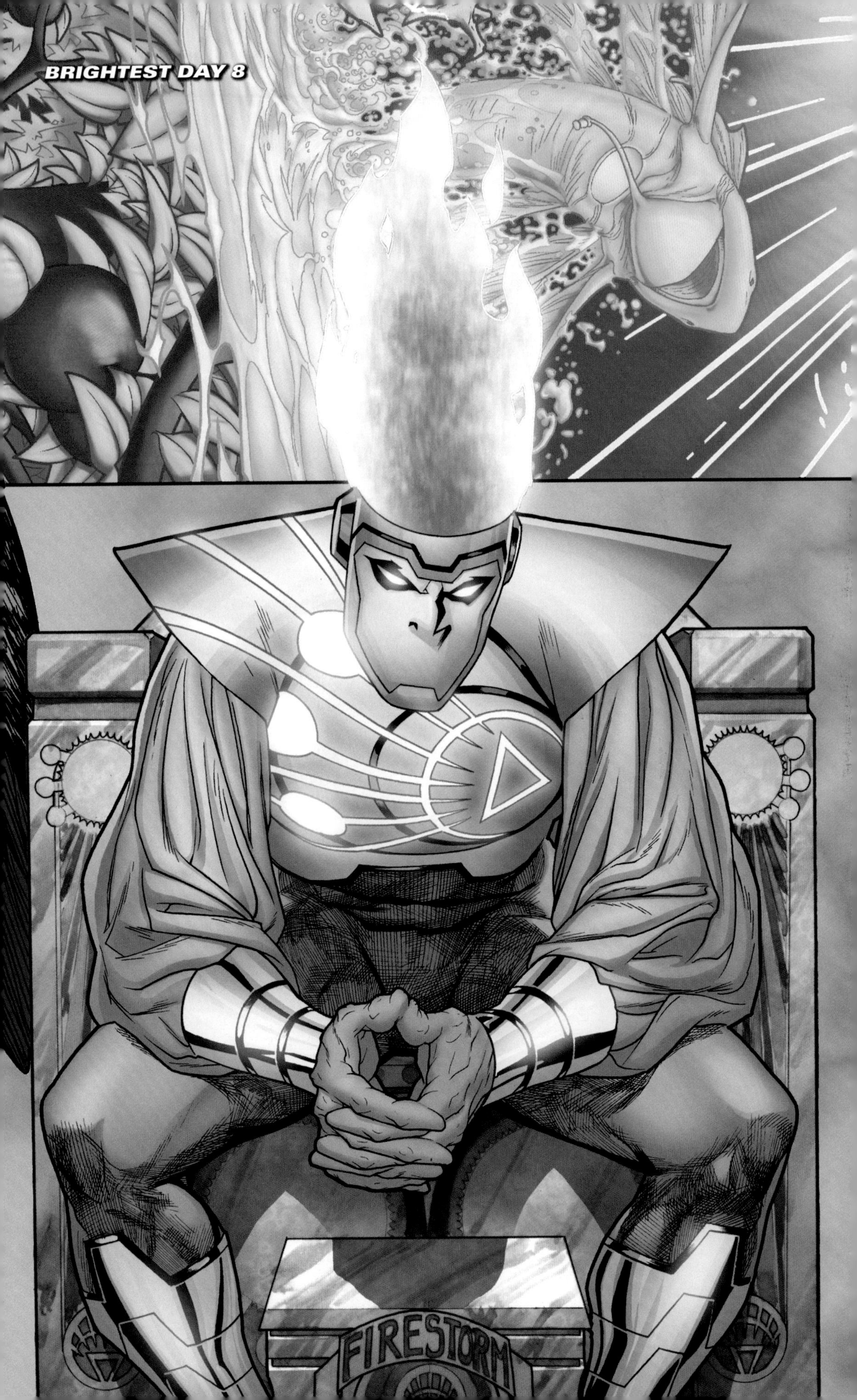
BRIGHTEST DAY 8
FIRESTORM

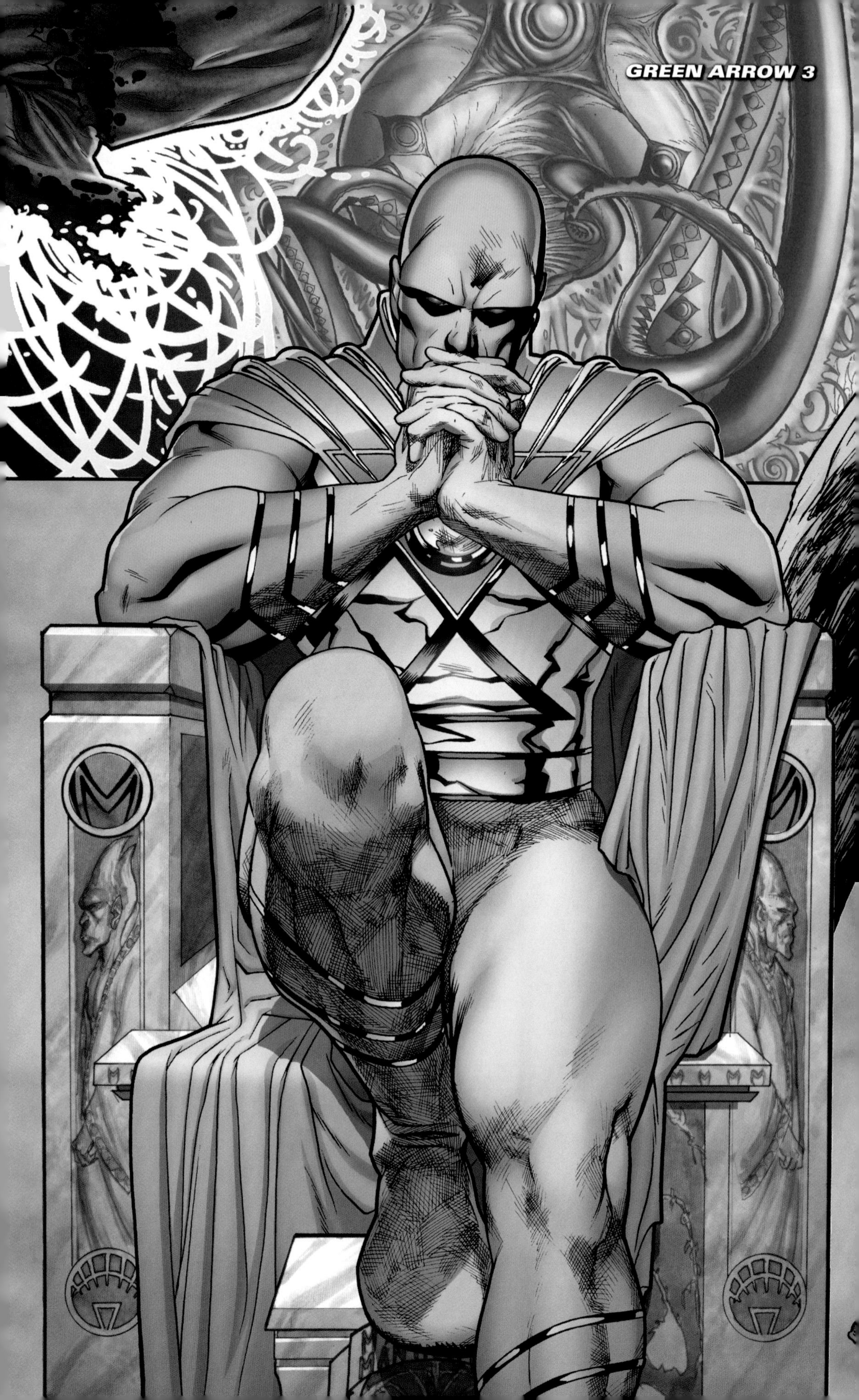
GREEN ARROW 3

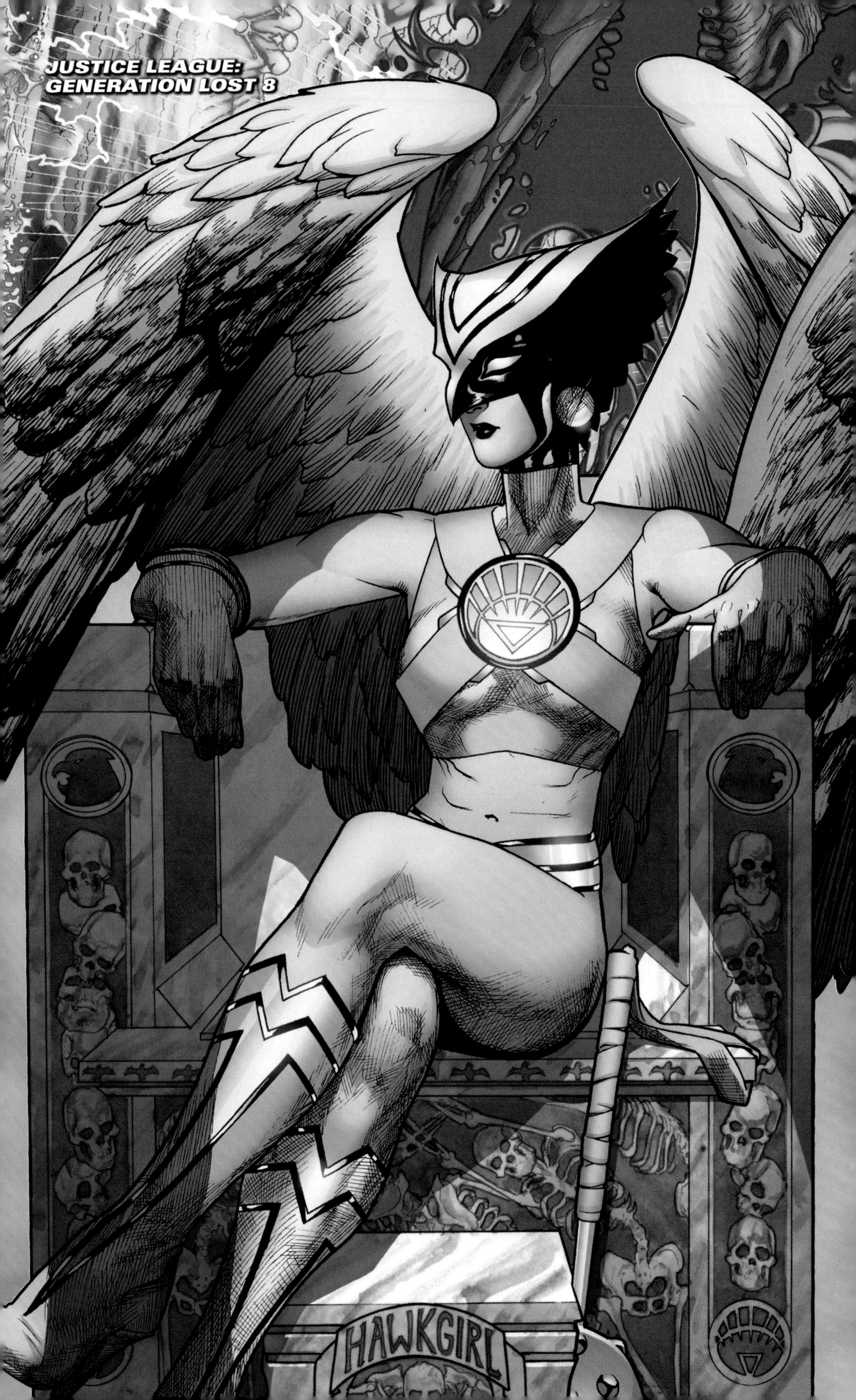
JUSTICE LEAGUE:
GENERATION LOST 8
HAWKGIRL

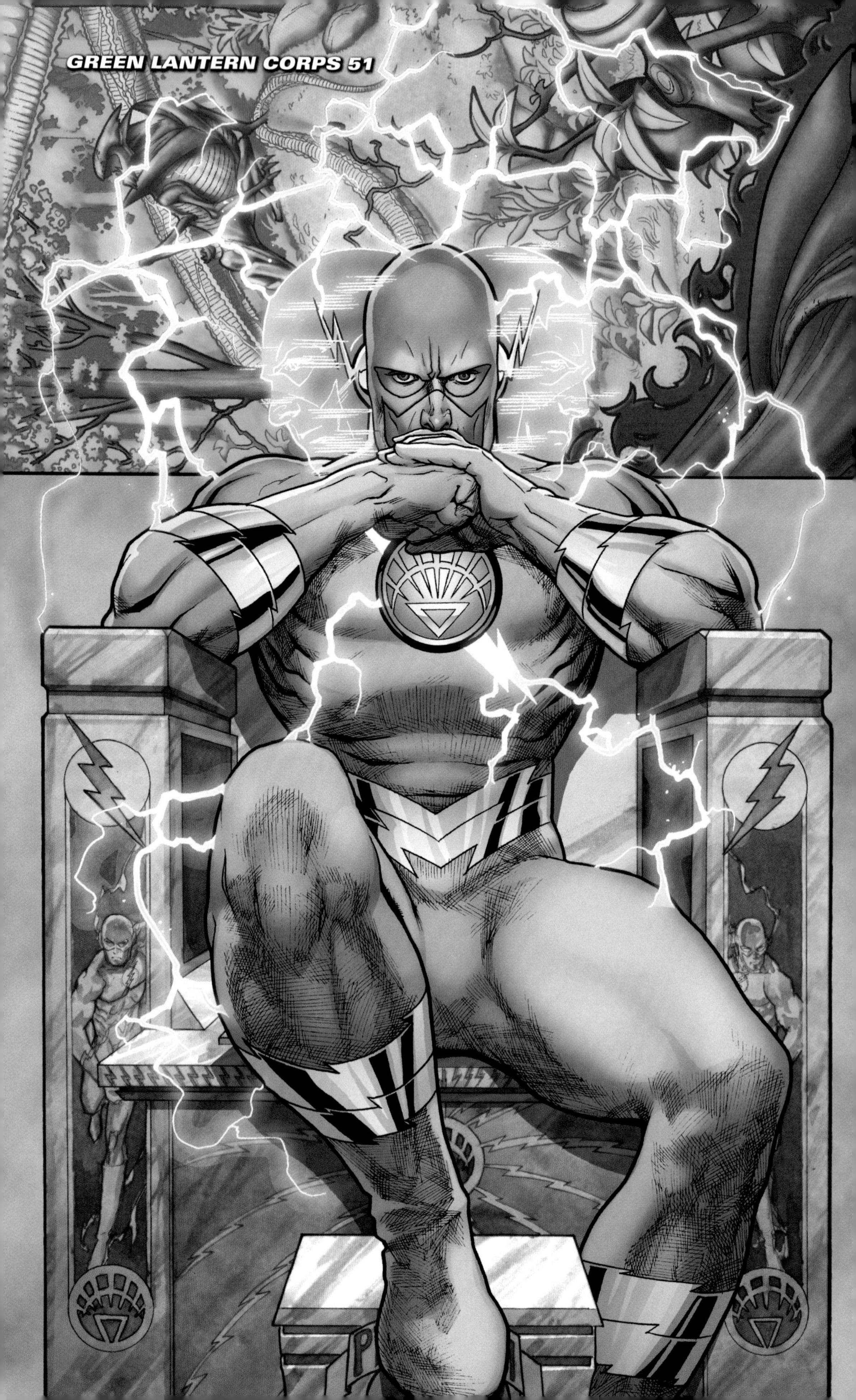
GREEN LANTERN CORPS 51

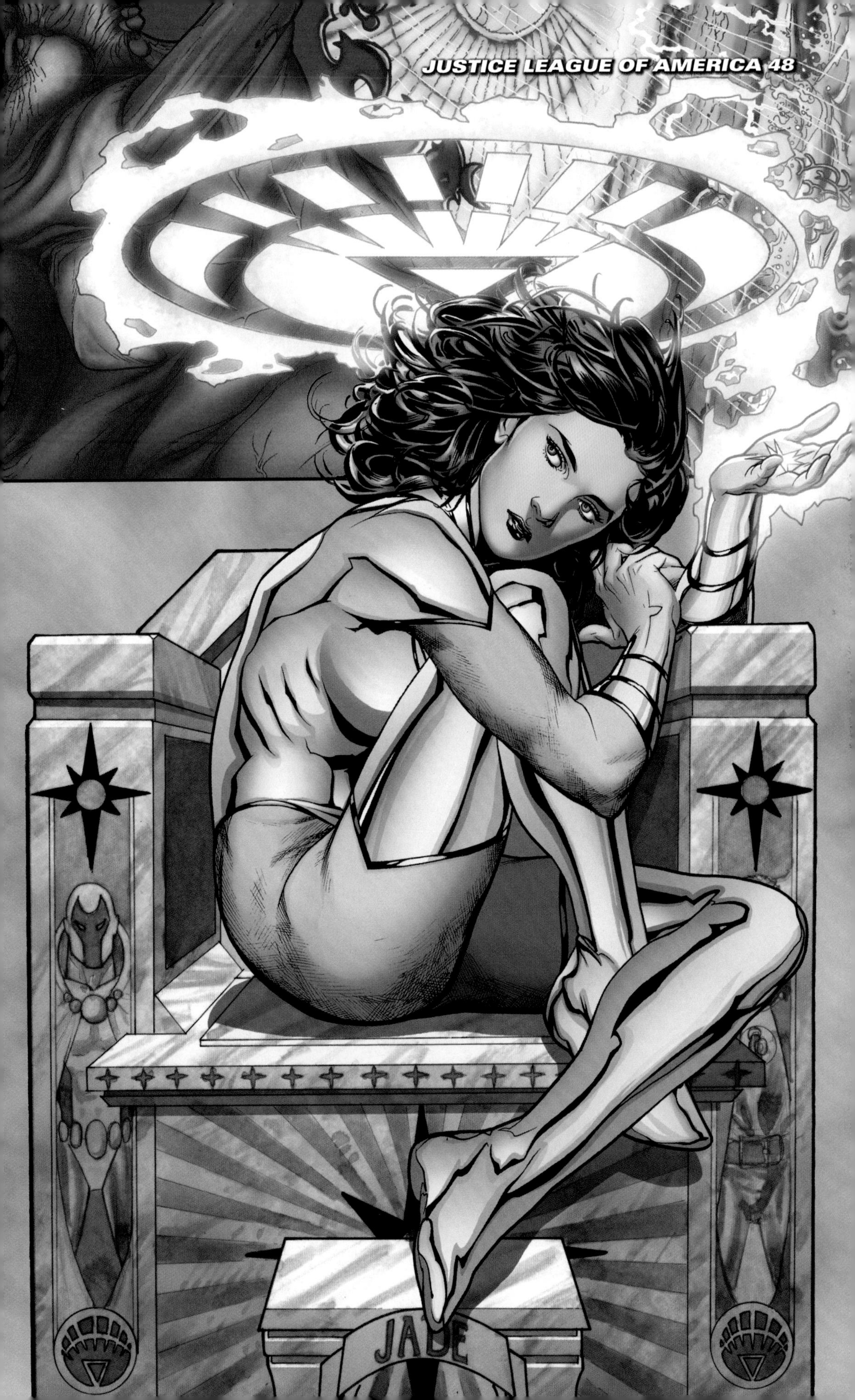
JUSTICE LEAGUE OF AMERICA 48
JADE

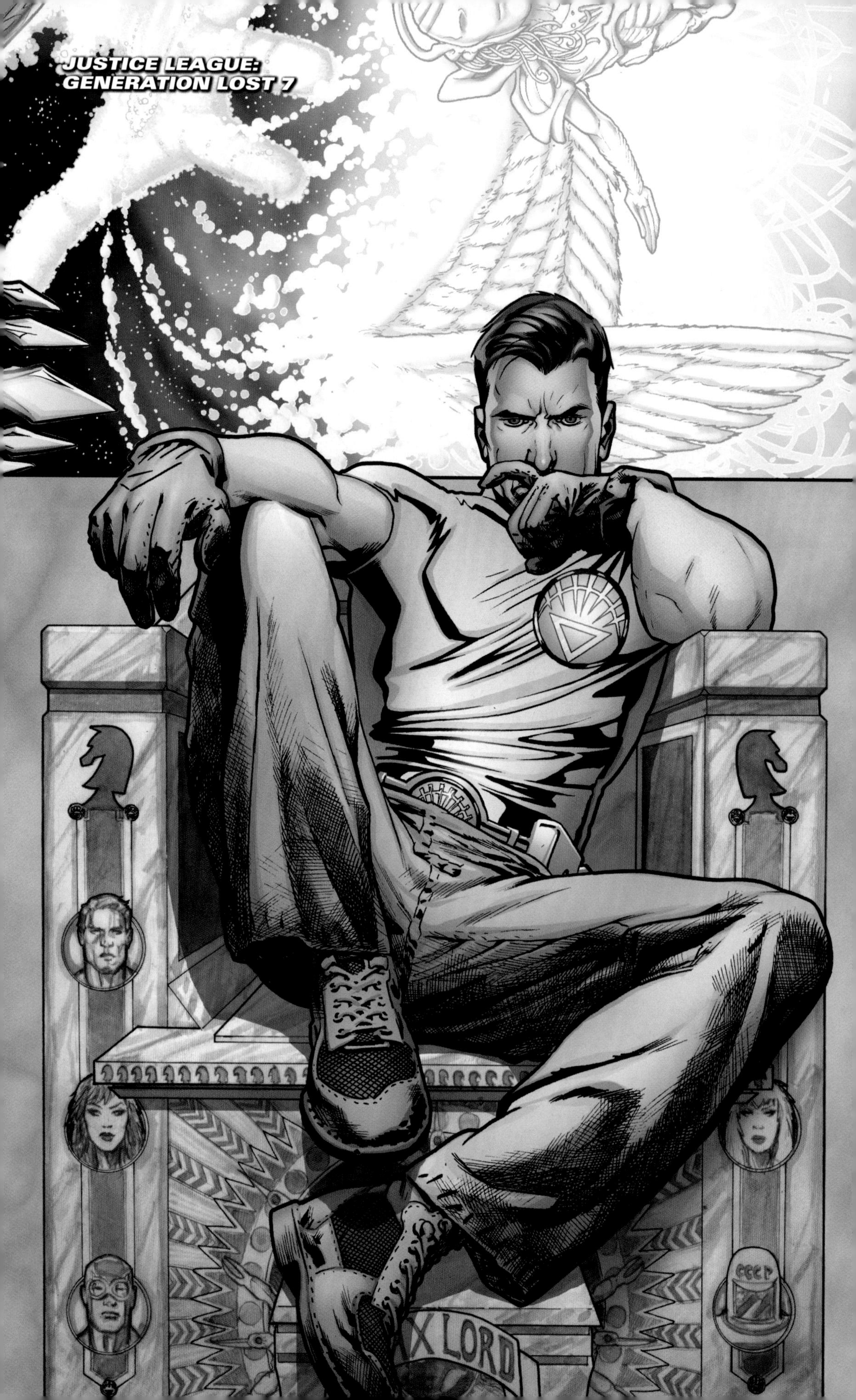
JUSTICE LEAGUE:
GENERATION LOST 7
X LORD

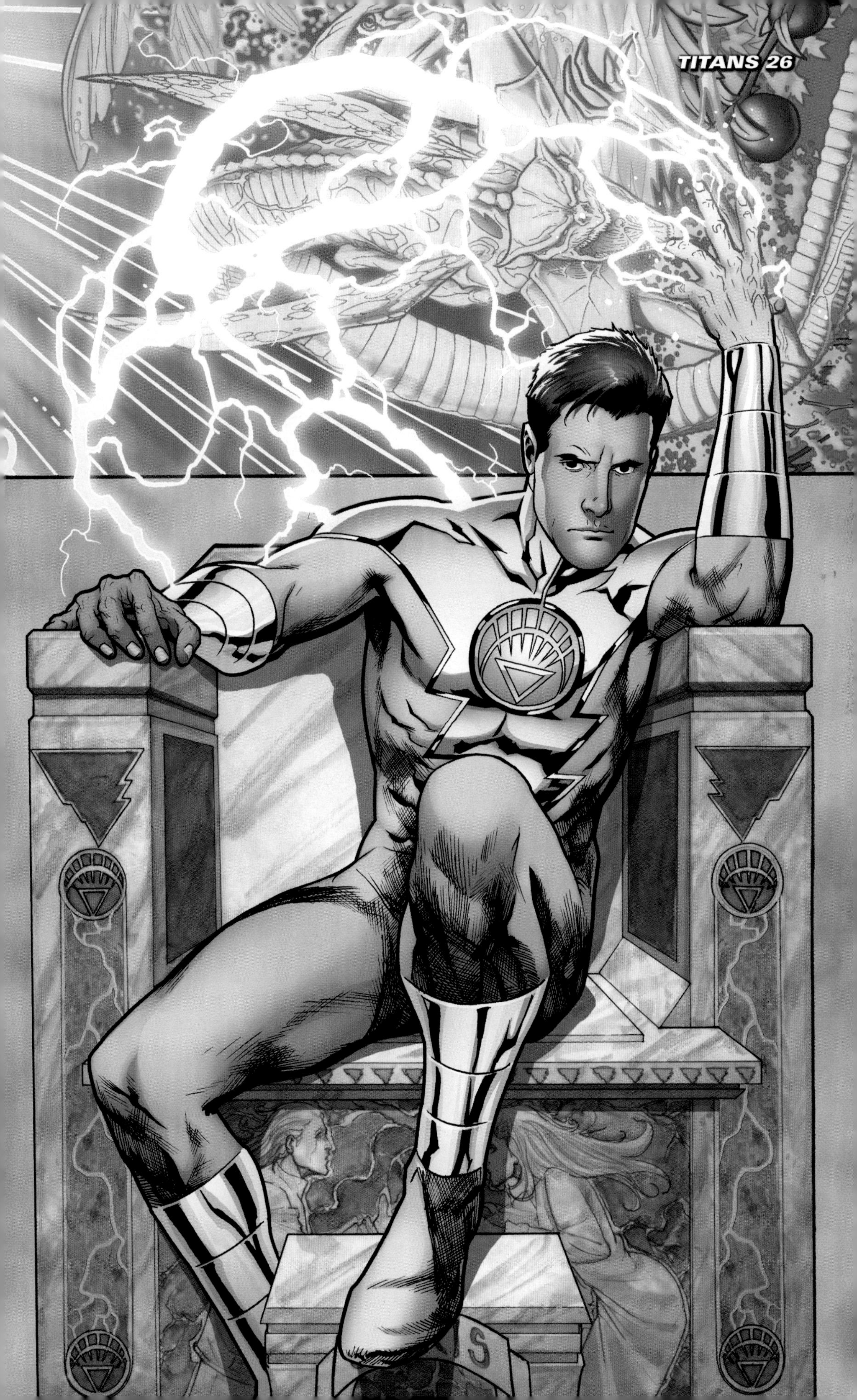
TITANS 26

THE FLASH 5

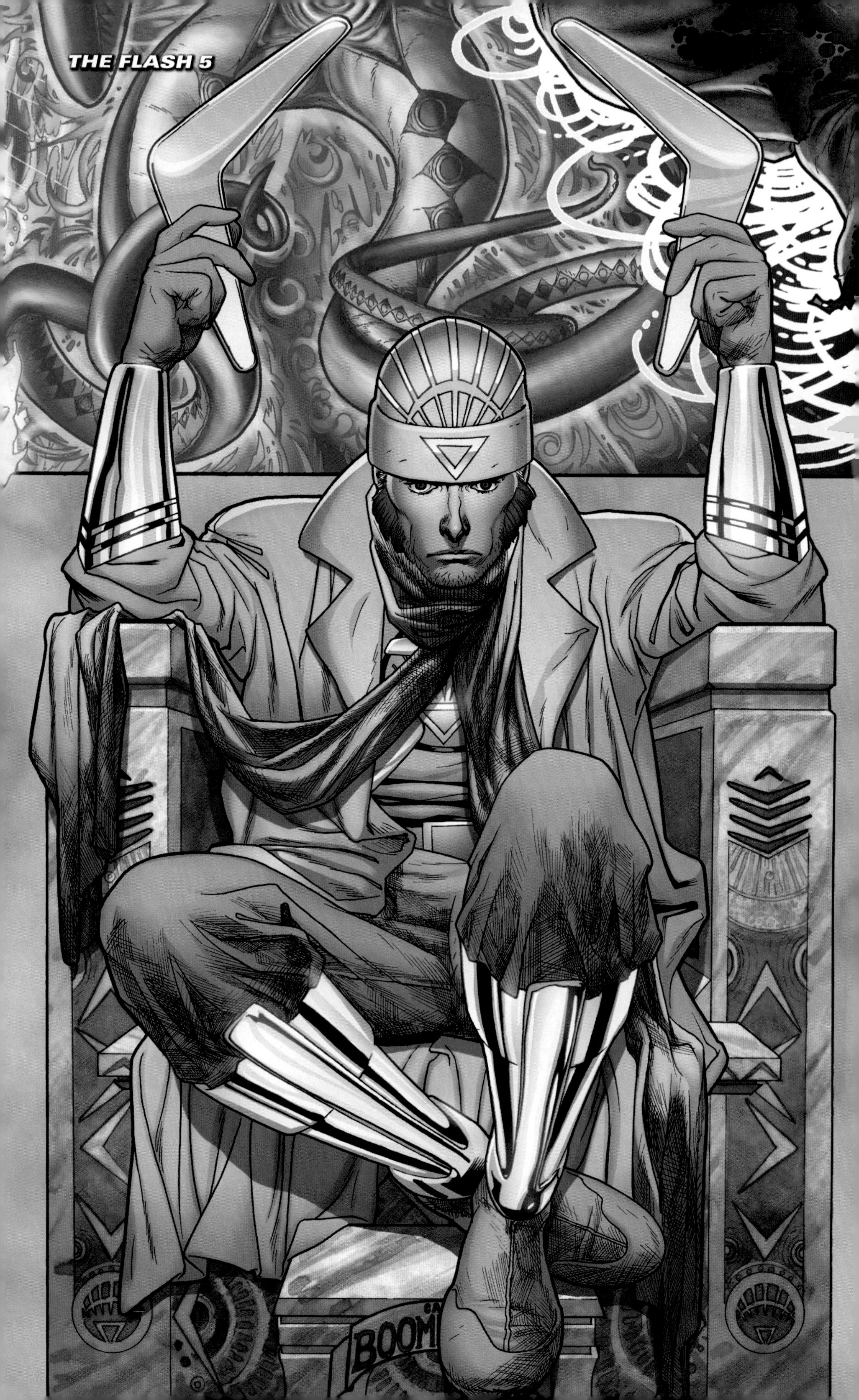
BOOM

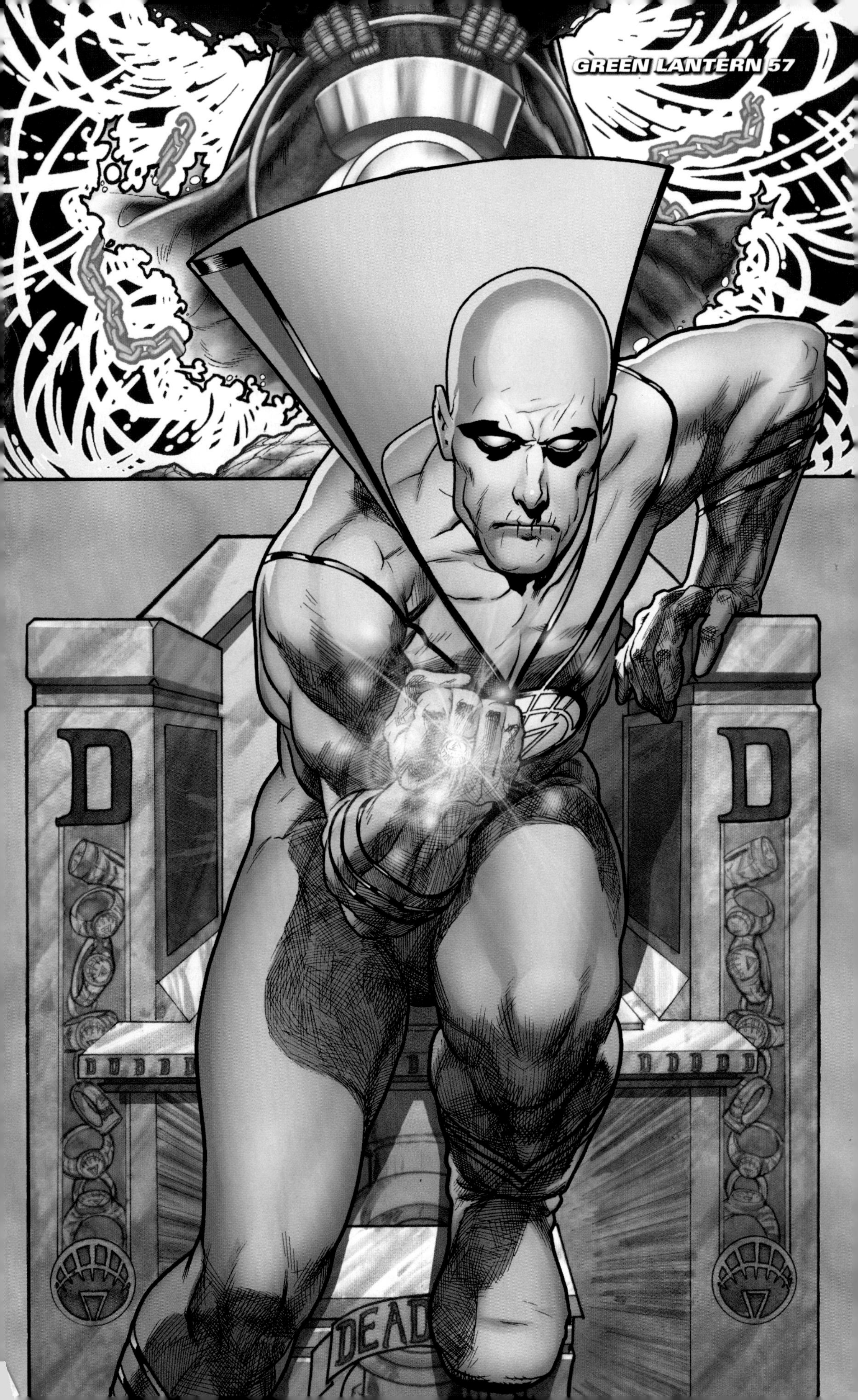
GREEN LANTERN 57
D
D
DEAD

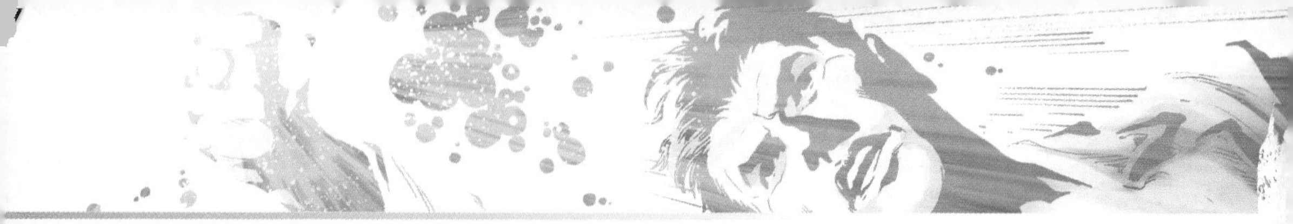

# BIOGRAPHIES

## GEOFF JOHNS

Geoff Johns is one of the most prolific and popular contemporary comic book writers. He has written highly acclaimed stories starring Superman, Green Lantern, the Flash, Teen Titans and the Justice Society of America. He is the author of the *New York Times* best-selling graphic novels GREEN LANTERN: RAGE OF THE RED LANTERNS, GREEN LANTERN: SINESTRO CORPS WAR, JUSTICE SOCIETY OF AMERICA: THY KINGDOM COME, SUPERMAN: BRAINIAC and BLACKEST NIGHT.

Johns was born in Detroit and studied media arts, screenwriting, film production and film theory at Michigan State University. After moving to Los Angeles, he worked as an intern and later an assistant for film director Richard Donner, whose credits include *Superman: The Movie, Lethal Weapon 4* and *Conspiracy Theory.*

Johns began his comics career writing STARS AND S.T.R.I.P.E. and creating Stargirl for DC Comics. Geoff received the Wizard Fan Award for Breakout Talent of 2002 and Writer of the Year for 2005 through 2008 as well as the CBG Writer of the Year 2003 through 2005, 2007 and 2008, and CBG Best Comic Book Series for JSA 2001 through 2005.

After acclaimed runs on THE FLASH, TEEN TITANS and the best-selling INFINITE CRISIS miniseries, Johns co-wrote a run on ACTION COMICS with his mentor, Donner. In 2006, he co-wrote 52, an ambitious weekly comic book series set in real time, with Grant Morrison, Greg Rucka and Mark Waid. Johns has also written for various other media, including the acclaimed "Legion" episode of SMALLVILLE and the fourth season of ROBOT CHICKEN. He wrote the story of the DC Universe Online massively multiplayer action game from Sony Online Entertainment LLC and has recently joined DC Entertainment as its Chief Creative Officer.

Johns currently resides in Los Angeles, California.

## PETER J. TOMASI

Peter J. Tomasi was an editor with DC Comics for many years where he proudly helped usher in new eras for GREEN LANTERN, BATMAN and JSA. He is now solely devoting all his time to writing comics and screenplays, having worked on such DC titles as GREEN LANTERN CORPS, BATMAN: BLACKEST NIGHT, THE OUTSIDERS, NIGHTWING, BLACK ADAM and the critically acclaimed graphic novel LIGHT BRIGADE, along with many other stories. His current projects include GREEN LANTERN: EMERALD WARRIORS and BATMAN AND ROBIN.

## IVAN REIS

Ivan Reis is a comic book artist born in 1976 in São Bernardo do Campo, São Paulo, Brazil. He started his US career in the '90s, on *Ghost* and *The Mask* for Dark Horse. After pencilling an issue of THE INVISIBLES for Grant Morrison, he started a long run on *Lady Death* for Chaos Comics, then did *The Avengers* and *The Vision*, with Geoff Johns, for Marvel. In 2004 Ivan began to work exclusively for DC. After illustrating high-profile series such as ACTION COMICS, INFINITE CRISIS and RANN-THANAGAR WAR, he started his now legendary run with Geoff Johns on GREEN LANTERN and BLACKEST NIGHT, with his inkers of choice, Oclair Albert and Joe Prado.

## PATRICK GLEASON

Patrick Gleason's career in comics has included work for Marvel and Image Comics. He is most noted for illustrating DC Comics' AQUAMAN, the relaunch of the Green Lantern Corps in the RECHARGE mini-series, and the regular ongoing GREEN LANTERN CORPS series. He is currently working on BATMAN AND ROBIN with Peter J. Tomasi.

## ARDIAN SYAF

Ardian Syaf is an Indonesian comic book artist. He has worked on *The Dresden Files* for Random House and BLACKEST NIGHT: BATMAN, SUPERMAN/BATMAN and GREEN LANTERN CORPS for DC. He is currently working on BIRDS OF PREY.

## SCOTT CLARK

Scott Clark has been working in the comic industry since the early '90s, for Image, Marvel, Aspen and Maximum Press, and most recently for DC on JUSTICE LEAGUE: CRY FOR JUSTICE.

## FERNANDO PASARIN

Fernando Pasarin is a Spanish artist who has worked on *Phenix* and *Strangers* for Semic France, and *Les Fils de la Louve* for Belgian publisher Le Lombard. He is currently working on GREEN LANTERN: EMERALD WARRIORS for DC Comics.

## JOE PRADO

Joe Prado started his career as a professional comic book artist in Brazil during the '90s, and has done hundreds of illustrations for RPG magazines and books. Six years ago he started to produce comics for the US market. His credits include ACTION COMICS, SUPERMAN, BIRDS OF PREY, GREEN LANTERN and THE WARLORD.